AUSTRALIAN URBAN POLICY

PROSPECTS AND PATHWAYS

AUSTRALIAN URBAN POLICY

PROSPECTS AND PATHWAYS

EDITED BY ROBERT FREESTONE,
BILL RANDOLPH AND WENDY STEELE

Australian
National
University

ANU PRESS

For Patrick Troy, 1936–2018

Australian
National
University

ANU PRESS

Published by ANU Press
The Australian National University
Canberra ACT 2600, Australia
Email: anupress@anu.edu.au

Available to download for free at press.anu.edu.au

ISBN (print): 9781760466299
ISBN (online): 9781760466305

WorldCat (print): 1421925745
WorldCat (online): 1421925474

DOI: 10.22459/AUP.2024

Cover design and layout by ANU Press

This book is published under the aegis of the Social Sciences editorial committee of ANU Press.

Published with the assistance of the Academy of Social Sciences in Australia.

ACADEMY OF
THE SOCIAL SCIENCES
IN AUSTRALIA

Contents

Part 6: Transitional needs and challenges

Part 7: Conclusion

List of figures

List of tables

Abbreviations

ABS	Australian Bureau of Statistics
ACT	Australian Capital Territory
AHURI	Australian Housing and Urban Research Institute
ALP	Australian Labor Party
ANU	The Australian National University
ASSA	Academy of Social Sciences in Australia
CBD	central business district
CHC	Commonwealth Housing Commission
COAG	Council of Australian Governments
CSHA	Commonwealth–State Housing Agreement
CSIRO	Commonwealth Scientific and Industrial Research Organisation
DCPs	Development Contribution Plans
DURD	Department of Urban and Regional Development
GCC	Greater Cities Commission
GDP	gross domestic product
GFC	Global Financial Crisis
GOD	greenspace-oriented development
GSC	Greater Sydney Commission
HERCON	National Heritage Convention
ICOMOS	International Council on Monuments and Sites
ICPs	Infrastructure Contribution Plans
ICT	information and communication technology
LGAs	local government areas

MCU	Major Cities Unit
NAHA	National Affordable Housing Agreement
NHHA	National Housing and Homelessness Agreement
NHS	National Housing Strategy
NSW	New South Wales
NZCH	net-zero carbon housing
OECD	Organisation for Economic Co-operation and Development
PIA	Planning Institute of Australia
PM&C	Department of the Prime Minister and Cabinet
PSS	planning support systems
SCaaS	smart city as a service
SDG	Sustainable Development Goal
SEIFA	Socio-Economic Indexes for Areas
SPI	Social Progress Index
TOD	transit-oriented development
UK	United Kingdom
UN	United Nations
UN-Habitat	United Nations Human Settlements Programme
UNDRIP	United Nations Declaration on the Rights of Indigenous Peoples
UNESCO	United Nations Educational, Scientific and Cultural Organization
UNSW	University of New South Wales
US	United States
VFT	Very Fast Train

Acknowledgement of Country

We, the authors, acknowledge the Traditional Owners on whose unceded lands we live, work, study, and play. We acknowledge the Aboriginal and Torres Strait Islander peoples of Australia have suffered the trauma and indignity of having their land taken from them without their consent, without a treaty, and without compensation. We acknowledge these matters are yet to be resolved. We pay our respects to your elders past and present. We also acknowledge that the Aboriginal and Torres Strait Islander peoples of Australia are among the world's oldest continuing cultures and maintain one of the oldest continuing forms of land tenure, land-use planning, and management. We acknowledge your continuing governance systems, diverse languages, customs, traditions, and rich knowledge of ecological systems, and the enduring connection and stewardship of Country that are integral to Aboriginal and Torres Strait Islander peoples' identity and culture and have been for thousands of generations. We are committed to learning to live together better on Country.

Acknowledgements

We thank the Academy of Social Sciences in Australia (ASSA), which, through its workshops program, was the principal enabler of the invited symposium entitled 'Australian Urban Policy: Achievements, Failures, Challenges', held on 26–27 August 2021 at the University of New South Wales (UNSW), at which early versions of papers that became the chapters in this book were presented and discussed. Nicholas Brown and Stephen Dovers (The Australian National University), Graeme Davison (Monash University), Peter Spearritt (University of Queensland), and David Wilmoth helped shape the early planning for the workshop. Staged at the height of the Covid-19 pandemic, what was projected as a traditional gathering of academic researchers transitioned to a fully online event. We thank Professor Chris Pettit, the Director of the UNSW City Futures Research Centre, which was the formal co-sponsor with ASSA of the workshop, for his continuing support. Aley Buxton and Xin Xia of City Futures provided valuable administrative and logistical assistance. We also acknowledge the Centre for Urban Research Unit at RMIT University, which hosted the Melbourne hub for the workshop, and Stephen Dovers and Ed Wensing for holding up the Canberra end. The transition from staging the workshop to a publishing enterprise through the continuing pandemic was enabled by ASSA and we thank its Director, Chris Hatherly, and Policy Analyst Isabel Ceron for their flexibility and assistance in enabling that to happen. Publication has also been supported by a small grant from the School of Built Environment at UNSW. At ANU Press, we acknowledge the input of Nathan Hollier, Elouise Ball, Sarah Sky and Teresa Prowse, along with peer-review feedback provided by the Social Sciences Editorial Board chaired by Professor Frank Bongiorno and two anonymous reviewers of what had become a hefty draft manuscript. Our thanks also to Jan Borrie for assisting with copyediting and indexing.

Contributors

Julian Bolleter is the Co-Director of the Australian Urban Design Research Centre (AUDRC) at the University of Western Australia and the Program Director of its Master of Urban Design course. Julian's research concerns the climate change adaptation of regional settlement patterns, urban areas, and open space. Julian is an experienced landscape architect and urban designer and has practised in Australia, the United States, the United Kingdom, and the Middle East; and has recently been appointed to the West Australian State Design Review Panel.

Alessandra Buxton is a planning researcher with a graduate degree in social research and policy from the University of New South Wales. She is a project officer at the City Futures Research Centre and is studying for a Master of Philosophy in the School of Built Environment, University of New South Wales.

Rebecca Clements is a Postdoctoral Research Fellow with the Henry Halloran Trust Infrastructure Governance Incubator at the University of Sydney. She is also completing a PhD at the University of Melbourne focused on parking policy in Japanese cities. Her research focuses on urban infrastructure and governance, transport, and parking approaches in Australia and East Asia. Her current work examines mobility justice and the right to the city through critical post-capital futures. She served as Victorian co-chair of the Australasian Early Career Urban Research Network for four years.

Amanda Davies is Professor and Head of the School of Social Sciences at the University of Western Australia, where she lectures and researches in human geography. With a disciplinary background in geography, Professor Davies' research focuses on Australia's population growth and distribution and patterns of demographic change. Her work also focuses on exploring the social, economic, and environmental issues related to rural repopulation.

Jago Dodson is Professor of Urban Policy in the Centre for Urban Research at RMIT University. Professor Dodson has an extensive record of research into housing, transport, urban planning, infrastructure, energy, and urban governance problems. He has contributed extensively to scholarly and public debates about Australian cities and has advised national and international agencies on urban policy questions. His books include *Planning After Petroleum: Preparing Cities for the Age Beyond Oil* (2016), *Australian Environmental Planning: Challenges and Future Prospects* (2014), *Shocking the Suburbs: Oil Vulnerability in the Australian City* (2008), and *Government Discourse and Housing* (2007).

Stephen Dovers FASSA is Emeritus Professor in the Fenner School of Environment and Society, College of Science, at The Australian National University; a senior associate with the firm Aither; and undertakes research into climate adaptation, disasters, and natural resource management. He co-authored the *Environment and Sustainability Policy* (2nd edn, 2013) and *The Handbook of Disaster Policies and Institutions* (2nd edn, 2013), and co-edited the volume *Climate, Energy and Water* (2015).

Hazel Easthope is Professor at the City Futures Research Centre at the University of New South Wales. Hazel has qualifications in sociology and human geography and researches urban studies and housing. Her research focuses on urban consolidation and the development, management, governance, and planning implications of apartment buildings and estates and the lived experiences of their residents. She is a leading researcher in this field, and is regularly consulted by industry, government, and peak body organisations in Australia and internationally.

Nicole Edwards is a Research Fellow in the Australian Urban Design Research Centre at the University of Western Australia. Her research integrates the disciplines of public health, geography, urban planning, and urban design, and is focused on the impact of the built environment on the health and wellbeing of urban and regional communities and the adaptation of public open spaces to withstand the impacts of climate change. Her research uses spatial analysis and public participatory mapping to integrate public open space distribution, park utilisation, and community wellbeing.

Niki Frantzeskaki is Chair Professor of Regional and Metropolitan Governance and Planning at Utrecht University, Faculty of Geosciences, the Netherlands. Niki's interests include environmental governance, urban sustainability transitions, urban experimentation, and innovation in cities with nature-based solutions. She has extensive international research experience with a portfolio of ongoing projects in Australia, Canada, and the United States. From 2019 to 2021, she was a research professor and director of the Centre for Urban Transitions at Swinburne University of Technology, Melbourne.

Robert Freestone FASSA FAHA is a Professor of Planning in the School of Built Environment at the University of New South Wales and a City Futures Research Centre Fellow. He is a former president of the International Planning History Society and co-author and editor of several books, including *Campus* (2023), *Designing the Global City* (2019), *Planning Metropolitan Australia* (2018), *Urban Nation: Australia's Planning Heritage* (2010), *Urban Planning in a Changing World* (2000), and *Spirited Cities* (2004).

Brendan Gleeson FASSA is an Honorary Professor in the Melbourne Centre for Cities at the University of Melbourne. He has qualifications in geography and urban planning and has made significant scholarly contributions to urban and social policy and environmental theory and policy. His most recent books are *Urban Awakenings, Disturbance and Enchantment in the Industrial City* (2020, with Sam Alexander), *Degrowth in the Suburbs* (2018, also with Alexander), and *The Urban Condition* (2014).

Nicole Gurran is Professor of Urban and Regional Planning and Director of the Henry Halloran Research Trust at the University of Sydney. She is an urban planner and policy analyst whose research focuses on comparative urban planning systems and approaches to housing and ecological sustainability. She has led and collaborated on a series of research projects on aspects of urban policy, housing, sustainability, and planning funded by the Australian Research Council, the Australian Urban and Housing Research Institute, and state and local governments.

Hayley Henderson is a Fellow at the Institute for Infrastructure in Society within the Crawford School of Public Policy at The Australian National University. She studies urban policymaking and governance in Australian and Latin American cities. Her research utilises comparative and mixed methods to examine the way state and societal actors work together in urban water management and urban revitalisation strategies.

Paula Hooper is a Healthway Research Fellow and Co-Director of the Australian Urban Design Research Centre within the School of Design at the University of Western Australia. Her multidisciplinary research work has studied the impact of the built environment and urban design on health and wellbeing with a strong focus on policy relevance and research translation with the goal of creating intelligent, community-informed urban design for future cities.

Matthew Kelly is a PhD candidate at the University of New South Wales, who is exploring the recognition and empowerment of Aboriginal peoples in the NSW planning system. Matt has been a sessional lecturer in the City Planning Program in the School of Architecture, Design and Planning for the past five years. Matt is an experienced urban planner, having worked for a leading multidisciplinary planning, urban design, and architecture firm, specialising in state-significant development applications and complex planning proposals in New South Wales.

Sophie-May Kerr is a Research Associate at the City Futures Research Centre at the University of New South Wales. She is a human geographer, who uses qualitative research methods to explore issues relating to housing and home. She is an advocate for city design, governance, and imaginaries that are inclusive of diversity and informed by the lived material and emotional complexities of residents' everyday lives. Sophie-May completed her PhD at the University of Wollongong in 2020.

Victoria Kolankiewicz is an urban historian and planning practitioner, who works as a strategic planner for the Victorian Department of Transport and Planning. Her doctoral research thesis, 'Leisure, pleasure, rubbish and rats: The planning of bluestone quarries and their after-use in Melbourne, 1835–2000' (University of Melbourne, 2020), examined the historical incapacity of planning mechanisms to adequately address urban quarrying.

Crystal Legacy is Associate Professor of Urban Planning at the University of Melbourne, where she is also the Deputy Director of the Informal Urbanism Research Hub. She lives on Wurundjeri Country, where she writes, teaches, and works with communities on urban transport politics, public participation, and the post-political city. She publishes in a range of academic journals, provides critical commentary in local and national media outlets, and works in solidarity with a range of community-based groups seeking climate justice in transport planning. Crystal is an editor of two journals, *Planning Theory and Practice* and *Urban Policy and Research*, and was the inaugural chair of the Australasian Early Career Urban Research Network.

James Lesh is an urban historian and heritage specialist. He is Director of Heritage Workshop, a conservation consultancy based in Melbourne. His research explores the theory and practice of heritage conservation in the twentieth and twenty-first centuries. He has published widely on Australian urban history. His publications include *Values in Cities: Urban Heritage in Twentieth-Century Australia* (2022) and the edited collection *People-Centred Methodologies for Heritage Conservation: Exploring Emotional Attachments to Historic Urban Places* (2021).

Vivienne Milligan PSM is an Honorary Professor at the City Futures Research Centre, University of New South Wales. She has had a 40-year career specialising in housing policy, working as a policymaker, program manager, consultant, educator, and researcher. In 2020, she co-authored (with Hal Pawson and Judith Yates) Australia's first major housing policy book in more than 25 years.

Kristy Muir is Professor of Social Policy in the Business School at the University of New South Wales. Her research has spanned housing, education, employment, social participation, disability, mental health, financial resilience, and wellbeing. She has published widely in policy, sociology, social work, history, and public health journals and in publicly accessible and popular media. She was formerly the CEO of the Centre for Social Impact and is the CEO of the Paul Ramsay Foundation.

Peter Newton FASSA is an Emeritus Professor in the Centre for Urban Transitions at the Swinburne University of Technology, Melbourne. Before that he was a Chief Research Scientist at the Commonwealth Scientific and Industrial Research Organisation (CSIRO). His areas of research interest are sustainable built environments, urban sustainability transitions (decarbonisation and regeneration), and sustainable consumption. His most recent books include *Migration and Urban Transitions in Australia* (2022), *Greening the Greyfields: New Models for Regenerating the Middle Suburbs of Low-Density Cities* (2022), *Decarbonising the Built Environment: Charting the Transition* (2019), and *Resilient Sustainable Cities: A Future* (2014).

David Nichols is Professor in Urban Planning in the Faculty of Architecture, Building and Planning at the University of Melbourne. His research interests include twentieth-century Australian planning and urban history as well as socio-historical, heritage, and popular culture issues. His authored and edited books include *The Alert Grey Twinkling Eyes of C.J. DeGaris* (2022),

Urban Australia and Post-Punk (co-edited with Sophie Perillo, 2020), *Trendyville* (co-authored with Renate Howe and Graeme Davison, 2014), and *The Bogan Delusion* (2011).

Hal Pawson is Professor of Housing Research and Policy at the University of New South Wales. He retains an Honorary Professor position at Heriot-Watt University, Edinburgh, where he was based until 2011. He was also a managing editor of the international journal *Housing Studies* from 2019 to 2023. His latest co-authored books are *Housing Policy in Australia: A Case for System Reform* (2021) and *The Private Rental Sector in Australia: Living with Uncertainty* (2021).

Chris Pettit is Director of the City Futures Research Centre, inaugural Professor of Urban Science, and PLuS Alliance Fellow at the University of New South Wales. He is Chair of the Board of Directors for Computational Urban Planning and Urban Management. He is a member of the Planning Institute of Australia's National Plantech Working Group, the advisory board for the Centre for Data Leadership, the Committee for Sydney's Smart Cities Taskforce, and the NSW Government Expert Advisory Group for Planning Evidence and Insights. His research is focused on the use of digital tools to support evidenced-based spatial planning.

Simon Pinnegar is Professor of City Planning at the University of New South Wales. He is also an Associate Director of the City Futures Research Centre, where his research interests include strategic spatial planning, city–region dynamics, and urban renewal and regeneration. Simon was previously a senior researcher and analyst in the UK Office of the Deputy Prime Minister.

Bill Randolph FASSA is Professor at the University of New South Wales. He stepped down as director at the end of 2020. At City Futures, he undertakes research specialising in housing policy, housing markets and affordability, urban renewal, and metropolitan planning policy issues. Bill has more than 40 years' experience as a researcher of housing and urban policy issues in the academic, government, nongovernmental, and private sectors. He was the inaugural convenor of the State of Australian Cities conference series and chair of the 2003 State of Australian Cities Conference.

Fatemeh Shahani is a Senior Strategic Planner at Darebin City Council in Melbourne and an Adjunct Research Fellow in urban sustainability and transition studies in the Centre for Urban Transitions, Swinburne

University of Technology, Melbourne. She holds a PhD in urban planning from La Trobe University and has experience in interdisciplinary areas such as policymaking, strategic planning, and urban sustainability.

Pranita Shrestha is a Postdoctoral Research Associate at the School of Architecture, Design and Planning at the University of Sydney. She is an urban planner and architect whose research focuses on housing affordability, informal housing markets, local rights-based heritage conservation, sustainable development, climate change, and disaster risk management. She has worked on several research projects in Europe, Asia, Africa, and Australia, funded by government and nongovernmental organisations and the Australian Research Council.

Peter Spearritt FAASA is an Emeritus Professor of History at the University of Queensland. He undertook his doctoral studies in the Urban Research Unit at The Australian National University. His book *Sydney's Century* (2000) won the NSW Premier's prize. His latest book is *Where History Happened: The Hidden Past of Australia's Towns and Places* (2018). He is a co-author of *Cities in a Sunburnt Country* (2022), drawing on an Australian Research Council Discovery project on the history and futures of capital city water supplies.

Marcus Spiller is Principal and Partner of SGS Economics & Planning and Associate Professor (Honorary) at the University of Melbourne. He has written extensively on housing policy, urban infrastructure funding, and intergovernmental relationships in the planning process. His books include *Australia's Metropolitan Imperative: An Agenda for Governance Reform* (with Richard Tomlinson, 2018) and *Urban Infrastructure: Finance and Management* (with Kath Wellman, 2012). Marcus co-founded SGS more than 30 years ago. It is an employee-owned company that publishes independent research in conjunction with its consulting work.

Wendy Steele is Professor of Sustainability and Urban Policy and leads the Critical Urban Governance research program in the Centre for Urban Research, RMIT University, Melbourne. Her recent books include *Planning Wild Cities: Human–Nature Relationships in the Urban Age* (2020), *Quiet Activism: Climate Action at the Local Scale* (2021), and *The Sustainable Development Goals and Higher Education: A Transformative Agenda?* (2021). She was a chair of the 2021 State of Australasian Cities Conference and President of the Australasian Cities Research Network.

Frank Stilwell FASSA is Professor Emeritus in Political Economy at the University of Sydney, where he began teaching in 1970. He is the author of 12 books on cities and regions, economic policy, and other issues in political economy, including *The Political Economy of Inequality* (2019). He has co-edited eight other books and, for the past 30 years, has been the coordinating editor of the *Journal of Australian Political Economy*.

Helen Sullivan is Professor and Dean of the College of Asia and the Pacific at The Australian National University. She is a public policy scholar whose work explores the nature of state–society relationships and their interaction with public policy systems. She is a Fellow of the Higher Education Academy, National Fellow of the Institute of Public Administration Australia, and past president of the Australian Political Studies Association.

Elizabeth Taylor is a Senior Lecturer in Urban Planning and Design at Monash University, Melbourne. Often using spatial and historical perspectives, her research develops understanding of long-term urban change and the role of policy settings in it. She is the author of *Dry Zones: Planning and the Hangovers of Liquor Licensing History* (2018). Her research interests include carparking policies, Australia's new city projects, and approaches to industrial land.

Elnaz Torabi is an adjunct member of Griffith University's Cities Research Institute. She has a background in architecture and urban and environmental planning research and practice. Her research explores urban resilience and adaptation to climate change in coastal cities. She has experience in integrated and adaptive infrastructure planning and climate change adaptation in local and state governments and is interested in water-resilient cities, strategic planning, and decision-making processes under deep uncertainty.

Laurence Troy is Senior Lecturer in Urbanism in the School of Architecture, Design and Planning at the University of Sydney. His research focus is on the relationship between precarious employment, housing, and citizenship, and the implications for patterns of urban settlement. Laurence's wider research focuses on urban renewal, the governance of urban change, the role of the higher-density multi-unit residential development sector in Australia in driving urban change, and funding models for social affordable housing.

Alexei Trundle is Associate Director (International) of the Melbourne Centre for Cities and is the Melbourne Postdoctoral Fellow for the University of Melbourne's Faculty of Architecture, Building and Planning.

He has a research background in urban climate change adaptation, with an interest in the application of climate-resilient development initiatives in Pacific Island cities. Since mid-2020, he has been chief investigator in a partnership with the City of Melbourne that is embedding the UN Sustainable Development Goals within the city's strategic planning framework. Alexei is also a scientific advisor to the UN Human Settlement Programme (UN-Habitat) in the Pacific.

Megan Weier is a Senior Research Fellow at the Centre for Social Impact at the University of New South Wales. Her work critically engages with ideas around measuring social progress, wellbeing, and program evaluation. She led the design and calculation of the first Australian Social Progress Index, and has worked with local and state governments to create metrics that help communities make decisions based on priority and equity considerations.

Ed Wensing FPIA (Life Fellow) FHEA is Honorary Research Fellow in the Centre for Aboriginal Economic Policy Research at The Australian National University, a City Futures Research Centre Fellow at the University of New South Wales, and Associate and Special Adviser with SGS Economics & Planning. An experienced planner, policy analyst, and academic, he has worked in government, the private and nongovernmental sectors, professional associations, and six Australian universities. His current research interests are in the intercultural contact zone between Indigenous peoples' rights and interests and the Crown's land tenures and land-use planning and environmental management systems.

Part 1: Introductory

1

Whither Australian urban policy?

Robert Freestone, Bill Randolph,
and Wendy Steele

Introduction

This book explores in overview the achievements, failures, and challenges of an assemblage of public policy areas unified by their urban context. It comes at a time when Australia must take seriously the prospects and implications of long-term population growth and development in economic, social, and environmental terms. This collection offers new ideas that challenge the established orthodoxy around Australian urban policy. Much evidence to date points to national initiatives lacking coherent responses to pressing concerns, with housing affordability, congestion, climate mitigation and adaptation, and social inclusion being prominent examples. Instead, political ideology, theoretical orthodoxy, and practical expediency too often seem to drive policy formulation. In this introduction, we establish the broad scope of erstwhile and projected urban policies, the evolution of thinking about urban policy, the enterprise that spawned this volume and its organisation, an intellectual debt, and the imperative of transcending business-as-usual thinking as we move into an uncertain future.

Rising to the urban policy question

Cities and urban regions may not obviously be an ascendant political priority in Australia at present, but they are the focus of diverse policies, procedures, and practices. Australia's 21 largest cities are where most of the population lives, generate some 80 per cent of national gross domestic product (GDP), and serve as international hubs for global exchange. In the early twenty-first century, Australian cities and regional towns are thus firmly on the public policy agenda, although not always in coherent, direct, and integrated ways.

For such an urbanised country, the lack of an explicit national urban policy focus is an outlier in the global context. Australian state and territory governments have recognised the nexus between urban development and nation-building since at least the 1940s. In contrast, Commonwealth Government engagement has been more equivocal and episodic in that period. But both left and right-of-centre political parties have expressed and acted on shifting imperatives for housing, environmental quality, employment, and infrastructure, particularly transport, in metropolitan settings. At the same time, private and community sector aspirations are now driving new directives designed to reshape and rescale the Australian 'urban nation' and its many discontents.

In many ways, the complexity and interconnectedness of urban-based challenges, together with the multi-scaled and often politically fractured governance framework in which such policy is determined, work against a unified response. This is compounded by a perception that 'urban' includes virtually all human activities at some scale and therefore does not need its own policy framework. Painter (1979) posited the 'impossibility' of urban policy on these grounds more than four decades ago. While the ambit and rationale of an Australian 'urban' policy are debated, there is little disagreement that in practice urban centres and major-city regions, in particular, have distinctive jurisdictional, economic, environmental, and cultural settings that warrant explicit recognition and attention. There have been numerous reports, inquiries, and manifestos involving government agencies, think tanks, and lobby groups that have underscored the critical importance of governments, and notably the Commonwealth Government, in factoring urbanisation and urbanism into policy matrices. And there has been no shortage of advice to government from researchers, professional bodies, think tanks, and industry groups across many specialised subfields and disciplines on specifically urban issues.

The degree to which academic research directly shapes the policy matrix is highly contingent on circumstance, despite urban studies being a constant preoccupation since at least the 1960s. The importance of evidence-based policy formulations remains widely accepted, if too often eschewed, by governments. However, there is also growing recognition that the transition to more sustainable futures for our city regions will require very different pathways to those that have come before. The challenge for the urban research–policy nexus is to shift the path dependency that is characteristic of so much urban policymaking and that is no longer 'fit for purpose' in the current climate of rapid and unpredictable change. This shift to evidence-*informed* policy builds in the need for creative disruption and experimentation as well as innovation to address societal challenges within the context of a deeply uncertain future.

The agenda for urban policy viewed at a national scale highlights many issues of concern. Without overreaching the definition of 'the urban', the need to recalibrate, re-engineer, and rethink policies is now apparent in many ways. Here is a partial list:

- Coping with the demonstrable, escalating, and unpredictable impacts of climate change.
- The increasing scale and complexity of Australia's major urban regions.
- Engaging with the ongoing struggle for truth, justice, and self-determination for Indigenous Australians.
- Struggles with the affordability of housing, supply of social housing, and homelessness.
- Contradictory transport planning, with motorway-led solutions remaining prominent.
- Accommodating fluctuating demographic trends and pressures, including immigration and internal migration in favour of regional areas.
- Erosion of greenspace and mounting pressure in parklands with urban intensification.
- Challenges to participatory, partnership, and collaborative governance.
- Entrenched issues of social inequality and marginalisation.
- Managing increasing density and complex urban renewal challenges across metropolitan areas.
- The problems of financing urban infrastructure and value capture.

- Shifting employment and labour market conditions.
- The balancing of development aspirations and ecological constraints.
- The limitations of traditional metropolitan planning frameworks.
- The resistance of the community and industry to reducing energy usage.
- The implications and challenges of 'smart city' thinking and technology.
- The lack of firm normative direction regarding a national settlement strategy.

Perhaps underlying this long-term failure to develop a coherent urban policy perspective is the fundamental fracture in the federal policy domain, which is constitutionally constrained and often politically unwilling to directly engage with urban-scale matters. Yet, it is this federal scale that is ultimately responsible for many of the policy decisions that impact our city regions and the state and territory policy domains that shoulder responsibility for managing the urban scale. Given this fragmentation of responsibilities, coupled with an overarching political consensus over the past 30 years that markets, not governments, are best placed to adjudicate economic and societal outcomes, it is not surprising that the urban policy realm has languished relative to other priority areas such as infrastructure.

So, as the Australian nation enters the third decade of the twenty-first century, and taking an overarching continental view, it is timely to consider what has been achieved by urban policy, where gaps and shortfalls exist in the policy matrix, and the needs and prospects for the future. Based on this triumvirate, three expansive questions are thus posed in this book:

- First, what has been delivered in demonstrably value-adding ways to enhance the prospects for productive, sustainable, and liveable cites?
- Second, what aspirations have fallen short or produced counterintuitive outcomes because of governance, financial, and political reasons?
- And third, and arguably most importantly, what can be identified as matters of emergent concern in both challenging existing and devising new policy settings to address the quality of life of Australian city regions into the mid to late twenty-first century?

There is a layering of past, present, and forthcoming in these areas of focus but the ultimate orientation is looking ahead to the nature, prioritisation, and interdependence of urban policies within a national framework that are equitable, sustainable, regenerative, and focused on a flourishing public realm.

Urban policy works at both integrative and sectoral levels. Given the complexity of the urban problematic and the crosscutting nature of urban issues—evident in the interdisciplinary range of contributions that follow— no review can be either exhaustive or definitive. But a diversity of policy approaches and initiatives, at times and in places interconnecting, must be reviewed to ensure the breadth of coverage captures the multidimensional nature of Australian city life. We are primarily interested in policy through a national lens, certainly, but also in problems expressed nationally and calling forth responses singly and cooperatively from other actors, states, local authorities, the private sector, and not-for-profit and community groups, as well as enhancing an interconnective 'line of sight' between them.

Looking back, looking forward

A Keynesian policy framework favouring 'big government' involvement in diverse social and economic policies defined the postwar reconstruction era that produced the 1945 Commonwealth–State Housing Agreement allied to urban planning obligations for the states. From the mid-1960s, Gough Whitlam, as leader of the federal opposition, steadily built a political and popular case for Commonwealth intervention to improve the efficiency and equity of urban development processes. At this time, Canberra, as designed and developed under the jurisdiction of the powerful National Capital Development Commission, became something of a national model city. William McMahon's Liberal government temporarily stole some of Labor's thunder with the launch of a National Urban and Regional Development Authority shortly before the federal election in 1972 that swept the Australian Labor Party (ALP) to power for the first time in more than two decades. Its urban agenda had electoral appeal and the subsequent establishment of the Department of Urban and Regional Development (DURD) marked a major pivot in the recognition that Australia was largely defined by its major urban areas and needed a policy framework, backed by ministerial heft.

In the event, the promise of DURD, and with it a national acceptance that Australia was essentially an urban nation, was short-lived. Over subsequent decades, federal engagement with cities policy has come and gone following the political inclinations of succeeding governments. Whitlam's major focus in 1972–75 was essentially on *'equitable cities'*. After a 15-year hiatus in which urban policy was largely sidelined, from 1991 to 1996, the Hawke–Keating governments revived an explicit dimension to public policy in a project-driven commitment to cross-governmental partnerships for the building of *'better cities'*. This avoided the more politically contentious issue of equity and pointed more towards technocratic and administrative innovation, capturing the rise of 'small government' neoliberalism.

In the following decade, the succeeding conservative government largely eschewed any explicit urban policy, leaving issues to the market and the states to manage. A return to intervention in urban matters resurfaced in the Rudd–Gillard Labor governments. They entrusted their *'triple bottom line* cities' urban policy, entitled *Our Cities, Our Future* (2011)—the first truly badged national urban policy, introduced by minister Anthony Albanese—to the Major Cities Unit (MCU) from 2008 to 2013, with a shift towards major infrastructure investment as an urban policy driver. The MCU was disbanded quickly after the return of a determinedly conservative government in 2011. However, between 2016 and 2022, the conservative Turnbull and Morrison governments more selectively focused on *'smart cities'* and infrastructure projects with a private–public partnership focus.

In an address to the *Australian Financial Review*'s Business Summit on 10 March 2021, then opposition leader Albanese stated that 'cities policy has been one of the abiding passions of my time in public life' and outlined six possible measures to 're-create cities policy in the wake of the [Covid-19] pandemic and the recession'—namely:

1. Deliver a new national urban policy framework.
2. Transform City Deals into genuine city partnerships.
3. Revitalise central business districts (CBDs).
4. Renew the independent role of Infrastructure Australia in urban planning.
5. Publish an annual state of the cities report.
6. Give local government a meaningful voice in national Cabinet.

There are slightly different versions of this 'joined-up vision' in the public domain, including on the ALP's policy page (ALP 2022). A spokesperson for the ALP's 2022 election manifesto, Giles (2022) provided a third version, which deletes the reference to CBDs, clarifies Infrastructure Australia as host of a new Australian Cities and Suburbs Unit (mentioned by Albanese), and proposes establishment of an 'Urban Policy Forum'. In the same month as Albanese's 2021 speech, the ALP met to determine its national platform ahead of the next federal election. The strongest single statement on cities related to public transport:

> Labor will build on the proud record of past Labor Governments which led a national effort to make our cities more productive, liveable and sustainable. We will ensure modern urban and transport planning practices, urban sustainability, and technology underpin all government investment decisions' including high-speed rail. (ALP 2021: 11)

Beyond these intentions, references are more scattered but link cities to other policy commitments addressing manufacturing jobs, water scarcity, and creating a low-emissions economy.

The election in March 2022 returned a Labor federal government under the prime ministership of Albanese. Fourteen months later, the Albanese government's second budget, in May 2023, finally confirmed movement in the urban policy space. It picked up some of the earlier promised elements including a new cities and suburbs unit, resurrecting state of the cities reporting, and new financial commitments for place-based infrastructure (Wiggins 2023).

Whatever the exact contours of the national urban policy that emerges, the past iterations reflect the mood and political realities of respective federal governments and their times. But the significance of cities and urban regions in national life has been regularly reaffirmed at the highest level through a succession of parliamentary committee and expert reports, reviews, statements, and guidelines that have striven towards more effective policy instruments for constructive intervention in market-driven urbanisation processes. Coordination with Australia's major urban governments, the states, and territories has been a major concern, particularly around infrastructure delivery.

The seeming fragility of national urban policy has, with a few notable and limited exceptions, been a consistent feature of the Australian policy context. The power of local politics has managed to obscure the basic fact that Australia was an urban nation long before much of the rest of the world caught up with what is now the defining feature of the global twenty-first century: mass urbanisation. Despite the prominence of national urban policies as key instruments for sustainable, liveable, and productive urban regions in various international frameworks of the United Nations and the Organisation for Economic Co-operation and Development (OECD), Australia has largely left the issue of how our urban systems should be best governed and the management strategies under which they need to flourish to the ever-changing predilections of successive state and territory governments. The states continue to offer shifting visions of possible urban futures based at least in part on local political expediencies and rivalries. Not surprisingly, the neoliberal turn has meant that much of what happens in our cities and towns has little to do with coherent policy per se, but a lot to do with facilitating the 'hidden hand' of the market and adapting to local pragmatic political sensibilities.

It is timely, therefore, to return to this fundamental issue at a time when the Australian urban system has gone through the almost existential shock of the Covid-19 pandemic that has threatened at times from 2020 to 2022 to derail—or at least recalibrate—the Australian urban prospect (Baum et al. 2022). At the height of the pandemic, with empty CBDs and an apparent flood of migrants to seachange and treechange towns, together with a collapse of the key driver of Australia's urban growth, international migration, it seemed as though the agglomeration attractions of our biggest cities might be due for a major reset. In the event, the rumours of the death of the city may have been premature, and the much-vaunted benefits of city living and ever greater urban density may not have completely lost their shine. But there could be a different mindset about their magnetism, as well as their capacity to survive, let alone thrive, in the post-Covid world that is increasingly impacted by the escalating climate emergency (Norman 2022).

The deeply embedded legacy issues—congestion, poor intraurban connectivity and car dependency, pollution, development pressures, unaffordable housing, emerging climate challenges, migration pressures, spatial employment mismatches, and growing urban inequality, among others—are still to be dealt with. All these are undergirded by a growing national consciousness of the legacy of settler-colonial development and the creation of Australian cities on unceded Indigenous land. Pathways to a more sustainable future will require considered and integrated approaches that will inevitably recall questions of equity as well as ecological integrity alongside the economies and diseconomies of agglomeration and productive efficiency.

On the other hand, despite talk about promoting a 'green Covid recovery', which would shift urban form and function towards a more sustainable climate-neutral setting, there are few signs this is happening at scale. Property markets have surged ahead, supported by short-term demand boosters (the 'traditional' policy response to economic downturns). CBDs appear to be hanging on to at least a good proportion of their workers, although the return to work has been hesitant in those sectors that have the choice to adopt new working practices. Hankering for the 'good old days' to return may not be unrealistic, but with them could come old policy settings and perspectives that are likely to prove inappropriate to new urban dynamics and pressures.

Given other distractions, there is every risk that government policy may seek to re-establish the status quo rather than think outside the box and set new policy directions that would impact on the path-dependent urban settings we had at the outset of the pandemic. The editors of and contributors to this volume are of the opinion that such a retreat to business as usual would be a major lost opportunity. The development of a coherent and integrated national urban policy framework, especially in relation to climate change, could be part of that opportunity. While many of the concerns discussed in individual chapters necessarily focus on state and local issues, there is every reason to look to Canberra for some form of national leadership on our cities and towns. This is not from some displaced nostalgia for long-past policy initiatives, but because the urban realm is such a central part of Australian national life. This collection provides some ideas for advancing rather than retreating.

The Australian urban policy workshop and its predecessors

This book had its origins in a workshop on 26–27 August 2021 held under the auspices of the Academy of Social Sciences in Australia (ASSA) and supported by the City Futures Research Centre at the University of New South Wales (UNSW) and the Centre for Urban Research at RMIT

University, Melbourne. The rationale was to offer a multi-voice, cross-disciplinary, policy-orientated, and nongovernmental forum on Australian urban policy. That sounds bespoke but, taking a longer view, a book like this is not without precedents.

There are many reminders of previous similar steps at the interface between academic research and urban policy. The first truly national conference capturing the interdisciplinary flavour of the emergent field of urban studies with presentations picking up on a variety of policy issues and implications was 'The Metropolis in Australia' in 1964. This was organised by the Social Sciences Research Council (SSRC, the predecessor of the ASSA) and held at The Australian National University (ANU). Noel Butlin appears to have been the prime mover and among the speakers were Max Neutze on transport, Mick Borrie on demographic trends, John Bayly on planning, Malcolm Hill on housing, and Ruth Atkins on urban government.

This pivotal event had two major consequences. First, it solidified a partnership between the SSRC and the Australian Planning Institute to establish a new council for urban affairs with a brief to promote 'awareness of urban problems and the possible contribution of research and education towards these problems'. This happened two years later with the establishment of the Australian Institute of Urban Studies. Second, it sowed the seed for the ANU Urban Research Unit/Program, which continued an annual series of urbanisation seminars for some years and by force of example begat similarly titled programs in other universities, although it was itself controversially terminated (Troy 1997).

Other notable events followed to establish a national mandate for urban research (Freestone et al. 2017). Thinking specifically of precedents for our venture, these include the Australian Institute of Political Science Summer School on 'Australian Cities: Chaos or Planned Growth' in Canberra in 1966 (Wilkes 1966); 'Toward Cities of the Twenty First Century', a 1970 joint venture between the Royal Australian Planning Institute, Royal Australian Institute of Architects, and Australian Institute of Landscape Architects (Canberra Forum 1970); the various conferences on urban strategies for Australia organised by the Australian Institute of Urban Studies in its heyday; and, into the twenty-first century, the Urban 45 summit on 'New Ideas for Australian Cities' held in Melbourne in 2007 (Atkinson et al. 2007), and Future Earth's 10-year urban strategy for sustainable development (O'Donnell et al. 2019). What was unusual in the 1960s and 1970s has become more commonplace, with countless workshops, seminars, and conferences sponsored by professional, industry, and research institutes, and nongovernmental organisations over the years. The flagship series remains the State of Australasian Cities conferences, held biennially since 2003 (most recently in Melbourne in 2021 and Wellington in 2023), with papers archived by the Analysis and Policy Observatory (APO 2022).

Publications have flowed from these gatherings and related initiatives to produce a rich and varied literature with no shortage of policy analyses and future scenarios. The present volume is just the latest in a procession of urban policy discourses. It captures the same valuation of research-driven expertise to disaggregate the complexity of contemporary and forward-looking urban problems into a set of meaningful targets and at the same time reassemble them into more than the sum of the parts. The greatest lesson from the interconnected cultures of urban research and policy since the 1960s is the need for informed, critical, and sustained dialogue that spans both disciplines and sectors.

While the perspectives informed by half a century of Australian urban scholarship are important, the need for new ideas about our changing urban system remains a pressing one. The chapters in this book are a showcase of both established and younger scholars who have taken up the challenge of undertaking research and developing policies that could guide and shape our cities and towns to make them a better fit for the challenges of the twenty-first century and beyond. Importantly, the chapters exhibit a wide range of perspectives, from a technocratic and/or objective professional policy and planning emphasis, to those advocating for increased democratic forums that foster community-centred deliberations on urban policy priorities and development. The editors would argue that this contrast enriches the potential areas for debate and the overall need for higher-level leadership within a transparent and consultative approach to address contested urban challenges.

So, what began as an earnest roundtable in the ASSA tradition of invited social science experts reflecting on future directions for urban policy in Australia has spawned a bigger and more public outcome. Facilitated by the online environment in which the workshop had to be conducted during the pandemic, the contributors grew in number and diversity to produce a spirited set of very individual contributions. Collectively, the contents represent an extensive stocktake of progress, with challenges to the status quo and ways forward opening on many fronts.

Structure of this book

The contributors include some of Australia's leading social scientists, academic thought leaders in urban policy, emerging urban scholars, and applied researchers and policy professionals active at the interface of academia and policy. Senior authors, early career researchers, and higher-degree research students are co-collaborators. The result is an extensive author list with an equal gender split and a spectrum of experience and expertise guaranteeing a distinctive set of outputs. Beyond their bearing in mind the three main questions articulated earlier (achievements, failures, challenges) and at a time when the pandemic was raising questions about long-term urban futures, contributors were given free rein to present their distinctive perspectives. The chapters reflect this, ranging from those with a specific policy focus to more open and reflective discussions of urban issues and policy implications at different scales.

There are 21 core chapters, variously singly and multi-authored. They are bookended by this introductory chapter and a short closing essay that attempts to pull together some of the key ideas that surface across the chapters. This introduction to the volume is followed immediately by two contributions cast as scene-setting. From a public policy perspective and ahead of diving more deeply into substantive topic areas, Hayley Henderson and Helen Sullivan present a typology of 'short-term' and 'long-term' alliances between urban researchers and policymakers. They explore the constraints on and opportunities for more effective and enduring partnerships, highlighting the different forms of research evidence that must inform policy. Reviewing history from the mid-2010s to 2020, Jago Dodson provides a policy narrative of initiatives at the Commonwealth level and reports an ongoing commitment—albeit a wavering one encased within the governance of federalism that ultimately devolves implementation to state and territory governments. Beyond this, the book is organised into five main sections providing a measure of thematic cohesion without denoting mutual exclusivity.

Sustainability, the environment, and conservation

First up is a quartet of papers focused primarily on environmental issues that ultimately inform many of the more functional matters subsequently discussed. Elnaz Torabi and Stephen Dovers tackle climate change—the primary existential crisis of our age. The accent here is on multi-scalar and jurisdictional processes of adaptation, highlighting the need for action over and beyond the limited 2015 National Climate Resilience and Adaptation Strategy. Similarly concerned with establishing a holistic multilateral response to the spectrum of environmental challenges, Alexei Trundle and Brendan Gleeson resist invention of a new set of targets in favour of adopting the United Nations' Sustainable Development Goals as an inclusive, readymade scaffold linking intranational capacity-building with international obligations. The next two chapters examine specific issues. Peter Spearritt considers the urgency of reducing reticulated water consumption on the world's driest inhabited continent through a mix of pricing and traditional harvesting initiatives. James Lesh articulates a key nexus between urban heritage and sustainability that is hampered by a leadership vacuum at the national government level.

Population, settlement, and urban form

The next section groups together contributions dealing with population distribution, spatial structure, and urban form. Amanda Davies applies a demographic lens to review recent national growth and relocation trends as a backdrop to any future population strategy and folds in the uncertain legacies of counter-urbanisation under Covid-19. Victoria Kolankiewicz, Elizabeth Taylor, and David Nichols also speculate on Covid's impact on regional settlement in a deeper historical dive into the prospects for more committed urban decentralisation policies. Simon Pinnegar takes us inside the big cities to reveal that urban renewal is better caricatured as developer-driven orthodoxy than a nuanced approach responsive to any fully formed urban policy. The implementation of the same density uplift is similarly critiqued by Hazel Easthope and Sophie-May Kerr, who make several recommendations to better realise the economic, environmental, and quality-of-life returns promised by compact city goals. Julian Bolleter, Nicole Edwards, and Paula Hooper canvass related issues in more traditional suburban settings and argue that a creative policy mix can simultaneously address issues of density, health, wellbeing, and effective greenspace provision.

Productivity and infrastructure

Economic development ('jobs and growth') has become a pervasive planning preoccupation, with the 'infrastructure turn' a major fixture of urban policy at all scales. In the first of two chapters in a section dealing with these issues, Chris Pettit and Alessandra Buxton take us inside the 'smart cities' bubble and the new technical armoury of 'datafication'. With a theme of national interest straddling the Morrison and Albanese governments, the expectation is for more sophisticated data analysis to better underpin urban policymaking for cities and suburbs. Marcus Spiller investigates approaches to funding urban infrastructure and the often-problematic outcomes when the Commonwealth Government wields its financial power to intervene directly in what should be state-driven projects. Recommendations are made for a more rational engagement according to the principles of subsidiarity.

Justice and wellbeing

Social and equity dimensions of urban life are considered explicitly in the five chapters in the next section, which turns from productivity to justice and wellbeing. With some 80 per cent of Indigenous Australians being urban-dwellers, Ed Wensing and Matthew Kelly call for a new space for negotiating the divide evident in urban land-use planning between Eurocentric and Aboriginal and Torres Strait Islander notions of property custodianship. Sensitive to both the data–policy nexus and the desirability of linking domestic benchmarks to international standards, as discussed in earlier chapters, Megan Weier and Kristy Muir advocate for a spatially granulated index of social progress to evaluate success in urban development. Housing stress is a major issue in that regard and the focus of the next three chapters. Laurence Troy identifies the historical turnaround in the fortunes of many outer suburbs, from bastions of homeownership delivering income security to increasingly precarious environments buffeted by shifting labour markets and a growing dependency on private rental housing. Hal Pawson and Vivienne Milligan call for a proper national housing policy leveraging the financial clout of the Commonwealth into strategic leadership to mitigate dysfunctionality and inequity. Nicole Gurran and Pranita Shrestha also portray a housing system in crisis, in the process absolving planning systems of the major blame apportioned by neoliberal critiques. They draw on lessons from the Covid-19 pandemic to identify several pathways towards a whole-of-system reform agenda.

Transitional needs and challenges

The final group of chapters could have been tagged to earlier sections but are separated here because they share a collective endorsement of a forward-looking theme that surfaces elsewhere—that is, collaborative transition planning around enlightened governance towards better urban futures. Setting their argument within the field of transport planning, but more broadly echoing a wider disenchantment with status quo policy processes, Crystal Legacy and Rebecca Clements approach the research–policy nexus with a paradigm-shifting call for a more partisan and inclusive challenge to technocratic orthodoxy. Niki Frantzeskaki, Peter Newton, and Fatemeh Shahani posit the three pathways of lifestyle changes, innovative infrastructure, and institutional reform in making a more decisive transition to low-carbon cities. In the final topic chapter, Frank Stilwell returns to the historical narrative of national urban policy as an instructive prelude to his vision of an Australian transition to a 'Green New Deal' that ties together some of the key issues highlighted in earlier chapters: equity, Indigenous knowledge and rights, a people's voice, housing reform, and sustainability. Our concluding chapter picks up on some of the same interdependencies that must underpin a regenerative and transformative urban policy agenda. Working collaboratively and across disciplines at the research–policy interface is critical to generating value where needed as part of the democratic process.

A 'light on the hill'

This volume has been inspired by the example of the late Emeritus Professor Patrick Troy AC (Macintyre 2000). He expended much energy and summoned considerable enthusiasm in attempting to understand complex urban challenges and promote coherent policy solutions. From his ANU base, Pat pushed, prodded, and cajoled often recalcitrant and unyielding policymakers and their political masters to take seriously our cities and the people who live and work in them. He also mentored, supported, and actively encouraged a generation of new urban researchers to take seriously the equity implications of cities and the role of urban policy. Several of the contributors to this book directly acknowledge the influence of his thinking about urban policy.

Ed Wensing, one of Pat's many fellow travellers, recalls Pat as a '"light on the hill" when it came to championing sound, evidence-based public policy on housing, infrastructure, transport, urban planning and development, and energy and water consumption' (Wensing 2018). He died in harness still plotting various books. One, with David Wilmoth, was set to explore six major public policy issues: housing, water supply, transport, inequality, education, and 'the poverty of planning'. These books will not happen, but this volume takes up the same challenge of multifaceted meanings of the urban policy imperative.

Indeed, reflecting Pat's all-encompassing interests, the contributions in this volume present a broad canvas of issues and ideas. As a result, taken superficially, it could be accused of incoherence, offering a mere smorgasbord of issues rather than attempting an integration for which we have implicitly called. We would argue that being broad in scope does not imply incoherence. Rather, the contributions are meant to highlight the range of interconnected issues that surface in urban contexts and need equally interconnected—'joined-up', in the jargon—policy responses. Moreover, the contributions are not equally weighted building blocks that would accumulate to a single holistic urban policy framework but reflect facets of the complex and fluid policy responses that would be needed in such an enterprise.

The workshop from which this book arose was based in no small way on Pat's modus operandi at ANU: bringing together thought leaders in policy-related fields to discuss and develop agendas and responses to urban problems that question orthodoxies underpinning current policy settings. He would undoubtedly have been an enthusiastic supporter of this initiative without ever thinking it was the last word; this is our position as well.

A dialogue on new directions

This book presents a range of informed views that point to the need for a new kind of urban policy framework for Australia, fit for the challenges of the twenty-first century and for Australian cities. Covid-19 may have started to shift the thinking on these issues. This collection aims to give this shift further traction. We hope it will act to challenge policymakers to start thinking outside the current policy box and to challenge voices who currently 'own' the ideas about cities and generate the 'evidence' on which much policy has been based, most of which is underwritten by quite explicit market sensibilities. The scope is topically wide-ranging, as now Prime Minister Anthony Albanese captured in 2021:

Cities policy embraces all the domains that affect prosperity and quality of life in our towns and cities—transport and infrastructure; housing; urban planning; economic development; industry and innovation policy; business and commerce; education, skills and training; policing and law enforcement; healthcare and social welfare. (Albanese 2021)

This book is neither a definitive manifesto nor a comprehensive blueprint, but rather a compendium of policy analyses, reviews, and prescriptions offered as a contribution to a continuing dialogue on the urban dimensions of public policy at a national level. We trust those in a position to frame future urban policies will respond positively to the findings in this volume to envisage truly transformational pathways to better equip Australia's urban places for the complex challenges that lie ahead. The development of the Albanese Labor Government's urban policy commitments given substance in the 2023 budget will be a central focus with the avowed intent to 'work with policy experts to develop "a vision for urban areas"' (Wiggins 2023).

References

Albanese, A. 2021. 'The Future of Our Cities.' Address to the Australian Financial Review's Business Summit 2021, Sydney, 10 March. Available from: anthonyalbanese.com.au/media-centre/the-future-of-our-cities-10-march-2021.

Analysis and Policy Observatory (APO). 2022. *Proceedings: 10th State of Australasian Cities National Conference, 1–3 December 2021*. Melbourne: APO. Available from: apo.org.au/search-apo/soac.

Atkinson, R., T. Dalton, B. Norman, and G. Wood, eds. 2007. *Urban 45: New Ideas for Australia's Cities*. Melbourne: RMIT University.

Australian Labor Party (ALP). 2021. *ALP National Platform: As Adopted at the 2021 Special Platform Conference*. March. Sydney: ALP. Available from: www.alp.org. au/about/national-platform/.

Australian Labor Party (ALP). 2022. *More Liveable Cities and Suburbs*. Sydney: ALP. Available from: www.alp.org.au/policies/more-livable-cities [page discontinued].

Baum, S., E. Baker, A. Davies, J. Stone, and E. Taylor. 2022. *Pandemic Cities: The COVID-19 Crisis and Australian Urban Regions*. Singapore: Springer. doi.org/ 10.1007/978-981-19-5884-7.

Canberra Forum. 1970. *Toward Cities of the Twenty-First Century. Proceedings of the Canberra Forum, 23–30 May 1970*. Canberra: Canberra Forum.

Department of Infrastructure, Transport, Regional Development, Communications and the Arts. 2022. *Corporate Plan 2022–2023.* Canberra: Commonwealth of Australia. Available from: www.infrastructure.gov.au/about-us/corporate-reporting/2022-23-corporate-plan.

Freestone, R., B. Randolph, and A. Wheeler. 2017. 'Defining and Refining the Research Agenda for Australian Cities.' In *A Research Agenda for Cities*, edited by J.R. Short, 249–65. London: Edward Elgar. doi.org/10.4337/9781785363429.00029.

Giles, A. 2022. 'National Urban Policy: ALP Statement.' *Urban Policy and Research* 40(3): 262–65. doi.org/10.1080/08111146.2022.2076828.

Macintyre, S. 2000. 'Patrick Troy: Public Good and the Intellectual.' *Urban Policy and Research* 18(2): 145–57. doi.org/10.1080/08111140008727829.

Norman, B. 2022. *Urban Planning for Climate Change.* London: Routledge.

O'Donnell, T., B. Webb, K. Auty, C. Ryan, E. Robson, M. Stafford Smith, and J. Dodson. 2019. *Sustainable Cities and Regions: 10 Year Strategy to Enable Urban Systems Transformation.* Canberra: Future Earth Australia, Australian Academy of Science.

Painter, M. 1979. 'Urban Government, Urban Politics and the Fabrication of Urban Issues: The Impossibility of Urban Policy.' *Australian Journal of Public Administration* 38(4): 335–46. doi.org/10.1111/j.1467-8500.1979.tb00877.x.

Troy, P.N. 1997. *The Urban Research Program 1966–1996.* Canberra: Urban Research Program, Research School of Social Sciences, The Australian National University.

Wensing, E. 2018. 'Memories and Condolences: Patrick Troy.' *The Canberra Times*, [Online]. Available from: www.legacy.com/amp/obituaries/canberratimes-au/189720836.

Wiggins, J. 2023. 'City Dwellers Promised "Thriving Suburbs" Under New Urban Policy.' *Australian Financial Review*, 10 May: B15.

Wilkes, J., ed. 1966. *Australian Cities: Chaos or Planned Growth?* Sydney: Angus & Robertson.

2

Uneasy bedfellows: Integrating urban research and policymaking in Australia

Hayley Henderson and Helen Sullivan[1]

Introduction

This chapter examines the urban research–policy nexus in Australia. It identifies why urban research and policymaking have made for uneasy bedfellows. The troubled relationship between the two is a longstanding area of debate globally and studies suggest that, while interest and imperatives exist for enhanced integration, operationalising it is fraught with doubts and obstacles (for example, Troy 2013; Hurley and Taylor 2016). This chapter suggests opportunities for better integration in the future.

The chapter begins with a brief assessment of *why* urban research should be integrated into policymaking. It then synthesises the main points of tension and barriers that exist in linking with urban research. Finally, it examines ways in which urban research is linked to practice in contemporary Australia and considers potential pathways for more deeply embedding these. Throughout, we acknowledge the challenge posed to both researchers and policy practitioners by the multifaceted idea of 'the urban', and account for this in our proposals for the future.

---

1   We would like to thank our colleagues Dr Kirsty Jones and Dr Ruth O'Connor for their thoughtful comments on an earlier draft of this chapter.

Why should urban research and policymaking be better integrated?

The relationship between academic researchers and policymakers is a perennial source of debate nationally and internationally (Davoudi 2006; Head 2015; Sullivan 2021). Advocates for closing the 'science–policy gap' or developing 'evidence-based policymaking' exist on both sides of the academic–practitioner divide, as do opponents. What unites all is the acknowledgement that academic and practitioner autonomy is essential for productive engagement.

Arguably, this debate is less pronounced in urban research given researchers' interest in contributing to the future of cities and their communities and policy practitioners' willingness to seek research when building an evidence base for policymaking. This is not to say that this relationship is unproblematic. Politics and power relations influence the questions to be asked and the parties that are listened to, meaning that some questions are not asked and some parties are not heard, with harmful consequences. As Flyvbjerg (1998: 226) highlights, 'power determines what counts as knowledge, [and] what kind of interpretation attains authority as the dominant interpretation'.

This problem is evident in several areas such as sustainability research and policy (for example, Alexander and Gleeson 2019), public health research and urban planning (for example, Lowe et al. 2019), and the relationship between research and practice involving Indigenous peoples and values in cities. Regarding the last, researchers including Wensing and Porter (2016) have highlighted the troubled relationship between planning and Indigenous peoples, including the 'complicity of planning' in perpetuating colonial processes in Australian cities (Porter 2017: 556). The evidence base that supports these claims has, as Porter laments, 'barely penetrated the consciousness of the vast majority of the professional planning community in Australia … [where] the industry largely operates under a settler-colonial business-as-usual model' (2017: 556). This disregard of Indigenous peoples' rights and interests in urban planning legislation and processes is a general theme across Australian states and territories but is particularly acute in southern states. It not only affects Indigenous peoples but also diminishes planning opportunities for a sustainable urban future based on traditional knowledge and culture. While there are acute challenges in bridging the divide between research on Indigenous issues and values and the practice of planning, this divide is a recurring issue across urban research subdisciplines.

There is also a common basis for supporting a closer connection between urban research and policymaking across subdisciplines: in principle, both are concerned with improving urban environments for a range of reasons, such as enhancing liveability, supporting more equitable development, driving efficient urban systems, or improving urban sustainability and resilience, among many others. Better integration between urban research and policymaking delivers more robust evidence to support these ends. While the pathways of integration and influence between research and policy are different, examples of successful integration demonstrate improved policymaking and urban outcomes.

For example, scholars researching the social determinants of health have demonstrated how cities impact population health outcomes, as well as how to design cities to support health and wellbeing outcomes through better public and active transport as well as high-quality open and greenspaces (for example, Barton et al. 2015; Giles-Corti et al. 2016). These Australia-based researchers have studied how, despite stated policy objectives, policy strategies and actions often are not informed by evidence and fail to promote 'healthy' cities—for example, by continuing to plan low-density, car-dependent residential neighbourhoods removed from key services, employment, and education (Lowe et al. 2019). Given the growing calls to integrate health-related evidence with urban policy, this group of scholars conducted an international review of liveability research and developed a definition of urban liveability for Australian cities with a range of indicators, which was used in a partnership with the then Victorian Department of Health and incorporated into the Victorian Public Health and Wellbeing Plan (2015–19) (Badland et al. 2014). The plan required local governments 'to prioritise planning for healthy and liveable communities' in their municipal public health plans, and evidence demonstrates that several Victorian local governments now employ the same 'research-based definition of liveability and/or use liveability indicators to benchmark and monitor policy progress' (Lowe et al. 2019: 131). This research provided health-based evidence to support the 'liveability' narrative that has existed in Melbourne since the Economist Intelligence Unit's Global Liveability Index ranked the city first in 2010. In particular, it served to articulate desirable policy goals to deliver measurable liveability outcomes and highlighted the liveability inequities experienced in the city. In this way, the researchers identified and responded to a 'policy window' of opportunity and delivered impactful research by creating a constructive partnership with a focus on research translation with the Department of Health (Lowe et al. 2019).

Why is it so hard?

If we accept that most urban researchers and practitioners are predisposed to better integration of research and policy, recent work suggests this does not translate into practice. Hurley and Taylor's (2016: 5) study of planning scholarship and policy reported that some urban policymakers considered research 'largely irrelevant' or difficult to access in ways that could be translated to practice through its design and methods. In addition, policymaking and project planning are often not designed to engage with active research.

The common barriers to integration affect research and policy of all kinds and include misalignment of priorities and time frames. The policy agenda is tied to issues relevant during cycles of government administration and adapts quickly to new questions as they arise. In contrast, research is not necessarily focused on issues relevant to current political debates and, for this reason, can be seen to lack currency in policymaking. This does not mean that research is not useful, but that it could find its use at a different time with a different government. Even where policy practitioners and researchers are aligned in terms of focus, the processes of decision-making in government and the time frames for action mitigate against the rhythms of research activity. This applies to both formative research—that is, research to shape urban policy or programs—and to summative research, which evaluates urban policy or programs. This can be overcome—for example, by drawing on existing research findings to take advantage of political or policy windows of opportunity and/or by expert adaptation of research designs, but it demands considerable commitment from both sides.

These common barriers are linked to what Head (2015: 10) terms supply and demand-side problems. The supply of academic research is influenced by ratings and rankings. Research is designed to produce academic outputs rather than outputs amenable to fast consumption by those in dynamic policy settings. So, even when researchers engage in topical and policy-related work, it may not be designed to interact iteratively with policymaking processes, and indeed academics may not be familiar with how policy works. There is a challenge to adequately respond to social and political conditions in early research design to support effective knowledge translation in future. Academics, even urban researchers, are discouraged from engaged research because their performance is measured by metrics associated with research outputs or income won, which compute more highly than advancing their field in practice—for example, as measured by policy change or participating in policy networks.

On the demand side, policymaking is often not designed to proactively engage researchers. Time pressure is often cited as a limit to learning from research or adopting new approaches that integrate research processes. Furthermore, new evidence and ideas can represent a threat to business as usual or 'lead to confusion' (Davoudi 2006: 18). Relationships between researchers and policy practitioners can be undone by competing interests and fluctuating politics. All policymaking is political, which places robust evidence in a broader context of managing stakeholder support, media portrayal, and risk. There are multiple sources of evidence, including what is available from formal research and informal and tacit knowledge. The political dimension of urban policy is well understood by urban researchers (for example, Forester 1982; Flyvbjerg 1998; Hillier 2002), as is the need to recognise the role of planners' values in their practice (Stretton 1970). In essence, evidence from scholarly research fits together and often competes with what Weiss (2001: 286) identifies as 'ideology, interests, institutional norms and practices, and prior information'. Factors like an individual's or an organisation's interests can undermine the prioritisation of other inputs in policymaking and, at times, research can be cherrypicked or disregarded to serve political objectives. Researchers also appreciate the risks of being marginalised when their work goes against the zeitgeist and of experiencing 'discomfort' (Hurley and Taylor 2016) at the way policymakers sometimes use their work. This discomfort can run both ways, as indicated above.

In addition to these general barriers, urban researchers and policymakers face a specific challenge in trying to build relationships and improve integration. This pertains to the need to navigate the multilevel governance arrangements for the planning and management of Australian cities. As well as networking and relationship management skills, researchers and practitioners must be able to work with bodies of knowledge and evidence that are complex and not easily amenable to interpretation. It is no accident that the now ubiquitous term 'wicked problems' was coined by two social planners in the United States (Rittel and Webber 1973). Adding the challenge of securing and maintaining a consistent line of problem definition, analysis, and action to the existing challenges of mismatched priorities and time frames makes it much harder to secure the kind of long-term coordination and bipartisan collaboration by policymakers required to sustain efforts.

What kind of research–policy linkages are produced?

The contemporary urban research–policy nexus is more multifaceted than in the 1960s and 1970s. This reflects changes in governance across liberal democracies that have reshaped the state, expanded the number of actors involved in policymaking (state and nonstate actors), and encouraged the development of new formal and informal linkages between them. Various programs of reform underpinned the reshaping of state–society relations, including the evidence-based policy movement (EBPM) that emerged in the 1970s (Head 2016) but gained strength in the 1990s. The EBPM is part of the broader project of state 'modernisation' in the United Kingdom as well as 'new instrumentalism' and corporate management frameworks adopted in Australian public management from the late 1980s (Jones and Seelig 2005), which encouraged a focus on measuring performance and results.

The rules of engagement characterising the contemporary Australian urban research and policy landscape differ from the past in some important ways. While a wider range of opportunities to connect exists—for example, through new policy networks and the use of valuable shared digital platforms—the application of New Public Management principles (Dent 2002) has reduced the scope of influence of scholars and inhouse research within the Australian Public Service in favour of a model that outsources urban policy analysis and design to private consulting firms. Nevertheless, there is a range of ways that scholarly research enters the mix of sources used in policy decision-making. In general, there is an 'instrumental' view or an 'enlightenment' view of the research–policy interface (Davoudi 2006). The former sees a utilitarian relationship between research and policy and tends to take a narrower focus and simplify the messiness associated with applying evidence in policymaking. The enlightenment view sees research more removed from the policy agenda and aiming 'to illuminate the landscape within which policy decisions have to be made' (Davoudi 2006: 16).

While the above separation is useful for understanding the urban research–policy interface, the following categorisation underscores two additional factors in our two groupings. First, we have focused on the relationship depth between research and practice. This, is turn, leads to shorter and longer-term categorisation lenses, which can change over time depending on the evolution of research relationships and new opportunities for closer engagement. Based on current practices, we have categorised the range of engagement between urban research and policymaking into two groups: lineal problem-solving and relational-oriented linkages. Each of these categories has five subgroups. They are described in Table 2.1.

Table 2.1 Urban policymaking and research links

Category	Type of link	Characteristics
Lineal problem-solving links	Traditional research	Policy actors as research subjects.
	Supervisor–student collaborations	Supervisors as facilitators. Students as agents of research translation.
	Research consultancies	Urban policy advice is outsourced by government to researchers, research consortiums, and other actors (i.e. private consultancies).
	Public commissions, inquiries, and reviews	Contracted or voluntary contributions by researchers to public processes of evaluation.
	Secondments, boards, or committees	Contracted or voluntary contributions by researchers to advisory roles.
Long-term strategies or relational links	Wilfully distant critical commentary	Targeted use of research to critique policy and shape public demands.
	Research–policy networks	Networks based on long-term relationships to coordinate joint activities, support mutual understanding, and build collective resources.
	Policy research institutes	Research centres designed to conduct policy-related studies with a focus on knowledge translation.
	Independent statutory and public research organisations	Public research agencies constituted through government legislation.
	Research partnerships	Planned collaboration from first stages of research design to research integration in policy.

Source: Authors' summary.

Lineal problem-solving approaches to the urban research–policy nexus

In this category, the integration of urban research and policymaking occurs to address a question over the short term that benefits or relies on the short-term or intermittent interaction between researchers and urban policy practitioners.

Traditional links made in the research process with policy actors as research subjects

In this first category, the aims and objectives of traditional research are likely to be theoretical and, while the research may be framed for policy relevance and take-up of findings may occur, it is not designed for research integration or knowledge transfer. Research leads to theory development and steers away from offering propositional results in favour of appraisals, critique, and theorisation. The link here is well-established and lies in the process of data collection: the research requires policymakers or other actors with influence over the policymaking process to participate—for example, through interviews, focus groups, or the Delphi technique. This relationship is short term and focused on data collection.

Some researchers may seek to shape the discussion of their findings to offer interpretations for applied relevance—for example, through placing greater emphasis on contextual factors. Furthermore, some may engage research participants more closely in data collection—for example, through ethnography. Regardless, research outputs are not predominantly designed for knowledge transfer and overwhelmingly include academic publications, though research briefings or general media opinion pieces with practical interpretations may be offered to widen dissemination and reach policymaking audiences.

From the traditional dissemination of research findings, and given conducive temporal and political factors, it is possible that deeper links between research and policy are developed on themes that become a focus of policymaking. In terms of these policy issues, there are likely to be areas of government that pay closer attention to traditional research outputs, such as inhouse research divisions, and consultants advising governments may utilise traditional research outputs in their applied work. Also, advocacy groups and the media may draw attention to research. Overall, this model of contact between urban research and policymaking is functional to pursuing scholarly objectives and sufficient to be leveraged in practice at times. Depending on shared interests and the research approach, including the method of communication with participants and levels of trust developed, initial research can evolve into closer partnerships over time.

Linkages made through supervisor–student collaboration

One significant space of connection between urban research and policymaking in Australia and abroad relates to the growing number of PhD candidates supervised within Australian universities. Many local and international students undertake their doctoral studies while still working or on leave from public service roles or from other policy-influential agencies, such as multilateral organisations or private consultancies. Some of these students receive scholarships with the purpose of facilitating knowledge transfer—for example, on Australian public policy issues (such as the Sir Roland Wilson Foundation, which is a partnership between The Australian National University, Charles Darwin University, and the Australian Public Service) or international aid (such as Australia Awards Scholarships, which are long-term awards administered by the Department of Foreign Affairs and Trade to emerging scholars from developing countries, predominantly from the Asia-Pacific).

Unique opportunities arise in these circumstances to build linkages between research and practice. These can come from the training and research opportunities provided within university settings facilitated by supervisors as well as the students' own ability to design policy-informed research or research focused on policy impact—for example, with opportunities for ethnographic or co-designed studies that utilise existing networks and relationships. Some doctoral theses will represent the culmination of a lineal, problem-solving research–practice relationship, while others can develop into a longer-term research–policy nexus in which the relationship is strong and the resources exist to collaborate.

Research consultancy

All three levels of government in Australia commission policy advisory work—a trend that has grown exponentially over recent decades given public service staffing caps and reductions associated with wider public management reforms. Increasingly, this work is awarded to private consultancies—predominantly to large firms but also to relatively small firms with expertise in urban policy. The expectation is that applied research is carried out efficiently and without the lengthy processes associated with traditional research (such as ethics approvals). Private consulting approaches to urban policy can offer rigorous advice based on extensive experience, expansive databases, strong actor relationships, and clear objectives on sustainability or equity, and are often realised by teams. It is not the task of this chapter to evaluate the outcomes of research conducted as part of this model; it is included in this typology because the practice of outsourcing creates relationships in public urban policymaking between state and nonstate advisory and management firms, as well as with academics.

In this regard, researchers from academia can be contracted by governments solely or in consortia with the private or nonprofit sectors to fulfill outsourced public policy advice. These 'boundary-spanning' scholars access policymaking by invitation or through competitive tender processes, which is common practice when researchers already work on a problem (such as housing or disaster management) and have experience applying and adapting their work to help solve it. Furthermore, urban policy scholars can be subcontracted by private consultants to provide specialist advice based on work they have undertaken or in which they have a track record—for example, in producing data, models, or other outputs that can support policymaking, or in applying specialist analytical skills. The involvement of academics is often an important part of urban policymaking given their specialist knowledge and skills. Many scholars aim to be directly involved in policy processes as part of their commitment to engaged research or service obligations and, in this regard, their involvement aligns with their ethics and principles regarding impact. In these instances, as in private consultancies, there is a need for research to be well connected to practice, from operating along stipulated (short) time frames to communicating results for policymaking purposes. Longer and more exploratory work does not tend to occur under this model given the risks it presents to both sides, as discussed above.

Special commissions of inquiry, reviews, and other public investigations

This category relates to the contributions of scholars made through royal commissions and other special commissions or parliamentary inquiries (such as the 2021 inquiries into homelessness in Victoria and housing affordability and supply in Australia), formal reviews and evaluations, and other public investigations. Urban policy and related research are relevant in numerous ways and can be brought to bear on formal processes of inquiry and reviews, from significant appointments to commissions or inquiries, via formal submission processes, or when called on to give expert evidence or contribute to background, issue, or assessment reports. Policy evaluations are frequently conducted by private consultancies and often scholarly research is used as a source of evidence in these evaluations on a diverse range of issues. While the nexus here between urban research scholars and policy is contractual and concentrated in time, the importance of these activities raises the esteem of research and researchers in terms of policy relevance and accountability.

Individual academics in policy advisory roles (secondments, boards, and committees)

Finally, in this category of shorter-term links between urban research and policy, it is relevant to recognise the significant service contributions, paid and voluntary, made by individual scholars. At times, high-level input from academics can be called on through their secondment into advisory roles or in forming part of policy committees or advisory boards, such as the ministerial planning advisory boards that are active across many states and territories in Australia. There is potential for research translation through deliberative engagement directly with policymakers in these environments, including the presentation and discussion of complex evidence through which the nuances and risks associated with policy issues can be measured in informal and formal ways. While their participation in these roles may be short—from one to four years, for example—their access to these roles and spaces of influence is due to the long-term cultivation of relationships and generation of empirical evidence and ideas that influence policy.

Long-term links, strategies, and relational approaches to the urban research–policy nexus

This section outlines some of the ways longer-term relationships are established between urban research and policymaking. These links range from arm's-length to highly integrated co-research or other methodologies that bind researchers and practitioners in urban policy. An important factor that distinguishes this category from the former is the depth of the link between research and practice. This relationship often evolves over the long-term, including more than one research project and with stronger ties to practice in different ways.

Wilfully distant approach to impact

Academics developing theory and offering commentary on matters of public policy may choose to do so less from a desire to integrate their research with practice and more from a wilfully distant position to influence through critique. While their methods do not engage practitioners or decision-makers involved in policymaking, their interventions can shape debates and public demands. Researchers in this category understand that rather than directly influencing a policymaking process in an instrumental way at a certain time, their work has the capacity to affect policy development in 'diffuse ways' over the long term, providing 'a background of empirical generalizations and ideas that creep into policy deliberations' (Weiss 1980: 381). Researchers may make contributions to democratic debate at a moment in time, though their impact is linked to knowledge and evidence built over the long term. Activist scholars may also subscribe to a view that distance from formal policymaking is important in pursuing their research with progressive social movements, with whom they are more likely to develop a longer-term relationship. Scholarship in this category is renowned for illuminating the urban policy and political landscape of decision-making, becoming a source of trusted and reliable critique by different actors.

Research–policy networks

Interconnections between urban research and policymaking can be built over time through research–policy networks. There are multiple contemporary examples of this, including the Research for Development Impact Network (RDI) (ACFID 2022), which is a network between practitioners and researchers working on international development themes, including poverty reduction; and, perhaps most significantly in contemporary urban research, the Australian Urban Research Infrastructure Network (AURIN and The University of Melbourne 2022), which is a national network of private sector researchers, policymakers, and data providers.

In general, with participants in such voluntary networks including researchers, policy advisers, data providers, analysts, and consultants, the networks grow or ebb and flow based on the relationships and trust built between members. Research–policy networks tend to emerge because of a topical policy issue and the links between members, as well as the success of their collective efforts, and are built through activities like networking events with informal information exchange, joint work on problems, and solutions through workshops, facilitated meetings, education sessions, and shared data platforms. As Head (2016) describes, working across the boundaries of professional groups and organisations in these ways can be crucial for good policy outcomes. These networks of researchers and practitioners foster long-term relationships through shared learning—for example, on the different types of values and practices within different organisations and the recognition and sharing of the different kinds of evidence used.

Policy research institutes

The purpose of policy research institutes is to influence policy and practice through the utilisation of specialised knowledge and skills. There are different models, including university-based institutes and nongovernmental research centres, which purposefully sit at the boundary of urban research and practice. The Australian Housing and Urban Research Institute (AHURI) is a clear case, which, in an example of the policy impact focus, espouses a mission to influence 'policy development across housing, homelessness, cities and urban issues by collaborating with a national network of university partners to deliver policy relevant peer-reviewed research that supports the decision making of all levels of government' (2020: 1). Another example is the Melbourne Institute (2020), which conducts economic and social policy research to develop 'an evidence base for effective policy reform', including the Household, Income and Labour Dynamics in Australia (HILDA) Survey funded by the Australian Government through the Department of Social Services. The policy impact orientation of such institutes means a focus on knowledge translation and integration, including acute attention to political questions and adoption of methodological approaches that deliver opportunities for influence (for example, embedded researchers). These institutes have a significant focus on partnerships and the communication of scientific knowledge for research impact.

Independent statutory and public research organisations

Since Federation, research agencies have been constituted through government legislation with the purpose of collecting and analysing data about social and economic trends, including those relevant to cities. Examples of these at the national level include the Commonwealth Scientific and Industrial Research Organisation (CSIRO), which was founded in 1949, the Australian Bureau of Statistics (ABS, in 1975), and the Australian Institute of Health and Welfare (1987). University-trained researchers work within these organisations to conduct independent research solely or in connection with university-based researchers, and their work is oriented to producing evidence that influences policy. The same public management reform agendas that have in recent decades led to staff caps and reductions hollowing out the capacity of the public sector have also affected the budgets and contracting possibilities, and thus research capabilities, of many publicly constituted and funded research agencies. Nevertheless, they continue to represent a major and necessary nexus between research and urban policymaking.

Co-research on urban policy matters (participatory action research, co-design, and co-production)

As Oliver and Cairney (2019: 7) found in their meta-review of the literature on policy impact, 'co-production is widely hailed as the most likely way to promote the use of research evidence in policy, as it would enable researchers to respond to policy agendas, and enable more agile multidisciplinary teams to coalesce around topical policy problems'. Co-research involves planned collaboration between researchers and policymakers from the beginning of a project or as part of the way entire research programs and institutes are designed.

This is a common approach in urban studies—for example, with research into housing affordability (for example, Whitzman 2017) and urban greening (Hurley et al. 2017); in multiple research projects housed within departments or institutes, such as the Healthy Liveable Cities Lab through which 'research is developed in partnership with stakeholders to inform best practice policy' (CUR 2021); or the ANU Institute for Infrastructure in Society, which has adopted a co-research approach to the study of social value and community engagement in Australia's infrastructure sector with the aim of improving policy and practices.

As a method, participatory research has existed since the 1940s and can be characterised generally by the focus on research impact on policy as well as a participatory and reflective approach to research. Researchers active in co-research describe the complexity and messiness of engaging organisations and managing interactions with stakeholders and influential actors (Whitzman 2017; Jones and Bice 2021). Partnerships created through combined funding arrangements and commitments linked to administration priorities may involve compromises in terms of agendas as well as the interpretation and use of evidence. The quality of the relationships between key figures in co-design partnerships is vital for research continuity and quality as they facilitate access to these different worlds of action.

Conclusion

This chapter has argued for the importance of better integration of urban research and policy and identified the common barriers that get in the way. Drawing on the Australian experience, it has proposed a categorisation of 10 contemporary experiences of interconnections between urban research and policymaking. These categories reflect the changing context for urban research and policy as well as the opportunities and obstacles encountered. In particular, the categories highlight the growing importance of intermediaries—institutions, actors, and processes—as bridges or boundary-spanners between urban researchers and policy (Head 2015; Bednarek et al. 2018; Sullivan 2021).

At the time of writing, opportunities to develop fruitful connections between urban research and policy seem more constrained than ever as national policy continues to erode support for social science and humanities research and the model of funding universities tied to international student income has collapsed under Covid-19 restrictions with no recovery alternatives offered. The university system has lost significant numbers of staff and remains under pressure, with continuing precarious employment conditions for early career and other academics. There is also the perennial issue of what is valued by universities in terms of research impact. While an ongoing commitment to evidence in informing policy supports research integration agendas, there are limits to the practicability of this in the current climate. In addition, it is important to highlight three challenges that universities and the public sector will need to address if they are to meet future challenges. These are not particular to urban research and policy but may be exacerbated given the complex and highly politicised nature of urban policymaking. Sullivan (2021) identifies these challenges as:

- *The lack of diversity in academia and the public service.* This is a challenge for both practitioners and academics; both work with frameworks of meaning and knowing that are shaped by the environment in which they emerged, but which may not reflect the same frameworks of the societies in which they are applied.

- *The national interest test/increasing government regulation.* The Commonwealth Government has become more interventionist in its regulation of universities. Emblematic of this stance is the National Interest Test as part of Australian Research Council funding. This was announced on 31 October 2018 by then Minister for Education Dan Tehan. In December 2021, the acting minister Stuart Robert rejected six peer-assessed and approved grants on the grounds that, in his view, they did not meet the National Interest Test, including as a project of direct relevance to urban research and policy. Other significant changes include the introduction of guidelines to counter foreign interference in Australian universities and a requirement that universities adopt a 'model code' to protect freedom of speech. These changes have the potential to limit the activities of universities and bind them more closely to government, effectively making them an arm of government. This limits the distance and independence necessary for both academics and public servants.

- *The robustness of higher education and the public service.* The policy academic–public servant relationship is predicated on both operating from positions of distinct identity, integrity, and independence. The power of the relationship arises from the additional value produced in their engagements. Undermining this on either side risks the production of that added value.

This chapter has identified strategies and pathways to building interconnections, despite these challenges, between urban research and policymaking in Australia. Collaborative approaches through co-research and the other relationships constituted between research and policy described above provide the strongest avenues for policy impact from research due to the extent of knowledge-sharing and the methods built into these approaches to adapt to contextual changes. Other options include institutionalising practices—for example, evaluation to be embedded in policy design—or nurturing the efforts and achievements of individual champions from the academy and the public service who have been trailblazers in policymaking. Across institutional and individual opportunities, critical reflection and debate about the direction of urban policy are necessary, as are administrative procedures that support research integration and the communication of research findings for practical application. Overall, for a productive urban policy and research interface, it is necessary to acknowledge and work with the practical factors that define limitations and enable integration.

References

Alexander, S., and B. Gleeson. 2019. *Degrowth in the Suburbs*. Singapore: Palgrave Macmillan. doi.org/10.1007/978-981-13-2131-3.

Australian Council for International Development (ACFID). 2022. *About the RDI Network*. Canberra: Research for Development Impact Network. Available from: rdinetwork.org.au/.

Australian Housing and Urban Research Institute (AHURI). 2020. *Policy Impact Statement 2020–2021*. Melbourne: AHURI. Available from: www.ahuri.edu.au/sites/default/files/documents/2021-12/AHURI-Policy-Impact-Statement-2020-2021_0.pdf.

Australian Urban Research Infrastructure Network (AURIN) and The University of Melbourne. 2022. *Australian Urban Research Infrastructure Network*. Melbourne: University of Melbourne. Available from: aurin.org.au/.

Badland, H., C. Whitzman, M. Lowe, M. Davern, L. Aye, I. Butterworth, D. Hes, and B. Giles-Corti. 2014. 'Urban Liveability: Emerging Lessons from Australia for Exploring the Potential for Indicators to Measure the Social Determinants of Health.' *Social Science & Medicine* 111: 64–73. doi.org/10.1016/j.socscimed.2014.04.003.

Barton, H., S. Thompson, S. Burgess, and M. Grant, eds. 2015. *The Routledge Handbook of Planning for Health and Well-Being: Shaping a Sustainable and Healthy Future*. London: Routledge. doi.org/10.4324/9781315728261.

Bednarek, A.T., C. Wyborn, C. Cvitanovic, R. Meyer, R.M. Colvin, P.F.E. Addison, S.L. Close, K. Curran, M. Farooque, E. Goldman, D. Hart, H. Mannix, B. McGreavy, A. Parris, S. Posner, C. Robinson, M. Ryan, and P. Leith. 2018. 'Boundary Spanning at the Science–Policy Interface: The Practitioners' Perspectives.' *Sustainability Science* 13: 1175–83. doi.org/10.1007/s11625-018-0550-9.

Davoudi, S. 2006. 'Evidence-Based Planning: Rhetoric and Reality.' *disP: The Planning Review* 42(165): 14–24. doi.org/10.1080/02513625.2006.10556951.

Dent, H. 2002. 'Consultants and the Public Service.' *Australian Journal of Public Administration* 61(1): 108–13. doi.org/10.1111/1467-8500.00265.

Flyvbjerg, B. 1998. *Rationality and Power: Democracy in Practice.* Chicago, IL: University of Chicago Press.

Forester, J. 1982. 'Planning in the Face of Power.' *Journal of the American Planning Association* 48(1): 67–80. doi.org/10.1080/01944368208976167.

Giles-Corti, B., A. Vernez-Moudon, R. Reis, G. Turrell, A.L. Dannenberg, H. Badland, S. Foster, M. Lowe, J.F. Sallis, M. Stevenson, and N. Owen. 2016. 'City Planning and Population Health: A Global Challenge. *The Lancet* 388(1062): 2912–24. doi.org/10.1016/S0140-6736(16)30066-6.

Head, B.W. 2015. 'Relationships between Policy Academics and Public Servants: Learning at a Distance?' *Australian Journal of Public Administration* 74(1): 5–12. doi.org/10.1111/1467-8500.12133.

Head, B.W. 2016. 'Toward More "Evidence-Informed" Policy Making?' *Public Administration Review* 76(3): 472–84. doi.org/10.1111/puar.12475.

Hillier, J. 2002. *Shadows of Power: An Allegory of Prudence in Land-Use Planning.* London: Routledge.

Hurley, J., and E.J. Taylor. 2016. 'Australian Early Career Planning Researchers and the Barriers to Research–Practice Exchange.' *Australian Planner* 53(1): 5–14. doi.org/10.1080/07293682.2015.1135813.

Hurley, J., E.J. Taylor, and K. Phelan. 2017. 'Collaboration with Caveats: Research–Practice Exchange in Planning.' *Planning Practice & Research* 32(5): 508–23. doi.org/10.1080/02697459.2017.1378971.

Jones, K., and S. Bice. 2021. 'Research for Impact: Three Keys for Research Implementation.' *Policy Design and Practice* 4(3): 392–412. doi.org/10.1080/25741292.2021.1936761.

Jones, A., and T. Seelig. 2005. *Understanding and Enhancing Research–Policy Linkages in Australian Housing: An Options Paper.* Final Report No. 79, 1 May. Melbourne: AHURI. Available from: www.ahuri.edu.au/research/final-reports/79.

Lowe, M., P. Hooper, H. Jordan, K. Bowen, I. Butterworth, and B. Giles-Corti. 2019. 'Evidence-Informed Planning for Healthy Liveable Cities: How Can Policy Frameworks Be Used to Strengthen Research Translation?' *Current Environmental Health Report* 6: 127–36. doi.org/10.1007/s40572-019-00236-6.

Melbourne Institute. 2020. *Melbourne Institute: Applied Economic & Social Research*. Melbourne: University of Melbourne. Available from: melbourneinstitute.uni melb.edu.au/.

Oliver, K., and P. Cairney. 2019. 'The Dos and Don'ts of Influencing Policy: A Systematic Review of Advice to Academics.' *Palgrave Communications* 5(21). doi.org/10.1057/s41599-019-0232-y.

Porter, L. 2017. 'Indigenous People and the Miserable Failure of Australian Planning.' *Planning Practice & Research* 32(5): 556–70. doi.org/10.1080/026 97459.2017.1286885.

Rittel, H.W.J., and M.M. Webber. 1973. 'Dilemmas in a General Theory of Planning.' *Policy Sciences* 4(2): 155–69. doi.org/10.1007/BF01405730.

RMIT Centre for Urban Research (CUR). 2021. *Healthy Liveable Cities Lab*. Melbourne: RMIT. Available from: cur.org.au/research-programs/healthy-liveable-cities-group/.

Stretton, H. 1970. *Ideas for Australian Cities*. Melbourne: Georgian House.

Sullivan, H. 2021. 'Reflecting on AJPA, 2015–2021: Revisiting the Relationship between Policy Academics and Public Servants—Distances from Learning.' *Australian Journal of Public Administration* 80(4): 652–60. doi.org/10.1111/1467-8500.12527.

Troy, P. 2013. 'Australian Urban Research and Planning.' *Urban Policy and Research* 31(2): 134–49. doi.org/10.1080/08111146.2013.793260.

Weiss, C. 2001. 'What Kind of Evidence in Evidence-Based Policy?' Paper presented to Third International Interdisciplinary Evidence-Based Policies and Indicator Systems Conference, Durham University, Durham, UK, July.

Wensing, E., and L. Porter. 2016. 'Unsettling Planning's Paradigms: Towards a Just Accommodation of Indigenous Rights and Interests in Australian Urban Planning?' *Australian Planner* 53(2): 91–102. doi.org/10.1080/07293682. 2015.1118394.

Whitzman, C. 2017. 'Participatory Action Research in Affordable Housing Partnerships: Collaborative Rationality, or Sleeping with the Growth Machine?' *Planning Practice & Research* 32(5): 495–507. doi.org/10.1080/02697459. 2017.1372245.

3

National policy for an urban nation: Establishing sustained Commonwealth attention to Australia's cities, 2008–2021

Jago Dodson

Introduction

Within a short period after European invasion, Australia had become an urban nation (Freestone 2010). Yet, despite occasional periods of interest in urban issues, including related concerns such as housing, there has never been a sustained period since Federation in 1901 during which the Commonwealth has continuously addressed urban questions. By 2022, however, the Commonwealth had for more than a decade maintained a largely continuous interest in urban affairs, including through a ministerial position and portfolio. It can now be reasonably argued that cities are a bipartisan Commonwealth policy concern.

This chapter adds to emerging reporting (Stace 2020) of Commonwealth urban policy in Australia since the late 2000s. It presents a critical narrative overview with four main aspects. First, historical Commonwealth attention to urban issues is surveyed within the context of international thinking on cities during the 2000s. Second, the chapter reviews the urban policy innovations arising from the 2007 election of the Rudd Labor Government and its successor Gillard Government in the period 2008–13, including discussion of Infrastructure Australia, the National Urban Policy, and the Council of Australian Governments (COAG) reform programs. Third, the chapter describes and assesses the urban policies of the Liberal-led Coalition Government of 2013–22, including preliminary efforts to establish a Liberal perspective on cities. This discussion focuses on the period from 2015 to the present, which has witnessed ongoing albeit uneven urban policy evolution. Fourth, the chapter concludes by arguing that urban policy is now substantially established, albeit weakly, within the Commonwealth suite of portfolios. This represents an advance on the preceding 112 years of Federation. The chapter further argues the need for greater attention to this changed policy diagram, including better periodic theorisation and stronger explanatory effort in relation to wider political and economic changes, alongside the need for greater empirical detail on policy development.

Policy precursors

At Federation in 1901, Australia was already an urban country, with most Australians living in cities and towns. The concentration of urban development around colonial administrative centres had produced dense settlement patterns by the late nineteenth century. Although housing was often of poor quality, the latter half of the nineteenth century saw urban improvements through public works such as water, sewerage, and drainage schemes, and railways and tramways that extended residential development beyond walking distance from commercial cores. In the Australian Constitution, responsibility for urban matters is assigned to the states without direct Commonwealth interest. Thus, the nascent town planning movement focused its efforts on state jurisdictions.

After World War II, the Commonwealth sought to restructure the Australian economy, financed housing construction, and encouraged urban planning regulation within its Keynesian national reconstruction program. Despite suburbanisation accelerating during the postwar period, the Commonwealth stepped back from active urban policy in the late 1950s, but returned via the Department of Urban and Regional Development (DURD) in 1972–75 to address suburban infrastructure backlogs, stabilising suburban land markets, and raising questions of population distribution imbalances (Lloyd and Troy 1981).

After 1975, the Commonwealth reverted to an uninterested stance on urban questions until the recession of the early 1990s motivated economic stimulus via the Building Better Cities Program (Neilson 2008). This scheme sought to enable post-industrial spatial restructuring via targeted urban renewal programs and infrastructure upgrades. With the recession fading in the late 1990s, the Commonwealth again withdrew from urban affairs, though intervening occasionally to support entry to homeownership.

A federal agenda for an urban nation

In the late 1990s new understandings emerged of the role of cities under globalisation. The removal of international trade barriers positioned cities as key nodes in global flows of goods and services, finance, telecommunications, and labour. In turn, urban conditions were seen to shape economic prospects. In 2008 the United Nations (UN 2008) declared that most of the world's population lived in cities and global economic agencies such as the World Bank and the Organisation for Economic Co-operation and Development (OECD) began to pay new attention to urbanisation. Scholarship informed and responded to the urban moment, producing a new urban literature on the role of cities in economic growth, and exhorting various policy measures to improve economic performance in the national interest (Brugmann 2009; Glaeser 2011; Hollis 2013). This 'urbanology', as Gleeson (2015) termed it, did not go unnoticed in Australia, with prominent local politicians reportedly communing over the new urban literature (Farrelly 2011).

Although urban policy languished on Commonwealth agendas for more than a decade after the Building Better Cities Program, growth pressures emerged among Australia's larger cities, as the effects of the 1990s recession wore off and global exchange increased. The larger globally exposed cities, such as Melbourne, Sydney, and those in South-East Queensland, faced the strongest pressures. NSW premier Bob Carr by 2000 claimed that 'Sydney is full up' (Mitchell 2000). State governments responded to growth with new metropolitan plans, such as the Melbourne 2030 strategy (Department of Infrastructure 2002), the South East Queensland Regional Plan (Office of Urban Management 2005), and Sydney's City of Cities strategy (Department of Planning 2005). Such state concerns filtered into national debates and in turn into party electoral platforms with, for example, the 2004 federal election platform of the Australian Labor Party

(ALP 2004) proposing a national infrastructure advisory council. Labor was elected in 2007, with Kevin Rudd as leader, on a platform promising action on infrastructure and urban problems with three main elements: the Infrastructure Australia agency, the Major Cities Unit, and the COAG national urban reform agenda (ALP 2007).

Infrastructure Australia was created as a statutory Commonwealth authority in late 2008 with a threefold mandate to: survey Australia's infrastructure needs, obtain and prioritise infrastructure project proposals presented by state governments, and advise on wider infrastructure and related policy, planning, and financing questions. As a statutory body, Infrastructure Australia was overseen by an independently appointed board and operated on a technocratic model, complementing other econocratic federal agencies such as the Productivity Commission, the Treasury, and the Reserve Bank of Australia.

The most prominent initial output from Infrastructure Australia was the *National Infrastructure Priorities* report (2009), which sought to assess the condition of Australian infrastructure and advise on principles and priorities for future procurement. Based on its audit, the agency prepared a list of priority infrastructure projects proposed by other federal agencies and the states to identify those with the highest national benefit that most justified the expenditure of federal funds. The Infrastructure Australia program can be viewed as a genuine policy innovation that brought greater formal scrutiny to federal involvement in major infrastructure projects. The agency quickly achieved a degree of technocratic authority in the urban sphere in Australia, despite its formal powers being little more than advisory.

A further institutional innovation was the Major Cities Unit (MCU). This small but active agency, overseen by Infrastructure Australia, was tasked with providing information and advice on urban and metropolitan issues. The MCU was prominent for its detailed State of Australian Cities series of reports (for example, MCU 2010) released annually between 2010 and 2015, depicting conditions in Australian cities across economic, social, and environmental domains. The MCU also supported internal coordination mechanisms within the Australian Public Service, including various committees operating across portfolios, and linking with external stakeholders. It was also tasked with supporting the development of the COAG national planning system agenda.

Labor's third urban policy element was national coordination of planning systems and urban strategies. In 2009, the Commonwealth initiated a process within the COAG to formulate a national perspective on cities that was to be agreed on by all states and territories. While the COAG had no formal constitutional status, it was sometimes useful as a mechanism for agreeing on issues of national significance. This process involved consultation among critical stakeholders as to what the national approach to urban and metropolitan planning should include. To support this objective, Labor promised funding to the states and territories if they aligned their metropolitan plans with the nationally agreed priorities. The COAG appointed a taskforce to review state government metropolitan plans to assess their alignment with the national objectives, after which it was anticipated that the harmonisation of state and territory urban plans with the COAG-agreed national objectives and criteria for future strategic planning of capital cities would be undertaken.

This COAG program was ambitious in both scale and scope, with the *National Planning Systems Principles* (COAG 2009) setting out a detailed national hierarchy of policy structures and instruments, from national urban policy objectives cascading down through state schemes and plans, effectively to the cadastral level, including building and site regulation (Figure 3.1). The intent was also idealistic, incorporating urban, environmental, and infrastructure planning, regulation, and delivery programs within a single national framework. That ambition deserves commendation for its optimism in confronting state planning system heterogeneity and differing electoral imperatives given the limited constitutional levers available to the Commonwealth to ensure compliance.

Environment and resource management	(Planning)	Infrastructure
National environmental and resource management priorities (Murray Darling, Great Barrier Reef, National Environmental Protection Measures)	**National urban policy and infrastructure investment priorities** (National Urban Policy, National Building Program, Building the Education Revolution)	**National infrastructure policies and priorities** Interstate rail, national highways, energy infrastructure, trade infrastructure, defence infrastructure, international airports
State environmental and resource management frameworks (Water resource and catchment management planning, coastal protection, state land development and allocation, forestry policy, mining and extractive resources)	**State legislative and operational frameworks** (State planning and infrastructure coordination legislation, state planning policies, state coastal management planning, state planning regulatory instruments, inspirational statements of strategic intent, e.g. "Q2", "our priorities in NSW")	**State infrastructure plans and policies** State infrastructure plans, key state roads, intra-state rail, education infrastructure, health infrastructure, ports, state energy policy, standards of service policy, competitive neutrality policy
Regional environmental and resource management (Catchment protection, regionally significant vegetation communities, regionally endangered species, regional extractive resources, regional open space and viewsheds)	**Regional plans (including metropolitan regional plans)** (Urban footprints, growth and density targets, integrated regional infrastructure plans, protection of regionally significant environmental and economic resources)	**Regional infrastructure delivery programs** Regional water supply, intra-state roads/rail/highways, ports, regional open space networks, energy infrastructure
Local environmental and resource management initiatives (Waterway protection, local bushland protection and acquisition, vegetation protection.)	**Local government/regional council planning schemes** (Local government strategic plans, local zoning and regulatory frameworks, identification of priority areas for infrastructure delivery, codes and standards)	**Local infrastructure planning and delivery programs** Local infrastructure programs (circulation networks, urban water cycle management programs, local open space networks
Neighbourhood initiatives (Healthy waterways partnerships, revegetation, amenity improvement)	**Local area and neighbourhood planning** (Local government structure plans/master plans, neighbourhood revitalisation)	**Neighbourhood infrastructure programs** Cycleways, local open space linked to regional open space
Site- or location-specific resource and environmental evaluations (Site/location environmental audits)	**Location-specific planning** (Centre plans, transit-oriented development, development-intensive centres, master plans, urban redevelopment areas)	**Collaborative location-specific infrastructure planning and provision** Infrastructure partnerships, joint funding
Development-related environmental and resource management outcomes (Codes developed around sustainability outcomes, impact assessments)	**Development assessment (individual/specific sites)** (Site-based zoning, development intents, codes)	**Infrastructure contributions frameworks and area-specific standards of service**
Site-specific environmental and resource management initiatives (Sustainable building design, water conservation standards)	**Built form** (Building, plumbing and site-drainage standards)	**Site-specific standards of service** Service connections, certification

Regional plans and local government planning schemes are key instruments for the spatial expression of integrated planning policy

Figure 3.1 COAG urban policy integration framework

Source: COAG (2009).

The 2011 National Urban Policy

In addition to the Infrastructure Australia program, establishing the MCU, and beginning the COAG reform program, the Australian Government began developing a national urban policy as an agreed national position on cities. This was undertaken via release of a background paper, *Our Cities: The Challenge of Change* (Australian Government 2010), and a discussion paper, *Our Cities: Building a Productive, Sustainable and Liveable Future* (DIT 2010), setting out options for future policy. Both documents were organised around three principal themes—productive cities, sustainable cities, and liveable cities—plus a further dimension of 'well-managed' cities (DIT 2010). The discussion paper was the more technical, assessing questions of productivity, sustainability, and liveability in greater detail than the background paper, though mainly by identifying issues and questions rather than specific policy proposals.

GOALS		OBJECTIVES	PRINCIPLES
	PRODUCTIVITY	1. Improve labour and capital productivity	Efficiency
		2. Integrate land use and infrastructure	Value for Money
		3. Improve the efficiency of urban infrastructure	
	SUSTAINABILITY	4. Protect and sustain our natural and built environments	Innovation
		5. Reduce greenhouse gas emissions and improve air quality	Adaptability
		6. Manage our resources sustainably	
		7. Increase resilience to climate change, emergency events and natural hazards	Resilience
	LIVEABILITY	8. Facilitate supply of appropriate mixed-income housing	Equity
		9. Support appropriate living choices	Affordability
		10. Improve accessibility and reduce dependence on private vehicles	
		11. Support community wellbeing	Subsidiarity
	GOOD GOVERNANCE	12. Improve the planning and management of our cities	Integration
		13. Streamline administrative processes	
		14. Evaluate progress	Engagement

Figure 3.2 National urban policy goals, objectives, and principles
Source: Redrawn from DIT (2011).

The eventual policy statement, *Our Cities, Our Future: A National Urban Policy for a Productive, Sustainable and Liveable Future* (DIT 2011), was released on budget night in May 2011. It set out a comprehensive agenda for Australian cities, including the rationale for a national urban policy; the need for coordination of the actions, roles, and responsibilities of different actors; and a set of principles, goals, and objectives. The policy was positioned as a complement to the sustainable population strategy (DSEWPaC 2011) that the government had previously released, translating that strategy to the urban context. The overarching intent of the urban policy was to 'guide policy development and public and private investment in cities' (DIT 2011: 18) via four goals—productivity, sustainability, liveability, and good governance—supported by 14 objectives, and 10 principles (Figure 3.2).

The release of the National Urban Policy was a significant moment in the development of urban policy in Australia. For the first time in the history since Federation, the Australian Government had undertaken a comprehensive program of urban policy preparation and development and had released a major and detailed systematic statement on the challenges of and responses to urbanisation at the national scale. This intention exceeded by a considerable breadth and depth the efforts of the Hawke–Keating governments' Building Better Cities Program of 1991–96 and the DURD program undertaken by the Whitlam Government in 1972–73. To the extent that it offered a comprehensive perspective on questions of urbanisation, its most comparable predecessor in federal action arguably was the 1944 Commonwealth Housing Commission report, although that document was overwhelmingly focused on housing provision and creating urban planning systems, rather than an all-encompassing focus on cities.

Despite its comprehensive scope, however, the National Urban Policy did not set out a detailed program of interventions with an implementation plan and funding. In this regard, the policy was weaker than its antecedents. Most of the policy consisted of discussion, affirmations, intentions, and directions. For example, in the case of integrating planning of land use and infrastructure, the main activities were further strategies to be jointly prepared with state governments. Some of the policies were set as terms and conditions for future federal expenditure, often involving further strategies and programs already under way or in development through frameworks and processes outside the National Urban Policy framework. For example, as one of the further initiatives to integrate land use and infrastructure, the policy proposed requiring 'as a condition of funding for the second

Nation Building Program, that each capital city has in place, by 2014, a 20-year freight strategy consistent with the *National Land Freight Strategy*' (DIT 2011: 31).

Viewed in this way, the National Urban Policy was as much a compilation and synthesis of existing relevant urban sectoral and related policy programs as it was an encapsulating policy reflecting a systematic understanding of urban processes. It belies a model of formulation in which a wide array of sectors is asked to pitch in existing or intended programs from their siloed portfolio domains, rather than a more sophisticated overarching comprehension of cities as interconnected urban systems. The form of the National Urban Policy raises some theoretical questions about the nature of urban policy: is 'the urban' merely a site where other sectoral policies and programs are brought together, or should policy be founded on an integrated conception of the urban process? The latter seems a stronger foundation.

Another way of considering the National Urban Policy is to recognise it as a necessary step on the path towards a more systematic federal engagement with urban issues, and one that occurred after nearly 15 years of near complete federal inattention to and inaction on cities. Thus, the three years from the installation of the Rudd Government in late 2007 through to the budget release of the National Urban Policy in mid-2011 involved building internal public sector capacity to govern on urban questions. This included the efforts on Infrastructure Australia, the MCU, and COAG, but also required coordination of divisions within existing portfolios such as transport and environment, through new governmental mechanisms. This internal public sector institutional development—perhaps more so than any specific policy action—is the substantive legacy of the 2011 National Urban Policy.

Another reason for a subdued view of the 2011 policy is its weak implementation. From 2011 to 2013, the government was grappling with the aftermath of the Global Financial Crisis, the consequences of the 2010 change in prime minister from Rudd to Julia Gillard, including the 2010 loss of electoral majority, plus a reinvigorated Liberal opposition. Amid such diversions and policy demands, it is not surprising that substantial implementation of the policy by 2013 was limited.

Liberal responses

The election of the Abbott Liberal–National Coalition in 2013 brought change in the Commonwealth approach to urban policy. There were initial signals that the Coalition might take an active interest in urban affairs. Before the 2013 election, the Liberal Party had placed Greg Hunt in the shadow urban portfolio. Hunt (2013: 255) argued for a strong Commonwealth role in 'encouraging a broadly agreed long-term vision for the basic shape and structure of our major metropolitan regions and in helping to create a road map to reach that vision'.

These roadmaps, Hunt argued, should be developed and implemented by integrated planning commissions over a 30-year time frame in cooperation with state governments. Although Hunt's proposal was rather optimistic, given the history of state and federal relations on cities, the overall approach of national policy alignment was broadly comparable with Labor's. While Labor preferred state technocratic coordination, the Liberal proposal emphasised a more corporatist multilevel model.

The Abbott Coalition Government elected in late 2013 was much less interested in cities than its shadow minister. In accordance with Coalition tradition, the infrastructure and transport portfolio that had overseen Labor's urban agenda was handed to the rural-oriented National Party under minister Warren Truss. The MCU was disbanded in 2013 (Thisleton 2013), though not without disquiet from urban sector representatives. The Planning Institute of Australia expressed its disappointment at the closure and urged continued policy development while the Property Council of Australia lamented the loss of intelligence on the urban dimensions of national productivity (Jewell 2013). The Grattan Institute think tank criticised the government for underestimating the contribution of cities to economic productivity (Jewell 2013).

The effect of the Abbott Government's actions was to slow the development of the content and institutions of federal urban policy. To the extent that urban policy continued to be developed, it was via the infrastructure agenda with two main streams. Principal among these was the continuation of Infrastructure Australia's program of infrastructure auditing, assessment, and prioritisation of projects—not all of which were urban. This task was complicated by Abbott's declaration that urban rail projects were not a federal concern, in contrast to roads, which were viewed as being of federal interest. This period included efforts to politicise infrastructure, as exemplified by the Victorian East West Link (EWL) toll road. The EWL, proposed by the Victorian Liberal Government to be built under the inner suburbs of Melbourne, was promised Commonwealth co-funding by the Coalition. Yet, the project's economic assessment produced a benefit–cost ratio of just 0.45, indicating a loss of $0.55 on every dollar invested (VAG 2015). This placed Infrastructure Australia in a difficult position and produced some technocratic contortions in which the agency released a 'high priority' list without the EWL plus a lesser 'priority list' including the EWL, with the government relying on the latter to justify its enthusiastic support. This bureaucratic discomfort was resolved at the 2014 Victorian election when the incoming Andrews Labor Government cancelled the EWL project.

A second prominent infrastructure feature of the Abbott era was the announcement of the preferred site for the second Sydney airport in 2015. The second airport is a large intervention in the economic geography of Australia's largest city, in terms of the scale of investment and employment impact, given the less high-skilled jobs profile of Sydney's western suburbs, where the airport will be built. This decision resolved a many-decades-long debate over the siting and initiating of the airport. While an airport is not strictly an urban policy or program, it can be reasonably understood as one, given the effect it will have on Sydney's spatial development and the wider urban interventions to support and serve it, such as via the City Deals Program, as discussed below, including new heavy rail lines.

Getting smart

In mid-2015, Abbott lost the Liberal leadership and was replaced as prime minister with Malcolm Turnbull, who had a background in merchant banking and digital entrepreneurship. Turnbull brought these interests to his prime ministership via a focus on economic productivity and digital innovation. Turnbull reshuffled the federal Cabinet, establishing a new Cities and Built Environment portfolio with its own minister, Jamie Briggs. This was the first time in the history of urban policy in Australia that a federal portfolio had a dedicated cities-focused minister separate from regional development. Although this was a relatively modest shift in policy direction within the Cabinet, from a symbolic perspective, it marked the moment when the recognition of cities as an important federal policy concern became a clear bipartisan position.

Since 2015, the Liberal Party—the dominant party within the Coalition—and the Labor Party have articulated policy positions on cities and urban development, albeit of varying coherence. This situation differs from most of Australia's federal history during which interest in urban affairs was largely a Labor Party preserve (Dodson 2013). Previous urban ministries had only been within Labor Cabinets. Both major parties in federal parliament have since maintained cities policies within their election platforms and have a cities ministerial portfolio or shadow portfolio. Indeed, while differing in tone, both parties have articulated broadly similar positions in focusing on infrastructure to support productivity and liveability.

Two main programs emerged from the 2015 Cabinet changes. The first was the *Smart Cities Plan* (PM&C 2016) and the second was the City Deals Program. The *Smart Cities Plan* was an attempt to link urban policy and productivity via digital transformation. The notion of smart cities had emerged from debates about digital technology, principally the internet, and urban productivity. This was reflected in the *Smart Cities Plan*, which was organised around the themes of 'smart investment, smart policy, and smart technology'. Regarding smart investment, the plan proposed creating opportunities for urban renewal by raising private capital, as well as drawing on value-capture mechanisms. The *Smart Cities Plan* also proposed 'city deals' to 'unlock public and private investment in key economic centres', as well as collecting city performance data. Last, the plan proposed to take full advantage of new transport, communications, and energy technologies, while leveraging open-data solutions for innovation. Substantively, the plan included a $50 million Smart Cities and Suburbs funding program, to enable local governments to apply digital transformation to built environments. Two rounds of this scheme had been run by 2019, funding projects such as 'digital choice-based letting' for public housing in Canberra and 'smart sports field planning, monitoring and management' at Wyndham City Council in Melbourne. A further feature of the *Smart Cities Plan* was the National Cities Performance Framework, a data dashboard that provided summary urban information at the city scale (PM&C 2016). The dashboard—discontinued in 2021—offered in digital format a version of the State of Australian Cities reports prepared by the MCU during 2009–13, though without the interpretative commentary provided by that unit.

Although the smart cities funding directly supported projects, the City Deals Program is arguably the more significant policy element of the *Smart Cities Plan*, given its attempt to coordinate the governance of spatial development in targeted locations. The city deals title borrows from devolution schemes in the United Kingdom (O'Brien and Pike 2019), in which the central government establishes spatial partnerships with devolved regional bodies and local governments. In Australia, the cognate jurisdictions are the states or territories and local governments. The purpose of the City Deals Program in Australia is to align the planning, investment, and governance of federal investment in urban regions. Initially, these efforts were focused on large regional cities, such as Townsville in Queensland, Geelong in Victoria, and Launceston, Tasmania. As the program has developed, it has begun to encompass the smaller of the major cities, such as Perth and Adelaide, and lately, western Sydney, South-East Queensland, and north-west Melbourne. By seeking to coordinate spatial development and distribute federal support, the City Deals Program has some resonance with the Australian Assistance Program undertaken as part of the Whitlam DURD program in 1972–75, and the urban redevelopment schemes of the 1991–96 Building Better Cities Program.

The Western Sydney City Deal (WSCD) serves as a useful exemplar of the City Deals Program. The Commonwealth and NSW governments, together with eight municipalities, agreed on 38 actions combining infrastructure, land-use development, and economic investment activities. For example, the WSCD commits to the North South Rail Link serving the land-use activity of the new Western Sydney airport 'Aerotropolis', accompanied by an investment attraction fund targeting major research and manufacturing companies, and universities. The deal has bespoke governance arrangements, including the Western City and Aerotropolis Authority (now part of a subsequent Western Parkland City Authority), established to serve as master planner and developer of the airport, and a dedicated Aerotropolis land-use and infrastructure plan (Department of Planning and Environment 2018) covering the City Deals region. While some of these activities require funding to implement, many require governance and planning coordination that otherwise might not have been immediately feasible between the three levels of government, particularly given federal responsibility for airports. While at the time of writing the WSCD plan is only in its third year of implementation, the annual progress report for 2021 identifies 11 of 38 commitments completed, including commencement of construction of the Sydney Metro–Western Sydney Airport railway line as well as land releases and various industrial training schemes (Australian Government 2021).

There has so far been only limited scholarly interest in the Australian City Deals Program, despite a growing body of UK literature on the preceding comparators there. Pill et al. (2020), for example, report that Australian policy interviewees considered the WSCD similar to the UK model, with positive assessments of the opportunities it presented, but recognised the complexity of spatial and institutional land-use and infrastructure coordination. Pill et al. (2020) noted, however, that the city deals generally had not been well aligned with strategic planning, particularly in relation to community engagement. They also argued in favour of a stronger effort to include affordable rental housing in the deals.

Population and parking

As the city deals were being rolled out from 2018, further debates were happening within the Coalition Government. Population growth had persisted during the 2010s because of high rates of net immigration to Australia. Cities such as Melbourne and Sydney grew at nearly 2 per cent per annum, placing pressure on urban policy, planning, and financing to provide infrastructure and housing. Although the Commonwealth Government controlled immigration levels, the pressures of accommodating this influx were experienced by the states, and mainly in the large cities. While the states were strained by this growth, they were broadly coping but also very welcoming of federal support. Given the increasing costs of servicing rapidly growing populations, a federal view developed that these growth pressures could in part be resolved by directing a greater proportion of population away from the major cities—principally Melbourne and Sydney—towards regional centres. Consequently, a policy agenda developed around population decentralisation and had, by early 2019, gathered some public momentum. This was initially pursued via a federal parliamentary inquiry that endorsed a population strategy including further investigation of decentralisation of population to regional cities (HoRSCIT 2018). By early 2019, the Commonwealth was promoting a national population plan, *Planning for Australia's Future Population* (PM&C 2019), which would elaborate this agenda. The eventual document, released in late March, was a thin and desultory volume, rushed in advance of the looming 2019 election, and scant of substantive policy content. Its main useful legacy has been to establish the national Centre for Population, which provides advice, evidence, and expertise on population issues and has produced a stream of data and discussion papers.

The period leading up to the May 2019 federal election was also notable for a further venture into urban policy by the Commonwealth Government in the form of a $600 million 'congestion-busting fund'. This scheme was intended to provide road widenings, intersection adjustments, and railway station carparking construction in suburban localities across Australian cities, though mainly in marginal seats in south-east Melbourne. The fund attracted official scrutiny, not least from the federal Auditor-General, who identified serious flaws in the scheme's design and governance—in particular, the prioritisation and selection of the carpark locations appeared principally political, rather than based on technical criteria relating to traffic volumes or benefit–cost analysis, and with negligible alignment with state land-use or transport planning policies (ANAO 2021). The scheme has been widely publicly ridiculed as a 'rort' (Mizen 2021). This scheme demonstrates the risks of a federal government involving itself in urban policy through ill-thought-out programs designed in haste remote from and with limited consideration of, or coordination with, state priorities, negligible technical or strategic guidance, and elevated electoral politicisation. Although the involvement of the federal government in urban policy is to be welcomed in general, program examples such as the congestion-busting fund offer a cautionary illustration of some of the potential weaknesses of policy developed poorly, remote from carefully determined city-level imperatives, and without systematic comprehension of strategic or operational urban needs.

Conclusion

This chapter has presented evidence that since 2008 Australia has increasingly cemented urban policy as an ongoing concern of the federal government. This consolidation and continuation have been marked by institutional innovation such as the establishment of the Infrastructure Australia agency. There has been information-gathering and development through the State of Australian Cities reports and National Cities Performance Framework. New governance arrangements have been tested through the COAG Reform Council and the City Deals Program. Various funding schemes have been pursued, such as the Smart Cities and Suburbs funding and, lately, the suburban carparks fund. Major long-term infrastructure has been funded, including the second Sydney airport. Each of these is indicative of policy progress, however episodic and uneven.

Yet, weaknesses remain. Federal relations remain largely unmodified, and the Covid-19 pandemic saw new fragmentary dynamics. The Rudd Government's COAG agenda and National Urban Policy, while useful, left little by way of permanent legacy. The longer-term benefits of the Smart Cities and Suburbs program are very hard to discern, while the carparking fund has been widely ridiculed. The Centre for Population is doing creditable, but mostly invisible and limited work on population including in cities. Infrastructure continues to be funded in a partly technocratic, partly political way, despite the worthy advisory efforts of its federal oversight agency. It is not clear whether the now defunct National Cities Performance Framework was actively used by decision-makers at any level of government, academia, or industry.

Despite these weaknesses, Australia has sustained more than a decade of urban policy at the national level. Though the substance of policy remains inadequate to the needs of an urban nation, this change is an important shift in the history of the federation. Cities are now a bipartisan federal concern, with a minister and portfolio. Thus, we should expect that policy capability within the Australian Public Service and the appreciation by future ministers of the importance of their portfolio will grow and strengthen over time. Yet, urban policy remains awkwardly, perhaps tenuously, positioned in Australia's constitutional relations, between the federal government, with the main fiscal power, and state and territory governments, with operational responsibility. At least the past 13 years have provided a bipartisan foundation for future improvements in the way this urban nation governs and manages its cities. Continued dedicated systematic effort involving programmatic structural, institutional, and fiscal innovation will be required to sustain and enhance Commonwealth policy on cities over the longer term. Meanwhile, further research is needed to understand the evolving nature of federal urban policy, theoretically, conceptually, and empirically, and within the context of wider economic, social, and environmental change. Finally, scholars will undoubtedly observe with interest the urban policy program of the Labor Government elected in mid-2022, which this chapter was unable to consider in detail.

References

Australian Government. 2010. *Our Cities: The Challenge of Change*. Background Paper. Canberra: Commonwealth of Australia.

Australian Government. 2021. *Western Sydney City Deal: Annual Progress Report 2021*. Canberra: Commonwealth of Australia. Available from: www.infrastructure.gov. au/sites/default/files/documents/western-sydney-progress-report-2021.pdf.

Australian Labor Party (ALP). 2004. *National Platform and Constitution*. Sydney: ALP.

Australian Labor Party (ALP). 2007. *National Platform and Constitution*. Sydney: ALP.

Australian National Audit Office (ANAO). 2021. *Administration of Commuter Car Park Projects within the Urban Congestion Fund*. Auditor-General's Report No. 47 2020–21. Canberra: ANAO.

Brugmann, J. 2009. *Welcome to the Urban Revolution: How Cities Are Changing the World*. New York, NY: Bloomsbury.

Council of Australian Governments (COAG). 2009. *National Planning Systems Principles*. Canberra: COAG.

Department of Infrastructure. 2002. *Melbourne 2030: Planning for Sustainable Growth*. Melbourne: Victorian Government.

Department of Infrastructure and Transport (DIT). 2010. *Our Cities: Building a Productive, Sustainable and Liveable Future*. Discussion Paper. Canberra: Commonwealth of Australia.

Department of Infrastructure and Transport (DIT). 2011. *Our Cities, Our Future: A National Urban Policy for a Productive, Sustainable and Liveable Future*. Canberra: Commonwealth of Australia. Available from: www.infrastructure australia.gov.au/sites/default/files/2019-06/Our_Cities_National_Urban_ Policy_Paper_2011.pdf.

Department of Planning. 2005. *City of Cities: A Plan for Sydney's Future*. Sydney: NSW Government.

Department of Planning and Environment. 2018. *Western Sydney Aerotropolis: Land Use and Infrastructure Implementation Plan—Stage 1 Initial Precincts*. Sydney: NSW Government.

Department of the Prime Minister and Cabinet (PM&C). 2016. *Smart Cities Plan*. Canberra: Commonwealth of Australia.

Department of Prime Minister and Cabinet (PM&C). 2019. *Planning for Australia's Future Population*. Canberra: Commonwealth of Australia.

Department of Sustainability, Environment, Water, Population and Communities (DSEWPaC). 2011. *Sustainable Australia, Sustainable Communities: A Sustainable Population Strategy for Australia.* Canberra: Commonwealth of Australia.

Dodson, J. 2013. 'Federal Policy for Australia's Cities: The 2011 National Urban Policy in Historical and Comparative Perspective.' Paper presented to Sixth State of Australasian Cities Conference, Sydney, 26–29 November.

Farrelly, E. 2011. 'Be Happy, Be More Interesting, Be Dense.' *Sydney Morning Herald*, 20 October.

Freestone, R. 2010. *Urban Nation: Australia's Planning Heritage.* Melbourne: CSIRO Publishing. doi.org/10.1071/9780643100138.

Glaeser, E.L. 2011. *Triumph of the City: How Our Greatest Invention Makes Us Richer, Smarter, Greener, Healthier, and Happier.* New York, NY: Penguin.

Gleeson, B. 2015. *The Urban Condition.* London: Routledge. doi.org/10.4324/9780203388174.

Hollis, L. 2013. *Cities Are Good For You: The Genius of the Metropolis.* New York, NY: Bloomsbury.

House of Representatives Standing Committee on Infrastructure and Transport (HoRSCIT). 2018. *Building Up & Moving Out: Inquiry into the Australian Government's Role in the Development of Cities.* Canberra: Parliament of the Commonwealth of Australia.

Hunt, G. 2013. 'Achieving the 30- and 50-Year Plans for Our Cities.' *Urban Policy and Research* 31(3): 255–56. doi.org/10.1080/08111146.2013.832844.

Infrastructure Australia. 2009. *National Infrastructure Priorities.* Sydney: Infrastructure Australia.

Jewell, C. 2013. 'Axing of Major Cities Unit widely condemned.' *The Fifth Estate*, [Sydney], 28 September. Available from: thefifthestate.com.au/articles/axing-of-major-cities-unit-widely-condemned/.

Lloyd, C., and P. Troy. 1981. *Innovation and Reaction: The Life and Death of the Federal Department of Urban and Regional Development.* Sydney: George Allen & Unwin.

Major Cities Unit (MCU). 2010. *State of Australian Cities 2011.* Sydney: MCU.

Mitchell, A. 2000. 'Shut the Gate.' *Sun Herald*, [Melbourne], 5 March: 1.

Mizen, R. 2021. 'Morrison's $660m Car Park Fund "Sports Rorts on An Industrial Scale".' *Australian Financial Review*, 28 June. Available from: www.afr.com/politics/federal/morrison-s-660m-car-park-fund-sports-rorts-on-an-industrial-scale-20210628-p58508.

Neilson, L. 2008. 'The "Building Better Cities" Program, 1991–96: A Nation-Building Initiative of the Commonwealth Government.' In *Australia Under Construction: Nation-Building Past, Present and Future*, edited by J. Butcher, 83–117. Canberra: ANU E Press. doi.org/10.22459/AUC.04.2008.08.

O'Brien, P., and A. Pike. 2019. '"Deal or No Deal?" Governing Urban Infrastructure Funding and Financing in the UK City Deals.' *Urban Studies* 56(7): 1448–76. doi.org/10.1177/0042098018757394.

Office of Urban Management. 2005. *South East Queensland Regional Plan 2005–2026.* Brisbane: Queensland Government.

Pill, M., N. Gurran, C. Gilbert, and P. Phibbs. 2020. *Strategic Planning, 'City Deals' and Affordable Housing.* Final Report No. 331. Melbourne: AHURI. doi.org/10.18408/ahuri-7320301.

Stace, S. 2020. 'Australian NUP: Lessons to Be Learnt.' In *Developing National Urban Policies*, edited by D. Kundu, R. Sietchiping, and M. Kinyanjui, 377–405. Singapore: Springer. doi.org/10.1007/978-981-15-3738-7_16.

Thisleton, R. 2013. 'Major Cities Unit Axed in Portfolio Reorganisation.' *Australian Financial Review*, 25 September.

United Nations (UN). 2008. 'Half of Global Population Will Live in Cities By End of this Year, Predicts UN.' *UN News*, 26 February. Available from: news.un.org/en/story/2008/02/250402-half-global-population-will-live-cities-end-year-predicts-un.

Victorian Auditor-General (VAG). 2015. *East West Link Project.* Melbourne: Victorian Government.

Part 2: Sustainability, the environment, and conservation

4

Climate change adaptation and resilience as a metapolicy framework

Elnaz Torabi and Stephen Dovers

Introduction

Whatever success is had with climate change *mitigation* (emission reductions), Australia's cities and towns will be severely impacted by already locked-in climate change. Social lives, environments, infrastructure, and economic flows will be disturbed, and current policy settings for *adaptation* to climate change are inadequate. We propose that thorough attention to living well with Australia's changing climate should underpin policy across jurisdictions, sectors, and portfolios, producing significant co-benefits aside from climate adaptation.

With bushfires, heatwaves, floods, severe storms, cyclones, and droughts, Australia is already experiencing longer, more severe, and/or more frequent events due to climate change (CSIRO and BOM 2020). The devastating bushfires and floods of 2019 and 2020, and more recent 2022 floods and 2023 heatwaves in the east of the country, show what a one-degree warmer Australia looks like, while the impacts of an expected three-degree warmer world by 2100 are beyond our lived experience (AAS 2021). The warnings of and evidence for severe or even catastrophic climate change impacts have become ever stronger (IPCC 2021; WMO et al. 2022).

Nearly 90 per cent of Australians live in cities, most in coastal areas vulnerable to sea-level rise and flooding (DCC 2009). One assessment identified more than A$226 billion (2008 replacement value) of commercial, industrial, road, rail, and residential assets at risk from a 1.1-metre rise in sea level (DCCEE 2011). The exposure of communities and changing perceptions of risk are impacting on the insurance and financial sectors, with perhaps one in every 19 property insurance premiums to become unaffordable by 2030 (AAS 2021).

Even if all international commitments under the Paris Agreement were to be met today, which is unlikely, we must deal with locked-in climate change. This highlights the importance of adaptation and of action to manage risks and protect communities and environments, and to exploit opportunities to enhance the resilience of our cities and societies.

There are synergies and opportunities (as well as tensions) between mitigation and adaptation, but also a commonality that must be made explicit. Both have profound social justice and equity dimensions: the costs of mitigation fall heavily on the poor, as do the impacts of climate extremes and the costs of adaptation. All policy responses must take that into account, to be just as well as effective. Calls for transformative adaptation to climate change that focus on justice and equity are increasing (FEA 2022).

Yet, Australia has been caught for decades now in a 'climate change policy impasse', both for mitigation and for adaptation (Brown and Dovers 2021). At the time of writing, a new national government indicates a greater level of action on mitigation at least, but the inheritance of inaction makes the task a challenging one. Alongside a poor record on climate policy, Australia's history of urban policy (for example, Ruming et al. 2017) has too often been one of flux, of eased regulation, and of poorly coordinated plans: strategic, structural, transport, metropolitan, open space, logistics, and others. Given its cross-sectoral scope, can we use adaptation as an integrating principle throughout urban policy and planning? That proposition, supported by the co-benefits of climate change adaptation and values delivered to the community (Table 4.1), is the central theme of this chapter.

This chapter addresses this question through the lens of resilience—a core concept of adaptation. We first assess the state of Australian adaptation policy, then describe the need for policy integration to address climate adaptation, and explore the usefulness of key adaptation concepts, especially resilience. We then combine resilience ideas with adaptation needs, followed by a series of broad policy recommendations. Our core proposition is that, through policy integration, climate adaptation should, and can, become a 'metapolicy principle' for decision-making and planning.

Adaptation and the Australian policy vacuum

Climate change *adaptation* for human systems is 'the process of adjustment to actual or expected climate and its effects, in order to moderate harm or exploit beneficial opportunities' (IPCC 2018: 542). Recently, the concept of *resilience* has become central in adaptation discourse and policy, and is defined as the

> capacity of social, economic and environmental systems to cope with a hazardous event or trend or disturbance, responding or reorganizing in ways that maintain their essential function, identity and structure while also maintaining the capacity for adaptation, learning and transformation. (IPCC 2018: 557)

Yet, resilience is a contested concept and there are challenges related to the nature of the societal values and policy goals that must be negotiated (Cañizares et al. 2021).

We focus on Australian climate change adaptation and the challenges and opportunities for vertical (between levels of government) and horizontal (across sectors/portfolios) *policy integration* using the concept of resilience. Our central argument is that adaptation cannot be regarded as a discrete issue, but rather should be considered a metapolicy principle and framework focusing on desired outcomes (that is, the co-benefits and community values to be delivered). Consider the *examples* of cross-sectoral and portfolio implications of adaptation and co-benefits in Table 4.1. Co-benefits are the added benefits of adaptation policy and broader values delivered to the community beyond the direct benefits achieved from addressing climate change.

Table 4.1 Climate change adaptation: Relevant policy sectors and co-benefits

Climate change adaptation issue	Examples of adaptation measures	Relevant policy sector/portfolio	Examples of co-benefits and values delivered to the community
Heatwaves	Urban greening, building insulation	Planning, open space management, building regulation	Urban amenity, walkability, biodiversity, public health, energy efficiency
Water scarcity (worsened droughts)	Water-sensitive urban design, efficiency standards, supply augmentation	Water, housing, open space management, infrastructure, development and building standards	Public health, biodiversity, urban cooling, avoided costs
Vulnerable remote communities	Improved employment connected to Country, better health, communication, and education services	Employment, industry, communications, health, environmental management	Improved economic, health, environmental, and cultural outcomes; national moral obligation to achieve
Sea-level rise, coastal storm surge	Ecosystem engineering (impact absorption, nature-based solutions), managed retreat, protective structures	Coastal and environmental management, planning, infrastructure, housing, tourism, fisheries	Coastal amenity and access, biodiversity, avoided costs and insurance, public safety
Inland flooding	Wetland creation (nature-based solutions), protective structures, house retrofits	Water management, open space management, environmental management, infrastructure, building regulation	Urban greening, recreational and visual amenity, biodiversity, public safety
Increased pressure on emergency management	Numerous: in recommendations of about 150 post-event reviews since 2009 (Cole et al. 2018), especially regarding risk mitigation	Emergency services, health, transport, communications, planning	Avoided deaths and asset and economic losses

Source: Author's summary.

The issues and benefits illustrated in Table 4.1 spread across metropolitan, regional, rural, and remote Australia, and national and indeed state policy would at the broadest level cover all these. However, following population concentration, the bulk of actions and benefits are in cities. In terms of the nation adapting to climate change, the interdependencies between 'city and country'—in food supply, social and cultural innovation, recreation, manufacturing capacity, water supply and use, and so on—warn against separate adaptation policy frameworks, even while place-specific demands must be attended to in subsidiary policies and actions.

The examples in Table 4.1 support two vital conclusions: 1) adaptation requires policy and action *across* multiple sectors and policy portfolios, and 2) many adaptation measures offer *co-benefits* in those sectors. Conclusion (1) requires coordinated action by all three levels of government and across portfolios within each level. Conclusion (2) offers the prospect of *no-regret* or *low-regret* adaptation measures, which are made more attractive where there are benefits other than climate adaptation. The impacts of a variable climate have been attended to less than they could have been in Australia to date (in water management, fire suppression, drought policy, coastal management, thermal performance of dwellings, urban open space and greening, and more): there are advantages in doing better (that is, focusing on the values and co-benefits), even in the absence of significant climate change. A third and critical point follows: proposed adaptation actions must be analysed, costed, and assessed for their effectiveness, like any other policy proposals. The existence of co-benefits—measured comprehensively (not just near-term economic benefits) and over extended periods—will often shift cost–benefit ratios positively in favour of climate change adaptation measures. These conclusions require a focus shift in adaptation policy to articulate the broader outcomes and values to be delivered to the community (for example, liveability, urban amenity, and public health). If these conclusions hold, along with the already noted strong scientific consensus on the severity of coming climate change, there is little excuse for not implementing much more vigorous adaptation measures across policy sectors and particularly the urban.

Australia has a federal governing system comprising the national (Commonwealth) government, six state and two territory governments (hereinafter, states), and local councils that are created, regulated, and largely financed under state legislation. The Commonwealth's powers are defined by the Australian Constitution and anything else is a residual power and thus the states' responsibility. This includes matters such as natural resource management, conservation, planning, and development, with aspects of land-use planning and development assessment delegated to local governments. Accordingly, much responsibility for disaster risk reduction and climate change adaptation falls on state governments (COAG 2011), which share responsibility for the identification of climate risk and incorporation into statutory and non-statutory decision-making with local governments. In this federal system, adaptation requires higher-level policy to establish consistent principles and, crucially, to support other levels of government and the nongovernmental sector, but implementation at local scales to ensure consistency with local geographical and economic contexts; local government has a key role.

A distinction must be drawn regarding climate change as a policy problem. The major focus of political debate has been *mitigation* (reducing emissions), and this remains an urgent challenge with serious implications for cities (and beyond the scope of this chapter). Yet, as a policy problem, given the intent and targets, there is a small number of systemic policy levers—carbon pricing, vehicle emission and technology standards, renewable energy targets, and so on—with reasonably predictable efficacy. It is a critical political failing that mitigation has been so poorly attended to nationally in Australia: it is politically difficult, but also urgent and tractable. *Adaptation* to the impacts of climate change, as a policy problem, is far messier, demanding consistent, broad policy settings but also endless variation in local adaptation actions according to the climate risks faced (coastal storm surges, bushfires, flooding, heatwaves, water supply, species at risk) across varied geographical and socioeconomic settings. There are few direct, systemic policy levers for adaptation. The intricacies of adaptation policy at all levels of government are well beyond the scope of this chapter, so coverage of issues and policy detail is kept largely to the general and illustrative.

The Australian Government does play a vital role, traditionally via the COAG and subsidiary arrangements, seeking policy coordination between governments. The COAG was replaced in 2020 with the loosely defined 'National Cabinet', involving reduced inclusion of local government. Other national organisations play key roles, including the CSIRO, the Bureau of Meteorology, Geoscience Australia, the (now vestigial) National Climate Change Adaptation Research Facility, and the recently (in 2021) established National Recovery and Resilience Agency, which was re-formed in 2022 as the National Emergency Management Agency.

Climate adaptation policy in Australia has been in a state of flux, overall and with respect to cities. While mitigation has been the focus of unproductive Australian debate for some time (the first emissions reduction proposal was submitted to the Cabinet in 1989) (Burgmann and Baer 2012), adaptation became topical only in 2006. Between 2007 and 2012, there was a rapid rise in adaptation policies and strategies at all levels of government (Howes and Dedekorkut-Howes 2017), followed by a period of decline as a result of changes of government; the national election of 2013 and some state elections (for example, Queensland in 2012) saw a shift from Labor to Liberal–National parties with climate-sceptical leaders. A timeline of national adaptation policy (and lack thereof) is presented in Table 4.2. The extensive list of documents in the table reflects the extent of the focus on adaptation relevant to each national government and the differences between them.

Table 4.2 A timeline of Australian national climate change adaptation policy, 1972–2023

Period/government	Climate change adaptation focus and key events	Key documents
1972–95 Whitlam Government (ALP) Fraser Government (Coalition) Hawke–Keating Government (ALP) Keating Government (ALP)	Global acknowledgement of the relationship between humans and the environment through the Stockholm Declaration (1962) First meeting of the Intergovernmental Panel on Climate Change (1988); rising scientific concern and public debate	*Report of a Committee on Climatic Change* (Australian Academy of Science 1976)
1996–2007 Howard Government (Coalition)	A growing focus on resourcing to address climate change at local, regional, and state scales Some states recognised the risk to properties and infrastructure from phenomena such as sea-level rise Need for better understanding of the levels of risk facing the whole nation	*Review of Australia's Ability to Respond to and Recover from Catastrophic Disasters* (Attorney-General's Department 2005) *Climate Change Impacts and Risk Management: A Guide for Business and Government* (Department of Climate Change and Energy Efficiency 2006)

Period/government	Climate change adaptation focus and key events	Key documents
2007 – June 2010 Rudd Government (ALP)	Establishment of the Department of Climate Change in 2007 (disbanded in 2013) Establishment of the National Climate Change Adaptation Research Facility Funding for programs by CSIRO Flagships, Geoscience Australia Garnaut review interim independent report (in 2008) submits that Australia is particularly vulnerable to the impacts of climate change and calls for effective climate policies Start of hearings on the impacts of climate change on coastal Australia by the House of Representatives, chaired by Jenny George MP, 2008 Department of Climate Change becomes Department of Climate Change and Energy Efficiency (2010)	*National Climate Change Adaptation Framework* (COAG 2007) *Garnaut Climate Change Review: Final Report* (2008) *Managing Our Coastal Zone in a Changing Climate: The Time to Act Is Now* (House of Representatives 2009) *Climate Change Risks to Australia's Coast: A First Pass National Assessment* (Department of Climate Change 2009) *Coastal Climate Change Advisory Committee: Issues and Options Paper* (Department of Planning and Community Development 2010) *Developing a National Coastal Adaptation Agenda: A Report on the National Coastal Climate Change Forum* (Department of Climate Change and Energy Efficiency 2010) *Adapting to Climate Change in Australia: An Australian Government Position Paper* (Department of Climate Change and Energy Efficiency 2010)

Period/government	Climate change adaptation focus and key events	Key documents
June 2010 – June 2013 Gillard Government (ALP) **June 2013 – September 2013** Rudd Government (ALP)	Multiparty Climate Change Committee created in 2010 (as required by the Labor–Greens agreement) Launch of the Climate Commission (2011) to provide expert advice and information to the public on climate change Establishment of the Coasts and Climate Change Council, an advisory body to the Minister for Climate Change and Energy Efficiency in 2009–11 Climate Change Authority and Australian Renewable Energy Agency formed in 2012 Coastal Adaptation Decision Pathways Program to provide funding for coastal councils Productivity Commission invited parties to register interest in an inquiry into regulatory and policy barriers to effective climate change adaptation Department of Climate Change is disbanded, with functions moving to other departments	*A Low Carbon and Resilient Urban Future: A Discussion Paper on an Integrated Approach to Planning for Climate Change* (Department of Climate Change and Energy Efficiency 2010) *National Strategy for Disaster Resilience* (COAG 2011) *Coastal Climate Change Risk — Legal and Policy Responses in Australia* (Department of Climate Change and Energy Efficiency 2011) *Climate Change Risks to Coastal Buildings and Infrastructure* (Department of Climate Change and Energy Efficiency 2011) *The Role of Regulation in Facilitating or Constraining Adaptation to Climate Change for Australian Infrastructure* (Department of Climate Change and Energy Efficiency 2012) *Barriers to Effective Climate Change Adaptation* (Productivity Commission 2012) *Adapting to Climate Change: An Australian Government Position Paper* (National Climate Change Adaptation Research Facility 2013) *Australia's Sixth National Communication on Climate Change: A Report Under the United Nations Framework Convention on Climate Change* (Department of Industry, Innovation, Climate Change, Science, Research and Tertiary Education 2013) *Climate Adaptation Outlook: A Proposed National Adaptation Assessment Framework* (Department of Industry, Innovation, Climate Change, Science, Research and Tertiary Education 2013)

Period/government	Climate change adaptation focus and key events	Key documents
2013–September 2015 Abbott Government (Coalition)	Dismantling of climate change programs Climate Commission abolished (later replaced with Climate Council funded by private donations) Little interest in pursuing the objectives of the Outlook Report (see above) COAG process fostering discussions on a national approach to climate change adaptation abolished In 2014 National Climate Change Adaptation Research Facility was funded to undertake the development of CoastAdapt tool to assist local councils (now ceased)	*National Disaster Funding Arrangements* (Productivity Commission 2014)
September 2015 – 2022 Turnbull/Morrison Government (Coalition)	National strategy for adaptation released (see below) Establishment of Coastal Risk Australia website in 2017 Establishment of OzCoasts website Establishment of Disaster and Climate Resilience Reference Group to integrate risk and resilience considerations into planning, policies, and programs of all government departments, in 2016	*National Climate Resilience and Adaptation Strategy* (Australian Government 2015) *Review of Climate Change Policies* (Department of Environment and Energy 2017) *National Climate Resilience and Adaptation Strategy 2021–2025*
May 2022 – Albanese Government (ALP) (In development)	Climate Risk and Opportunity Management Program; National Climate Risk Assessment; new National Adaptation Policy Office in 2023	National Adaptation Plan

Sources: Based on Talberg et al. (2016), Thom (2018), and government announcements.

Australian states and territories have undergone policy reversals. In Queensland, a shift to a Liberal National Party of Queensland (LNP) government in 2012 'systematically dismantled the forward-looking climate policies of previous governments, leaving Queensland unprepared' (DEHP 2016: 2), while the subsequent Labor government brought climate change back on to the policy agenda with a focus on adaptation. With a change of government in Victoria, the sea-level rise benchmark of 0.8 metres by 2100 (established in 2008) was revised to 0.4 metres (Gurran et al. 2013) and later moved back to the 0.8-metre mark; similar shifts occurred in New South Wales. In the absence of national leadership and direction, state sea-level rise benchmarks and responses are patchy and inconsistent (Dedekorkut-Howes et al. 2020).

Why does this matter? In policy domains with a national profile, multiple cause–effect linkages, cross-portfolio implications, shared jurisdictional responsibilities, required policy instruments, and varied implementation scales, *strategic* or *framework* policies (Samnakay 2017) are a commonly employed response, especially in federal systems. Strategic plans provide the same broader logic and structure for the urban realm within which subsidiary plans and instruments can operate in a coherent fashion. The need for strong yet flexible strategic policy is not fulfilled in Australia nationally by the previous and current strategies (Australian Government 2015, 2021) or in many state jurisdictions.

The lack of consistent long-term national and state adaptation policies and therefore consistent metrics and direction inevitably makes adaptation at the local level challenging. This results in vastly different responses across local jurisdictions—for example, neighbouring councils facing similar challenges but with different adaptation responses and planning benchmarks. It can lead to maladaptation or undermine actions—for example, when the lack of policy and action by one council undermines adaptation efforts in adjacent councils (Dedekorkut-Howes et al. 2020). This puts additional pressure on councils which rarely have the resources, capacities, and political support to address climate change but are viewed as responsible for climate adaptation (Nalau et al. 2021). Framing adaptation as a local government issue and responsibility comes with a high risk of failure, as, at the coalface of adaptation, local governments face competing planning agendas and deal with local politics, community demands, and development pressures. Some adaptation actions, such as managed retreat, have large political risk that goes beyond local governments (Gibbs 2016), but most importantly, the lack of clear adaptation leadership from higher levels leaves many communities at risk, financially burdening governments at all levels and exposing them to litigation risks. Many adaptation actions—such as major waterway regeneration, dwelling insulation, or flood-proofing—are capital-intensive and unachievable without higher-level mandates, enabling, and funding.

Lack of adaptation policy direction from the higher levels (especially when not a high priority on state government agendas) could also be an opportunity for local governments to make a difference, but this is highly influenced by having local community and political support and effective leadership. Queensland's Sunshine Coast Regional Council has a history of environmental leadership and climate action, as reflected in local policies that are well integrated and prioritise building resilience and adaptation (Torabi et al. 2017). Similarly, Noosa Shire Council—formerly part of the Sunshine Coast—is known for its climate change leadership and declared a climate emergency in 2019, putting adaptation and mitigation at the top of its policy response (Wellington 2019). Yet, with Australian local governments existing entirely within the power of state legislation, local government adaptation actions can be undermined by state governments, such as the case of Queensland Government intervention in Moreton Bay Regional Council's planning scheme, demanding it remove references to sea-level rise to protect 'resident rights' (Solomons and Willacy 2014).

With a future highly impacted by climate change and a system of governance that struggles with wicked and complex problems (Daley et al. 2021), Australia is in desperate need of policy leadership on adaptation.

The need for adaptation policy integration

Climate change adaptation poses challenges for policymakers as it involves a high level of uncertainty over the degree of impact and timing. However, it also presents opportunities to rethink the way we plan and manage our cities and regions—the potential of significant co-benefits illustrated in Table 4.1. Adaptation aligns well with existing areas of planning and decision-making and offers considerable synergies. The challenges of adaptation policy are to embed core concepts within development priorities, strategies, and plans. This entails modifying or updating frameworks such as local planning schemes and/or developing new climate change strategies.

What is important is the level of interaction between different policies in supporting the desired outcome and their collective performance (Torabi et al. 2017).

Adaptation must be integrated vertically (between levels of government) and horizontally (across different sectors within a jurisdiction) in policy and planning to be effective. Vertical integration is common in many policy sectors (but not well achieved in adaptation) through means such as intergovernmental task forces, strategic policy frameworks, ministerial councils, coordinated regulation and statutes, and shared information systems. The means are familiar also for horizontal integration (across one government): strategic policies, state planning policies, interdepartmental committees or task forces, parliamentary inquiries, insertion of statutory objects in relevant policy sectors, or placement of responsibilities within a central agency rather than a line department. An analogous situation exists in the closely related area of emergency management, where the vast bulk of recommendations from the (very many) post-event inquiries target the operations of specialist emergency management agencies, whose role is primarily response, not other policy sectors that have the capacity to reduce future vulnerability (such as land-use planning, infrastructure development, and communications) (Cole et al. 2018). Arguments for 'mainstreaming' disaster risk reduction across policy sectors resonate with our arguments here regarding adaptation (see Dovers 2022; and associated commentaries).

Adaptation policy integration has been elusive, and we note that environmental policy integration has struggled for many years (Ross and Dovers 2008). There is a tendency to consider climate change an 'environmental' issue rather than a social, economic, or land-use planning one (Measham et al. 2011), thus forcing competition with other (usually more prominent) community needs such as housing and road upgrades. Climate change considerations are found in land-use plans, disaster management plans, and/or stand-alone climate change strategies, yet their level of focus, horizontal integration across different sectors (for example, infrastructure, agriculture, health, and development), and vertical integration under higher-level policy are fraught with challenges. Three key considerations exacerbate this problem:

- Fuzziness of key concepts: for example, the significance and meaning of resilience and adaptation vary substantially between policy documents at all levels as policymakers interpret the terms according to their interests or expertise, or as interchangeable with other paradigms such as sustainability.
- Varying degrees of understanding of and planning for different climate impacts: for example, climate adaptation is better understood and planned for in the context of rapid-onset events such as floods, than of droughts or the urban heat island effect.
- The challenge of embedding uncertainty and long-term impacts in policies and plans that have a short-term horizon.

These three issues contribute to a situation in which existing higher-order adaptation policies do not instruct, enable, or empower actions that can be taken with a recognised mandate and confidence. This is reminiscent of the failure to implement, in the 1990s, the then-prominent metapolicy imperative of ecologically sustainable development across and through all levels of government. The aspiration was strong, but the policy principles were vague, clear empowerment of actors and organisations lacking, implementation pathways not explicit, an institutional base absent, and policy instruments to enable action missing (Dovers 1992). Strategic policy frameworks are common yet strangely underexamined, however, insights from recent work on the attributes of more successful ones could inform adaptation policy (Samnakay 2021). The 2015 and 2021 national climate adaptation strategies (Australian Government 2015, 2021) would not rate highly against criteria such as acceptance of national leadership, clear objectives, use of well-designed policy instruments, or evaluation of outcomes.

Resilience: A silver bullet?

Resilience has become a focus of planning and policy, especially when adapting to climate change, moving far from its origins in ecology with Holling's (1973) work (Cañizares et al. 2021). In Australia, national policies on disasters and climate adaptation include the term, and both in New South Wales (Resilience NSW; now the NSW Reconstruction Authority) and federally (National Recovery and Resilience Agency), it is in the title of new government organisations.

Resilience has been defined as a city's ability to: 1) bounce back to its previous state (static urban resilience); 2) adjust to shocks or stresses and minimise disruption by reorganisation (socioecological resilience); and 3) learn, adapt, and transform (evolutionary resilience) (Handmer and Dovers 1996; Davidson et al. 2016). Depending on the scale and severity of shocks or stresses and the nature of the urban system, enhancing resilience could involve all these characteristics. To be flood resilient, for example, a city might withstand floods by building levees or seawalls (robustness), accommodating floodwaters (adaptability), and/or shifting from 'fighting water' to 'living with water' (transformability) (Restemeyer et al. 2015).

In an urban context, enhancing resilience provides a more positive policy framing than reducing vulnerability (McEvoy et al. 2013). Resilience encourages thinking about adaptation with a long view and delineates the transitions and transformations that can happen when the ability to adapt is overwhelmed or has reached a limit (Nelson 2011). The strategy of 'adaptation pathways' has become prominent (for example, Barnett et al. 2014), where well-designed and coordinated actions are sequenced over time to allow a buildup of adaptive measures.

Despite its popularity, resilience is challenging to define and operationalise, with this lack of a clear definition and understanding giving it 'a chameleon-like quality' (Bulkeley and Tuts 2013: 654). Existing definitions of resilience are generally situated on a spectrum ranging from 'returning to a previous (exact) state' to 'maintaining the same state and identity by adjusting structure and/or bouncing forward and transforming to new states' (Torabi et al. 2021). Some policy definitions consider resilience a synonym for other concepts such as vulnerability, sustainability, or adaptation (Meerow and Newell 2016). While some of these synonyms are normative positive concepts, the desirability of resilience depends on the identification of 'resilience of what to what' and for whom (Carpenter et al. 2001).

The application of a concept rooted in ecological models to social systems such as cities has been criticised for its lack of focus on politics, power, and equity issues (Cote and Nightingale 2012). Power, politics, and conflict are at the heart of resilience, impacting on the distribution of burdens and benefits—the winners and losers of resilience and adaptation policy (Davoudi et al. 2012). Every resilience decision involves trade-offs for balancing action across time, space, and sectors (Chelleri et al. 2015). In addressing these trade-offs, Meerow et al. (2016) raise critical questions to consider: *who* determines what is desirable, *what* networks and sectors are included, *when* is the time to act, *where* should actions be focused or prioritised, and *why* should specific goals be considered? The question of *how* resilience could become a politically acceptable and viable policy principle remains challenging.

In policy, resilience is often used as a general term—a synonym for future-proofing, without clarity as to what it means and how it should be achieved (Davoudi et al. 2012). This leads to ad hoc policymaking in which resilience actions (and adaptation) are non-deliberate, implicit, and even unfit for the local context (Wardekker et al. 2021). For example, there are differences in the policy framing of resilience as 'quick recovery' to a previous state as opposed to adaptative recovery or transformation to different, more sustainable states. There are also policy differences focusing on resilience in general (against anything) versus specific disturbances (Matyas and Pelling 2015).

The translation of a general resilience policy principle into practical planning interventions is difficult. In line with the dominant (and politically acceptable) engineering view of resilience as 'bouncing back', in practice, building resilience and adaptation to climate change often focuses on measures to build back and a quick return to an equilibrium. This typically entails fast-tracked infrastructural solutions (levees, seawalls, rebuilding in flood-prone locations, etc.) as opposed to more transformational measures that promote societal change. There is also often a siloed focus on elements or sectors of cities such as communities, infrastructure, ecosystems, or the economy as the focus of resilience policy and, depending on the context, there are differences in what aspect of resilience (for example, flexibility, redundancy, diversity) should be improved and what aspect should be prioritised (Wardekker et al. 2021). There is a patchy history of strategic or higher-order plans for Australian cities: an open space plan laid over a transport plan, within a strategic land-use plan not connected to the infrastructure plan, at odds with a nature conservation plan, and so on. Can an approach to living well in Australia's current and future climate be an integrating strategy that brings such plans together, providing local decision-makers and social actors with broad but flexible guidance for actions accounting for the near and longer terms and across jurisdictions and sectors?

From resilience to adaptation policy integration

Despite being contested, resilience is a useful concept in climate adaptation policy. The inherent flexibility of the concept can enhance its function as a 'boundary object' that connects multiple sectors and stakeholders (Brand and Jax 2007). Davoudi et al. (2012: 309) highlight the power-laden nature of resilience as an opportunity to allow 'values to be identified, choices to be made, and political pathways to be identified'. Critically approached, 'resilience' can force explicit discussions about what matters, to whom, for whom, where, and when. This is key to understanding and consideration of values that can be delivered via policy.

We propose that, when framed in the context of resilience, climate adaptation could become a metapolicy framework focusing on best-value community outcomes through better integration across sectors and institutional levels and consideration of policy co-benefits across sectors and levels. This is a recommendation easier said than done, however, consideration of two critical issues could prove helpful. First, there is a need for clear delineations of adaptation and resilience (sometimes used interchangeably) for decision-making to better understand policy intentions. For example, adaptation is often associated with new conditions and forward-looking expectations to alter a system to accommodate anticipated climate change and seek opportunities and new benefits, while resilience is sometimes considered as withstanding a hazard and a return to pre-disturbance conditions (CRS 2021). Noting the distinctions between the two terms can help clarify policy implications: what are we seeking to achieve? Using these terms interchangeably can create confusion and uncertainty. For example, managed retreat of development and infrastructure from high-risk areas as an adaptation approach (O'Donnell 2022) is at odds with the 'bouncing back' understanding of resilience. Clear translation of key policy principles in higher-order policies and statutes can drive the direction and longevity of subsidiary policies, plans, and actions.

Second, in line with resilience thinking, adaptation policy should consider the whole socio-ecological system, focusing on cross-sectoral integration of resilience goals and outcomes, not on separate parts of the system. Treating the elements of the system (such as a city) separately—conceptually or in policies and plans—can undermine resilience by leading to larger disasters in the long term (Bettencourt and West 2010). Similarly, adaptation policy that ignores the links between urban and rural systems will inevitably overlook important material, energy, and service flows. One way to enhance such policy integration is through the consideration of the dimensions of resilience when framing policy. These dimensions are physical/infrastructural, natural, economic, institutional, and social (Ribeiro and Gonçalves 2019). When framed by its dimensions, resilience can be a crosscutting concept, extending across organisational silos and bringing stakeholders together around a shared vision (Torabi et al. 2021). The key is interpreting resilience as concerning the capacities of a system (ecosystem, community, city) to continue to provide key outcomes (energy supply, water, employment, social connection) in the face of change, but not necessarily in the same manner as before—being able to benefit from disturbance and change rather than simply resist, defend, or recover (Cañizares et al. 2021), and realising the co-benefits that expand beyond. Resilience thus becomes closer to adaptation.

Policy recommendations

To bring the preceding arguments together, we propose several broad policy propositions. The first is bold: adaptation and resilience to climate change should be a fundamental structural consideration across policy and planning instruments. The imperative to adapt is clear, the cross-sectoral linkages are strong and demand integration, the cost of not adapting is significant, and the potential co-benefits are abundant. Strategic plans, structural plans, sectoral policies, and the like should not include subsidiary or tangential accommodation of climate change adaptation, but rather be reviewed and revised to be consistent with long-term purposeful adaptation. In planning terms, adaptation becomes a 'superior' plan and principle—one that focuses on delivering broader values and benefits to the community.

How to achieve such a commitment? We propose the following broad policy initiatives, most of which have precedents that are noted and some of which are explored in the cross-sectoral case studies in Brown and Dovers (2021) that provide lessons for climate policy (and refer to other iterations of measures equalling a transformative adaptation response—for example, FEA 2022). These reforms are not fanciful or unachievable in our political and legal system:

- Clarifying meaning and definitions to enable better policy framing of what disturbances the policy should focus on, what future scenarios to anticipate, defining levels of acceptable risk, and enabling a shift from the reactive 'predict and plan' approach to more adaptive approaches. Clarity of intent and trade-offs are core to effective policy.

- Robust strategic policy frameworks at national and state levels, developed in a coordinated fashion, with consistent, broad scope and pathways, policy principles, and general objectives, while allowing flexibility in implementation. Such policies would exhibit known policy success criteria such as those proposed by Samnakay (2021), drawing on other, previous policy reform experiences.

- Development of agreed necessary measures nationally, and formulation in policy and regulation of these at state level, to provide local government with a mandate and support to take strong and consistent adaptation measures across all sectors and levels. (A precedent at state level is sea-level rise benchmarks, noting that these have problematically been changed.)

- A review of relevant statutes and major policies at national and state levels, to identify and recommend reforms in cases where adaptation is discouraged, not enabled, or could be encouraged. (Precedent: National Competition Policy legislative review.)

- Institutional mechanisms nationally and at state level to provide information, drive and monitor policy integration and implementation, and measure success. (Precedent: National Water Commission's research and information monitoring roles for the National Water Initiative, before its disestablishment in 2014, and likely re-establishment by the new national government.)

- Insertion of nondiscretionary obligations on relevant agencies (health, transport, planning, infrastructure, etc.) to explicitly consider climate change adaptation and resilience as core concerns in policy and decision-making, principally but not only via statutory objects in enabling legislation. (Precedent: Inclusion of principles of ecologically sustainable development in multiple statutes after the 1992 national strategy for ecologically sustainable development).

- Within the above, an explicit requirement to account for the distributional and equity implications of both climate impacts and possible adaptation measures in policy.

- Development of widely promulgated methods for assessing the costs and benefits of adaptation measures, over long time frames, and considering environmental, social, and economic aspects, providing decision-makers such as local councils with an authoritative basis for regulation and investment. (Precedent: The work of Infrastructure Australia.)
- Adequate resourcing where implementation of adaptation measures consistent with strategic policies falls to local government or other local or regional actors, consistent with the principle of subsidiarity. (Precedents: Many, across national and state grant and funding programs.)
- Significant research and development coordination and support, linking research, policy, and practice. (Precedent: The productive and collaborative National Climate Change Adaptation Research Facility, when properly funded.)

Conclusion

Is such a strong, coordinated, long-term policy response possible in an era in which proactive policy reform is difficult (Brown and Dovers 2021; Daley et al. 2021), the 2022 election of an apparently more reformist government notwithstanding? Once upon a time, Australia's governments decided that our economy and society had to be more open to the world, competitive, and efficient. They drove massive policy change via the National Competition Policy suite of measures, and changed the nation profoundly with a determined, robust policy approach (Curran and Hollander 2002). In the same era, Australia recognised the need to achieve ecological sustainability, undertook much work, promised much, and failed to create or implement a believable policy response. Those were social and political choices.

In the twenty-first century, climate change demands we embrace change and adapt the way we live and how we organise and manage our cities. Should we decide we want to live well in Australia's currently changing and very different future climate, the political, institutional, informational, and policy capacity are available for the task. It is a choice.

In this chapter, we have proposed climate change adaptation as a metapolicy principle and framework for better integration of urban and planning policy across all levels of government (vertical integration) and different sectors and portfolios (horizontal integration). While contested, the concept of resilience provides opportunities for systems thinking and holistic consideration of all elements of our cities. Framing climate change adaptation through the lens of resilience provides opportunities to benefit from change (rather than simply resisting it) and realise co-benefits that go beyond adaptation. This would underpin the sustainability of our cities.

References

Australian Academy of Science (AAS). 2021. *The Risks to Australia of a 3°C Warmer World*. Canberra: AAS.

Australian Government. 2015. *National Climate Resilience and Adaptation Strategy 2015*. Canberra: Commonwealth of Australia.

Australian Government. 2021. *National Climate Resilience and Adaptation Strategy 2021–2025*. Canberra: Commonwealth of Australia.

Barnett, J., S. Graham, C. Mortreux, R. Fincher, E. Waters, and A. Hurlimann. 2014. 'A Local Coastal Adaptation Pathway.' *Nature Climate Change* 4(12): 1103–8. doi.org/10.1038/nclimate2383.

Bettencourt, L., and G. West. 2010. 'A Unified Theory of Urban Living.' *Nature* 467(7318): 912–13. doi.org/10.1038/467912a.

Brand, F.S., and K. Jax. 2007. 'Focusing the Meaning(s) of Resilience: Resilience as a Descriptive Concept and a Boundary Object.' *Ecology and Society* 12(1): 23. doi.org/10.5751/ES-02029-120123.

Brown, N., and S. Dovers, eds. 2021. *Principles of Effective Policy Reform: Lessons for Australia's Climate Change Policy Impasse*. Canberra: Academy of the Social Sciences in Australia.

Bulkeley, H., and R. Tuts. 2013. 'Understanding Urban Vulnerability, Adaptation and Resilience in the Context of Climate Change.' *Local Environment* 18(6): 646–62. doi.org/10.1080/13549839.2013.788479.

Burgmann, V., and H.A. Baer. 2012. *Climate Politics and the Climate Movement in Australia*. Melbourne: Melbourne University Press.

Cañizares, J.C., S.M. Copeland, and N. Doorn. 2021. 'Making Sense of Resilience.' *Sustainability* 13(15): 8538. doi.org/10.3390/su13158538.

Carpenter, S., B. Walker, J.M. Anderies, and N. Abel. 2001. 'From Metaphor to Measurement: Resilience of What to What?' *Ecosystems* 4(8): 765–81. doi.org/10.1007/s10021-001-0045-9.

Chelleri, L., J.J. Waters, M. Olazabal, and G. Minucci. 2015. 'Resilience Trade-Offs: Addressing Multiple Scales and Temporal Aspects of Urban Resilience.' *Environment and Urbanization* 27(1): 181–98. doi.org/10.1177/0956247814550780.

Cole, L., S. Dovers, M. Gough, and M. Eburn. 2018. 'Can Major Post-Event Inquiries and Reviews Contribute to Lessons Management?' *Australian Journal of Emergency Management* 33(2): 34–39.

Commonwealth Scientific and Industrial Research Organisation (CSIRO) and Bureau of Meteorology (BOM). 2020. *State of the Climate 2020*. Canberra: Commonwealth of Australia.

Congressional Research Service (CRS). 2021. 'Climate Change: Defining *Adaptation* and *Resilience*, with Implications for Policy.' *In Focus*, May. Washington, DC: CRS. Available from: sgp.fas.org/crs/misc/IF11827.pdf.

Cote, M., and A.J. Nightingale. 2012. 'Resilience Thinking Meets Social Theory: Situating Social Change in Socio-Ecological Systems (SES) Research.' *Progress in Human Geography* 36(4): 475–89. doi.org/10.1177/0309132511425708.

Council of Australian Governments (COAG). 2011. *National Strategy for Disaster Resilience*. Canberra: Attorney-General's Department.

Curran, G., and R. Hollander. 2002. 'Changing Policy Mindsets: ESD and NCP Compared.' *Australasian Journal of Environmental Management* 9(3): 158–68. doi.org/10.1080/14486563.2002.10648556.

Daley, J., B. Matthews, and R. Anderson. 2021. *Gridlock: Removing Barriers to Policy Reform*. Grattan Institute Report 2021-08. Melbourne: Grattan Institute.

Davidson, J.L., C. Jacobson, A. Lyth, A. Dedekorkut-Howes, C.L. Baldwin, N.J. Ellison, N.J. Holbrook, M.J. Howes, S. Serrao-Neumann, L. Singh-Peterson, and T.F. Smith. 2016. 'Interrogating Resilience: Toward a Typology to Improve its Operationalization.' *Ecology and Society* 21(2): 27. doi.org/10.5751/ES-08450-210227.

Davoudi, S., K. Shaw, L.J. Haider, A.E. Quinlan, G.D. Peterson, C. Wilkinson, H. Fünfgeld, D. McEvoy, and L. Porter. 2012. 'Resilience: A Bridging Concept or a Dead End? "Reframing" Resilience: Challenges for Planning Theory and Practice. Interacting Traps: Resilience Assessment of a Pasture Management System in Northern Afghanistan. Urban Resilience: What Does it Mean in Planning Practice? Resilience as a Useful Concept for Climate Change Adaptation? The Politics of Resilience for Planning: A Cautionary Note.' *Planning Theory & Practice* 13(2): 299–333. doi.org/10.1080/14649357.2012.677124.

Dedekorkut-Howes, A., E. Torabi, and M. Howes. 2020. 'Planning for a Different Kind of Sea Change: Lessons from Australia for Sea Level Rise and Coastal Flooding.' *Climate Policy* 21(2): 152–70. doi.org/10.1080/14693062.2020. 1819766.

Department of Climate Change (DCC). 2009. *Climate Change Risks to Australia's Coast: A First Pass National Assessment.* Canberra: Commonwealth of Australia. Available from: www.climatechange.gov.au/~/media/publications/coastline/cc-risks-full-report.pdf.

Department of Climate Change and Energy Efficiency (DCCEE). 2011. *Climate Change Risks to Coastal Buildings and Infrastructure: A Supplement to the First Pass National Assessment.* Canberra: Commonwealth of Australia.

Department of Environment and Heritage Protection (DEHP). 2016. *Advancing Climate Action in Queensland: Making the Transition to a Low Carbon Future.* Brisbane: Queensland Government.

Dovers, S. 2022. 'Mainstreaming Disaster Risk Reduction, Seriously?' *Australian Journal of Emergency Management* 37(2): 20–28.

Future Earth Australia (FEA). 2022. *A National Strategy for Just Adaptation.* Canberra: Australian Academy of Science. Available from: www.futureearth. org.au/publications/national-strategy-just-adaptation-0.

Gibbs, M. 2016. 'Why is Coastal Retreat So Hard to Implement? Understanding the Political Risk of Coastal Adaptation Pathways.' *Ocean and Coastal Management* 130: 107–14. doi.org/10.1016/j.ocecoaman.2016.06.002.

Gurran, N., B. Norman, and E. Hamin. 2013. 'Climate Change Adaptation in Coastal Australia: An Audit of Planning Practice.' *Ocean and Coastal Management* 86: 100–9. doi.org/10.1016/j.ocecoaman.2012.10.014.

Handmer, J.W., and S.R. Dovers. 1996. 'A Typology of Resilience: Rethinking Institutions for Sustainable Development.' *Organization & Environment* 9(4): 482–511. doi.org/10.1177/108602669600900403.

Holling, C.S. 1973. 'Resilience and Stability of Ecological Systems.' *Annual Review of Ecology and Systematics* 4: 1–23. doi.org/10.1146/annurev.es.04.110173. 000245.

Howes, M., and A. Dedekorkut-Howes. 2017. 'The Adaptation Roller-Coaster: Planning for Climate Change on the Gold Coast, Queensland.' Paper presented to Eighth State of Australasian Cities National Conference, Adelaide, 28–30 November. Available from: apo.org.au/node/178686.

Intergovernmental Panel on Climate Change (IPCC). 2018. 'Annex I: Glossary.' [Matthews, J.B.R., ed.]. In *Global Warming of 1.5°C. An IPCC Special Report on the Impacts of Global Warming of 1.5°C Above Pre-Industrial Levels and Related Global Greenhouse Gas Emission Pathways, in the Context of Strengthening the Global Response to the Threat of Climate Change, Sustainable Development, and Efforts to Eradicate Poverty*, edited by V. Masson-Delmotte, P. Zhai, H.-O. Pörtner, D. Roberts, J. Skea, P.R. Shukla, A. Pirani, W. Moufouma-Okia, C. Péan, R. Pidcock, S. Connors, J.B.R. Matthews, Y. Chen, X. Zhou, M.I. Gomis, E. Lonnoy, T. Maycock, M. Tignor, and T. Waterfield, 541–62. Cambridge, UK: Cambridge University Press. doi.org/10.1017/9781009157940.008.

Intergovernmental Panel on Climate Change (IPCC). 2021. 'Summary for Policymakers.' In *Climate Change 2021: The Physical Science Basis. Contribution of Working Group I to the Sixth Assessment Report of the Intergovernmental Panel on Climate Change*, edited by V. Masson-Delmotte, P. Zhai, A. Pirani, S.L. Connors, C. Péan, S. Berger, N. Caud, Y. Chen, L. Goldfarb, M.I. Gomis, M. Huang, K. Leitzell, E. Lonnoy, J.B.R. Matthews, T.K. Maycock, T. Waterfield, O. Yelekçi, R. Yu, and B. Zhou. Cambridge, UK: Cambridge University Press. Available from: www.ipcc.ch/report/ar6/wg1/downloads/report/IPCC_AR6_WGI_SPM_final.pdf.

McEvoy, D., H. Fünfgeld, and K. Bosomworth. 2013. 'Resilience and Climate Change Adaptation: The Importance of Framing.' *Planning Practice and Research* 28(3): 280–93. doi.org/10.1080/02697459.2013.787710.

Matyas, D., and M. Pelling. 2015. 'Positioning Resilience for 2015: The Role of Resistance, Incremental Adjustment and Transformation in Disaster Risk Management Policy.' *Disasters* 39(s1): 1–18. doi.org/10.1111/disa.12107.

Measham, T.G., B.L. Preston, T.F. Smith, C. Brooke, R. Gorddard, G. Withycombe, and C. Morrison. 2011. 'Adapting to Climate Change through Local Municipal Planning: Barriers and Challenges.' *Mitigation and Adaptation Strategies for Global Change* 16: 889–909. doi.org/10.1007/s11027-011-9301-2.

Meerow, S., and J.P. Newell. 2016. 'Urban Resilience for Whom, What, When, Where, and Why?' *Urban Geography* 40(3): 309–29. doi.org/10.1080/02723638.2016.1206395.

Meerow, S., J.P. Newell, and M. Stults. 2016. 'Defining Urban Resilience: A Review.' *Landscape and Urban Planning* 147: 38–49. doi.org/10.1016/j.landurbplan.2015.11.011.

Nalau, J., E. Torabi, N. Edwards, M. Howes, and E. Morgan. 2021. 'A Critical Exploration of Adaptation Heuristics.' *Climate Risk Management* 32: 100292. doi.org/10.1016/j.crm.2021.100292.

Nelson, D.R. 2011. 'Adaptation and Resilience: Responding to a Changing Climate.' *Wiley Interdisciplinary Reviews: Climate Change* 2(1): 113–20. doi.org/10.1002/wcc.91.

O'Donnell, T. 2022. 'Managed Retreat and Planned Retreat: A Systematic Literature Review.' *Philosophical Transactions of the Royal Society B: Biological Sciences* 377(1854). doi.org/10.1098/rstb.2021.0129.

Restemeyer, B., J. Woltjer, and M. van den Brink. 2015. 'A Strategy-Based Framework for Assessing the Flood Resilience of Cities: A Hamburg Case Study.' *Planning Theory and Practice* 16(1): 45–62. doi.org/10.1080/14649357.2014.1000950.

Ribeiro, P.J.G., and L.A.P.J. Gonçalves. 2019. 'Urban Resilience: A Conceptual Framework.' *Sustainable Cities and Society* 50(May): 101625. doi.org/10.1016/j.scs.2019.101625.

Ross, A., and S. Dovers. 2008. 'Making the Harder Yards: Environmental Policy Integration in Australia.' *Australian Journal of Public Administration* 67: 245–60. doi.org/10.1111/j.1467-8500.2008.00585.x.

Ruming, K., G. Nicole, P.J. Maginn, and G. Robin. 2017. 'Australian Planning System Reform: Tinkering at the Edges or Instrumental Change?' In *The Routledge Handbook of Australian Urban and Regional Planning*, edited by N. Sipe and K. Vella, 98–109. New York, NY: Routledge. doi.org/10.4324/9781315748054-9.

Samnakay, N. 2017. 'Thinking Strategically in Federal Policy: Defining the Attributes of High-Level Policies.' *Australian Journal of Public Administration* 76(1): 106–21. doi.org/10.1111/1467-8500.12199.

Samnakay, N. 2021. 'A Framework for Analysing and Informing Australia's Strategic National Resource Management Policies.' *Australasian Journal of Environmental Management* 28(3): 267–86. doi.org/10.1080/14486563.2021.1959427.

Solomons, M., and M. Willacy. 2014. 'Jeff Seeney Orders Moreton Bay Regional Council to Remove References to Climate Change–Derived Sea Level Rises from Regional Plan.' *ABC News*, 9 December. Available from: www.abc.net.au/news/2014-12-09/seeney-removes-climate-change-references-from-council-plan/5954914.

Talberg, A., S. Hui, and K. Loynes. 2016. *Australian Climate Change Policy to 2015: A chronology.* Parliamentary Library Research Papers 2015–16, [Updated 5 May]. Canberra: Parliament of the Commonwealth of Australia. Available from: www.aph.gov.au/About_Parliament/Parliamentary_Departments/Parliamentary_Library/pubs/rp/rp1516/Climate2015.

Thom, B. 2018. 'Climate Change Adaptation in Australia: A Loss of Momentum.' *Pearls and Irritations*, 28 February. Available from: johnmenadue.com/bruce-thom-climate-change-adaptation-a-loss-of-momentum/.

Torabi, E., A. Dedekorkut-Howes, and M. Howes. 2017. 'Not Waving, Drowning: Can Local Government Policies on Climate Change Adaptation and Disaster Resilience Make a Difference?' *Urban Policy and Research* 35(3): 312–32. doi.org/10.1080/08111146.2017.1294538.

Torabi, E., A. Dedekorkut-Howes, and M. Howes. 2021. 'A Framework for Using the Concept of Urban Resilience in Responding to Climate-Related Disasters.' *Urban Research & Practice* 15(4): 561–83. doi.org/10.1080/17535069.2020.1846771.

Wardekker, A., B. Wilk, V. Brown, C. Uittenbroek, H. Mees, P. Driessen, M. Wassen, A. Molenaar, J. Walda, and H. Runhaar. 2021. 'A Diagnostic Tool for Supporting Policymaking on Urban Resilience.' *Cities* 101(2020): 10269. doi.org/10.1016/j.cities.2020.102691.

Wellington, T. 2019. 'Why This South-East Queensland Council Declared a "Climate Emergency".' *Brisbane Times*, 27 July. Available from: www.brisbanetimes.com.au/national/queensland/why-this-south-east-queensland-council-declared-a-climate-emergency-20190724-p52acd.html.

World Meteorology Organization (WMO), United Nations Environment Programme (UNEP), Intergovernmental Panel on Climate Change (IPCC), United Nations Office for Disaster Risk Reduction (UNDRR), Global Carbon Project (GCP), and UK Met Office. 2022. *United in Science 2022: A Multi-Organization High-Level Compilation of the Most Recent Science Related to Climate Change, Impacts and Responses*. Geneva: WMO. Available from: library.wmo.int/index.php?lvl=notice_display&id=22128#.YyFhxnauY2w.

5

The UN Sustainable Development Goals: Australia's de facto national urban policy?

Alexei Trundle and Brendan Gleeson

Introduction

The 2030 Agenda for Sustainable Development forms the centrepiece of the United Nations' global development framework, setting out 17 Sustainable Development Goals (SDGs) and 169 associated targets, to be reported on and achieved by all 193 UN member states by 2030. Elevated within this global agreement is an 'urban' goal (SDG11), which aims to 'make cities inclusive, safe, resilient and sustainable' through 10 city-focused targets and 15 associated indicators. This global agreement, to which Australia is a signatory, arguably represents the country's highest-level commitment to urban policymaking and sustainability, with many of the additional targets contained within the other 16 SDGs also requiring extensive urban transformation if they are to be achieved nationally.

Implementation of the 2030 Agenda by the Australian Government was lackadaisical, patchwork, and tokenistic during the first five-year period of its enactment (2015–20). Australia—along with several other economically developed countries—has struggled to integrate the SDGs with both foreign aid programs and domestically focused policy frameworks.

Despite nominally taking a 'whole-of-government' approach, the primary responsibility for implementing and reporting on the SDGs has fallen on the Department of Foreign Affairs and Trade, with limited support or engagement from other relevant agencies such as the Australian Bureau of Statistics (ABS) and the Department of the Prime Minister and Cabinet (PM&C) (Pawar et al. 2020).

This lack of institutional integration and analysis is reflected in Australia's slow progress towards the targets contained within each of the 17 goals. A recent global benchmarking report found only 35 per cent of the targets with available indicator data were 'on track' for achievement by 2030, while Australia's overall progress continued to lag the OECD average (Allen et al. 2020: 528). Implementation of SDG11 has been even more limited, both domestically and within Australia's international development programs and policy (Allen et al. 2020).

These results are despite an accelerating uptake of the 2030 Agenda by local and state governments, as well as civil society organisations and corporations (Giles-Corti et al. 2020). The State of Victoria's updated metropolitan planning strategy, *Plan Melbourne 2017–2050*, for example, commits the entire metropolitan area of Australia's second-largest city to monitoring and reporting against the SDG Framework (DELWP 2017). At another scale, the Melbourne City Council has directly integrated the SDGs into its own strategic planning framework (City of Melbourne 2022). The 2030 Agenda is also being taken up by nongovernmental entities. In 2019, 48 per cent of the 150 largest companies listed on the Australian Stock Exchange (the ASX150) reported against the SDGs (up from 37 per cent in 2018), while in 2020 a consortium of 52 chief executive officers (CEOs) from across civil society, academia, and the business sector petitioned the Australian Government to 'build back better' by framing its Covid-19 recovery plan around the targets contained within the 2030 Agenda.

This chapter argues that the SDGs present an unprecedented opportunity to align local, state, and national governments' urban planning processes within Australia, in partnership with communities, the private sector, and academia. While complex, consideration of sustainable urban development within this more holistic—and globally relevant—frame can bring to light broader synergies and trade-offs across the often-disparate agendas of urban stakeholders and decision-makers. Rather than continuing to search for the 'Holy Grail' of a standalone, detailed, and well-resourced National Urban

Policy, alignment with the 2030 Agenda is proposed to provide an alternative advocacy position that can draw on existing bipartisan Commonwealth commitments to transformative urban sustainability.

Planning for sustainable cities in a neoliberal age

Two decades ago, Gleeson (2000) observed that strategic urban governance in Australia had been all but dismantled in line with the ascendency of neoliberalism but faced a turning tide as subnational governments— particularly the states of Victoria and New South Wales—renewed their interest. This was far from the first attempt to reconfigure the citadels of Australian modernity and non-primary economic production (Ruming et al. 2010). However, the need to develop new models to 'govern cities in the age of globalization' (Gleeson 2000: 270) was for the first time being defined not by concern for the immediate environmental condition of the cities themselves, but by the urban age's collective implications for environmental sustainability writ large.

Despite these positive subnational signs, Australian urban governance and policy at the Commonwealth level progressed little over the first two decades of the twenty-first century. Neoliberal urbanism marched on in the face of growing awareness of the exceedance of planetary boundaries and a deeper understanding of the spatial and temporal implications of the Anthropocene. At the halfway point of this period, the late Patrick Troy noted in his review of Australian urban research and planning that 'sober analysis of urban issues has been replaced by the influence peddlers and "admen" who campaign for various developers', with little concern among political leaders for 'serious, informed exploration of alternative approaches to the social, locational or environment consequences of the way Australian Cities are developed and managed' (Troy 2013: 147). Urban inequality has relatedly continued to grow—a microcosm of the global stratification of wealth, as the meta-feudal structures of global corporations consolidate power at the expense of the retreating state.

Australia's local governments and municipalities, however, align poorly with this narrative of a disengaged and increasingly privatised neoliberal nation. Contrary to the persistent stereotypes of local governments as delegated purveyors of roads, rates, and rubbish (alongside more political criticisms of incumbency to developer interests and party politics), the twenty-first-century turn in urban Australia has seen a resurgence of municipal advocacy and activism, including in relation to environmental issues (Brown 1992; de Vries 2021). This is especially evident within progressive electoral geographies where municipal policies, investments, and activities diverge from Commonwealth and state consensus, in areas ranging from the celebration of Australia Day on 26 January to the installation of cycle paths and the provision of affordable housing.

Most prominent within these local urban agendas is the push for emissions reduction and climate action more broadly, which has occurred concurrently with nearly a decade of sustained national policy failure and persistent criticism on the global scale (Robiou Du Pont et al. 2017; Hadfield and Cook 2019). This subnational insurrection has been by no means limited to Australia, with similar movements evident in the city governments of other climate 'laggards', such as Vancouver, Canada, and New York City in the United States (Jones 2013). It also reaches far beyond the domains of the inner-city 'elites', with nearly 100 Australian local governments, representing more than 8 million primarily urban citizens, declaring a climate emergency by mid-2020 (Chou 2021; Oke et al. 2021).

Broader conceptualisations of sustainable urban development and policy, however, continue to lack cohesion at any level of Australian government. Municipalities are yet to consolidate efforts around a recognised sustainability framework, while states and territories remain focused on energy and transport infrastructure initiatives, and the Commonwealth continues to demonstrate limited interest in furthering sustainable urban form and policy. The example of climate action, nonetheless, provides a template for a wider consideration of the leadership role that Australian cities can play in driving a national urban sustainability agenda within and beyond Australia (Acuto et al. 2021)—a provocation on which we expand here through the lens of the SDGs.

Cities and urban planning within the 2030 Agenda

The inclusion of an 'urban' goal (SDG11) within the 2030 Agenda was heralded as a victory for urban planning and policy at the global scale, recognising the world's majority urban population and the disproportionate flows of resources, waste, and associated means of production contained within and drawn on by cities (Simon et al. 2015; Barnett and Parnell 2016). This aspect of the transition from the more narrowly defined Millennium Development Goals (MDGs) was dually significant, representing both a new acknowledgement within the UN system of the role of subnational governments in development and the wider shift in conceding that 'in an urban world, cities can be pathways to sustainable development' (Parnell 2016: 529). SDG11 also sat outside the 2030 Agenda's broader coupling of the socioeconomically centred Millennium Declaration's objectives with planetary boundaries and cycles (Griggs et al. 2013), reflecting a deeper geography characteristic of the Anthropocene (Gandy 2018).

As a singular goal, SDG11 provides a formidable policy framework for sustainable urbanisation on its own. Within the overarching objective of making 'cities and human settlements inclusive, safe, resilient, and sustainable' are a further 10 targets and 15 associated indicators for measuring progress. As shown in Table 5.1, these targets encompass a diverse characterisation of urban sustainability and its contemporary detractors at the global scale, ranging from housing affordability and greenspace, to supply chains and carbon emissions.

Table 5.1 Targets within the 'urban' Sustainable Development Goal 11

11.1	By 2030, ensure access for all to adequate, safe, and affordable housing and basic services, and upgrade slums.
11.2	By 2030, provide access to safe, affordable, accessible, and sustainable transport systems for all, improving road safety — notably, by expanding public transport, with special attention to the needs of those in vulnerable situations, women, children, persons with disabilities, and older persons.
11.3	By 2030, enhance inclusive and sustainable urbanisation and capacity for participatory, integrated, and sustainable human settlement planning and management in all countries.
11.4	Strengthen efforts to protect and safeguard the world's cultural and natural heritage.
11.5	By 2030, significantly reduce the number of deaths from, the number of people affected by, and substantially decrease the direct economic losses relative to global gross domestic product caused by disasters, including water-related disasters, with a focus on protecting poor and vulnerable people.
11.6	By 2030, reduce the adverse per capita environmental impact of cities, including by paying special attention to air quality and municipal and other waste management.

11.7	By 2030, provide universal access to safe, inclusive, and accessible green and public spaces — in particular, for women and children, older persons, and persons with disabilities.
11.a	Support positive economic, social, and environmental links between urban, peri-urban, and rural areas by strengthening national and regional development planning.
11.b	By 2020, substantially increase the number of cities and human settlements adopting and implementing integrated policies and plans towards inclusion, resource efficiency, mitigation and adaptation to climate change, and resilience to disasters, and develop and implement, in line with the Sendai Framework for Disaster Risk Reduction 2015–30, holistic disaster risk management at all levels.
11.c	Support least-developed countries, including through financial and technical assistance, in building sustainable and resilient buildings utilising local materials.

Source: UN (2014).

SDG11 alone therefore constitutes a transformative urban agenda that, if fully implemented globally by 2030, would radically shift the global development trajectory towards sustainability, and indeed address a broader array of urban concerns in areas such as social services and governance. With the world's urban population projected to double by the middle of this century (Trundle et al. 2019), there is the potential to 'embed' these ideals within yet-to-be-built urban areas and through the retrofitting of existing urban areas and the upgrading of the informal housing of the world's more than 1 billion informal urban inhabitants (French et al. 2021).

The 2030 Agenda's other 16 goals are also inextricably intertwined with cities and urban governance to varying extents. As illustrated in Figure 5.1, global assessments by local government peak bodies and multilateral organisations such as the United Nations Human Settlements Programme (UN-Habitat) and United Cities and Local Governments (UCLG) have identified that roughly two-thirds of the 169 SDG targets require input and implementation by local governments (UCLG 2015; GTLRG et al. 2016). These range from managing conditions associated with road-related deaths and injuries (Target 3.6 under the good health and wellbeing goal, SDG3) to the leadership of cities in areas such as climate action (SDG13) and energy consumption and associated emissions (SDG7).

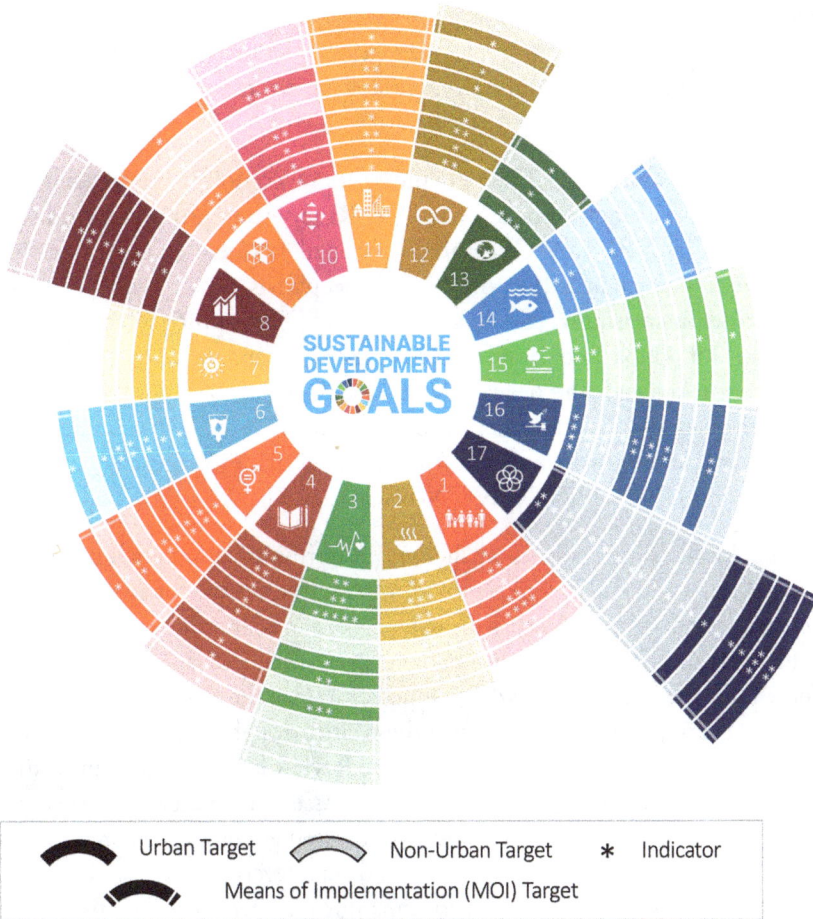

Figure 5.1 Urban-relevant SDG targets
Source: Trundle et al. (2021).

The Voluntary Local Review movement: Localising the global goals

The ability to 'localise' the scope of nationally focused targets further broadens the potential application of the 2030 Agenda within cities, contingent on jurisdiction, urban form, and geographic context. Localisation is a central component of city-scale adaptation and application of the SDGs, allowing city actors to scope goals, targets, and indicators to their local context. No specific definition of localisation is provided within the 2030 Agenda, its guidance documentation, or its implementation frameworks. However, it is defined here as the process of adapting, implementing, and monitoring the SDGs at a subnational level, including by nongovernmental actors, to contribute to the achievement of the 2030 Agenda.

Localisation efforts by cities are increasingly consolidating around the concept of a Voluntary Local Review (VLR) reporting process. Introduced in tandem by New York City and a cohort of Japanese cities of differing size and typology in 2018, the VLR concept has subsequently evolved, with cities increasingly taking a 'whole of SDGs' approach, referred to as 'VLR2.0' (Pipa and Bouchet 2020: 11). Recent guidelines for SDG localisation through the development of a VLR have emerged at regional scales in Europe, North America, and the Asia-Pacific, with frameworks also under development in Latin America and Africa (Siragusa et al. 2020; UCLG and UN-Habitat 2020; UN-ESCAP 2020).

While localisation presents challenges in terms of comparability across jurisdictions and scales, it also provides a tangible avenue for ensuring local relevance and compatibility with existing urban planning frameworks, all under the umbrella of the 'common language' of the SDGs. As of mid-2021, more than 160 cities either had developed or were in the process of developing a VLR (Narang Suri et al. 2021). Of these cities, roughly half had done so as part of the New York City Voluntary Local Review Declaration, committing to presenting their VLR to the UN General Assembly in New York (Narang Suri et al. 2021). VLR development is also being conducted concurrently by local governments at metropolitan and state levels in Brussels, Belgium, and Para, Brazil, respectively—additions not reflected in the figures above (UCLG and UN-Habitat 2020). Within the Asia-Pacific, this figure already includes cities in China, Malaysia, Solomon Islands, Kiribati, Taiwan, the Philippines, and Japan, with the City of Melbourne the sole Australian signatory to date (NYC-OIA 2021).

The City of Melbourne's approach—developed in partnership with the University of Melbourne and Monash University—was designed to not only 'localise' the SDGs and associated targets and indicators, but also ensure that these localisation efforts could be compared with other jurisdictions. Alignment with national metrics and frameworks also means that municipal-scale implementation can be 'scaled up' in line with metropolitan, state, national, and even regional commitments. This localisation approach was enshrined within the Melbourne Principles, through which local stakeholders adapted the suite of global targets within each of the SDGs to suit jurisdictional needs and capabilities, in line with each target's international and national themes. Indicator selection, meanwhile, similarly prioritised comparability and scalability where 'like for like' data could not be found that were consistent with the internationally determined SDG indicator framework.

A parallel SDG benchmarking report developed by the university partners as part of the project demonstrated the value in this approach. Extending the VLR, the benchmarking report ensured that the City of Melbourne's SDG progress could be compared with 700 member cities of the Sustainable Development Solutions Network (SDSN) across Europe and the United States, the more than 650 cities reporting SDG data to the OECD, and 22 other Australian municipalities (drawing primarily on data derived from the ABS) (Briggs et al. 2022). The last comparison, summarised in Figure 5.2, demonstrates the potential for knowledge exchange on SDG implementation and progress at subnational scales, as well as the variation in SDG progress even within a single national context, Australia.

Despite the City of Melbourne being the only Australian city to have publicly committed to developing a VLR to date, a growing number of local governments have begun to engage with the SDGs outside—or, in several cases, as a precursor to involvement within—the VLR movement. The City of Sydney's Sustainable Sydney 2030 strategy embedded goals within its Social Sustainability Policy and Action Plan, focusing on goals 3, 8, 10, 11, 16, and 17 (City of Sydney 2018: 8), while the metropolitan-scale Greater Sydney Commission (now the Greater Cities Commission) has been tasked by the state government to 'consider and integrate' the 2030 Agenda as part of its monitoring and evaluation framework (Holloway 2017). In addition to the City of Melbourne, the metropolitan municipalities of Casey and Whitehorse, and other Victorian cities and towns including Bendigo, Geelong, and Warrnambool have participated in participatory action research programs led by RMIT University, Monash University, and the University of Melbourne, aimed at building institutional capacity and city-to-city networks for taking the next step towards SDG localisation (Leavesley 2021). Like Sydney's plan, *Plan Melbourne 2017–2050* aligns monitoring and evaluation of the implementation of the metropolitan planning strategy with the SDGs (DELWP 2017).

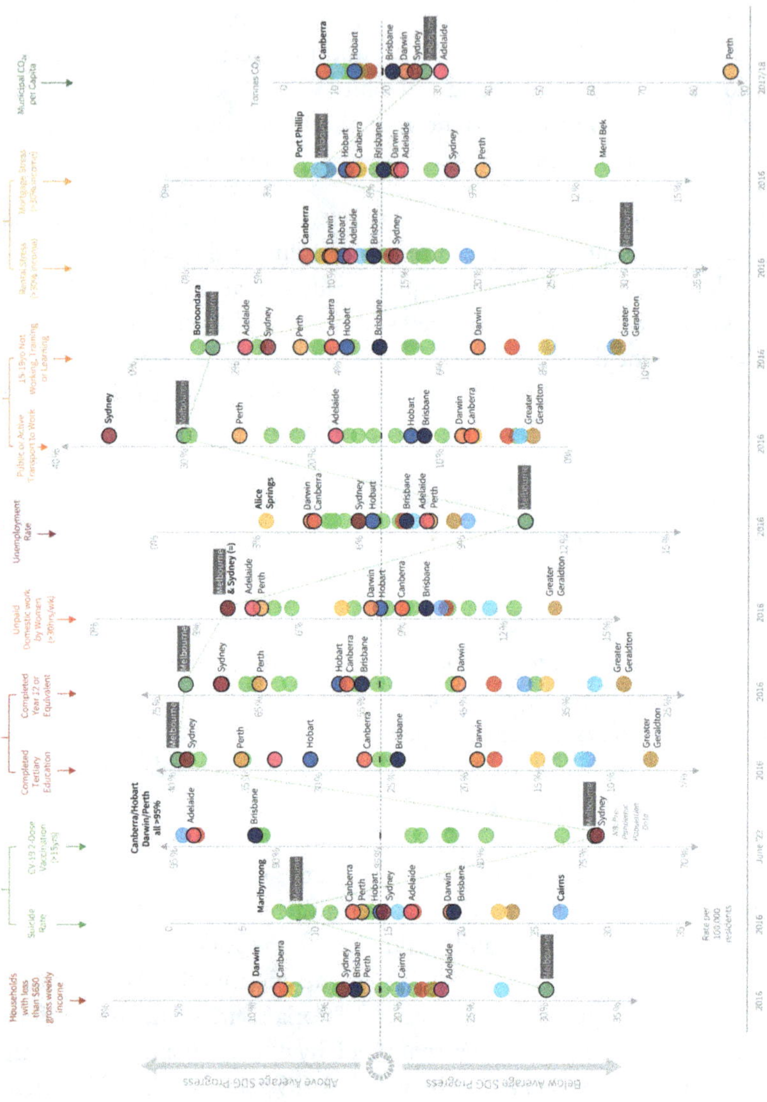

Figure 5.2 Australian city SDG indicator benchmark data
Source: Reproduced from Briggs et al. (2022), with permission.

The diversity of these approaches highlights the multifaceted nature of the 2030 Agenda—an attribute that we argue is a strength rather than a weakness of SDG localisation, albeit one that results in some limitations and complexities in scalability and comparability. Rather than simply situating the SDGs within strategic or environmental planning, their consideration within areas such as community planning—for example, the City of Newcastle—and economic development, as is the case in the Peri-Urban Group of Rural Councils at Melbourne's metropolitan fringe, demonstrates the potential to drive sustainability from locally relevant institutional leverage points (City of Newcastle 2018; Potts 2020). Elsewhere this has enabled key shortcomings of the 2030 Agenda to be addressed. For instance, the Yawuru people of Broome, Western Australia, have developed culturally relevant wellbeing indicators—a process that has been put forward as an example of how Indigenous values, perspectives, and knowledge can be better considered within the indicator framework of the SDGs (Yap and Watene 2019).

Planning for urban sustainability in 'can-do capitalism' Canberra

According to departmental responses to a recent senate inquiry into the implementation, awareness, and measurement of the SDGs in Australia, the Department of Foreign Affairs and Trade was 'actively engaged in more than two years of consultations and negotiations to shape the 2030 Agenda and ensure that the issues that the 2030 Agenda covers aligns [*sic*] with Australia's national interests and challenges faced in our region' (FADTC 2019: 4). The bipartisan Foreign Affairs, Defence and Trade Committee devoted an entire chapter of its 190-page report to partnerships with other levels of government, emphasising the now defunct COAG as a suitable mechanism for aligning local, state, and national SDG implementation strategies and reporting. While the importance of engaging local governments was a feature of the report, specific consideration of urban issues, policies, and considerations within the 2030 Agenda was notably absent.

Australia, as a signatory to the United Nations' New Urban Agenda, committed to developing a National Urban Plan at the UN Conference on Housing and Sustainable Urban Development (Habitat III) in 2016, 'in accordance with the UN-Habitat's *International Guidelines on Urban and Territorial Planning* (Schindler et al. 2018: 48). In its official statement at this vicennial global event, Australia's then Permanent Representative to the United Nations, Ambassador Gillian Bird, acknowledged the intersection between the New Urban Agenda and SDG11, emphasising the influence of urbanisation on Australia's overseas aid program, and the domestic inequalities exhibited in our cities (AMUN 2016).

Australia's first National Urban Policy, however, had been replaced with the *Smart Cities Plan* only six months before Habitat III, with the former left to languish after the fall of the Rudd–Gillard government in 2013 (Burton and Dodson 2016). The latter, as acknowledged by Ambassador Bird, is more 'a vision statement for cities, with a focus on Smart Policy; Smart Investment, and Smart Technology' (AMUN 2016: 5), with resultant city deals applied in a patchwork fashion rather than through the lens of national planning. As noted by Burton, a cynical observer would argue the *Smart Cities Plan* is a 'continuation of an Australian tradition of taking an ad hoc approach to federal urban policy making in which the politics of the pork barrel are preferred to anything more systematic and evidence based' (2017: 10).

Thus, although the past decade has seen an unprecedented level of bipartisan interest in urban management in Australia, the common ground has been situated squarely within the remit of 'contemporary neoliberal urbanism', with 'smart cities' and 'city deals' designed as tools for accelerating economic production with little consideration to social and environmental needs and necessary recalibrations (Gleeson 2018: 206). Despite being referenced strongly in Australia's 2018 VLR, there is little evidence that city deals and the 2016 *Smart Cities Plan* are generating significant progress towards SDG11 or, indeed, the 2030 Agenda as a whole, either implicitly or through more explicit policy alignment (Hu 2020; Stace 2020).

The SDGs—and, indeed, international development—are not immune to such criticisms. The 2030 Agenda is a product of negotiations not only driven by member states but also influenced by powerful global corporations, as well as multilateral champions of these neoliberal ideologies, not least the Bretton Woods Institutions. Although the inclusion of deeper social and environmental considerations in the MDGs' successor was heralded as a shift from the ascendant neoliberalism of the 1990s at the time of the SDGs' inception (Koehler 2015), the centrality of corporate interests within the 2030 Agenda's 'means of implementation', particularly SDG17, the 'partnerships' goal, remains a point of contention (Briant Carant 2017; Weber 2017). However, when coupled with the partisan Australian political context, this apparent contradiction with strategic, transformative government intervention can equally be argued to present a unique platform for bipartisanship in engagement with both national and global urban development processes.

Rainbow-washing or scaffolding? Building SDG literacy

As with the formulation of urban policy more broadly, a key barrier to city or state engagement with the 2030 Agenda is the multifaceted nature of the concept of sustainable development itself. In practice, comprehensive engagement with the SDGs requires a significant investment of time and resources in familiarising institutional representatives, partners, stakeholders, and—if the participatory ethos of the 2030 Agenda is to be followed in full—the public with the SDGs, as well as their subsidiary targets and indicators (Fritz et al. 2019). The difficulties associated with this deployment process can be seen in the earlier iterations of city-scale SDG localisation and VLR development, where local governments selected a subset of or a singular SDG for use within their existing strategic planning environment (Pipa 2019; Narang Suri et al. 2021).

Early efforts by nonstate entities to engage with the SDGs have therefore sustained considerable criticism of their transformative potential, drawing on the precedence and narratives of greenwashing, compounded by the intertwinement of the 2030 Agenda with corporate interests and engagement with the United Nations more broadly (Gupta and Vegelin 2016; Langford 2016). The study of corporate SDG measurement and disclosure of SDG progress in Australia, for instance, found that while 48 per cent of ASX150 companies mentioned the SDGs in their annual corporate sustainability reports in 2019, only five set quantitative or qualitative targets in line with these broader narratives and linkages (Subramaniam et al. 2020: 20). There is therefore legitimate concern that the continuing uptick in interest in and deployment of the SDGs is little more than 'rainbow-washing', centred on the sustainability branding of the SDG 'wheel' and 17 distinctively coloured sustainability squares (Weber and Weber 2020).

A more optimistic perspective, however, would posit that familiarisation with and integration of 17 high-level goals, mapping and calibration of 169 targets, and measurement of more than 200 associated indicators require a gradual and ongoing process of institutional learning and change. It is in this space—enhancing SDG literacy, supporting methodological standardisation, and compiling subnational contributions and initiatives—that the Commonwealth is most sorely needed despite limited substantive engagement to date. In many ways, the potential alignment of local, state, and national efforts around shared SDG interests represents a more structured form of the 'city deals' framework, with the added benefits of both national and international comparability.

It is from this baseline that local governments and their state and federal counterparts will have the potential to scaffold both institutional learning and engagement with the 2030 Agenda. Such a process will also distil difficulties in the comparison and aggregation of indicator data (Simon et al. 2015) and the trade-offs and co-benefits that become contextually evident in SDG implementation (Zinkernagel et al. 2018; Pipa and Bouchet 2020). With SDG literacy in the Australian public lagging significantly behind the global average, as well as that of many other countries in our region (Boyon 2019), federal government engagement through the lens of urban reinvigoration has the potential to provide a new and globally coherent vision for sustainable development in Australia.

Conclusion

The period 2020–30 has been dubbed a 'Decade of Action' to deliver the global goals, with the '10 years to transform our world' intersecting with critical thresholds in greenhouse gas emissions reduction, geopolitical manoeuvring, and the continuing polarisation and socioeconomic upheaval of the Covid-19 pandemic. Australia, however, sits at dual policy impasses, with national urban policy and international development policy having been articulated with minimal national vision through the past two terms of federal government, beyond a responsiveness to subnational and bilateral needs and initiatives. As a result, trends towards worsening urban inequality and socioeconomic fragmentation have continued (Butcher et al. 2021), while the economic and social opportunities presented by the global transformations already occurring in the middling stages of the twenty-first century continue to pass Australia by (Hatfield-Dodds et al. 2015; Newton et al. 2019).

The 2030 Agenda is undoubtedly imperfect, complicated, and fraught by the multilateral bodies and member state interests from which it has emerged. Key limitations include only indirect consideration of LGBTIQ+ rights and the weak recognition of indigenous peoples (Starrs et al. 2018; Yap and Watene 2019). However, the ability to 'localise' the targets within each goal presents an opportunity to strengthen the 2030 Agenda itself, and address these and other considerations, drawing on a broader cross-section of stakeholders and perspectives outside the tight bounds of multilateralism and the consensus of UN member states.

As argued by Australia's current prime minister, 'when it comes to our cities, legislators need vision. It's not enough to simply respond to the pressures of development and population growth as they arise' (Albanese 2017: 14). The SDGs provide a coherent urban vision that is not only globally agreed, but also has bipartisan federal support both in application within our own cities and, through that, for our international development initiatives. As with all global commitments, the question that arises is the willingness to implement meaningful change locally to address these lofty ambitions, as well as the financial commitment to assist their achievement by less developed countries within our region. Engagement with the more concrete targets and measurement through associated indicators are the keys to the success of the 2030 Agenda in both cases.

As cities have demonstrated through unilateral climate action and greenhouse gas mitigation efforts, subnational government is asserting itself as a new force in international diplomacy, governance, and development more broadly (Moallemi et al. 2020; Mokhles and Davidson 2021). In bringing the SDGs to the forefront of efforts to establish and formalise a new national urban policy, Australia can simultaneously resolve the anti-urban bias in both its international and its domestic policy frameworks, while generating a deeper alignment of our three-tier system of government, with minimal additional intervention at the federal level. This would realise a de facto urban policy that commits us to leaving no citizen—urban or otherwise—behind.

References

Acuto, M., A. Kosovac, D. Pejic, and T.L. Jones. 2021. 'The City as Actor in UN Frameworks: Formalizing "Urban Agency" in the International System?' *Territory, Politics, Governance* 11(3): 519–36. doi.org/10.1080/21622671.2020.1860810.

Albanese, A. 2017. 'Better Cities Need Greater Vision.' *Planning News*, [Victoria], 43(9): 14–15.

Allen, C., M. Reid, J. Thwaites, R. Glover, and T. Kestin. 2020. 'Assessing National Progress and Priorities for the Sustainable Development Goals (SDGs): Experience from Australia.' *Sustainability Science* 15(2): 521–38. doi.org/10.1007/s11625-019-00711-x.

Australian Mission to the United Nations (AMUN). 2016. 'Statement on the New Urban Agenda.' Statement delivered to HABITAT III: The United Nations Conference on Housing and Sustainable Urban Development, Quito, Ecuador, 19 October. New York: AMUN. Available from: unny.mission.gov.au/files/unny/Habitat%20III%20-%20Statement%20on%20the%20New%20Urban%20Agenda%20%2019%20October%202016.pdf.

Barnett, C., and S. Parnell. 2016. 'Ideas, Implementation and Indicators: Epistemologies of the Post-2015 Urban Agenda.' *Environment & Urbanization* 28(1): 87–98. doi.org/10.1177/0956247815621473.

Boyon, N. 2019. *United Nations Sustainable Development Goals: Global Attitudes Towards Its Use and Regulation August 2019.* Ipsos Survey for the World Economic Forum Conducted in August 2019 Wave of Global Advisor. Paris: IPSOS. Available from: www.ipsos.com/en/awareness-united-nations-sustainable-development-goals-highest-emerging-countries.

Briant Carant, J. 2017. 'Unheard Voices: A Critical Discourse Analysis of the Millennium Development Goals' Evolution into the Sustainable Development Goals.' *Third World Quarterly* 38(1): 16–41. doi.org/10.1080/01436597.2016.1166944.

Briggs, J., A. Trundle, J. Boulton, M. Acuto, C. Allen, and J. Thwaites. 2022. *Global SDG Cities Benchmarking Report 2022. SDGs for Melbourne.* Melbourne: Melbourne Centre for Cities, University of Melbourne. doi.org/10.26188/20459880.

Brown, V.A. 1992. 'Roads, Rates and Rubbish Are Environmental Issues: The Environmental Policy Role of Local Government.' *Urban Policy and Research* 10(2): 41–44. doi.org/10.1080/08111149208551494.

Burton, P. 2017. 'Is Urban Planning in Australia Hindered by Poor Metropolitan Governance?' *Urban Science* 1(34): 1–14. doi.org/10.3390/urbansci1040034.

Burton, P., and J. Dodson. 2016. 'Australian Cities: In Pursuit of a National Urban Policy.' In *Australian Public Policy: Progressive Ideas in the Neoliberal Ascendency*, edited by C. Millier and L. Orchard, 245–62. Bristol, UK: Policy Press. doi.org/10.2307/j.ctt1ggjk39.20.

Butcher, S., M. Acuto, and A. Trundle. 2021. 'Leaving No Urban Citizens Behind: An Urban Equality Framework for Deploying the Sustainable Development Goals.' *One Earth* 4(11): 1548–56. doi.org/10.1016/j.oneear.2021.10.015.

Chou, M. 2021. 'Australian Local Governments and Climate Emergency Declarations: Reviewing Local Government Practice.' *Australian Journal of Public Administration* 80(3): 613–23. doi.org/10.1111/1467-8500.12451.

City of Melbourne. 2022. *United Nations Sustainable Development Goals: City of Melbourne Voluntary Local Review 2022*. Melbourne: City of Melbourne in partnership with the Melbourne Centre for Cities, University of Melbourne, and the Monash Sustainable Development Institute, Monash University. Available from: www.melbourne.vic.gov.au/SiteCollectionDocuments/un-sustainable-goals-voluntary-local-review.pdf.

City of Newcastle. 2018. *Newcastle 2030: Community Strategic Plan 2018–2028*, Newcastle, NSW: Newcastle City Council. Available from: www.newcastle.nsw. gov.au/Newcastle/media/Documents/Engagements/Completed/3119-CSP-Strategy-FINAL-WEB.pdf.

City of Sydney. 2018. *A City for All: Towards a Socially Just and Resilient Sydney— Social Sustainability Policy and Action Plan 2018–2028*. Sydney: City of Sydney. Available from: www.cityofsydney.nsw.gov.au/strategies-action-plans/social-sustainability-policy-action-plan.

Department of Environment, Land, Water and Planning (DELWP). 2017. *Plan Melbourne 2017–2050: Metropolitan Planning Strategy*. Melbourne: Victorian Government. Available from: www.planmelbourne.vic.gov.au/__data/assets/ pdf_file/0007/377206/Plan_Melbourne_2017-2050_Strategy_.pdf.

de Vries, S. 2021. 'The Power of Procedural Policy Tools at the Local Level: Australian Local Governments Contributing to Policy Change for Major Projects.' *Policy and Society* 40(3): 414–30. doi.org/10.1080/14494035.2021.1955471.

Foreign Affairs, Defence and Trade References Committee (FADTC). 2019. *United Nations Sustainable Development Goals (SDG)*. Report, February. Canberra: Parliament of the Commonwealth of Australia. Available from: www.aph.gov. au/Parliamentary_Business/Committees/Senate/Foreign_Affairs_Defence_and _Trade/SDGs/Report.

French, M., A. Trundle, I. Korte, and C. Koto. 2021. 'Climate Resilience in Urban Informal Settlements: Towards a Transformative Upgrading Agenda.' In *Climate Resilient Urban Areas*, edited by R. de Graaf-van Dinther, 129–53. Cham, Switzerland: Palgrave Macmillan. doi.org/10.1007/978-3-030-57537-3_7.

Fritz, S., L. See, T. Carlson, M. Haklay, J.L. Oliver, D. Fraisl, R. Mondardini, M. Brocklehurst, L.A. Shanley, S. Schade, U. Wehn, T. Abrate, J. Anstee, S. Arnold, M. Billot, J. Campbell, J. Espey, M. Gold, G. Hager, S. He, L. Hepburn, A. Hsu, D. Long, J. Masó, I. McCallum, M. Muniafu, I. Moorthy, M. Obersteiner, A.J. Parker, M. Weisspflug, and S. West. 2019. 'Citizen Science and the United Nations Sustainable Development Goals.' *Nature Sustainability* 2(10): 922–30. doi.org/10.1038/s41893-019-0390-3.

Gandy, M. 2018. 'Cities in Deep Time.' *City* 22(1): 96–105. doi.org/10.1080/13604813.2018.1434289.

Giles-Corti, B., M. Lowe, and J. Arundel. 2020. 'Achieving the SDGs: Evaluating Indicators to be Used to Benchmark and Monitor Progress Towards Creating Healthy and Sustainable Cities.' *Health Policy* 124(6): 581–90. doi.org/10.1016/j.healthpol.2019.03.001.

Gleeson, B. 2000. 'New Challenges, New Agendas for Australia's Cities.' *International Planning Studies* 5(3): 269–71. doi.org/10.1080/713672859.

Gleeson, B. 2018. 'The Metropolitan Condition.' In *Planning Metropolitan Australia*, edited by S. Hamnett and R. Freestone, 195–211. London: Routledge. doi.org/10.4324/9781315281377-9.

Global Taskforce of Local and Regional Governments (GTLRG), United Nations Development Programme (UNDP), and UN-Habitat 2016. *Roadmap for Localizing the SDGs: Implementation and Monitoring at Subnational Level.* New York, NY: UN Department of Economic and Social Affairs. Available from: sustainabledevelopment.un.org/content/documents/commitments/818_11195_commitment_ROADMAP%20LOCALIZING%20SDGS.pdf.

Griggs, D., M. Stafford-Smith, O. Gaffney, J. Rockström, M.C. Öhman, P. Shyamsundar, W. Steffen, G. Glaser, N. Kanie, and I. Noble. 2013. 'Sustainable Development Goals for People and Planet.' *Nature* 495(7441): 305–7. doi.org/10.1038/495305a.

Gupta, J., and C. Vegelin. 2016. 'Sustainable Development Goals and Inclusive Development.' *International Environmental Agreements: Politics, Law and Economics* 16(3): 433–48. doi.org/10.1007/s10784-016-9323-z.

Hadfield, P., and N. Cook. 2019. 'Financing the Low-Carbon City: Can Local Government Leverage Public Finance to Facilitate Equitable Decarbonisation?' *Urban Policy and Research* 37(1): 13–29. doi.org/10.1080/08111146.2017.1421532.

Hatfield-Dodds, S., H. Schandl, P.D. Adams, T.M. Baynes, T.S. Brinsmead, B.A. Bryan, F.H.S. Chiew, P.W. Graham, M. Grundy, T. Harwood, R. McCallum, R. McCrea, L.E. McKellar, D. Newth, M. Nolan, I. Prosser, and A. Wonhas. 2015. 'Australia is "Free to Choose" Economic Growth and Falling Environmental Pressures.' *Nature* 527(7576): 49–53. doi.org/10.1038/nature16065.

Holloway, A. 2017. 'Localising Global Goals in Australia's Global City: Sydney.' *WIT Transactions on Ecology and the Environment* 226(1): 181–91. doi.org/10.2495/SDP170161.

Hu, R. 2020. 'Australia's National Urban Policy: The Smart Cities Agenda in Perspective.' *Australian Journal of Social Issues* 55(2): 201–17. doi.org/10.1002/ajs4.104.

Jones, S. 2013. 'Climate Change Policies of City Governments in Federal Systems: An Analysis of Vancouver, Melbourne and New York City.' *Regional Studies* 47(6): 974–92. doi.org/10.1080/00343404.2011.585150.

Koehler, G. 2015. 'Seven Decades of "Development", and Now What?' *Journal of International Development* 27(6): 733–51. doi.org/10.1002/jid.3108.

Langford, M. 2016. 'Lost in Transformation? The Politics of the Sustainable Development Goals.' *Ethics and International Affairs* 30(2): 167–76. doi.org/10.1017/S0892679416000058.

Leavesley, A. 2021. Sustainable Transitions in Cities: Local Transformation in an Urbanising World. MC-ENV thesis, University of Melbourne.

Moallemi, E.A., S. Malekpour, M. Hadjikakou, R. Raven, K. Szetey, D. Ningrum, A. Dhiaulhaq, and B.A. Bryan. 2020. 'Achieving the Sustainable Development Goals Requires Transdisciplinary Innovation at the Local Scale.' *One Earth* 3(3): 300–13. doi.org/10.1016/j.oneear.2020.08.006.

Mokhles, S., and K. Davidson. 2021. 'A Framework for Understanding the Key Drivers of Cities' Climate Actions in City Networks.' *Urban Climate* 38(July): 100902. doi.org/10.1016/j.uclim.2021.100902.

Narang Suri, S., M. Miraglia, and A. Ferrannini. 2021. 'Voluntary Local Reviews as Drivers for SDG Localisation and Sustainable Human Development.' *Journal of Human Development and Capabilities* 22(4): 725–36. doi.org/10.1080/1945 2829.2021.1986689.

Newton, P., D. Prasad, A. Sproul, and S. White, eds. 2019. *Decarbonising the Built Environment: Charting the Transition.* Singapore: Springer. doi.org/10.1007/978-981-13-7940-6.

New York City Mayor's Office for International Affairs (NYC-OIA). 2021. List of Signatories to the New York City Voluntary Local Review Declaration. Unpublished.

Oke, C., S.A. Bekessy, N. Frantzeskaki, J. Bush, J.A. Fitzsimons, G.E. Garrard, M. Grenfell, L. Harrison, M. Hartigan, D. Callow, B. Cotter, and S. Gawler. 2021. 'Cities Should Respond to the Biodiversity Extinction Crisis.' *npj: Urban Sustainability* 1(11). doi.org/10.1038/s42949-020-00010-w.

Parnell, S. 2016. 'Defining a Global Urban Development Agenda.' *World Development* 78: 529–40. doi.org/10.1016/j.worlddev.2015.10.028.

Pawar, M., D. O'Sullivan, B. Cash, R. Culas, K. Langat, A. Manning, N. Mungai, J. Rafferty, S. Rajamani, and W. Ward. 2020. 'The Sustainable Development Goals: An Australian Response.' *International Journal of Community and Social Development* 2(4): 374–93. doi.org/10.1177/2516602620983716.

Pipa, T. 2019. 'Shaping the Global Agenda to Maximize City Leadership on the SDGs: The Experiences of Vanguard Cities.' *Brief*, June. Washington, DC: Brookings Institution. Available from: www.brookings.edu/wp-content/uploads/2019/06/City-leadership-on-the-SDGs.pdf.

Pipa, T., and M. Bouchet. 2020. *Next Generation Urban Planning: Enabling Sustainable Development at the Local Level Through Voluntary Local Reviews (VLRs)*. Report, February. Washington, DC: Brookings Institution. Available from: www.brookings.edu/wp-content/uploads/2020/02/Next-generation-urban-planning_final.pdf.

Potts, G. 2020. *Peri Urban Group of Rural Councils: Economic Development Strategy (Draft)*. 4 January. Ballan, Vic. Available from: www.mrsc.vic.gov.au/files/assets/public/council/our-council/meeting-attachments/2020/06/24/ordinary/ordinary-council-meeting-2020-06-24-pe4-attachment-peri-urban-group-of-rural-councils-economic-development-strategy-draft-review.pdf.

Robiou Du Pont, Y., M.L. Jeffery, J. Gütschow, J. Rogelj, P. Christoff, and M. Meinshausen. 2017. 'Equitable Mitigation to Achieve the Paris Agreement Goals.' *Nature Climate Change* 7(1): 38–43. doi.org/10.1038/nclimate3186.

Ruming, K., A. Tice, and R. Freestone. 2010. 'Commonwealth Urban Policy in Australia: The Case of Inner Urban Regeneration in Sydney, 1973–75.' *Australian Geographer* 41(4): 447–67. doi.org/10.1080/00049182.2010.519694.

Schindler, S., D. Mitlin, and S. Marvin. 2018. 'National Urban Policy Making and Its Potential for Sustainable Urbanism.' *Current Opinion in Environmental Sustainability* 34: 48–53. doi.org/10.1016/j.cosust.2018.11.006.

Simon, D., H. Arfvidsson, G. Anand, A. Bazaz, G. Fenna, K. Foster, G. Jain, S. Hansson, L.M. Evans, N. Moodley, C. Nyambuga, M. Oloko, D.C. Ombara, Z. Patel, B. Perry, N. Primo, A. Revi, B. Van Niekerk, A. Wharton, and C. Wright. 2015. 'Developing and Testing the Urban Sustainable Development Goals Targets and Indicators: A Five-City Study.' *Environment and Urbanization* 28(1): 49–63. doi.org/10.1177/0956247815619865.

Siragusa, A., P. Vizcaino, P. Proietti, and C. Lavalle. 2020. *European Handbook for SDG Voluntary Local Reviews*. EUR 30067. Luxembourg: Publications Office of the European Union. doi.org/10.2760/670387.

Stace, S. 2020. 'Australian NUP: Lessons to Be Learnt.' In *Developing National Urban Policies: Ways Forward to Green and Smart Cities*, edited by D. Kundu, R. Sietchiping, and M. Kinyanjui, 377–405. Singapore: Springer. doi.org/10.1007/978-981-15-3738-7_16.

Starrs, A.M., A.C. Ezeh, G. Barker, A. Basu, J.T. Bertrand, R. Blum, A.M. Coll-Seck, A. Grover, L. Laski, M. Roa, Z.A. Sathar, L. Say, G.I. Serour, S. Singh, K. Stenberg, M. Temmerman, A. Biddlecom, A. Popinchalk, C. Summers, and L.S. Ashford. 2018. 'Accelerate Progress: Sexual and Reproductive Health and Rights for All—Report of the Guttmacher–Lancet Commission.' *The Lancet* 391(10140): 2642–92. doi.org/10.1016/S0140-6736(18)30293-9.

Subramaniam, N., R. Mori, jr, S. Akbar, S. Ji, and H. Situ. 2020. *SDG Measurement and Disclosure 2.0: A Study of ASX150 Companies*. Research Report, August. Melbourne: RMIT University. Available from: www.unaa.org.au/wp-content/uploads/2020/08/UNAA-RMIT-ASX-150-SDG-Report.pdf.

Troy, P. 2013. 'Australian Urban Research and Planning.' *Urban Policy and Research* 31(2): 134–49. doi.org/10.1080/08111146.2013.793260.

Trundle, A., B. Barth, and D. McEvoy. 2019. 'Leveraging Endogenous Climate Resilience: Urban Adaptation in Pacific Small Island Developing States.' *Environment and Urbanization* 31(1): 53–74. doi.org/10.1177/0956247818816654.

Trundle, A., J. Briggs, and M. Acuto. 2021. *UN SDG Target and Indicator Urban Relevance Wheel*. [Dataset]. Melbourne: University of Melbourne. doi.org/10.26188/16599293.

United Cities and Local Governments (UCLG). 2015. *The Sustainable Development Goals: What Local Governments Need to Know*. Barcelona, Spain: UCLG. Available from: www.citiesalliance.org/sites/default/files/publications/UCLG%202015%20The_sdgs_what_localgov_need_to_know.pdf.

United Cities and Local Governments (UCLG) and United Nations Human Settlements Programme (UN-Habitat). 2020. *Guidelines for Voluntary Local Reviews. Volume 1: A Comparative Analysis of Existing VLRs*. Barcelona, Spain: UCLG. unhabitat.org/guidelines-for-voluntary-local-reviews-volume-1-a-comparative-analysis-of-existing-vlrs.

United Nations (UN). 2014. *Transforming Our World: The 2030 Agenda for Sustainable Development*. A/RES/70/1. New York: United Nations. Available from: sustainabledevelopment.un.org/content/documents/21252030%20Agenda%20for%20Sustainable%20Development%20web.pdf.

United Nations Economic and Social Commission for Asia and the Pacific (UN-ESCAP). 2020. *Asia-Pacific Regional Guidelines on Voluntary Local Reviews: Reviewing Local Progress to Accelerate Action for the Sustainable Development Goals.* ST/ESCAP/2918. Bangkok: United Nations Economic and Social Commission for Asia and the Pacific. Available from: www.unescap.org/sites/default/d8files/knowledge-products/Asia-Pacific%20Regional%20Guidelines%20on%20VLRs_0.pdf.

Weber, H. 2017. 'Politics of "Leaving No One Behind": Contesting the 2030 Sustainable Development Goals Agenda.' *Globalizations* 14(3): 399–414. doi.org/10.1080/14747731.2016.1275404.

Weber, H., and M. Weber. 2020. 'When Means of Implementation Meet Ecological Modernization Theory: A Critical Frame for Thinking about the Sustainable Development Goals Initiative.' *World Development* 136: 105129. doi.org/10.1016/j.worlddev.2020.105129.

Yap, M.L.M., and K. Watene. 2019. 'The Sustainable Development Goals (SDGs) and Indigenous Peoples: Another Missed Opportunity?' *Journal of Human Development and Capabilities* 20(4): 451–67. doi.org/10.1080/19452829.2019.1574725.

Zinkernagel, R., J. Evans, and L. Neij. 2018. 'Applying the SDGs to Cities: Business As Usual Or A New Dawn?' *Sustainability* 10(9): 1–18. doi.org/10.3390/su10093201.

6

Potable water: Pay more, use less

Peter Spearritt[1]

Introduction

Many Australian cities and towns struggle to maintain a potable water supply that can keep up with unfettered demand, especially when households pay so little for the water they consume. Throughout the twentieth century, water consumption increased exponentially, among both industry and suburban-dwellers. Agriculture remains the largest user of both potable water from publicly owned water storages and non-potable water from rivers and artesian sources (Cook et al. 2022).

Droughts and suburban growth drove huge new dams, aquifer tapping, and a variety of sewage and stormwater disposal systems. In the twenty-first century, all the mainland state capitals embraced desalination plants in a knee-jerk reaction to the Millennium Drought, which varied from city to city over the period 2003–10. In this chapter, I offer counter policy propositions: that the most effective way to cut potable water use is to charge more for water, but also reduce connection charges, rewarding those

---

1   The arguments developed here draw on many discussions with Anne Gilmore and George Wilkenfeld, and my colleagues on an Australian Research Council–funded study of capital city water supplies, reported in *Cities in a Sunburnt Country: Water and the Making of Urban Australia* (Cook et al. 2022)—namely, Margaret Cook, Lionel Frost, Andrea Gaynor, Jenny Gregory, Ruth Morgan, and Martin Shanahan.

consumers who use water carefully. And second, that water tanks should be mandated for all new dwellings and retrofitted for existing dwellings where possible.

The Millennium Drought

Australia is the world's driest inhabited continent. This has produced a settlement pattern in which 80 per cent of people live within 60 kilometres of the coast in large cities that enjoy annual rainfall of between 500 and 2,000 millimetres, so we only worry about our urban water supply in times of drought. Indigenous peoples understood the relationship between rainfall, topography, climate, and heat. They learnt how to find natural supplies of water and methods of active water collection for dry spells— a skill that European 'explorers' did not always acquire.

Before the 1960s, many Australian households still had one relative 'on the land'—usually relying on tank water. It was a rude shock when staying with family or friends on farms to be instructed not to leave the tap running while brushing your teeth. Even city-dwellers often experienced extreme water shortages and water restrictions, sometimes with supply turned off for hours a day because of lack of water and inadequate water pressure (Cook et al. 2022).

During the postwar housing shortage in the late 1940s, Indigenous residents at La Perouse, on Botany Bay, in Sydney—some in mission housing, others in shacks they had built themselves—had just one public tap from which to access water. This, of course, is still the case in thousands of shanty towns and refugee camps around the world.

The Millennium Drought and the dramatic media coverage of climate change—from floods to bushfires—have undermined public confidence in the ability of governments to maintain water supply and protect houses from fire. With the 2019–20 fire season destroying not just isolated rural properties but also the main streets of smaller country towns, and reaching outer suburbs, the public is alarmed.

When Pat Troy set out to organise a public seminar about the millennium water crisis as part of the Academy of Social Science's annual symposium for 2007, he sought out disinterested scholars from economics, geography, history, law, and environmental studies. Published under the title *Troubled*

Waters: Confronting the Water Crisis in Australia's Cities (Troy 2008), the book produced from the symposium represented a contribution to a debate that until then had been dominated by the various water bureaucracies, from semi-autonomous statutory authorities to state government departments and the federal government. Before then, university-based water research concentrated on rural water and the ongoing saga of the Murray–Darling Basin. Urban water suddenly attracted some Australian Research Council (ARC) funding, including the Murdoch University National Centre for Excellence in Desalination, the very title of which presupposed the optimum solution to the urban water crisis. Short-lived (2010–16), it took a remarkably uncritical approach to assessing the pros and cons of desalination plants. The Cooperative Research Centre for Water Sensitive Cities (CRCWSC, 2012–21) was a much more broadly based research operation at Monash University and the University of Queensland, undertaking important research into water conservation at the local scale. However, arguably intimidated by some of its water bureaucracy backers, it skirted hard-hitting analysis of policy failures, especially quick-fix solutions, because that necessitated criticism of almost every state government. The CRCWSC commissioned Laing and Walter to study the Victorian Government's water reform attempts, but the full report remains unpublished, with some of the findings included in a shorter scholarly article (Laing and Walter 2020).

Dam certainty

In the land of droughts and flooding rains, urban water supply enters public consciousness only when there is not enough to keep up with demand, or the heavens open and whole suburbs and regional towns are engulfed by floods (Cook 2019). Between the 1920s and the 1980s, every capital city built additional dams and reservoirs—some quite small, some huge (Cook et al. 2022). Warragamba Dam in western Sydney (built from 1948 to 1960) holds almost four times the amount of water held by the five dams built south-west of the city centre between 1907 and 1941 (Cook and Spearritt 2021).

Dams, groundwater, and other harnessed sources of potable water appeared to be sufficient for our growing cities. State governments and/or water bureaucracies implemented water restrictions only in times of drought—most notably, banning sprinkler use and trying to persuade households that gardens and lawns should be rethought, with more emphasis on native plantings. Graduated charges for water use were introduced, but in most jurisdictions the penalty rates for excessive use remain modest. In the 1980s, the Brisbane City Council, the only metropolitan-wide council in a capital city, abandoned the installation of water meters, and actually buried several hundred thousand new meters—a popular move by a vast council whose householders could leave their sprinklers on day and night, with no economic penalty. Their water rates were simply calculated on unimproved capital value, not their water usage, which remained unmeasured. Water conservation plans for the Gold Coast in the mid-1990s reminded people not to flush their cigarettes down the toilet—a handy form of rubbish disposal, especially for smokers attempting to hide their habit from the rest of their household (Spearritt 2008).

During the Millennium Drought, governments finally started creating policies and incentives to permanently reduce household and business consumption. The Commonwealth Government passed the *Water Efficiency and Labelling Standards (WELS) Act 2005*, with mandatory water efficiency standards and labelling for toilets and showers, and later washing machines and dishwashers. Finally, consumers could see how much water new appliances would use, as they had been able to do for energy since 1986 (Australian Government 2021).

At the metropolitan level, the most thoroughgoing conservation policies were implemented in Brisbane, with financial incentives to install water tanks and water-saving appliances, shower timers (four minutes) distributed to every household, and regulations changed so laundry water could be used on the garden, which became safer with the development of ecologically friendly detergents. Businesses, schools, airports, warehouses—any structures with good roof capacity—were encouraged to collect rainwater for their own use. Brisbane got per capita consumption down to 112 litres per day in 2008–09—lower than in any other capital city (Walton and Hume 2011). Water tanks were mandated for new dwellings in Brisbane, Adelaide, and Melbourne. Perth, with the highest household consumption, never mandated water tanks for new dwellings nor demanded business water plans. Perth has never heeded the late George Seddon's advice to 'fear the hose' (Morgan 2015).

The desalination quick fix: We had to 'build something big'

Desalination plants built between 2006 and 2012 were a quick fix for governments anxious to show they were doing something about increasing the potable water supply during urban droughts. The first cab off the rank was Perth (at Kwinana in 2006), servicing a city that has never tried very hard to convince its citizens to use less water.

Desalination plants were quick but expensive to build, with multinational firms Degremont and Veolia at the ready to design and advise the local construction industry. Capital city electors could be reassured that their state governments were doing something in the face of the urban drought. State Labor governments in Queensland, New South Wales, and Victoria commissioned 'desal' plants in quick succession. The Tugun plant, abutting the Gold Coast Airport, remains in government ownership, and has been mothballed for much of the time since its opening in 2009. The Kurnell plant in Sydney (built in 2010), with renewable energy offsets from the Capital Wind Farm at Bungendore more than 200 kilometres away, became an exercise in 'green sophistry'. If the same amount of money and electrical energy had been invested in water recycling plants, using stormwater and/or wastewater, Australia would have an environmental achievement of which to be proud. Kurnell, too, has spent much of its life mothballed, occasionally made operational, not least to deflect attention from its enormous cost. The plant is partly owned by the Ontario Teachers' Pension Fund, and substantial payments are required whether the plant is mothballed or not (O'Hanlon and Spearritt 2020). The Wonthaggi plant, east of Melbourne, like Kurnell, is a public–private partnership, with a locked-in contract and huge annual payments. It has had only minimal use.

Auditors-general in the three eastern states expressed concerns about how these plants were financed and the enormous ongoing costs. The Productivity Commission's *National Water Reform 2020*, released in September 2021, points out that the Millennium Drought posed 'water security risks to most major cities', but concludes that 'a lack of effective planning and poor execution resulted in rushed investments into desalination' (PC 2021: 164). As one senior bureaucrat told Laing and Walter (2020), they experienced great pressure to 'build something big'.

Curbing water use

In a society in which increased consumption is viewed as economic progress by both the Labor and the Coalition parties, water, like electricity, is seen as a public right, and should not be too expensive. Private swimming pools are almost universally admired, even though they represent highly visible instances of conspicuous consumption. Twelve per cent of Australian households had a pool in 2007, according to the most recent ABS survey. Very few suburban houses with inground pools have enough tank capacity to fill them. A variety of online mapping tools provide ample empirical evidence of this, and now that we have better data on house prices by locality, what a topic it would be for a PhD in conspicuous consumption and its environmental impacts.

On the Gold Coast, high-rollers, having failed in their illegal attempt to colonise the surf beaches in front of their properties, instead build pools and grandiose entertainment areas, as do hundreds of apartment blocks and resort complexes, from Cairns and Port Douglas in the north, to Perth in the west. Many of the most egregious examples of pools are literally a couple of minutes' walk from the beach. Meanwhile, only a small proportion of golf courses currently collect enough water to keep their 'greens' green. Some jurisdictions have changed their habits, so the ACT Government, for instance, stopped soaking many of its parks and verges on its grandiose road system to keep them green in summer, which was a common practice until the late 1980s (Wright 1987).

Can recycling and tank capacity be ramped up?

Australian city and town-dwellers are used to getting safe drinking water at the turn of a tap, so the idea of recycled water remains anathema to many. The conspiracy theorists had a field day with recycling fears, and the 'Poowoomba' anti-recycling campaign run in Toowoomba, Queensland, during the Millennium Drought still resonates with many. That proposal involved highly treated wastewater being returned to a storage dam and checked again before going to households (Hurlimann and Dolnicar 2010). Brochures attacking recycled water (analogous to anti-vaccination propaganda) were widely distributed in Brisbane during the drought, when the state government was about to embrace a major recycled water initiative for South-East Queensland. The Bligh state government lost its nerve, much to the dismay of the scientific advisors who had worked on the scheme (Spearritt and Head 2010; Head 2014). Then it rained, so, as usual, the government simply breathed a sigh of relief and turned its focus to the January 2011 floods, when water shortage fears promptly vanished (Cook 2019).

There is more recycling of water happening than the public realises, as water authorities and bulk suppliers have been increasingly careful about what they say about how they treat and deploy wastewater (Radcliffe 2015). As long as we do not have more of the *E. coli* water-quality scares that engulfed Sydney in 1998, we may continue down this softly, softly path (Sheil 2000). Treating and making better use of stormwater are increasingly common, as is the creation of wetlands, not just in older suburbs (for example, the low-lying, sandy hinterlands west of the Frankston railway line on Port Phillip Bay in Melbourne, and underneath the Westgate Bridge), but also in new housing estates throughout suburban Australia, where wetlands, to cope with runoff, are a selling point—environmentally sound and 'green'. Some housing developments now have a potable supply and a separate recycled supply for garden watering, with different-coloured supply pipes, as do some universities, belatedly doing something practical on their own campuses. Water reuse and solar power are easily implemented instruments of sustainability for large institutional and commercial establishments. Both save money and create much less angst than cutting back on carparking, which is such a money pot for airports, hospitals, and universities.

Ever since the Millennium Drought there has been a marked increase in the take-up of water tanks on suburban blocks in Australia's towns and cities, and there is a growing body of research on the costs and benefits of tanks (Gardiner 2010; Moy 2012). By 2013, according to the most recent ABS survey, 28 per cent of urban households had tanks, with Brisbane (47 per cent), Adelaide (44 per cent), and Melbourne (31 per cent) the leaders. We do not have good data on the mean and medium capacity of those tanks or how they relate to the catchment of the available roof area (ABS 2013). Key variables include annual rainfall—higher in Queensland and NSW coastal cities—and its distribution over the year. Roof size can be an issue, although most detached houses and even townhouses have a lot of roof space. Tanks are relatively cheap, especially poly tanks, and plumbing to laundry, toilet, and shower is usually straightforward as it does not entail the extra costs of filtering for water purity. There is a legal requirement for excess water from house roofs to go to the public gutter in most but not all cities. Some urban jurisdictions, including the NSW Blue Mountains and Townsville in Queensland, require stormwater on new builds to be held on the property to reduce erosion. Downpipes on houses, carports, and even apartment blocks can be readily diverted to a garden tank. Most local government areas in Australia allow for installation of a tank up to 10,000 litres without a development application. Tank water must be pressurised for indoor use, but with the rapidly growing take-up of household solar panels—now found on more than one-quarter of all dwellings—many tank users pay little or nothing for electric pump use.

The more dams lobby

Electors have long been enticed by the promise of large capital works, from bridges and dams to the Snowy Mountains Hydroelectric Scheme. When Australia's biggest urban dams were being built, including Warragamba (Sydney), Wivenhoe (Brisbane), and Thompson (Melbourne), metropolitan water authorities and state governments could readily afford to borrow funds, not least because of their guaranteed cash flows from residential and commercial water and sewerage connection charges, which were usually calculated on the unimproved capital value of land. Throughout Australia, residents of rural towns regarded a safe and reliable water supply as their right, so scores of water storages were built, even for quite small settlements (Lloyd 1988). Such projects now come under much more scrutiny, from their capital cost to their environmental impacts. The federal Labor government's intervention, in 2009, to prevent the Traveston Dam being built on the Mary River near Gympie in Queensland, on environmental grounds, marked a new era in cost–benefit analysis for assessing major dams. In response, Labor premier Anna Bligh threatened to build a series of desalination plants on the Gold and Sunshine coasts (Head 2014).

Expanding coastal cities are now demanding additional water storages to service their growing suburbs. In northern New South Wales, with a sharp increase in demand for new housing blocks, the strident real estate lobby is demanding a new dam, just south of Nimbin. Environmental experts and passionate locals have been modelling the likely cost of alternatives, from demand management to new water sources, to avoid the proposed 50-gigalitre Dunoon Dam at a guestimate cost of $200 million (White 2020). The Rous County Council provides bulk water to a population of 100,000 in the shires of Ballina, Byron, Lismore, and Richmond Valley, but billing is managed by the constituent shire councils. The average yearly rainfall across the whole area is between 1,500 and 2,000 millimetres, and several cities and towns experience regular flooding, including the disastrous floods of March 2022. Over the past decade, the 14,000-megalitre Rocky Creek Dam near Lismore has never fallen below 80 per cent capacity, reflecting a high annual rainfall in a subtropical catchment. The area served has 47,000 rateable properties, mostly detached houses or businesses with extensive roofing (Rous County Council 2021). An unknown proportion already has tanks. If the Rous County Council simply gifted 7,000–8,000-litre tank capacity to 30,000 detached dwellings connected to town water, which has been estimated at a bulk-buy cost of $3,000 per property, including pump and connection to toilet, shower, and laundry, the total cost would amount to $90 million—less than half the likely capital cost of the new dam. When you add in the destruction to Indigenous sites, endangered species, and some pristine forests, the dam becomes even less enticing, except to those who want to make money out of subdividing and selling productive rural land for housing blocks, hobby farms, and the insatiable demands of the lucrative short-term tourist trade.

Regrettably, most local councils still harken after a bigger rate base and unceasing new building as a sign of economic growth. The Rous County Council does not have the funds to give away so many tanks, but nor does it have the funds to build the dam. In the past, such dams were built by state departments of public works. At present Rous modestly subsidises tank installation if connected to toilet and laundry. An expanded subsidy scheme, under which householders bore some of the cost, along with rigorous building regulations mandating 7,000–8,000-litre capacity for new detached dwellings and townhouses—still the dominant form in the service area—would be vastly cheaper than another dam. Unfortunately, while the NSW Government–mandated Building Sustainability Index (BASIX) building code demands a tank for new dwellings, most have a small capacity of about 1,500–2,000 litres.

Slimline tanks can usually fit near the toilet and laundry, with minimal plumbing expense. Households with gardens can usually find a spot for a 5,000-litre-plus round tank. And there must be a lot more pressure on businesses—from shopping malls to bowling clubs and breweries—to make the most of the storage capacity within their ample roof space, which would send a great message to the community. We must avoid the slippery tendency of politicians to promise 'water forever', as they usually do at dam openings, or the equally implausible promise of 'drought-proofing'—always popular terms employed by Labor, Liberal, and particularly National Party politicians (Cook et al. 2022).

The rising cost of electricity—especially because of peak price spikes— has now convinced many clubs and a wide variety of manufacturing, wholesaling, and retailing establishments to install roof-top solar and battery storage. If businesses feared higher water charges as much as they worry about the cost of electricity, they would also be much more inclined to install substantial tanks. Even Sydney Water now boasts that the extensive native gardens at its Warragamba Dam recreation area are only watered with onsite tank water.

Charge more for potable water: Change household and business rating regimes

Most householders regularly complain about their energy bills and their council rates. If they live in localities that are cold in winter, energy bills are front of mind. If they install solar, they usually know what their feed-in tariff is and regret that it is now falling sharply. When it comes to council rates and charges, I have only encountered a handful of people who regularly check what proportion of their rates or water bills is taken up by charges for access to water and sewerage. In most jurisdictions in Australia, the wastewater access charge is often six times the water access charge, so sewerage connection is costing many households more than $1,000 a year, while the potable water consumed is often only a couple of hundred dollars. In some towns and cities, council rate notices include water use, while in others the amount of water used is billed separately, by either a local council or a large corporate body, such as Sydney Water.

At between $2.50 and $3 a kilolitre, the real charge for potable water consumed is tiny. As many commentators have pointed out, most of us think nothing about paying a thousand times as much per litre for fancy bottled mineral water, whether it is from Italy or Tasmania. The clear consumer message is that there is no pressing financial reason to conserve water. And when their storages are full, most water authorities lose interest in preaching restraint to their customers. There are important equity concerns about the price of water, but the connection charges are invariably many multiples of the usage charge. Why not change the pricing structure? The regimes we have inherited reflect attempts to recoup construction and maintenance costs of dams, water pipelines, water-quality checks, and sewage disposal (Neutze 1997). Water bills are so hard to understand that, like insurance, it is just something for which householders cough up. Why not change the ratios dramatically, to indicate to households that if they can constrain their potable water use, they will reap real financial rewards? At present, the only way to feel better about your high connection charges is to use more water, put on your sprinkler (when there are no restrictions), flush the toilet often, and take longer showers, so at least you think you are getting your money's worth.

Dams are a lot more difficult to site and fund than desalination plants, which are usually plonked on government-owned land abutting sea inlets and outlets. With a greater understanding of environmental impacts, not just on the immediate environment, but also on the catchment area, dams are the ultimate political hot potato, except for the National Party, which always regards them as a winner. And, with belated but growing recognition that most dam proposals involve flooding culturally important Indigenous sites, dams usually remain in the too-hard basket. Raising dam walls is easier—now done twice at the Hinze Dam in the Gold Coast hinterland. The proposal to raise the Warragamba Dam wall would defeat the purpose of having retention capacity when there is torrential inflow. Upstream flooding would be temporary, not permanent, but undoubtedly cause permanent damage to World Heritage–listed ecosystems and Indigenous sites. Sydney Water has been arguing that the raised wall will lower the flood risk for existing residents, while opponents are suspicious that the primary aim is to allow more suburban development on the floodplain, and so put more people in danger, as well as risking the World Heritage status of the Blue Mountains National Park (McIlroy 2019; Cox 2022).

Conclusion

If we cannot dampen demand for potable water and make more use of recycled water, not least greywater for gardens, we face a future in which, given the capital cost and the environmental damage caused by new dams, we will end up with more and more desalination plants cluttering our urban coastlines, consuming vast amounts of power. And then you must add minerals to the desalinated product so that it tastes like water.

Almost all state and federal government policies promote greater consumption of goods and services as central to our economic wellbeing, whether it is water, electricity, larger houses with more bathrooms, or upgrading our televisions. Federal government action has effectively reduced smoking—notably, by banning advertising—while high excise taxes help pay for the burden smokers place on the public health system. The Australian Medical Association has called for a sugar tax, pointing out that most of us do not realise how much sugar we consume in processed foods and soft drinks—analogous to our water usage in that it is a type of hidden consumption.

Only one major political party, The Greens, is prepared to question rampant consumption, with the left of the ALP unable to persuade the rest of the party that not all consumption is good for the nation (Hamilton and Denniss 2005). Both the Coalition and the ALP uncritically champion developers and the industry that builds houses and apartments, warehouses, casinos, and shopping malls. Such activity is lauded as the surest sign of jobs and economic growth, leading us out of the pandemic. Getting people to use less water and think more about how they use water and energy in such a consumerist society could be as difficult as getting Australia to become a republic.

References

Australian Bureau of Statistics (ABS). 2013. *Environmental Issues: Water Use and Conservation*. March. Canberra: ABS.

Australian Government. 2021. *Water Rating: Legislation*. [Last modified 18 August]. Canberra: Commonwealth of Australia. Available from: www.waterrating.gov.au/about/legislation.

Cook, M. 2019. *A River with a City Problem: A History of Brisbane Floods*. Brisbane: University of Queensland Press.

Cook, M., and P. Spearritt. 2021. 'Water Forever: Warragamba and Wivenhoe Dams.' *Australian Historical Studies* 52(2): 211–26. doi.org/10.1080/1031461X.2021.1882513.

Cook, M., L. Frost, A. Gaynor, J. Gregory, R.A. Morgan, M. Shanahan, and P. Spearritt. 2022. *Cities in a Sunburnt Country: Water and the Making of Urban Australia*. Cambridge, UK: Cambridge University Press. doi.org/10.1017/9781108917698.

Cox, L. 2022. 'Raising Warragamba Dam Wall Flouts Australia's World Heritage Obligations, Scientists Warn.' *The Guardian*, [Australia], 2 February. Available from: www.theguardian.com/australia-news/2022/feb/02/raising-warragamba-dam-wall-flouts-australias-world-heritage-obligations-scientists-warn.

Dolnicar, S., and A. Hurlimann. 2015. 'Australians' Water Conservation Behaviours and Attitudes.' *Australasian Journal of Water Resources* 14(1): 43–53. doi.org/10.1080/13241583.2010.11465373.

Frost, L., and M. Shanahan. 2021. 'Domesticating Water: How Initial Choices Shaped Water Networks in Three Australian Cities.' *Australian Historical Studies* 52(2): 171–88. doi.org/10.1080/1031461X.2020.1862879.

Gardiner, A. 2010. 'Do Rainwater Tanks Herald a Cultural Change in Household Water Use?' *Australasian Journal of Environmental Management* 17: 100–11. doi.org/10.1080/14486563.2010.9725255.

Hamilton, C., and R. Denniss. 2005. *Affluenza: When Too Much is Never Enough*. Sydney: Allen & Unwin.

Head, B.W. 2014. 'Managing Urban Water Crises: Adaptive Policy Responses to Drought and Flood in Southeast Queensland, Australia.' *Ecology and Society* 19(2): 33. doi.org/10.5751/ES-06414-190233.

Hurlimann, A., and S. Dolnicar. 2010. 'When Public Opposition Defeats Alternative Water Projects: The Case of Toowoomba, Australia.' *Water Research* 44(1): 287–97. doi.org/10.1016/j.watres.2009.09.020.

Laing, M., and J. Walter. 2020. 'Partisanship, Policy Entrepreneurs and the Market for Ideas: What We Can Learn from Policy Failure?' *Australian Journal of Political Science* 55(1): 122–34. doi.org/10.1080/10361146.2019.1686120.

Lloyd, C.J. 1988. *Either Drought or Plenty: Water Development and Management in NSW*. Sydney: Department of Water Resources.

McIlroy, J. 2019. 'Hundreds March to "Give a Dam" in Blue Mountains.' *Green Left*, [Sydney], Issue 1225, 13 June. Available from: www.greenleft.org.au/content/hundreds-march-give-dam-blue-mountains.

Morgan, R. 2015. *Running Out? Water in Western Australia*. Perth: University of Western Australia Press.

Moy, C. 2012. 'Rainwater Tank Households: Water Savers or Water Users?' *Geographical Research* 50(2): 204–16. doi.org/10.1111/j.1745-5871.2011.00720.x.

Neutze, M. 1997. *Funding Urban Services: Options for Physical Infrastructure*. Sydney: Allen & Unwin.

O'Hanlon, S., and P. Spearritt. 2020. 'From Water Engineers to Financial Engineering: Water Provision in Australia's East Coast Capital Cities, 1945–2015.' *Journal of Urban History* 46: 98–112. doi.org/10.1177/0096144217692985.

Productivity Commission (PC). 2021. *National Water Reform 2020*. Inquiry Report No. 96. Canberra: Productivity Commission.

Radcliffe, J.C. 2015. 'Water Recycling in Australia: During and After the Drought.' *Environmental Science: Water Research & Technology* l: 554–62. doi.org/10.1039/C5EW00048C.

Rous County Council. 2021. *Future Water for Our Region*. Lismore, NSW: Rous County Council. Available from: rous.nsw.gov.au.

Sheil, C. 2000. *Water's Fall: Running the Risks with Economic Rationalism*. Sydney: Pluto Press.

Spearritt, P. 2008. 'The Water Crisis in Southeast Queensland: How Desalination Turned the Region into Carbon Emission Heaven.' In *Troubled Waters: Confronting the Water Crisis in Australia's Cities*, edited by P. Troy, 19–36. Canberra: ANU E Press. doi.org/10.22459/TW.06.2008.02.

Spearritt, P., and B. Head. 2010. 'Water Politics.' In *A Climate for Growth*, edited by B. Gleeson and W. Steele, 88–107. Brisbane: University of Queensland Press.

Troy, P., ed. 2008. *Troubled Waters: Confronting the Water Crisis in Australia's Cities*. Canberra: ANU E Press. doi.org/10.22459/TW.06.2008.

Walton, A., and M. Hume. 2011. 'Creating Positive Habits in Water Conservation: The Case of the Queensland Water Commission and the Target 140 Campaign.' *International Journal of Nonprofit and Voluntary Sector Marketing* 16: 215–24. doi.org/10.1002/nvsm.421.

White, S. 2020. Submission to Rous County Council future water plan, September. Unpublished.

Wright, T. 1987. 'Smaller Parks, Less Watering in ACT.' *The Canberra Times*, 27 October.

7

Saving heritage policy: The past and future of conservation in the Australian city

James Lesh[1]

Introduction

In 2021, the NSW Government initiated a review of the *Heritage Act 1977* (NSW). The framing of the review expressed confusion about the purpose of heritage policy and administration. The accompanying discussion paper identified no fewer than 19 questions (Standing Committee on Social Issues 2021a). These questions were not based on a depth of knowledge of the challenges facing the governance and management of heritage places. Rather, tensions between traditional and evolving outlooks on heritage appeared throughout the paper and in the subsequent parliamentary review report (Standing Committee on Social Issues 2021b).

Conservation has long privileged the retention of traditional heritage values: historic, aesthetic, and scientific significance. Emerging viewpoints equally foreground the social, economic, and environmental capacities of conservation. Similar challenges appear in policy initiatives and decision-

1   Thank you to Cameron Logan, Hannah Lewi, Helen Lardner, Natica Schmeder, Richard Mackay, Robert Freestone, Ursula de Jong, and Paul Ashton for their assistance with this paper.

making conducted across national, state, and local jurisdictions. This is evidence of duplication and fragmentation in urban heritage policymaking, while broader philosophical and strategic issues remain unresolved.

Australian urban heritage is at a major juncture. Since the early 2000s, the capacity for authorities to pursue innovative heritage policy and to facilitate sophisticated conservation outcomes has been eroded. Heritage governance has not been responsive to evolving professional and community expectations for the historic environment. After the closure of the Australian Heritage Commission (1975–2004), the nation has had no effective national leadership in urban heritage. This devolution agenda, making state and local authorities exclusively responsible for urban heritage, while professional and voluntary bodies uphold conservation standards, has generated issues. The authorities and bodies are disparate and under-resourced. Traditional outlooks and approaches have become entrenched (Sullivan 2015). For instance, the capacity for urban heritage to advance social, economic, and environmental sustainability has not been substantively recognised in the Australian context, raising questions about the continuing relevance of heritage conservation.

As background, this chapter first maps the national policy environment for urban heritage that has formed since the mid-2000s. The body of the chapter then provides three areas for augmenting federal government leadership related to national coordination, review frameworks, and sustainability transitions. A theme throughout is the longstanding policy precedents established by the former Australian Heritage Commission, which continue to be adopted within national, state, and local heritage policy. Many of these precedents now act as barriers to advancing heritage governance and management. Comparative examples are drawn from across Australia's cities, from overseas jurisdictions, and from intragovernmental and nongovernmental bodies: the United Nations Educational, Scientific and Cultural Organization (UNESCO) and the International Council on Monuments and Sites (ICOMOS). Opportunities exist for renewed national (and state) leadership, revised policy frameworks, and broader sustainability transitions, aligned with evolving political, social, and economic imperatives.

Background

Heritage conservation provides models for perceiving, valuing, and safeguarding the inherited physical environments and embodied social relations that make up our cities. Heritage has long been recognised for its contribution to cultural identity and community wellbeing. It is also increasingly identified as a potential driver of economic growth and environmental benefit (DAWE 2011). In Australia, state and local authorities have the leading role in identifying, managing, and interpreting urban heritage places and guiding public and private property owners in how to sustain the significance of their heritage places. In conjunction with heritage practitioners, national authorities have facilitated the frameworks, guidelines, and principles that shape how conservation is done to areas and buildings by state and local authorities and private sector consultants. However, these frameworks have been effectively frozen since the close of the twentieth century.

Australia's existing model of urban heritage governance was largely established between the 1960s and the 1980s—'the heroic period of conservation' (Harwood and Powers 2004: 9) and an era remarkable for the intensity and innovativeness of heritage activism, policymaking, and practice (Lesh 2023). During the 1950s, municipal authorities introduced urban conservation measures, which became more strategic and sophisticated from the 1970s. State authorities, beginning with Victoria in 1974 and concluding with Tasmania in 1995, passed dedicated state heritage legislation. Following the federal government's Inquiry into the National Estate (1973–74), the Australian Heritage Commission was established, in 1975 (Veale and Freestone 2012; Lesh 2019a).

Heritage authorities and managers enshrined their overarching objective as conserving and promoting cultural significance, meaning the aesthetic, historic, scientific, and social values of heritage places. This objective and these four values were enshrined in national legislation from 1975. Each value had distinctive genealogies in both the national and the global histories of conservation. The primary focus of urban heritage was aesthetic and historic significance. This values-based approach was recorded in the Burra Charter (1979), the de facto national guidelines and conservation principles. The Burra Charter was revised in 1981, 1988, 1999, and 2013. Since 1999, the full title of the Burra Charter has been 'The Australia ICOMOS Charter for Places of Cultural Significance'. The Australian chapter of ICOMOS holds custodianship over it. Problematically, this late-twentieth-century institutional landscape was destabilised with the closure of the Australian Heritage Commission in 2004.

Today, Australia's national governance arrangements for urban heritage are legislated under the *Environment Protection and Biodiversity Conservation Act 1999 (EPBC Act)*, administered by what is now the Department of Climate Change, Energy, the Environment and Water (Boer and Wiffen 2005). The *EPBC Act* creates the National Heritage List (NHL), which comprises 120 places, along with the Commonwealth Heritage List (CHL) (DAWE 2021). Metropolitan Sydney has the largest number of NHL items, with 11 listings, followed by metropolitan Melbourne, with eight. The CHL recognises 390 places owned or controlled by the federal government in areas such as defence, maritime safety, communications, and customs. The two federal lists incorporate Indigenous, historic, and natural sites. In contrast, state and territory legislation creates separate lists for each of these three heritage management categories.

Historic heritage typically means post-contact architectural, planning, and built heritage, and has been distinguished from both pre- and post-contact First Peoples' heritage places. The awkward nomenclature of 'historic heritage' came about because Indigenous culture was once conceived of as prehistoric—in contrast with historic heritage. Designation on any statutory heritage list generates legal obligations for property owners and managers to protect the cultural significance and historic fabric of their heritage assets. At a national level, competitive grants programs provide financial assistance to property owners to support recognition, conservation, preservation, and community engagement objectives. Some funding is also reserved for ad hoc projects conducted by heritage consultants and by professional and voluntary bodies and for supporting representation at international heritage meetings.

A purpose of the *EPBC Act* is to meet Australia's obligations under the UNESCO World Heritage Convention (1972). Expert advice is provided to the federal government by the Australian World Heritage Advisory Committee. As of 2023, Australia had 20 World Heritage List inscriptions—heritage places recognised for their outstanding universal value for present and future generations of humanity (in addition to their national significance and thus appearing on national, state, and local lists). Of these designations, three are in urban contexts: Melbourne's Royal Exhibition Building (inscribed in 2004), the Sydney Opera House (2007), and Australian convict sites (2010). The last is a serial listing comprising 11 individual sites, including Fremantle Prison in Western Australia; Hobart's Cascades Female Factory; Sydney's Hyde Park Barracks, Old Government House, and Domain; and Kangaroo Island, 112 kilometres south-west of Adelaide. It is expected that the planners, architects, landscape architects, archaeologists, engineers, and historians managing national heritage places hold substantive professional expertise through longstanding experience and professional esteem. Expertise is also demonstrated through membership of and standing in specialist professional bodies, such as the Australian Institute of Architects, the Planning Institute of Australia, and Australia ICOMOS, which is both a domestic professional body for heritage professionals and an international nongovernmental advisory body to UNESCO. Volunteer-led and minimally resourced, Australia ICOMOS operates based on the interests of its membership and promotes the Burra Charter's values-based approach.

The federal government minimises its involvement in urban heritage (Department of the Environment 2015). Its primary role extends to administrating the two national lists. The Australian Heritage Council (2004–) provides independent expert advice to the government and the Department of Climate Change, Energy, the Environment and Water about national heritage places. It also offers input on strategy and policy. Its 10 expert members are appointed by the federal government and have included politically affiliated individuals. The former Australian Heritage Commission was an independent statutory body with broad legislative powers. In contrast, the council chiefly has only an advisory role. Its strategic remit, responsibilities, resources, and capabilities are minimal. It also has a negligible professional or public profile in advancing urban conservation. Its (unsuccessful) public opposition to the $500 million redevelopment of the Australian War Memorial in Canberra was a notable exception.

Another national body is the Heritage Chairs and Officials of Australia and New Zealand (HCOANZ), a committee that meets twice a year. The HCOANZ is the singular standing arrangement for coordinating urban heritage policy across Australian jurisdictions. It also has no major strategic function, again having minimal responsibilities, resources, and capabilities. Ultimately, the minister and the department decide whether to pursue initiatives and take on the advice offered by the national advisory groups, state and local authorities, and professional and voluntary bodies. While noting some of the issues and challenges facing urban heritage, the federal government has made no commitment to acting in the area (Department of the Environment 2015), including after the release of the *State of the Environment* report (McConnell et al. 2021).

For managing individual national heritage places, ad hoc cross-departmental and/or cross-jurisdictional committees are often formed. NHL sites appear on the relevant state register, which often has the effect of producing municipal or local protections, too. NHL sites are owned or controlled by state or local governments, corporate entities, or individuals, making them a state planning responsibility. Membership of the ad hoc committees may also include private sector heritage professionals, who ultimately manage and maintain Australia's heritage places, following the issuance of permits and guidance by the relevant authorities. Responsibilities under the *EPBC Act* for national urban heritage places are frequently delegated to state agencies, further minimising federal involvement. Bilateral agreements are also prepared for World Heritage sites, where the federal government has the strongest statutory responsibility. All these factors mean the federal government does not have a depth of heritage, architectural, historical, or archaeological knowledge.

In contrast, the former Australian Heritage Commission had both an operational and a strategic remit. It was responsible for compiling the Register of the National Estate (1975–2007)—a master national heritage list ultimately comprising 13,000 places across Australia. It paralleled the US National Register of Historic Places—now with 95,000 places—which has been administered by the National Park Service since 1966. Unlike the current national lists, however, the Register of the National Estate had little power to enforce conservation measures. The commission also coordinated state and local authorities; issued grants to property owners, professional bodies, and community groups; coordinated education programs tailored for primary, secondary, and tertiary education, professional, and generalist audiences; arranged specialist events and seminars; commissioned research and policy reports; and communicated best-practice frameworks and approaches (Yencken 1982).

The commission facilitated platforms for the exchange of heritage knowledge among not only national, state, and local authorities, but also professionals and community groups. It supported the operation of Australia ICOMOS, including its preparation of the Burra Charter in 1979. Neither Australia ICOMOS nor the state-based national trusts have had the capacity to facilitate the continuation of these networks, which have thus ruptured with the retirement of an earlier generation of practitioners. The commission's environmental and First Nations advocacy meant it attracted strong criticism, especially from the mining and development sectors (Ashton and Cornwall 2006). Although less adversarial in the sphere of urban heritage—which, after all, is a state and local planning responsibility— the commission once had the authority, independence, and resources to further conservation in Australia's cities. Its closure followed a report of the Productivity Commission (2006), an independent federal advisory body, which cited issues of duplication and complexity among jurisdictions as part of a broader neoliberal argument for curtailing heritage regulations across Australia.

Policy areas for future consideration

The institutional structures for urban heritage governance that formed in Australia in the 1970s assumed a strong and continuing leadership role for the federal government. As a federation of states and territories, Australia followed especially the Canadian and the US models. According to the Committee of Inquiry into the National Estate (1974: 281):

> Central Government action in these countries and elsewhere emphasises the depth and extent of the research and investigation work carried out nationally and the considerable skills which national governments have assembled to do this work.

The same observation could be made today: in contrast with Australia, across the world, central governments continue to play a major role in shaping conservation. Agencies such as Heritage New Zealand, Historic England, and the US National Park Service have the same responsibilities as the former Australian Heritage Commission: policymaking, coordination, standards, research, and education, with involvement from multijurisdictional authorities, practitioners, community groups, and individuals. Re-establishing the commission in Australia seems unlikely and may be undesirable (Wesley 1996), but its former leadership role and responsibilities could be taken up by the federal government. Three specific opportunities for national policy development in urban heritage are now considered.

National coordination

The federal government could take up the opportunity to harmonise urban heritage policymaking across jurisdictions. Within the existing legislation, the relevant area of the public service (currently the Department of Climate Change, Energy, the Environment and Water) could be appropriately resourced and staffed for strategic initiatives and site administration. The Australian Heritage Council and the HCOANZ could be allocated strategic responsibilities and resourced with their own secretariats. Both actions would provide an opportunity to consolidate heritage expertise within the federal government and share knowledge across jurisdictions, to benchmark and improve decision-making and, thus, urban heritage outcomes.

Due to the foundational role played by the Australian Heritage Commission, policy frameworks and legislative models across Australia's state and local jurisdictions are still broadly similar. The values-based approach promoted by the Burra Charter incorporates conservation principles that guide the decision-making of national, state, and local authorities (as well as those of private sector practitioners). Since the 1970s, the state legislation protecting urban heritage has taken two forms: dedicated heritage law administered by state heritage agencies, and heritage provisions within planning laws administered by municipal councils. Separate legislation addresses natural and First Nations heritage including in cities.

For protecting places of local significance under planning laws, guidance and advice used to be provided to municipal councils by both national and state authorities. This responsibly has now been entirely devolved to state authorities. Some states offer municipalities funding for heritage work, but this funding has not kept up with the increased expectations for heritage protection placed on municipalities by state authorities and local communities. Strategic municipal heritage planning tasks are commonly outsourced to private sector consultants. Everyday decisions are then made by generalist council planners or officers. Other than in well-resourced, central-city contexts, few municipalities have a dedicated heritage planner. Depending on the jurisdiction, municipalities may engage a specialist heritage consultant, perhaps on a part-time basis. A lack of leadership, expertise, and resources has consistently produced uneven local heritage outcomes (Lewis 1999; Logan 2007).

State heritage agencies vary in their composition, size, and capacity, and are typically minimally resourced for strategic projects. Their primary focus is managing state heritage lists, which are incrementally increasing in length, as new places are recognised as significant. The growing identification and protection of mid and late twentieth-century heritage places are creating further responsibilities (and have the potential to inspire novel ways of addressing colonial and nineteenth-century heritage places). Continuing the important work of the Australian Heritage Commission, some state agencies occasionally commission thematic research studies to capture groups of places around a typology, use, period, style, person, or issue. Yet, just six such studies, in only three state jurisdictions, were commissioned between 2016 and 2021 (McConnell et al. 2021). Furthermore, these studies are limited within jurisdictional borders, so cannot have a truly comparative, national, or international scope, which limits their potential insights, especially given the interconnectivity between Australian cities and with the global urban world over at least the past two centuries. Both architectural typological and historical thematic comparative analyses across heritage places suffer from similar limitations.

In addition to facilitating new and updating existing listings, the state agencies are responsible for enforcing protections and ensuring reliable and consistent decision-making on development applications for designated places. These applications are most often brought by heritage practitioners on behalf of property owners. Recent development booms across Australia's cities have produced substantial workloads for both heritage authorities and practitioners. Arbitration of heritage decision-making occurs at heritage councils or specialist planning courts. Other tasks pursued by state authorities include heritage promotion, education, and grants administration, along with providing cross-governmental policy input when heritage might be impacted (related to, for instance, infrastructure projects or disaster recovery).

The institutional landscape of Australian urban heritage governance had settled by the 1990s and has not substantively evolved since. From a structural perspective, an assumption remains that the federal government has a leadership and coordinating role in support of state and municipal authorities. In other words, even after the closure of the Australian Heritage Commission, the state agencies continue to have limited policymaking functions and pursue minimal cross-jurisdictional activities. As a result, meaningful reform in legislation and policy has been restrained. The NSW Government's response to the *Heritage Act 1977* review, and the creation of the Victorian *Heritage Act 2017* and the West Australian *Heritage Act 2018* introduced only incremental legislative and policy changes, despite the passage of two decades since their previous iterations and substantive changes in the urban heritage landscape. Heritage reform agendas have not meaningfully engaged with the growing body of critical scholarship, grey literature, and popular commentary concerning urban heritage, which questions the foundations of the traditional heritage management of the mid to late twentieth century (Smith 2006; Harrison 2013).

Reviewing frameworks

Another reason for the lack of urban heritage reform is that related policy reviews have never seriously questioned the longstanding national frameworks. An opportunity thus exists for Australia to conduct a comprehensive strategic review. The Australian Heritage Strategy (Department of the Environment 2015) explicitly identified the development of national standards as a priority, but meaningful steps have not been taken towards this—due to the lack of national funding and enthusiasm. The existing frameworks shaping policy and practice date to the late twentieth century. The early intention was to 'review them every twelve months' (AHC 1988: 13). Consolidation occurred after the first and only National Heritage Convention, in Canberra in 1998. It involved 220 people, including authorities, practitioners, First Peoples, and community representatives. According to the Australian Heritage Commission (1997: 32), the objective was to agree on 'a practical and consistent framework ... for systematically identifying, assessing, interpreting and managing heritage places'.

In 2000, the federal government implemented the nine National Heritage Convention (HERCON) criteria (Table 7.1). Criteria A to D concerned historic value and importance, rarity, instructiveness, exceptionality, and representativeness. Criterion E referred to aesthetic value. In parallel, Criterion F noted creative or technical achievement, linked to scientific or archaeological value. Criterion G is social value. Criterion H identified prominent people or groups of people. Criterion I introduced Indigenous significance, which was also replicated in the Burra Charter from 1999. This new criterion has not been widely adopted in the state and local urban heritage context, due to Indigenous heritage having its own enabling legislation. State and municipal authorities largely followed the national lead by adopting the HERCON criteria.

As noted, the criteria map on to specific heritage values, such as historic or aesthetic significance. This assumes minimal interaction or overlap between the different heritage values identified for places and prevents authorities from considering a wider array of cultural or social values in decision-making—contrary to contemporary and critical heritage approaches. Other aspects of the national heritage framework include the Burra Charter (2013), last substantively updated in 1999, and the Australian Historic Themes (2001, 2022). The benefit of the 2022 update to the Australian Historic Themes framework will be limited by the fact that they have not been mapped on to the previous, 2001, version (on which thousands of national, state, and local listings depend), or endorsed by state or local authorities, heritage practitioners, academic and professional historians, or community bodies. Meanwhile, historians continue to question the capacity of thematic approaches to meaningfully conserve the historic and social values of heritage places (Davison 2000, 2013). Despite the desirability of regular revisions and review, the national urban heritage framework—comprising criteria, principles, and themes—has not been substantively revised since the 1998 National Heritage Convention.

Table 7.1 National Heritage Criteria, 2000

Criterion A	The place has outstanding heritage value to the nation because of its importance in the course, or pattern, of Australia's natural or cultural history.
Criterion B	The place has outstanding heritage value to the nation because of its possession of uncommon, rare, or endangered aspects of Australia's natural or cultural history.
Criterion C	The place has outstanding heritage value to the nation because of its potential to yield information that will contribute to an understanding of Australia's natural or cultural history.
Criterion D	The place has outstanding heritage value to the nation because of its importance in demonstrating the principal characteristics of: 1) a class of Australia's natural or cultural places; or 2) a class of Australia's natural or cultural environments.
Criterion E	The place has outstanding heritage value to the nation because of its importance in exhibiting aesthetic characteristics valued by a community or cultural group.
Criterion F	The place has outstanding heritage value to the nation because of its importance in demonstrating a high degree of creative or technical achievement from a particular period.
Criterion G	The place has outstanding heritage value to the nation because of its strong or special association with a community or cultural group for social, cultural, or spiritual reasons.
Criterion H	The place has outstanding heritage value to the nation because of its special association with the life or works of a person, or group of persons, of importance in Australia's natural or cultural history.
Criterion I	The place has outstanding heritage value to the nation because of its importance as part of Indigenous tradition.

Source: Adapted from Environment Protection and Biodiversity Conservation Regulations, Reg. 10.01A National Heritage criteria (Act s. 325D), 2000.

State authorities have pursued heritage policymaking to both implement the national framework and address evolving heritage priorities. For instance, many state authorities have individually prepared supplementary guidance for the HERCON criteria, often taking the form of thresholding processes for inclusion in state registers. The goal of the guidance and thresholding is to produce consistent and expedient heritage outcomes for property owners and communities. An unintended effect has been to contribute additional complexity to decision-making. Such guidance is supplementary to the HERCON criteria and is not uniform across Australia.

Moreover, the national heritage framework is not comprehensively implemented. After its adoption for listing decisions, the framework is then rarely used in assessing development applications, shaping conservation works, or guiding site interpretation. This produces a remarkable disconnect between listings (and their variable statements of significance) and subsequent governance and management activities. Every state and local authority has a unique process for making decisions about the extent of allowable physical change to heritage places.

Alongside the thematic research studies, state and local authorities have commissioned policy guidance and pursued activities to address further contemporary heritage challenges. But the guidance and activities operate as subsidiary to existing frameworks. Consequently, the national framework prepared by the Australian Heritage Commission continues to unevenly structure the actions of authorities, private sector consultants, and professional bodies. There is no body equipped to undertake occasional or periodic reviews of existing arrangements. A lack of sustained knowledge exchange across jurisdictions—and between urban, design, planning, and heritage professionals—also means duplication of strategic policy initiatives. Only national coordination will overcome these various challenges.

Sustainability transitions

A third major opportunity for Australian urban heritage policymaking is to recognise social, economic, and environmental sustainability as core objectives. This would follow the UN Sustainable Development Goals (2015) and the UN-Habitat Urban Agenda, both of which identify the protection of cultural heritage as fundamental to making cities and human settlements inclusive, safe, resilient, and sustainable (Labadi and Logan 2016). For conservation, sustainability means embracing: social diversity, inclusion, and participation (Lesh 2019b); economic viability and regeneration (Mason 2008); and environmental benefits of material reuse and embodied energy (Crawford 2011).

The lack of strategic policy development in Australian urban heritage since the close of the twentieth century suggests that national authorities will need to take an active role to achieve this objective. For instance, as noted, at a state level, historic, First Peoples, and natural heritage places are considered under separate heritage legislation and within separate heritage lists. This has contributed to notable limitations in the recognition of First Peoples' knowledge in urban heritage legislation, policy, and practice (Lewi 2005; Porter 2017; Logan and Simanowsky 2019). A more cohesive regime for Indigenous and non-Indigenous urban heritage would mean that a place or landscape could be simultaneously protected for its diversity of cultural and natural values for a range of Indigenous and non-Indigenous communities.

A challenge preventing sustainability transitions relates to competing interpretations of the Burra Charter and its values-based conservation approach, which is effectively universally endorsed by authorities. When the values-based approach was first developed by the Australian Heritage Commission and Australia ICOMOS, the significance of urban heritage places was assumed to be objective, static, and fixed in the past. Architectural and historical knowledge bound to historic fabric, structures, and buildings were taken to be sufficient for achieving best-practice project outcomes. A new interpretation of the values-based approach has emerged since the 1990s, following engagements with Australia's values-based model in Asia, Europe, and North America. These international engagements were motivated by the methodological approach of the Australian model and how it systematically evaluates traditional historic and aesthetic values and provides conceptual openings for social and other emergent values.

Although not fully implemented in any domestic or international jurisdictions, critical interpretations of the values-based approach explicitly take the cultural significance of places to be dynamic, contextual, and contested. Heritage significance is treated as dynamically produced by people over time in dialogue with historic environments, rather than inherent to historic or early fabric (Muñoz Viñas 2005; Orbaşli 2017). The contemporary outlook also places fewer restrictions on the kinds of expertise and knowledge that can be adopted in decision-making (Wells and

Stiefel 2018; Madgin and Lesh 2021) and perceives social, economic, and environmental values as having a central role in conservation (Avrami et al. 2019; Gibson and Pendlebury 2009).

Across Australian jurisdictions, legislation, policy, and frameworks operate as barriers to adopting an innovative heritage outlook and so pursuing sustainability objectives for the historic environment (cf. Guzmán et al. 2017). Heritage policy and practice, in their reliance on dated assumptions, tend to conflate early or old fabric with cultural significance (Byrne et al. 2001; Ireland et al. 2020). They then emphasise the retention of early fabric over the conservation of cultural significance (Waterton et al. 2006). The conflation of significance and fabric can be traced back to narrow readings of the late nineteenth-century philosophy of conservative repair exemplified by the approach of the British Society for the Protection of Ancient Buildings, which was adopted across the world, with its sanctioning in the Venice Charter in 1964. These were the international conservation principles on which the twentieth-century Burra Charter was based.

Contemporary conservation theory recognises that efforts should instead be directed towards protecting the historic fabric from various periods specifically contributory to cultural significance. Progressive conservation models also recognise that cultural significance can be sustained or even enhanced by interfering with both historic and early fabric. Frequently, conserving old fabric has been privileged over sustaining cultural significance, compromising the ongoing, viable, and safe use of heritage places, and thus diminishing the potentially positive contribution of conservation to cities and communities. A contemporary approach foregrounding cultural significance suggests heritage places should be conserved because they are important for cities, people, culture, economies, and the environment, and operate as social repositories of historic, aesthetic, and scientific values. In fact, sophisticated conservation and design interventions could enhance cultural significance. The conservation strategy of adaptive reuse, for instance, has unrealised potential for enhancing heritage places by foregrounding community and environmental benefits (Mitchelhill et al. 2021).

A notable instance of governance weakness occurred in Ballarat, Victoria, amid the pursuit of innovative urban heritage protections. The City of Ballarat embraced the Historic Urban Landscape Recommendation (2011), becoming a pilot city for this UNESCO initiative (Bandarin and van Oers 2012). Yet, after using the approach to capture diverse and creative responses to places, no conservation measures could ultimately be implemented within the existing state heritage and planning frameworks. The project was more successful in terms of community engagement with heritage places and cultural change in favour of broader heritage priorities within the municipality (Fayad and Buckley 2019); and, potentially, paving the way for a nomination of the Victorian Goldfields to the World Heritage List.

Case studies such as Ballarat and the NSW *Heritage Act 1977* review point to the urgent need to interrogate the assumptions underlying legislation and policy, to stress-test frameworks and approaches for the twenty-first century, and to evolve policy and legislation for present-day urban priorities and heritage approaches. Instead of adopting a proactive and innovative approach to heritage policymaking, jurisdictions have weakened existing protections, eroded the independence of advisory bodies, and increased ministerial intervention. Public cynicism towards conservation combined with the effective lobbying of sections of the property and development sectors has enabled these regressive trends. A sophisticated approach to heritage policymaking would recognise development as a key enabler of conservation, emphasise the social and cultural capital accrued by corporations from protecting heritage places, and strengthen the financial and economic incentives for conservation. A model would be the US Historic Preservation Tax Incentive, extended to corporations and individual property owners.

A strategic national policy agenda in urban heritage is required. Australia could look to the United Kingdom. After more than five years of high-level policy work, in conjunction with the commercial, university, and community sectors, the Historic Environment Policy for Scotland (Historic Environment Scotland 2019) was released. It foregrounds sustainability as fundamental to the retention of heritage places and their cultural significance—an idea that has figured in revised planning legislation and national infrastructure policy, which promotes a principle of 'reuse first' of existing assets. In Australia, both the 2021 and the 2016 State of the Environment reports identify only disparate sustainability efforts in some jurisdictions (McConnell et al. 2021; Mackay 2017). In Victoria in 2021, the Heritage and Climate Change (Heritage Council of Victoria) initiative and consultation activities related to the Built Environment Climate Change Adaptation Action Plan 2022– 2026 identified the threats to historic buildings and structures posed by climate change. This kind of policymaking is necessary to ensure the future of heritage places and promotes a relationship between sustainability and heritage. But such policymaking also has not achieved its potential due to the narrow focus on mitigating the risks and threats to traditional heritage values within existing frameworks—in contrast with, for example, a broader 'reuse first' principle or tying sustainability to social justice (Avrami 2022). Bolder cross-jurisdictional policymaking across Australia's cities could recognise and then realise the positive and diverse opportunities offered for conservation by sustainability transitions.

Conclusion

During the 1973 Victorian state election campaign, Liberal premier Rupert Hamer (1973) proposed:

> The concepts of conservation and preservation, whether related to historic buildings, national parks, tourist attractions, industrial areas or the myriad other quality of life activities, demand the exercise of imagination, creativity and most importantly, flexibility. The restraints of money, time, qualified people and opportunity are more pressing in the quality of life issues than in most others.

Introducing innovative heritage protections, for Hamer (1969, 1973), improved what today is called liveability and has produced the concept of 'gross national wellbeing'. But, he noted, heritage could only bring about such attractive benefits through investment in sophisticated public administration rather than 'dogmatic inflexible policies' (Hamer 1973).

Half a century later, the continued intensity of development across Australia's cities means there is a need for the ongoing evaluation of the most appropriate ways of managing the inevitably of change to heritage places, while maximising the continuation of cultural significance and the protection of historic fabric (Madgin 2020). Yet, as David Yencken (2019: 216), the inaugural chairman of the Australian Heritage Commission, identified, 'national heritage is seen as a second-order concern, a long way behind other great matters of state'. He called on Australia to initiate an independent citizen inquiry into heritage, in the model of the Inquiry into the National Estate. Since the 2000s, the experiment with minimal federal government involvement in urban heritage has resulted in underperforming national, state, and municipal governance systems.

The challenges for urban heritage in Australia's cities are similar but are not being strategically tackled. At present, standards, criteria, and frameworks across jurisdictions broadly align with each other. But continued national inaction risks jurisdictions conducting the necessary reforms on an independent basis, inevitably splintering the policy landscape. Instead, a national body, agency, or group could pursue strategic projects, centralise policy and management knowledge, and facilitate cross-jurisdictional coordination. A strong case also exists for the federal government to enable and empower the sustainability transition for urban heritage. The relevance of urban heritage for future generations, and its capacity to contribute to cities, economies, society, and culture, will ultimately depend on the success of this transition.

References

Ashton, P., and J. Cornwall. 2006. 'Corralling Conflict: The Politics of Australian Federal Heritage Legislation Since the 1970s.' *Public History Review* 13: 53–65. doi.org/10.5130/phrj.v13i0.244.

Australian Heritage Commission (AHC). 1988. *Annual Report*. Canberra: AHC.

Australian Heritage Commission (AHC). 1997. *Australia's National Heritage: Options for Identifying Heritage Places of National Significance*. Discussion Paper. Canberra: AHC.

Avrami, E., ed. 2022. *Preservation, Sustainability, and Equity*. New York, NY: Columbia University Press.

Avrami, E., S. Macdonald, R. Mason, and D. Myers, eds. 2019. *Values in Heritage Management: Emergent Approaches and Research Directions*. Los Angeles, CA: Getty Conservation Institute.

Bandarin, F., and R. van Oers. 2012. *The Historic Urban Landscape: Managing Heritage in An Urban Century*. 2nd edn. Hoboken, NJ: John Wiley. doi.org/ 10.1002/9781119968115.

Boer, B., and G.J. Wiffen. 2005. *Heritage Law in Australia*. Melbourne: Oxford University Press.

Byrne, D., H. Brayshaw, and T. Ireland. 2001. *Social Significance*. Discussion Paper. Sydney: NSW National Parks and Wildlife Service.

Committee of Inquiry into the National Estate. 1974. *Report of the National Estate: Report of the Committee of Inquiry into the National Estate*. Canberra: AGPS.

Crawford, R. 2011. *Life Cycle Assessment in the Built Environment*. London: Spon Press. doi.org/10.4324/9780203868171.

Davison, G. 2000. 'Heritage: From Patrimony to Pastiche.' In *The Use and Abuse of Australian History*, 110–30. Sydney: Allen & Unwin.

Davison, G. 2013. 'My Heritage Trail.' In *Australian History Now*, edited by A. Clark and P. Ashton, 181–97. Sydney: NewSouth Publishing.

Department of Agriculture, Water and the Environment (DAWE). 2011. *Australian Heritage Strategy: Commissioned Essays*. Canberra: Commonwealth of Australia. Available from: www.environment.gov.au/heritage/australian-heritage-strategy/past-consultation/comissioned-essays.

Department of Agriculture, Water and the Environment (DAWE). 2021. *Heritage Places and Lists*. Canberra: Commonwealth of Australia. Available from: www.awe.gov.au/parks-heritage/heritage/heritage-places.

Department of the Environment. 2015. *Australian Heritage Strategy*. Canberra: Commonwealth of Australia.

Fayad, S., and K. Buckley. 2019. 'The Transformational Power of the HUL Approach: Lessons from Ballarat, Australia, 2012–2017.' In *Reshaping Urban Conservation: The Historic Urban Landscape Approach in Action*, edited by A. Pereira Roders and F. Bandarin, 123–48. Singapore: Springer. doi.org/10.1007/978-981-10-8887-2_7.

Gibson, L., and J.R. Pendlebury. 2009. *Valuing Historic Environments*. Farnham, UK: Ashgate.

Guzmán, P.C., A.R.P. Roders, and B.J.F. Colenbrander. 2017. 'Measuring Links between Cultural Heritage Management and Sustainable Urban Development: An Overview of Global Monitoring Tools.' *Cities* 60: 192–201. doi.org/10.1016/j.cities.2016.09.005.

Hamer, R.J. 1969. 'Who Pays for Conservation in Housing Development?' In *Conservation and Development: Who Said You Can't Have Both?*, edited by Town and Country Planning Association of Victoria, 17–22. Melbourne: Town and Country Planning Association.

Hamer, R.J. 1973. 'Political Views on Preservation: The Liberal View.' *Trust News*, [Victoria], May: 4.

Harrison, R. 2013. *Heritage: Critical Approaches*. London: Routledge.

Harwood, E., and A. Powers, eds. 2004. *The Heroic Period of Conservation*. London: Twentieth Century Society.

Historic Environment Scotland. 2019. *Historic Environment Policy for Scotland*. Edinburgh: Historic Environment Scotland.

Ireland, T., S. Brown, and J. Schofield. 2020. 'Situating (In)significance.' *International Journal of Heritage Studies* 26(9): 826–44. doi.org/10.1080/13527258.2020.1755882.

Labadi, S., and W. Logan, eds. 2016. *Urban Heritage, Development and Sustainability: International Frameworks, National and Local Governance*. London: Routledge. doi.org/10.4324/9781315728018.

Lesh, J. 2019a. 'Social Value and the Conservation of Urban Heritage Places in Australia.' *Historic Environment* 31(1): 42–62.

Lesh, J. 2019b. 'The National Estate (and the City), 1969–75: A Significant Australian Heritage Phenomenon.' *International Journal of Heritage Studies* 25(2): 113–27. doi.org/10.1080/13527258.2018.1475406.

Lesh, J. 2023. *Values in Cities: Urban Heritage in Twentieth Century Australia*. New York, NY: Routledge. doi.org/10.4324/9780429352713.

Lewi, H. 2005. 'Whose Heritage? The Contested Site of the Swan Brewery.' *Fabrications* 15(2): 43–61. doi.org/10.1080/10331867.2005.10525210.

Lewis, M. 1999. *Suburban Backlash: The Battle for the World's Most Liveable City*. Melbourne: Bloomings Books.

Logan, C., and A. Simanowsky. 2019. 'Unsettled: The Afterlife of the Newcastle Post Office.' *Fabrications* 29(1): 37–59. doi.org/10.1080/10331867.2019.1541510.

Logan, W.S. 2007. 'Reshaping the "Sunburnt Country": Heritage and Cultural Politics in Contemporary Australia.' In *Geographies of Australian Heritages: Loving a Sunburnt Country?*, edited by R. Jones and B.J. Shaw, 207–23. Aldershot, UK: Ashgate. doi.org/10.4324/9781351157520-13.

McConnell, A., J. Terri, C. Zena, and I. Cresswell. 2021. *Australia: State of the Environment 2021—Heritage*. Independent report to the Australian Government Minister for the Environment. Canberra: Commonwealth of Australia. doi.org/10.26194/7w85-3w50.

Mackay, R. 2017. *Australia State of the Environment 2016: Heritage*. Canberra: Department of the Environment and Energy.

Madgin, R. 2020. 'Urban Heritage and Urban Development.' In *Concepts of Urban-Environmental History*, edited by S. Haumann, M. Knoll, and D. Mares, 235–82. Bielefeld, Germany: Transcript. doi.org/10.1515/9783839443750-016.

Madgin, R., and J. Lesh, eds. 2021. *People-Centred Methodologies for Heritage Conservation: Exploring Emotional Attachments to Historic Urban Places*. London: Routledge. doi.org/10.4324/9780429345807.

Mason, R. 2008. 'Be Interested and Beware: Joining Economic Valuation and Heritage Conservation.' *International Journal of Heritage Studies* 14(4): 303–18. doi.org/10.1080/13527250802155810.

Mitchelhill, J., H. Lewi, and C. Logan. 2021. 'Adaptive Histories: The Role of Architectural Historians in Urban Redevelopment Outcomes.' In *Proceedings of the Society of Architectural Historians Australia and New Zealand. Volume 37: What If? What Next? Speculations on History's Futures*, edited by K. Hislop and H. Lewi, 488–99. Perth: SAHANZ.

Muñoz Viñas, S. 2005. *Contemporary Theory of Conservation*. Oxford, UK: Elsevier.

Orbaşli, A. 2017. 'Conservation Theory in the Twenty-First Century: Slow Evolution or a Paradigm Shift?' *Journal of Architectural Conservation* 23(3): 157–70. doi.org/10.1080/13556207.2017.1368187.

Porter, L. 2017. 'Heritage Management.' In *Planning in Indigenous Australia: From Imperial Foundations to Postcolonial Futures*, edited by S. Jackson, L. Porter, and L.C. Johnson, 195–213. New York, NY: Routledge. doi.org/10.4324/978131 5693668-13.

Productivity Commission. 2006. *Conservation of Australia's Historic Heritage Places*. Productivity Commission Inquiry Report No. 37, 6 April. Canberra: Productivity Commission. Available from: www.pc.gov.au/inquiries/completed/ heritage/report/heritage.pdf. doi.org/10.2139/ssrn.925774.

Smith, L. 2006. *Uses of Heritage*. New York, NY: Routledge. doi.org/10.4324/ 9780203602263.

Standing Committee on Social Issues. 2021a. *Review of NSW Heritage Legislation*. Discussion Paper, April. Sydney: NSW Parliament. Available from: www. heritage.nsw.gov.au/assets/A-Review-of-Heritage-Legislation-discussion-paper.pdf.

Standing Committee on Social Issues. 2021b. *Review of the Heritage Act 1977*. Report No. 59, October. Sydney: Legislative Council, NSW Parliament. Available from: www.parliament.nsw.gov.au/lcdocs/inquiries/2814/Report%20No.%2059% 20-%20Standing%20Committee%20on%20Social%20Issues%20-%20Review %20of%20the%20Heritage%20Act%201977.pdf.

Sullivan, S. 2015. 'Does the Practice of Heritage As We Know It Have a Future?' *Historic Environment* 27(2): 110–17.

Veale, S., and R. Freestone. 2012. 'The Things We Wanted to Keep: The Commonwealth and the National Estate 1969–1974.' *Historic Environment* 24(3): 12–18.

Waterton, E., L. Smith, and G. Campbell. 2006. 'The Utility of Discourse Analysis to Heritage Studies: The Burra Charter and Social Inclusion.' *International Journal of Heritage Studies* 12(4): 339–55. doi.org/10.1080/13527250600727000.

Wells, J.C., and B. Stiefel, eds. 2018. *Human-Centered Built Environment Heritage Preservation: Theory and Evidence-Based Practice*. New York, NY: Routledge.

Wesley, R. 1996. The Australian Heritage Commission: A Vain Hope? The Role, Function and Operation of the Australian Heritage Commission 1975–1995. MA thesis, University of Tasmania, Hobart.

Yencken, D. 1982. *The National Estate in 1981: A Report of the Australian Heritage Commission*. Canberra: AGPS.

Yencken, D. 2019. *Valuing Australia's National Heritage*. Melbourne: Future Leaders.

Part 3: Population, settlement, and urban form

8

Changing Australia's settlement geography: The repopulation of regional cities and towns

Amanda Davies

Introduction

Australia's population has grown by 5 million over the past two decades. This population growth has been described as unexpected, unprecedented, and unplanned. Driving such characterisations are the frequently reported occurrences of unmet demand for infrastructure and services across Australia's capital and regional cities resulting from population growth. From increasing travel times for commuters and escalating housing costs to overcrowded classrooms and extended waiting times for emergency medical services, reports that characterise the negative impacts of population growth are all too common. While these set out the negative impacts for city-dwellers and their lifestyles, it is the promise of the city lifestyle and employment opportunities that continues to attract people to move to cities.

With Australia's population forecast to grow by another 10 million people over the next two decades, this chapter considers how this population growth can be accommodated. It is not a fait accompli that major cities will need to be spatially expanded to accommodate population growth. Reflecting on recent settlement patterns that show that capital cities have been experiencing net internal population decline for years (ABS 2021c), it is argued that it is time to question the adage that everyone wants to live in the city. While there is no doubt that rural to urban migration has been a dominant trend in Australia for many decades, times have changed and the factors that once drove rural to urban migration have also shifted. The liveability and employment opportunities in smaller regional cities and towns have diversified and expanded, diminishing the relative 'pull factors' of capital and large cities.

This chapter examines these issues and considers how Australia's public health response to Covid-19 is shaping population growth and the potential implications for Australia's settlement geography. In particular, the chapter considers potential implications of the normalisation of working from home and how changing perceptions of the relative safety of highly populous and high-density environments could have longer-term impacts for Australia's population geography.

Australia's population growth

The 'growing pains' being experienced in Australia's major cities, such as extended commuting times and shortages of affordable housing, have led to claims that population growth has been unmanaged or poorly managed. In reality, Australia's population growth is highly managed. To better understand this, it is useful to consider the component parts of population growth: international migration and natural change (births and deaths).

International migration

With approximately 66 per cent of Australia's population growth the result of international migration, at the macro-scale, Australia's population growth has long been regulated (ABS 2018). Australia's migration program regulates the number of migrants who move here. Through visa categories, the program also regulates the initial destination for some migrants (Tan et al. 2019; Department of Home Affairs 2021). Before the Covid-19 pandemic, Australia's population was forecast to grow by another 10 million people over the decade from 2019, with population growth projected to be 0.9–1.4 per cent per annum (ABS 2018). International migration was projected to make up between 56 per cent and 66 per cent of this growth, with population growth from international migration alone projected to be 0.7–1.1 per cent per annum (ABS 2018).

Australia's public health response to Covid-19 resulted in the national border being closed for some time to most travellers and international migrants. As a result, population forecasts are being recalculated to accommodate this much reduced migration flow. The population forecasts underpinning the 2021–22 federal budget drew on an assumption that a small level of international travel to Australia, particularly for international students, would begin in late 2021. It was also assumed that broader international travel and permanent migration to Australia would resume from mid-2022. Based on these assumptions, net overseas migration was forecast to be 21,600 for 2021–22, increasing to 95,900 during 2022–23, and further increasing to 201,100 during 2023–24 (Love and Spinks 2021).

Natural change: Births and deaths

While a lot of attention is given to the implications of international migration on Australia's population growth, natural change—from births and deaths—is also an important factor. First, Australia's fertility rate is below replacement level, which is not a new trend: it has been the case since 1976 (with the replacement rate considered to be 2.1 births per woman) (ABS 2021a). Between 2009 and 2019, the fertility rate decreased from 1.97 to 1.66 (ABS 2021a). Second, Australia's standardised death rate is approximately 5.3 deaths per 1,000 standard population (ABS 2021b). The death rate has steadily declined from the 1970s and the gap between the death rates for males and females has also been reduced. In 1979, the death rate for males was 13.4 and for females it was eight. By 2019, it had reduced to 6.3 for males and 4.4 for females (ABS 2021b).

So, why are births and deaths interesting? While international migration accounted for approximately 65 per cent of Australia's population growth (before Covid-19), natural increase makes up the rest. Natural increase occurs when there are more births than deaths over a period. In Australia, as the fertility rate and the mortality rate have decreased (and the population has aged as a result), the contribution of natural increase to population growth has lessened; however, it remains an important factor. Importantly, there is geographic unevenness in birth and death rates across Australia, which has implications for localised variations in population growth and resulting service demand—an issue addressed further below.

The ABS's population projections produce three models to account for low, medium, and high-growth scenarios. Across these, there is relatively little variability in the mortality and fertility rates, which reflects the 'normal state' in which trends in mortality and fertility are slow-moving. Essentially, unless there is a significant or catastrophic event, it is safe to assume Australia will continue to see below replacement fertility rates and an ageing of the population.

The question then becomes: is Covid-19 a significant or catastrophic event that will result in changes to the fertility or mortality rates? At the time of writing, Australia was managing the pandemic in such a way that there had been little impact on the overall fertility and mortality rates. Provisional mortality statistics for the period from January 2020 until April 2021 indicate excess mortality, with the number of deaths 5.6 per cent higher than expected (ABS 2022). Above average deaths were recorded between May 2020 and September 2020 and correlate with Covid-19 infections (ABS 2022). However, this variation is not sufficient to result in a change in life expectancy or the longer-term standardised death rate.

Some media reports indicated there could be a 'Covid baby boom' (for example, Boseley 2021; Street et al. 2021). Moving beyond the headlines, however, there is no robust evidence for this. Reports of baby booms point to increasing numbers of babies being born in some areas, but such trends can readily be explained by the overall population growth and demographic shift occurring in these places. This noted, the Australian Centre for Population (2020) projected a minor decline in the nation's birthrate because of the decline in international migration and suggested that some families would defer their decision to have children due to Covid-19.

Reforecasting Australia's population growth

The impact of Australia's public health response to Covid-19 had immediate impacts on the size and growth trajectory of the Australian population, which was approximately 4 per cent smaller than it was projected to be by mid-2021 (Centre for Population 2020). The sharp decline in international immigration has necessitated the revision of population forecasts, with Australia's population growth expected to have slowed in 2020 by the equivalent of three years. However, at the time of writing, reforecasts assumed that international migration would recover by mid to late 2022, and there would be little change in mortality rates because of Covid-19. With many unknowns remaining about the impact of the virus on human health and mortality, and uncertainties about the resumption and continuity of international travel and migration, it is plausible that population forecasts will need to be further revised.

From the rural drift to the city exodus

The past few decades have seen Australia's capital cities and surrounding metropolitan regions grow in terms of population, spatial coverage, and arguably, socioeconomic and cultural complexity. Indeed, since 1960, the share of Australians living in urban areas has increased from 82 per cent to 90 per cent, and more than two-thirds of the population is based in a capital city (Infrastructure Australia 2018). Furthermore, approximately 65 per cent of Australia's population lives in a city with more than 1 million people and another 10 per cent lives in a medium-sized city of between 100,000 and 1 million (PM&C 2019).

The rural to urban transition of Australia's population has been extensively explored in academic scholarship, with research highlighting the impacts of both the structural changes to employment in primary industries and the contraction of government-provided services in small and medium-sized settlements as drivers of outmigration from rural and remote areas (Davies and Tonts 2010; Argent et al. 2014; Smailes et al. 2014; Argent and Tonts 2015; Plummer et al. 2018). In contrast, it has been recognised that the concentration of government services and the diversification of employment and lifestyle opportunities in large urban areas and cities have underpinned the growth of those places.

But is Australia's rural drift now ending; are we seeing a population turnaround? While this question is not new, and counter-urbanisation trends have been reported for more than two decades (Tonts and Greive 2002; Gurran 2008; Argent et al. 2013), it has attracted considerable media attention since the Covid-19 pandemic (see, for example, Terzon 2021). Indeed, it has been suggested that the pandemic will result in an exodus from cities (Davies 2021b). Underpinning this suggestion are several issues and trends related to housing, working arrangements, and international migration patterns that have been bundled together. To work out what changes in population distribution are occurring and could occur in the near term, it is critical to accurately establish what the internal migration trends were before Covid-19.

Until the pandemic, Australia had an average per annum net population growth of 1.6 per cent over the previous decade, however, as noted above, this growth was spatially unevenly distributed (Centre for Population 2020). In a nutshell, the largest cities had the highest growth rates and very small settlements typically had the lowest. It is this unevenness in distribution and the impacts on services, infrastructure, employment, and housing that have generated considerable concern for both large and small settlements.

With Australia's largest capital cities experiencing significant population growth rates in recent years, at a macro-level, it could seem that these large cities are experiencing similar development patterns. However, in examining the component parts of population growth for these large cities, there is considerable difference in the drivers of growth. Table 8.1 shows net interstate and net intrastate migration for the three largest capital cities for the period 2015 to 2019. The table also shows the net international migration to the respective states for these capital cities (further spatial breakdown is not available) for 2015 to 2019.

Greater Sydney has been losing population to other parts of New South Wales and other states since at least 2001 (ABS 2020b). Greater Melbourne has been losing population to other parts of Victoria for approximately two decades but gaining from other states since 2008. In contrast, Greater Brisbane has been gaining population through both intrastate and interstate migration. While Greater Brisbane has had net positive interstate migration for more than two decades, it has only had net positive intrastate migration since 2015.

Population movement—or churn—between or within states is not unusual. Australia has, in broad terms, a particularly mobile population (Bernard et al. 2017). About 40 per cent of the population changes address at least once within a five-year period (PC 2014). However, since the 1990s, the level of internal migration within Australia has fallen, driven by a 25 per cent decline in long-distance moves between cities and regions between 1991 and 2016. For those moving between states, the decline was smaller, however, it was still significant, at 16 per cent. Importantly, there is variability in the type and frequency of movement across demographic groups (Smailes et al. 2014; Bernard et al. 2017; Borsellino 2020; Davies and Prout Quicke 2021). Indeed, a recent analysis of internal migration patterns in Australia confirmed that despite absolute and relative growth in the number of people aged 65 and over between 1981 and 2016, there had been no concurrent increase in mobility within this group. In fact, migration intensity fell from 9 per cent in 1976–81 to 7 per cent in 2011–16 (Borsellino 2020).

Table 8.1 Component parts of population growth for Sydney, Melbourne, and Brisbane, 2015–2019

Year	Greater Sydney			Greater Melbourne			Greater Brisbane		
	Net intrastate migration	Net interstate migration	Net overseas migration	Net intrastate migration	Net interstate migration	Net overseas migration	Net intrastate migration	Net interstate migration	Net overseas migration
2015	–13,687	–5,856	72,840	–5,533	13,335	64,190	3,458	3,395	19,480
2016	–15,591	–8,410	96,200	–8,026	16,983	82,910	5,671	6,466	32,430
2017	–18,160	–13,439	94,930	–12,645	15,439	87,130	5,056	9,494	27,640
2018	–17,019	–15,345	92,890	–14,637	12,760	89,540	3,219	10,160	33,740
2019	–13,995	–14,473	79,280	–11,569	11,021	85,060	6,903	10,044	33,920
Total	**–78,452**	**–57,523**	**436,140**	**–52,410**	**69,538**	**408,830**	**24,307**	**39,559**	**147,210**

Sources: ABS (2019–20) for net overseas migration; and ABS (2020b) for intrastate and interstate migration.

Providing insight into how demographic characteristics can impact population distribution, Borsellino (2020) also found that those aged 65 and over typically moved from highly urban and remote areas to 'middle-density' regions. This finding reflects the findings of Davies and James (2011), who identified that older people who moved were likely to move away from remote rural areas, which typically have limited services to support individuals as they move into late old age. Davies and James (2011) also found that older people were more likely to select high amenity and well-serviced 'lifestyle' destinations for their retirement.

Importantly though, Borsellino's (2020) analysis reveals how internal migration patterns are not static and do change in response to social, economic, and environmental factors. Given the migration trends of the 1980s and 1990s, it has become a truism that retirees head to high-amenity 'retirement' destinations of the north coast of New South Wales and South-East Queensland. However, the data reveal that from the early 2000s these areas and the peripheries of capital cities have become less popular as destinations for those aged 65 and over. In contrast, regional cities adjacent to capital cities are emerging as the new retirement destinations (Borsellino 2020).

Covid-19 and the so-called city exodus

Since the onset of the Covid-19 pandemic, Australia's capital cities have recorded their largest losses of population on record. Despite this, for the financial year 2019–20, the population of Australia's capital cities still grew by 1.4 per cent. Approximately 160,000 international migrants moved to Australia and into its capital cities and there was also a natural population increase of approximately 110,000 persons. However, during this initial period, capital cities experienced a net loss of 54,800 people to internal migration (Table 8.2). This sparked considerable public interest, leading to concerns about a 'city exodus' and a related housing shortage in regional areas.

Table 8.2 Quarterly net internal migration for Australian capital cities, March 2020 to March 2021

City	March 2020	June 2020	Sept. 2020	Dec. 2020	March 2021	Total, March 2020 – June 2021
Sydney	–8,087	–6,378	–7,782	–9,317	–8,169	**–39,733**
Melbourne	–2,163	–7,994	–7,445	–8,491	–8,273	**–34,366**
Brisbane	1,874	3,189	3,215	4,770	3,274	**16,322**
Adelaide	–446	–181	–334	–247	59	**–1,149**
Perth	–72	408	1,388	1,794	1,554	**5,072**
Hobart	–166	–42	–162	–92	–289	**–751**
Darwin	–562	–202	8	259	–139	**–636**
Canberra	–520	243	–135	699	138	**425**
Total	**–10,142**	**–10,957**	**–11,247**	**–10,625**	**–11,845**	**–54,816**

Source: ABS (2021c).

Drilling further into the initial migration data, there was considerable unevenness across capital cities. Brisbane experienced substantive growth during the Covid-19 period, with nearly 5,000 new residents in the December 2020 quarter alone. Greater Perth moved from a net loss to a net gain—the latter typically only experienced during periods of mining construction and expansion in Western Australia. Canberra and Darwin also enjoyed quarters of net population growth, with Adelaide moving into net growth in the March 2021 quarter. Overall, considering the net population decline of Australia's capital cities, the greatest contributors to the 'city exodus' were Sydney and Melbourne.

Since March 2020, Sydney lost between 8,000 and 9,000 residents (net) each quarter. For Sydney, the net loss experienced since the pandemic has been a little larger than in previous years, but not substantively, and it does not exceed quarterly population losses recorded in the 2000s. However, for Melbourne, the story is a little different. While the overall net loss is less than that for Sydney, the change experienced was more significant. In the March quarter, Melbourne had a net loss of just 2,163 residents; however, by the December 2020 quarter, this had increased to a loss of approximately 8,500 and a further 8,200 by the March 2021 quarter (ABS 2021c). While the cause of the unprecedented outmigration from Melbourne is not provided by the ABS data, the observed increase does align with the periods of extended lockdown that were experienced in that city.

The data for internal migration during the Covid-19 period are showing the emergence of some interesting trends—including that Australians continue to be highly mobile despite lockdowns and border closures. However, the data are not yet showing an exodus from our cities. Indeed, while Greater Melbourne lost population to intrastate and interstate localities, the remainder of Victoria also lost population to interstate migration—and the loss from regional Victoria was, proportionally, more severe than that for Melbourne (ABS 2021c). Therefore, in Victoria, people are not leaving Melbourne for the country; they are leaving Victoria all together.

The data for Queensland since March 2020 are also interesting. Non-metropolitan Queensland experienced a significant upswing in net interstate migration (ABS 2021c). While it is not possible to determine from the regional migration data who is moving where in the regional areas of each state, drawing on population data from the 2016 census, it is anticipated that much of this population growth was concentrated in the populous Gold and Sunshine coasts. Indeed, the fastest-growing areas outside capital cities are those that offer sophisticated urban settings.

Overall, the introduction of public health measures in response to Covid-19 has increased movement away from some capital cities, but not all. Furthermore, during the pandemic, Perth, in the state that was subject to the strictest border controls, was recording arrivals at a level not seen since the last mining boom. At the time of writing, the data on regional migration are not sufficiently reliable to comment on whether Covid-19 will cause a longer-term disruption to the established migration flows between cities and between cities and regions, but the change observed is sufficient to warrant increased policy attention to internal population mobility.

Post Covid-19 and rural repopulation

Across Australia for some decades now, the populations of regional cities and large towns have been growing, largely through internal population redistribution. Urban areas adjacent to capital cities have expanded, become more urbane, and emerged as major cities in their own right. Smaller towns, particularly those with high amenity values, have attracted population. Population growth has resulted in these places transforming to become major hubs, some with all the trappings, including unmet demand for infrastructure and services. As these places have grown and transformed, their appeal to different demographic groups has also shifted, in turn impacting on in and outmigration trends.

Past trends in population movements typically provide the basis for future projections. However, as populations change (for example, grow, decline, age, and increase or decrease in average wealth), the factors that drive these flows also change. For example, while the sleepy coastal communities of the NSW central and northern coasts were once highly desirable to retirees and, conversely, lost young people through outmigration, these places have transformed into more dynamic urban settlements and now attract a more diverse working-age demographic. Therefore, it is important to consider how places are changing in response to population growth (and related demographic change) and how these changes, in turn, impact the push and pull characteristics of places for different demographics.

With the above in mind, in considering how the Covid-19 pandemic could shape Australia's population geography, there are two issues of particular interest:

- the normalisation of working from home arrangements in workplaces
- changing perceptions about the relative safety of highly populous and high-density environments.

As a result of the Covid-19 public health measures, many employers have enabled staff to work remotely, most commonly from home. The ABS's Household Impacts of Covid-19 Survey found that between 30 and 40 per cent of respondents had worked from home as a response to the pandemic (ABS 2020a). The uptake in working from home, while positioned as a short-term and 'emergency measure', could have longer-term implications for Australia's population distribution. Indeed, one estimate suggests that more than 65 per cent of those able to work from home indicated they expected this to continue more regularly after the pandemic (Lennox 2020a).

A major barrier to rural in-migration in Australia has been the lack of diverse employment opportunities available in smaller settlements (Davies 2008; Argent et al. 2013). Indeed, this remains one of the major drivers of outmigration. This is a well-recognised issue and, as such, the potential utility of advancements in internet communications for enabling rural-dwellers to access more diverse employment opportunities is also appreciated (Davies 2021a).

It has been argued that information and communication technology innovations could be a panacea for small rural communities, with workers able to live in rural areas with limited local employment but access remote employment opportunities. However, there has not been broad uptake of fully online remote working due to a complex of factors, including the urban–rural digital divide, the costs associated with upgrading employers' internal systems to support working from home, and required changes in workplace organisational cultures and management frameworks (Davies 2021a). However, there are signs that these barriers to broader participation in remote working are being addressed. First, the pandemic necessitated workplaces to rapidly develop supportive organisational frameworks to enable staff to work from home—and, in so doing, removed one of the major initial barriers to a broader-scale and longer-term transition. Second, workers have become more familiar with navigating working from home arrangements—for themselves and their colleagues—meaning another significant barrier to longer-term change is being overcome.

What remains unknown is whether employers and employees will continue to engage in working from home arrangements over the longer term. While it has been demonstrated that such arrangements are possible as a short-term arrangement, whether they are preferable as a permanent arrangement is not yet known. On this matter, considering the initial impact of the shift of some Australian workplaces to working from home in 2020, Lennox (2020b) found that those who worked from home would be more prepared to undertake longer commutes to a central workplace if these were less frequent.

Also of interest to considerations of Australia's population geography over the longer term is the question of how people's preparedness to live in highly populated and dense environments could shift. Reports abound about city-dwellers moving out for the relative safety of country areas (Malatzky et al. 2020). Despite regional areas often having limited healthcare services, and certainly very limited medical facilities for dealing with any Covid-19 outbreak, they have been positioned as safer as they are less populous with lower population densities. This repositioning of country areas as safer, desirable lifestyle destinations could go some way to addressing another significant barrier to rural in-migration: the perception that rural areas are in decline and offer limited social and cultural opportunities compared with major-city counterparts.

Conclusion

There are many uncertainties about how Australia's population geography will be impacted by Covid-19 and the related public health responses. However, it can be concluded that without a recovery in international migration, Australia's population growth will sharply decline, the population will age, and the population will become less ethnically diverse. It can be concluded that as the characteristics of places change, migration flows will also respond and adjust. If highly dense environments emerge as places where people are at greater risk of disease, it is plausible that more people will move to less dense environments. This could be within the city (suburbanisation) or moves from the city to smaller regional settlements. However, it is also plausible that if the health crisis is prolonged, there will be increased in-migration to larger settlements with advanced tertiary healthcare resources. If the current temporary remote working arrangements in some sectors are broadly normalised in the longer term, it is plausible that there will be a disruption to the centralising of employment (and education) in major cities and, in turn, shifts in the established patterns of population distribution.

While the pandemic is throwing up uncertainties about the implications for population growth and distribution, the decrease in net international migration, the increase in net outmigration from some capital cities, and the increase in migration to some regional areas have drawn attention to the precarity of Australia's overall population growth, city growth, and spatial distribution. As Australia adapts to Covid-19, it will be particularly important to give attention to developing improved agility in the policies and planning for growing and changing populations. Population growth in cities should not be assumed a fait accompli and, likewise, the growth of some regional settlements should not be interpreted as a shift to counter-urbanisation. As the implications of Covid-19 become clearer, population projections should be regularly reviewed. Within this, careful attention must be given to any shifts in the demographic character of a population as the result of changes in population growth and distribution.

References

Argent, N., and M. Tonts. 2015. 'A Multicultural and Multifunctional Countryside? International Labour Migration and Australia's Productivist Heartlands.' *Population, Space and Place* 21(2): 140–56. doi.org/10.1002/psp.1812.

Argent, N., M. Tonts, R. Jones, and J. Holmes. 2013. 'A Creativity-Led Rural Renaissance? Amenity-Led Migration, the Creative Turn and the Uneven Development of Rural Australia.' *Applied Geography* 44: 88–98. doi.org/10.1016/j.apgeog.2013.07.018.

Argent, N., M. Tonts, and A. Stockdale. 2014. 'Rural Migration, Agrarian Change, and Institutional Dynamics: Perspectives from the Majority World.' *Population, Space and Place* 20(4): 299–302. doi.org/10.1002/psp.1827.

Australian Bureau of Statistics (ABS). 2018. *Population Projections, Australia, 2017 (Base) — 2066.* Catalogue no. 3222.0, 22 November. Canberra: ABS. Available from: www.abs.gov.au/statistics/people/population/population-projections-australia/2017-base-2066.

Australian Bureau of Statistics (ABS). 2019–20. *Migration, Australia (2019–20 Financial Year).* Catalogue no. 3412.0. Canberra: ABS. Available from: www.abs.gov.au/statistics/people/population/migration-australia/latest-release.

Australian Bureau of Statistics (ABS). 2020a. *Household Impacts of COVID-19 Survey (Detailed release June 2020).* Canberra: ABS. Available from: www.abs.gov.au/statistics/people/people-and-communities/household-impacts-covid-19-survey/detailed-release-june-2020.

Australian Bureau of Statistics (ABS). 2020b. *Regional Internal Migration Estimates, Provisional (September 2020).* Catalogue no. 3412.0.55.005. Canberra: ABS. Available from: www.abs.gov.au/statistics/people/population/regional-internal-migration-estimates-provisional/sep-2020.

Australian Bureau of Statistics (ABS). 2021a. *Births, Australia (2021)*. Catalogue no. 3301.0. Canberra: ABS. Available from: www.abs.gov.au/statistics/people/population/births-australia/latest-release.

Australian Bureau of Statistics (ABS). 2021b. *Deaths, Australia (2021)*. Catalogue no. 3302.0. Canberra: ABS. Available from: www.abs.gov.au/statistics/people/population/deaths-australia/latest-release.

Australian Bureau of Statistics (ABS). 2021c. *Regional Internal Migration Estimates, Provisional (March 2021)*. Catalogue no. 3412.0.55.005. Canberra: ABS. Available from: www.abs.gov.au/statistics/people/population/regional-internal-migration-estimates-provisional/mar-2021.

Australian Bureau of Statistics (ABS). 2022. *Provisional Mortality Statistics (Jan–Nov 2022)*. Catalogue no. 3303.0.55.004. Canberra: ABS. Available from: www.abs.gov.au/statistics/health/causes-death/provisional-mortality-statistics/latest-release.

Bernard, A., P. Forder, H. Kendig, and J. Byles. 2017. 'Residential Mobility in Australia and the United States: A Retrospective Study.' *Australian Population Studies* 1(1): 41–54. doi.org/10.37970/aps.v1i1.11.

Borsellino, R. 2020. 'The Changing Migration Patterns of the 65+ Population in Australia, 1976–2016.' *Australian Population Studies* 4(1): 4–19. doi.org/10.37970/aps.v4i1.60.

Boseley, M. 2021. 'Is There a Covid Baby Boom? Experts Disagree but Australia's Maternity Wards Are Straining.' *The Guardian*, [Australia], 6 June. Available from: www.theguardian.com/australia-news/2021/jun/06/is-there-a-covid-baby-boom-experts-disagree-but-australias-maternity-wards-are-straining.

Centre for Population. 2020. *2020 Population Statement*. Canberra: Commonwealth of Australia. Available from: population.gov.au/publications/statements/2020-population-statement.

Davies, A. 2008. 'Declining Youth In-Migration in Rural Western Australia: The Role of Perceptions of Rural Employment and Lifestyle Opportunities.' *Geographical Research* 46(2): 162–71. doi.org/10.1111/j.1745-5871.2008.00507.x.

Davies, A. 2021a. 'COVID-19 and ICT-Supported Remote Working: Opportunities for Rural Economies.' *World* 2: 139–52. doi.org/10.3390/world2010010.

Davies, A. 2021b. 'Has COVID Really Caused an Exodus from Our Cities? In Fact, Moving to the Regions Is Nothing New.' *The Conversation*, 15 February. Available from: theconversation.com/has-covid-really-caused-an-exodus-from-our-cities-in-fact-moving-to-the-regions-is-nothing-new-154724.

Davies, A., and A. James. 2011. *Geographies of Ageing: Social Processes and the Spatial Unevenness of Population Ageing*. Abingdon, UK: Ashgate.

Davies, A., and S. Prout Quicke. 2021. 'Population Mobility, "Usual Residence" and the Census: The Case of Australia's Grey Nomads.' *Australian Population Studies* 5(1): 9–17. doi.org/10.37970/aps.v5i1.76.

Davies, A., and M. Tonts. 2010. 'Economic Diversity and Regional Socioeconomic Performance: An Empirical Analysis of the Western Australian Grain Belt.' *Geographical Research* 48(3): 223–34. doi.org/10.1111/j.1745-5871.2009.00627.x.

Department of Home Affairs. 2021. *Migration Program Planning Levels*. Canberra: Commonwealth of Australia. Available from: immi.homeaffairs.gov.au/what-we-do/migration-program-planning-levels.

Department of the Prime Minister and Cabinet (PM&C). 2019. *Planning for Australia's Future Population*. Canberra: Commonwealth of Australia.

Gurran, N. 2008. 'The Turning Tide: Amenity Migration in Coastal Australia.' *International Planning Studies* 13(4): 391–414. doi.org/10.1080/1356347 0802519055.

Infrastructure Australia. 2018. *Future Cities: Planning for Our Growing Population*. Reform Series, February. Sydney: Infrastructure Australia. Available from: www.infrastructureaustralia.gov.au/sites/default/files/2019-06/future-cities-paper-web.pdf.

Lennox, J. 2020a. 'More Urban Sprawl While Jobs Cluster: Working from Home Will Reshape the Nation.' *The Conversation*, 19 August. Available from: theconversation.com/more-urban-sprawl-while-jobs-cluster-working-from-home-will-reshape-the-nation-144409.

Lennox, J. 2020b. *More Working from Home Will Change the Shape and Size of Cities*. CoPS Working Paper No. G-306, August. Melbourne: Centre of Policy Studies, Victoria University. Available from: www.copsmodels.com/ftp/work papr/g-306.pdf.

Love, S., and H. Spinks. 2021. *Immigration: Budget Review 2020–21 Index*. Canberra: Parliament of the Commonwealth of Australia. Available from: www.aph.gov.au/About_Parliament/Parliamentary_Departments/Parliamentary_Library/pubs/rp/BudgetReview202021/Immigration.

Malatzky, C., J. Gillespie, D.L. Couch, and C. Cosgrave. 2020. 'Why Place Matters: A Rurally-Oriented Analysis of COVID-19's Differential Impacts.' *Social Sciences & Humanities Open* 2(1): 100063. doi.org/10.1016/j.ssaho.2020.100063.

Plummer, P., M. Tonts, and N. Argent. 2018. 'Sustainable Rural Economies, Evolutionary Dynamics and Regional Policy.' *Applied Geography* 90: 308–20. doi.org/10.1016/j.apgeog.2017.01.005.

Productivity Commission (PC). 2014. *Geographic Labour Mobility Research Report.* Canberra: Productivity Commission.

Smailes, P., T. Griffin, and N. Argent. 2014. 'Demographic Change, Differential Ageing, and Public Policy in Rural and Regional Australia: A Three-State Case Study.' *Geographical Research* 52(3): 229–49. doi.org/10.1111/1745-5871.12067.

Street, J., C. Fitzsimmons, and D. Prosser. 2021. '"Oh, COVID Baby": New Mums, Midwives Deliver Verdicts on Regional "Baby Boom", Demographers Not So Sure.' *ABC News*, 28 February. Available from: www.abc.net.au/news/2021-02-28/covid-baby-boom-regional-midwives-agree-demographers-say-maybe/13189694.

Tan, G., A. Cebulla, A. Ziersch, and A. Taylor. 2019. 'Australia's State Specific and Regional Migration Schemes: Exploring Permanent and Temporary Skilled Migration Outcomes in South Australia.' *Australian Population Studies* 3(2): 16–28. doi.org/10.37970/aps.v3i2.50.

Terzon, E. 2021. 'ABS Data Confirms a City Exodus during COVID, With Biggest Internal Migration Loss on Record.' *ABC News*, 2 February. Available from: www.abc.net.au/news/2021-02-02/abs-data-confirms-city-exodus-during-covid/13112868.

Tonts, M., and S. Greive. 2002. 'Commodification and Creative Destruction in the Australian Rural Landscape: The Case of Bridgetown, Western Australia.' *Geographical Research* 40(1): 58–70. doi.org/10.1111/1467-8470.00161.

9

Prospects and policies for new urban settlements in Australia

Victoria Kolankiewicz, Elizabeth Taylor, and David Nichols

Introduction

This chapter examines the state of play of decentralisation development in Australia, reappraising past visions and realised schemes, and exploring possibilities for these to shape Australia's urban and rural futures. We consider responses to the 2020–22 Covid-19 pandemic, which have resulted in a de-urbanisation that is novel for recent decades and has reversed some of the metropolitan primacy and growth rates that underscored established Australian planning discourse and practice. Reflecting the range of decentralisation discourse itself, we consider claims to recentre cities or to create 'new' cities, including schemes both speculative and realised, and reflect on the diverse fates of greenfield versus proximate satellite city schemes.

In the almost 50 years since the plans of the Department of Urban and Regional Development (DURD) for new Australian cities collapsed with (as it transpired) only Albury–Wodonga and Macarthur in south-western Sydney undeniably fruitful outcomes, it appears the concept of the purpose-built greenfield 'new city' has barely reared its head in Australian policy. While the Morrison Government was supportive in principle of shifting Australia's population away from a metropolitan primacy model, only token programs were proposed. In fact, no federal government since Paul Keating's (1991–96) has committed specific funds to any paradigm-shifting enterprise.

As is so often the case, the cause of new-city development has been muddled by a confusion of terms—the question, for instance, of whether 'satellite cities' are necessarily purpose-built or merely economic dependents and, additionally, whether such cities are glorified dormitory suburbs or whether their 'satellite' nature is a mere geographical signifier of their relative position to a primate city while they nonetheless operate with a high degree of self-sufficiency. 'New cities' also pose definitional problems, particularly as so many thus designated are enhanced and expanded versions of towns. Questions of whether major infill or perimeter city expansion—adding effectively to metropolitan primacy, rather than decentralisation per se—qualifies as new-city building are also in the eye of the beholder.

Contemporary examples of real estate–driven new-city claims abound. Greater Springfield, a metropolitan fringe locality in Brisbane, serves as one illustrative example. With its (state government–provided) railway station promising a 30-minute trip to the Brisbane CBD, a (federally funded) university campus, and technology emphasis, the suburb is effectively a purposefully nominated new city developed by private enterprise and fully supported by multiple tiers of government (King and Fagan 2018). In New South Wales, and initiated at a state government level, the 'Western Sydney Aerotropolis', more recently rebranded Bradfield (itself possibly a temporary name), is in the urban fringe locality of Badgerys Creek. Bradfield is being promoted as the hub of a 'new third city' in the wider Sydney region and illustrates the magnetism of major infrastructure in promoting urban development. The new-city idea is also regularly evoked in the form of privately instigated proposals aligned with interstate high-speed railway development, indicating to the cynically minded the existence of a 'proposal industry'. All remain unrealised, however much they are widely publicised in their scoping stages as settlement schemes linked to very-fast-train routes, most recently in the Consolidated Land and Rail Australia (CLARA) scheme. At the same time, in Victoria, with Melbourne shortly to surpass Sydney in population, major development corporations continue to posit their own visions for 'new cities' perched on the edges of the metropolis's growth regions.

The prospects for a significant reset of urban settlement policies are perhaps constrained by experience: unrealised new-city schemes posited as having the potential to develop autonomously but later absorbed, with little acknowledgement of faded idealism, into contiguous capital cities. Familiar issues prevail with these progressive visions: how to persuade new residents to relocate, suffering not only the privations of pioneers in a growing region but also, potentially, the problems of decline and promises unfulfilled?

Such questions reverberate within current federal and state policy environments and the overarching expectation that inaction will lead to the degradation of urban quality of life. While urban policies in Australia's cities retain consolidation strategies for directing growth to specified corridors, paired with increasing infill densities, discontent brewing around the sustainability and liveability of major cities echoes the concerns that underscored DURD's growth centre announcements in the 1970s.

Decentralisation and new towns

One hundred years ago, it might have seemed that a major remaking of the still new nation of Australia was just around the corner. The Country Party, which remains (rebranded as the Nationals) the third major force in Australian politics, was formed in 1920 in part to engender the redistribution of Australia's population and to arrest the 'drift' of country-dwellers to the city. Decentralisation was soon declared a 'plank' of the new party (The Age 1922).

While the attractions of the city were, for many, indisputable, at the same time, the apparently arbitrary nature of Australia's urban growth was hard to justify. The small number of large inland towns, much less cities, was similarly problematic in the eyes of many, and the establishment of Canberra as the nation's inland capital city was in many respects symbolic of a national resolution to conquer the continent rather than merely huddle on its shores.

Had Canberra's success come sooner than it did the nation could have been faster to establish more new inland cities; instead, the merits or otherwise of a significant urban redistribution have gone on to carry outsized discursive weight. Of course, there have been numerous new centres established across Australia in relation to industrial ports and extraction industry enterprises. The 'new town' of Elizabeth was a South Australian Government enterprise designed along British postwar lines. In Victoria, the unusual false start of Sunbury Satellite Town (1959) led to charges of fraud and misrepresentation on the part of the vendor, Payne's Properties. Yet, whatever mistakes Payne's made in execution, the state government came to the opinion that the project's core premise was correct: the small town of Sunbury was ideally located to serve as a growth centre (Kolankiewicz et al. 2022). Sunbury and nearby Melton were chosen for expansion as satellite cities while at a similar time, on the other side of Melbourne, local government was aspiring to take a lead role in urban development. Aware of an interest in funnelling growth into a region extending out from the south-eastern industrial centre of Dandenong, the council of the outer suburban area of Berwick endorsed the recommendations of the planning firm Loder and Bayly. Aspiring to physical and functional separation from Melbourne, the novel proposal would reject the dominant patterns of suburbanisation seen in the wake of postwar settlement, reinforcing the decentralised township as an opportunity for experimental urbanisation. Ultimately the local government–led Berwick 'Metrotown' plans were shelved and Berwick's subsequent growth followed a more conventional pathway.

South Australia, the state that has never lost its sense of (and pride in) its social experiment origins (Hutchings and Bunker 1986), was prospective home in the late 1980s and 1990s to the unrealised Multifunction Polis (MFP), which was slated as a Japanese-funded high-tech smart city. The project was a victim of not only racism and fear of international control but also scepticism regarding the Labor government's 'clever country' rhetoric, but it was a financial downturn in the sponsor country that saw the MFP take a definitive dive. The city—which, at least in cartoonists' minds, appeared to be a self-contained cross between Silicon Valley and a medieval monastery—became instead a suburb of Adelaide, renamed Mawson Lakes, and characterised as a knowledge and technology-oriented housing development.

Such proposals at both state and local government levels were joined by federal investment in expanded urban areas in five Australian locations, under the (in)famous DURD growth centre proposals, two of which, Albury–Wodonga and Macarthur, were substantially established. Another, Bathurst–Orange in New South Wales, was barely embarked on; Monarto and Salvado in Western Australia left even less evidence of their advocates' ambitions.

Since the 1980s, urban policy in Australia has been characterised by consolidation strategies for increasing the infill densities of major cities and directing urban growth to expanding designated corridors—sometimes absorbing previous new-city projects. The major exception to this rule is a frequently expressed interest in a form of decentralisation to regions effected primarily by obliging public servants to disperse from major cities. The 2018 *Building Up & Moving Out* report (House of Representatives Standing Committee on Infrastructure, Transport and Cities 2018: 49 passim), for instance, dedicated a section to debates about this process 'as a potential catalyst for growth', adding that it had 'to be done in a sustained and coordinated way' (p. xxxviii). Released a month later, the Planning Institute's *Through the Lens: The Tipping Point* report decried the lack of cohesive strategy at a national level, opining that without a coherent plan, 'all jurisdictions will be disadvantaged when making resource allocation decisions and planning for basic enabling infrastructure' (PIA 2018: 24).

In short, the experimental initiatives in 1970s and 1980s Australia entailing the creation of new cities by government agencies—in part because they are so often represented as 'ill-fated'—have given rise to a negative outlook on such strategies. The quick rise and demise of DURD, in particular, seems to have only consolidated an Australian urban policy resolve to adhere to metropolitan primacy and the 'path dependency' critiqued by Troy (1999: 165). Bolleter et al. (2021b: 1020) concluded that had DURD been able to operate in ways

> less centralist in its *modus operandi*, more nimble in its responses to counter urbanization trends, and with Federal Government funding sustained and private sector investment more skilfully leveraged— the gap between planned and achieved Growth Centre populations may have been closed even more ... [R]edistribution of the national urban population could have been made more secure.

The turn of the century

The last decade of the twentieth century saw many of the disasters predicted by advocates of new regional centres come to pass, prompting a revisiting of past visions. While these were facilitated by government policy—notably, on taxation—they were the result not of state government visions, but of market-led activities. Sydney real estate prices, for instance, soared to levels inconceivable in the 1980s, and Melbourne followed suit in the early twenty-first century. Pressures on existing population centres saw their peripheries, and beyond, developed to meet growing need—again, undertaken by market interests aided by governmental decisions such as growth boundary shifts and the use of first-homeowner grants. In 1999–2000, the Victorian City of Casey—covering, in part, the Berwick region—and the Shire of Melton were two of the biggest growth areas in the nation, with the expansion of both typified by the subdivision of agricultural land for housing. Queensland's Gold Coast saw far and away the greatest increase (Wade 2004), offering, as Andrew Leach (2018: 142) has pointed out, 'an infrastructure based on … the paradoxical stance of offering an urbanised experience of "getting away from" the city'. A reappraisal of DURD growth centres found several had come close to their anticipated populations but had been eclipsed by the sheer scale of growth in larger urban conglomerations (Bolleter et al. 2021b).

In this context, ideas for shifting, stemming, or competing with the forces of global cities had come to seem almost quaint by the turn of the twenty-first century. A cynic could be forgiven for imagining that the MFP was the last attempt to create an entirely new metropolis for Australia. Yet, some important success stories of new-city development hide in plain sight. The Northern Territory's Palmerston, initially conceived as 'Darwin East', has, over 40 years, become a self-governing settlement of 18 suburbs and a city centre, with a population of more than 34,000 people. The city of Joondalup, in Western Australia, was developed in the late 1980s by the state government on land close to the region intended as the DURD city of Salvado. Businessman Maha Sinnathamby's Greater Springfield, mentioned above, is, however, the outstanding example: in late 2013, railway access was extended to the area with a dedicated spur line (Josey and Burton 2014). It now has a population comparable with Palmerston's and local government is eager to capitalise on growth potential. In 2011, Ipswich City Council announced the development of the new satellite city of Ripley, 17 kilometres west of Springfield, to increase its population from 400 to 120,000 (Urban Land Development Authority 2011). It is expected Springfield's railway line will be extended to Ripley.

Looking at these examples, it seems reasonable to conclude that while autonomous new cities, by definition, do not 'just happen' at a high level of settlement policy, they are nonetheless promoted under the radar across the nation. Whereas twentieth-century government agencies, at state or federal level, could have been brought into existence through political braggadocio seeking to nation-build through city construction, we now see a lower-key and uncoordinated process merged with private development and marketing. This is, perhaps, the legacy of a historical lesson learnt: that grand pronouncements should be resisted. Governments and private interests alike have come to eschew modernist cure-alls for urban ills, and instead hope to create or encourage new urban areas in a more subtle fashion—one validated by market forces better equipped to take on risk. A strong impulse in both the marketing of and the rationale for the new city in Australia is green living and sustainable urbanism, with the additional (related) appeal of a second 'quality of life' string to the new-city dream.

Schemes led by rail and air

The Australian nation-state grew and prospered in the second half of the nineteenth century under the modernising and clarifying influence of railways. New visions for urban and rural futures arose in the wake of this national skeleton. The notion that the next shot in the arm for population redistribution could come from railway technology is at the very least a nod to tradition. Australia's original railway networks were developed by colonial governments interested in ratifying their capitals and, by default or design, drew population away from regional sea and river ports. The twentieth century saw a shift to contracted rail networks and later to infrastructure supporting car ownership.

A change was first signalled in 1984 with the development of the Very Fast Train (VFT) project, initially proposed by Paul Wild of CSIRO, nurtured by the federal government, then picked up by private enterprise, which nonetheless abandoned it in the face of later governmental uninterest (indeed, disincentive). More recently, proposals for a Melbourne–Canberra–Sydney–Brisbane railway suggest the possibility of rail-based redistribution, with new-city options proximate to the rail route. The CLARA scheme proposes bullet trains through south-eastern Australia, with strings of 'new towns' near (but not in) Nagambie and Shepparton in Victoria, anticipating land value uplift. The CLARA consortium received federal government seed funding. Federal government fast-rail proposals, however, amount to little more than varying degrees of scoping reports over recent decades (Terril et al. 2020).

Before CLARA, the High Speed Rail Study was initiated by the Rudd Labor Government in 2008 and the phase one report was tabled in parliament in 2011 by then transport minister Anthony Albanese. It takes seriously the impact of a new rail line operating services at up to 350 kilometres per hour in hitherto remote environments, with justification from both ecological and economic standpoints. 'Development benefits' were considered for each potential route, but the defining principle of each was primarily the ease of construction, line length, and issues of terrain—that is, the favoured locations for new developments fell naturally as new beads on a string between the four cities in need of service—notwithstanding that 'capital city satellites, within 150 kilometres [of existing state capitals], such as Wollongong and the Gold Coast, are growing faster than coastal, inland or capital cities' (AECOM 2011: 23). 'Workaround' routes to take in remote areas, such as the NSW towns of Moree or Tamworth–Armidale, were considered, perhaps for reasons of political sensitivity. Their inclusion would, however, add hours to the rail journeys regardless of how 'high speed' they were, negating a core element of the project: competition with air travel. South to north, the primary regions in New South Wales identified for growth via a new high-speed rail line included Wagga Wagga, the Southern Highlands, the Central Coast, and Coffs Harbour (AECOM 2011: 78). The report notes that at its Queensland end, the high-speed railway (HSR) would pass near three places already designated as urban development areas by the state government: Flagstone, Yarrabilba, and Ripley (AECOM 2011). The considerable route planning notwithstanding, the HSR project was terminated by the Abbott Government in 2013. A dedicated advisory group was abolished in November of that year, among 21 non-statutory bodies considered redundant or out of alignment with federal policy (Thosmen 2013).

The HSR project has a descendant in the 2015 CLARA proposal, which would cover a much shorter distance, Melbourne–Canberra–Sydney, but harbours greater ambition for demographic change in Australia. The CLARA plan is, the journal *Foreground* notes, 'radically' different from previous proposals as 'the largest "value capture" initiative ever proposed by a commercial developer' (Gupta 2017). It proposes 'to build the world's most liveable, sustainable, and connected cities in Victoria and New South Wales and connect them by a world-class high-speed rail' (CLARA 2021). Stations—and, therefore, urban expansion—lie between the three large urban centres, the first and last being Melbourne and Sydney, respectively. The scheme is premised on private settlement schemes. New centres embrace Strathbogie (population 300) and Shepparton (population 51,000), both in Victoria, and unnamed, vaguely positioned, and designated 'new smart cities' between Canberra and Sydney. The CLARA plan, while supported in scoping stages, relies on access to a protected rail corridor that remains elusive. Federal and state funding in Victoria for regional train infrastructure has meanwhile bolstered commuter-oriented train services in the interests of extant regional cities and towns such as Bendigo, Ballarat, and Geelong (the last long heralded as a growth centre and now serving unofficially as such, particularly in light of its affordability relative to Melbourne's), which at least until the Covid-19 pandemic were serving as dormitory suburbs of Melbourne—highlighting the ambiguity in what is meant by new, recentralised, or decentralised, and to whom (Denham 2017).

Fast-rail projects—interstate and intranational—are traditionally set up in opposition to air travel nodes. Bradfield presents, therefore, an additional 'strand' of urban growth. This development aligns with the concept of Sydney as a polycentric conurbation: the new Aerotropolis region, with a population at the time of writing of less than 300, is to become commensurate with the subcentres of Penrith and Parramatta. The positioning of 'three cities' enfolds the new within the old. The region is conceived of as 'a Parkland City in the true sense, with a dense urban neighbourhood focused on both the new metro station and Wianamatta–South Creek [waterway] system' (DPE 2021).

Congestion, consolidation, and beyond: Urban discontents revisited

While urban policies in Australia's cities retain consolidation strategies for directing urban growth to corridors and increasing infill densities, twenty-first-century discontent with the sustainability and liveability of major cities echoes the concerns that underscored DURD's growth centre announcements in the 1970s. Dredging up past visions has seen decentralisation narratives in Australia turn to new settlements in response to population pressures in major cities, and ideas of acting as a 'relief valve'. Moreover, new settlements have been put forward as responses to cities' growing pains. DURD cities were rooted in this analysis: travel times, liveability, and housing quality were all identified as urban ills to be designed out in new decentralised settlements.

Traffic congestion was one of the 'deteriorating conditions' (Pennay 2005: 273) cited in calls for decentralisation and new-town initiatives in Australia through the 1960s and 1970s (Neutze 1971; Logan and Wilmoth 1975;

Ravallion 1975; Stein 2012). Reviewing the impetus for the 1972 federal designation of Albury–Wodonga as a growth centre, Stein (2012: 22) summarised these, suggesting that 'most researchers state that at a certain point the advantage in an agglomeration changes and diseconomies of scale prevail', including travel time: '[A]s the size of the city increases traffic congestion [and] time lost traveling from home to work ... become problems.' To Neutze (1971, 1988), traffic and travel time were part of the case for developing middle-sized cities and town centres in Australia. The minimisation of travel, while realised at the scale of Albury–Wodonga, did not substantively shift patterns for major cities. Travel, congestion, and transport in the twenty-first century reassert themselves as central planning and government concerns—apparent in, for example, the 20 (or 30)–minute neighbourhood aspiration. In Victoria, precinct structure plans continue to aspire to local employment as a solution to travel time costs. Yet, at least before Covid-19, surveys of residents reported it being 'a fantasy to get employment around the area' (Nicholls et al. 2018).

Australian urban consolidation and densification strategies since the 1980s have been mainly concerned with growth. Growth corridor suburbs in Melbourne by the early 2000s were adding tens of thousands of new residents each year, underscoring rapid recalibration of strategic plans. Ideas for supporting regions occupied incremental territory such as differential incentives for first-homebuyer grants outside metropolitan areas. Decentralisation schemes to 'ease the burden' and 'reinvigorate' regional areas by relocating public servants or other attractions—most recently seen in the bayside regional centre of Geelong in Victoria—have been eclipsed by larger patterns of urban growth.

How the Australian nation can negotiate the dispersal of growth is largely informed, and in turn constrained, by past efforts. The absence of an illustrative, powerful, and ultimately successful precedent—aside from Canberra—casts doubt on the capacity of the public and private sectors alike to provide new conduits for urban and population increase, let alone to craft appealing and valid new urban places and centralities. Perhaps the limitations and constraints that led to the failure of past policies are too often emphasised. These have been, at worst, wholly unfulfilled, such as in the case of Monarto, and at best, either partly complete, such as Albury–Wodonga, or fully absorbed into an existing metropolitan area, such as the Melton–Sunbury satellites in Melbourne. We ponder how contemporary attempts at decentralisation can negate public and political apprehension based on the historical outcomes of such policy. This is especially relevant in an age in which the quality of urban life is seen to degrade against markers of housing affordability, congestion, pollution, and the intensification of infill development.

Despite falling off higher-level policy agendas, there is a continuity in public (and developer) narratives, with calls and claims for new cities persisting over decades and centuries in Australia, in varying forms, as a response to urban discontent; hence the discursive role of CLARA-like proposals as the 'best of both worlds'. Steve Bracks and Pat McNamara's *Victoria's future state: Why decentralisation should be our priority* (2018) discusses an assembly of political, private, and academic interests, proposing a self-described 'fourth option'. This entails a vision for the state in which 'via a planned and long-term (30-plus year) decentralisation program Victoria grows its existing regional cities and develops new ones in order to divert future growth out of Melbourne and across our state'. It indicates a demonstrable reliance on the private sector not only to fund and coordinate such efforts, but also to absorb risk.

As it stands, attempts to purposefully relocate or recentre populations are ad hoc and stumbling. In May 2015, then minister for agriculture and deputy prime minister Barnaby Joyce announced that the Australian Pesticides and Veterinary Medicines Authority (APVMA) would be relocated from Canberra to regional Australia—specifically, a city within his seat, Armidale. The move, Joyce claimed, would 'contribute about $16 million a year to the local economy, and would lead to an additional 200 jobs' (Thomas 2015). Costing the nation more than $25 million, the move, Joyce advised, would be the first of at least three relocations 'to boost regional economics and put researchers closer to rural industries' (Barbour 2016). Less than three years later, it was revealed that more than half of APVMA's close to 200 employees, including 33 regulatory scientists, had resigned. As of May 2018, only two staff members had relocated. An initial relocation offer of $30,000 was upgraded to $55,000 (Conifer and McKinnon 2018). Reliance on a monetary incentive fails to appreciate the relationship between lifestyles and urbanity, and how the 'critical mass' of existing cities is germane to the identities, lifestyles, and cultural practices of their residents (van Diepen and Musterd 2009). This perhaps indicates what townships presently receiving the decentralisation treatment lack.

If he had been one to engage with the history of similar initiatives, Joyce could have validly pointed to a tradition of requiring public servants to move—most notably, the populating of Canberra itself, the city *from* which

Joyce was now insisting the APVMA employees move. Other initiatives such as the Victorian Government's relocation of the Traffic Accidents Commission (TAC) to Geelong, announced in 2005 and effected in 2009, was less prescriptive (the TAC's headquarters was moved from Melbourne, but employees were not required to do so) but nonetheless followed a decentralisation principle (TAC 2009). Approximately 650 TAC employees worked in the commission's new headquarters and 190 staff chose to live locally.

Like other shelved or demoted visions, the CLARA plan so far exists in the realm of VFT corridors, Monarto or Berwick new towns, and the MFP as initially conceived: visions assembled, sometimes by private developers, in turn either unrealised or absorbed without ceremony into the prevailing urban fabric. Decades of settlement planning have in practice focused on a duality of intense growth (largely from migration, both overseas and interstate) and attempts at strategic management of this growth. Whether the effects of Covid-19—which in the short term appear to be haphazardly realising long-held aspirations for regional population redistribution—will fundamentally shift the prevailing state of settlement policy and discourse in the longer term remains to be seen.

Conclusion

The influence of the pandemic and government responses to it in Australian cities is unfolding at the time of writing. Almost immediately, Covid-19 reignited a rift between proponents and critics of density as a planning instrument, calling into question its continued relevance in an era characterised by social distancing and remote working. This in turn has prompted contemplation of new visions of how we could one day live and work. Many of the features promoted as desirable urban qualities have been recast as problematic: high-rise living, major (crowded) events, global connections, lively urban spaces, and public transport. Initial evidence of altered migration patterns runs counter to recent decades of growth. To some, the bullet train has been rebadged as an 'economic game changer' for the post-Covid-19 world (Terrill et al. 2020). Schemes like CLARA, which promote diffused and scaled-down new towns, could fit a mooted new appetite for smaller cities, yet these still fundamentally rely on a model of primacy and growth (and office work) that seems unfeasible in post-Covid settings. Even the pandemic-based demise of air travel could yet undermine, or at least delay, Sydney's 'third city' in the same ways commentators have deemed VFTs and bullet trains as unfeasible technology on which to base settlements (Terrill et al. 2020).

Planning professionals, in the main, have supported (or acquiesced to the reality of) controlled growth in major urban areas. Bolleter et al. (2021a) found Australian planning professionals were reconsidering plausible or desirable schemes for 'smaller, self-contained cities'. Such issues bring to light the carrot-and-stick approach of the construction and population of new cities and major urban areas. Housing prices are notoriously high in state capitals, leaving new homeowners in peripheral greenfield suburbs as isolated from the city centre as regional residents, while simultaneously subjected to the growing pains of new suburban development (Buxton et al. 2020). Yet, both state and federal governments in the early twenty-first century seem to regard passivity as the best practice in a nation that maintains a high percentage of homeownership and, therefore, little impetus to challenge the status quo when it comes to desirable 'destinations'. It has until recently appeared that if a change is to come, it will only be incremental and subtle. Reflecting on past Australian projects with new-city aspirations that have sought from varying distances to unsettle the centres that so quickly after colonisation gained primate-city status, any new schemes—from the distant to the satellite-proximate—will enter the uncertain discursive territory of what new, separate, and even 'city' mean and look like beyond a marketing vision.

In 2020–21, Covid-19 and associated policies reignited debates about suburban versus infill housing, and there is some evidence that planning professionals are reappraising the desirability if not the plausibility of new self-contained cities. Planning in the 1970s was informed by a view that post-industrial technology would shorten or remove the need for travel, that society 'would be less reliant on personal interaction for work, education and leisure', and thus there would be 'freedom from some of the constraints of transportation' (Maunsell & Partners 1975: 19). If the DURD's new cities have shown us anything, it is that we cannot consider new cities in terms of the years they were established or proposed. Only with the Covid-19 pandemic was the mid-1970s dream of working from home realised—via public health order: one central premise of the resistance to new cities, the chiaroscuro of distance from the established 'big smoke', finally laid bare.

References

AECOM. 2011. *High Speed Rail Study: Phase 1.* Prepared for the Department of Infrastructure and Transport. Sydney: AECOM.

The Age. 1922. 'The Elections: Coalition with Liberals.' *The Age*, [Melbourne], 20 October: 8.

Barbour, L. 2016. 'Relocation of Australian Pesticides and Veterinary Medicines Authority to Cost Taxpayers $25.6m.' *ABC News*, 25 November. Available from: www.abc.net.au/news/2016-11-25/pesticides-veterinary-medicines-authority-allowed-to-relocate/7996372.

Bolleter, J., N. Edwards, R. Cameron, A. Duckworth, R. Freestone, S. Foster, and P. Hooper. 2021a. 'Implications of the Covid-19 Pandemic: Canvassing Opinion from Planning Professionals.' *Planning Practice & Research* 37(1): 13–34. doi.org/10.1080/02697459.2021.1905991.

Bolleter, J., R. Freestone, R. Cameron, G. Wilkinson III, and P. Hooper. 2021b. 'Revisiting the Australian Government's Growth Centres Programme 1972–1975.' *Planning Perspectives* 36(5): 999–1023. doi.org/10.1080/02665433.2021.1885479.

Bracks, S., and P. McNamara. 2018. 'Victoria's Future State: Why Decentralisation Should Be Our Priority.' Paper prepared for the Balance Victoria online initiative, August. Melbourne: Balance Victoria. Available from: www.balancevictoria.com.au/_files/ugd/eb9113_0f14eaf5574a4e00a664cfeabc86da5a.pdf.

Buxton, M., G. Falk, J. Holdsworth, M. Scott, and S. Thorne. 2020. *Growing Pains: The Crisis in Growth Area Planning.* September. Melbourne: Charter 29. Available from: static1.squarespace.com/static/5f44419b29831038122b3e30/t/5f51c5bcf8d6a26d14879946/1599194601572/Charter+29+Report+200904+as+printed+and+mailed.pdf.

Conifer, D., and M. McKinnon. 2018. 'Barnaby Joyce's Push for Armidale Relocation of Pesticides Regulator Sees Staff Exodus.' *ABC News*, 29 March. Available from: www.abc.net.au/news/2018-03-29/barnaby-joyce-push-for-armidale-relocation-sees-staff-exodus/9599774.

Consolidated Land and Rail Australia Pty Ltd (CLARA). 2021. *The CLARA Plan: Overview.* Melbourne: CLARA. Available from: clara.com.au/the-clara-plan/overview/.

Denham, T. 2017. 'Metro-Bound Commuting And Regional Development: Evidence from Victoria.' Paper presented to State of Australasian Cities Conference, Adelaide, 28–30 November. Available from: apo.org.au/node/178811.

Department of Planning and Environment (DPE). 2021. *Aerotropolis Core, Badgerys Creek and Wianamatta–South Creek Precincts.* Sydney: NSW Government. Available from: www.planning.nsw.gov.au/Plans-for-your-area/Priority-Growth-Areas-and-Precincts/Western-Sydney-Aerotropolis/Aerotropolis-Core-Badgerys-Creek-and-Wianamatta-South-Precincts.

Forster, C. 1990. 'The South Australian New Cities Experience: Elizabeth, Monarto and Beyond.' *Australian Planner* 28(3): 31–36. doi.org/10.1080/07293682. 1990.9657470.

Gupta, E. 2017. 'Trains Have Always Catalysed New Towns and Column Inches. Australia's HSR Is No Exception.' *Foreground*, 15 February. Accessed from: www.foreground.com.au/transport/trains-and-new-towns-have-always-been-linked-australias-hsr-is-no-exception/ [page discontinued].

House of Representatives Standing Committee on Infrastructure, Transport and Cities. 2018. *Building Up & Moving Out: Inquiry into the Australian Government's Role in the Development of Cities.* Canberra: Parliament of the Commonwealth of Australia.

Hutchings, A., and R. Bunker, eds. 1986. *With Conscious Purpose: A History of Town Planning in South Australia.* Adelaide: Wakefield Press in association with Royal Australian Planning Institute (South Australian Division).

Josey, P., and T. Burton. 2014. 'Novel Alliance Completes Springfield's New Rail Link in Queensland, Australia.' *Proceedings of the Institution of Civil Engineers: Civil Engineering* 167(1): 40–47. doi.org/10.1680/cien.12.00039.

King, M., and D. Fagan. 2018. *Greater Springfield: Australia's Newest City.* Brisbane: University of Queensland Press.

Kolankiewicz, V., E. Taylor, and D. Nichols. 2022. '"Where Will All the New Citizens Live?" The Satellite Development of Sunbury, Victoria 1959–1970.' *Australian Historical Studies* 53(2): 242–65. doi.org/10.1080/1031461X.2022. 2040551.

Leach, A. 2018. *Gold Coast: City and Architecture.* London: Lund Humphries.

Logan, M.I., and D. Wilmoth. 1975. 'Australian Initiatives in Urban and Regional Development.' In *National Settlement Strategies East and West*, edited by H. Swain, 119–79. Laxenburg, Austria: International Institute for Applied Systems Analysis.

Maunsell & Partners. 1975. *New Structures for Australian Cities: Main Report.* Canberra: Cities Commission.

Neutze, M. 1971. *Decentralisation: Theory, Policy and Practice.* Monograph No. 12. Melbourne: Australian Agricultural Economics Society Victorian Branch.

Neutze, M. 1988. *Planning as Urban Management: A Critical Assessment.* Urban Research Unit Working Paper No. 6. Canberra: The Australian National University.

Nicholls, L., K. Phelan, and C. Maller. 2018. '"A Fantasy to Get Employment Around the Area": Long Commutes and Resident Health in An Outer Urban Master-Planned Estate.' *Urban Policy and Research* 36(1): 48–62. doi.org/10.1080/08111146.2017.1308859.

Pennay, B. 2005. *Making a City in the Country.* Sydney: UNSW Press.

Planning Institute of Australia (PIA). 2018. *Through the Lens: The Tipping Point.* Canberra: PIA.

Ravallion, M. 1975. 'Urban Problems, Public Policies and Social Structure.' *Australian Quarterly* 47(4): 7–19. doi.org/10.2307/20634810.

Stein, C. 2012. The Growth and Development of Albury–Wodonga 1972–2006: United and Divided. PhD thesis, Macquarie University, Sydney.

Terrill, M., G. Moran, T. Crowley, and M. Marcus. 2020. *Fast Train Fever.* Grattan Institute Report No. 2020-07, May. Melbourne: Grattan Institute.

Thomas, K. 2015. 'Agriculture Minister Identifies Armidale as Priority Location for Australian Pesticides and Veterinary Medicines Authority.' *ABC News*, 20 May. Available from: www.abc.net.au/news/2015-05-20/agriculture-minister-identifies-armidale-as-priority-location-f/6482652.

Thosmen, J. 2013. 'Where to for High Speed Rail After Advisory Group Abolished.' *ABC Local*, 13 November.

Transport Accident Commission (TAC). 2009. 'TAC Relocation a Major Boost to Geelong Economy.' Media release, 26 February. Melbourne: TAC. Available from: www.tac.vic.gov.au/about-the-tac/media-room/news-and-events/2009-media-releases/tac-relocation-a-major-boost-to-geelong-economy.

Troy, P. 1999. 'The Future of Cities: Breaking Path Dependency.' *Australian Planner* 36(3): 162–70. doi.org/10.1080/07293682.1999.9665751.

Urban Land Development Authority. 2011. *Ripley Valley Development Scheme.* Brisbane: Queensland Government.

van Diepen, A.M.L., and S. Musterd. 2009. 'Lifestyles and the City: Connecting Daily Life to Urbanity.' *Journal of Housing and the Built Environment* 24: 331–45. doi.org/10.1007/s10901-009-9150-4.

Wade, M. 2004. 'What Impudence … Melbourne Dares to Outgrow Big Sister.' *Sydney Morning Herald*, 7 July: 11.

10

In absentia: Urban renewal policy in the Australian city

Simon Pinnegar

Introduction

Australia's cities and its communities live through both incremental and, at times, significant change. While a stuttered timeline of initiatives shares some of the historical narrative that has driven regeneration imperatives internationally, contemporary urban renewal activity presents as the poster child for the deficiencies—and indeed vacuum—of urban policy that nominally guides development in our large cities. Whether through public housing estate renewal policies based on 'asset recycling', speculative activity through rezoning of vital industrial and employment lands, or the simple alignment of 'highest and best use' decisions with highest 'value' for return to government treasuries or developer profit, current urban renewal settings reflect neoliberalism's concentrated efforts to replace planning in the public interest with planning as a 'deal-maker' (Rogers and Gibson 2021). Exposing the limitations of urban renewal through feasibility-driven intensification and 'hypotrophy' (Gleeson 2018), this chapter seeks to recast the impetus for, and objectives of, regeneration in ways that better acknowledge and accord with the diversity of contexts, markets, and coalitions of interest in Australia's variegated suburban landscapes.

High-profile spaces of urban 'transformation' aligned with global-city aspirations and imperatives such as Sydney's Barangaroo (Harris 2018) and Melbourne's Fishermans Bend (Shaw 2018) are not the focus here, not least because focusing attention on these highly contentious and contested sites risks overshadowing the more pervasive rollout of market-led logic under the guise of 'urban renewal' across wider metropolitan geographies. Rather, this chapter laments the absence of a more considered civic, peopled dimension to urban renewal narratives in the Australian context and how this lack feeds through—or does not—into broader urban policy goals. With urban policy somewhat absent, the drivers and outcomes of renewal activity expose more fundamental tensions that define the nexus between development processes, the planning systems that seek to negotiate those processes, and the communities invariably caught up (but also participating) in the middle. They also act to reinforce observations highlighted through a rich legacy of urban thinkers—including Hugh Stretton, Leonie Sandercock, and Maurice Daly—wherein questions of land, ownership, and property rights have underpinned, and continue to drive, the dynamics of the Australian city.

To help develop this argument, this chapter highlights two contemporary debates that capture how the determination and enactment of development rights enabled through land policy frame policy logics of urban development across Greater Sydney. The first is perhaps an unlikely catalyst for the heated discussion that has ensued, with the future of industrial and employment lands across the city acting as a site of significant contestation and making explicit the stakes and interests at play in relation to uplift 'created' through renegotiating development rights within under-pressure and worn-down planning frameworks. A second lens looks at the positioning of urban renewal settings and principles within recent strategic planning frameworks setting out directions for the Western Parkland City, which is the geographical focus for much of western Sydney's expected population growth to 2056 (GSC 2018a). Of particular interest is how assumptions tied to 'infrastructure-led' rezoning and densification translate (or not) from higher-value land markets in the city's east to more disadvantaged geographies in the west. Each of these debates offers some insight into tensions at play when the primacy of growth-dependent imperatives risks crowding out the potential for alternative approaches to renewal.

Arguing that a more nuanced, *peopled* understanding of suburban renewal is required, the chapter moves on to explore and open different frames in which urban change can be envisaged and negotiated, involve a wider range of stakeholders, interests, and models, and deliver more inclusive outcomes.

Sydney provides the principal arena in which these debates are contextualised, but the issues discussed, and the challenges and opportunities that arise, resonate across Australia's major cities.

Limitations of market-driven logic, I: The great industrial land 'grab'

Perhaps more so than any other lens, recent debate about the future of industrial and employment lands captures the tensions and contestation at the heart of renewal discourse, and how the absence of effective urban policy leaves our cities to the limitations of unfiltered residential property–led economic development. Australian cities have not been alone in the sustained and indeed deepening pressure placed on protecting these vital, often strategically positioned land assets, with similar 'global-facing' post-industrial cities experiencing commensurate challenges (Wolf-Powers 2005; Ferm and Jones 2016, 2017; Grodach and Martin 2020). The industrial lands debate, not only in its arguments, but also in how those arguments are played out, captures—in multiple dimensions—the further evisceration of urban planning's legitimacy to *plan*.

Sydney has seen a significant shift towards a predominantly knowledge-sector economy over the past two decades, and the relative contribution of industrial, manufacturing, and urban services employment has seen a decline as professional, health, and education sector roles have flourished. As those 'traditional' sectors have retreated, the zoned lands on which they sit—often in high-value, highly accessible parts of the city—have come under intense pressure and been the subject of significant developer interest. In a fast-growing city chasing high housing supply targets, the case for these valuable geographies to be rezoned to 'highest and best use' in the name of urban renewal has been robustly pursued by the property development lobby.

When the Greater Sydney Commission (GSC; now the Greater Cities Commission), the city's strategic planning agency, sought to put the brakes on both formal and informal pressures with the release of its 'retain and manage' policy in *A Metropolis of Three Cities* (GSC 2018a) and discussed in a companion Thought Leadership Paper, *A Metropolis that Works* (GSC 2018b), the gloves came off. Although prosaically signalling a precautionary, 'no regrets' approach in the face of rezoning pressures, initial reactions from the vociferous Urban Taskforce (Johnson 2019), representing developer interests, were predictable. They also foreshadowed the forward line of attack to be deployed. Much of the public-facing record of this stoush unfolded on the online newspaper *The Fifth Estate*, where traded barbs, rights of reply, and reader comments provided an energetic snapshot of the battlelines drawn.

In response, the GSC's senior trio—the Chief Commissioner, Deputy Chief Commissioner, and CEO (the top 'troika', as provocatively labelled by Johnson 2019)—did something rarely seen in Sydney: they dared to suggest that cities could not be planned 'simply on the basis of allowing all land to be left to the "efficiencies" of the market and "highest and best financial use"' (Turnbull et al. 2019). Supporters of the GSC's stance highlighted the crucial role played by industrial lands in cities repositioning for the future in terms of their embedded local networks with other key job sectors (Gill 2019). Opponents enlisted the tried and tested technique of asserting one-dimensional truisms and casting binaries, devaluing the sites as underutilised, static inhibitors—yesterday's geographies—holding back a positive future framed by flexibility and productivity (Craig 2019; Williams 2019; Cikuts et al. 2020). The argument followed that rather than protection from market forces, what these spaces needed was *opening* to market-driven innovation and investment.

The most predatory elements of the *flexibility* and 'for the future' pitch drew on and coopted the mantra of mixed-use development and a simplistic reading of Jane Jacobs' railings against 'single use' zoning (Johnson 2019). Why retain our employment lands as old-fashioned static land-use 'zones' when the future is 'activated, vibrant, walkable, caffeinated' (Katz and Wagner 2014)? In reality, the concept of 'retain and manage' calls out and seeks to stem more base, speculative pressures: stripped down to the machinations of metropolitan land markets and planning systems with sufficient vulnerabilities to be 'gamed', advocating mixed use acts as a trojan horse for the bigger prize—the insertion of residential uses into these often prime-positioned city locations. Despite the barrage, 'retain and manage' provided the timely sense check intended, enabling local authorities to embed a precautionary approach to industrial land futures in their local strategic planning statements prepared over the subsequent 18 months.

However, growth machine and booster interests were far from spent and, by the 2020–21 NSW budget update, the state government was vowing to 'speed up the state's approval assessment times and lift the ban on mixed-use developments on dilapidated industrial land' (Yap 2020). The NSW Productivity Commission provided further ammunition for the government to overturn its own policy, with a recommendation to 'evaluate the retain-and-manage approach to managing industrial and urban services land in Greater Sydney against alternative approaches [and] to identify what would maximise net benefits to the State' (2021: 303). A robust mix of pressure from the development lobby—spurred on by the Productivity Commission's recommendation—and the fact that the policy proponent, the GSC, was also to lead the review of its own policy, reflected the often reactive, laden context within which urban policy debate and settings struggle to take and retain hold.

Although the review process provided the setup for a quiet dismantling of 'retain and manage', its findings—underpinned by a series of draft guiding principles, consultation with a breadth of stakeholders, and several international expert voices echoing arguments raised in *A Metropolis that Works*—acted to reassert the policy's important role in providing certainty and helping reduce unproductive land speculation. Chinks in the armour have been opened through recognition that transition to alternative uses could involve 'mixed uses and in some cases may allow for some types of residential use' (GCC 2022: 10), and the opportunity to revisit (and thus undermine) 'retain and manage' will come with the refreshing of the metropolitan plan to extend across its wider six-cities remit. These potential fissures were arguably modest in an otherwise significant—and reassuring—reassertion of existing policy. The fight for Sydney's industrial lands in the name of urban renewal presents as an all too rare example of evidence-based pushback against the rent-seekers.

Limitations of market-driven logic, II: From Mount Druitt to Luxford

A second lens into the current logic driving urban renewal narratives is provided by recent strategic planning activity focused on the design and delivery of Greater Sydney's Western Parkland City and new Aerotropolis. Early signals suggest that the guiding policy logic essentially cuts and pastes the same infrastructure-led, uplift-through-densification handbook rolled out in higher-value markets to the east, rather than fostering different approaches to steward progressive and resilient regeneration across the existing and new communities that will make up the Western Parkland City in the coming decades. In the initial stages of strategic thinking shaping *A Metropolis of Three Cities*, the western component of Sydney's new triptych was provocatively defined as a networked 'metropolitan cluster' with echoes of a new Randstad or Y-plan-era Canberra. This suggested a distributed urban form, centring much of the anticipated growth on the existing western Sydney cities of Penrith, Liverpool, Fairfield, and Campbelltown—home to some of Australia's most diverse and disadvantaged urban communities.

By the time the metropolitan plan was released in 2018, the pitch that the Parkland City's future structure and form would evolve as a networked cluster remained, but the Aerotropolis—an economic hub to be built adjacent to the Western Sydney Airport currently under construction— had strengthened its presence as a new jobs-rich focus within the existing network of cities. Reinforcement of the new core was locked in through the strategic and statutory powers given to the newly established Western Parkland City Authority, whose spatial remit is more tightly focused on lands to be developed around the airport than the wider geographies of the Western Sydney Planning Partnership that provided the initial governance frame for the Parkland City.

This rebalancing of spatial interest from brownfield to greenfield was cemented with the economic analysis supporting development of the GSC's Place Infrastructure Compact covering the Parkland City, in which two scenarios—capturing different options in terms of geographical focus and sequencing of long-term growth—were evaluated (GSC 2019, 2020; SGS Economics and Planning 2020). While both scenarios envisage growth over the 30 to 40 years distributed throughout the wider Parkland City, the 'Thriving Aerotropolis' scenario concentrates early energy on the new core, while the 'Thriving Metropolitan Cluster' sees a greater proportion of development activity around existing strategic centres and through 'infill' in the north in the Greater Penrith and Eastern Corridor.

'Thriving Aerotropolis' came out as the preferred scenario based on the fact that it would 'create far better equity outcomes for workers in the Western Parkland City with more jobs near where people live', trading off the more efficient, lower-cost alternative scenario (GSC 2020: 65). Indeed, the GSC goes to some lengths to support economic 'efficiency' arguments directing energies into the 'new' rather than 'existing' urban areas on the basis that broader, intergenerational benefits for all offer the better prize in the long run. While providing sufficient momentum to the jobs-generating hopes vested in the new airport follows the dominant infrastructure-led development narratives, such an approach inevitably privileges certain geographies over others, and defers investment and urban renewal interest in areas of arguably greater need.

A spotlight here on Mount Druitt, in the heart of the Greater Penrith and Eastern Corridor between Blacktown and Penrith, illustrates the gaps that emerge within this guiding logic. Delving into the supporting contextual data and evidence base (GSC 2019) uncovers a rebranding of the Radburn estates laid out by the Housing Commission in the 1970s and 1980s to the north of Mount Druitt Centre as 'Luxford', in honour of the principal road that weaves through the neighbourhoods making up one of the last significant concentrations of public housing in Sydney. The area's future renewal 'potential' will come into focus in the longer term, 'when Sydney Metro is delivered' through completion of the missing link between the current terminating station at Tallawong on the North West Line and St Marys, where the Western Sydney Airport Line will initially join the T1 heavy rail line (GSC 2020: 21). The econometric analysis maps out a potential doubling of households in Luxford through asset recycling—in this case, the public land on which sits the current Land and Housing Corporation portfolio—once viability kicks in. Analysis suggests potential for 20,000 new dwellings post 2036, yet only 5,000 of these will return to the public housing ledger after 'transformation'.

While the narrative contextualising Luxford's future renewal trajectory seeks to acknowledge the need to act in the best interests of current tenants and the wider community—notably, improving access to opportunities through greater connectivity—the policy parameters within which those considerations will be made are tightly constrained. Recently published research by the Australian Housing and Urban Research Institute (AHURI) captures the limiting knowledge frames within which public housing estate renewal policies in Australia are positioned, drawing on the notion of 'advocacy coalition frameworks' within which deep core policy beliefs act to reinforce a series of nested logics (Weible and Sabatier 2007; Nygaard et al. 2021). These beliefs—assumptions tied to infrastructure-led planning, density uplift, and mixed-tenure provision guided by a '30/70' public/private split—act to crowd out alternatives. The application of efficiency or equity considerations based on long-term, region-wide 'potential' (the efficiency element), as seen in the Place Infrastructure Compact analysis, firmly ties the narrative and timing of Luxford's 'staged' renewal to economic cycles and market feasibility, rather than more locally driven and determined need (the equity element).

Unsettling the assumptions and expectations framing renewal discourse and debate

> The overarching political strategy shaping the city continues to be the pursuit of *growth first* ... They prioritise 'highest and best use' as the criterion for land use decisions, roll forward gentrification and create (frequently privatized) spaces for elite consumption. (Mayer 2017: 173)

Both lenses—the pressure on industrial lands and the positioning of the 'need' for urban renewal within market-driven logic—highlight the challenges tied to staking sufficient claim on value generated through the planning process and, in particular, rezoning. The opportunity to secure public 'goods' has, time and again, been relinquished—most notably, in the failure to capture value at the outset and instead fuel intense land speculation. Whether played out in the rezoning fiasco of Fishermans Bend (Millar et al. 2015; Dunstan 2018; Shaw 2018), or the publication of indicative rezoning plans akin to a developers' charter in the early stages of Sydney's Sydenham–Bankstown Urban Renewal Corridor (DPE 2015; Troy et al. 2020), the story of who benefits is a sorry tale:

> Why even have a department labelled 'Planning'. Why pretend? Because, in all of these rezonings, all these rampaging clumpages from Blacktown to Bondi Junction, and within all the fluff and bother that surrounds them, there's really just a single idea, a single descriptor, a single methodology. The single methodology, cloaked as 'market forces', is let rip. (Farrelly 2021)

While Elizabeth Farrelly's journalistic commentary sometimes flairs towards polemic, her observations of the parlous state of planning in the city often cut to the chase with a curt incisiveness. The exasperation expressed in the above quotation was triggered by release of masterplan proposals for Blackwattle Bay (including the soon-to-be-vacated Sydney Fish Markets site), which falls within the Pyrmont Peninsula Place Strategy (DPIE 2020, 2021b). The strategic planning process, and the inevitability of the end product, repeats a monotone renewal template being stamped out across Australian cities. The right noises are made about design and place, the sequencing of necessary infrastructure, and affordable housing contributions stretching existing City of Sydney provisions towards 5 per cent.

Such place strategies are very much in vogue. Polished in their aspiration and vision, they provide an effective framework for enabling good urban design as a key ingredient in city-building (and *re*building). However, the concern with the reassertion of a 'design and place' narrative (GANSW 2017; DPIE 2021b) is that the maxims of enabling good urban design and a focus on producing 'liveable' places—without considered counter checks and balances—translate into an increasing degree of design determinism (Knox and Schweitzer 2010). While a positive direction, 'placemaking' arguably serves as an amenable shield, deflecting questions about the deep-seated and more fundamental levers at play in a market-led, growth-dependent planning system and the inequities that those settings entrench. Design-led assurances of 'density done well' (Toderian 2013) sound like a win-win but tend to leave growth-machine interests and treasury-determined imperatives shaping our cities largely unchallenged. As skilfully deployed in Sydney's industrial land heist outlined above and demonstrated to great effect through the inclusion of residential uses in the recently released Draft Macquarie Park Place Strategy (DPIE 2021a), 'mixed use' and the pitch for it as activator of *static, single-use* employment land into *thriving, connected* places have proved a wonderful foil in the push to rezone.

The greater spatial sophistication that could be inferred from the promotion of 'place-based' approaches does not translate into renewal models that reflect and respond to the variegated nature of land and housing markets, and the diversity of community social, economic, and environmental needs. The 'single methodology' called out by Farrelly acts to exacerbate rather than mitigate market failure and, as discussed in the context of Mount Druitt/Luxford, renewal through uplift tends to reinforce existing spatial inequities. The conditions must be right; this one size fits all only 'works' in some contexts: it relies on land values ready to be *re*capitalised, on local market demand being able to support significant densification, on a certain scale of development, and, in turn, developers capable of negotiating complex planning requirements.

Where those factors align, and where state-led gentrification is unashamedly being pursued, the uplift-through-densification model serves a purpose, albeit delivering a rather vanilla product that only partially lives up to the boosters' promise. Away from those higher-value markets, even where favourable rezoning occurs, the model struggles if local demand and affordability constraints limit the likely price points of the new supply (Pinnegar and Randolph 2012; Pinnegar et al. 2020). An unmediated market-led approach dependent on leveraging certain land values builds in a waiting game until those conditions are met, and policy interest is placed on hold until the market determines it can happen. Layered approaches to urban renewal in Bankstown or Blacktown cannot simply use the pattern book of inner Sydney's Green Square. It is not simply a matter of turning up the density dial.

So, where to from here? Critical urban scholars have been forensic and compelling in exposing the many limitations of neoliberal economic and fiscal frameworks but attempts to carve out alternative directions have struggled to gain traction, even where the inadequacies of business as usual are all too apparent. Arguably much of the thrust of academic debate and applied research, seeking to eke out measures within the post-political frames of the neoliberal city, has exercised considerable intellectual energy with frustratingly little impact 'on the ground'. Academics have researched, again and again, the causes and consequences of housing affordability constraints in our major cities, and chased the complex, contestable crumbs that could be enabled through hard-fought inclusionary zoning measures or value-capture mechanisms. It is wrong to paint this as a modern planning dilemma; indeed, planning in its overarching rationale has since its earliest foundations grappled with how to quantify, allocate, and make use of the 'unearned increment' or distribute 'betterment levies'. Yet, contemporary settings have shifted *who* determines the 'rules of the game', and planning's most powerful lever—land policy, and the capacity to innovate through allocation and determination of land use—has been progressively undermined.

Rather than ensure public benefit flows through value created by land-use planning decisions, our strategic planning processes have typically shown their 'best hand' upfront. Before mechanisms to capture planning-generated dividends are put in place, the market has already acted: developers speculatively move in, pay prices reflective of expected yields on likely future rezoning, and much of that windfall flows to the landowner. On purchase, feasibility calculations, expected yields, and required rates of return ensure that developers are focused on maximising gains based on the parameters established in determining the price paid for that land. With the lion's share of the value enabled by the planning system banked by the original owner, planners are left with 'busy work' (and, arguably, affordable housing policy over the past 15–20 years accords well with this label) trying to extract some public benefit on terms that by that stage are firmly dictated by the economic feasibility spreadsheets of developers with site-specific goals. This is not urban renewal, but urban redevelopment that is more complicated than it needs to be, which delivers outcomes less successful than desired, and produces inequities in the share of the spoils. Nor does it constitute policy. In the face of continual political deferral, the response has been calls for ever more sophisticated models and toolkits, based on ever more robust evidence bases. It has been a masterclass in kicking the can down the road.

Towards more inclusive frameworks for suburban renewal

Despite the limitations created, and inequities fuelled, by the strong market dependencies embedded within Australian planning systems, any changes that seek to reset the negotiation of development rights will be hard fought. The Victorian Government's proposed windfall tax to begin in July 2023 (SRO 2021) will warrant close attention, not least with the lines of attack already heavily broadcast (HIA 2021; PCA 2021; Young 2021). The Housing Industry Association (HIA 2021) astutely points out that the 'windfall tax', which will introduce an effective tax rate of up to 50 per cent of value uplift instigated by a planning decision, 'is only a windfall for the Victorian Government'. Indeed, that is the point and, as Spiller (2021) reminds us, reflects the fact that 'rights on how land may be used or developed is reserved by the community through planning laws'.

In the face of the predictable ire of developer and property peak bodies, Australia has a tradition of compromising away opportunities to reclaim planning's capacity to engage in progressive and fair land policy. In practice, any prospect of reform in relation to recasting renewal futures is likely to be more incremental in nature. It is also likely to emerge through acknowledging and mediating the expectations in the 'unspoken Australian *right* to make easy money out of land' (Spiller 2021) and a demand for innovative ways of negotiating the interplay between landowners' property and associated bundles of rights to develop, which blur planning's spatial remit. It also points to the need for contextual and meaningful engagement with the Australian heartlands (Gleeson 2006), in not only social, economic, environmental, and built-form terms, but also with the varied interests representing local stakeholders, alliances, and neighbourhood growth and anti-growth coalitions to recast the renewal narrative.

While notions of private property confer a distinct set of assumptions tied to bounded space, the determination, conferral, and exercising of development rights reflect rather more hybrid enactments between 'private' and 'public' (Ostrom 1990; German and Keeler 2010). Property and rights 'to develop' operate within a spatial context beyond the cadastre over which planning interests span (Blomley 2016). Those scalar tensions between the individual and a notion of proximate, community, and wider interests underpin the need to understand 'property as a set of political and legal relations to urban social relations' (Blomley 2004: xv). We struggle with the territorial mismatch that exists between the spaces where development risk and reward accrue and the wider geographies that contextualise and frame the allocation of those rights.

The tensions at play here reflect somewhat paradoxical aims, but they also potentially point to sites of innovation. There are novel ways to think about capturing the nexus between individual and wider community (collective) interests that enable a greater diversity of approaches to urban renewal and commensurate opportunities to open to different actors, agencies, and interests. A bleeding of individual rights into collective decision-making is increasingly seen in the shift to the compact city—for example, strata apartment owners already occupy these blurred spaces (Randolph and Easthope 2014). Similarly, there has been an increase in activity driven by 'multilaterally dependent' relationships driving collective sales, where neighbours come together to contemplate an 'en bloc' response to developer interest in their homes (or, more accurately, the land on which those homes sit) after a rezoning to higher density (Knight Frank 2017). The ability of local owners to productively engage as a collective affects their individual property rights; conversely, these negotiations also shape broader urban outcomes and signal a conceptual shift in the role of government as an arbiter and steward of change.

Promoting alternative models and frameworks that have the potential to better reconcile individual and collective and private and public interests in development rights and managing urban change is not a call to simply replace our one-size-fits-all, growth-dependent *hard densification* template with a more bottom-up approach. While in some cases density is not the answer, or at least should not be the driving determinant of interventions, the pressures and opportunities presented by population growth in our major cities mean that intensification is an inevitable part of our suburban renewal futures. As such, the pitch is to open the *business* of densification (Debrunner et al. 2020) to a more diverse array of actors, with different drivers, capable of reflecting a wider range of interests, representing that individual/collective nexus, and in so doing, stimulating more diverse outcomes.

Key to such consideration is understanding and giving agency to residents and owners in both the shaping and the business of neighbourhood futures. Valuable insights can be drawn from attempts to provide fairer models for individuals impacted by processes of eminent domain—for example, Heller and Hills' (2008: 1470) advocacy for the idea of land assembly districts, which 'create a mechanism by which neighbors can bargain effectively for a share of the neighborhood's "assembly value"'. The challenge set for a more thoughtful, inclusive urban policy framework is to support and work across a range of approaches, enabling a spectrum to coexist from the financialised to more progressive growth outcomes (Wijburg 2020).

What might this look like? Interest in *soft* densification processes (Pinnegar et al. 2015; Touati-Morel 2015; Bibby et al. 2020) captures the cumulative significance of more incremental acts of neighbourhood change. Alternative land policy instruments such as land readjustment—seen, for example, in Japan (Sorensen 2007, 2011) and the Netherlands (Muñoz Gielen 2016; Meijer and Jonkman 2020)—highlight possible frameworks by which public agencies seek to coordinate interests and steward public benefit outcomes from rezoning or urban restructuring within otherwise primarily market-led contexts. These mechanisms are guided by the principle of existing owner and resident interests being embedded in the renewal outcomes devised. For many decades, Vienna has supported a policy of 'gentle renewal', facilitated by Wohnfonds, a citywide, neighbourhood-based government agency that acts as a broker and partner across the breadth of renewal activity (Bauer 2019; Lawson and Ruonavaara 2019). Its remit includes social housing renewal as well as partnering with private entities—notably, individual and collective homeowners—to renovate and refurbish existing dwellings. Subsidy, including for private dwelling renewal, is a vital part of the mix, enabling the city government to direct investment towards sustainable urban transitions.

These varied compacts between communities, developers, and government in different jurisdictions will give rise to different institutional logic and levels of engagement. Both land adjustment models and Wohnfonds capture longstanding practices within their respective planning and urban policy contexts that are hard to translate to the market-led imperatives guiding redevelopment in Australian cities. But these examples *do* provide some real pointers that are instructive: they highlight that neighbours are prepared to work together and demonstrate how individual and collective interests can be coordinated and how partnerships, in an inclusive sense, can accommodate a diversity of renewal responses. They also demonstrate why it is worth having *urban* policy.

Conclusion

Having the wrong policy in place is one thing; the vacuum created by the absence of policy is another. It creates a void to be filled, and the most vocal and single-minded find themselves well-placed in such circumstances to define the terms of engagement. Capitulation to developer pressure to rezone increasingly scarce industrial land to mixed use (read: high-density residential) reinforces perceptions—perhaps deservedly—that state governments treat their cities as development plays. Even in relation to government-led renewal of public housing estates, the frameworks proffered in the guise of Victoria's Public Housing Renewal Program or New South Wales's Communities Plus are little more than a redevelopment model with an overdependency on density as enabler (Pawson and Pinnegar 2018; Kelly and Porter 2019). When the gaze shifts to facilitating renewal in predominantly private sector geographies, a similar lack of nuance is observed. The subject sites of renewal, and the pathways laid out to facilitate redevelopment, bear a blinkered relationship to need, questions of community good, or joined-up policy solutions committed to enhancing wellbeing, housing affordability, and security.

In place of encompassing *urban* policy, we have recourse to, and ever more polished advocacy of, a series of hard-to-dispute truisms that guide urban renewal discourse, such as the win-win of mixed-use development and the importance of placemaking, as canvassed in this chapter. These considerations are by no means to be dismissed: they are crucial components of effective city-building. However, in the absence of commitment to accountable urban policy shaping how our governments engage in our cities, they risk deflecting the harder questions that get to the heart of the matter. In making the case for this re-engagement, our task is to reignite a tradition of telling a more holistic, nuanced, and *peopled* story of our cities, in all their complexity, brilliance, and glorious limitations, in the spirit of Stretton, Sandercock, Gleeson, and Troy, and to reconnect with the processes that have shaped, and continue to shape, Australian urban environments.

The clues about what will shape and drive more inclusive and contextually informed urban renewal policy are there, embedded within the diversity of institutions and the outcomes of our rich and diverse suburban geographies, which over time have demonstrated an incredible capacity to respond to and accommodate change. Those patchwork and diverse landscapes reflect the range of individual, collective, and hybrid processes and partnerships at play over time, and provide insight into how contemporary negotiation of development rights between individual and collective interests could be framed. Crucially, they will need to develop a concord that accommodates the Australian psyche, logic, and expectations tied to property as much as build institutions and intermediaries capable of opening the business of densification and foster a more multilayered, peopled process. Rather than applying pro-/anti-growth labels to either side of the dichotomy, the opportunity is there to facilitate more inclusive growth coalitions that provide residents and communities with a stake in the renewal dividend and deliver the diversity of renewal outcomes our cities need.

Postscript

The Greater Sydney (and subsequently Greater Cities) Commission was ultimately a short-lived experiment in Sydney's metropolitan planning history. In late 2023, the NSW government announced that its strategic planning functions would be returned to the Department of Housing, Planning and Infrastructure, and the GCC was formally dissolved on 1 January 2024. The author declares an interest as a Visiting Academic at the Commission during 2017/2018, including contributions to the industrial lands paper *A Metropolis that Works* (GSC, 2018b) discussed in this chapter.

References

Bauer, S. 2019. 'Gentle Urban Renewal in Vienna.' Presentation to International Social Housing Festival, Lyon, France, 5 June.

Bibby, P., J. Henneberry, and J. Halleux, J. 2020. 'Under the Radar? "Soft" Residential Densification in England 2001–2011.' *Environment and Planning B: Urban Analytics and City Science* 47(1): 102–18. doi.org/10.1177/2399808318772842.

Blomley, N. 2004. *Unsettling the City: Urban Land and the Politics of Property.* New York, NY: Routledge. doi.org/10.4324/9780203499801.

Blomley, N. 2016. 'The Boundaries of Property: Complexity, Relationality, and Spatiality.' *Law & Society Review* 50(1): 224–55. doi.org/10.1111/lasr.12182.

Cikuts, L., B. Craig, and T. Ward. 2020. *Unlocking Sydney's Employment Lands: Is Flexibility the Way of the Future?* Research Paper, June. Sydney: Ethos Urban. Available from: ethosurban.com/insights/unlocking-sydneys-employment-lands-is-flexibility-the-way-of-the-future/research-paper-unlocking-sydneys-employment-lands-is-flexibility-the-way-of-the-future/.

Craig, B. 2019. 'Managing Sydney's Industrial Land: Striking the Balance.' *The Fifth Estate*, [Sydney], 14 May. Available from: thefifthestate.com.au/innovation/industrial/managing-sydneys-industrial-land-striking-the-balance/.

Debrunner, G., A. Hengstermann, and J. Gerber. 2020. 'The Business of Densification: Distribution of Power, Wealth and Inequality in Swiss Policy Making.' *Town Planning Review* 91(3): 259–81. doi.org/10.3828/tpr.2020.15.

Department of Planning and Environment (DPE). 2015. *Sydenham to Bankstown: Urban Renewal Corridor Strategy*. October. Sydney: NSW Government. Available from: greatercities.au/strategic-planning/industrial-lands.

Department of Planning, Industry and Environment (DPIE). 2020. *Pyrmont Peninsula Place Strategy*. Sydney: NSW Government.

Department of Planning, Industry and Environment (DPIE). 2021a. *Draft Macquarie Park Place Strategy*. Sydney: NSW Government.

Department of Planning, Industry and Environment (DPIE). 2021b. *Explanation of Intended Effect: Blackwattle Bay State Significant Precinct*. Sydney: NSW Government.

Dunstan, J. 2018. 'Fishermans Bend Developers Face Height Restrictions Under New Planning Rules.' *ABC News*, 5 October. Available from: www.abc.net.au/news/2018-10-05/fishermans-bend-height-restrictions-concern-developers/10339988#:~:text=Under%20the%20new%20planning%20framework,10%20metres%20from%20the%20street.

Farrelly, E. 2021. 'This City Vision Starts with a Fallacy and Ends with the Towering Phallus.' *Sydney Morning Herald*, 10 July. Available from: www.smh.com.au/national/nsw/this-city-vision-starts-with-a-fallacy-and-ends-with-the-towering-phallus-20210708-p5885o.html.

Ferm, J., and E. Jones. 2016. 'Mixed Use "Regeneration" of Employment Land in the Post-Industrial City: Challenges and Realities in London.' *European Planning Studies* 24(10): 1903–36. doi.org/10.1080/09654313.2016.1209465.

Ferm, J., and E. Jones. 2017. 'Beyond the Post-Industrial City: Valuing and Planning for Industry in London.' *Urban Studies* 54(4): 3380–98. doi.org/10.1177/0042098016668778.

German, L., and A. Keeler. 2010. '"Hybrid Institutions" Applications of Common Property Theory Beyond Discrete Property Regimes.' *International Journal of the Commons* 4(1): 571–96. doi.org/10.18352/ijc.108.

Gill, J. 2019. 'The Truth about Jobs of the Future is That They Are Complex and Need Integrated Land Use.' *The Fifth Estate*, [Sydney], 4 April. Available from: thefifthestate.com.au/urbanism/planning/the-truth-about-jobs-of-the-future-is-that-they-are-complex-and-need-integrated-land-use/.

Gleeson, B. 2006. *Australian Heartlands: Making Space for Hope in Our Suburbs.* Sydney: Allen & Unwin.

Gleeson, B. 2018. 'The Metropolitan Condition.' In *Planning Metropolitan Australia*, edited by S. Hamnett and R. Freestone, 195–211. London: Routledge. doi.org/10.4324/9781315281377-9.

Government Architect NSW (GANSW). 2017. *Better Placed: An Integrated Design Policy for the Built Environment in New South Wales.* Sydney: NSW Government.

Greater Cities Commission (GCC). 2022. *Industrial Lands 'Retain and Manage' Policy Review.* Review Findings Paper, June. Sydney: GCC.

Greater Sydney Commission (GSC). 2018a. *A Metropolis of Three Cities.* Sydney: GSC.

Greater Sydney Commission (GSC). 2018b. *A Metropolis that Works.* TLP 2018-1. Sydney: GSC.

Greater Sydney Commission (GSC). 2019. *Growth Infrastructure Compact #2 Greater Penrith to Eastern Creek Investigation Area: Baseline Infrastructure and Services Assessment.* Sydney: GSC.

Greater Sydney Commission (GSC). 2020. *Making the Western Parkland City: Initial Place-Based Infrastructure Compact (PIC) Area.* Draft PIC Report. Sydney: GSC.

Grodach, C., and D. Martin. 2020. 'Zoning in On Urban Manufacturing: Industry Location and Change among Low-Tech, High-Touch Industries in Melbourne, Australia.' *Urban Geography* 42(4): 458–80. doi.org/10.1080/02723638.2020.1723329.

Harris, M. 2018. 'Barangaroo: Machiavellian Megaproject or Erosion of Intent?' In *Urban Regeneration in Australia: Policies, Processes and Projects of Contemporary Urban Change*, edited by K. Ruming, 311–32. London: Routledge. doi.org/10.4324/9781315548722-6.

Heller, M., and R.M. Hills. 2008. 'Land Assembly Districts.' *Harvard Law Review* 121(6): 1465–527. Available from: harvardlawreview.org/print/vol-121/land-assembly-districts/.

Housing Industry Association (HIA). 2021. 'From Lockdown to Lock Out Victoria Introduces Another Tax.' Media release, 12 November. Canberra: HIA. Available from: hia.com.au/our-industry/newsroom/economic-research-and-forecasting/2021/11/from-lockdown-to-lock-out--victoria-introduces-another-tax.

Johnson, C. 2019. 'Chris Johnson: The Case for Mixed Use with Employment Land.' *The Fifth Estate*, [Sydney], 1 April. Available from: thefifthestate.com.au/urbanism/planning/chris-johnson-the-case-for-mixed-use/.

Katz, B., and J. Wagner. 2014. *The Rise of Innovation Districts: A New Geography of Innovation in America*. Washington, DC: Brookings Institution.

Kelly, D., and L. Porter. 2019. *Understanding the Assumptions and Impacts of the Victorian Public Housing Renewal Program. Final Report*. Melbourne: RMIT Centre for Urban Research.

Knight Frank. 2017. 'Collective Sales for Residential Development.' *Market Insight*, September. Sydney: Knight Frank. Available from: kfcontent.blob.core.windows.net/research/1331/documents/en/collective-sales-for-residential-development-september-2017-4941.pdf.

Knox, P., and L. Schweitzer. 2010. 'Design Determinism, Post-Meltdown: Urban Planners and the Search for Policy Relevance.' *Housing Policy Debate* 20(2): 317–27. doi.org/10.1080/10511481003738617.

Lawson, J., and H. Ruonavaara. 2019. *Land Policy for Affordable and Inclusive Housing: An International Review*. Espoo, Finland: Smart Land Use Policy for Sustainable Urbanization (Smartland), Aalto University. Available from: smartland.fi/wp-content/uploads/Land-policy-for-affordable-and-inclusive-housing-an-international-review.pdf.

Mayer, M. 2017. 'Whose City? From Ray Pahl's Critique of the Keynesian City to the Contestations Around Neoliberal Urbanism.' *Sociological Review* 65(2): 168–83. doi.org/10.1111/1467-954X.12414.

Meijer, R., and A. Jonkman. 2020. 'Land-Policy Instruments for Densification: The Dutch Quest for Control.' *Town Planning Review* 91(3): 239–58. doi.org/10.3828/tpr.2020.14.

Millar, R., C. Lucas, and B. Preiss. 2015. 'Report Slams Matthew Guy on Rezoning of Fishermans Bend.' *The Age*, [Melbourne], 20 October. Available from: www. theage.com.au/national/victoria/report-slams-matthew-guy-on-rezoning-of-fishermans-bend-20151019-gkcyrv.html.

Muñoz Gielen, D. 2016. 'Proposal of Land Readjustment for the Netherlands: Analysing its Effectiveness from an International Perspective.' *Cities* 53: 78–86. doi.org/10.1016/j.cities.2016.02.001.

NSW Productivity Commission. 2021. *Productivity Commission White Paper 2021: Rebooting the Economy*. Sydney: NSW Government. Available from: www.productivity.nsw.gov.au/sites/default/files/2021-06/Productivity%20 Commission%20White%20Paper%202021.pdf.

Nygaard, C., S. Pinnegar, E. Taylor, I. Levin, and R. Maguire. 2021. *Evaluation and Learning in Public Housing Urban Renewal*. Final Report No. 358, 15 July. Melbourne: AHURI. Available from: www.ahuri.edu.au/research/final-reports/ 358. doi.org/10.18408/ahuri51226.

Ostrom, E. 1990. *Governing the Commons: The Evolution of Institutions for Collective Action*. Cambridge, UK: Cambridge University Press. doi.org/10.1017/CBO 9780511807763.

Parliament of Victoria. 2018. *Inquiry into the Public Housing Renewal Program*. Legal and Social Issues Committee. Melbourne: Victorian Government Printer.

Pawson, H., and S. Pinnegar. 2018. 'Regenerating Australia's Public Housing Estates.' In *Urban Regeneration in Australia: Policies, Processes and Projects of Contemporary Urban Change*, edited by K. Ruming, 311–32. London: Routledge. doi.org/ 10.4324/9781315548722-15.

Pinnegar, S., and B. Randolph. 2012. *Renewing the West: Prospects for Urban Regeneration in Sydney's Western Suburbs*. Research Paper No. 13. Sydney: City Futures Research Centre, University of New South Wales.

Pinnegar, S., B. Randolph, and R. Freestone. 2015. 'Incremental Urbanism: Characteristics and Implications of Residential Renewal Through Owner-Driven Demolition and Rebuilding.' *Town Planning Review* 86(3): 279–301. doi.org/10.3828/tpr.2015.18.

Pinnegar, S., B. Randolph, and L. Troy. 2020. 'Decoupling Growth from Growth-Dependent Planning Paradigms: Contesting Prevailing Urban Renewal Futures in Sydney, Australia.' *Urban Policy and Research* 38(4): 321–37. doi.org/ 10.1080/08111146.2020.1795636.

Property Council of Australia (PCA). 2021. 'Property Industry Slams Tax Hikes to Jobs, Investment, And Homeownership Dreams of Victorians.' Press release, 15 May. Sydney: Property Council of Australia. Available from: www.propertycouncil. com.au/Web/Content/Media_Release/VIC/2021/Property_industry_slams_ tax_hikes_as_blow_to_jobs__investment__and_homeownership_dreams_of_ Victorian.aspx.

Randolph, B., and H. Easthope. 2014. 'The Rise of Micro-Government: Strata Title, Reluctant Democrats and the New Urban Vertical Polity.' In *Public City: Essays in Honour of Paul Mees*, edited by B. Beza and B. Gleeson, 210–24. Melbourne: Melbourne University Press.

Rogers, D., and C. Gibson. 2021. 'Unsolicited Urbanism: Development Monopolies, Regulatory-Technical Fixes and Planning-As-Deal-Making.' *Environment and Planning A: Economy and Space* 53(3): 525–47. doi.org/ 10.1177/0308518X20952421.

SGS Economics and Planning. 2020. *Western Sydney Growth Infrastructure Compact Program Land Use Scenario Forecasts, March 2020.* Summary Report prepared for Greater Sydney Commission. Sydney: SGS Economics and Planning. Available from: www.sgsep.com.au/assets/main/SGS-Economics-and-Planning_appendix _3_-_western_sydney_pic_land_use_scenarios_forecasts.pdf.

Shaw, K. 2018. 'Murky Waters: The Politics of Melbourne's Waterfront Regeneration Projects.' In *Urban Regeneration in Australia: Policies, Processes and Projects of Contemporary Urban Change*, edited by K. Ruming, 135–58. London: Routledge. doi.org/10.4324/9781315548722-7.

Sorensen, A. 2007. 'Consensus, Persuasion, and Opposition: Organizing Land Readjustment in Japan.' In *Analyzing Land Readjustment: Economics, Law, and Collective Action*, edited by Y. Hong and B. Needham, 89–114. Cambridge, MA: Lincoln Institute of Land Policy.

Sorensen, A. 2011. 'Evolving Property Rights in Japan: Patterns and Logics of Change.' *Urban Studies* 48(3): 471–91. doi.org/10.1177/0042098010390241.

Spiller, M. 2021. 'Windfall Tax Break Backlash Misunderstands Property Rights.' *Insights*, 25 June. Sydney: SGS Economics and Planning. Available from: www. sgsep.com.au/publications/insights/windfall-tax-backlash-misunderstands- property-rights.

State Revenue Office Victoria (SRO). 2021. 'Proposed Windfall Gains Tax.' News release, 12 October. Melbourne: SRO. Available from: www.sro.vic.gov.au/news/ proposed-windfall-gains-tax.

Toderian, B. 2013. 'TODERIAN: Density Done Well.' *Spacing: Canadian Urbanism Uncovered*, [Toronto], 10 April. Available from: spacing.ca/national/2013/04/10/toderian-density-done-well/.

Touati-Morel, A. 2015. 'Hard and Soft Densification Policies in the Paris City Region.' *International Journal of Urban and Regional Research* 39(3): 603–12. doi.org/10.1111/1468-2427.12195.

Troy, L., B. Randolph, S. Pinnegar, L. Crommelin, and H. Easthope. 2020. 'Vertical Sprawl in the Australian City: Sydney's High-Rise Residential Development Boom.' *Urban Policy and Research* 38(1): 18–36. doi.org/10.1080/08111146.2019.1709168.

Turnbull, L., G. Roberts, and S. Hill. 2019. 'GSC On Why We Can't Leave City Planning to the Efficiencies of the Market.' *The Fifth Estate*, [Sydney], 26 March. Available from: thefifthestate.com.au/urbanism/planning/gsc-on-why-we-cant-leave-city-planning-to-the-efficiencies-of-the-market/.

Weible, C., and P. Sabatier. 2007. 'A Guide to the Advocacy Coalition Framework.' In *Handbook of Public Policy Analysis: Theory, Politics and Methods*, edited by F. Fischer, G. Miller, and M. Sidney, 189–220. Boca Raton, FL: CRC Press.

Wijburg, G. 2020. 'The De-Financialization of Housing: Towards A Research Agenda.' *Housing Studies* 36(8): 1276–93. doi.org/10.1080/02673037.2020.1762847.

Williams, T. 2019. 'Tim Williams: Why We Need to Plan Our Cities for the Jobs of the Future.' *The Fifth Estate*, [Sydney], 18 March. Available from: thefifthestate.com.au/urbanism/planning/why-we-need-to-plan-cities-for-the-jobs-of-the-future/.

Wolf-Powers, L. 2005. 'Up-Zoning New York City's Mixed-Use Neighborhoods: Property-Led Economic Development and the Anatomy of a Planning Dilemma.' *Journal of Planning Education and Research* 24(4): 379–93. doi.org/10.1177/0739456X04270125.

Yap, N. 2020. 'NSW Reviews Industrial Land Use, Injects $812m in Social Housing.' *Australian Property Journal*, 17 November. Available from: www.australianpropertyjournal.com.au/2020/11/17/nsw-reviews-industrial-land-use-injects-812m-in-social-housing/.

Young, G. 2021. 'Victorian "Windfall Tax" Kicks Entrepreneurs and Home Buyers.' *Australian Financial Review*, 8 June. Available from: www.afr.com/policy/tax-and-super/victorian-windfall-tax-kicks-entrepreneurs-and-home-buyers-20210608-p57z53.

11

Addressing the unanticipated consequences of compact city policies

Hazel Easthope and Sophie-May Kerr

Introduction

Promoting the compact city, which is characterised by 'dense and proximate development patterns, built-up areas linked by public transport systems, and accessibility to local services and jobs' (OECD 2012: 19), has become planning orthodoxy in Australia. The metropolitan plans of major cities around the country support increasing urban density and the efficiencies of urban infrastructure provision associated with them. In 2015, for the first time in Australia's history, construction began on more attached than detached properties (ABS 2020), and the size of developments has been increasing (Rosewall and Shoory 2017).

In this respect, compact city policies have delivered the numbers, especially in the eastern states of Queensland, New South Wales, and Victoria (ABS 2020). But they have also resulted in a series of largely unanticipated and unintended consequences (Troy 2013) related to the idiosyncrasies of the dominant form of apartment housing provision in the country. The rapid growth in speculative development of strata-titled apartment buildings in Australia has brought with it a series of challenges, including the widespread incidence of building defects (Shergold and Weir 2018), poorly maintained buildings (Easthope et al. 2012), insufficient or delayed infrastructure provision (Easthope et al. 2020a), and land fragmentation that hinders future redevelopment at higher densities (Easthope and Randolph 2021). Addressing such challenges requires substantial policy and regulatory responses, especially at the state and municipal levels. Scholars have cautioned that, if governments do not adequately respond to these issues, compact city policies could fail to meet their objectives (Troy 1996).

Compact city policies were realised in Australia in large part thanks to the introduction of strata-title ownership. This has important consequences for the nature and outcomes of urban consolidation nationally. Strata is not just houses stacked on top of each other, and the delivery of strata apartments differs from delivery of other dwelling types, in physical, legal, social, and financial senses. Two important reasons for this are that strata-titled apartments are usually delivered as speculative developments and that the properties are both interconnected and separately owned. The rapid increase in strata development has been accompanied by the concurrent growth in new private systems of urban governance (in the form of strata corporations), with responsibilities for managing both built form and social relations. The growing dominance of these local private governance bodies presents its own challenges, but it also offers opportunities for improved urban governance (Easthope 2019).

This chapter outlines the unanticipated consequences of the realisation of compact city policies through the provision of speculative strata-title developments and outlines an agenda for action, focused on improving the quality of life in Australian compact cities in the remainder of the twenty-first century. We begin by tracing the delivery of the compact city, highlighting a profit-driven speculative development process. The chapter then outlines the consequences of this development model on apartment design and quality, alongside the challenges that have emerged in relation to collective governance in strata-titled buildings. The following section proposes an agenda for action that includes recommendations for building better apartment housing and neighbourhoods, capitalising on the potential of collective governance frameworks, and mitigating land fragmentation. In the conclusion, we argue that interventions in the existing housing supply system are needed for Australian cities to better deliver on the social, economic, and environmental promises of the compact city.

Promoting and delivering the compact city

In recent decades, Australian strategic metropolitan plans have focused on urban consolidation and compact city policies (Randolph 2006; Bunker 2014; Troy et al. 2020). The compact city objective is promoted as an efficient means of accommodating growing urban populations and is often cast as a solution for lower-carbon, more affordable housing (McFarlane 2016). Although the social, economic, and environmental benefits of compact cities continue to be debated (Troy 2013; Sharam et al. 2015; Easthope 2019), Australia has witnessed unprecedented growth in higher-density housing, with strategic planning policies 'each anticipating more growth than the last' (Troy et al. 2020: 22). The shift towards more compact housing has revolutionised Australian cities (Randolph 2006), with impacts on both housing supply and market dynamics.

Delivery of the compact city relied in large part on the introduction of strata-title legislation, and most privately owned apartments are now strata titled (Easthope and Randolph 2009; Easthope et al. 2020b). Strata-title legislation, which facilitates ownership of individual apartments along with shared ownership of common property, dates to the early 1960s. Although the Government of New South Wales had previously discussed similar reforms to property law, property developer Dick Dusseldorp of Lend Lease is largely credited with encouraging the shift to strata title, which he saw as a more tradeable and attractive commodity than its predecessor, company title (Easthope 2019). Under company title, individuals owned shares in the property as a whole and banks were wary about approving loans because of the risk that other shareholders might block the sale of the unit in the case of mortgage default. As a result, banks would usually charge higher interest rates than for typical mortgages on detached houses. The introduction of strata title removed the associated risk and made apartments more accessible (with a mortgage), broadening the market of potential owners considerably, and making apartments a more tradeable commodity (Easthope 2019).

Within the broader contexts of the neoliberalisation of government policy (Jacobs 2019) and housing financialisation (Aalbers 2008), apartment development in Australia has become as much about economic development as about meeting housing supply requirements (Troy et al. 2020). The fact that almost all strata-titled apartments are now delivered as speculative developments (Troy et al. 2020) also has implications for the purchaser profile of new buildings (Sharam et al. 2015) and there is a much higher proportion of investor ownership in apartments than in other residential property in Australia. The most recent census data revealed that almost half (48 per cent) of all private apartments in Australia were rented while just over one-quarter (26 per cent) were owner-occupied (Easthope et al. 2020b). Targeting of apartment sales at offshore investors has also contributed to this owner profile (Rogers 2017; Ma 2021).

Since 2010, Australian apartment construction has boomed. Most of this growth has been concentrated in large cities and has predominantly occurred in New South Wales (Sydney), Victoria (Melbourne), and Queensland (Brisbane) (Rosewall and Shoory 2017). By 2020, there were 340,601 strata schemes across Australia, comprising 2,869,845 individual lots (Easthope et al. 2020b), and the total insured value of strata properties across the country in 2020 was more than $1 trillion. The growth in apartment construction was especially rapid in the early part of the 2010s but began to slow in 2018 (the decline starting before the Covid-19 pandemic), with explanations including oversupply and a reduction in interested investors shaped by changes to domestic and foreign investment policies and tightened lending practices for investors (Denman and Chittenden 2019; Ma et al. 2019; Ma 2021). Covid-19 brought further uncertainty to the investor market in early 2020 (Ellis 2020a). As the property market regained momentum throughout the year, professionals in the property industry attributed an increase in sales to owner-occupiers and first homebuyers rather than investors (Ellis 2020b, 2020c).

The unanticipated consequences of the compact city

The rapid growth of speculative development of strata-titled apartment buildings in Australia has been accompanied by a series of challenges that have required substantial policy and regulatory responses, especially at the state and municipal levels.

Consequences of speculative development

Strata-title legislation was introduced in Australia to promote private investment in apartment housing. It has been very successful in doing that in quantitative terms but less so when it comes to the quality of the investment product and the quality of the housing delivered (Shergold and Weir 2018; NSW Government 2019). Viewing apartments as assets before homes has meant apartments have often been overlooked as spaces of meaning, belonging, and everyday life (Baxter 2017). Speculative developments tend to target the investor market, which is perceived to be less concerned with amenity and design than are aspiring owner-occupiers (Sharam et al. 2018). Developers focus on off-the-plan sales (as a risk-mitigation measure) and look to sell and then move on as quickly as possible (Sharam et al. 2015). Rather than producing for a single client, developers produce apartments for a disparate group of clients who have little oversight over the design or construction of their properties and often do not have access to the information or experience to be expert consumers (Lambert 2015). In a sector plagued with design and quality issues, this is problematic (Public Accountability Committee 2020). Multiple reviews of the building and construction industry have highlighted problems with government regulation and compliance as well as conflicts of interest (Lambert 2015; Shergold and Weir 2018; NSW Government 2019; Public Accountability Committee 2020), which have allowed profit-seeking and cost-shifting activity to go largely unchecked.

This has resulted in serious failures in newly constructed buildings, with building defects resulting in financial, social, and health costs for both residents and owners (James 2007; Firing et al. 2016; Shergold and Weir 2018; Johnston and Reid 2019; NSW Government 2019; Crommelin et al. 2021). The rectification of defects can be extremely difficult in strata-titled properties (Easthope et al. 2012). Common problems relate to the developer and/or builder holding control of the scheme and delaying the rectification works or the developer and/or builders no longer operating and therefore not taking responsibility for remedy of the defects (Easthope et al. 2012). There is also evidence of developers not disclosing the details of defects to purchasers because defective work either has not been identified or has been concealed, and buyers typically cannot access adequate information about building quality to make an informed decision about whether to purchase a property (Crommelin et al. 2021). Resolving defects is incredibly costly in terms of investigation and remediation of the works themselves as well as legal fees and other professional advice (Crommelin et al. 2021).

As well as concerns about the quality of construction, unit and building *design* quality have important impacts on liveability for residents. Speculative developments targeting an investor market are typically not built with diverse end-users in mind. Research examining developer assumptions has shown apartment developments are often built for a narrow resident profile—

namely, young professionals and empty-nesters (Fincher 2004). Developers' socially constructed ideas about the life course and 'who should be housed where' have a direct impact on the built form, resulting in apartments that tend to not cater to the needs of diverse households including families with children, multigenerational households, and larger households (Fincher 2004; Liu et al. 2013; Kerr et al. 2018). Failure to recognise the long-term needs of diverse households in apartment developments jeopardises the social sustainability of compact city models into the future (Randolph 2006).

Speculative development trends also impact on neighbourhood amenity. With insufficient funding available to local councils for growing amenity and infrastructure needs, local governments increasingly enter into agreements with developers to fund neighbourhood improvements (Allan et al. 2006). Negotiations between local governments and for-profit developers may include local councils allowing increases in permitted development densities and building heights on development sites in exchange for increases in developer contributions to community infrastructure (Easthope et al. 2020a). While this model can support valuable community infrastructure, it is not without controversy, and public infrastructure does not always reflect the community's best interests or preferences, instead deferring to developer feasibility calculations (Easthope et al. 2020a).

Consequences of interconnected and separately owned properties and the necessity for collective governance

Strata-title properties are both interconnected and separately owned (Altmann et al. 2018). Individual apartments within a complex are interdependent in both a physical and a legal sense and this can lead to tensions between individual rights and collective responsibility (Easthope 2019). Owners are required to collectively make decisions relating to the governance and management of their development (Johnston and Too 2015). At the same time, they have reduced autonomy over the individual changes they can make and what they can do in their own dwellings (Sherry 2013).

This means that the realisation of the compact city in Australia has required residents to adjust to new forms of governance. There is a multitude of governance challenges associated with collective decision-making, especially in relation to maintenance, repair, and upgrades to buildings. Changes to resident profiles, differing priorities, and differing financial capacities to afford maintenance and improvement costs—all provide examples of this (Miezis et al. 2016; Loschke and Easthope 2017; Easthope 2019). These tensions are further complicated by the high incidence of building defects (discussed above), particularly when they pose health and safety concerns to residents (Easthope 2019) and when there is a lack of guidance to assist residents navigate participatory decision-making (Crommelin et al. 2021).

Further to this, separate ownership of individual apartments and shared ownership of common property result in land fragmentation that can hinder future redevelopment at higher densities. When buildings are too old or have been allowed to fall into disrepair, decisions about redevelopment and/or collective sale must be made by unanimous consent, or (in many Australian jurisdictions) by a super-majority of owners (Crommelin et al. 2020). Separate ownership makes this decision difficult. If a unanimous or super-majority vote cannot be reached, redevelopment can be stalled, and if the super-majority vote is reached, minority owners face the prospect of navigating legal challenges through the courts. The makeup of owners can also change during this process as individuals or development companies motivated by profit gradually purchase units within a development, increasing their share in decision-making (Easthope and Randolph 2021). Due to the complexity of the governance challenges of owner-led redevelopment, the most feasible option for redevelopment often is collective sale to developers (Easthope and Randolph 2021). Research by Troy and colleagues (2015) in Sydney has demonstrated that such developer-led speculative redevelopment is likely to result in either densification (increasing land fragmentation) or gentrification (including displacement of renters who can no longer afford to live in the new developments).

An agenda for action

The cooption of strata title development for speculative profit has often been to the detriment of good housing and local planning outcomes. In this section, we propose an agenda for action and discuss some ways in which strata title can be utilised to facilitate alternative approaches and outcomes.

Responding to speculative development

Building better housing

For the compact city model to be successful and to improve the safety and functionality of apartments, improved minimum standards for apartment construction and design are needed (Public Accountability Committee 2020).

Considering the widescale incidence of defects in the Australian apartment market, improving the effectiveness of compliance and enforcement systems for the building and construction industry across Australia is imperative (Shergold and Weir 2018). The NSW Government has begun taking steps in the right direction, announcing a series of reforms in 2019, including the appointment of a Building Commissioner, an overhaul of compliance reporting, requiring building practitioners with reporting obligations to be registered, and ensuring an industry-wide duty of care to homeowners (NSW Government 2019). The aim of the strategy is to 'produce more trustworthy buildings through a more customer focused, ethical, sustainable, innovative and digitally enabled construction industry' (Crommelin et al. 2021: 13). It is too early to determine to what extent such reforms will succeed in ensuring the delivery of better apartment buildings. Ensuring improvements across the apartment market will necessitate a long-term commitment on the part of state and territory governments to sustain regulatory oversight. Even with such regulatory commitment, the wide-scale incidence of defective apartments already in the housing stock means that this issue will undermine the market for years to come (Crommelin et al. 2021).

As well as construction quality, there is a need for more attention to the design quality of apartments in Australia. While apartment design regulation and guidance exist in some Australian jurisdictions (for example, NSW Government 2002; DELWP 2017), there is a need for design guidance that recognises the diversity of apartment residents (Fincher 2004; Kerr et al. 2020). Recognising that apartments are occupied not just by singles and empty-nesters, design standards should prioritise flexibility and focus on apartments as homes for diverse households (Baxter 2017; Easthope 2019). In particular, better apartment design to meet the needs of families with children has been raised by multiple Australian commentators (Fincher 2004; Easthope and Tice 2011; Nethercote and Horne 2016;

Reid et al. 2017; Andrews et al. 2018; Kerr et al. 2018, 2020) and there are international precedents for such guidance (City of Toronto 2017; City of Vancouver 2020).

There is also great potential in the delivery of apartment housing outside the speculative strata-title model, which can take many forms. Speculative but non–strata-titled developments, such as purpose-built rental housing (build-to-rent), can avoid some of the challenges associated with lack of purchaser oversight at the handover stage because purchasers of these properties tend to have more oversight at the development stage (Pawson et al. 2019). Non-speculative developments including public, social, and affordable housing, and collective self-organised and other not-for-profit housing development bring with them benefits associated with prioritising housing as a home. In addition, while strata title was introduced in Australia to support speculative development of apartment housing, it can also be used effectively for non-speculative housing development. This can include mixed-tenure development with increased supply of public and affordable housing (with support through inclusionary zoning) (Judith Stubbs and Associates 2017), not-for-profit development (Moore and Doyon 2018), and collective self-organised developments (Palmer 2020). There are benefits of using strata for these types of development: cross-subsidy (Gurran et al. 2018), the ease of obtaining mortgages (in the case of owner-led development), and readymade governance structures (Randolph and Easthope 2007; Easthope and Kerr forthcoming).

Building better neighbourhoods

Controversy about speculative developers funding neighbourhood infrastructure (for example, due to lack of public transparency and questions about whether developers are acting in the best interests of the public or for their own marketing gain) (Crommelin et al. 2017) highlights the need for better-resourced and coordinated action by local and state planning authorities to ensure adequate (and flexible) neighbourhood service provision. This includes the importance of negotiating infrastructure provision at the outset of development and planning a staged process for infrastructure provision in precinct-level projects. Current models often require demand to be demonstrated (that is, they require residents to move in) before new infrastructure is planned, financed, approved, and built, resulting in a significant time-lag after residents move in before vital community amenity is available (Easthope et al. 2020a). A better approach would see services and infrastructure delivered before population growth. Power and information imbalances between local government officials and developers can also lead to uncertainty about community needs being prioritised. Better outcomes are recognisable in circumstances in which the community is engaged in precinct planning and where community spaces are provided early in the development process for residents to come together (Easthope et al. 2020a). For positive neighbourhood outcomes to become more widespread, this requires better resourcing of government service and infrastructure provision. A recent example of this can be seen in the NSW Government's decision to lift rate caps to help councils raise the revenue required to meet the infrastructure needs of growing populations (OLG 2021).

Responding to interconnected and separately owned properties and the need for collective governance

Capitalising on the potential of collective governance

The introduction of strata title in the 1960s created new local governance structures that brought with them both challenges and opportunities. Earlier we outlined some of the challenges of collective decision-making and reduced individual autonomy within the home. However, there is also great potential within collective governance frameworks. An agenda for action must prioritise supporting, and leveraging, the governance capacity of strata corporations. Strata allows for and can facilitate collective action at a local scale. This is especially important for community development and resilience. This is evidenced through condominium governance structures that have helped facilitate disaster preparedness (Becker & Poliakoff Hurricane Recovery Team 2014), provided intergenerational support (TTN Caring Collaborative 2011), and, more recently, facilitated information-sharing and practical and social support as part of the Covid-19 response (Easthope and Kerr forthcoming).

There is potential for strata committees to develop partnerships with local governments and not-for-profit organisations to support community cohesion and development (Easthope 2019). However, an important factor working against this is the high level of resident mobility, resulting from large proportions of renters in strata-titled properties (reflecting high investor ownership) alongside poor rental regulations (Hulse et al. 2011). Rental reforms to improve resident stability are essential for realising the potential to leverage local governance capacity within strata (Easthope 2016). Providing alternative options for renters (such as build-to-rent) could be an important part of the solution (Pawson et al. 2019).

Mitigating land fragmentation

Poor-quality building in combination with poor maintenance (sometimes because of market incentives to redevelop) creates pressure for strata property redevelopment. At present, to redevelop strata buildings usually requires an increase in units to offset the costs of demolition and rebuilding (Easthope and Randolph 2021). This results in larger developments and increases fragmentation of landownership. Yet, there are limits to the feasibility of this model. In some settings, apartments cannot feasibly be redeveloped under existing market conditions or due to physical constraints (Easthope and Randolph 2021). The challenges associated with redevelopment highlight the importance of constructing good-quality buildings in the first place and ones that can be easily upgraded; and promoting upgrading as an alternative to rebuilding to mitigate (or slow) the land fragmentation problem. Owner-led upgrades may include adding units on the roof, onsite energy generation, facade replacements, basements, and balconies (Easthope and Randolph 2021). Collective ownership provides opportunities to share costs and deliver larger projects because of the larger number of owners contributing to the costs. However, for these benefits to be realised, the challenges of collective governance and decision-making must be addressed (Loschke and Easthope 2017).

Government can be an important partner in supporting strata corporations to navigate large decisions such as building upgrades or sustainability improvements. By way of example, the City of Sydney's Smart Green Apartments program involves the municipal government working with strata corporations to improve the water and energy efficiency of their buildings (City of Sydney n.d.). Residents benefit from reduced utility bills alongside assistance with governance and communications, while the municipal government, through partnering with strata corporations, harnesses existing governance structures in strata developments to achieve its own sustainability targets (City of Sydney n.d.). Recognition of the governance potential of strata owner corporations points to a largely untapped potential for municipal and state governments to work alongside these local urban governance bodies in achieving collective goals, such as the maintenance and upgrading of existing buildings as an alternative to demolition and rebuilding.

Land fragmentation can also be mitigated through the provision of purpose-built rental housing under single ownership, including private build-to-rent and social rental housing (Easthope and Randolph 2021). Easthope and Randolph (2021) note that at scale this could reduce the proportion of renters in strata-titled properties, with important implications for the governance of those buildings and the turnover of their residents (as renters tend to move more often).

Conclusion

Compact city policies in Australia have delivered when it comes to the numbers, but they have done so at great cost to urban communities. The main mechanism for their delivery has been the speculative development of strata-titled apartment buildings. The combination of speculative development and strata-title ownership has contributed to serious and unanticipated consequences, including the delivery of poor-quality apartment buildings in under-resourced neighbourhoods that act as a barrier to effective future urban densification.

Responding to these challenges will require sustained government and community commitment. It will also require a shift in the narrative of urban consolidation from one focused primarily on delivering housing supply to one focused on the suitability of the housing being built and its ability to cater to the diverse needs of its residents over the longer term.

We are not calling for an end to speculative development or to strata-title ownership. Rather, we see the need for four main interventions in the existing housing supply system to help Australian cities better deliver on the social, economic, and environmental promises of the compact city. They are:

1. Improved federal and state/territory government regulation and enforcement of construction and design quality of new apartment buildings.
2. Better resourcing of local and state/territory government services and infrastructure provision and reduced influence of private interests in determining the nature and timing of that provision.
3. Federal, state/territory, and local government support for more diverse forms of housing provision (including build-to-rent, social housing, not-for-profit, and owner-led development), some of which could be speculative (for example, private build-to-rent), while some could benefit from utilising strata ownership.

4. Recognition of the governance potential of strata owner corporations and a commitment on the part of local and state/territory governments to support and leverage this potential.

We have primarily relied on the market to deliver compact city policies in Australia. While market-led development has resulted in the successful delivery of large numbers of apartments, the quality of homes and urban spaces delivered has not been as successful. The difficulties we now find are born of the context of the neoliberalisation of government policy and the financialisation of housing. This has played out in the context of the speculative delivery of strata-titled properties in Australian cities. The resulting shortfalls are significant and will remain part of the urban landscape for years to come. Undoing the damage will not be easy and rests in large part on the willingness and capacity of governments (at all levels) to step in to provide better regulatory oversight, resourcing, and support for alternative models of housing and local service provision. There is a silver lining: the incredible growth of strata owner corporations that has resulted from the realisation of compact city policies. These governance structures provide an important local resource that, if properly leveraged, can help deliver improved urban outcomes in the future.

References

Aalbers, M.B. 2008. 'The Financialization of Home and the Mortgage Market Crisis.' *Competition & Change* 12(2): 148–66.

Allan, P., L. Darlison, and D. Gibbs. 2006. *Are Councils Sustainable? Final Report: Findings and Recommendations.* Independent Inquiry into the Financial Sustainability of NSW Local Government, May. Sydney: Local Government and Shires Associations of NSW. Available from: our.wollongong.nsw.gov.au/530/widgets/1132/documents/359.

Altmann, E., P. Watson, and M. Gabriel. 2018. 'Environmental Restriction in Multi-Owned Property.' In *Multi-Owned Property in the Asia-Pacific Region: Rights, Restrictions and Responsibilities*, edited by E. Altmann and M. Gabriel, 119–36. London: Palgrave Macmillan. doi.org/10.1057/978-1-137-56988-2_7.

Andrews, F., E. Warner, and B. Robson. 2018. 'High-Rise Parenting: Experiences of Families in Private, High-rise Housing in Inner City Melbourne and Implications for Children's Health.' *Cities and Health* 3(1–2): 158–68. doi.org/10.1080/23748834.2018.1483711.

Australian Bureau of Statistics (ABS). 2020. *Building Activity*. Catalogue no. 8752.0. Canberra: ABS.

Baxter, R. 2017. 'The High-Rise Home: Verticality as Practice in London.' *International Journal of Urban and Regional Research* 41(2): 334–52. doi.org/10.1111/1468-2427.12451.

Becker & Poliakoff Hurricane Recovery Team. 2014. *Hurricane Preparedness and Recovery Guide for Community Associations*. Fort Lauderdale, FL: Becker & Poliakoff. Available from: www.condoassociation.com/hubfs/Disaster%20 Recovery%20Guide.pdf.

Bunker, R. 2014. 'How Is the Compact City Faring in Australia?' *Planning Practice & Research* 29(5): 449–60. doi.org/10.1080/02697459.2014.945376.

City of Sydney. n.d. *Smart Green Apartments*. Sydney: City of Sydney. Available from: www.cityofsydney.nsw.gov.au/environmental-support-funding/smart-green-apartments.

City of Toronto. 2017. *Growing Up: Planning for Children in New Vertical Communities*. Toronto: City of Toronto. Available from: www.toronto.ca/city-government/planning-development/planning-studies-initiatives/growing-up-planning-for-children-in-new-vertical-communities/.

City of Vancouver. 2020. *High-Density Housing for Families with Children Guidelines*. Land Use and Development Policies and Guidelines. Vancouver, BC: City of Vancouver. Available from: guidelines.vancouver.ca/guidelines-high-density-housing-for-families-with-children.pdf.

Crommelin, L., H. Easthope, and L. Troy. 2017. *Equitable Density: The Place for Lower-Income and Disadvantaged Households in a Dense City. Report 2: The Neighbourhood Scale*. Sydney: City Futures Research Centre, University of New South Wales. Available from: cityfutures.be.unsw.edu.au/research/projects/equitable-density-place-lower-income-and-disadvantage-households-dense-city/.

Crommelin, L., H. Easthope, L. Troy, and B. Randolph. 2020. 'A New Pathway to Displacement? The Implications of Less-Than-Unanimous Strata Renewal Laws for Vulnerable Residents.' *Australian Planner* 56(4): 261–69. doi.org/10.1080/07293682.2020.1854798.

Crommelin, L., S. Thompson, M. Loosemore, H. Yang, C. Buckle, and B. Randolph. 2021. *Cracks in the Compact City: Tackling Defects in Multi-Unit Strata Housing*. Sydney: University of Technology Sydney & City Futures Research Centre, University of New South Wales. Available from: cityfutures.ada.unsw.edu.au/documents/670/Defects_final_report_for_publication_HSGP9LW.pdf.

Denman, A., and P. Chittenden. 2019. 'Episode 2: How to Maximise Gross Realisation, Play the Long Game and Know When to Say No.' *Property Marketing Podcast*, [Transcript]. Available from: www.propertymarketingpodcast.com.au/peter-chittenden/.

Department of Environment, Land, Water and Planning (DELWP). 2017. *Apartment Design Guidelines for Victoria*. Melbourne: Victorian Government. Available from: www.planning.vic.gov.au/__data/assets/pdf_file/0030/80994/Apartment-Design-Guidelines-for-Victoria_August-2017.pdf.

Easthope, H. 2016. 'Losing Control at Home?' In *Place and Placelessness Revisited*, edited by R. Freestone and E. Liu, 108–19. New York, NY: Routledge.

Easthope, H. 2019. *The Politics and Practices of Apartment Living*. Cheltenham, UK: Edward Elgar. doi.org/10.4337/9781786438089.

Easthope, H., L. Crommelin, L. Troy, G. Davison, M. Nethercote, S. Foster, R. van den Nouwelant, A. Kleeman, B. Randolph, and R. Horne. 2020a. *Improving Outcomes for Apartment Residents and Neighbourhoods*. Final Report 329. Melbourne: AHURI. doi.org/10.18408/ahuri-7120701.

Easthope, H., and S.M. Kerr. forthcoming. 'Condominium Living.' In *Housing, the Home and Society: Research Handbook*, edited by K. Jacobs, K. Flanagan, J. Verdouw, and J. De Vries. Cheltenham, UK: Edward Edgar.

Easthope, H., and B. Randolph. 2009. 'Governing the Compact City: The Challenges of Apartment Living in Sydney, Australia.' *Housing Studies* 24(2): 243–59. doi.org/10.1080/02673030802705433.

Easthope, H., and B. Randolph. 2021. 'Condominiums Aren't Forever: Governance, Redevelopment, and Implications for the City.' In *Condominium Governance and Law in Global Urban Context*, edited by R. Lippert and S. Treffers, 217–33. London: Routledge. doi.org/10.4324/9781003141600-17.

Easthope, H., B. Randolph, and S. Judd. 2012. *Governing the Compact City*. Sydney: City Futures Research Centre, University of New South Wales. Available from: cityfutures.ada.unsw.edu.au/documents/43/Governing_the_Compact_City_FINAL_REPORT.pdf.

Easthope, H., S. Thompson, and A. Sisson. 2020b. *2020 Australasian Strata Insights*. Sydney: City Futures Research Centre, University of New South Wales & Strata Community Association. Available from: cityfutures.be.unsw.edu.au/research/projects/2020-australasian-strata-insights/.

Easthope, H., and A. Tice. 2011. 'Children in Apartments: Implications for the Compact City.' *Urban Policy and Research* 29(4): 415–34. doi.org/10.1080/08111146.2011.627834.

Ellis, J. 2020a. 'Investorist Market Update with IBuildNew and IBuyNew Group.' *Investorist Market Update*, [Podcast], 15 April.

Ellis, J. 2020b. 'How are the Nations Best Channel Managers Working Through COVID-19?' *Investorist Market Update*, [Podcast], 29 April.

Ellis, J. 2020c. 'Investorist Market Update with REINSW.' *Investorist Market Update*, [Podcast], 16 June. Available from: vimeo.com/429837300.

Fincher, R. 2004. 'Gender and Life Course in the Narratives of Melbourne's High-Rise Housing Developers.' *Australian Geographical Studies* 42(3): 325–38. doi.org/10.1111/j.1467-8470.2004.00278.x.

Firing, M., O. Laedre, and J. Lohne. 2016. 'Main Challenges Found in the Handover of a Shopping Centre in Norway.' *Social and Behavioral Sciences* 226: 100–7. doi.org/10.1016/j.sbspro.2016.06.167.

Gurran, N., C. Gilbert, K. Gibb, R. van den Nouwelant, A. James, and P. Phibbs. 2018. *Supporting Affordable Housing Supply: Inclusionary Planning in New and Renewing Communities*. Final Report 297. Melbourne: AHURI. doi.org/10.18408/ahuri-7313201.

Hulse, K., V. Milligan, and H. Easthope. 2011. *Secure Occupancy in Rental Housing: Conceptual Foundations and Comparative Perspectives*. Final Report 170. Melbourne: AHURI.

Jacobs, K. 2019. *Neoliberal Housing Policy: An International Perspective*. London: Routledge. doi.org/10.4324/9780429425523.

James, B. 2007. *Children and Young People's Housing Experiences: Issues and Scoping*. Wellington: Centre for Housing Research Aotearoa New Zealand. Available from: www.researchgate.net/publication/293695283_Children_and_Young_People's_Housing_Experiences_Issues_and_Scoping.

Johnston, N., and S. Reid. 2019. *An Examination of Building Defects in Multi-Owned Properties*. Research Report, June. Melbourne: Deakin University. Available from: www.griffith.edu.au/__data/assets/pdf_file/0030/831279/Examining-Building-Defects-Research-Report.pdf.

Johnston, N., and E. Too. 2015. 'Multi-Owned Properties in Australia: A Governance Typology of Issues and Outcomes.' *International Journal of Housing Markets and Analysis* 8(4): 451–70. doi.org/10.1108/IJHMA-02-2015-0005.

Judith Stubbs and Associates. 2017. *Best Practice in Multi-Tenure Development. Part A: Australian Case Studies.* Report prepared for NSW Federation of Housing Associations Inc. under the NSW Community Housing Industry Development Strategy, July. Bulli, NSW: Judith Stubbs and Associates. Available from: communityhousing.org.au/wp-content/uploads/2018/07/PART-A-AUSTRALIAN-CASE-STUDIES-170703.pdf.

Kerr, S.M., C. Gibson, and N. Klocker. 2018. 'Parenting and Neighbouring in the Consolidating City: The Emotional Geographies of Sound in Apartments.' *Emotion, Space and Society* 26: 1–8. doi.org/10.1016/j.emospa.2017.11.002.

Kerr, S.M., N. Klocker, and C. Gibson. 2020. 'From Backyards to Balconies: Cultural Norms and Parents' Experiences of Home in Higher-Density Housing.' *Housing Studies* 36(3): 421–43. doi.org/10.1080/02673037.2019.1709625.

Lambert, M. 2015. *Independent Review of the Building Professionals Act 2005.* Final Report, October. Sydney: NSW Government. Available from: www.fairtrading. nsw.gov.au/__data/assets/pdf_file/0017/604520/Independent-review-of-the-Building-Professionals-Act-2005.pdf.

Liu, E., H. Easthope, I. Burnley, and B. Judd. 2013. 'Multigenerational Households in Australian Cities: Evidence from Sydney and Brisbane at the Turn of the Twenty-First Century.' Presented to Seventh Australasian Housing Researchers' Conference, Fremantle, Western Australia, 6–8 February.

Loschke, S.K., and H. Easthope. 2017. 'How Adaptive Redesign and Participatory Approaches Can Transform Ageing Housing.' In *From Conflict to Inclusion in Housing: Interaction of Communities, Residents and Activists. Volume 1*, edited by G. Cairns, G. Artopoulos, and K. Day, 71–86. London: UCL Press. doi.org/ 10.2307/j.ctt1xhr55k.11.

Ma, X. 2021. 'Chinese Housing Policy, Capital Switching and the Foreign Real Estate Investment "Boom and Bust" in Australia.' *International Journal of Housing Policy* 21(3): 451–63. doi.org/10.1080/19491247.2020.1814191.

Ma, X., Z. Zhang, Y. Han, and X.-G. Yue. 2019. 'Sustainable Policy Dynamics: A Study on the Recent "Bust" of Foreign Residential Investment in Sydney.' *Sustainability* 11(20): 5856. Available from: www.mdpi.com/2071-1050/11/ 20/5856. doi.org/10.3390/su11205856.

McFarlane, C. 2016. 'The Geographies of Urban Density: Topology, Politics and the City.' *Progress in Human Geography* 40(5): 629–48. doi.org/10.1177/ 0309132515608694.

Miezis, M., K. Zvaigznitis, N. Stancioff, and L. Soeftestad. 2016. 'Climate Change and Buildings Energy Efficiency: The Key Role of Residents.' *Environmental and Climate Technologies* 17(1): 30–43. doi.org/10.1515/rtuect-2016-0004.

Moore, T., and A. Doyon. 2018. 'The Uncommon Nightingale: Sustainable Housing Innovation in Australia.' *Sustainability* 10(10): 3469. Available from: www.mdpi.com/2071-1050/10/10/3469. doi.org/10.3390/su10103469.

Nethercote, M., and R. Horne. 2016. 'Ordinary Vertical Urbanisms: City Apartments and the Everyday Geographies of High-Rise Families.' *Environment and Planning A* 48(8): 1581–98. doi.org/10.1177/0308518X16645104.

NSW Government. 2002. *State Environmental Planning Policy No. 65—Design Quality of Residential Apartment Development (2002 EPI 530).* Sydney: NSW Government. Available from: legislation.nsw.gov.au/view/html/inforce/2021-02-12/epi-2002-0530#statusinformation.

NSW Government. 2019. *NSW Government Response to the Shergold Weir Building Confidence Report.* February. Sydney: Better Regulation Division, Department of Finance, Services and Innovation. Available from: www.fairtrading.nsw.gov.au/__data/assets/pdf_file/0007/451375/Response-to-Shergold-Weir-Building-Confidence-Report.pdf.

Office of Local Government (OLG). 2021. *Local Government Rating Reform: Review of the Rate Peg Methodology.* Sydney: NSW Government. Available from: www.olg.nsw.gov.au/councils/policy-and-legislation/local-government-rating-reform/.

Organisation for Economic Co-operation and Development (OECD). 2012. *Compact City Policies: A Comparative Assessment.* OECD Green Growth Studies. Paris: OECD Publishing. doi.org/10.1787/9789264167865-en.

Palmer, J.S. 2020. 'Realising Collective Self-Organised Housing: A Network Agency Perspective.' *Urban Policy and Research* 38(2): 101–17. doi.org/10.1080/08111146.2020.1730785.

Pawson, H., C. Martin, R. van den Nouwelant, V. Milligan, K. Ruming, and M. Melo. 2019. *Build to Rent in Australia: Product Feasibility and Affordable Housing Contribution.* Sydney: Landcom. Available from: apo.org.au/sites/default/files/resource-files/2019-07/apo-nid246516.pdf.

Public Accountability Committee. 2020. *Regulation of Building Standards, Building Quality and Building Disputes. Final Report.* Report 6, April. Sydney: Parliament of NSW. Available from: www.parliament.nsw.gov.au/lcdocs/inquiries/2540/PAC%20-%20Regulation%20of%20building%20standards%20quality%20disputes%20-%20Final%20report%20-%20Report%20no%206.pdf.

Randolph, B. 2006. 'Delivering the Compact City in Australia: Current Trends and Future Implications.' *Urban Policy and Research* 24(4): 473–90. doi.org/10.1080/08111140601035259.

Randolph, B., and H. Easthope. 2007. 'Governing the Compact City: The Governance of Strata Titled Developments in Sydney.' Paper presented to Sustainable Urban Areas International Conference, Rotterdam, Netherlands, 25–28 June. Available from: www.researchgate.net/profile/Bill-Randolph/publication/267771580_W 19_-_The_Sustainable_City_%27Governing_the_Compact_City%27_The_ governance_of_strata_title_developments_in_Sydney/links/54c6a4d30cf22d 626a35114e/W19-The-Sustainable-City-Governing-the-Compact-City-The-governance-of-strata-title-developments-in-Sydney.pdf.

Reid, S., K. Lloyd, and W. O'Brien. 2017. 'Women's Perspectives on Liveability in Vertical Communities: A Feminist Materialist Approach.' *Australian Planner* 54(1): 16–23. doi.org/10.1080/07293682.2017.1297315.

Rogers, D. 2017. *The Geopolitics of Real Estate: Reconfiguring Property, Capital and Rights*. London: Rowman & Littlefield.

Rosewall, T., and M. Shoory. 2017. 'Houses and Apartments in Australia.' *Reserve Bank of Australia Bulletin*, June Quarter. Sydney: RBA. Available from: rba.gov. au/publications/bulletin/2017/jun/pdf/bu-0617-1-houses-and-apartments-in-australia.pdf.

Sharam, A., L. Bryant, and T. Alves. 2015. *Making Apartments Affordable: Moving from Speculative to Deliberative Development*. Melbourne: Swinburne Institute for Social Research. Available from: eprints.qut.edu.au/90144/.

Sharam, A., M. Byford, B. Karabay, S. McNelis, and T. Burke. 2018. *Matching Markets in Housing and Housing Assistance*. Final Report 307, 22 November. Melbourne: AHURI. doi.org/10.18408/ahuri-5315301.

Shergold, P., and B. Weir. 2018. *Building Confidence: Improving the Effectiveness of Compliance and Enforcement Systems for the Building and Construction Industry Across Australia*. Canberra: Commonwealth of Australia. Available from: www.industry.gov.au/sites/default/files/July%202018/document/pdf/building_ ministers_forum_expert_assessment_-_building_confidence.pdf.

Sherry, C. 2013. 'Lessons in Personal Freedom and Functional Land Markets: What Strata and Community Title Can Learn from Traditional Doctrines of Property.' *The University of New South Wales Law Journal* 36(1): 280–315.

The Transition Network (TTN) Caring Collaborative. 2011. *Creating a Vertical Village in a High-Rise Building*. New York: TTN. Available from: silo.tips/ download/creating-a-vertical-village-in-a-high-rise-building.

Troy, L., B. Randolph, L. Crommelin, H. Easthope, and S. Pinnegar. 2015. *Renewing the Compact City: Economically Viable and Socially Sustainable Approaches to Urban Development*. Final Report, November. Sydney: City Futures Research Centre, University of New South Wales. Available from: cityfutures.ada.unsw.edu.au/documents/694/Renewing_the_Compact_City_-_Final_Report_ThT j7eX.pdf.

Troy, L., B. Randolph, S. Pinnegar, L. Crommelin, and H. Easthope. 2020. 'Vertical Sprawl in the Australian City: Sydney's High-Rise Residential Development Boom.' *Urban Policy and Research* 38(1): 18–36. doi.org/10.1080/08111146.2019.1709168.

Troy, P. 1996. *The Perils of Urban Consolidation*. Sydney: The Federation Press.

Troy, P. 2013. 'Consolidation Policy and its Effects on the City.' Paper presented to Sixth State of Australasian Cities Conference, Sydney, 26–29 November. Available from: apo.org.au/node/59764.

12

In GOD we trust: Tracking density, greenspace, and wellbeing in Australian cities

Julian Bolleter, Nicole Edwards, and Paula Hooper[1]

Introduction

Australian urbanist Patrick Troy played a significant role in highlighting the relevance of the cities–policy nexus through formative publications, including *The Politics of Urban Growth* (Parker and Troy 1972), *Australian Cities* (Troy 1995), and *The Perils of Urban Consolidation* (Troy 1996). In contradistinction to contemporary planning orthodoxies, Troy was a prominent critic of urban consolidation. He railed against drives for densification, which he regarded as a 'massive and sustained attack on the form of Australia's cities' (Troy 2004: 117). To Troy, such 'misguided' drives overlooked the evidence that the desire for a house and garden (that is, the 'Australian dream') remained the preference for a vast proportion of Australians due to the appeal of 'green and secluded neighbourhoods', where families could enjoy 'fresh air, a pleasant view and a shady garden' (2004: 119). Troy attributed this 'blindness' to community preferences to the ideologically determined policy for higher-density living, which reflected 'a curious coalition of intellectuals and aesthetes who had long expressed disdain for the suburban life' (2004: 122).

---

1 This chapter draws on material from previous publications: Bolleter and Ramalho (2014, 2019b); and Bolleter et al. (2022).

Troy's sentiments resonate with current attitudes stemming from the global Covid-19 pandemic—a crisis that prompted a revaluation of oft-scorned spacious and verdant suburbia. Such quintessential suburbs offer onsite disposal of organic waste, generation of energy, collection of rainwater, production of food, the use of vegetation to create cool microclimates, and allowed residents to lock down with more privacy and ample access to open spaces and nature during Covid-19 outbreaks (Bolleter et al. 2021). Accordingly, home gardens are a significant factor in residents' quality of life (Syme et al. 2001). Moreover, the psychological benefits of the home garden have been well documented (Kaplan, in Syme et al. 2001). Nevertheless, urban commentary and policy have largely understated or ignored suburbia's possibilities for adaptation (Gleeson 2008).

The pandemic appears to have dramatically reshaped lifestyle and dwelling preferences, which will significantly affect urban policy in Australia and elsewhere. For example, in the Plan My Australia Community Survey (n = 1,008), conducted from May to November 2020, the Australian Urban Design Research Centre found that 56 per cent of respondents were less willing to live in an apartment and 38 per cent were less willing to travel by public transport since the onset of the pandemic in Australia (Bolleter et al. 2021). In a related survey, the Plan My Australia Experts Survey (n = 284), conducted from February to April 2020, many respondents noted that a dispersed population within cities 'is an added protection', reduces transmission, and increases liveability during lockdowns (Bolleter et al. 2021).

Moreover, shifting work patterns favour suburban expansion. Of course, the degree to which such sentiments will linger is unknown. Regardless, recent data from the ABS (2021) highlight the continued demand for detached housing, with private sector house approvals soaring to a record high. The quintessential suburban lifestyle has continuing allure, which is explained in part by the problems that bedevil compact city policies in Australia.

Against this backdrop, our chapter explores the triple ambitions of managing increasing density, reversing the erosion of greenspace, and bolstering human wellbeing through greenspace-oriented development (GOD). Through urban densification around upgraded suburban parks, GOD seeks to conserve the best of suburbia but render it more sustainable and compact. Furthermore, we believe that GOD can reconcile the push from state and territory governments for urban density in a way that also resonates with Troy's aspirations for housing set within gardens that provide a cool microclimate, grow food, accommodate waste, and provide a natural setting for daily life (Troy 2004)—aspirations prescient of current post-Covid-19 attitudes. Through GOD, we can have our cake and eat it, too!

First, the chapter considers the issues associated with current transit-oriented development (TOD) densification policies and surveys the resulting urban morphologies. Subsequently, we consider related concerns about greenspace provision and speculate on the broader impacts on resident health and wellbeing. The chapter then draws on alternative models for delivering density, greenspace, and health and wellbeing, such as GOD. Finally, the chapter proposes potential policy implications.

Issues in current densification policy

We acknowledge that suburban expansion faces several longstanding issues, including the sterilisation of agriculturally productive (Seto et al. 2000) and biodiverse land (Radeloff et al. 2010), service and public transport infrastructure costs (Bento et al. 2005; Brownstone and Golob 2009), and the concentration of socioeconomic vulnerabilities on the city's fringes (Nechyba and Walsh 2004; Sturm and Cohen 2004; Dodson and Sipe 2008; Zhao and Kaestner 2010). Sprawl has also been correlated with adverse health effects, including worrying levels of obesity, high blood pressure, hypertension, and chronic disease (Ewing et al. 2003). The real and perceived negative impacts of sprawl have understandably spurred the pursuit of infill development by Australian state and territory governments to consolidate new development in existing urban areas. The compact city model emphasises the intensification of urban development and activity, creates limits to urban development, encourages land-use mix, and focuses on the importance of mass transit and urban design quality (Bibri et al. 2020). TOD is the recurring spatial planning strategy that most notably integrates these goals to increase urban density and enhance public transport connectivity (Jabareen 2006; Ibraeva et al. 2020).

TOD has varied applications in Australia but essentially aims to concentrate urban activity in high-intensity mixed-use precincts centred on highly accessible transport nodes to increase public transport use and deliver urban infill (Curtis 2012). Proponents claim that TOD delivers an abundance of benefits, including boosting the viability of public transportation (Hagan 2017), the mobility of low-income households, the delivery of local services, reducing car dependency, and constraining energy consumption and greenhouse gas emissions (CNU 2016). Advocates also propose that TOD in existing urban areas increases urban density and sustainable transport options for cities dealing with traffic congestion and ballooning urban footprints. Finally, supporters of TOD believe it will stimulate a diversity of local employment opportunities and kindle knowledge diffusion and thus economic growth—all of which contribute to a higher quality of life for residents (OECD 2012).

Delivering urban infill correlated with transport is a *sine qua non* in Australian urban policy across all levels of government. Since the 1980s, urban consolidation has become a firmly established orthodoxy in Australian spatial planning theory and practice (Bolleter and Ramalho 2019b). However, the results have been patchy and debated, and suburbia dominates as the major housing frontier (Gordon 2016). Achievements have been selective and the reality of urban development in Australian cities contrasts starkly with the TOD vision, which is echoed in community resistance to the Australian planning system's facilitation of higher density as the preferred urban form (Lewis 1999). There exists a 'divergence between the compact city imagined in metropolitan plans and what is occurring on the ground in Australian cities' (Gray et al. 2010: 336). As Forster (2006) posits, this reductive vision of TOD-driven metropolitan sustainability is starkly contradicted by the morphologies of our cities that stubbornly remain differentiated and dispersed instead of tidily multi-nucleated.

Despite the promotion of TOD in Australia's capital cities, full implementation has proven elusive (Goodman and Moloney 2004; Kelly and Donegan 2015; Bunker et al. 2017; Burton 2017; Goodman 2017). This situation endures despite such policies being in operation in some cities since the 1980s (Murphy 2012). Furthermore, the 2021 census revealed that only 10.3 per cent of all Australians lived in apartments, although this number is rising (ABS 2022). The evidence illustrates that, despite the promotion and agendas of planners and policymakers, the suburban home remains most desired by families (Elliot 2017). As a result, a truly 'back to the city' future, as imagined by retro-urbanists, seems highly unlikely short of imposing heavy-handed planning regimes (Berger et al. 2017: 10).

The challenges confronting TOD have resulted in a 'missing middle' in Australian cities, where the 'middle' refers to high-quality medium-density multi-unit or clustered housing types. Instead, Australian cities tend to be polarised between high-rise, high-density apartments in areas of high land value and small-scale, low-density infill in middle-ring suburbs. Regarding the latter, a substantial proportion of infill development occurs through the piecemeal carving up of backyards. Planners refer to this as 'background' infill: small projects yielding less than five generally semidetached survey strata, single-storey group dwellings gathered around a space-hungry communal driveway leading to private garages (Bolleter 2016). Despite decades of TOD dreaming, developers deliver a substantial portion of infill in this ad hoc, background manner (Newton et al. 2011).

Compromised greenspace provision

The push for higher-density living through TOD represents a fundamental shift in how Australians live. Apartment residents typically have less private space and, when it is provided, there is often limited communal space in the building complex. A significant concern for densifying cities, especially in the inner city, is the underprovision of open space (Searle 2011). In inner-city areas and those flagged for urban consolidation, an ongoing debate remains around how much public open space is needed as densities increase and private open spaces decrease (that is, through the loss of the back garden). These concerns often presume that residents will need to compensate for limited access to private open spaces by using public open spaces such as parks more frequently—a notion referred to as the 'compensation hypothesis' (Byrne et al. 2010).

Unsurprisingly, background infill development provides a mere fragment of the bountiful garden area in a 'classic' quarter-acre block (Seddon 1994). The open space in background infill is typically narrow, effectively useless, and residual, generated through the unthinking application of minimum setbacks between lot lines and building edges (Bolleter 2016). In addition, a proclivity for private carparking adjoining private dwellings means that, in many cases, more lot area is dedicated to the parking and movement of cars than to living and garden space for humans (Bolleter 2016).

A worrying side-effect of background infill has been a decimation of urban forests in middle-ring suburbs despite the critical role of trees in supporting urban liveability and sustainability (Bolleter and Ramalho 2019b). Background infill development has slashed urban forest cover because most trees grow on private land (Brunner and Cozens 2013). Such trees are reduced to providing the 'trimmings to the designed urban environment and are afforded little or no protection against the exigency of meeting development aspirations' (Brunner and Cozens 2013: 232). The apparent shortage of greenspace and the degradation of urban forests associated with compact city policy have many potential ramifications for human health and wellbeing.

Human health and wellbeing implications

A lack of suitably designed greenspace is worrying because contact with 'nature' in greenspaces plays a crucial role in bolstering urban liveability, health, and wellbeing. Various models have been proposed to explain the observed relationship between greenspace and health. For example, Hartig et al. (2014) suggested four principal and interacting pathways through which nature or greenspace contribute to health: by promoting physical activity (for example, recreational walking); by reducing exposure to stress factors and providing an environment for physiological and mental recovery that yields coping resources to deal with the stress of life; by promoting social interaction and a sense of community; and by providing a healthy, comfortable environment (for example, better air quality and thermal comfort than nearby built spaces).

Others such as Lachowycz and Jones (2013) emphasised physical activity, engagement with nature, relaxation, and social activities and interactions as major pathways to health. Moreover, Villanueva et al. (2015) proposed a model emphasising respiratory health and resilience to heat-related illness, social capital and cohesion, and physical activity. Finally, Lee et al. (2015a) hypothesised three main mechanisms for health benefits: providing opportunities for physical activity, recovery from stress and attention fatigue, and facilitation of social contact. Regardless of the model, these pathways lead to multiple health and wellbeing benefits that play out across a lifespan (Astell-Burt et al. 2014).

The importance of parks and their health benefits were underscored by Covid-19. To bolster mental and physical health during extended lockdowns, urban residents often sought refuge in parks (Larson et al. 2021). City-dwellers were more likely than others to suffer health impacts from the pandemic and greenspaces presented respite from virus transmission risk and lonely—or conversely crowded—home lockdowns. Indeed, adults who maintained outdoor activity in greenspaces during the pandemic reported better health outcomes than those confined to interior environments (Larson et al. 2021). So, what forms of health benefits do well-designed parks offer?

The provision of attractive, open greenspaces, such as parks, or recreational spaces, such as sports ovals, provide important places for people to engage in physical activity (Giles-Corti et al. 2005). While increased urban density can *per se* promote walkability in contrast with low density, car-dependent neighbourhoods (Giles-Corti et al. 2012; Udell et al. 2014), recreational walking and physical activity in greenspaces help to combat sedentary lifestyles and are associated with a reduction in obesity, heart disease, and several types of cancer, and extended lifespans (Bell et al. 2008; Yelenik and Levine 2011; Pereira et al. 2013). In this way, physical activity in green settings, such as walking or running in the park, is more restorative than conducting the same activity in the built environment (Marselle et al. 2013).

Evidence of how the presence of parks can stimulate activity is provided by a recent study of 11,000 residents in Brisbane that found that park users were 35 per cent more likely to meet the physical activity guidelines compared with those who indicated they did not regularly use a park (Hooper et al. 2020). The park's size was also positively associated with participation in physical activity, with users of larger-sized parks spending more time doing vigorous activity and engaging in more activity sessions than non-users.

A lack of access to parks is also an indirect environmental determinant of obesity. The pathway through which parks are hypothesised to impact obesity is thought to be by encouraging physical activity. Indeed, several studies have found that higher levels of neighbourhood parks are associated with lower levels of obesity in children (Bell et al. 2008). Furthermore, a systematic review of 60 studies from the United States, Canada, Australia, Aotearoa New Zealand, and Europe on the relationships between parks and obesity indicators revealed that 68 per cent of papers correlated access to parks with reduced obesity. Nonetheless, these relationships could be modified by age and socioeconomic status (Lachowycz and Jones 2011).

There is consensus and well-documented evidence that urban environments with greenspaces, such as urban parks, are critical restorative environments for urban-dwellers (Astell-Burt et al. 2014). Indeed, active and passive recreation in good-quality greenspaces reduce stress and the psychological toll of urban living (de Vries et al. 2013; Peschardt and Stigsdotter 2013; Tyrväinen et al. 2014; Bratman et al. 2015), improve mental health (Francis et al. 2012) and attention restoration (Nordh et al. 2009), and play a crucial role in the cognitive development of children (Dadvand et al. 2015). Moreover, urban parks and other greenspaces provide children with unique opportunities for risk-taking, discovery, creativity, mastery and control, strengthening the sense of self, inspiring basic emotional states, and enhancing psychological restoration (Bowler et al. 2010). Furthermore, different greening solutions, such as green roofs, within built precincts can also positively affect attention restoration and stress reduction (for example, Lee et al. 2015b).

Parks and other greenspaces are also crucial as settings that engender social interaction and the development of social ties (Chiesura 2004). Indeed, good-quality parks provide a forum for socialising with friends and neighbours, thus improving social ties (Kaźmierczak 2013). For example, in Chicago, parks were found to mitigate stress indirectly by fostering social support (Fan et al. 2011). Studies have also found that people with better-quality streetscape vegetation felt their neighbourhood was calmer and more cohesive, which was related to improved self-reported health (de Vries et al. 2013).

So, what type of parks play the most prominent role in human health and wellbeing? The literature affirms that biodiversity plays a crucial role. Fuller et al. (2007) and Dallimer et al. (2012) revealed that greater perceived richness of plants and birds in urban parks and greater habitat diversity were associated with increased psychological benefits to park users. More recently, Carrus et al. (2015) and Marselle et al. (2016) showed that this association is mediated by the perceived restorative quality of parks with those characteristics. In other words, perceived biodiversity and naturalness (Marselle et al. 2016) enhance people's perceptions of the restorative effect of greenspaces. In Berlin, Palliwoda et al. (2017) concluded that a considerable proportion of leisure activities undertaken by park users were linked to biodiversity—in particular, individual plant species, with some species sought after for consumption and decoration, and others for simple *in situ* observation and experience.

Urban biodiversity also allows people to engage with nature and learn about the natural world meaningfully. As cities sprawl more than ever before, people are less likely to primarily experience nature in the places where they live and work (Miller and Hobbs 2002). Connection with nature in urban areas is thus key to preventing the extinction of the experience of nature (Miller 2005). Below, we set out one mechanism for conflating the benefits of biodiversity and urban density in our cities: GOD.

Introducing greenspace-oriented development

With compact city policies often detrimental to greenspace provision, an alternative pathway more in tune with such needs warrants consideration. We advance the idea of GOD, which prioritises sustainable suburban renewal around open spaces in reasonable proximity to public transport (Bolleter and Ramalho 2019b). Many planning and design movements have sought to marry urban morphologies and green systems in recent decades (Bolleter and Ramalho 2019b). For example, 'green urbanism' proposes a 'city that maximises landscapes, gardens, biodiversity, and green infrastructure' (Lehmann 2010: 212). Similarly, 'landscape urbanism' foregrounds landscape as the 'ultimate system to which all goes, and from which all comes, a template for urbanism' (Weller 2006: 67).

Our model spins off TOD, but while TOD correlates urban densification with mass transit hubs, GOD correlates urban densification with significant upgraded parks within a 5-minute cycle or 15-minute walk of public transport in middle-ring suburbs (Figures 12.1 and 12.2). At its core, a GOD approach builds on the well-recognised importance of parks in delivering a cornucopia of health and wellbeing benefits to urban-dwellers. The central spatial idea is to develop the walkable catchment of upgraded parks (about 400 metres) with new medium-density infill development addressing the perceived 'missing middle' in Australian cities. Thus, the positive aspects of suburban development (that is, access to open space) are woven together with those of urban districts (that is, mid-rise development, access to public transport, facilities, and good urban design) (Bolleter and Ramalho 2019b).

While Australia's middle-ring suburbs have a typically generous provision of parks, many offer minimal amenity and experience of biodiversity and are underutilised (Byrne and Sipe 2010). Indeed, local governments often swathe this ubiquitous element of the suburban landscape with irrigated turf and a scattering of lonely trees. Moreover, while the middle-ring park design caters for organised active team sports, other passive recreation and wildlife habitat functions are given scant attention (Byrne and Sipe 2010). As a result, these parks are often sparsely occupied, especially on weekdays. A GOD approach could act as a catalyst for redesigning these often-denuded suburban landscapes (Bolleter and Ramalho 2019b).

Figure 12.1 Public open space before being upgraded according to GOD

Source: Bolleter and Ramalho (2019b).

Figure 12.2 After GOD: Urban densification correlated with upgraded parks

Source: Bolleter and Ramalho (2019b).

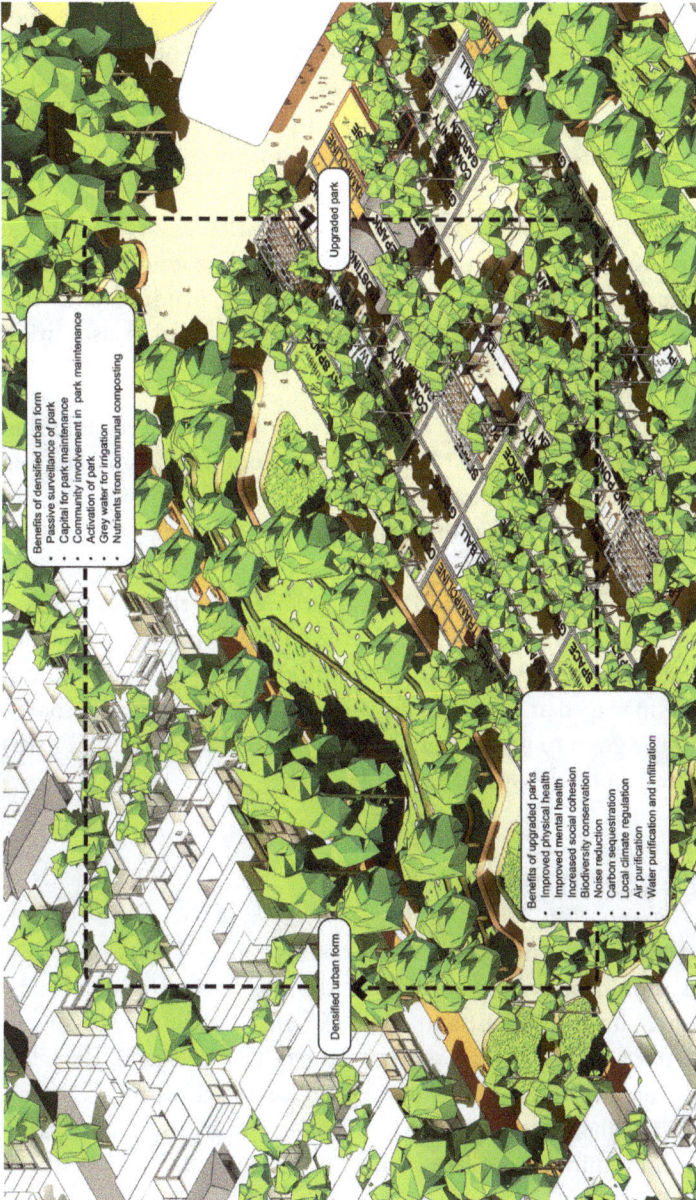

Benefits of densified urban form
- Passive surveillance of park
- Capital for park maintenance
- Community involvement in park maintenance
- Activation of park
- Grey water for irrigation
- Nutrients from communal composting

Benefits of upgraded parks
- Improved physical health
- Improved mental health
- Increased social cohesion
- Biodiversity conservation
- Noise reduction
- Carbon sequestration
- Local climate regulation
- Air purification
- Water purification and infiltration

Upgraded park

Densified urban form

Figure 12.3 Upgraded public open space

This can provide a range of human health and wellbeing, ecological, and economic benefits to adjacent residents, while densified urban precincts surrounding parks also offer crucial benefits to the utility of the parks

Source: Bolleter and Ramalho (2019b).

We base the association between urban densification and public open space on three fundamental principles. First, these spaces can provide physical (van Dillen et al. 2012) and mental (Astell-Burt and Feng 2019) health benefits, increase the likelihood of walking (Giles-Corti et al. 2005), reduce land surface temperature (Yu et al. 2018), and 'compensate' residents living in medium-density settings for a relative lack of private greenspace (Chiesura 2004; Haaland and van den Bosch 2015) (Figure 12.3). Second, well-designed, adjacent, densified urban precincts can offer significant benefits to parks themselves, such as increased local rates and taxes that local governments can direct towards park upgrades and maintenance, more people to activate the park, and concomitant increases in public safety due to passive surveillance (Udell et al. 2014). Third, by promoting the socioeconomic rejuvenation of nearby urban areas (for example, LaFarge 2014; Ryu and Kwon 2016)—namely, by increasing surrounding property values (Crompton 2005; Brander and Koetse 2011; Panduro and Veie 2013)—quality parks can foster urban redevelopment and densification (Mell 2009; Newton et al. 2011).

This use of upgraded parks to leverage the densification in middle-ring suburbs is a strategy that has been largely absent from Australian planning for urban densification. However, the idea of correlating density and greenspace is not new. Readers should note the work of others in the GOD space, including the Greater Sydney Commission (now the Greater Cities Commission), and Rod Simpson (2018) in particular, in their planning to correlate urban density with greenspace in 'parkland-oriented development'. We also note Newton's work exploring how informal background infill can be strategically managed at the precinct level to provide high-quality shared spaces and a finer grain to pedestrian circulation and interconnection paths beyond the street line (Newton et al. 2011).

Policy recommendations

In grappling with the thorny issue of densifying Australian suburbs, policymakers should be attentive to those who live in Australia's cities to understand their needs, desires, and fears, rather than blindly striving to deliver infill development or transit use targets (Bolleter and Ramalho 2019b). This situation has (to some degree) occurred with TOD—an approach that might have convinced planners but has not necessarily convinced communities (Bolleter and Ramalho 2019a). As Troy

(2004: 125) rightly cautioned us, the pursuit of 'architectural and lifestyle fashions imported from other cultures that are not grounded in the lived experience or aspirations of most Australians' will only waste planners' time and government funding. The enduring popularity of the 'suburban dream' in Australia and entrenched community resistance to urban infill attest to this. Robert Bruegmann (2017: 36) reinforces the importance of working with rather than against the prevailing sensibilities:

> To make a real contribution to the emerging urban pattern, it would probably help for architects, planners, and public policymakers to move away from their fixation on the forms of the past, traditional aesthetic notions, and attempts to build cities to accommodate existing technology and ways of life.

Moreover, we must acknowledge that cities are human systems first and built physical environments second. Unfortunately, planning experts often use the 'built environment' rubric inappropriately to direct discussion and urban planning. As Gleeson et al. (2010: 7) remind us: '[C]ontemplation of the built environment is surely critical but should flow from, and not precede, this appreciation.' To this end, planners could benefit from thinking about how a preferred suburban lifestyle can be serviced with alternative, sustainable forms of transport rather than how alternative ways of living can be made to conform with existing transport systems.

Farrelly (2021: 55) also identifies in our TOD fixation a 'prioritisation of the "going" over the "being" [in which] lies an overweening impatience, a focus on efficiency and a near-universal obsession with utility as the highest good'. Moreover, Fishman (1982) explains how the mission to organise the city around speed and efficiency allowed urban planning to be seen as a science, not an art—a situation that has manifested in an emphasis on transport connectivity over the creation of 'place'. In this way, great places need a train less than a train needs a great place (Quednau 2018). For this reason, urban planners and designers should cogently, firmly, and enduringly reflect the design principles and imperatives that will maximise the potential of TODs—and GODs—as authentic community places.

To this end, TOD planning should be subject to a fine-grained analysis of the lived experience of residents (Bolleter and Ramalho 2019b). According to the various state and territory policies across Australia, there are more than 300 TOD-driven activity centres identified for infill development nationwide (Bolleter and Weller 2013). Planners and policymakers could benefit from a national review to see whether planning is achieving the policy objectives for activity centres—particularly for open space provision and health and wellbeing indicators (Bolleter and Ramalho 2019b).

Conclusion

This chapter has noted the ongoing popularity of suburbia, which the Covid-19 pandemic has reinforced. To partly explain this popularity, we have scoped the problems bedevilling the implementation of compact city policies in Australia—none of which would have surprised Patrick Troy. While the existing literature identifies the myriad challenges associated with TOD, given the pandemic, urban policy would benefit from an overarching critical appraisal of both the implementation of TOD and the viable complementary strategies that resonate with the contemporary aspirations of Australian society. The chapter presented a complementary policy model for delivering density, greenspace, and health and wellbeing through GOD. This focus on delivering an appealing, healthy, green urban environment is even more critical in our Covid age. We argue that, through GOD, density need not be inimical to quality greenspace and health and wellbeing—an inherited notion that Patrick Troy held dear and that remains lodged in the minds of many Australians.

References

Astell-Burt, T., and X. Feng. 2019. 'Association of Urban Green Space with Mental Health and General Health Among Adults in Australia.' *JAMA Network Open* 2(7): e198209. doi.org/10.1001/jamanetworkopen.2019.8209.

Astell-Burt, T., R. Mitchell, and T. Hartig. 2014. 'The Association between Green Space and Mental Health Varies Across the Lifecourse: A Longitudinal Study.' *Journal of Epidemiology and Community Health* 68(6): 578–83. doi.org/10.1136/jech-2013-203767.

Australian Bureau of Statistics (ABS). 2021. 'Dwelling Approvals Fall, But Private Houses Reach New High.' Media release, 1 June. Canberra: ABS. Available from: www.abs.gov.au/media-centre/media-releases/dwelling-approvals-fall-private-houses-reach-new-high.

Australian Bureau of Statistics (ABS). 2022. '2021 Census Count Includes Australians Living on Wheels and Water, But Most of Us Still Firmly on Land.' Media release, 28 June. Canberra: ABS. Available from: www.abs.gov.au/media-centre/media-releases/2021-census-count-includes-australians-living-wheels-and-water-most-us-still-firmly-land#:~:text=The%202021%20Census%20separately%20identified,us%20now%20live%20in%20apartments.

Bell, J.F., J.S. Wilson, and G.C. Liu. 2008. 'Neighborhood Greenness and 2-Year Changes in Body Mass Index of Children and Youth.' *American Journal of Preventive Medicine* 35(6): 547–53. doi.org/10.1016/j.amepre.2008.07.006.

Bento, A.M., M.L. Cropper, A.M. Mobarak, and K. Vinha. 2005. 'The Effects of Urban Spatial Structure on Travel Demand in the United States.' *Review of Economics and Statistics* 87(3): 466–78. doi.org/10.1162/0034653054638292.

Berger, A., J. Kotkin, and C. Guzman. 2017. 'Introduction.' In *Infinite Suburbia*, edited by A. Berger, J. Kotkin, and C. Guzman, 10–23. Cambridge, MA: MIT Press.

Bibri, S.E., J. Krogstie, and M. Kärrholm. 2020. 'Compact City Planning and Development: Emerging Practices and Strategies for Achieving the Goals of Sustainability.' *Developments in the Built Environment* 4: 100021. doi.org/10.1016/j.dibe.2020.100021.

Bolleter, J. 2016. 'Background Noise: A Review of the Effects of Background Infill on Urban Liveability in Perth.' *Australian Planner* 10(4): 265–78. doi.org/10.1080/07293682.2016.1245201.

Bolleter, J., N. Edwards, R. Cameron, A. Duckworth, R. Freestone, S. Foster, and P. Hooper. 2021. 'Implications of the Covid-19 Pandemic: Canvassing Opinion from Planning Professionals.' *Planning Practice & Research* 37(1): 13–34. doi.org/10.1080/02697459.2021.1905991.

Bolleter, J., and C. Ramalho. 2014. 'The Potential of Ecologically Enhanced Urban Parks to Encourage and Catalyze Densification in Greyfield Suburbs.' *Journal of Landscape Architecture* 9(3): 54–65. doi.org/10.1080/18626033.2015.968418.

Bolleter, J., and C. Ramalho. 2019a. 'GOD Save Us: Greenspace-Oriented Development Could Make Higher Density Attractive.' *The Conversation*, 18 November. Available from: theconversation.com/god-save-us-greenspace-oriented-development-could-make-higher-density-attractive-126204. doi.org/10.1007/978-3-030-29601-8_3.

Bolleter, J., and C. Ramalho. 2019b. *Greenspace-Oriented Development: Reconciling Urban Density and Nature in Suburban Cities.* London: Springer. doi.org/10.1007/978-3-030-29601-8.

Bolleter, J., C. Ramalho, and R. Freestone. 2022. 'Greenspace Oriented Development.' *LA+* (Spring): 53–59.

Bolleter, J., and R. Weller. 2013. *Made in Australia: The Future of Australian Cities.* Perth: University of Western Australia Press.

Bowler, D., L.M. Buyung-Ali, T.M. Knight, and A.S. Pullin. 2010. 'A Systematic Review of Evidence for the Added Benefits to Health of Exposure to Natural Environments.' *BMC Public Health* 10(456). Available from: bmcpublichealth. biomedcentral.com/articles/10.1186/1471-2458-10-456. doi.org/10.1186/1471-2458-10-456.

Brander, L.M., and M.J. Koetse. 2011. 'The Value of Urban Open Space: Meta-Analyses of Contingent Valuation and Hedonic Pricing Results.' *Journal of Environmental Management* 92(10): 2763–73. doi.org/10.1016/j.jenvman. 2011.06.019.

Bratman, G.N., G.C. Daily, B.J. Levy, and J.J. Gross. 2015. 'The Benefits of Nature Experience: Improved Affect and Cognition.' *Landscape and Urban Planning* 138: 41–50. doi.org/10.1016/j.landurbplan.2015.02.005.

Brownstone, D., and T.F. Golob. 2009. 'The Impact of Residential Density on Vehicle Usage and Energy Consumption.' *Journal of Urban Economics* 65(1): 91–98. doi.org/10.1016/j.jue.2008.09.002.

Bruegmann, R. 2017. 'The Anti-Suburban Crusade.' In *Infinite Suburbia*, edited by A. Berger, J. Kotkin, and C. Guzman, 26–37. Cambridge, MA: MIT Press.

Brunner, J., and P. Cozens. 2013. '"Where Have All the Trees Gone?" Urban Consolidation and the Demise of Urban Vegetation: A Case Study from Western Australia.' *Planning Practice & Research* 28(2): 231–55. doi.org/10.1080/ 02697459.2012.733525.

Bunker, R., R. Freestone, and B. Randolph. 2017. 'Sydney: Growth, Globalization and Governance.' In *Planning Metropolitan Australia*, edited by S. Hamnett and R. Freestone, 84–108. London: Routledge. doi.org/10.4324/9781315281377-4.

Burton, P. 2017. 'South East Queensland: Change and Continuity in Planning.' In *Planning Metropolitan Australia*, edited by S. Hamnett and R. Freestone, 156–77. London: Routledge. doi.org/10.4324/9781315281377-7.

Byrne, J., and N. Sipe. 2010. *Green and Open Space Planning for Urban Consolidation: A Review of the Literature and Best Practice.* Urban Research Program Issues Paper 11. Brisbane: Griffith University.

Byrne, J., N. Sipe, and G. Searle. 2010. 'Green Around the Gills? The Challenge of Density for Urban Green-Space Planning in SEQ.' *Australian Planner* 47(3): 162–77. doi.org/10.1080/07293682.2010.508204.

Carrus, G., M. Scopelliti, R. Lafortezza, G. Colangelo, F. Ferrini, F. Salbitano, M. Agrimi, L. Portoghesi, P. Semenzato, and G. Sanesi. 2015. 'Go Greener, Feel Better? The Positive Effects of Biodiversity on the Well-Being of Individuals Visiting Urban and Peri-Urban Green Areas.' *Landscape and Urban Planning* 134: 221–28. doi.org/10.1016/j.landurbplan.2014.10.022.

Chiesura, A. 2004. 'The Role of Urban Parks for the Sustainable City.' *Landscape and Urban Planning* 68: 129–38. doi.org/10.1016/j.landurbplan.2003.08.003.

Congress for the New Urbanism (CNU). 2016. *The Charter of the New Urbanism.* Washington, DC: CNU. Available from: www.cnu.org/who-we-are/charter-new-urbanism.

Crompton, J.L. 2005. 'The Impact of Parks on Property Values: Empirical Evidence from the Past Two Decades in the United States.' *Managing Leisure* 10(4): 203–18. doi.org/10.1080/13606710500348060.

Curtis, C. 2012. 'Transitioning to Transit-Oriented Development: The Case of Perth, Western Australia.' *Urban Policy and Research* 30(3): 275–92. doi.org/10.1080/08111146.2012.665364.

Dadvand, P., M.J. Nieuwenhuijsen, M. Esnaola, J. Forns, X. Basagaña, M. Alvarez-Pedrerol, I. Rivas, M. López-Vicente, M. De Castro Pascual, J. Su, M. Jerrett, X. Querol, and J. Sunyer 2015. 'Green Spaces and Cognitive Development in Primary Schoolchildren.' *Proceedings of the National Academy of Sciences* 112(26): 7937–42. doi.org/10.1073/pnas.1503402112.

Dallimer, M., K.N. Irvine, A.M.J. Skinner, Z.G. Davies, J.R. Rouquette, L.L. Maltby, P.H. Warren, P.R. Armsworth, and K.J. Gaston. 2012. 'Biodiversity and the Feel-Good Factor: Understanding Associations between Self-Reported Human Well-Being and Species Richness.' *Bioscience* 62(1): 47–55. doi.org/10.1525/bio.2012.62.1.9.

de Vries, S., S.M.E. van Dillen, P.P. Groenewegen, and P. Spreeuwenberg. 2013. 'Streetscape Greenery and Health: Stress, Social Cohesion and Physical Activity as Mediators.' *Social Science and Medicine* 94: 26–33. doi.org/10.1016/j.socscimed.2013.06.030.

Dodson, J., and N. Sipe. 2008. *Unsettling Suburbia: The New Landscape of Oil and Mortgage Vulnerability in Australian Cities.* Urban Research Program Research Paper No. 17. Brisbane: Griffith University. Available from: griffith.rl.talis.com/items/04D0CDA5-689F-BEFE-788B-50DB1149C818.html.

Elliot, R. 2017. 'Australia's Misplaced War on the Australian Dream.' In *Infinite Suburbia*, edited by A. Berger, J. Kotkin, and C. Guzman, 104–13. Cambridge, MA: MIT Press.

Ewing, R., T. Schmid, R. Killingsworth, A. Zlot, and S. Raudenbush. 2003. 'Relationship between Urban Sprawl and Physical Activity, Obesity, and Morbidity.' *American Journal of Health Promotion* 18(1): 47–57. doi.org/10.4278/0890-1171-18.1.47.

Fan, Y., K.V. Das, and Q. Chen. 2011. 'Neighborhood Green, Social Support, Physical Activity, and Stress: Assessing the Cumulative Impact.' *Health & Place* 17(6): 1202–11. doi.org/10.1016/j.healthplace.2011.08.008.

Farrelly, E. 2021. *Killing Sydney: The Fight for a City's Soul.* Sydney: Picador.

Fishman, R. 1982. *Urban Utopias in the Twentieth Century: Ebenezer Howard, Frank Lloyd Wright, and Le Corbusier.* Cambridge, MA: MIT Press.

Forster, C. 2006. 'The Challenge of Change: Australian Cities and Urban Planning in the New Millennium.' *Geographical Research* 44(2): 173–82. doi.org/10.1111/j.1745-5871.2006.00374.x.

Francis, J., L.J. Wood, M. Knuiman, and B. Giles-Corti. 2012. 'Quality or Quantity? Exploring the Relationship between Public Open Space Attributes and Mental Health in Perth, Western Australia.' *Social Science & Medicine* 74(10): 1570–77. doi.org/10.1016/j.socscimed.2012.01.032.

Fuller, R.A., K.N. Irvine, P. Devine-Wright, P.H. Warren, and K.J. Gaston. 2007. 'Psychological Benefits of Green-Space Increase with Biodiversity.' *Biology Letters* 3(4): 390–94. doi.org/10.1098/rsbl.2007.0149.

Giles-Corti, B., M.H. Broomhall, M. Knuiman, C. Collins, K. Douglas, K. Ng, A. Lange, and R.J. Donovan. 2005. 'Increasing Walking: How Important is Distance To, Attractiveness, and Size of Public Open Space?' *American Journal of Preventive Medicine* 28(2)[Supp. 2]: 169–76. doi.org/10.1016/j.amepre.2004.10.018.

Giles-Corti, B., K. Ryan, and S. Foster. 2012. *Increasing Density in Australia: Maximising the Health Benefits and Minimising the Harm.* Melbourne: National Heart Foundation of Australia. Available from: www.heartfoundation.org.au/getmedia/91efe665-707f-4be1-839f-07461b79d05d/Increasing-density-in-Australia-Evidence-Review-2012.pdf.

Gleeson, B. 2008. 'Waking from the Dream: Towards Urban Resilience in the Face of Sudden Threat.' *Urban Studies* 45(13): 2653–68. doi.org/10.1177/0042098008098198.

Gleeson, B., J. Dodson, and M. Spiller. 2010. *Metropolitan Governance for the Australian City: The Case for Reform.* Urban Research Program Issues Paper 12. Brisbane: Griffith University.

Goodman, R. 2017. 'Melbourne: Growing Pains for the Liveable City.' In *Planning Metropolitan Australia*, edited by S. Hamnett and R. Freestone, 59–83. London: Routledge. doi.org/10.4324/9781315281377-3.

Goodman, R., and S. Moloney. 2004. 'Activity Centre Planning in Melbourne Revisited.' *Australian Planner* 41(2): 47–54. doi.org/10.1080/07293682.2004. 9982353.

Gordon, D.L.A. 2016. 'Is Australia a Suburban Nation?' *Blogged Environment*, 30 June. Available from: www.alexandrinepress.co.uk/blogged-environment/ australia-suburban-nation.

Gray, R., B. Gleeson, and M. Burke. 2010. 'Urban Consolidation, Household Greenhouse Emissions and the Role of Planning.' *Urban Policy and Research* 28(3): 335–46. doi.org/10.1080/08111146.2010.490618.

Haaland, C., and C.K. van den Bosch. 2015. 'Challenges and Strategies for Urban Green-Space Planning in Cities Undergoing Densification: A Review.' *Urban Forestry & Urban Greening* 14(4): 760–71. doi.org/10.1016/j.ufug.2015.07.009.

Hagan, S. 2017. 'Metabolic Suburbs or the Virtue of Low Densities.' In *Infinite Suburbia*, edited by A. Berger, J. Kotkin, and C. Guzman, 468–77. Cambridge, MA: MIT Press.

Hartig, T., R. Mitchell, S. de Vries, and H. Frumkin. 2014. 'Nature and Health.' *Annual Review of Public Health* 35: 207–28. doi.org/10.1146/annurev-publ health-032013-182443.

Hooper, P., S. Foster, N. Edwards, G. Turrell, N. Burton, B. Giles-Corti, and W.J. Brown. 2020. 'Positive HABITATS for Physical Activity: Examining Use of Parks and Its Contribution to Physical Activity Levels in Mid-to Older-Aged Adults.' *Health & Place* 63: 102308. doi.org/10.1016/j.healthplace.2020.102308.

Ibraeva, A., G.H. de A. Correia, C. Silva, and A.P. Antunes. 2020. 'Transit-Oriented Development: A Review of Research Achievements and Challenges.' *Transportation Research Part A: Policy and Practice* 132(C): 110–30. doi.org/ 10.1016/j.tra.2019.10.018.

Jabareen, Y.R. 2006. 'Sustainable Urban Forms: Their Typologies, Models, and Concepts.' *Journal of Planning Education and Research* 26(1): 38–52. doi.org/ 10.1177/0739456X05285119.

Kaźmierczak, A. 2013. 'The Contribution of Local Parks to Neighbourhood Social Ties.' *Landscape and Urban Planning* 109: 31–44. doi.org/10.1016/j.landurb plan.2012.05.007.

Kelly, J.-F., and P. Donegan. 2015. *City Limits: Why Australian Cities Are Broken and How We Can Fix Them*. Melbourne: Melbourne University Press.

Lachowycz, K., and A.P. Jones. 2011. 'Green-Space and Obesity: A Systematic Review of the Evidence.' *Obesity Reviews* 12(5): e183–89. doi.org/10.1111/ j.1467-789X.2010.00827.x.

Lachowycz, K., and A.P. Jones. 2013. 'Towards a Better Understanding of the Relationship between Green-Space and Health: Development of a Theoretical Framework.' *Landscape and Urban Planning* 118: 62–69. doi.org/10.1016/ j.landurbplan.2012.10.012.

LaFarge, A. 2014. *On the High Line: Exploring America's Most Original Urban Park*. London: Thames & Hudson.

Larson, L.R., Z. Zhang, J.I. Oh, W. Beam, S.S. Ogletree, J.N. Bocarro, K.J. Lee, J. Casper, K.T. Stevenson, J.A. Hipp, L.E. Mullenbach, M. Carusona, and M. Wells. 2021. 'Urban Park Use during the COVID-19 Pandemic: Are Socially Vulnerable Communities Disproportionately Impacted?' *Frontiers in Sustainable Cities* 3: 710243. doi.org/10.3389/frsc.2021.710243.

Lee, A.C.K., H.C. Jordan, and J. Horsley. 2015a. 'Value of Urban Green Spaces in Promoting Healthy Living and Well-Being: Prospects for Planning.' *Risk Management and Healthcare Policy* 8: 131–37. doi.org/10.2147/RMHP.S61654.

Lee, K.E., K.J.H. Williams, L.D. Sargent, N.S.G. Williams, and K.A. Johnson. 2015b. '40-Second Green Roof Views Sustain Attention: The Role of Micro-Breaks in Attention Restoration.' *Journal of Environmental Psychology* 42: 182–89. doi.org/10.1016/j.jenvp.2015.04.003.

Lehmann, S. 2010. *The Principles of Green Urbanism: Transforming the City for Sustainability*. London: Earthscan.

Lewis, M.B. 1999. *Suburban Backlash: The Battle for the World's Most Liveable City*. Melbourne: Bloomings Books.

Marselle, M., K. Irvine, and S. Warber. 2013. 'Walking for Well-Being: Are Group Walks in Certain Types of Natural Environments Better for Well-Being Than Group Walks in Urban Environments?' *International Journal of Environmental Research and Public Health* 10(11): 5603–28. doi.org/10.3390/ijerph10115603.

Marselle, M., K.N. Irvine, A. Lorenzo-Arribas, and S.L. Warber. 2016. 'Does Perceived Restorativeness Mediate the Effects of Perceived Biodiversity and Perceived Naturalness on Emotional Well-Being Following Group Walks in Nature?' *Journal of Environmental Psychology* 46: 217–32. doi.org/10.1016/j.jenvp.2016.04.008.

Mell, I.C. 2009. 'Can Green Infrastructure Promote Urban Sustainability?' *Proceedings of the Institution of Civil Engineers: Engineering Sustainability* 162(1): 23–34. doi.org/10.1680/ensu.2009.162.1.23.

Miller, J.R. 2005. 'Biodiversity Conservation and the Extinction of Experience.' *Trends in Ecology and Evolution* 20(8): 430–34. doi.org/10.1016/j.tree.2005.05.013.

Miller, J.R., and R.J. Hobbs. 2002. 'Conservation Where People Live and Work.' *Conservation Biology* 16(2): 330–37. doi.org/10.1046/j.1523-1739.2002.00420.x.

Murphy, P. 2012. 'The Metropolis.' In *Planning Australia: An Overview of Urban and Regional Planning*, edited by S. Thompson and P. Maginn, 155–79. Melbourne: Cambridge University Press. doi.org/10.1017/CBO9781139197205.011.

Nechyba, T.J., and R.P. Walsh. 2004. 'Urban Sprawl.' *Journal of Economic Perspectives* 18(4): 177–200. doi.org/10.1257/0895330042632681.

Newton, P., S. Murray, R. Wakefield, C. Murphy, L.-A. Khor, and T. Morgan. 2011. *Towards a New Development Model for Housing Regeneration in Greyfield Residential Precincts*. Final Report No. 171, 28 July. Melbourne: AHURI. doi.org/10.1016/j.ufug.2009.06.003.

Nordh, H., T. Hartig, C.M. Hagerhall, and G. Fry. 2009. 'Components of Small Urban Parks That Predict the Possibility for Restoration.' *Urban Forestry & Urban Greening* 8(4): 225–35.

Organisation for Economic Co-operation and Development (OECD). 2012. *Compact City Policies: A Comparative Assessment*. OECD Green Growth Studies. Paris: OECD Publishing. doi.org/10.1787/9789264167865-en.

Palliwoda, J., I. Kowarik, and M. von der Lippe. 2017. 'Human–Biodiversity Interactions in Urban Parks: The Species Level Matters.' *Landscape and Urban Planning* 157: 394–406. doi.org/10.1016/j.landurbplan.2016.09.003.

Panduro, T.E., and K.L. Veie. 2013. 'Classification and Valuation of Urban Green Spaces: A Hedonic House Price Valuation.' *Landscape and Urban Planning* 120: 119–28. doi.org/10.1016/j.landurbplan.2013.08.009.

Parker, R.S., and P.N. Troy, eds. 1972. *The Politics of Urban Growth*. Canberra: ANU Press.

Pereira, G., H. Christian, S. Foster, B.J. Boruff, F. Bull, M. Knuiman, and B. Giles-Corti. 2013. 'The Association between Neighborhood Greenness and Weight Status: An Observational Study in Perth, Western Australia.' *Environmental Health* 12(1): 49. doi.org/10.1186/1476-069X-12-49.

Peschardt, K.K., and U.K. Stigsdotter. 2013. 'Associations between Park Characteristics and Perceived Restorativeness of Small Public Urban Green Spaces.' *Landscape and Urban Planning* 112: 26–39. doi.org/10.1016/j.landurbplan.2012.12.013.

Quednau, R. 2018. 'Why Walkable Streets Are More Economically Productive.' *Strong Towns*, [Brainerd, MN], 18 January. Available from: www.strongtowns.org/journal/2018/1/16/why-walkable-streets-are-more-economically-productive.

Radeloff, V.C., S.I. Stewart, T.J. Hawbaker, U. Gimmi, A.M. Pidgeon, C.H. Flather, R.B. Hammer, and D.P. Helmers. 2010. 'Housing Growth in and Near United States Protected Areas Limits Their Conservation Value.' *Proceedings of the National Academy of Sciences* 107(2): 940–45. doi.org/10.1073/pnas.0911131107.

Ryu, C., and Y. Kwon. 2016. 'How Do Mega Projects Alter the City to Be More Sustainable? Spatial Changes Following the Seoul Cheonggyecheon Restoration Project in South Korea.' *Sustainability* 8(11): 1178. Available from: www.mdpi.com/2071-1050/8/11/1178. doi.org/10.3390/su8111178.

Searle, G. 2011. 'Urban Consolidation and the Inadequacy of Local Open Space Provision in Sydney.' *Urban Policy and Research* 29(2): 201–8. doi.org/10.1080/08111146.2011.576650.

Seddon, G. 1994. 'The Australian Back Yard.' In *Australian Popular Culture*, edited by I. Craven, 22–35. Cambridge, UK: Cambridge University Press.

Seto, K.C., R.K. Kaufmann, and C.E. Woodcock. 2000. 'Landsat Reveals China's Farmland Reserves, But They're Vanishing Fast.' *Nature* 406(6792): 121. doi.org/10.1038/35018267.

Simpson, R. 2018. 'AILA: Starting with Landscape.' Presentation to Parliamentary Friendship Group for Better Cities, 181128. Available from: www.aila.org.au/common/Uploaded%20files/_AILA/Submission%20Library/181128_AILA_rod%20simpson_images_lores.pdf.

Sturm, R., and D.A. Cohen. 2004. 'Suburban Sprawl and Physical and Mental Health.' *Public Health* 118(7): 488–96. doi.org/10.1016/j.puhe.2004.02.007.

Syme, G., M. Fenton, and S. Coakes. 2001. 'Lot Size, Garden Satisfaction and Local Park and Wetland Visitation.' *Landscape and Urban Planning* 56: 161–70. doi.org/10.1016/S0169-2046(01)00179-7.

Troy, P., ed. 1995. *Australian Cities: Issues, Strategies and Policies for Urban Australia in the 1990s*. Melbourne: Cambridge University Press. doi.org/10.1017/CBO 9780511597183.

Troy, P. 1996. *The Perils of Urban Consolidation*. Sydney: The Federation Press.

Troy, P. 2004. 'Saving Our Cities with Suburbs.' In *Griffith Review: Dreams of Land*, edited by J. Schultz, 115–27. Brisbane: Griffith University.

Tyrväinen, L., A. Ojala, K. Korpela, T. Lanki, Y. Tsunetsugu, and T. Kagawa. 2014. 'The Influence of Urban Green Environments on Stress Relief Measures: A Field Experiment.' *Journal of Environmental Psychology* 38: 1–9. doi.org/10.1016/j.jenvp.2013.12.005.

Udell, T., M. Daley, B. Johnson, and R. Tolley. 2014. *Does Density Matter? The Role of Density in Creating Walkable Neighbourhoods*. Discussion Paper. Melbourne: National Heart Foundation of Australia. Available from: www.heartfoundation.org.au/getmedia/d0bd5c9f-e8fd-444e-8be5-00966ba902fc/Heart_Foundation __Does_density_matter.pdf.

van Dillen, S.M.E., S. de Vries, P.P. Groenewegen, and P. Spreeuwenberg. 2012. 'Green-Space in Urban Neighbourhoods and Residents' Health: Adding Quality to Quantity.' *Journal of Epidemiology and Community Health* 66(6): e8. doi.org/10.1136/jech.2009.104695.

Villanueva, K., H. Badland, P. Hooper, M.J. Koohsari, S. Mavoa, M. Davern, R. Roberts, S. Goldfeld, and B. Giles-Corti. 2015. 'Developing Indicators of Public Open Space to Promote Health and Well-Being in Communities.' *Applied Geography* 57: 112–19. doi.org/10.1016/j.apgeog.2014.12.003.

Weller, R. 2006. 'Global Theory, Local Practice.' *Kerb* (15): 66–71.

Yelenik, S.G., and J.M. Levine. 2011. 'The Role of Plant–Soil Feedbacks in Driving Native-Species Recovery.' *Ecology* 92(1): 66–74. doi.org/10.1890/10-0465.1.

Yu, Z., X. Guo, Y. Zeng, M. Koga, and H. Vejre. 2018. 'Variations in Land Surface Temperature and Cooling Efficiency of Green Space in Rapid Urbanization: The Case of Fuzhou City, China.' *Urban Forestry & Urban Greening* 29: 113–21. doi.org/10.1016/j.ufug.2017.11.008.

Zhao, Z., and R. Kaestner. 2010. 'Effects of Urban Sprawl on Obesity.' *Journal of Health Economics* 29(6): 779–87. doi.org/10.1016/j.jhealeco.2010.07.006.

Part 4:
Productivity and
infrastructure

13

Mobilising smart city infrastructure in the Australian context

Chris Pettit and Alessandra Buxton

Introduction

In a rapidly urbanising world, there is critical need for more evidenced-based decision-making to plan more liveable, productive, resilient, and sustainable cities. Recently we have witnessed the rise of digital disruption, smart cities, big data, data science, machine learning, artificial intelligence (AI), and much more. Such data and technology innovations offer possibilities to accelerate data-supported city solutions. Moreover, with the advent of open data, the Internet of Things, and co-design methodologies, we can begin to view and analyse our precincts and cities as living laboratories. These technology-inspired solutions promise pathways to a digital utopia but do such solutions result in better planned cities and communities? A recent survey by Daniel and Pettit (2021) of planners in Australia attempted to understand how they utilise data and technology, with the results indicating the current use of smart city technology in professional practice continues to be low.

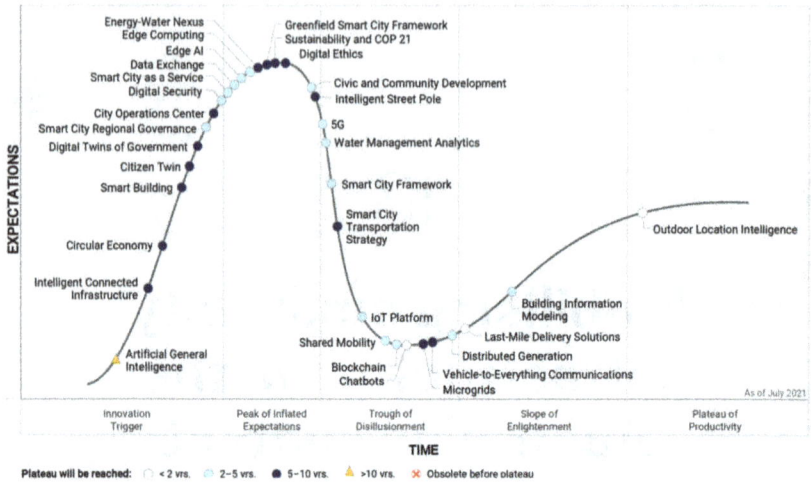

Figure 13.1 Gartner Hype Cycle: Smart city technology and solutions, July 2021

Source: © 2022 Gartner Inc. and/or its affiliates. All rights reserved.

The concept of smart cities has been driven by the information and communication technology (ICT) sector and has left in its wake opportunities and challenges for urban planners and policymakers to consider. In ICT circles, the Gartner Hype Cycle is widely used in understanding past, current, and emerging trends and disruptions in technology. This is done by looking at five key phases in a technology's life: the innovation trigger, the peak of inflated expectations, the trough of disillusionment, the scope of enlightenment, and the plateau of productivity (Gartner 2021). When we examine the Gartner Hype Cycle for 2021, we see that 'smart cities' and related terms feature significantly (Figure 13.1). Both 'smart city framework' and 'smart city transportation strategy' have peaked and are now in the trough of disillusionment. However, 'smart city as a service' (SCaaS) and 'smart buildings' are within the innovation cycle. The concept of SCaaS embraces the idea of open data platforms/portals, which are discussed later in this chapter.

While we live in a rapidly urbanising world, that world is also rapidly digitising. The smart city concept is synonymous with big data, digitisation, and digital disruption. This chapter will critically examine the role of data and technology-supported solutions to urban challenges, focusing predominantly on the Australian context. The chapter begins with a critique of smart cities from various perspectives followed by a brief international history. We then dive into the state of play in Australia, outlining key

250

government planning and policy initiatives. The chapter then looks at some data technology and methodologies for co-design that are considered fundamental building blocks for the smart city. We next focus on four key themes that are anchor tenants to Australia's *Smart Cities Plan*: open data, dashboards, planning support systems (PSS), and the concept of 'PlanTech'. The chapter concludes by reflecting on the smart city journey and how the wise use of data and technology can support urban policymaking and ultimately more liveable, sustainable, and prosperous cities.

The promise of smart cities

In examining the rise of the smart city in recent times it is important to start with a definition, so what is a smart city? The name itself implies a city that is 'not dumb' (Williams 2016); however, it has morphed into a catch-all term for city-related data and technology and, as such, has numerous interpretations and definitions. Some define smart cities as those that aim to enhance and inform innovative strategies to influence their socioeconomic, logistic, ecological, and competitive performances (Kourtit et al. 2012), while some focus on the technological and engineering aspects of cities before defining them as 'smart' (Allwinkle and Cruickshank 2011; Lazaroiu and Roscia 2012). Others consider smart cities as those that can be monitored and regulated in real time using advanced ICT, including data portals, sensors, and dashboards (Townsend 2013). Ultimately, defining what a smart city is depends on one's point of view. The overarching theme, however, is that the data and technology are encapsulated in the concept of a smart city, which also links to human and business capital with such technologies (Harrington 2016).

The term 'smart city' has a fictional air (Batty et al. 2012). Yet, this fiction has become a reality as technologies and cities have evolved in the past decade in how they access data and use ICT to be more effective, equitable, sustainable, and liveable (Nam and Pardo 2011). But what is it that makes these cities smart? Is it the innovative use of technology to monitor our cities or is it the application of this ever-shifting sphere of data to urban and social policy? As the concept of the smart city has grown in popularity in the policy sector, the focus has been on the role of ICT infrastructure in creating a smart city rather than on smart cities as drivers of social and urban growth (Caragliu et al. 2011). There is a divide among the academic, government, and business literature in respect to the ideological theories underpinning each smart city idea (Kitchin 2015). Academics are said to present their smart city ideals as pragmatic and non-ideological; businesses present their initiatives as city and citizen-oriented, albeit financially vested in deregulation and privatisation; whereas local and national governments appear to positively endorse the smart city as a path to socioeconomic progress and secure and sustainable cities (Kitchin 2015). Regardless of the diverging opinions in articulating the smart city, it is evident they represent a constantly shifting multidisciplinary field that is shaped by technological and urban development (Angelidou 2015) the objective of which is to provide improvement rather than stagnancy or regression.

A brief history of smart cities

In mapping the history of smart cities, it is best to begin with the concept's growth in popularity. In the 1980s, the notion of implementing technological networks within cities led to the conception of terms such as 'wired cities', 'cybercities', 'information cities', 'intelligent cities', and 'digital cities' (Angelidou 2015: 98). However, many of these expressions represented a distant future rather than a reality (Batty 2012). It was not until technology accelerated in the 1990s that these terms held relevance and ICT featured in visions of future cities (Angelidou 2015).

The hype of the smart city grew in the 1990s, with the Smart Cities World Forum in 1997 estimating there would be about 50,000 smart cities across the world by 2007 (Saunders and Baeck 2015). While this prediction was far from the reality, funding and interest in the smart city concept have only grown since, with increases in smart city initiatives, academic literature, conferences, and consultancies (Kitchin 2015). Amsterdam was arguably the first city to be labelled 'smart', with its 1994 creation of De Digitale Stad ('Digital City') to promote internet usage (GlobalData 2020). It was not until the mid-2000s, however, that significant research and investment into smart cities were seen. In the subsequent decade, smart cities started popping up around the world, with many countries launching pilot programs—most notably, India's '100 Smart Cities Mission' (GlobalData 2020). Interest in the smart city has continued to grow over the past decade, with Google Trends illustrating interest peaking around 2015 (Figure 13.2). A similar trend can be seen in the context of peer-reviewed texts. Smart cities entered the vernacular around 2003 and mentions rapidly grew between 2016 and 2021, peaking in 2019, not long after its popularity as a search term on Google (Figure 13.3).

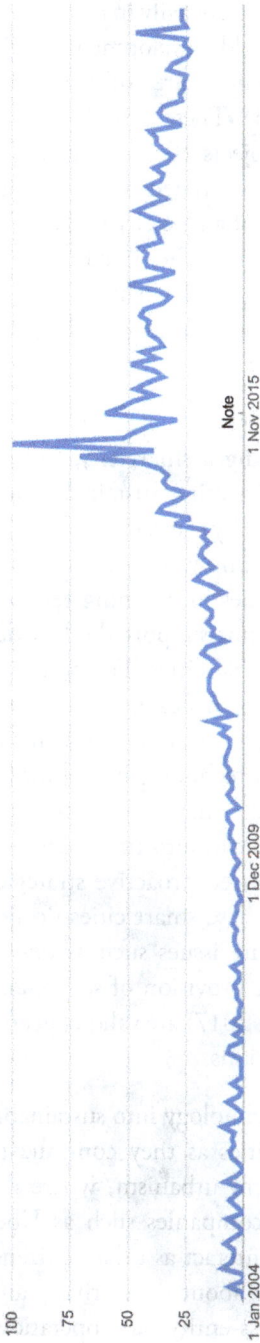

Figure 13.2 Google Trends: Smart cities, 2004–2021

Source: Google Trends (trends.google.com/).

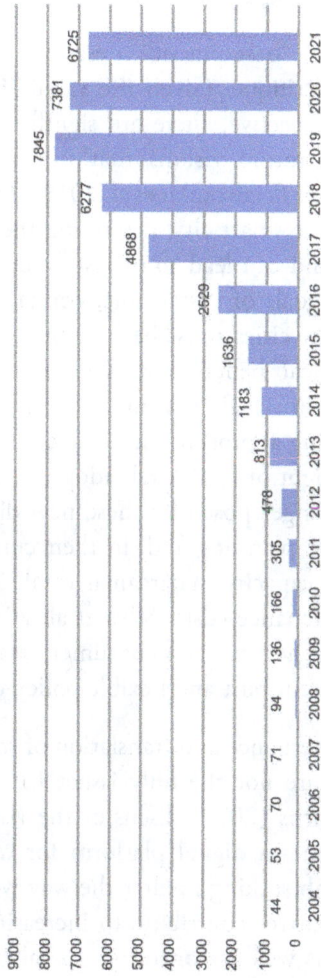

Figure 13.3 Publications on smart cities: Scopus search for the terms 'smart' and 'cities'

no. = 40,674 documents

Source: Scopus (www.scopus.com).

It is important to note that smart city pilot projects and countrywide initiatives are not without criticism. Cities such as Songdo in North Korea and Masdar in the United Arab Emirates have featured heavily in discussions about smart cities (Kitchin 2015). These greenfield developments, built from scratch through public–private partnerships, are decked with multitudes of digital infrastructure (Kitchin 2015). These early initiatives have been criticised in the media as 'failed' projects (Greenfield 2013) and 'Chernobyl-like' (Pettit and White 2018). It is argued that, from an aesthetic perspective, these cities lack the 'essence' of a true city and appear static and easily replicable (Keeton 2015). In contrast, other literature cites these developments as examples of best practice (Yigitcanlar et al. 2019) and empirical evidence showing the near-completed Songdo as popular with residents (Yang 2020).

Despite the 'best practice' description, these cities are subject to further necessary critique. Given the variability in defining a smart city, from a policy perspective, there are significant gaps in creating sustainable and attainable future visions that integrate with a city's existing planning mechanisms (Yigitcanlar et al. 2019). To articulate simply, by not adequately defining the smart city, describing these future cities in planning terms is difficult and can lead to infrastructure that does not support the broader planning goals of sustainable, equitable, and liveable cities. Furthermore, these smart cities must be humanised, rather than so heavily focused on technological benefits, so the urban citizen receives tangible benefits (Neubert 2021). By placing so much emphasis on technological solutions, a misleading approach can be taken in building the smart city, as planners can lose sight of the overall adoption of smart policies into the smart city. The challenges posed by these new digital cities need proactive strategies to improve planning and, in their current state, these smart cities do not have that capacity (Yigitcanlar et al. 2019). Future issues such as design and maintenance costs (Silva et al. 2018) and the provision of secure and sustainable networks for consumer data (Baig et al. 2017) are valid concerns that require robust and flexible policy-driven solutions.

Urban governance and translation of smart city technology into sustainable planning are not the only issues facing smart cities as they continue to evolve. Barns (2020) discusses the rise of platform urbanism, where the city becomes a digital platform for technology companies such as Uber and Airbnb seeking to alter the way we live and interact as urban citizens. Such initiatives contribute to increasing concerns about data privacy and security, as well as constituting challenges in cross-entity data operations

(Xiao et al. 2018). There are growing concerns about panoptic surveillance, corporate and technocratic governance, widening inequalities, social profiling, and much more (Kitchin 2015) that do not benefit the citizens of smart cities. Such issues point to a greater need to not only embed the practices of urban planning into smart cities, but also address policy concerns so these cities are truly being shaped for citizens rather than for private gain, efficiency, and productivity.

As such, the elements of transparency, accountability, citizen participation, and equity should be front and centre for the planners and policymakers involved in shaping the smart city dialogue.

Smart cities in Australia

While Australia has not been a leader in smart cities, there have been initiatives from both an investment and a policy perspective to make major and regional cities smarter. In 2016, the federal government announced its *Smart Cities Plan* to prioritise projects that met economic and social objectives such as affordable housing, healthy environments, accessibility, and jobs, as well as driving smarter city policies (PM&C 2016). In this plan, the government pledged to invest $50 million in both public and private smart city projects (PM&C 2016).

From this $50 million, 82 smart city projects around Australia have been funded, 62 of which are complete (Australian Government 2021). Analysis of these projects, generated through a word cloud, found the most common descriptive terms were 'data', 'community', 'technology', 'council', 'sensor', and 'smart technology' (Figure 13.4). Notably missing from this search were terms such as 'governance', 'policy', 'planning', and 'sustainability' that would imply a relationship between these projects and urban planning. However, we identify the prevalence of (1) open data and smart technology. The latter encapsulates technology including (2) city dashboards and digital planning tools, also known as (3) planning support systems. These three themes are further critiqued later in this chapter.

It is clear from this basic search that existing smart city projects have focused their energy on being technologically savvy but have not provided clear evidence of applying smart city objectives to urban planning and local and state policy. While ours was only an elementary search, the early findings demonstrate a disconnect between the smart city and sustainable urban planning and policymaking.

Figure 13.4 Word cloud of all plans funded by the 2016 Smart City Plan
Source: Created by authors.

State governments have implemented smart city initiatives, such as the NSW Department of Planning, Industry and Environment's 2020 Smart Places Strategy, which has a $45 million associated accelerator fund, and a $656 million scheme focusing on smart technologies in regional Victoria (Booth 2020). New South Wales also has its own open data strategy. While other states and territories do not have smart city initiatives, all Australian capital cities have some sort of smart city project either completed or under development. These have been driven predominantly by local councils in partnership with institutions, organisations, or private investors (Australian Government 2020). Prime examples of these include the Greater Sydney Commission's '30-minute city', the City of Sydney's Digital City, the Smart Connected Brisbane Network, 'Switching on Darwin', Melbourne's smart litter and free wi-fi projects, and Adelaide's multiple smart city initiatives. Smart projects are not limited to major cities and there are important initiatives in regional Australia such as in Byron Bay, Newcastle, and Wollongong in New South Wales, and Townsville and Ipswich in Queensland.

Many of the projects would not be attainable without the involvement of peak industry and professional bodies such as the Smart Cities Council Australia and New Zealand, Australian Smart Communities Association, and the Planning Institute of Australia (PIA). Each of these organisations has curated research and dialogue to provide invaluable insight for governments and planners to assist with a smart city agenda and digitally connected communities. The cooperation between organisations such as these is critical as they connect a range of leading consultancy firms and experts who can better prepare planners and inform policy on the challenges of smart cities and how digital technology can be used to inform smarter and more sustainable cities.

Responses to the Covid-19 pandemic highlighted that data and technology are increasingly important to sustain a smart city and connected communities. Whether it be cloud computing for running analytics, city models, or simulations, dashboards for reporting on Covid-19 incidents (Johns Hopkins University & Medicine 2021), or simply video-conferencing facilities enabling people to connect to work, study, and play, technology permeates every aspect of Australians' lives. With isolation and general 'connectedness' affected so highly, there are unique opportunities for smart technology and urban planning to bring communities together both physically and virtually. Projects such as the 20-Minute Neighbourhood in Melbourne (Department of Planning and Transport 2021) and the 15-minute neighbourhood in Paris (Yeung 2021) are increasingly relevant in the era of Covid-19 as local mobility is becoming more of a focus and necessity (Praharaj et al. 2020). As planners focus on the future of our cities, it is important to factor in the changing world in which we now live and the role smart urban planning can play to facilitate more connected communities.

Smart city data and technology

In this section, we introduce some of the key data and technology innovations associated with the rise of the smart city, focusing on evidence-based digital tools including open data, dashboards, and PSS as key areas where Australia has focused innovation and adoption of smart technology.

Open data

In 2017, *The Economist* reported that data were the new oil of our age. In the context of smart cities, data fuel innovation through the digital economy. Data are also the fuel that powers spatial analysis, machine learning, and other such techniques enabling urban analysts to form deeper understandings of the form and function of cities. Data and subsequent analytics shared openly can support more transparent government decision-making. Since the beginning of the millennium, we have witnessed the global explosion of open data. The Open Data Barometer is one index that measures the level of data openness across the world. Interestingly, the barometer reports Australia as the third-highest ranking country in open data maturity, behind only Canada and the United Kingdom, and ahead of the United States (World Wide Web Foundation 2018). Each chapter of a recent book, *Open Cities | Open Data* (Hawken et al. 2020), delves into the possibilities of a greater understanding of our built environment, enabled through the modelling and visualisation of open data.

Over the past decade, we have seen the creation of the Australian Urban Research Infrastructure Network, which provides urban researchers access to more than 3,000 datasets to support data-driven investigations of housing, mobility, health, and other urban issues (Sinnott et al. 2014; Pettit et al. 2017). Similarly, the National Map (available from: nationalmap.gov.au/) provides open access to a growing array of digital datasets and city open data portals, both in academia and in local government—see, for example, RMIT's Australian Urban Observatory (available from: auo.org.au/about/), City Data at the University of New South Wales (available from: citydata. be.unsw.edu.au/), and the open data portals of the City of Melbourne (available from: data.melbourne.vic.gov.au/) and Brisbane City Council (available from: www.data.brisbane.qld.gov.au/). All these data are powering a new generation of digital planning tools, including dashboards and PSS, as outlined below. However, while a significant number of city databases are opening to support evidenced-based planning and policymaking, there is much work to be done in ensuring databases are complete, accurate, and discoverable. The Australian Research Data Commons has established the FAIR Data principles to assist data custodians to better manage their data assets (available from: ardc.edu.au/resources/working-with-data/fair-data/). The four key principles are: findable, accessible, interoperable, and reusable (FAIR).

City dashboards

With a growing array of open and big data being created as a key ingredient of the smart city, we have seen the emergence of dashboards. The dashboard metaphor is sourced from the car dashboard, which essentially provides the driver with real-time information to make decisions as they navigate their journey. Smart city dashboards have been defined as 'graphic user interfaces which comprise a combination of information and geographical visualization methods for creating metrics, benchmarks, and indicators to assist in monitoring and decision-making' (Pettit and Leao 2018: 1). Two notable examples are the London Dashboard (Gray et al. 2016) and the City of Sydney's dashboard (Pettit et al. 2017).

In the context of city planning, dashboards have been created to support the transparency of decision-making. For example, the Greater Cities Commission has a dashboard for reporting on how Sydney is performing against a set of key directions, including metrics on housing, jobs, efficiency, and resilience (available from: www.greater.sydney/dashboard). However, the challenge with such a dashboard is understanding for whom it is designed. Who is using this dashboard to make planning and policy decisions, or is this just for government transparency and accountability? The purpose of such dashboards must be made very clear, and need human-centred designs for their intended users, be they residents, planners, or policymakers (Lock et al. 2019). There are other challenges for such dashboards in the provision of real-time or near real-time data to support government decision-making. The Covid-19 pandemic underscored the need for up-to-date data to support evidenced-based planning and decision-making. The Australia-wide Covid-19 Property Market Dashboard provides an example of a real-time dashboard bringing together information from a range of sources to provide a comprehensive understanding of the impact of the pandemic on the Australian property market (City Futures Research Centre 2022).

Planning support systems

Digital planning tools to support both operational and strategic planning are commonly referred to as PSS. There is a wide body of literature on PSS that pre-dates and integrates with smart city discourse (Geertman et al. 2017, 2019, 2021). With the emergence of smart cities and the advent of more openly available data, PSS are becoming more targeted to support urban planning and policymaking. Examples of PSS tools applied in Australia include What-If, Envision, CommuntiyViz, and more recently, the RAISE Toolkit (Leao et al. 2021; Pettit et al. 2018, 2020). The RAISE Toolkit has been developed to support planners and policymakers to explore value-uplift scenarios for new train stations (Pettit et al. 2020). The toolkit enables the user to drag and drop a new train station, calculate the value uplift associated with this new infrastructure, then rezone the adjacent land, and calculate further value uplift. Value capture is a key policy objective in Australia's *Smart Cities Plan* (PM&C 2016) and such evidence-based digital planning tools offer much promise. However, there remain challenges for wide adoption of such tools as the best way to capture property value uplift is not widely agreed across government and the processes of determining new transport infrastructure and rezoning are highly complex and is often political.

While much work has been done on data modelling and visualisation, 'planning support theatres' have appeared to bring together key actors to access smart city toolkits. However, such facilities have typically not been built to support strategic or collaborative planning endeavours. More recently, we have seen the emergence of technology-supported spaces dedicated to urban planning and design activities. The iHub Facility at Swinburne University connects several similar facilities, at Monash University, Curtin University, the University of Queensland, and the University of New South Wales. The City Analytics Lab at the University of New South Wales serves both as a node to the iHub Facility and a standalone planning support theatre where participants can interact with an array of dashboards and digital planning tools via frameworks such as geodesign to envision future cities and support urban policymaking (Pettit et al. 2019). Punt et al. (2020) report on the strengths and weaknesses of planning support theatres, highlighting the promise of such physical spaces for bringing together different stakeholders assisted by digital tools to explore different planning scenarios and policy options. Globally, we see a trend towards such installations enabling urban policymaking supported by geodesign, co-design, and co-production methodologies.

The emergence of PlanTech

Smart cities have emerged primarily through a strong technology push from the ICT sector with the likes of IBM, Cisco, and other multinational corporations driving the agenda. However, the planning profession has recently started to think critically about the opportunities for data and technology with the emergence of PlanTech. With similar ambitions to PSS, PlanTech refers to the latest wave of technology and its specific application to supporting urban planning tasks. However, unlike PSS, which have been driven by academics, PlanTech is being championed by the planning profession. The Planning Institute of Australia has set up a PlanTech National Working Group and in July 2021 launched 10 guiding principles for PlanTech (PIA 2021):

1. Planners must be prepared for wide-reaching change in their day-to-day work.

2. Planners must be central to the design of digital planning infrastructure.

3. Digital planning infrastructure must be public infrastructure built with open technology.

4. Ambitious programs can be implemented to improve social and environmental outcomes.

5. Outcomes for communities and places must be considered alongside the efficiency of approval processes in the development of digital planning systems.

6. Ethics, accountability, and transparency must be built into digital decision systems.

7. Digital planning applications should be developed in a human-centric way.

8. Communication of planning content and processes to non-planners should be reimagined.

9. Collaboration should be prioritised in the development of underlying digital planning infrastructure.

10. A culture of innovation and sharing should be promoted.

The emergence of PlanTech is a global phenomenon, with planning institutes in Aotearoa New Zealand, the United Kingdom, the United States, and others embracing this agenda—one that is being driven by planners for planners. However, a recurring challenge identified by planning institutes and by the Academy of the Social Sciences in Australia (Hatherley et al. 2022) pertains to workforce issues associated with levels of 'digital literacy'. Planners and urban policymakers must know how to properly utilise data infrastructure and big data to ensure evidenced-based decision-making and social systems thinking occur in shaping our future cities.

Conclusion

In this chapter, we have discussed the rise of the smart city and what is means for city planning and policymaking in Australia. There are both opportunities and challenges surfacing through the data and technological dimensions of the smart city concept. Much of what has transpired in Australia around smart cities, as funded through the federal government's

Smart Cities and Suburbs Program, has been focused on technologically enabled demonstrators centred on the efficiency of how cities are managed, rather than how they are strategically planned and governed.

In the context of the federal *Smart Cities Plan* (PM&C 2016), we have focused on four areas to illustrate what has been undertaken in Australia, including a significant move to open data, the creation of city dashboards, the maturing of digital planning tools, and the emergence of the PlanTech movement, which offers much promise in putting planners in the driver's seat in determining the future of data and technology solutions.

In conclusion, it is worthwhile revisiting the Gartner Hype Cycle (Figure 13.1), which identifies smart city as a service nearing the peak of the innovation cycle. Open data platforms, as discussed in this chapter, are a key element of SCaaS. Worth noting in the hype cycle is the emergence of smart-city regional governance as a trigger for innovation. The term 'smart urban governance'—the movement away from technology-driven governance, which is often seen in smart cities—has also recently entered the vernacular (Jiang et al. 2020). Alongside PlanTech, it offers a promising alternative to the technocratic vision of smart cities to help bridge the implementation gap in the adoption of smart technology toolkits in planning practice and policymaking. The goal, however, is how data and technology can be better harnessed to assist in planning more liveable, equitable, and inclusive Australian cities.

References

Allwinkle, S., and P. Cruickshank. 2011. 'Creating Smart-er Cities: An Overview.' *Journal of Urban Technology* 18(2): 1–16. doi.org/10.1080/10630732.2011.60 1103.

Angelidou, M. 2015. 'Smart Cities: A Conjuncture of Four Forces.' *Cities* 47: 95–106. doi.org/10.1016/j.cities.2015.05.004.

Australian Government. 2020. *Smart Cities and Suburbs Program.* Canberra: Commonwealth of Australia. Available from: business.gov.au/grants-and-programs/smart-cities-and-suburbs-program#:~:text=The%20Smart%20Cities %20and%20Suburbs,based%20solutions%20to%20urban%20challenges.

Australian Government. 2021. *Smart Collaboration Platform.* Canberra: Commonwealth of Australia. Accessed from: www.infrastructure.gov.au/cities/smart-cities/collaboration-platform/ [page discontinued].

Baig, Z.A., P. Szewczyk, C. Valli, P. Rabadia, P. Hannay, M. Chernyshev, M. Johnstone, P. Kerai, A. Ibrahim, K. Sansurooah, N. Syed, and M. Peacock. 2017. 'Future Challenges for Smart Cities: Cyber-Security and Digital Forensics.' *Digital Investigation* 22: 3–13. doi.org/10.1016/j.diin.2017.06.015.

Barns, S. 2020. *Platform Urbanism: Negotiating Platform Ecosystems in Connected Cities*. Singapore: Palgrave Macmillan. doi.org/10.1007/978-981-32-9725-8.

Batty, M. 2012. 'Smart Cities, Big Data.' *Environment and Planning B: Planning and Design* 39(2): 191–93. doi.org/10.1068/b3902ed.

Batty, M., K.W. Axhausen, F. Giannotti, A. Pozdnoukhov, A. Bazzani, M. Wachowicz, G. Ouzounis, and Y. Portugali. 2012. 'Smart Cities of the Future.' *The European Physical Journal Special Topics* 214(1): 481–518. doi.org/10.1140/epjst/e2012-01703-3.

Booth, E. 2020. 'Victoria Invests in Regional Digital Infrastructure.' *Council*, [Melbourne], 1 December. Available from: councilmagazine.com.au/victoria-invests-in-regional-digital-infrastructure/.

Caragliu, A., C. Del Bo, and P. Nijkamp. 2011. 'Smart Cities in Europe.' *Journal of Urban Technology* 18(2): 65–82. doi.org/10.1080/10630732.2011.601117.

City Futures Research Centre. 2022. *Value Australia: COVID-19 Australian Property Market Dashboard*. Sydney: City Futures Research Centre, University of New South Wales. Available from: frontiersi.com.au/value-australia/.

Daniel, C., and C. Pettit. 2021. 'Digital Disruption and Planning: Use of Data and Digital Technology by Professional Planners, and Perceptions of Change to Planning Work.' *Australian Planner* 57(1): 50–64. doi.org/10.1080/07293682.2021.1920995.

Department of Planning and Transport. 2021. '20-Minute Neighbourhoods.' In *Plan Melbourne 2017–2050*. Melbourne: Victorian Government. Available from: www.planning.vic.gov.au/guides-and-resources/strategies-and-initiatives/20-minute-neighbourhoods.

Department of the Prime Minister and Cabinet (PM&C). 2016. *Smart Cities Plan*. Canberra: Commonwealth of Australia. Available from: ssroc.nsw.gov.au/wp-content/uploads/2016/06/Smart_Cities_Plan.pdf.

The Economist. 2017. 'The World's Most Valuable Resource Is No Longer Oil, But Data.' *The Economist*, [London], 6 May. Available from: www.economist.com/leaders/2017/05/06/the-worlds-most-valuable-resource-is-no-longer-oil-but-data.

Gartner. 2021. *Hype Cycle for Smart City Technologies and Solutions, 2021*. Gartner Research, 21 July. Stamford, CT: Gartner. Available from www.gartner.com/en/documents/4003854-hype-cycle-for-smart-city-technologies-and-solutions-2021.

Geertman, S., A. Allan, C. Pettit, and J. Stillwell. 2017. *Planning Support Science for Smarter Urban Futures*. Cham, Switzerland: Springer International Publishing. doi.org/10.1007/978-3-319-57819-4.

Geertman, S., A. Allan, Q. Zhan, and C. Pettit. 2019. *Computational Urban Planning and Management for Smart Cities*. Cham, Switzerland: Springer International Publishing. doi.org/10.1007/978-3-030-19424-6.

Geertman, S.C.M., C. Pettit, R. Goodspeed, and A. Staffans. 2021. *Urban Informatics and Future Cities*. The Urban Book Series 1. Cham, Switzerland: Springer International Publishing. doi.org/10.1007/978-3-030-76059-5.

GlobalData. 2020. 'History of Smart Cities: Timeline. GlobalData Thematic Research.' *Verdict*, [London], 28 February. Available from: www.verdict.co.uk/smart-cities-timeline/.

Gray, S., O. O'Brien, and S. Hügel. 2016. 'Collecting and Visualizing Real-Time Urban Data Through City Dashboards.' *Built Environment* 42(3): 498–509. doi.org/10.2148/benv.42.3.498.

Greater Cities Commission. 2021. 'PI 2: 30-Minute City.' In *The Pulse of Greater Sydney 2020*. Sydney: Greater Cities Commission. Available from: greatercities.au/strategic-planning/monitoring/pulse-2020.

Greenfield, A. 2013. *Against the Smart City (The City Is Here for You to Use. Book 1)*. London: Do Projects.

Harrington, A. 2016. 'What is a Smart City?' *The Fifth Estate*, [Sydney], 7 March. Available from: thefifthestate.com.au/columns/spinifex/what-is-a-smart-city/.

Hatherley, C., I. Ceron, and C. Jones. 2022. *Australia's Data-Enabled Research Future: The Social Sciences*. Canberra: Academy of the Social Sciences in Australia.

Hawken, S., H. Han, and C. Petti. 2020. *Open Cities | Open Data: Collaborative Cities in the Information Era*. Singapore: Palgrave Macmillan. doi.org/10.1007/978-981-13-6605-5.

Jiang, H., S. Geertman, and P. Witte. 2020. 'Smart Urban Governance: An Alternative to Technocratic "Smartness".' *GeoJournal* 9(4): 1–17. doi.org/10.1007/s10708-020-10326-w.

Johns Hopkins University & Medicine. 2021. *COVID-19 Dashboard by the Centre for Systems Science and Engineering (CSSE) at Johns Hopkins University.* Coronavirus Resource Centre. Baltimore, MD: Johns Hopkins University & Medicine. Available from: coronavirus.jhu.edu/map.html.

Keeton, R. 2015. 'When Smart Cities Are Stupid.' Rotterdam, Netherlands: International New Town Institute. Available from www.newtowninstitute.org/spip.php?article1078.

Kitchin, R. 2015. 'Making Sense of Smart Cities: Addressing Present Shortcomings.' *Cambridge Journal of Regions, Economy and Society* 8(1): 131–36. doi.org/10.1093/cjres/rsu027.

Kourtit, K., P. Nijkamp, and D. Arribas. 2012. 'Smart Cities in Perspective: A Comparative European Study by Means of Self-Organizing Maps.' *Innovation* 25(2): 229–46. doi.org/10.1080/13511610.2012.660330.

Lazaroiu, G.C., and M. Roscia. 2012. 'Definition Methodology for the Smart Cities Model.' *Energy* 47(1): 326–32. doi.org/10.1016/j.energy.2012.09.028.

Leao, S.Z., R. van den Nouwelant, V. Shi, H. Han, S. Praharaj, and C.J. Pettit. 2021. 'A Rapid Analytics Tool to Map the Effect of Rezoning on Property Values.' *Computers, Environment and Urban Systems* 86: 101572. doi.org/10.1016/j.compenvurbsys.2020.101572.

Lock, O., T. Bednarz, S.Z. Leao, and C. Pettit. 2019. 'A Review and Reframing of Participatory Urban Dashboards.' *City, Culture and Society* 20: 100294. doi.org/10.1016/j.ccs.2019.100294.

Nam, T., and T. Pardo. 2011. 'Conceptualizing Smart City with Dimensions of Technology, People, and Institutions.' *Proceedings of the 12th Annual International Digital Government Research Conference: Digital Government Innovation in Challenging Times, June 2011*, 282–91. doi.org/10.1145/2037556.2037602.

Neubert, H. 2021. 'Smart Cities Should Be Human Cities.' *Dialogue Issue 33*. San Francisco, CA: Gensler. Available from: www.gensler.com/publications/dialogue/33/smart-cities-should-be-human-cities.

Pettit, C., and S. Leao. 2018. 'Planning Smart, Healthy, and Accessible Cities.' *Shashwat* 4: 121–23.

Pettit, C.J., A. Bakelmuna, S.N. Lieskeb, S. Glackinc, K. Hargrovesd, G. Thomsond, H. Shearere, H. Diaf, and P. Newman. 2018. 'Planning Support Systems for Smart Cities.' *City, Culture and Society* 12: 13–24. doi.org/10.1016/j.ccs.2017.10.002.

Pettit, C.J., S. Hawken, C. Ticzon, S.Z. Leao, A.E. Afrooz, S.N. Lieske, T. Canfield, H. Ballal, and C. Steinitz. 2019. 'Breaking Down the Silos Through Geodesign: Envisioning Sydney's Urban Future.' *Environment and Planning B: Urban Analytics and City Science* 46(8): 1387–404. doi.org/10.1177/2399808318812887.

Pettit, C.J., S.N. Lieske, and M. Jamal. 2017. 'CityDash: Visualising a Changing City Using Open Data.' In *Planning Support Systems and Smart Cities, Lecture Notes in Geoinformation and Cartography*, edited by A. Geertman, J. Ferreira, jr, R. Goodspeed, and J. Stillwell, 337–53. Berlin: Springer. doi.org/10.1007/978-3-319-57819-4_19.

Pettit, C.J., Y. Shi, H. Han, M. Rittenbruch, M. Foth, S. Lieske, R. van den Nouwelant, P. Mitchell, S. Leao, B. Christensen, and M. Jamal. 2020. 'A New Toolkit for Land Value Analysis and Scenario Planning.' *Environment and Planning B: Urban Analytics and City Science* 47(8): 1490–507. doi.org/10.1177/2399808320924678.

Pettit, C.J., A. Tice, and B. Randolph. 2017. 'Using An Online Spatial Analytics Workbench for Understanding Housing Affordability in Sydney.' In *Seeing Cities through Big Data: Research, Methods and Applications in Urban Informatics*, edited by P. Thakuriah, N. Tilahun, and M. Zellner, 233–55. Cham, Switzerland: Springer International Publishing. doi.org/10.1007/978-3-319-40902-3_14.

Pettit, H., and C. White. 2018. 'A Glimpse into the Future? $39 Billion High-Tech Smart City in South Korea Turns into a "Chernobyl-Like Ghost Town" After Investment Dries Up.' *Daily Mail*, [London], 28 March. Available from: www.dailymail.co.uk/sciencetech/article-5553001/28-billion-project-dubbed-worlds-Smart-City-turned-Chernobyl-like-ghost-town.html.

Planning Institute of Australia (PIA). 2021. *PIA PlanTech Principles*. Canberra: PIA. Available from: www.planning.org.au/planningresourcesnew/plantech-pages/pia-plantech-principles.

Praharaj, S., D. King, C. Pettit, and E. Wentz. 2020. 'Using Aggregated Mobility Data to Measure the Effect of COVID-19 Policies on Mobility Changes in Sydney, London, Phoenix, and Pune.' *Findings*, 20 October. doi.org/10.32866/001c.17590.

Punt, E., S.C.M. Geertman, A.E. Afrooz, P.A. Witte, and C.J. Pettit. 2020. 'Life is a Scene and We Are the Actors: Assessing the Usefulness of Planning Support Theatres for Smart City Planning.' *Computers, Environment and Urban Systems* 82: 101485. doi.org/10.1016/j.compenvurbsys.2020.101485.

Saunders, T., and P. Baeck. 2015. *Rethinking Smart Cities from the Ground Up*. June. London: Nesta. Available from: media.nesta.org.uk/documents/rethinking_smart_cities_from_the_ground_up_2015.pdf.

Silva, B.N., M. Khan, and K. Han. 2018. 'Towards Sustainable Smart Cities: A Review of Trends, Architectures, Components, and Open Challenges in Smart Cities.' *Sustainable Cities and Society* 38: 697–713. doi.org/10.1016/j.scs.2018.01.053.

Sinnott, R.O., C. Bayliss, A. Bromage, G. Galang, G. Grazioli, P. Greenwood, A. Macaulay, L. Morandini, G. Nogoorani, M. Nino-Ruiz, M. Tomko, C. Pettit, M. Sarwar, R. Stimson, W. Voorsluys, and I. Widjaja. 2014. 'The Australia Urban Research Gateway.' *Concurrency and Computation: Practice and Experience* 27(2): 358–75. doi.org/10.1002/cpe.3282.

Townsend, A. 2013. *Smart Cities: Big Data, Civic Hackers, and the Quest for A New Utopia*. New York, NY: W.W. Norton.

Williams, T. 2016. 'Smart Cities Need Smart Governance: Discuss!' *The Fifth Estate*, [Sydney], 17 May. Available from: thefifthestate.com.au/columns/spinifex/smart-cities-need-smart-governance-discuss/.

World Wide Web Foundation. 2018. *The Open Data Barometer*. Washington, DC: World Wide Web Foundation. Available from: opendatabarometer.org/.

Xiao, Z., X. Fu, and R.S.M. Goh. 2018. 'Data Privacy: Preserving Automation Architecture for Industrial Data Exchange in Smart Cities.' *IEEE Transactions on Industrial Informatics* 14(6): 2780–91. doi.org/10.1109/TII.2017.2772826.

Yang, C. 2020. 'Historicizing the Smart Cities: Genealogy as a Method of Critique for Smart Urbanism.' *Telematics Informatics* 55: 101438. doi.org/10.1016/j.tele.2020.101438.

Yeung, P. 2021. 'How "15-Minute Cities" Will Change the Way We Socialise.' *Worklife*, [BBC], 5 January. Available from: www.bbc.com/worklife/article/20201214-how-15-minute-cities-will-change-the-way-we-socialise.

Yigitcanlar, T., H. Han, Md. Kamruzzaman, G. Ioppolo, and J. Sabatini-Marques. 2019. 'The Making of Smart Cities: Are Songdo, Masdar, Amsterdam, San Francisco and Brisbane the Best We Could Build?' *Land Use Policy* 88: 2–11. doi.org/10.1016/j.landusepol.2019.104187.

14

Funding urban infrastructure: What role for the Commonwealth Government?

Marcus Spiller[1]

Introduction

Notwithstanding its lack of a constitutional mandate in city and regional planning, the Commonwealth Government has sporadically intervened in urban infrastructure funding almost from the inception of the federation. In so doing, it has applied policy ideas ranging from the visionary to the farcical. Ideally, federal funding of state, territory, and local governments should be premised on mitigating vertical fiscal imbalances, advancing horizontal fiscal equalisation, and nudging these jurisdictions to make investment and program choices that align with national objectives. Subsidiarity should provide the touchstone principle for any such policy.

This chapter discusses why and how the Commonwealth Government could involve itself differently in the funding of infrastructure to support Australia's major cities. It begins with a brief account of the current arrangements for funding urban infrastructure across Australia's trilevel system of governance, using growth areas in metropolitan Melbourne as a case study. A proposed typology of urban infrastructure assets follows,

---

1   This chapter draws on material from a range of consultants' reports and independently produced publications from SGS Economics & Planning Pty Ltd. All sources are cited.

providing a framework for analysing roles for the federal, state and territory, and local governments in infrastructure provision based on subsidiarity principles. The discussion then moves to a critique of Commonwealth Government involvement in urban infrastructure funding, referencing these principles and the development of national urban policy since Federation. The paper concludes with some propositions for reform of Commonwealth policy.

Funding urban infrastructure: Melbourne's greenfield areas

Perhaps surprisingly, it is difficult to establish from the Australian literature the cost of providing urban infrastructure. Reported figures vary substantially depending on the scope and purpose of the studies in question.

Spiller and Forrest (2017) estimate that, depending on the infrastructure assets included, the Victorian State Government outlays about $50,000 for every new home in Melbourne's greenfield growth areas to supply arterial roads, schools, public transport links, healthcare facilities, and other regional-level infrastructure, as well as part-funding of local facilities like sport and recreation centres. At $50,000 per dwelling over 30 years, the state government can expect to invest $11 billion in present value terms to set up this infrastructure for growth areas. This investment excludes creation of trunk electricity, water supply, and sewerage infrastructure, which is now provided by private or government-owned businesses and funded mainly by recurrent charges. The $11 billion cost is partly offset by the government's Growth Area Infrastructure Charge (GAIC), which is levied on landowners when farmland is rezoned for housing development. The GAIC produces about $6,100 per dwelling; the remainder is paid by the general taxpayer.

Spiller and Forrest (2017) further estimate that on top of the state government's outlays, municipal councils in Melbourne's growth areas will deliver local infrastructure programs at the rate of about $38,000 per home, amounting to a present-value investment of $8 billion over 30 years. This investment covers mainly 'offsite' infrastructure for greenfield developers— that is, assets and facilities not typically built by the developer as part of the land subdivision process. Offsite infrastructure can include subarterial roads, community facilities, and open space 'embellishments' such as pavilions and public toilets.

These capital outlays on the part of growth area councils are in part defrayed via statutory Development Contribution Plans (DCPs) or Infrastructure Contribution Plans (ICPs) put together under the aegis of the Victorian Planning Authority. DCP/ICP levies currently vary between different growth areas, but average $23,000 per dwelling. The balance between these receipts and the cost to councils is funded through local rates and transfers from other spheres of government. About two-thirds of growth area council revenues, net of development contributions, come from rates.

The cost of several infrastructure items supporting growth areas is not included in the combined total of $88,000 per dwelling above. These include the value of onsite infrastructure, including local roads and pathways, local parks and built-in water-cycle management assets, as well as the cost of extending power, water, and telecommunications infrastructure.

Infrastructure Victoria (2019) estimates the total cost of infrastructure to support greenfield development in Melbourne to be between $126,000 and $259,000 per dwelling, excluding lot infrastructure and public open space. Differences in the cost of completing onsite civil works and drainage, which are strongly influenced by landform, soil conditions, and local infrastructure capacity, account for much of the variation in the total cost of infrastructure supply (Table 14.1).

Table 14.1 Estimated cost of supplying urban infrastructure for Melbourne's greenfield growth areas (A$)

	Low	High	Medium
Lot infrastructure	445,465	445,465	445,465
Transport	45,703	45,703	45,703
Civil works and drainage	24,643	106,651	50,463
Sewerage	6,332	23,232	10,983
Water supply	4,097	15,464	10,289
Electricity	7,470	21,220	9,665
Gas	2,780	3,430	3,105
Telecommunications	2,979	5,966	3,791
Community infrastructure	14,616	18,100	14,616
Emergency services	817	817	817
Health infrastructure	1,200	1,200	1,200
Education infrastructure	14,900	17,600	16,400
Public open space[ab]	5,000	5,000	5,000

[a] Includes englobo land value and housing construction cost.

[b] Author's estimates.

Source: Infrastructure Victoria (2019).

Table 14.2 provides an overview of current funding arrangements using the infrastructure categories applied by Infrastructure Victoria (2019). Assuming the cost of providing major roads is divided 40/40/20 between state taxes, development contributions, and local rates, and the cost of providing community infrastructure is shared 50/50 between development contributions and local rates, a broad funding mix can be discerned as follows:

- 30 per cent of the cost of providing infrastructure, other than lot infrastructure, in growth areas is funded through developers building roads, pathways, drains, etc. onsite and transferring these assets for free to councils
- 20 per cent from cash or in-kind development contributions for 'offsite' assets
- 20 per cent from recurrent user charges levied by utility companies on households after they have taken up occupancy of the new community
- 20 per cent from general state revenues
- 10 per cent from local rates.

This funding mix is the product of significant policy changes over the past five decades, not only in Victoria but also across the nation. Since the late 1960s, there has been a rebalancing of funding sources, first, to require developers to complete all onsite infrastructure before lots can be registered and sold, and second, to require developers to make cash or in-kind contributions to the provision of shared offsite infrastructure. 'Traditional' methods of paying for infrastructure, through taxes and recurrent user charges, now account for only about half the total funding task.

It is noteworthy that the federal government is not a baseload player in the funding of growth area infrastructure, leaving aside high-level tax-sharing agreements, such as the division among states and territories of goods and services tax (GST) receipts and other untied transfers.

The Commonwealth has sporadically injected itself into the infrastructure funding area over the decades, however, it has not been a consistent and reliable presence in this facet of urban policy, no doubt reflecting its lack of a constitutional mandate to be involved in such matters (Tomlinson and Spiller 2018).

Table 14.2 Principal funding sources by infrastructure type

Lot infrastructure	Wholly funded by developer
Transport	Major arterial roads are typically funded by the state government. The Growth Area Infrastructure Charge (GAIC), which is a betterment tax, provides a small offset.
	Other arterial roads are funded from development contributions (DCPs/ICPs) with top-ups from council funds. DCP/ICP charges are apportioned to development proponents based on share of usage.
Civil works and drainage	Typically built and transferred by the developer as part of the subdivision process.
Sewerage	Mainly funded from recurrent charges levied on households post occupancy of the development.
Water supply	Mainly funded from recurrent charges levied on households post occupancy of the development.
Electricity	Mainly funded from recurrent charges levied on households post occupancy of the development.
Gas	Mainly funded from recurrent charges levied on households post occupancy of the development.
Telecommunications	Mainly funded from recurrent charges levied on households post occupancy of the development.
Community infrastructure	Provided mainly by local government and funded via development contributions (DCPs/ICPs), local rates, state government transfers, and occasional Commonwealth Government transfers.
Emergency services	Provided and funded by state government through general tax revenue.
Health infrastructure	Provided and funded by state government through general tax revenue.
Education infrastructure	Provided and funded by state government through general tax revenue.
Public open space	Local and district parks funded mainly through DCPs/ICPs and similar mandated development contributions.

Source: Author's summary.

While the Commonwealth lacks a direct urban policy mandate, it is wont to get involved simply because it has acquired the fiscal muscle to do so. Moreover, how city growth is managed, including the funding of infrastructure, has major implications for national economic, social, and environmental outcomes for which the Commonwealth is held accountable.

The Commonwealth can and should be involved in urban infrastructure funding. The question is how it can make its best contribution. A good place to start is to appreciate that some infrastructure investments are of greater national consequence than others.

Not all infrastructure is equal

The typology of urban infrastructure projects that is embedded in official national guidelines for integrated transport and land-use planning (ATAP Steering Committee 2016) has three categories: strategic, structural, and follower infrastructure. Their characteristics, as set out in the Australian Transport Assessment and Planning guidelines, are as follows:

- *Strategic infrastructure:* Strategic or 'city-shaping' infrastructure is almost exclusively in the transport domain and is distinguished by its power to alter relative accessibility across the metropolis (for example, the Melbourne City Loop underground railway or Sydney's M7 Motorway). These investments drive where people live and where businesses locate. They create new agglomeration economies, boosting productivity (Spiller et al. 2012).

- *Structural infrastructure:* Structural or district infrastructure represents higher-order or trunk facilities, networks, and nodes (excluding strategic infrastructure) that form a region's urban framework. It includes arterial roads and district public transport connections. These items are distinguished by their subregional service catchments and relatively high cost.

- *Follower infrastructure:* Follower infrastructure includes services and facilities with localised service catchments. While vital to community wellbeing, business efficiency, and placemaking, local infrastructure neither shapes development patterns nor provides an overarching structure for settlement and industry development. It provides services into a suburb or neighbourhood once the area has been enabled by investment in higher-order infrastructure initiatives.

Neither structural nor follower infrastructure has a significant enough impact on relative accessibility to influence the shape of the city.

A fourth category of infrastructure could be warranted: 'national projects'. The primary justification for these investments would be facilitation of national trade and integration in line with the federation commitment made by the states and territories. Moreover, because they are premised on linking major Australian urban centres and economic hubs, they are likely to have settlement pattern–shaping potential. A fast train link between Melbourne and Sydney, for example, could profoundly redistribute urban growth along its corridor as well as in the two anchor metropolises.

Table 14.3 Funding principles by infrastructure category

Infrastructure type	Function	Funding principles
National infrastructure	National economic integration. Regional equalisation. (Potentially) shapes settlement patterns at the interregional level.	Funded from national tax pool, reflecting the national integration mandate of these investments.
Strategic infrastructure	Shapes metropolitan and intra-metropolitan settlement patterns in line with strategic plans. Services urban growth.	Funded from metropolitan/regional tax pool, recognising dispersed benefits of these investments. Significant funding via value capture also warranted, recognising the nexus between the success of these projects and the value of development rights awarded through the planning system.
Structural infrastructure	Services urban growth at the subregional level. Provides a basis for '20-minute' neighbourhoods.	Similar to strategic infrastructure.
Follower infrastructure	Services local urban growth. Provides for walkability.	Funded from user charges and development contributions, apportioned based on share of usage, to enable efficient price signalling and application of cost impact mitigation to manage unsequenced urban growth (Spiller et al. 2012).

Source: Author's summary.

Differences in function and reach evident across this now four-part typology of infrastructure point to some broad principles for an appropriate funding mix. Bearing in mind a wider discussion about the respective roles of the various spheres of governance in the federation based on the subsidiarity doctrine (see below), a conclusion that could be drawn from Table 14.3 is that the Commonwealth's role in funding infrastructure should diminish as one descends the various asset categories. One could also conclude that it is only in the first category that the Commonwealth is mandated and competent to make project choices. In all other categories, such decisions should be left to those spheres of government that are more competent, in the subsidiarity sense. In any case, federal government involvement in funding infrastructure should be clearly premised on national interest. Contemporary Commonwealth involvement in such matters is a far cry from this, with no less than Commonwealth ministers making direct choices about where structural and follower infrastructure projects should occur, including, latterly, commuter carparks and changing pavilions for sporting clubs.

Before addressing how this situation could be redressed, a review of the 'evolution' of the Commonwealth's role in urban infrastructure is useful.

Commonwealth Government involvement in urban infrastructure

The Commonwealth Government has a long history of involvement in infrastructure funding, but it is characterised by a stop–start nature and erratic shifts in policy emphasis (Table 14.4). The lack of a constitutional mandate to frame and direct Commonwealth activity in infrastructure funding is evident, with 'advances' in urban policy contingent on the vagaries of the electoral cycle. For example, the Turnbull Government's City Deals Program began with reasonably sound public policy foundations, broadly following the model established in the United Kingdom under which Westminster invests in additional infrastructure for a partner region (for example, Greater Manchester) with part of the investment returned via higher tax revenues generated by a more productive urban structure. Despite the program's ambition, relatively few City Deals have been struck over the past five years, with the possible exception of the western Sydney agreement, which is, arguably, premised on optimising national returns from the Commonwealth's stake in the second metropolitan airport; the 'national interest' rationale for other City Deals is not particularly evident. Some deals appear to have a narrow focus on specific projects, such as the Townsville stadium, which would not meet the criteria for 'city-shaping infrastructure' discussed above.

Arguably the most coherent and comprehensive view of the role of the Commonwealth in urban infrastructure was prosecuted by the Whitlam Government of 1972–75. However, in hindsight, its urban program looks like a historical aberration, with successive federal governments pursuing idiosyncratic, small-scale, and opportunistic initiatives focused on near-term political gain. Notwithstanding its strong intellectual underpinnings and laudable scope, even the Whitlam Government's urban agenda now looks ham-fisted. Precious little attention was paid to the subsidiarity principle as the Commonwealth often sought to bypass the states in fixing the problems of the cities. Failure to work within a federal constitutional framework could have put paid to the Commonwealth's ambitions even if the political turbulence of the time had not brought the early demise of the Whitlam Government.

Table 14.4 Selected events in the Commonwealth Government's involvement in infrastructure funding

Event, program, or policy initiative	Major expenditure target
Main Roads Development Act 1923 (Cwth)	Specific-purpose payments to state and territory governments for transport projects begin.
1933 establishment of Commonwealth Grants Commission	Expansion of specific-purpose payments to states and territories.
1972 establishment of Commonwealth Department of Urban and Regional Development (DURD)	Formation of DURD is part of the Whitlam Government's (1972–75) agenda to expand special-purpose assistance to the states and territories across several priority areas, including urban and regional planning and urban public transport. Initiatives of DURD include the Sewerage Backlog Program, the Area Improvement Program, Australian Assistance Plan, land commissions, growth centres, and the Urban Rehabilitation Program.
Grants Commission Act 1973 (Cwth)	Extends the role of the Commonwealth to funding local government urban programs. Regional organisations established to make funding bids to the Commonwealth with the Grants Commission assessing applications.
1975 Fraser Government reforms of Commonwealth–state financial relations	Fraser Coalition Government abandons DURD and its programs. The flow of Commonwealth revenue to local initiatives is managed on a hands-off tax-sharing basis linked to population levels. State grants commissions determine the intrastate allocation of funding to individual local government authorities based on a mix of population share and need.
1991–96 Building Better Cities Program	Better Cities funds distributed to state and territory governments under the (officially untied) General Purpose Capital Grants framework but tied to the achievement of urban development targets in the funded precincts and regions. Formal intergovernmental agreements struck to secure these outcomes.
Local Government Financial Assistance Act 1995 (Cwth)	Commonwealth assistance intended for local government adjusted so that the states and territories are funded on a per capita basis while subsequent sharing of these funds across councils is determined partially on a per capita basis and partially based on equalisation.

Event, program, or policy initiative	Major expenditure target
2000 Roads to Recovery Bill	This specific-purpose road funding program introduced by the Howard Government allocated funds to councils based partly on population and partly on length of roads.
2001 Sustainable Regions Program	This modest ($100 million) program provides Commonwealth assistance for community infrastructure and facilities in targeted locations.
2008 formation of Infrastructure Australia	In line with its election promise to 'depoliticise' Commonwealth funding of roads and other infrastructure projects, the Rudd Labor Government establishes Infrastructure Australia to provide the government with strategic and independent advice on how the Commonwealth can best deploy its capital outlays on roads, rail, water, and other projects of national interest.
2008 new federalism and the Global Financial Crisis	The Rudd Government attempts to reframe Commonwealth–state financial relations with a greater emphasis on untied transfers and national agreements on outcomes. The Global Financial Crisis prompts major stimulus spending on the part of the Commonwealth, including bringing forward many infrastructure projects.
2011 National Urban Policy	The Gillard Government reintroduces a discrete Commonwealth focus on national urban policy; however, while overall policy frameworks are articulated, spending on infrastructure is modest compared with earlier Commonwealth forays into this area. Some of the Gillard Government's programs include the Suburban Jobs Initiative, Managed Motorways Program, and Sustainable Regional Development Program — all of which involved a budgeted spend of less than $200 million.
2016 City Deals Program	The Turnbull Coalition Government, as part of its 'Smart Cities' agenda, seeks to leverage its financial contribution to infrastructure projects to achieve more coordinated planning and urban development in designated urban corridors and towns deemed to be of strategic significance. The City Deals Program broadly follows the model established in the United Kingdom, under which Westminster invests in additional infrastructure for a partner region (e.g. Greater Manchester) with part of the investment returned via higher tax revenues generated by a more productive urban structure. Despite its ambition, only a handful of City Deals have been struck or are in prospect in Australia, and some appear to have a narrow focus on single projects, such as the Townsville stadium.
Contemporary Commonwealth policy	Tax-sharing to benefit local government and national road and rail funding continues, as does the City Deals Program. Otherwise, current policy is characterised by seemingly ad hoc grant programs focused on lower-order infrastructure categories, with ministers, as distinct from independent assessments, determining where and when projects will be delivered.

Source: Author's summary.

History suggests the general failure of the Commonwealth to successfully intervene in urban infrastructure funding is in part attributable to wanton disregard for good governance principles in framing federal programs. The next section canvasses what these principles could be.

Directions for reform

The literature points to three circumstances in which transfers of funds from central to subnational governments would be warranted: correction for vertical fiscal imbalance, correction for horizontal fiscal imbalance, and pursuit of national priorities (SGS 2011).

Vertical fiscal imbalance occurs when a tier of government is charged with responsibility for delivering services but does not have the revenue-raising power to fund these functions. Transfers from higher spheres of governance are typically offered as a remedy, but such transfers are not without their drawbacks. They can lead to a dilution of accountability in the delivery of public services in that subnational governments may blame poor performance on the inadequacy of funding transfers from central governments, while central governments claim the transfers are appropriate and the inefficiency of subnational governments is to blame. Generally, a preferred solution to the vertical fiscal imbalance problem is to increase the revenue-raising powers of local (that is, non-central) governments, though this can diminish the central government's capacity to manage macroeconomic stability.

Horizontal fiscal imbalance describes the situation in which interjurisdictional differences cause disparities in subnational governments' abilities to raise revenue to fund local expenditure. This can result in service-level variations that are deemed to be out of step with broader community expectations or perceptions of fairness. This idea was adopted early in the fiscal federalism literature and remains one of the most compelling arguments for intergovernmental transfers in Australia (see, for example, CGC 2021). Intergovernmental transfers are seen as a way of 'equalising' local governments, so each has roughly the same ability to service their jurisdictions.

Both the fiscal equalisation principles built into Australia's GST revenue allocation arrangements and the various forms of income tax–sharing with local government applied by the Australian Government since the 1970s (Table 14.4) provide examples of policy responses to address horizontal fiscal imbalance.

Advancement of national objectives is the third premise for central governments to transfer funds for infrastructure to other spheres of governance. Without central government intervention, project and program choices made by subsidiary governments may not align sufficiently or at all with outcomes that are preferred across the Australian community or in terms of Australia's international treaty obligations.

According to this argument, suboptimal levels of service will be supplied if provision is left entirely to state, regional, or local governments, as the spillover benefits to the nation are ignored in the local government's decisions or set aside due to local funding limits. Consequently, central governments provide funding to ensure that the desired levels of service are achieved across the country.

Accompanying these fiscal principles for funding transfers between central and other governments is the touchstone concept of subsidiarity (Moran 2014). This holds that nothing should be decided at a higher level of authority if the matter in question can be resolved at a lower level competently and without compromise to the choices open to the higher-order authorities.

Subsidiarity in the context of the current discussion of interjurisdictional transfers implies, first, that each sphere of government within a federated system should be able to stand on its own feet and enjoy a high degree of self-determination for those issues falling within its scope of competency. This, in turn, implies a relatively high degree of fiscal autonomy, including in revenue-raising powers. To have some spheres of governance dependent on, or beholden to, other spheres for the resources to fund decisions within their competency can lead to confusion about accountability, as discussed above.

Second, the subsidiarity principle implies that non-central governments are seen as partners rather than the mere foot-soldiers of a central government that is providing funds to address horizontal fiscal imbalance or national priorities. The central government is entitled to be clear about *what* is to be achieved via the interjurisdictional funding program. Indeed, sound public finance practice requires that expected outcomes are spelled out and readily discoverable. Having said this, *how* these outcomes are to be achieved with the resources on offer should be a matter for recipient governments to determine.

Apart from fostering a more efficient public finance system with clearer accountabilities, the application of subsidiarity could be expected to deliver a variety of other benefits. A potential gain is a more informed and engaged electorate in all spheres of government, thereby promoting better policymaking. Another is innovation in public service delivery, with different jurisdictions free to develop new and potentially more efficient methodologies to address community needs.

What are the potential practical impacts of these principles in future iterations of Commonwealth involvement in urban infrastructure funding? They would see the Commonwealth:

- working with the states and territories within the subsidiarity paradigm to resolve questions of vertical and horizontal fiscal imbalance in their own right—that is, outside any specific national urban agenda
- articulating a clear and, as far as possible, measurable vision for how it wants cities to develop in the national interest, touching on such matters as emissions abatement, water sustainability, biodiversity retention and rehabilitation, efficient labour markets and productivity, improved health outcomes, and social inclusion
- being clear about what it sees as the essential governance, institutional, and public finance reforms required to achieve these urban transformations in the national interest, with such reforms potentially including the creation of metropolitan governments and the broad-based and systematic capture of value created through regulated development rights (Spiller et al. 2017)
- harmonising its own investments, recurrent programs, and regulations with this urban development vision
- after the above, deploying untied but outcome-agreed funding programs to nudge state and local government investment, recurrent programs, and regulations towards the national vision for urban development.

Conclusion

The Commonwealth Government will inevitably loom large in urban policy and infrastructure funding in part because of its fiscal heft. It collects 81 per cent of the nation's total taxes including the GST, which is cycled back to the states and territories with adjustments for horizontal fiscal imbalances, and 61 per cent of all taxes excluding the GST (ABS 2023).

However, beyond its constitutional role in facilitating interjurisdictional trade and integration, including through provision of transport infrastructure, the Commonwealth has no authority to intervene in settlement patterns and city planning. Historically, this has not deterred the Commonwealth from involving itself in urban policy. As noted, this is due in part to this sphere's financial muscle. It also reflects the profound nexus between the shape of the cities and Australia's ability to fulfil nationally shared goals and international obligations, including those relating to emissions abatement.

This combination of motive and opportunity has seen the Commonwealth pursue a multiplicity of urban infrastructure funding programs, albeit often without a clearly stated rationale, and typically with a lack of consistency from one government to the next. These programs have ranged from the Whitlam Government's attempts to effectively sideline the states in remaking cities to a procession of electorate-specific infrastructure grants in which the Australian Government has involved itself in localised infrastructure.

This history suggests that the Commonwealth does its best work in urban policy when it sets clear national objectives for urban performance across all dimensions of sustainability and leaves the 'how-tos' to the states and territories. In this context, the Commonwealth uses its fiscal power not to override the superior competency of the states and territories in urban planning, but to nudge these jurisdictions towards priorities shared across the Australian community. This will require restraint and respect from future administrations in Canberra.

References

Australian Bureau of Statistics (ABS). 2023. *Taxation Revenue, Australia (2020–21 Financial Year)*. Canberra: ABS. Available from: www.abs.gov.au/statistics/economy/government/taxation-revenue-australia/latest-release.

Australian Transport Assessment and Planning (ATAP) Steering Committee. 2016. *Australian Transport Assessment and Planning Guidelines. F0.2 Integrated Transport & Land Use Planning*. Canberra: Department of Infrastructure and Regional Development. Available from: www.atap.gov.au/sites/default/files/f02_integrated _transport_and_land_use_planning.pdf.

Commonwealth Grants Commission (CGC). 2021. *Horizontal Fiscal Equalisation in the Australian Federation*. Fact Sheet. Canberra: CGC. Available from: www. cgc.gov.au/sites/default/files/2021-11/fs04_horizontal_fiscal_equalisation.pdf.

Infrastructure Victoria. 2019. *Infrastructure Provision in Different Development Settings: Metropolitan Melbourne. Volume 2: Technical Appendix.* April, revised August. Melbourne: Infrastructure Victoria. Available from: infrastructure victoria.com.au/resources/infrastructure-priorities-for-the-regions.

Moran, T. 2014. 'Governments, Subsidiarity and Saving the Federation.' In *A Federation for the 21st Century*, edited by Committee for Economic Development of Australia (CEDA), 157–64. Melbourne: CEDA.

SGS Economics & Planning (SGS). 2011. Funding Growth Areas in a National Urban Policy. Unpublished background paper prepared for National Growth Areas Alliance. Melbourne: SGS Economics & Planning.

Spiller, M., and B. Forrest. 2017. *Better Value from Greenfield Urban Infrastructure in Victoria*. Melbourne: SGS Economics & Planning.

Spiller, M., A. Spencer, and P. Fensham. 2017. *Value Capture Through Development Licence Fees*. SGS Occasional Paper. Melbourne: SGS Economics & Planning.

Spiller, M., P. Thakur, and K. Wellman. 2012. 'Principles and Systems for Coordination of Infrastructure Investment Across Portfolios.' In *Urban Infrastructure: Finance and Management*, edited by K. Wellman and M. Spiller, 259–84. Chichester, UK: Wiley-Blackwell. doi.org/10.1002/9781118401637.

Tomlinson, R., and M. Spiller. 2018. *Australia's Metropolitan Imperative: An Agenda for Governance Reform*. Melbourne: CSIRO Publishing. doi.org/10.1071/9781486307975.

Part 5:
Justice and
wellbeing

15

Voice, treaty, truth: Planning for coexistence in Australia's cities and towns

Ed Wensing and Matthew Kelly[1]

Introduction

Australia has not come to terms with the fact that all its settlements, towns, and cities are on the stolen lands of the Aboriginal and Torres Strait Islander peoples who owned and occupied this land for many thousands of years before colonisation by the British in 1788 (Wensing 2019b).

Aboriginal and Torres Strait Islander peoples continue to assert they never ceded their sovereignty, their land was stolen from them without consent, and extinguishment is alien to their law and custom. Under Aboriginal law and custom, the settler state's assertion of ownership and sovereignty over land has no legitimacy. Their persistent desire is that the two systems of law and custom relating to land be accorded an equal and non-discriminatory status. This position is supported by various international human rights instruments and recent developments in Australia (Wensing 2019b).

---

1   Pat Troy and co-author Ed Wensing knew each other for more than 45 years. In the closing years of his life, Pat attended many of Ed's formal PhD presentations at The Australian National University and gave Ed considerable encouragement and support for his research into land justice for the Aboriginal and Torres Strait Islander peoples of Australia. In a conversation with Ed in early 2018, Pat said he wished he had focused on the rights and interests of the Aboriginal and Torres Strait Islander peoples in our cities and regions earlier in his career, and he asked to whom he should talk about their water rights because of his more recent research into water consumption.

This chapter discusses why urban policy—here focused on land-use planning—matters to Aboriginal and Torres Strait Islander peoples, considers the historical legacies and current practices of planning, and outlines a model for coexistence in planning based on respect and parity between two different systems of land rights and interests, land use, and tenure. Given the denial and dispossession that Aboriginal and Torres Strait Islander peoples have endured since colonisation and the lack of respect for their rights, interests, values, and world views, they have politely requested to be advised, in the Introduction, if the names of deceased Aboriginal or Torres Strait Islander persons are mentioned. With due respect, Aboriginal and Torres Strait Islander people are advised that this chapter contains the names of deceased persons.

Why urban policy and land-use planning matter

Pat Troy, like Max Neutze, was dedicated to the development of the social sciences and to issues of national importance in Australia, especially the development of policy affecting the way we live in and use our cities (Troy 2000). While much of his work on urban policy did not delve into the rights and interests of the Aboriginal and Torres Strait Islander peoples of Australia, in his book *Accommodating Australians*, Troy (2012: 1) endorsed Peter Read's (2000) edited volume on the history of Australian Indigenous housing, noting that the provision of housing had been used by governments 'for a variety of political ends' and to 'settle and control people who have lived and freely moved in this country for millennia'. The concluding chapter in Read's collection was written by Will Sanders (2000), who had worked on Aboriginal housing issues while at the Urban Research Program at The Australian National University in the 1980s (Sanders 1984, 1990). In 2000, Troy concluded that 'a more complete explanation' of the Commonwealth's focus on accommodation of the Aboriginal and Torres Strait Islander population was 'still needed'.

One of Troy's peers at the Urban Research Program, Max Neutze (2000: 203), recognised that Aboriginal and Torres Strait Islander land rights did exist and that First Australians 'are responsible for the land and have an obligation to look after it' (citing Rowley 1978). He appreciated that the Aboriginal and Torres Strait Islander peoples' relationship to land is not one of simple ownership as understood in modern Western societies, and that their relationship and obligations to land cannot be avoided because their spirituality, culture, and social life depend on the land (Neutze 2000). He argued that, at least in theory, equity and environmental and efficiency objectives could be achieved by coordinating the decisions of public and private producers of urban space through land-use planning (Neutze 2000).

Land, land use, and planning are essentially about the relationships between people and land, and the uses to which land and resources can be put, in both urban and non-urban contexts. Planning is an ongoing process of setting objectives, exposing connections, presenting alternatives and their likely consequences, guiding and making choices, monitoring and reviewing progress, and revisiting the objectives and outcomes in a timely manner. The contribution of planning therefore lies in optimising the connections and linkages, the functional as much as the visual, within a structured landscape (Wensing and Small 2012). The essence of planning is not in the individual elements of society, economy, environment, or culture, but in their combination and interactions with each other. As Johnson (2018: 41) puts it, planning is 'a purposeful intervention' aimed at 'formulating a better future', echoing Throgmorton's (1992: 17) maxim that 'good planning is persuasive storytelling about the future' and Jackson's (1997: 226) assertion that any future narrative 'must be a new story, not the kind of fiction which legitimised terra nullius and rationalised unjust and racist land use decisions'.

Planning's praxis includes zoning and development controls that shape the environment (Wensing 2019a). Our land-use planning and development systems operate by requiring compliance with permitted uses set out in land-use zoning plans and through planning permits or development assessment processes. As Spiller (2021) argues, the only right that property owners have is the right to continued enjoyment of lawfully sanctioned uses of their land, and to trade in the land, within these limits, if they so wish. This right cannot be taken away without compensation, as we see when governments compulsorily acquire property for roads, airports, hospitals, and other public purposes. Every other right as to how land may be used or developed is reserved by the community through planning laws.

In Australia, land administration and land-use planning are essentially public functions within each state and territory, which have their own unique laws for administering land tenure and regulating the use and enjoyment of land for present and future generations. The rationale and legitimacy of land-use planning are largely based on maintaining or improving the common good, on the assumption that the Crown holds ultimate control over all land in Australia, including the power to grant or transfer land in whatever form of tenure it decides, and to control what landholders do with their land (Wensing 2019a; Spiller 2021). Planning matters to everyone because it affects everyone's everyday lives, including Aboriginal and Torres Strait Islander peoples because most of them live in our major cities and their proximate inner regional areas (Wensing and Porter 2015).

The state's control over what landowners (public and private) can or cannot do must be seriously questioned after the High Court of Australia's decision in *Mabo (No. 2)* (1992) because the Crown now shares its interests in land with native titleholders. That most certainly applies in circumstances where native title exists or may exist under the Commonwealth *Native Title Act 1993*. However, Aboriginal and Torres Strait Islander peoples' rights and interests still apply elsewhere, including on private land, because Aboriginal cultural heritage is regulated under different legislation (Wensing 2021a).

Why urban policy and land-use planning matter to Australia's Indigenous peoples

Law and culture are deeply entwined, shaping each other (Nolan 2011). Our laws reflect the culture in which they were made and reinforce that culture once made. Whether the law is just or unjust, it also shapes behaviour (Tapsell 2014). That is the problem in Australia (Wensing 2021a): urban policy and land-use planning law continue to curtail Aboriginal and Torres Strait Islander peoples' rights to economic self-determination.

For more than two centuries, the existence of the Aboriginal and Torres Strait Islander peoples of Australia was denied, they were alienated and dispossessed from their lands, and forcibly relocated to missions and reserves. The law and the judiciary have played 'an important, but hardly creditable, part in the interaction between Aborigines and white society' (Cranston 1974: 60). These laws confined Aboriginal people to reserves or missions to which many had no cultural connection, deprived them of their civil rights, and sought to justify their supposed inferiority (Cranston 1974).

The material and geographical manifestations of Aboriginal cultures that developed over 65,000 years are being rapidly destroyed by mining companies, urban development, and public infrastructure, such as roads and other public works, and our regulatory regimes fail to prevent their destruction (Langton 2020; Wensing 2021a).

It was not until *Mabo (No. 2)* that Aboriginal and Torres Strait Islander peoples were accorded any legal recognition of their pre-existing land rights and interests. In many respects, our laws are still playing 'catchup' after *Mabo (No. 2)*. The High Court's decision was as much about the substance of the Meriam people's claim to their ancestral lands in the Torres Strait as it was about the essence of a system of Aboriginal and Torres Strait Islander law and custom, including rights to their ancestral lands and waters (Wensing 1999, 2016). While the *Native Title Act 1993* deals with the former, we have not really come to terms with the wider implications of the latter for the way we deal with land and cultural heritage matters more generally. This is principally why mistakes like the destruction of Juukan Gorge in Western Australia occur (Wensing 2021a).

Other international and domestic imperatives are also driving a greater focus on the dysfunctional relationship between law and culture in relation to indigenous peoples' land and development rights. At the international level, in 2007, the UN General Assembly adopted the United Nations Declaration on the Rights of Indigenous Peoples (UNDRIP). Declarations are adopted by the General Assembly because they are considered universally applicable (Amnesty International 2022). While Canada, Australia, Aotearoa New Zealand, and the United States originally opposed the declaration, all four have since reversed their opposition (Wensing 2021b). While the UNDRIP may not be a direct source of law (UN 2013), it carries considerable normative weight and legitimacy. It was 30 years in the making, compiled in consultation with, and the support of, Indigenous peoples worldwide (Daes 2008), and it reflects 'an important level of consensus at the global level about the content of indigenous peoples' rights' (UN 2013: 16). It also 'reflects the needs and aspirations of Indigenous peoples' (Eide 2006: 157), as well as the concerns of states (Wensing 2019a).

The UNDRIP expresses rights and, in so doing, explains how Indigenous peoples want nation-states (and others) to conduct themselves in relation to matters that affect their rights and interests (Wensing 2019b). Most importantly, it enshrines the inextricably linked principles of self-determination and free, prior, and informed consent. There is therefore an expectation by indigenous peoples and others that the UNDRIP imposes obligations on states and third parties to conform to the standards expressed in the declaration when it comes to making decisions that affect their rights and interests, including in land. Therefore, nation-states can no longer make decisions affecting indigenous peoples by imposition, but rather have a duty to consult with them based on free, prior, and informed consent when dealing with matters that will affect their rights and interests (Wensing 2021b). Where an activity impacts on the rights of an Indigenous group, attention should be given to whether the group's free, prior, and informed consent was obtained, 'which is determined by reference to the relevant international standards and not whether the arrangement is valid under Australian domestic law' (Southalan 2016: 902–3). In many respects, the UNDRIP therefore establishes a moral and ethical compass to guide urban policy and land-use planning.

At the domestic level, the most significant development is the Uluru Statement from the Heart, which emerged from the First Nations National Constitutional Convention at Uluru, in the Northern Territory, in May 2017 (Figure 15.1). The Uluru Statement resulted from a series of dialogues around the country with Aboriginal and Torres Strait Islander peoples about constitutional reform. It is the most recent of several declarations that Aboriginal and Torres Strait Islander Peoples have made about their rights and interests over the past 80 years (Wensing 2019b). It is also the most profound statement because it outlines the issues they want the nation to address, and how.

The Uluru Statement contains three key elements: voice, treaty, and truth (Davis 2017). First, is a constitutionally enshrined Aboriginal and Torres Strait Islander Voice to parliament, whose functions are to be determined by the parliament but would involve the supervision of Section 51 (xxvi) (the parliament's power to make laws for the people of any race) and Section 122 (the parliament's power to make laws for the territories) of the Australian Constitution. The second element is a *makarrata* or treaty. *Makarrata* is a Yolngu word from north-eastern Arnhem Land that is sometimes translated as 'things are all right again after a conflict' or 'coming together after a struggle' (Hiatt 1987: 140). Third, a Makarrata Commission created by legislation will enable localised truth-telling on a First Nations basis, using geographical areas identified by Aboriginal and Torres Strait Islander peoples based on language or clan ancestry and connections to Country, rather than regions determined by the state (Davis and Williams 2021).

STATEMENT FROM THE HEART

We, gathered at the 2017 National Constitutional Convention, coming from all points of the southern sky, make this statement from the heart:

Our Aboriginal and Torres Strait Islander tribes were the first sovereign Nations of the Australian continent and its adjacent islands, and possessed it under our own laws and customs. This our ancestors did, according to the reckoning of our culture, from the Creation, according to the common law from 'time immemorial', and according to science more than 60,000 years ago.

This sovereignty is a spiritual notion: the ancestral tie between the land, or 'mother nature', and the Aboriginal and Torres Strait Islander peoples who were born therefrom, remain attached thereto, and must one day return thither to be united with our ancestors. This link is the basis of the ownership of the soil, or better, of sovereignty. It has never been ceded or extinguished, and co-exists with the sovereignty of the Crown.

How could it be otherwise? That peoples possessed a land for sixty millennia and this sacred link disappears from world history in merely the last two hundred years?

With substantive constitutional change and structural reform, we believe this ancient sovereignty can shine through as a fuller expression of Australia's nationhood.

Proportionally, we are the most incarcerated people on the planet. We are not an innately criminal people. Our children are aliened from their families at unprecedented rates. This cannot be because we have no love for them. And our youth languish in detention in obscene numbers. They should be our hope for the future.

These dimensions of our crisis tell plainly the structural nature of our problem. This is the torment of our powerlessness.

We seek constitutional reforms to empower our people and take a rightful place in our own country. When we have power over our destiny our children will flourish. They will walk in two worlds and their culture will be a gift to their country.

We call for the establishment of a First Nations Voice enshrined in the Constitution.

Makarrata is the culmination of our agenda: the coming together after a struggle. It captures our aspirations for a fair and truthful relationship with the people of Australia and a better future for our children based on justice and self-determination.

We seek a Makarrata Commission to supervise a process of agreement-making between governments and First Nations and truth-telling about our history.

In 1967 we were counted, in 2017 we seek to be heard. We leave base camp and start our trek across this vast country. We invite you to walk with us in a movement of the Australian people for a better future.

Figure 15.1 The Uluru Statement from the Heart

Source: Referendum Council (2017b). Reproduced with permission.

The Uluru Statement was issued to the people of Australia as an invitation 'to walk with us in a movement of the Australian people for a better future' (Referendum Council 2017b) because it is the people of Australia who vote to change the constitution (Davis and Williams 2021). The election of a federal Labor government in May 2022 has breathed new life into the Uluru Statement from the Heart. On election night on 21 May, Labor leader Anthony Albanese began his victory speech by stating: 'I begin by acknowledging the traditional owners of the land on which we meet. I pay my respects to their elders past, present and emerging. And on behalf of the Australian Labor Party, I commit to the *Uluru Statement from the Heart* in full' (ABC News 2022). On 30 July 2022 at the annual Garma Festival on Yolngu Country in north-eastern Arnhem Land, in the Northern Territory, Prime Minister Albanese outlined the Australian Government's commitment to holding a referendum to enshrine an Indigenous Voice to Parliament in Australia's Constitution (Albanese 2022). Details about the implementation of the other key elements of the statement are still being worked on.

The Uluru Statement is relevant to city and regional planning because, as Professor Mick Dodson, a Yawuru man from Broome in the Kimberley region of Western Australia and Australia's first Aboriginal and Torres Strait Islander Social Justice Commissioner, states:

> No consent was given to the colonisers to occupy and settle this land. What the colonisers did was wrong in so many ways. And the nation-state continues to refuse to address these wrongs comprehensively within a human rights framework ... We can fix your problem. Sit down and talk to us about it. Let's negotiate our way through this. (Personal communication with Ed Wensing, 16 October 2016)

These assertions apply to our cities and regions as much as to rural and remote Australia (Wensing and Porter 2015).

Both the UNDRIP and the Uluru Statement represent significant shifts in the recognition of Indigenous peoples' rights and interests (Davis and Williams 2021). Consequently, there have been significant shifts in public sentiment towards better accommodation of their rights and interests in urban policy and city and regional planning (Porter and Arabena 2018; Mayfield and Porter 2020).

What must change therefore are our approaches to engagement with Aboriginal and Torres Strait Islander peoples and their land rights and interests in city and regional contexts. Our current approaches are deeply flawed because we continue to focus on reconciliation and inclusion. While those approaches have been necessary and good, it is now time to shift the focus to reparation, restitution, and redistribution of power and resources.

Historical legacies and current practices

It is an uncomfortable truth that planning is an instrument that was, and still is, used to solidify the colonial claim to land (Blatman-Thomas 2019). Land is at the centre of Indigenous–settler-state relations (Harris 2004) and planning is inextricably linked to acts of colonisation because it structures the relationship between people and land and land use (Wensing and Small 2012).

The use of planning technologies (mapping, naming, bounding, surveying) and spatial practices (regulating land uses, the location of people, housing, and industry) enabled colonial claims in land to be recorded, ratified, and managed under the laws of the United Kingdom. Rendering Aboriginal peoples 'invisible' was the intended outcome, and these technologies and practices were highly effective at achieving this (Byrne 2003; Blatman-Thomas and Porter 2019).

Indigenous peoples' autonomy in the colonial landscape was 'spatially controlled or constrained' by the 'colonial cadastral grid' (Byrne 2003: 170), which formalised the taking of land, resources, and places that were granted as property by the colonial state. The act of transferring 'land' to 'property' was a 'physical and conceptual transformation' (Jackson et al. 2017: 228) and remains highly destructive to the 'people, languages, relationships, knowledge, understanding and cultures whose belonging together make Country' (Howitt 2019: 197).

The legacies of planning's complicity in the colonial project create implications for our contemporary practice. Blatman-Thomas and Porter (2019) argue that the settler-colonial order can never become 'post' because it is endlessly recomposed. While planning systems are only one component of the settler-colonial apparatus, and therefore cannot resolve all issues within their domain, planning systems can be mobilised to 'alter the basic distribution of public power within the settler state' (Lino 2017: 386) and facilitate respect and inclusion of Indigenous customary rights and interests in land.

Despite the recognition of the land rights and interests of Aboriginal and Torres Strait Islander peoples in *Mabo (No. 2)* and the enactment of the *Native Title Act 1993*, the extent to which the various planning statutes and systems around Australia take account of Aboriginal and Torres Strait Islander peoples' rights and interests is still woefully inadequate (Wensing 2017). Only three jurisdictions incorporate provisions relating to Aboriginal and Torres Strait Islander peoples' rights and interests in land (Table 15.1). In New South Wales, the relevant provisions in the *Environmental Planning and Assessment Act 1979* are only applicable to land that has been granted to Aboriginal people under that state's *Aboriginal Land Rights Act 1983*. In Victoria, the relevant provisions in the *Planning and Environment Act 1987* are only applicable where agreements have been reached under the *Traditional Owner Settlement Act 2010*.

Table 15.1 Recognition of Aboriginal and Torres Strait Islander peoples' rights and interests in Australian planning legislation

Jurisdiction	Statute	Incorporates Aboriginal and Torres Strait Islander peoples' rights and interests?
Cwth (Australian Capital Territory only)	*Australian Capital Territory (Planning and Land Management) Act 1988*	No.
Australian Capital Territory[a]	*Planning and Development Act 2007*	No.
New South Wales	*Environmental Planning and Assessment Act 1979*	Yes, but only where the local Aboriginal land council is the landowner under the *Aboriginal Land Rights Act 1983* (NSW).
Northern Territory	*Planning Act 2015*	No.
Queensland	*Planning Act 2016*	Yes. Applies to all entities performing functions under the Act throughout Queensland.
South Australia	*Planning, Development and Infrastructure Act 2016*	No.
Tasmania	*Land Use Planning and Approvals Act 1993*	No.
Victoria	*Planning and Environment Act 1987*	Yes, but only where agreements have been reached under the *Traditional Owner Settlement Act 2010* (Vic.).
Western Australia	*Planning and Development Act 2005*	No.

[a] There are two primary planning statutes for the Australian Capital Territory. When the Commonwealth granted the ACT self-government in 1989, it enacted legislation that retained control over designated areas in the territory (as defined in the National Capital Plan; NCA 2016: 8–10) and imposed a level of oversight over land-use planning by the territory government in the remainder.

Source: Wensing (2017 [updated]).

In contrast, and for the first time in the history of planning law in Australia, the Queensland *Planning Act 2016* includes a provision that requires all entities performing functions under it to perform them in a way that advances the purposes of the Act. Significantly, the purposes of the Act include 'valuing, protecting and promoting Aboriginal and Torres Strait Islander knowledge, culture and tradition' and 'conserving places of cultural heritage significance' (s.5[2][d], [e]). This provision applies throughout Queensland and does not depend on the existence of native title, a heritage listing, a site of significance being entered on a register, or a land grant or transfer to Aboriginal or Torres Strait Islander peoples. The onus of taking Aboriginal and Torres Strait Islander peoples' knowledge, culture, and tradition into account is placed on the entity undertaking certain planning functions under the Act. The provision also gives Aboriginal and Torres Strait Islander peoples the opportunity to be proactive rather than reactive. For these reasons, it sets a very significant precedent for other jurisdictions to follow (Wensing 2018). The planning statutes in the Australian Capital Territory, Northern Territory, South Australia, Tasmania, and Western Australia contain no provisions relating to the land rights and interests of Aboriginal and Torres Strait Islander peoples.

Australia's planning laws are only just beginning to provide opportunities for Aboriginal and Torres Strait Islander peoples to be integrally involved in land-use decision-making on their ancestral Country. There is still a long way to go to stop reinforcing a culture of denial and dispossession of Australia's Aboriginal and Torres Strait Islander peoples.

Thirty years have elapsed since the *Native Title Act 1993* was enacted, 16 years since the UNDRIP was endorsed by the UN General Assembly, and five years since the Uluru Statement from the Heart was released. Since the release of the Uluru Statement, at least four jurisdictions are taking steps in the direction of treaty developments (Victoria, the Northern Territory, Queensland, and Tasmania). The Victorian Parliament passed Australia's first treaty law, the *Advancing the Treaty Process with Aboriginal Victorians Act 2018*, which established the First Peoples' Assembly of Victoria and the Yoorrook Justice Commission to formally recognise historical wrongs and address ongoing injustices for Aboriginal Victorians (Williams 2020). There is little doubt that land and water justice will be matters for negotiations at some stage (Wensing 2021b, 2021c).

A model for coexistence in planning

> There are two laws. Our covenant and white man's covenant, and we want these two to be recognised … We are saying we do not want one on top and one underneath. We are saying that we want them to be equal.
>
> —David Mowaljarlai, Elder, Ngarinyin people, Western Australia, 1997 (via personal communication with Ed Wensing from Kado Muir, a traditional man from the deserts of Western Australia, 1999)

> What Aboriginal people ask is that the modern world now makes the sacrifices necessary to give us a real future. To relax its grip on us. To let us breathe, to let us be free of the determined control exerted on us to make us like you. And you should take it a step further and recognise us for who we are, and who you want us to be. Let us be who we are—Aboriginal people in a modern world—and be proud of us. Acknowledge that we have survived the worst of what the past has thrown at us, and we are here with our songs, our ceremonies, our land, our language, our people—our full identity. What a gift this is that we can give you, if you choose to accept us in a meaningful way. (Yunupingu 2016)

The failure to recognise Aboriginal and Torres Strait Islander peoples' sovereignty and rights to self-determination and free, prior, and informed consent is at the heart of the discourse about land rights and land-tenure reforms. The current situation is underpinned by an entrenched belief among governments that Aboriginal and Torres Strait Islander cultures are incompatible with economic development and that native title must be extinguished or somehow suppressed.

The recognition of Aboriginal and Torres Strait Islander peoples' land rights and interests as being at least equal, if not superior, to the Crown's land rights and interests is the unfinished business of the colonisation of Australia by the British. It is the unfinished business of a whole series of insurgent and official interventions over many decades: the land rights campaigns from the 1960s through to the 1990s, Canberra's Tent Embassy (Foley and Anderson 2006; Foley et al. 2014), the Royal Commission into Aboriginal Deaths in Custody (RCADC 1991), the Social Justice Strategy promised by prime minister Paul Keating as the third prong of the Australian Government's response to the High Court of Australia's decision in *Mabo (No. 2)* (ATSIC 1995), the National Inquiry into the Separation of Aboriginal and Torres Strait Islander Children from their

Families (HREOC 1997), the Final Report of the Council for Aboriginal Reconciliation, the (Sydney) Harbour Bridge Walk (CAR 2000), the review by the Australian Law Reform Commission (ALRC 2015) of the *Native Title Act 1993*, the Final Report of the Referendum Council, and the Uluru Statement from the Heart (Referendum Council 2017a, 2017b).

Land is an integral component of Aboriginal and Torres Strait Islander peoples' being and wellbeing. Their obligation to care for and nurture their ancestral Country for present and future generations is an integral and inherent part of their law and custom. This obligation cannot be extinguished by the Australian State, which explains why Aboriginal and Torres Strait Islander peoples see extinguishment as 'repugnant' (Yu 2016: 2). Aboriginal peoples' connections to and responsibilities for Country remain over our capital cities and major regional centres, even though many of the native title claims over our capital cities have been unsuccessful for a variety of reasons (Wensing and Porter 2015). At stake is a long-sought reconfiguration of power relations between two culturally different societies (Wensing 2019b).

If property in land is an essential component of any society, and how that society controls, uses, and transmits its property determines the wellbeing of its citizens and ultimately the planet, then the elements of land rights and interests, land use, and land tenure constitute the points of commonality in property. By separating these three constitutive elements, it is possible to ascertain how they are applied in different cultural domains to manage who owns the land, what use is made of the land, and how transmission or tenure are managed, including over time and through generations. The elements of rights, interests, use, and tenure can form a basis for comparing and managing interactions between Indigenous and Western systems of property.

It is time to move beyond mere recognition of divergence to viewing the two culturally distinct systems of law and custom on a level playing field, interacting with each other on matters of mutual concern with relatively equal autonomy through agreement-making, rather than hierarchically and in adversarial fashion through the courts.

The model presented below gives practical resolution to the equality of which Galarrwuy Yunupingu spoke. The conceptual model in Figure 15.2 places the two systems of law and custom side by side with their three constitutive elements operating separately, but consecutively.

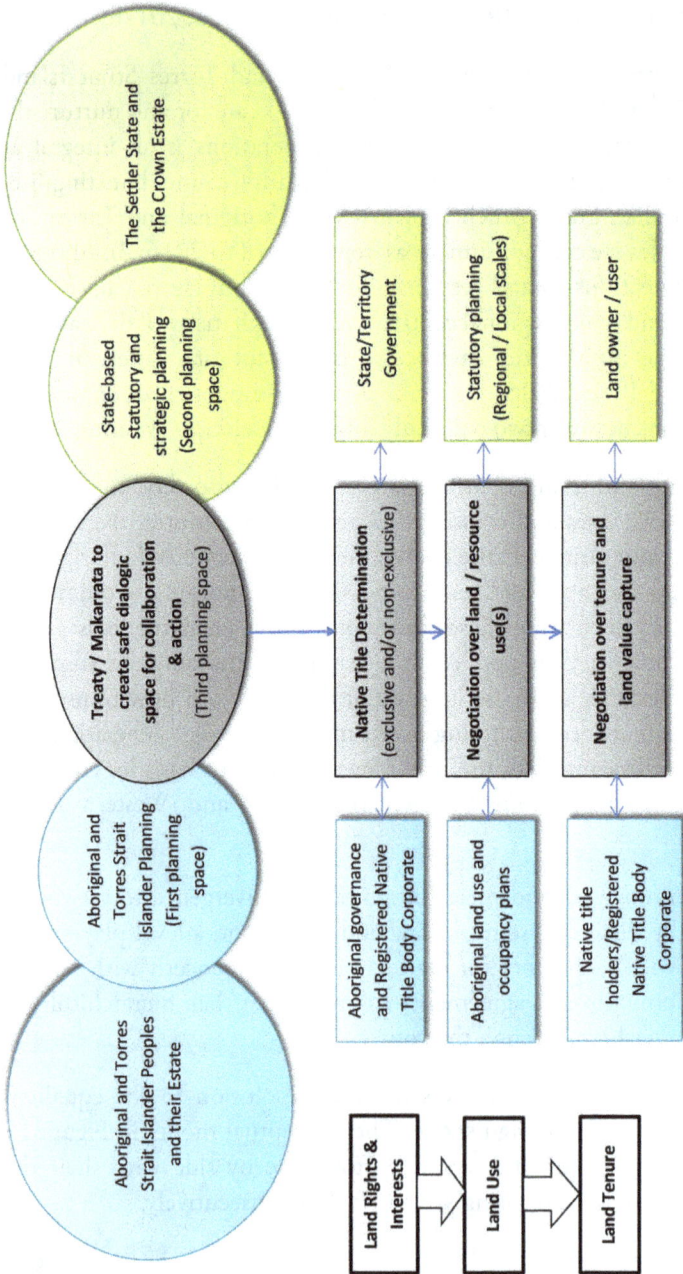

Figure 15.2 Model for parity and coexistence between Indigenous and settler-state land rights and interests, land use, and land tenure

Source: Adapted from Wensing (2019b).

The top layer in Figure 15.2 shows 'three sites of/for planning' (Matunga 2017). On the left-hand side are the Aboriginal and Torres Strait Islander peoples and the Indigenous estate, which includes land subject to native title, land grants, transfers, reserves, and other arrangements enabling Aboriginal and Torres Strait Islander peoples to own, manage, or control land. On the right-hand side are the settler state and the Crown estate, which includes land held by the Crown or the public 'such that the sovereign power has the ultimate right to make grants in land or leases over land' (Porter 2017: 61), except native title rights and interests.

Moving inwards from the left-hand side is Aboriginal and Torres Strait Islander planning—the first planning space—something they have done for thousands of years and continue to do (Howitt and Lunkapis 2010). Moving inwards from the right-hand side is state-based statutory and strategic planning—the second planning space—which includes the state-based planning and environmental management statutes. In the middle is what Matunga (2017: 644) refers to as the third planning space, 'where the coloniser and colonised, oppressed and oppressor can come together to dialogue reconciliation, emancipation, collaboration and collective action for the future'. This middle space becomes a dialogic space for collaborative planning and action.

Placing the two sovereigns on the same level opens the assumptions and predilections underpinning their relations (Wensing 2019b). Matunga (2013: 4) asserts that 'planning' as an activity 'isn't owned by the West, its theorists, or practitioners' but is a 'universal human function with an abiding and justifiable concern for the future'. Indigenous planning is a legitimate form of planning and must be recognised through formal institutional and statutory connectors with settler-state-based planning. Planning across all three spaces is critical to our collective future.

Figure 15.2 also shows that the model can be further expanded into each of the three constitutive layers, as follows:

- The top layer deals with rights and interests in land, especially the continued existence of native title rights and interests as per the *Native Title Act 1993* with all its merits or demerits.
- The middle layer deals with land use and planning and this is where Indigenous planning can be seen as having equal status with state-based planning.

- The bottom layer deals with tenure, the instrumentation used to register interests in land, any dealings with land, and its transactional value for taxation purposes as well as collateral for finance.

The model is aimed at enabling a more equitable coexistence of rights and interests based on mutual respect and justice. The primary goal is to remove the necessity for Aboriginal and Torres Strait Islander peoples to sever their cultural connections with, and responsibilities for, their ancestral lands through extinguishment of their rights and interests against their will. The model is about restitution and reparation of Aboriginal peoples' landownership and decision-making over their ancestral lands on their terms without outside interference and based on free, prior, and informed consent, consistent with Articles 18 and 19 in the UNDRIP (UN 2007).

The dialogic space in the middle is an 'intercultural contact zone' between two systems relating to property in land (Wensing 2019b: 14). While an intercultural contact zone may be an emergent and unpredictable space, it can also be a space where concerns are raised and the parties work together, creatively and collaboratively, based on mutual respect, reciprocity, and justice. A key ingredient is for the parties to come to the negotiating table as equals, and not with one side always having some form of superiority over the other (Wensing 2019b).

The model has the potential to make a valuable contribution to planning and governance *if* the parties are prepared to consider a different kind of relationship based on parity, mutual respect, reciprocity, and a willingness to negotiate over land rights and interests, land use, and land tenure. The 'if' is emphasised here because the model rests on a significant paradigm shift in the relationships between Aboriginal and Torres Strait Islander peoples and the nation-state over land rights and interests, land use, and land tenure. As the Uluru Statement from the Heart states, Aboriginal and Torres Strait Islander peoples' aspirations are 'for a fair and truthful relationship with the people of Australia and a better future for our children based on justice and self-determination' (Referendum Council 2017b).

Conclusion

The time is now right for Australia to shrug off its inheritance of denial and dispossession, its lack of political will, and refusal to make a long-lasting commitment to justice for Aboriginal and Torres Strait Islander peoples, especially as they relate to our cities and regions. We should respond to the invitation in the Uluru Statement from the Heart and walk with Australia's First Nations peoples towards a better future. The truth is that successive governments have failed Aboriginal and Torres Strait Islander peoples in the past. We cannot erase the past, but we can change the future. We can, and should, do better, because continuing failure in this space is no longer an option.

Postscript

The Australian voting public rejected the insertion of an Aboriginal and Torres Strait Islander Voice to Parliament in Australia's Constitution in the referendum that was held in October 2023. This outcome should not be seen as meaning that Voice, Treaty, Truth do not have a role to play in urban policy and planning. Quite the contrary, it reinforces the need for Voice, Treaty and Truth-telling, especially at the local or regional scales. A stronger system of implicit recognition of the prior and continuing ownership of all land and waters in Australia by Aboriginal and Torres Strait Islander peoples under traditional law and custom is required to embed their consideration in conventional and contemporary land use and environmental planning systems. Otherwise, we remain a nation built on the stolen lands of the Aboriginal and Torres Strait Islander peoples who owned and occupied these lands for thousands of years before colonisation.

References

ABC News. 2022. 'Read Incoming Prime Minister Anthony Albanese's Full Speech After Labor Wins Federal Election.' *ABC News*, 22 May. Available from: www.abc.net.au/news/2022-05-22/Anthony-albanese-acceptance-speech-full-transcript/101088736.

Aboriginal and Torres Strait Islander Commission (ATSIC). 1995. *Recognition, Rights and Reform: A Report to Government on Native Title Social Justice Measures.* Canberra: ATSIC.

Albanese, A. 2022. 'Address to Garma Festival.' Gulkula, Northern Territory, 30 July. Available from: www.pm.gov.au/media/address-garma-festival.

Amnesty International. 2022. *10 Ways to be a Genuine Ally to First Nations Communities.* 2 July. Sydney: Amnesty International Australia. Available from: www.amnesty.org.au/10-ways-to-be-an-ally-to-indigenous-communities/.

Australian Human Rights Commission (AHRC). 2016a. *Indigenous Property Rights*. Sydney: AHRC. Available from: www.humanrights.gov.au/our-work/aboriginal-and-torres-strait-islander-social-justice/projects/indigenous-property-rights.

Australian Human Rights Commission (AHRC). 2016b. *Indigenous Property Rights Network: Guiding Rights and Principles for Process and Outcomes*. Sydney: AHRC. Available from: humanrights.gov.au/sites/default/files/Indigenous%20Property%20Rights%20Guiding%20Principles%20-%20FINAL%202016.pdf.

Australian Law Reform Commission (ALRC). 2015. *Connection to Country: Review of the Native Title Act 1993 (Cth)*. ALRC Report 126. Sydney: ALRC.

Blatman-Thomas, N. 2019. 'Reciprocal Repossession: Property as Land in Urban Australia.' *Antipode* 51(5): 1395–415. doi.org/10.1111/anti.12570.

Blatman-Thomas, N., and L. Porter. 2019. 'Placing Property: Theorizing the Urban from Settler Colonial Cities.' *International Journal of Urban and Regional Research* 43(1): 30–45. doi.org/10.1111/1468-2427.12666.

Byrne, D.R. 2003. 'Nervous Landscapes: Race and Space in Australia.' *Journal of Social Archaeology* 3: 169–93. doi.org/10.1177/1469605303003002003.

Council for Aboriginal Reconciliation (CAR). 2000. *Reconciliation: Australia's Challenge*. Final Report of the Council for Aboriginal Reconciliation to the Prime Minister and the Commonwealth Parliament, December. Canberra: CAR. Available from: www5.austlii.edu.au/au/orgs/car/finalreport/index.htm.

Cranston, R. 1974. 'The Aborigines and the Law: An Overview.' *University of Queensland Law Journal* 8: 60–78.

Daes, E. 2008. 'An Overview of the History of Indigenous Peoples: Self-Determination and the United Nations.' *Cambridge Review of International Affairs* 21(1): 7–26. doi.org/10.1080/09557570701828386.

Davis, M. 2017. 'Self-Determination and the Right to be Heard.' In *A Rightful Place: A Road Map to Recognition*, edited by S. Morris, 119–46. Melbourne: Black Inc.

Davis, M., and G. Williams. 2021. *Everything You Need to Know about the Uluru Statement from the Heart*. Sydney: NewSouth Publishing.

Eide, A. 2006. 'Rights of Indigenous Peoples: Achievements in International Law during the Last Quarter of a Century.' *Netherlands Yearbook of International Law* 37: 155–212. doi.org/10.1017/S0167676806001553.

Foley, G., and T. Anderson. 2006. 'Land Rights and Aboriginal Voices.' *Australian Journal of Human Rights* 12(3): 83–108. doi.org/10.1080/1323238X.2006.11910814.

Foley, G., A. Schaap, and E. Howell, eds. 2014. *The Aboriginal Tent Embassy: Sovereignty, Black Power, Land Rights and the State*. London: Routledge. doi.org/10.4324/9780203771235.

Harris, C. 2004. How Did Colonialism Dispossess? Comments from An Edge of Empire.' *Annals of the Association of American Geographers* 94(1): 165–82. doi.org/10.1111/j.1467-8306.2004.09401009.x.

Hiatt, L.R. 1987. 'Treaty, Compact, Makaratta …?' *Oceania* 58(2): 140–44. doi.org/10.1002/j.1834-4461.1987.tb02266.x.

Howitt, R. 2019. 'Unsettling the Taken (For Granted).' *Progress in Human Geography* 44(2): 193–215. doi.org/10.1177/0309132518823962.

Howitt, R., and G.J. Lunkapis. 2010. 'Coexistence: Planning and the Challenge of Indigenous Rights.' In *The Ashgate Research Companion to Planning Theory: Conceptual Challenges for Spatial Planning*, edited by J. Hillier and P. Healey, 109–33. Farnham, UK: Ashgate.

Human Rights and Equal Opportunity Commission (HREOC). 1997. *Bringing Them Home: Report of the National Inquiry into the Separation of Aboriginal and Torres Strait Islander Children from their Families*. Final Report, April. Sydney: HREOC. Available from: www.humanrights.gov.au/publications/bringing-them-home-report-1997.

Jackson, S. 1997. 'A Disturbing Story: The Fiction of Rationality in Land Use Planning in Aboriginal Australia.' *Australian Planner* 34(4): 221–26. doi.org/10.1080/07293682.1997.9657792.

Jackson, S., L. Porter, and L. Johnson. 2017. *Planning in Indigenous Australia: From Imperial Foundations to Postcolonial Futures*. London: Routledge. doi.org/10.4324/9781315693668.

Johnson, L.C. 2018. 'Australian Planning Texts and Indigenous Absence.' In *Planning in Indigenous Australia: From Imperial Foundations to Postcolonial Futures*, edited by S. Jackson, L. Porter, and L. Johnson, 34–51. London: Routledge. doi.org/10.4324/9781315693668-3.

Johnson, L.C., L. Porter, and S. Jackson. 2018. 'Reframing and Revising Australia's Planning History and Practice.' *Australian Planner* 54(4): 225–33. doi.org/10.1080/07293682.2018.1477813.

Langton, M. 2020. 'The Destruction of the Juukan Gorge Caves: A Cultural Property Crime in Moral Terms.' *The Saturday Paper*, [Melbourne], No. 319, 19–25 September.

Lino, D. 2017. 'Thinking Outside the Constitution on Indigenous Constitutional Recognition: Entrenching the Racial Discrimination Act.' *Australian Law Journal* 91: 381–85.

Matunga, H. 2013. 'Theorising Indigenous Planning.' In *Reclaiming Indigenous Planning*, edited by R. Walker, T. Jojola, and D. Natcher, 3–32. Montreal, Qc: McGill-Queen's University Press.

Matunga, H. 2017. 'A Revolutionary Pedagogy of/for Indigenous Planning.' *Planning Theory & Practice* 18(4): 639–66. doi.org/10.1080/14649357.2017. 1380961.

Mayfield, P., and L. Porter. 2020. *Urban Planning and Design Professions: Situational Analysis of Current Engagement Practices with Indigenous Communities Within Australia and Steps Towards Deepening Engagement Practices.* National Environmental Science Program. Sydney: Clean Air and Urban Landscapes Hub. Available from: nespurban.edu.au/wp-content/uploads/2020/10/Situational-Analysis.pdf.

National Capital Authority (NCA). 2016. *National Capital Plan. December 1990. Volume 1.* Canberra: Commonwealth of Australia.

Neutze, M. 2000. 'Economics, Values and Urban Australia.' In *Equity, Environment, Efficiency: Ethics and Economics in Urban Australia*, edited by P. Troy, 196–222. Melbourne: Melbourne University Press.

Nolan, J.L. 2011. *Legal Accents, Legal Borrowing.* Princeton, NJ: Princeton University Press.

Porter, L. 2017. 'Dispossession and Terra Nullius: Planning's Formative Terrain.' In *Planning in Indigenous Australia: From Imperial Foundations to Postcolonial Futures*, edited by S. Jackson, L. Porter, and L.C. Johnson. New York, NY: Routledge. doi.org/10.4324/9781315693668-5.

Porter, L., and L. Arabena. 2018. *Flipping the Table: Toward an Indigenous-Led Urban Research Agenda.* National Environmental Science Program. Sydney: Clean Air and Urban Landscapes Hub. Available from: nespurban.edu.au/wp-content/uploads/2018/11/interim-report-flipping-the-table-toward-an-indigenous-led-research-agenda.pdf.

Read, P., ed. 2000. *Settlement: A History of Indigenous Housing in Australia.* Canberra: AIATSIS.

Referendum Council. 2017a. *Final Report of the Referendum Council.* 30 June. Canberra: Commonwealth of Australia. Available from: www.referendum council.org.au/sites/default/files/report_attachments/Referendum_Council_Final_Report.pdf.

Referendum Council. 2017b. *Uluru Statement from the Heart.* Statement on the First Nations National Constitutional Convention, 26 May. Canberra: Commonwealth of Australia. Available from: www.referendumcouncil.org.au/sites/default/files/2017-05/Uluru_Statement_From_The_Heart_0.PDF.

Rose, D.B. 1996. *Nourishing Terrains: Australian Aboriginal Views of Landscape and Wilderness.* Canberra: Australian Heritage Commission.

Rowley, C.K. 1978. *A Matter of Justice.* Canberra: Australian National University Press.

Royal Commission into Aboriginal Deaths in Custody (RCADC). 1991. *Royal Commission into Aboriginal Deaths in Custody: Final Reports. National Reports: Vols 1–5. Regional Reports: Vols 1–4.* Adelaide: RCADC. Available from: www.austlii.edu.au/au/other/IndigLRes/rciadic/.

Sanders, W. 1984. 'Aboriginal Town Camping, Institutional Practices and Local Politics.' In *Australian Urban Politics: Critical Perspectives*, edited by J. Halligan and C. Paris. Melbourne: Longman Cheshire.

Sanders, W. 1990. 'Reconstructing Aboriginal Housing Policy for Remote Areas: How Much Room to Manoeuvre?' *Australian Journal of Public Administration* 49(1): 38–50. doi.org/10.1111/j.1467-8500.1990.tb02250.x.

Sanders, W. 2000. 'Understanding the Past, Looking to the Future: The Unfinished History of Australian Indigenous Housing.' In *Settlement: A History of Indigenous Housing in Australia*, edited by P. Read, 237–48. Canberra: AIATSIS.

Southalan, J. 2016. 'Human Rights and Business Lawyers: The 2011 Watershed.' *Australian Law Journal* 90: 889–907.

Spiller, M. 2021. 'Windfall Tax Backlash Misunderstands Property Rights.' *Sourceable*, 15 June. Available from: sourceable.net/windfall-tax-backlash-misunderstands-property-rights/.

Tapsell, K. 2014. *Potiphar's Wife: The Vatican's Secret and Child Sexual Abuse.* Adelaide: ATF Press. doi.org/10.2307/j.ctt163t8c3.

Throgmorton, J.A. 1992. 'Planning as Persuasive Story Telling about the Future: Negotiating An Electric Power Rate Settlement in Illinois.' *Journal of Planning Education and Research* 12: 17–31. doi.org/10.1177/0739456X9201200103.

Troy, P., ed. 2000. *Equity, Environment, Efficiency: Ethics and Economics in Urban Australia*. Melbourne: Melbourne University Press.

Troy, P. 2012. *Accommodating Australians: Commonwealth Government Involvement in Housing*. Sydney: The Federation Press.

United Nations (UN). 2007. *Declaration on the Rights of Indigenous Peoples*. General Assembly Resolution 61/295. New York, NY: United Nations. Available from: legal.un.org/avl/pdf/ha/ga_61-295/ga_61-295_ph_e.pdf.

United Nations (UN). 2013. *Report of the Special Rapporteur on the Rights of Indigenous Peoples*. General Assembly Sixty-Eighth session, A/68/317. New York, NY: United Nations. Available from: unsr.jamesanaya.org/docs/annual/2013-ga-annual-report-en.pdf.

United Nations Global Compact. 2015. *Business Community Affirms That Respect for Human Rights is a Key Contribution to Sustainable Development: Statement in Support of UN Guiding Principles and Sustainable Development Goals*. November. New York, NY: United Nations. Available from: www.unglobalcompact.org/docs/issues_doc/human_rights/business-statement-supporting-GPs-SDGs.pdf.

United Nations Human Rights Council (UNHRC). 2011a. *Guiding Principles on Business and Human Rights: Implementing the United Nations 'Protect, Respect and Remedy' Framework. Report of the Special Representative of the Secretary-General on the Issue of Human Rights and Transnational Corporations and Other Business Enterprises, John Ruggie*. UN Doc. A/HRC/17/31, 21 March. Geneva: UNHRC. Available from: www2.ohchr.org/english/bodies/hrcouncil/docs/17session/A.HRC.17.31_en.pdf.

United Nations Human Rights Council (UNHRC). 2011b. *Human Rights and Transnational Corporations and Other Business Enterprises*. Resolution adopted by the Human Rights Council, UN Doc. A/HRC/RES/17/4, 6 July. Geneva: UNHRC. Available from: business-humanrights.org/sites/default/files/media/documents/un-human-rights-council-resolution-re-human-rights-transnational-corps-eng-6-jul-2011.pdf.

Wensing, E. 1999. *Comparing Native Title and Anglo-Australian Land Law: Two Different Timelines, Two Different Cultures and Two Different Laws*. Discussion Paper No. 25. Canberra: The Australia Institute.

Wensing, E. 2016. *The Commonwealth's Indigenous Land Tenure Reform Agenda: Whose Aspirations, and for What Outcomes?* AIATSIS Research Report, 1 July. Canberra: AIATSIS. Available from: aiatsis.gov.au/sites/default/files/research_pub/the-commonwealths-indigenous-land-tenure-reform_2.pdf.

Wensing, E. 2017. Indigenous Rights in Planning: Continuing Cultural Blindness or Racial Prejudice ... Or Both? Unpublished research paper.

Wensing, E. 2018. 'Indigenous Rights and Interests in Statutory and Strategic Land Use Planning: Some Recent Developments.' *James Cook University Law Review* 24: 169–90.

Wensing, E. 2019a. 'A Planner's Response to the Uluru "Statement from the Heart".' Paper presented to Planning Institute of Australia National Congress, Gold Coast, Qld, 16 May.

Wensing, E. 2019b. Land Justice for Indigenous Australians: How Can Two Systems of Land Ownership, Use and Tenure Coexist with Mutual Respect Based on Equity and Justice? PhD thesis, The Australian National University, Canberra.

Wensing, E. 2021a. 'The Destruction of Juukan Gorge: Lessons for Planners and Local Governments.' *Australian Planner* 56(4): 241–48. doi.org/10.1080/0729 3682.2020.1866045.

Wensing, E. 2021b. 'Indigenous Peoples' Human Rights, Self-Determination and Local Governance: Part 1.' *Commonwealth Journal of Local Governance* 24: 98–123. doi.org/10.5130/cjlg.vi24.7779.

Wensing, E. 2021c. 'Indigenous Peoples' Human Rights, Self-Determination and Local Governance: Part 2.' *Commonwealth Journal of Local Governance* 25: 1–28. doi.org/10.5130/cjlg.vi25.8025.

Wensing, E., and L. Porter. 2015. 'Unsettling Planning's Paradigms: Toward a Just Accommodation of Indigenous Rights and Interests in Australian Urban Planning?' *Australian Planner* 53(2): 91–102. doi.org/10.1080/07293682. 2015.1118394.

Wensing, E., and G. Small. 2012. 'A Just Accommodation of Customary Land Rights in Land Use Planning Systems.' Paper presented to the Tenth International Urban Planning and Environment Association Symposium, University of Sydney, Sydney, 24–27 July.

Williams, G. 2020. 'Delivering Truth and Justice for Aboriginal Victorians.' Media release by Minister for Aboriginal Affairs, Victoria, 11 July. Melbourne: Department of the Premier. Available from: www.premier.vic.gov.au/delivering-truth-and-justice-aboriginal-victorians.

Yu, P. 2016. 'Keynote Address.' Northern Development Conference, Darwin, 20 June.

Yunupingu, G. 2016. 'Rom Watangu: The Law of the Land.' *The Monthly*, July.

16

Towards a social progress index for urban liveability, productivity, and sustainability

Megan Weier and Kristy Muir

Introduction

Over the past three decades Australia has experienced enviable and unprecedented economic growth, yet our social progress has not kept pace. Social progress is key if we are to create urban areas for the future that are liveable, productive, and sustainable.

This chapter examines social progress as a concept, what it means for helping to understand and address social inequities, how we are going as a country, and why tracking and focusing on it at local, state, national, and international levels are important for urban policy now and into the future. The social progress index is suggested as a suitable instrument for operationalising these imperatives.

Problems and issues

Australia has an undeniably successful economic track record. Until the recent Covid-19 pandemic, Australia experienced 29 years of continuous economic growth, with gross domestic product (GDP) increasing on average every year since 1991 (ABS 2020). Economic growth has been of significant concern for all recent Australian governments, with the previous federal Liberal–National Coalition in particular prioritising policies that ensured the economy was kept strong and a focus for Covid-19 recovery (Frydenberg and Birmingham 2020).

Economic success, however, does not always accurately reflect the lived experience of communities. While Australian GDP has displayed ongoing growth, there are many areas of socioeconomic inequality, including housing stress and unemployment, that are increasing among certain groups and geographical areas (AIHW 2020). Globally, there are numerous instances of economic development initiatives that have actively harmed the social progress of society and its citizens (Costanza et al. 2009). Australia has its own examples. Mining company Rio Tinto's May 2020 detonation of explosives at Juukan Gorge, Western Australia, for example, resulted in the destruction of 46,000-year-old cave shelters that were of personal, community, national, and international significance for the culture and history of the Puutu Kunti Kurrama and Pinikura peoples and Indigenous peoples more widely (Joint Standing Committee on Northern Australia 2020).

The value of a strong economy is tied to urban development: new housing and infrastructure have positive implications for employment and population growth and, ultimately, should contribute to a more efficient and productive economy. A challenge for sustainable and progressive urban development is to think about development beyond, say, just provision of housing to consciously plan developments that surround affordable and accessible housing with adequate social services, medical care, and education, while also ensuring developments are environmentally sustainable.

Economic indicators are critical to society's progress, but to accurately understand and measure the progress of a society, there must be initiatives that include indicators outside the economy. In particular, by measuring components of progress that are more explicitly social and environmental, it is possible to correlate findings with economic indicators to determine the relationship between the two.

Numerous policy frameworks have been advocated for cities and urban locations to be 'productive, liveable, and sustainable'. In 2011, the Australian Government published its National Urban Policy, reflecting the 'Australian Government's intention to improve the productivity, sustainability and liveability of major urban centres' (DIT 2011: 7). This framework is a cohesive approach responding to 'the need to improve productivity growth; provide affordable and accessible housing; create safe community spaces; meet the needs of a growing and aging population; ensure an inclusive and cohesive society; and address the implications of climate change'.

These three tenets—liveability, productivity, and sustainability—have since driven policy frameworks and advocacy for urban planning more generally. In 2011, the Victorian State Government partnered with the University of Melbourne 'to create evidence to inform public policy that can build healthy, liveable and sustainable communities in Victoria and beyond' (Lowe et al. 2013: 5). The Australian Sustainable Built Environment Council (ASBEC 2013) developed a plan of action for 'productive, liveable and sustainable cities for Australia'. In 2021, this framework was still being used by the Greater Cities Commission and the NSW Department of Planning and Environment to inform district plans and set a direction for Greater Sydney 2056 (Department of Environment and GSC 2017; Greater Cities Commission 2021).

The Australian Social Progress Index (SPI), the analytical focus of this chapter, is a holistic framework that can inform the planning of urban developments that are liveable, productive, and sustainable. It can also be used to track the extent to which urban spaces are delivering against indicators for people and communities.

Social Progress Index as a concept

Recognising the limits of considering only economic measures as indicators of progress, the SPI was first used in 2013 as a complementary indicator for development and progress within society. The nonprofit Social Progress Imperative defines social progress as

> the capacity of a society to meet the basic human needs of its citizens, establish the building blocks that allow citizens and communities to enhance and sustain the quality of their lives, and create the conditions for all individuals to reach their full potential. (Stern et al. 2018: 3)

Based on this definition, the SPI comprises three broad 'dimensions' of social progress: basic human needs, foundations of wellbeing, and opportunity. Four underlying components for each dimension speak to the concepts the data are trying to capture. When deciding which indicators to include, the Social Progress Imperative has developed what are termed 'universally important questions' to help conceptualise a shared SPI framework (Figure 16.1). The index scores each included jurisdiction from zero to 100, and ranks them relative to one another, based on the outcome indicators that are included in the SPI's calculation. A jurisdiction is generally doing better at achieving social progress the closer to 100 are its scores.

The SPI has been calculated at a global level annually since 2013. The 2020 index captured 163 countries, using indicators collected and held by global agencies. Using the same framework and methodology, 'subnational' indexes have been developed for individual countries such as India and the United States (Kapoor and Debroy 2019; Social Progress Imperative 2018b), transnational jurisdictions such as the European Union (Annoni and Bolsi 2020), and local government districts (LBBD 2021). Paraguay was the first national government to adopt the SPI as part of its 2030 development plan, and index findings directed spending that resulted in an increase in internet access and a reduction in child stunting over four years. The SPI for Costa Rica Tourism Destinations provides key social indicators for the country's main tourist areas and has triggered discussions about the relationship between tourism and social progress (Social Progress Imperative 2018a). Subnational indexes allow for granularity (for example, by cutting data by state or community categories), as well as identification of indicators that are politically or contextually important for that jurisdiction when conceptualising each of the SPI domains. In 2018 and 2019, we led the development of an Australian iteration of the SPI, using locally relevant indicators and data (Weier et al. 2020).

BASIC HUMAN NEEDS	FOUNDATIONS OF WELLBEING	OPPORTUNITY
Nutrition & Basic Medical Care Do people have enough food to eat and are they receiving basic medical care?	**Access to Basic Knowledge** Do people have access to an educational foundation?	**Personal Rights** Are people's rights as individuals protected?
Water & Sanitation Can people drink water and keep themselves clean without getting sick?	**Access to Information & Communications** Can people freely access ideas and information from anywhere in the world?	**Personal Freedom & Choice** Are people free to make their own life choices?
Shelter Do people have adequate housing with basic utilities?	**Health & Wellness** Do people live long and healthy lives?	**Inclusiveness** Is no one excluded from the opportunity to be a contributing member of society?
Personal Safety Are people safe?	**Environmental Quality** Does the environment support societal well-being?	**Access to Advanced Education** Do people have access to the world's most advanced knowledge?

Figure 16.1 Social Progress Index framework
Source: Stern et al. (2018). Reproduced with permission.

Australia's social progress

The first Australian SPI was calculated as a time series, comparing states and territories on overall social progress and its related domains between 2015 and 2018 (CSI 2020). The index is calculated from publicly available outcome data that can be addressed by changes to policy or programs to yield better outcomes (such as the estimated homelessness rate or the proportion of people who feel safe using public transport). Datapoints were converted to standardised scores using identified 'best-case' and 'worst-case' scenarios. Wherever possible, these scenarios were based on state, national, or international goals, such as New South Wales's commitment to reduce homelessness by 50 per cent, or targets set out in the United Nations' Sustainable Development Goals. Where no relevant goals were identified, historical datapoints were used. The use of best and worst-case scenarios standardises the index and component scores, but also serves as an advocacy tool that demonstrates there is always room for improvement in how programs and services are delivered.

Due to data availability, the index could only be calculated at a state/ territory level of granularity, using 52 indicators that included survey responses, administrative data, and environmental data such as air-quality ratings (Figure 16.2). This results in a 'smoothing out' of statistics that cannot reflect the diversity of outcomes experienced dependent on location. However, an examination of results between 2015 and 2018 provides insight into Australia's development in social progress. All states and territories had higher overall social progress scores in 2018 than in 2015. The Australian Capital Territory ranked first each year, while Western Australia and the Northern Territory ranked seventh and eighth, respectively.

The Australian Capital Territory is the smallest geographic jurisdiction in Australia, comprising only one major city. Western Australia and the Northern Territory, in contrast, have the highest proportions of residents living in remote and very remote areas, including the highest proportions of residents who are Aboriginal or Torres Strait Islander and/or living in a remote community. This distribution of the population has implications for the availability of appropriate and supportive services that can be easily accessed. As the indicators included in the SPI rely on outcome data, the results suggest that access to appropriate care and services is not equitably distributed across jurisdictions.

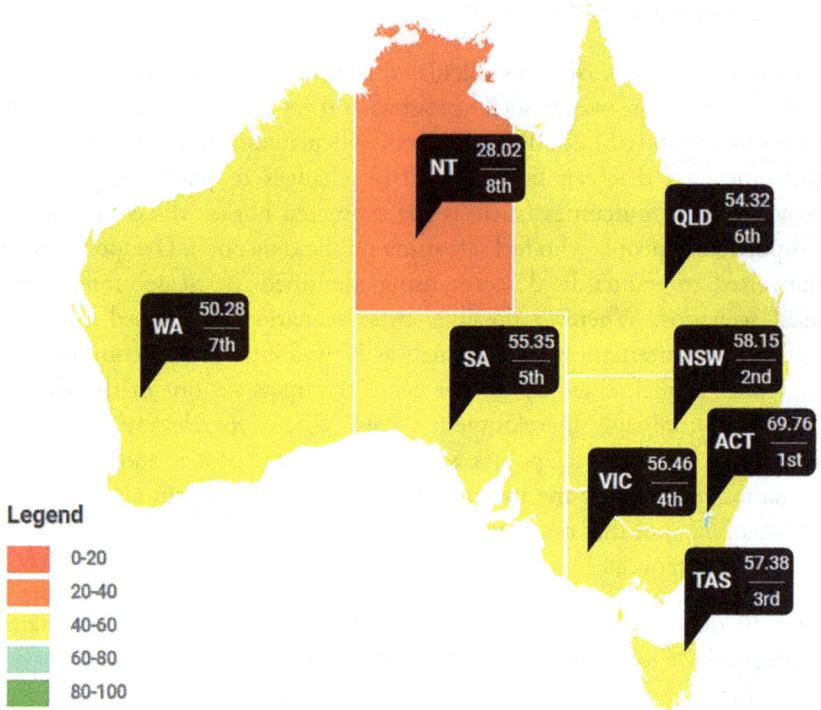

Figure 16.2 Australian Social Progress Index 2018 scores and rankings
Source: CSI (2020). Reproduced with permission.

Based on the included indicators, several components received mid-range scores (between 40 and 60 out of 100) across each state and territory that suggest average performance compared with stated national goals. Access to information and communication was one of the lowest-scoring components across the entire index, alongside personal freedom and choice, inclusiveness, and the accessibility of advanced education. While these components of social progress are not at first glance directly the responsibility of urban policy more generally, the indicators used to calculate the scores, and the universal guiding questions for these components, highlight the need for a multi-lens approach to urban planning. Developments must provide housing and access to amenities and infrastructure, but to be truly liveable, they must also be designed in ways that help to address social inequities and improve quality of life for all residents (Manaugh et al. 2015; Tahmasbi et al. 2019).

Helping to understand and address inequities

Even before the economic impacts of the Covid-19 pandemic, income inequality was a matter of policy concern and priority. Despite relatively high average household incomes by international standards, Australia's wealth is unequally distributed. It has been estimated that in 2018 the top 20 per cent of households held 90 times the amount of wealth of the bottom 20 per cent (Davidson et al. 2020). The fact that more than half of household wealth is held in property demonstrates the role that urban development can play in contributing to and helping to address social inequities.

Ensuring urban planning considers employment opportunities and income levels is critical, but it is not sufficient to help determine whether an urban area is liveable, productive, and sustainable. The Australian SPI demonstrates that for overall progress to improve, policies, programs, and services must be designed with inclusivity and equity in mind. A similar approach can be taken to urban planning. The SPI's framework and universally important questions create a structure for a variety of stakeholders to join in planning urban development, by considering factors such as:

- Is the planned housing inclusive of social and affordable housing?
- Is there adequate infrastructure to support fast internet connections?
- Are there schools and other education centres close by?
- Is there easy access to health and welfare services?
- Are parks, shopping centres, and other public spaces designed to ensure that people feel safe and included?
- What is the environmental impact of the development, and how can the development ensure it is using environmentally sustainable design?

Influencing future social progress in urban areas

With improved technological capabilities it has become possible to draw on diverse data sources to create multidimensional community profiles or 'social atlases' (.id community 2021) that can provide snapshot insights into small-area community differentiation, education levels, employment, and family composition. This also builds on earlier work by social scientists (Vinson 2009; Vinson et al. 2015) using administrative and geographic datasets. While understanding demographic profiles through mechanisms such as the census is vital for directing funding and services, they cannot provide insight into the social outcomes that are a result of urban design or service delivery. A statewide SPI cannot identify the complexities or areas of challenge for urban areas undergoing development. More disaggregated data, which are collected consistently across jurisdictions and at least at the scale of local government areas (LGAs), should be a long-term goal for understanding the priorities for developing progressive and sustainable societies.

This will require data that can identify the policy and program needs of communities. As a starting point, existing indexes, such as Socio-Economic Indexes for Areas (SEIFA), can be used to determine and prioritise need levels in different communities. However, as demonstrated by others (for example, Saunders 2008; Lim et al. 2011), the use of SEIFA alone to identify low socioeconomic status or other indicators of individual disadvantage is not necessarily accurate, nor does it consider the ways in which policy application may be producing or increasing disadvantage. Using a measure such as the SPI, which is based on the outcomes of policies or programs, would help to determine which social planning activities are contributing to disadvantage. The SPI methodology can then be used to determine localised social progress. This would inform the design of urban developments in responding to the needs of communities, address gaps where they exist, capitalise on structures and services contributing to positive outcomes, and track social progress over time to ensure urban areas continue to evolve, adapt, and improve.

Designing future liveable, productive, and sustainable urban areas: Sydney's west as an example

'As part of Sydney's growth, a city the size of Adelaide and Canberra combined is being built now in Sydney's west' (UNSW et al. 2017). So, how can we make sure future opportunities are available to all our citizens? How do we make sure that all young people have equity of access to the jobs and other opportunities of the future? How do we make sure these urban areas are liveable, productive, and sustainable?

The Western Sydney City Deal and other initiatives, like the new airport (Collins 2021), offer unparalleled opportunities for growth and evolution. The Greater Cities Commission (2021) is endeavouring to implement the 'Greater Sydney Region Plan: A Metropolis of Three Cities' at a district level with the aspiration of 'liveability, productivity, and sustainability'. Given the opportunities and investments currently under way, now is the time to ensure that we maximise equity of opportunity in all aspects of this major development commitment.

Based on the commission's districts, the areas of growth in the west of Sydney include four Central City LGAs and eight Western Parkland City LGAs (Table 16.1). The original inhabitants of the lands identified herein are the Bidjigal, Cabrogal, Darkinjung, Dharawal, Dharug, Gundungura, Gweagal, and Tharawal peoples.

Table 16.1 Greater Sydney Region Plan: District boundaries in the west

Central City LGAs	Western City LGAs
Blacktown	Blue Mountains
Cumberland	Hawkesbury
Parramatta	Penrith
The Hills	Camden
	Campbelltown
	Liverpool
	Fairfield
	Wollondilly

Source: Department of Planning and Environment (2021).

Yet, if social progress goals are to be achieved, urban planning must not only aim for increased equity, but also address inequities that are already entrenched. To determine social need, indicators such as SEIFA from ABS Census estimates are used as proxies for determining disadvantage. One subindex of SEIFA, the Index of Relative Socio-Economic Disadvantage, illustrates that communities in many western Sydney LGAs are faring worse than other areas in Australia and New South Wales (Table 16.2). These scores are based on population factors such as the proportion of households on low incomes, private dwellings with no internet connection, and the proportion of people with a long-term health condition or disability.

Table 16.2 Western Sydney district indexes of relative socioeconomic disadvantage

Area	2016 index	Percentile within Australia[a]
Blacktown City	986	37
Blue Mountains City	1,045	73
Camden Council	1,056	80
Campbelltown City	950	21
City of Canterbury-Bankstown	935	17
City of Parramatta	1,039	69
Cumberland Council	929	15
Fairfield City	856	6
Hawkesbury City	1,028	62
Liverpool City	952	22
Penrith City	999	44
The Hills Shire	1,107	98
Wollondilly Shire	1,043	72
Western Sydney (LGA)	978	33
Greater Sydney	1,018	56
New South Wales	1,001	45
Australia	1,002	46

[a] Percentile ranking provides an approximate position of this locality in a ranked list of all Australian localities. Higher percentile rankings indicate there are fewer locations that are less socioeconomically disadvantaged than that area.

Source: .id community (2020). Compiled from ABS Census of Population and Housing 2016.

As this profile shows, these areas have higher levels of disadvantage compared with Greater Sydney. Yet, this analysis is based primarily on household or individual-level factors, rather than demonstrating disadvantage that is created through inadequate access to services or social support. Given the sheer growth and economic investments occurring in this region, now is the time to ensure that disadvantage is reduced (rather than compounded) in all aspects of urban planning and service provision. This includes leveraging and building on existing infrastructure and services and focusing on geographical areas showing indicators of disadvantage, as discussed below.

Table 16.3 Key demographics of western Sydney communities

	Median age	Aboriginal or Torres Strait Islander population (%)	Households with children (%)	Households with 6 or more residents (%)	Unemployment rate (%)	Born overseas (%)	Language other than English spoken at home (%)
Blacktown City	33	2.8	59.4	7.7	7.3	40.4	41.0
Blue Mountains City	44	2.4	40.5	2.7	4.7	16.8	6.0
Camden Council	33	2.5	57.3	5.6	4.1	17.6	14.4
Campbelltown City	34	3.8	54.2	6.7	7.9	31.4	30.3
City of Canterbury-Bankstown	35	0.7	52.9	7.9	8.2	44.0	60.1
Cumberland Council	32	0.6	53.1	9.7	9.5	52.2	65.6
Fairfield City	36	0.7	60.2	11.0	10.5	53.9	70.7
Hawkesbury City	38	3.7	48.4	5.0	4.3	12.3	5.9
Liverpool City	33	1.5	59.5	8.8	7.5	40.7	51.9
City of Parramatta	34	0.7	47.5	3.9	7.0	49.5	52.0
Penrith City	34	3.9	51.4	5.5	5.7	21.6	16.8
The Hills Shire	38	0.5	61.4	5.7	4.6	35.1	31.8
Wollondilly Shire	37	3.2	52.9	6.2	4.0	11.8	5.6
Western Sydney (LGA)	35	1.8	54.4	7.1	7.1	38.6	43.6
Greater Sydney	36	1.5	45.8	4.0	7.1	27.6	25.1
Australia	38	2.9	40.7	3.4	6.9	26.3	20.8

Source: .id community (2020). Compiled from ABS Census of Population and Housing 2016.

Based on projections from the previous ABS Census (.id community 2020), there are an estimated 2.59 million people living in the western Sydney LGAs. In general, people living in western Sydney are younger and more likely to have children, be unemployed, be born overseas, and speak a language other than English at home compared with the rest of New South Wales and Australia (.id community 2020). As Table 16.3 shows, cultural diversity—including the proportion of residents who are Aboriginal and/or Torres Strait Islander—varied greatly across LGAs.

Disadvantage has increased in these areas in recent times with the proportion of people on social security rising at a higher rate than the Greater Sydney and NSW averages. It increased from 4.8 per cent in March 2020 to 8.4 per cent in January 2021, compared with 6.6 per cent of the population in Greater Sydney and 7.6 per cent across all New South Wales (DSS 2021). The role western Sydney plays in delivering social services was demonstrated in one of the largest outbreaks of Covid-19 cases in Australia, with the majority of infections occurring in western Sydney LGAs (NSW Health 2021). It is speculated that spread occurred in these areas in large part because of the higher proportion of residents who were employed in 'essential' services or insecure work and were therefore less likely to be able to work from home or stay home when unwell. The proportion of households with six or more residents is also higher in these communities of concern, contributing to family spread of infections.

While many of these communities face significant challenges, the right planning, services, supports, and infrastructure can mitigate the impacts and help create equity of opportunity for children, families, and communities. There is great opportunity especially given the high proportion of children and young people in these areas.

Continuing the tracking of advantage and disadvantage through SEIFA over time is important, but it does not directly assist communities or policymakers to make refined changes to social issues and determine where and whether they are making a difference to social progress. Extending the calculation of the Australian SPI to a community level could assist because it would not only provide a high-level globally, nationally, state, and (potentially) community comparable index, it would also provide granularity for practical application. While community-level indexes have not yet been calculated within Australia, we are beginning work with local councils that use the SPI framework and its universally important questions to help guide planning and prioritisation, but also to directly identify the anticipated outcomes that can be measured over time to evaluate whether a social progress mindset in urban planning yields its anticipated outcomes.

In the case of planning for Sydney's west, this could involve: access to safe, affordable, and appropriate housing; ensuring environmental sustainability is addressed in planning within households and across the community; ensuring that educational opportunities and health services are available, accessible, appropriate, and acceptable across the life cycle; ensuring that food scarcity is addressed and people can access three nutritious meals a day; addressing domestic and family violence; ensuring that inclusion is addressed in regard to physical infrastructure, community belonging, and lack of stigma; and addressing digital inclusion through hardware, skills, data availability, and capability. A planning approach based on SPI principles means we would be building in not just jobs, but also the opportunity to access those jobs, and setting up children and young people with the skills and resources to support them to make the most of the opportunities from the future growth in these districts. In the long term, a community-level calculation of an SPI could act as a complement to SEIFA scores everywhere, identifying where individual disadvantage is compounded by poor outcomes from inaccessible or inappropriate service delivery.

Conclusion

Australia has experienced remarkable and unparalleled economic growth since the 1970s. Yet, there are great disparities between this growth and our social progress, demonstrating that tracking economic growth alone is not sufficient to understand how we are faring as a society. At federal and state levels, urban policy frameworks are embracing urban design approaches that support productive, liveable, and sustainable outcomes. However, design alone is insufficient. We must also be able to understand whether and where we are making social progress. Are we meeting basic human needs, establishing the building blocks that allow citizens and communities to enhance and sustain the quality of their lives, and create the conditions for all individuals to reach their full potential?

The SPI has promise. Social progress as a concept, and the SPI, was first used in Australia in 2018–19 with nationally relevant indicators and data. There is a significant opportunity for the SPI to be further adapted to measure social progress at a smaller scale. The issues accompanying growth in Sydney's west are one such opportunity, in an area in which social progress is at a crossroads. Urban designers and policymakers could use the components of the social progress framework to ensure that basic human needs, foundations of wellbeing, and opportunity are built into infrastructure and social scaffolding within communities.

There are of course challenges in using the SPI in a design and evolution process. For example, government responsibilities exist at local, state, and federal levels (requiring better integration and coordination); there are major gaps in the tracking and reporting of data; and results must be acted on by different players across government, business, not-for-profit, and community sectors in addition to individuals in the community. In selecting indicators at a community level, we also considered the annual availability of data, granularity, the adequacy of the sample sizes, and the reliability and transparency of the data collection processes. There are current limitations because of a lack of consistent environmental indicators, irregular collection of social indicators, and the 'deficit approach' of available Indigenous indicators. Finally, it will be important to also examine socio-spatial equity within communities.

Nonetheless, the social progress framework is a potentially positive tool for urban policy and the SPI can measure changes over time to see where and whether design and interventions are making a difference and can be used to adapt and apply changes with real-time, community-based responsiveness.

References

Annoni, P., and P. Bolsi. 2020. *The Regional Dimension of Social Progress in Europe*. Brussels: European Commission.

Australian Bureau of Statistics (ABS). 2020. *Australian System of National Accounts (2019–20 Financial Year)*. Catalogue no. 5204.0. Canberra: ABS. Available from: www.abs.gov.au/statistics/economy/national-accounts/australian-system-national-accounts/2019-20.

Australian Institute of Health and Welfare (AIHW). 2020. *Australia's Welfare 2019: In Brief*. Catalogue no. AUS 227. Canberra: AIHW.

Australian Sustainable Built Environment Council (ASBEC). 2013. *Productive, Liveable and Sustainable Cities for Australia: A Call to Action*. Sydney: ASBEC.

Centre for Social Impact (CSI). 2020. *Amplify Social Impact: Australian Social Progress Index*. Sydney: CSI. Available from: amplify.csi.edu.au/social-progress-index/.

Collins, A. 2021. 'First Look at What Sydney's Third City Centre Will Look Like as Work to Begin this Year.' *ABC News*, 15 June, [Updated 16 June]. Available from: www.abc.net.au/news/2021-06-15/bradfield-city-gets-1bn-for-western-sydney-airport-development/100215240.

Costanza, R., M. Hart, S. Posner, and J. Talberth. 2009. *Beyond GDP: The need for new measures of progress*. The Pardee Papers No. 4, January. Boston, MA: The Frederick S. Pardee Center for the Study of the Longer-Range Future, Boston University. Available from: www.bu.edu/pardee/files/documents/PP-004-GDP.pdf.

Davidson, P., B. Bradbury, M. Wong, and T. Hill. 2020. *Inequality in Australia. Part 1: Overview*. Sydney: Australian Council of Social Service & University of New South Wales. Available from: povertyandinequality.acoss.org.au/wp-content/uploads/2020/09/Inequality-in-Australia-2020-Part-1_FINAL.pdf.

Department of Environment and Greater Sydney Commission (GSC). 2017. *A Liveability Framework for Sydney*. Sydney: NSW Department of Environment and Greater Sydney Commission. Available from: greatercities.au/sites/default/files/2023-07/Liveability%20Framework_March2017.pdf.

Department of Infrastructure and Transport (DIT). 2011. *Our Cities, Our Future: A National Urban Policy for a Productive, Sustainable and Liveable Future*. Canberra: Commonwealth of Australia.

Department of Planning and Environment. 2021. 'Greater Sydney Districts.' In *A Metropolis of Three Cities*. Sydney: NSW Government. Available from: greatercities.au/strategic-planning/region-plans/metropolis-three-cities.

Department of Social Services (DSS). 2021. *JobSeeker Payment and Youth Allowance Recipients: Monthly Profile*. Canberra: Commonwealth of Australia. Available from: data.gov.au/data/dataset/jobseeker-payment-and-youth-allowance-recipients-monthly-profile.

Frydenberg, J., and S. Birmingham. 2020. *Mid-Year Economic and Fiscal Outlook 2020–21*. Canberra: Commonwealth of Australia. Available from: archive.budget.gov.au/2020-21/myefo/download/myefo-2020-21.pdf.

Greater Cities Commission. 2021. *Western City District Plan*. Sydney: Greater Cities Commission. Available from: www.greater.sydney/western-city-district-plan.

.id community. 2020. 'Population and Dwellings.' In *Western Sydney (LGA): Community Profile*. Melbourne: .id Consulting. Available from: profile.id.com.au/cws/population?WebID=230.

.id community. 2021. *Find Your Social Atlas ....* Melbourne: .id Consulting. Available from: atlas.id.com.au/.

Joint Standing Committee on Northern Australia. 2020. *Never Again: Inquiry into the Destruction of 46,000 Year Old Caves at the Juukan Gorge in the Pilbara Region of Western Australia. Interim Report.* Canberra: Parliament of the Commonwealth of Australia. Available from: parlinfo.aph.gov.au/parlInfo/download/committees/reportjnt/024579/toc_pdf/NeverAgain.pdf;fileType=application%2Fpdf.

Kapoor, A., and B. Debroy. 2019. 'GDP Is Not a Measure of Human Well-Being.' *Harvard Business Review*, 4 October. Available from: hbr.org/2019/10/gdp-is-not-a-measure-of-human-well-being.

Lim, P., S. Gemici, J. Rice, and T. Karmel. 2011. 'Socioeconomic Status and the Allocation of Government Resources in Australia: How Well Do Geographic Measures Perform?' *Education and Training* 53(7): 570–86. doi.org/10.1108/00400911111171977.

London Borough of Barking and Dagenham (LBBD). 2021. *Social Progress Index.* Barking, UK: LBBD. Available from: www.lbbd.gov.uk/social-progress-index.

Lowe, M., C. Whitzman, H. Badland, M. Davern, D. Hes, L. Aye, I. Butterworth, and B. Giles-Corti. 2013. *Liveable, Healthy, Sustainable: What Are the Key Indicators for Melbourne Neighbourhoods?* Place, Health and Liveability Research Program Research Paper 1, May. Melbourne: University of Melbourne.

Manaugh, K., M.G. Badami, and A.M. El-Geneidy. 2015. 'Integrating Social Equity into Urban Transportation Planning: A Critical Evaluation of Equity Objectives and Measures in Transportation Plans in North America.' *Transport Policy* 37: 167–76. doi.org/10.1016/j.tranpol.2014.09.013.

NSW Health. 2021. *COVID-19 in NSW.* Sydney: NSW Government. Available from: www.health.nsw.gov.au/Infectious/covid-19/Pages/stats-nsw.aspx.

Saunders, P. 2008. 'Measuring Wellbeing Using Non-Monetary Indicators: Deprivation and Social Exclusion.' *Family Matters* 78: 8–17. doi.org/10.3316/informit.101058957127508.

Social Progress Imperative. 2018a. Social Progress Imperative, Index & Network. Washington, DC: Social Progress Imperative. Unpublished internal document.

Social Progress Imperative. 2018b. *Social Progress Index: US States Methodology Summary.* Washington, DC: Social Progress Imperative.

Stern, S., A. Wares, and T. Epner. 2018. *2018 Social Progress Index Methodology Summary.* Washington, DC: Social Progress Imperative.

Tahmasbi, B., M.H. Mansourianfar, H. Haghshenas, and I. Kim. 2019. 'Multimodal Accessibility-Based Equity Assessment of Urban Public Facilities Distribution.' *Sustainable Cities and Society* 49: 101633. doi.org/10.1016/j.scs.2019.101633.

University of New South Wales (UNSW), Sydney Water, and Low-Carbon Living Cooperative Research Centre. 2017. *Cooling Western Sydney: A Strategic Study On the Role of Water in Mitigating Urban Heat in Western Sydney*. Sydney: Sydney Water Corporation. www.sydneywater.com.au/content/dam/sydneywater/documents/cooling-western-sydney.pdf.

Vinson, T. 2009. *Social Inclusion: Markedly Socially Disadvantaged Localities in Australia—Their Nature and Possible Remediation*. Social Inclusion Research Paper Series, No. 2. Canberra: Department of Education, Employment and Workplace Relations.

Vinson, T., M. Rawsthorne, A. Beavis, and M. Ericson. 2015. *Dropping Off the Edge: Persistent Communal Disadvantage in Australia*. Melbourne: Jesuit Social Services and Catholic Social Services Australia.

Weier, M., I. Saunders, L. Etuk, and P. Krylova. 2020. *Methodology Report: Social Progress Index Australia*. Sydney: Centre for Social Impact and Social Progress Imperative. Available from: amplify.csi.edu.au/documents/42/SPI_Methodology_Final.pdf.

17

Housing, income, and precarity: The Australian suburban settlement in an age of uncertainty

Laurence Troy[1]

Introduction

'Social citizenship' was one of the defining concepts of the 'welfare society' (Marshall 1950) that prevailed in many OECD countries in the decades after 1945. In Australia, Castles (1985, 1998) has argued that housing, and specifically homeownership, was an essential feature of the postwar welfare model that connected high wages with supportive welfare policies, enabling households to secure their own homes, and was epitomised in the concept of the postwar 'social settlement' (Kelly 1994; Randolph 2020). For Gleeson (2006), this social settlement underpinned the expansion of the nation's system of urban settlements in the postwar period, and he argues that the resulting 'suburban settlement' reflected the unique social and economic compromise that made Australia a relatively egalitarian nation during the twentieth century. Burke and Hulse (2010: 826) noted: 'In Australia it is probably more appropriate to talk in terms not of an ownership value but a *suburban* ownership value' (emphasis added).

---

1   This work was supported by the Australian Research Council (DP210102002).

However, the 'great unsettling' of the past 30 years has seen Australia's suburban settlement rapidly crumbling (Gleeson 2006; Stebbing and Spies-Butcher 2016), with a reversal of the postwar pattern of urban socio-spatial structure: the so-called urban inversion (Ehrenhalt 2012; Randolph 2017). The suburbs are now increasingly associated with areas of disadvantage while the inner city has gentrified.

During this time, Australia also witnessed a historically significant generational change in housing opportunities. For example, homeownership among 25- to 34-year-olds declined from more than 60 per cent in 1981 to 45 per cent in 2016, with ownership rates for this cohort in the bottom income quintile falling from 60 per cent to a little more than 20 per cent over this period (Daley and Coates 2018). For the first time since World War II, many younger Australians now face the prospect of a lifetime of 'housing precarity' as private renters rather than homeowners—the so-called Generation Rent (Hulse and Burke 2015; Hoolachan et al. 2017; Pawson et al. 2017). Adkins et al. (2021) go further and suggest that property asset wealth—increasingly concentrated among the older population—is now the defining feature of inequality in Australian society.

In parallel with changes to housing outcomes, structural changes in labour markets reflecting shifting policy goals and global economic imperatives have led to the increasing prevalence of 'precarious' or insecure and casual employment, especially in younger cohorts, both in Australia and internationally (Standing 2014; Stanford 2017; Rahman and Tomlinson 2018). Non-standard employment now accounts for nearly half of all jobs and has a bigger impact on women and the young (Melbourne Institute 2019). Insecurity and low wage inflation have resulted in wages declining in real terms, especially for younger cohorts compared with earlier generations (Bagshaw 2018; Rahman and Tomlinson 2018). Recently, high rates of overall inflation have only compounded the effects of low wage growth. Cumulatively, these changes in both income and housing security potentially mark a significant rupture in the postwar Australian social settlement and point to a generational shift in housing and employment pathways for those navigating the transition to independent living.

This chapter argues that the disintegration of these two interrelated pillars of Australia's postwar suburban settlement—homeownership and income security—is impacting on patterns of urban settlement. The chapter is broadly separated into two parts: the first outlines the conceptual and historical framing of the housing question and patterns of urban settlement in Australia in relation to wider ideas of social citizenship. The second part empirically explores some of the changes in dwelling and tenure outcomes across Australia, with a focus on Australia's largest city, Sydney. This section argues that the Australian suburban settlement of the twentieth century has given way to *the precarious city*—an emergent socio-spatial structure based on living and employment insecurity and wealth polarisation.

Social citizenship and property ownership

Marshall (1950) long ago put forward the proposition that 'citizenship' consisted of more than the civil and political liberties commonly associated with that term—the right to vote, freedom of speech, the right to own property, and the right to justice—and extended to the concept of 'social citizenship'. The last incorporated socially acceptable norms of economic welfare and security, which Marshall saw as a necessary condition of securing both formal and substantive rights in the domain of political and civil citizenship (Holston and Appadurai 1999). This idea is also reflected in wider discussions about liberal rights that ask 'without adequate conditions for the use of freedom, what is the value of freedom' (Waldron 1993: 6)? Such has been the influence of the concept of 'social citizenship' that welfare state ideas of the postwar period became deeply embedded in the Keynesian economic orthodoxy that drove the 'long boom' in Australian postwar development (Jessop 1995).

While the implementation of welfare state regimes across the developed world has varied significantly (Esping-Andersen 1990), Castles (1985) argues that Australia and Aotearoa New Zealand are wage-earners' welfare states and are unique in the Western context. Importantly, he argues that a core pillar of Australia's model of social citizenship is the ability to purchase one's own home. Consequently, postwar bipartisan support for maintaining wage levels and limited increases in taxation was partly driven by the need for working households to afford mortgage payments (Paris et al. 1993; Kemeny 2005; Gleeson 2006; Jacobs 2015). By the mid-1950s, this uniquely Australian model of delivering social citizenship inextricably tethered employment conditions and policy to the delivery of homeownership as the principal welfare security mechanism (Kemeny 1983; Troy 2012), particularly in retirement (Yates and Bradbury 2010). Political commentator Paul Kelly argued that the relationship between relatively high wages backed by a wage arbitration system, in return for a smaller role for government in taxation and welfare spending, was part of the Australian 'social settlement' (1994). This denoted an informal agreement between labour and capital, across class and political parties, that enshrined ideals of income, justice, employment, and security.

While this debate was perhaps not explicitly about housing, Castles (1998), Kemeny (1983), and others have argued that housing was a central issue. As far back as 1944, the Commonwealth Housing Commission wrote, 'We consider that a dwelling of good standard and equipment is not only the need but the right of every citizen' (quoted in Troy 2012: vi), making explicit the connection between citizen's rights and material standards of living. The housing program that was rolled out during this period did not immediately privilege homeownership. However, the election of the Menzies Government in 1949 marked a shift in focus and arguably embedded homeownership as the central element of modern Australian society. It was the pivotal element in Prime Minister Robert Menzies' broad pitch on what Australia should look like socially, economically, and politically:

> One of the best instincts in us is that which induces us to have one little piece of earth with a house and a garden which is ours; to which we can withdraw, in which we can be among our friends, into which no stranger may come against our will. (Menzies 1942)

In this context, homes became the centrepiece of middle-class Australia, embodying middle-class values for a middle-class society. It was an idea that was built around national patriotism, which 'inevitably springs from the instinct to defend and preserve our own homes' (Menzies 1942). As Harvey (2008) suggested, it was about disciplining labour as a protection against the notional rise of socialism and, if nothing else, turning the population into good consumers to fuel the long boom. In other words, housing and housing policy were simultaneously about the *rights of citizens*, the *model society*, and the *model economy*.

This broad social and economic compact had its roots in our cities, which at this time were set to embark on a sustained period of continuous growth. Gleeson (2006: 13) argues that the Australian social settlement 'was a stabilising order with deep foundations in the cities and their suburbs. It contributed immensely to the strength of the nation's system of urban settlements, and to the healthy growth of its offspring, the suburbs.' The 'suburban settlement' was born and, in a broad sense, underpinned a unique political and economic compact in contributing to make Australia a relatively egalitarian nation during the twentieth century (Gleeson 2006)

Precarious employment and homeownership

While urban scholars have been quick to point to the urban roots of the social settlement, what is perhaps glossed over is the role of employment in supporting the shape of Australian cities. One of the consequences of labour market reforms driven by neoliberal policies globally over the past several decades has been to undermine established employment practices and high wages (Harvey 2005). In the contemporary context, the rise of the 'gig economy' (Friedman 2014; Stanford 2017) signifies a shift to more 'flexible' work arrangements in which employment is undertaken on a temporary, time-limited, contract, and/or 'zero-hours contract' basis (Pennycook et al. 2013).

Notwithstanding that such practices have long existed (Stanford 2017), the resurgence of flexible or non-standard work practices has been crystallised in the concept of the 'precariat' (employees characterised by economic insecurity), which has undermined the work–life expectations of citizens (Standing 2014). In many ways, the recent focus on precarious employment is an extension of established theories on dualism or segmentation in the labour market, which contrast job outcomes in 'primary' sectors with those in 'secondary' sectors, especially in larger global cities (Sassen 1991; Ryan 2018). The secondary market is characterised by workers in low-paid, insecure, and low-status jobs with few career prospects, while primary-group members benefit from high skills, higher wages, good contract conditions, and career prospects. The increasing bifurcation of employment between these two broad groups highlights the structural recomposition of employment that has occurred after the postwar long boom since the 1980s.

But while growing income inequality has become a major economic concern globally (for example, Stiglitz 2012), recent literature on housing rarely *explicitly* explores the rise of labour market restructuring and precarious employment and its connection to changes in homeownership opportunities. A recent report by the Grattan Institute (Daley and Coates 2018), for example, highlights the disproportionate increase in housing costs over the past decade for younger generations in the lowest income quintile in comparison with higher income groups in the same generations. This valuable observation, connecting housing experiences to income, nevertheless stops short of investigating underlying structural changes in employment conditions as a cornerstone of the 'wage-earner welfare' state.

However, the recent intensification of housing unaffordability in major cities, coupled with declines in real wages and insecurity for many on lower incomes, potentially signals a major break in the established notion of a long-term housing career inevitably involving mortgage-supported homeownership linked to stable employment opportunities, both of which, as noted above, were essential pillars of the postwar consensus on social citizenship (Malpass 2008; Yates and Bradbury 2010; Acolin et al. 2016). This calls into question the basis of the ongoing policy frameworks and the assumed household career trajectories that still adhere to asset-based welfare prescriptions.

The 'great unsettling': Financialisation and the re-emergence of private rental

Gleeson (2006) makes the case that the long boom bringing full employment, high wages, and a supportive policy context helped deliver the modern suburbs we know today. Since the 1980s, however, there has been an 'unsettling' driven by a broad neoliberalisation of the economy and urban processes (Gleeson and Low 2000; Adkins et al. 2021). Deregulation of banking and finance, weakening of the industrial relations system, economic globalisation, and the withdrawal and privatisation of government services have all radically reshaped the economic landscape in which households are operating.

The impact on cities has been well documented. Randolph (2020), for example, argues that mid-ring and fringe suburbs, far from being centres of opportunity and relative wealth equality, have become repositories of disadvantage. The 'urban inversion' or the 'great unsettling' has seen once 'aspirational' suburbs increasingly isolated from the employment and wealth–generating opportunities that have concentrated in and near the urban core. At the same time, this core has been all but emptied of low-income and disadvantaged households who have increasingly been pushed to the suburbs (Randolph and Tice 2017). There they have been accommodated in new urban housing markets to match the realities of employment insecurity—for example, the development of a suburban lower-value private rental market (Pawson et al. 2015; Hulse and Reynolds 2018).

Recent research has centred on the favourable tax treatment of investors and the role of the rental investor market in the deterioration in housing affordability in Australia's cities (Pawson and Martin 2021), with loans to investors in 2016 accounting for more than 50 per cent of new mortgage finance for the first time in Australia's postwar history (Adkins et al. 2021). Hulse and Reynolds (2018) have termed this process 'investification', which captures both the involvement of individual 'mum and dad' investors in the process supported by favourable taxation arrangements and its role in underpinning the suburbanisation of disadvantage.

This could have long-term impacts. The apparent shift in housing careers means that the spectre of a growing proportion of Generation Rent reaching retirement age with limited housing assets has the potential to place a considerable burden on a system that relies on property ownership in old age to underpin a reasonable living standard (Yates and Bradbury 2010; Beer and Faulkner 2011; Stebbing and Spies-Butcher 2016). Recent first-time buyers who have managed to secure property ownership are now increasingly relying on family wealth to do so and, as Stebbing and Spies-Butcher (2016) note, the current trajectory of housing opportunity is generating a system in which inheritance and *inter vivos* gifts become essential supports for securing homeownership for first-time buyers, further entrenching wealth class divides in Australia and elsewhere (Forrest and Yip 2013; Christophers 2018). Increasingly, younger generations have found themselves locked out of owner-occupied housing and facing a political economic system that is 'locked into' asset-price inflation and property investing as necessary to maintaining the Australian economy (Konings et al. 2021). Housing policy has arguably shifted from one of *home*ownership in the twentieth century to one of *property* ownership in the twenty-first. Consequently, Maclennan et al. (2021: 5) have noted that homeownership in Australia has 'transitioned from a wealth spreading to a wealth concentrating institution'.

While these developments have been seen as inequalities generated in and by housing markets, they have not been directly connected to wider concerns about social citizenship and models of society. Thus, a key plank of the postwar suburban settlement has been significantly undermined, with those unable to invest in property, for whatever reason, effectively excluded from asset accumulation and now reliant on renting from those who can. This brings into question two of the central elements of Australia's long-established welfare model: secure employment with high wages and homeownership. It also raises important questions about the shape of urban settlement in Australian cities and a new urban social-spatial model that embeds inequality at its heart.

The rise of the precarious city

If the suburban settlement and *homeownership* of the twentieth century embodied a commitment to social citizenship and some level of socioeconomic equality, how is the shift to *property ownership* and increasing socioeconomic inequality reshaping or being shaped by Australian cities? Experiences of this change have varied across the country as expressed by the range of ownership rates. For example, while approximately 70 per cent of Perth households are homeowners, the figure for Sydney is 61 per cent (ABS 2021), with house price inflation also geographically contingent.

Australia's largest cities of Sydney and Melbourne have been at the forefront of the 'investification' process and have experienced some of the sharpest declines in homeownership over the past decade. For the first time, during 2015, finance commitments to residential investors exceeded those of owner-occupiers in New South Wales (ABS 2016b), showing an increasing dominance of investor owners within the housing market. While these are NSW trends, anecdotally, this is likely to be concentrated in Sydney, as reflected in the underlying rates of owner-occupation in Sydney compared with the rest of New South Wales. This change is not only about a decline in homeownership and a rise in private rental, but also a story of indebtedness of households broadly.

Figures 17.1a and 17.1b show the dominant housing tenure across Sydney since 2001, when outright ownership represented the largest group of households in most areas. There has since been a gradual shift to mortgaged households through the 2000s in the outer-ring suburbs and to renter households in much of the inner and middle-ring suburbs. The higher dwelling prices have been driving higher levels of debt, but also the leveraging of existing property ownership to support investment in additional property has been an important part of rising rates of mortgaged households (Allon and Parker 2016). Generous tax concessions have been capitalised into rising property prices, further inflated by cheap housing finance, with an inevitable impact on falling homeownership rates among the young (Daley and Coates 2018). Those locked out of homeownership underlie the trend towards renter households emerging as the largest cohort in large parts of the city (Pawson et al. 2017; Konings et al. 2021).

2001

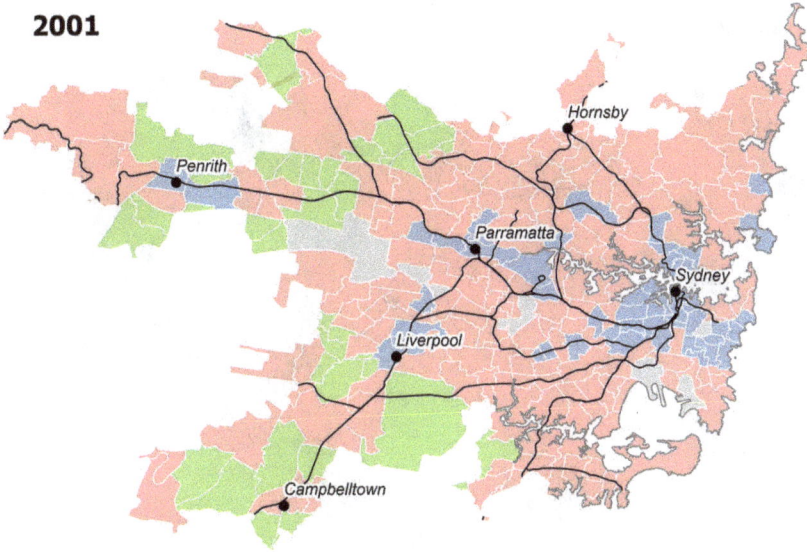

2006

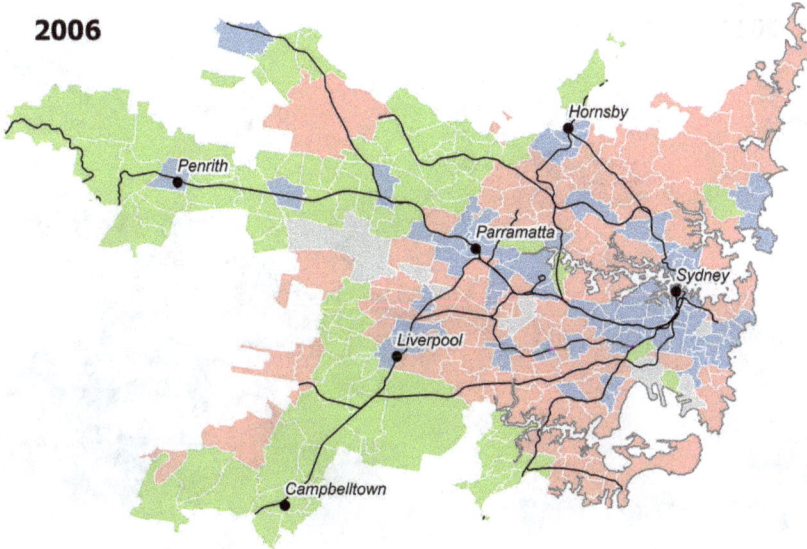

Own | N/A
Purchasing | — Train Line
Renting

0   10   20
Kilometres

**Figure 17.1a Dominant housing tenure in Sydney by Statistical Area
Level 2, 2001–2006**

Source: ABS (2011).

2011

2016

Own		N/A	
Purchasing		— Train Line	
Renting			

0   10   20
Kilometres

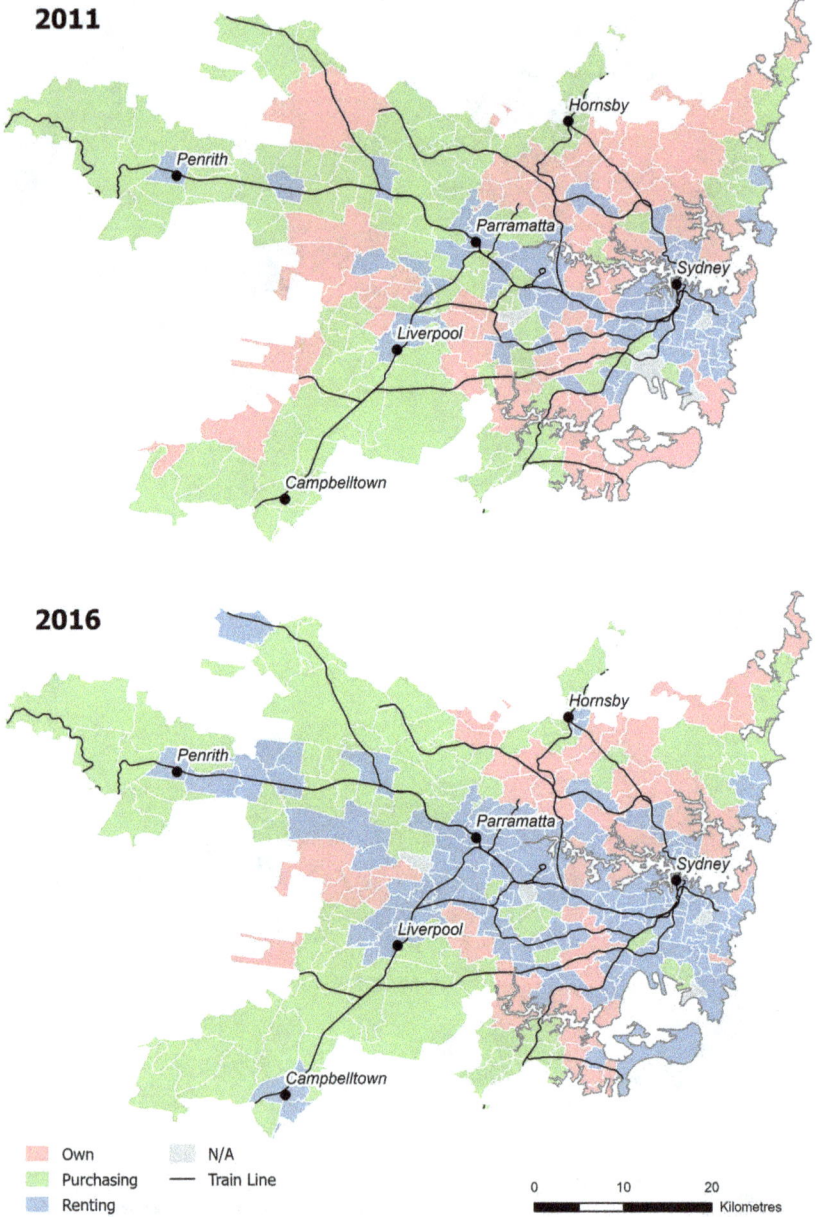

Figure 17.1b Dominant housing tenure in Sydney by Statistical Area Level 2, 2011–2016

Source: ABS (2016a).

Table 17.1 Tenure breakdown by dwelling type in three Australian capital cities, 2016

	Greater Sydney		Greater Melbourne		Greater Brisbane	
	Flats (3+ storeys)	All other dwellings	Flats (3+ storeys)	All other dwellings	Flats (3+ storeys)	All other dwellings
Owner occupied	29.6%	63.3%	21.5%	61.8%	24.4%	58.1%
Private rental	46.6%	19.2%	48.5%	20.9%	47.7%	25.1%
Public/ community housing	4.5%	4.2%	6.2%	1.9%	4.8%	3.2%
Other tenure (including visitor-only)	10.1%	6.6%	11.5%	6.6%	10.3%	6.5%
Unoccupied	9.2%	6.8%	12.3%	8.8%	12.8%	7.1%
Total dwellings	436,787	1,397,385	184,741	1,631,965	81,464	809,545
Investment ownership[a]	65.9%	32.6%	72.3%	36.3%	70.8%	38.7%

[a] Includes private rental, other tenure, and unoccupied dwellings.

Source: ABS (2016a).

As argued elsewhere (Konings et al. 2021), financial logic is driving this change, but there is also a physical transformation underpinning this shift. The location of renter households along rail transport corridors is instructive as to the nature of this transformation. Apartments have been the dominant form of new housing development in Sydney for the past three decades and while there has been dispersal across the region, there has been considerable concentration of this type of housing along railway corridors. The high-density boom of the mid-2000s and mid-2010s delivered predominantly 'investor-grade' rental accommodation across larges parts of Sydney (Troy et al. 2020). In 2016, the census revealed some stark differences in tenure breakdown across housing types. Two-thirds of all apartments are in investor ownership compared with just one-third in other dwelling types. This concentration is even more apparent in Melbourne and Brisbane, at 72 per cent and 70 per cent, respectively (Table 17.1).

Given that nearly 80 per cent of new development in Sydney is taking this form, this points to an emerging housing system predicated on investor-driven logic. When we overlay this with a new generation of would-be homeowners, that trend is starker. Focusing on the key household-formation demographic of 25- to 34-year-olds, a more nuanced picture emerges.

From 2006 to 2016 in Sydney, there was a net decline in the number of households who owned houses, with the biggest jump in dwelling type and tenure being rented apartments (Table 17.2). The only city in Australia to experience substantial net growth in the number of households in the 25- to 34-year-old demographic who own houses was Perth. When examining the gain in tenure-dwelling share, all cities showed a decline in owned houses while the biggest gains were in rented apartments, except for Adelaide and Perth, where it was in rented houses (Table 17.3). In other words, the key transition across the largest Australian cities is not just of movement away from homeownership generally, but also movement away from owned *houses*, to rented *apartments*. There is also a geographic pattern to this that emerges in Sydney, whereby the dominant tenure for this household-formation cohort in large parts of the central and mid-ring suburbs is rental apartments, while in outer suburbs it is owned houses, with some notable exceptions around the key centres of Bankstown, Blacktown, Fairfield, and Liverpool (Figure 17.2).

Table 17.2 Capital city change in tenure of 25–34-year-olds (household heads), 2006–2016

	Houses		Apartments (3+ storeys)		Total	
	Owned	Rented	Owned	Rented	Owned	Rented
Greater Sydney	−9,811	−71	7,223	29,645	−2,579	29,577
Greater Melbourne	1,930	28,161	5,880	22,984	7,806	51,147
Greater Brisbane	347	15,269	1,484	8,875	1,835	24,142
Greater Adelaide	−341	8,453	194	994	−141	9,454
Greater Perth	15,430	16,272	1,122	4,098	16,556	20,380

Source: ABS (2016a).

Table 17.3 Capital city change in share of tenure of 25–34-year-olds (household heads), 2006–2016 (per cent)

	Houses		Apartments (3+ storeys)	
	Owned	Rented	Owned	Rented
Greater Sydney	−7	−3	2	9
Greater Melbourne	−10	2	2	7
Greater Brisbane	−9	3	1	5
Greater Adelaide	−8	6	0	1
Greater Perth	−5	3	1	2

Source: ABS (2016a).

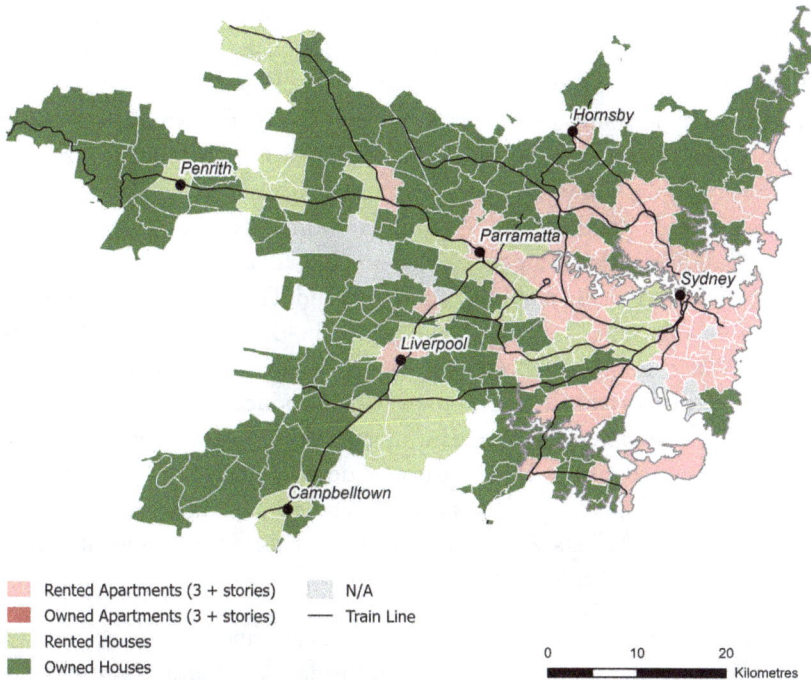

Figure 17.2 Dominant tenure and dwelling type for households headed by 25–34-year-olds, 2016

Source: ABS (2016a).

Geographic differences partly reflect the nature of housing supply, in that where new housing development is in the form of houses, owner-occupation seems to follow, compared with areas in which apartments are being built, where rental follows. But there are fundamentally different drivers of the apartment and house markets: in houses, it is still by and large owner-occupation, whereas in apartments it is investment. The vertical shift reshaping the future of Australia's larger cities is one rooted in an investment or financialised logic supported by national taxation policies that provide exceptional tax incentives for investment in private rental as a way of building household wealth. While this is not necessarily intentional, it has come at the price of driving broad social inequality. Whereas postwar suburban settlement was rooted in some commitment to social equality and wealth distribution, the key process driving change in the twenty-first century is premised on inequality and concentration of wealth.

These observations are not about fetishising the form of housing but are nonetheless critical to understanding the changing nature of urban settlement. This is an important side note to compact city conversations that are quick to point out the amenity benefits of inner-city living, yet fail to recognise that the emergent experience, in Sydney at least, is *suburban* apartment living. There are considerable challenges to apartment living (Easthope and Randolph 2009) and apartment construction broadly, where building defects are rife (Crommelin et al. 2021), design lacks basic consideration for children (Easthope and Tice 2011), and there are often poor outcomes for low-income households (Easthope et al. 2020, 2022). While policy interventions can certainly address many of these challenges, the current situation potentially introduces a range of inequities in housing outcomes for those in apartments. As noted above, this is principally a recognition that apartment development is being driven by speculative development practices that both reflect and are impacting on the financialisation (Aalbers 2016) of housing and the polarisation of wealth through property (Adkins et al. 2021).

Returning to the wider national policy debate about housing and its connections to the models of social citizenship and wealth accumulation, that conversation has not caught up with the housing reality emerging in our largest cities. It is still framed by old ideas about Australia as a nation of suburban house owners and the benefits of owner-occupation extending into retirement, whereas the prospectus for the locked-out generation is one of precarity, insecurity, and uncertainty. Some domains of housing policy have attempted to address the insecurities of the rental experience by advocating longer leases, ending no-grounds evictions, and generally pushing the power imbalance back towards tenants.

Likewise, another key area of policy debate is focused squarely on the provision of social housing as a welfare good of last resort. At the other end of the spectrum, there is a long history of research to address the challenges of attaining homeownership and interventions that are designed to assist first-time buyers. Indeed, the only consistent strand of policy and shared commitment across party lines over the past 30 years has been a focus on assisting younger generations to buy homes through various grants and concession schemes. This research, while valuable, risks normalising rental as a long-term option, solidifying social and affordable housing as a residual welfare good, and adding more liquidity into housing markets, reinforcing the very inequalities that make housing problematic in the first place.

Conclusion

A key claim of this chapter is that housing has been a central feature of Australia's model of citizenship over the past 70 years. If high and secure wages and low welfare spending were the centrepiece of the Australian social settlement that defined the second half of the twentieth century, housing is what made this a solid compact. The suburban settlement gave rise to a unique model of social citizenship that was woven into the very fabric of Australian society and culture. Its demise marked the beginning of a transition in which housing and *homeownership* shifted to *property ownership* as a foundation pillar of the Australian settlement. This has been enabled by a decisive shift in the socio-spatial structure of Australia's largest cities.

Insecure, short-term, and underemployment, with low or no wage inflation, has delivered an increasing sense of precarity in the working lives of the younger generation in particular. This has been matched by the arrival of increasingly precarious living arrangements with much higher rates of private rental, and indebtedness for those who do manage homeownership. This fusion of precarious employment and precarious living is driving a new form of urban change: arise the *precarious city*. The dominant experience now is one not of suburban homeownership, but defined by rental in higher density, and increasingly suburban, apartment living.

The wealth dimension that is embedded in changes to housing pathways is now opening new, or perhaps reintroducing old, social fault lines along which property wealth is the key driver of class difference and socioeconomic inequality. Recognising that well-endowed homeowners, and particularly those with multiple properties, have been the direct beneficiaries of government policy and concessions over a long period is key to expanding the public discussion beyond that of residual welfare support. By understanding the wealthy as key beneficiaries of public policy, even proponents of neoliberal policy would recognise and support that this represents an unfair distortion of free markets. Perhaps the key challenge for urban and housing scholarship broadly is to reposition equality, and specifically wealth equality, as a normative judgement with which to frame both scholarship and advocacy. Future housing policy, then, ought to begin by situating specifics on wealth inequalities and ideas of social citizenship within a housing system framework in which government is seen as intervening in all parts of the housing market. That being the case, housing policy and advocacy could look to arguments about social citizenship and seeing housing as a key enabler of civil and political citizenship and all the rights and responsibilities this may entail, to frame future housing policy ambition.

References

Aalbers, M. 2016. *The Financialization of Housing: A Political Economy Approach*. New York, NY: Routledge. doi.org/10.4324/9781315668666.

Acolin, A., L.S. Goodman, and S.M. Wachter. 2016. 'A Renter or Homeowner Nation?' *Cityscape* 18(1): 145–58.

Adkins, L., M. Cooper, and M. Konings. 2021. 'Class in the 21st Century: Asset Inflation and the New Logic of Inequality.' *Environment and Planning A: Economy and Space* 53(3): 548–72. doi.org/10.1177/0308518X19873673.

Allon, F., and J. Parker. 2016. 'Building on Sand? Liquid Housing Wealth in an Era of Financialisation.' In *Housing and Home Unbound: Intersections in Economics, Environment and Politics in Australia*, edited by N.T. Cook, A. Davison, and L. Crabtree, 56–71. London: Routledge.

Australian Bureau of Statistics (ABS). 2011. *Census of Population and Housing (2011)*. Canberra: ABS.

Australian Bureau of Statistics (ABS). 2016a. *Census of Population and Housing (2016)*. Canberra: ABS.

Australian Bureau of Statistics (ABS). 2016b. *Housing Finance, Australia (April 2016)*. Catalogue No. 5609.0. Canberra: ABS. Available from: www.abs.gov.au/ausstats/abs@.nsf/7d12b0f6763c78caca257061001cc588/76afb21c982098edca257fea00176844!OpenDocument.

Australian Bureau of Statistics (ABS). 2021. *Census of Population and Housing (2021)*. Canberra: ABS.

Bagshaw, E. 2018. 'Full-Time Median Earnings Grow by Just 1.5 Per Cent.' *Sydney Morning Herald*, 26 February. Available from: www.smh.com.au/politics/federal/full-time-median-earnings-grow-by-just-1-5-per-cent-20180226-p4z1rk.html.

Beer, A., and D. Faulkner. 2011. *Housing Transitions through the Lifecourse: Needs, Aspirations and Policy*. Bristol, UK: Policy Press. doi.org/10.46692/9781847429360.

Burke, T., and K. Hulse. 2010. 'The Institutional Structure of Housing and the Sub-Prime Crisis: An Australian Case Study.' *Housing Studies* 25(6): 821–38. doi.org/10.1080/02673037.2010.511161.

Castles, F.G. 1985. *The Working Class and Welfare: Reflections on the Political Development of the Welfare State in Australia and New Zealand, 1890–1980.* Sydney: Allen & Unwin in association with Port Nicholson Press.

Castles, F.G. 1998. 'The Really Big Trade-Off: Home Ownership and the Welfare State in the New World and Old.' *Acta Politica* 33(1): 5–19.

Christophers, B. 2018. 'Intergenerational Inequality? Labour, Capital, and Housing Through the Ages.' *Antipode* 50(1): 101–21. doi.org/10.1111/anti.12339.

Crommelin, L., S. Thompson, H. Easthope, M. Loosemore, H. Yang, C. Buckle, and B. Randolph. 2021. *Cracks in the Compact City: Tackling Defects in Multi-Unit Strata Housing.* Final Project Report, October. Sydney: City Futures Research Centre, University of New South Wales.

Daley, J., and B. Coates. 2018. *Housing Affordability: Re-Imagining the Australian Dream.* Melbourne: Grattan Institute.

Easthope, H., L. Crommelin, S.-M. Kerr, L. Troy, R. van den Nouwelant, and G. Davison. 2022. 'Planning for Lower-Income Households in Privately Developed High-Density Neighbourhoods in Sydney, Australia.' *Urban Planning* 7(4): 1–16. doi.org/10.17645/up.v7i4.5699.

Easthope, H., L. Crommelin, L. Troy, G. Davison, M. Nethercote, S. Foster, R. van den Nouwelant, A. Kleeman, B. Randolph, and R. Horne. 2020. *Improving Outcomes for Apartment Residents and Neighbourhoods.* Final Report No. 329, 28 May. Melbourne: AHURI. doi.org/10.18408/ahuri-7120701.

Easthope, H., and B. Randolph. 2009. 'Governing the Compact City: The Challenges of Apartment Living in Sydney, Australia.' *Housing Studies* 24(2): 243–59. doi.org/10.1080/02673030802705433.

Easthope, H., and A. Tice. 2011. 'Children in Apartments: Implications for the Compact City.' *Urban Policy and Research* 29(4): 415–34. doi.org/10.1080/08111146.2011.627834.

Ehrenhalt, A. 2012. *The Great Inversion and the Future of the American City.* New York, NY: Vintage.

Esping-Andersen, G. 1990. *The Three Worlds of Welfare Capitalism.* Cambridge, UK: Polity Press.

Forrest, R., and N. Yip. 2013. *Young People and Housing: Transitions, Trajectories and Generational Fractures.* New York, NY: Routledge. doi.org/10.4324/9780203095096.

Friedman, G. 2014. 'Workers Without Employers: Shadow Corporations and the Rise of the Gig Economy.' *Review of Keynesian Economics* 2(2): 171–88. doi.org/10.4337/roke.2014.02.03.

Gleeson, B. 2006. *Australian Heartlands: Making Space for Hope in the Suburbs.* Sydney: Allen & Unwin.

Gleeson, B., and N. Low. 2000. 'Revaluing Planning: Rolling Back Neo-Liberalism in Australia.' *Progress in Planning* 53(2): 83–164. doi.org/10.1016/S0305-9006(99)00022-7.

Harvey, D. 2005. *A Brief History of Neoliberalism.* Oxford, UK: Oxford University Press. doi.org/10.1093/oso/9780199283262.003.0010.

Harvey, D. 2008. 'The Right to the City.' *New Left Review* 53(September–October): 23–40.

Holston, J., and A. Appadurai. 1999. 'Introduction: Cities and Citizenship.' In *Cities and Citizenship*, edited by J. Holston, 1–18. Durham, NC: Duke University Press. doi.org/10.2307/j.ctv11cw70j.4.

Hoolachan, J.E., K. McKee, T. Moore, and A.M. Soaita. 2017. '"Generation Rent" and the Ability to "Settle Down": Economic and Geographical Variation in Young People's Housing Transitions.' *Journal of Youth Studies* 20(1): 63–78. doi.org/10.1080/13676261.2016.1184241.

Hulse, K., and T. Burke. 2015. 'Private Rental Housing in Australia: Political Inertia and Market Change.' In *Housing in 21st Century Australia: People, Practices and Policies*, edited by R. Dufty-Jones and D. Rogers, 139–52. Aldershot, UK: Ashgate.

Hulse, K., and M. Reynolds. 2018. 'Investification: Financialisation of Housing Markets and Persistence of Suburban Socio-Economic Disadvantage.' *Urban Studies* 55(8): 1655–71. doi.org/10.1177/0042098017734995.

Jacobs, K. 2015. 'A Reverse Form of Welfarism: Some Reflections on Australian Housing Policy.' *Australian Journal of Social Issues* 50(1): 53–68. doi.org/10.1002/j.1839-4655.2015.tb00334.x.

Jessop, B. 1995. 'The Regulation Approach, Governance and Post-Fordism: Alternative Perspectives on Economic and Political Change?' *Economy and Society* 24(3): 307–33. doi.org/10.1080/03085149500000013.

Kelly, P. 1994. *The End of Certainty: Power, Politics and Business in Australia.* Sydney: Allen & Unwin.

Kemeny, J. 1983. *The Great Australian Nightmare: A Critique of the Home-Ownership Ideology.* Melbourne: Georgian House.

Kemeny, J. 2005. '"The Really Big Trade-Off" between Home Ownership and Welfare: Castles' Evaluation of the 1980 Thesis, and a Reformulation 25 Years On.' *Housing, Theory and Society* 22(2): 59–75. doi.org/10.1080/140360905 10032727.

Konings, M., L. Adkins, G. Bryant, S. Maalsen, and L. Troy. 2021. 'Lock-In and Lock-Out: COVID-19 and the Dynamics of the Asset Economy.' *Journal of Australian Political Economy* 87(Winter): 20–47.

Maclennan, D., J. Long, and C. Leishman. 2021. *Housing Wealth and the Economy: All That Glitters Is Not Gold.* Sydney: City Futures Research Centre, University of New South Wales.

Malpass, P. 2008. 'Housing and the New Welfare State: Wobbly Pillar or Cornerstone?' *Housing Studies* 23(1): 1–19. doi.org/10.1080/0267303070173 1100.

Marshall, T. 1950. *Citizenship and Social Class, and Other Essays.* Cambridge, UK: Cambridge University Press.

Melbourne Institute. 2019. *Living in Australia: A Snapshot of Australian Society and How It Is Changing Over Time.* Melbourne: Melbourne Institute.

Menzies, R. 1942. 'The Forgotten People.' Speech, [Radio broadcast], 22 May. Available from: www.menziesrc.org/the-forgotten-people.

Paris, C., A. Beer, and W. Sanders. 1993. *Housing Australia.* Melbourne: Macmillan. doi.org/10.1007/978-1-349-15160-8.

Pawson, H., K. Hulse, and L. Cheshire. 2015. *Addressing Concentrations of Disadvantage in Urban Australia.* Melbourne: AHURI.

Pawson, H., K. Hulse, and A. Morris. 2017. 'Interpreting the Rise of Long-Term Private Renting in a Liberal Welfare Regime Context.' *Housing Studies* 32(8): 1062–84. doi.org/10.1080/02673037.2017.1301400.

Pawson, H., and C. Martin. 2021. 'Rental Property Investment in Disadvantaged Areas: The Means and Motivations of Western Sydney's New Landlords.' *Housing Studies* 36(5): 621–43. doi.org/10.1080/02673037.2019.1709806.

Pennycook, M., G. Cory, and V. Alakeson. 2013. *A Matter of Time: The Rise of Zero-Hours Contracts.* London: The Resolution Foundation.

Rahman, F., and D. Tomlinson. 2018. *Cross Countries: International Comparisons of Intergenerational Trends.* Intergenerational Commission Report, February. London: The Resolution Foundation. Available from: www.resolution foundation.org/app/uploads/2018/02/IC-international.pdf.

Randolph, B. 2017. 'Emerging Geographies of Suburban Disadvantage.' In *The SAGE Handbook of New Urban Studies*, edited by J.A. Hannigan and R. Greg, 159–78. London: SAGE. doi.org/10.4135/9781412912655.n11.

Randolph, B. 2020. 'Dimensions of Urban Segregation at the End of the Australian Dream.' In *Handbook of Urban Segregation*, edited by S. Musterd, 76–100. London: Edward Elgar. doi.org/10.4337/9781788115605.00012.

Randolph, B., and A. Tice. 2017. 'Relocating Disadvantage in Five Australian Cities: Socio-Spatial Polarisation under Neo-Liberalism.' *Urban Policy and Research* 35(2): 103–21. doi.org/10.1080/08111146.2016.1221337.

Ryan, P. 2018. 'Primary and Secondary Labour Markets.' In *The New Palgrave Dictionary of Economics*, 10728–31. London: Palgrave Macmillan. doi.org/10.1057/978-1-349-95189-5_1617.

Sassen, S. 1991. *The Global City: New York, London, Tokyo*. Princeton, NJ: Princeton University Press.

Standing, G. 2014. *A Precariat Charter: From Denizens to Citizens*. London: Bloomsbury. doi.org/10.5040/9781472510631.

Stanford, J. 2017. 'The Resurgence of Gig Work: Historical and Theoretical Perspectives.' *The Economic and Labour Relations Review* 28(3): 382–401. doi.org/10.1177/1035304617724303.

Stebbing, A., and B. Spies-Butcher. 2016. 'The Decline of a Homeowning Society? Asset-Based Welfare, Retirement and Intergenerational Equity in Australia.' *Housing Studies* 31(2): 190–207. doi.org/10.1080/02673037.2015.1070797.

Stiglitz, J.E. 2012. *The Price of Inequality: How Today's Divided Society Endangers Our Future*. New York, NY: W.W. Norton.

Troy, L., B. Randolph, S. Pinnegar, L. Crommelin, and H. Easthope. 2020. 'Vertical Sprawl in the Australian City: Sydney's High-Rise Residential Development Boom.' *Urban Policy and Research* 38(1): 18–36. doi.org/10.1080/08111146.2019.1709168.

Troy, P.N. 2012. *Accommodating Australians: Commonwealth Government Involvement in Housing*. Sydney: The Federation Press.

Waldron, J. 1993. *Liberal Rights: Collected Papers, 1981–1991*. Cambridge, UK: Cambridge University Press.

Yates, J., and B. Bradbury. 2010. 'Home Ownership as a (Crumbling) Fourth Pillar of Social Insurance in Australia.' *Journal of Housing and the Built Environment* 25(2): 193–211. doi.org/10.1007/s10901-010-9187-4.

18

Towards a national housing policy for the 2020s

Hal Pawson and Vivienne Milligan

Introduction

The start of the 2020s sees Australia remaining close to the top of the global housing unaffordability league (Demographia 2020). The country's growing international notoriety on this score is reflected domestically in the way that controversy over housing policy has formed a prominent flashpoint in four of the past six federal elections (2007–22)—after a long period of relative electoral obscurity.

Rising stress affecting Australia's housing system is manifest in numerous ways. Central to these is the long-run trajectory for house prices to rise ahead of incomes, increasingly restricting access to homeownership to high-income households and those benefiting from family wealth. Homeownership among young adults (aged 25–34 years)—a key measure of concern—has fallen from 61 per cent to 43 per cent since 1981 (Whelan et al. 2023). Meanwhile, the proportion of low-income households facing unaffordable housing costs rose from 35 per cent to 43 per cent over the decade to 2017–18 (ABS 2019). Moreover, rising mortgage debt is the main factor propelling Australia's overall household debt-to-income ratio close to the top of the developed-country ranking (OECD 2021). Indeed, there are growing calls for recognition that such housing system outcomes represent an impost on Australia's economic performance, as well as its population welfare (Daley et al. 2018; Maclennan et al. 2018, 2021).

Despite the importance of this issue and its rising popular prominence, a national housing policy or plan to address attendant challenges has been absent since the postwar reconstruction schemes of the Curtin Government. The Commonwealth Government's largely disengaged stance on housing for much of the ensuing period was a key component of Pat Troy's (1978) critique of the nation's divergence from 1945 aspirations for postwar urban planning. A central consideration in this discussion is the status and positioning of housing within the governance and institutions of the Australian federation.

The main aim of this chapter, therefore, is to assess the case for a national housing policy and to suggest how such a framework could be justified and positioned. The chapter begins by briefly exploring the relevant constitutional considerations that underlie debates about the governance of housing policy in Australia. Next, it assesses the Commonwealth Government's role in housing policy during the postwar period, highlighting some discontinuities and critical moments. This leads to a review of recent developments in the ongoing contestation around the attribution of governmental responsibility for housing matters. Against this context and history, the chapter attempts to define the challenges that a 2020s national housing policy—or housing strategy—would appropriately address, and the institutional reforms needed to deliver this.

Housing policy in Australia: Constitutional status and complexity

Critical to any consideration of housing policy in Australia is the nation's federal governance structure as underpinned by the Australian Constitution. Given that the specified areas of national government competence (Section 51) designate no powers to legislate on housing or urban issues, the nation's founding charter is conventionally understood as assigning responsibility for housing, and urban-related decision-making, and any necessary intervention to state and territory governments (hereinafter 'states'). Thus, the comment of a former federal transport and urban development minister, John Sharp, that there is 'no clear rationale or constitutional basis' for Commonwealth Government involvement in urban matters (quoted in Simons 2011).

On this understanding, therefore, whatever housing priorities (if any) are favoured at the national level, directly relevant interventions or regulations can be implemented only by the lower tiers of government (Parkin 1992). However, there is no legal bar to the Commonwealth's active interest in the housing system, including an interest in (although not control over) the direct delivery of housing services. Indeed, the federal government has maintained significant housing funding agreements with the states throughout the entire postwar period and has regularly initiated explicit interventions in the housing system.

Beyond this, as argued by Winter (2015), there is in fact a range of constitutionally prescribed Commonwealth policy responsibilities that impact on the housing system. Most importantly, these include banking (for example, housing finance regulation), taxation (including property-associated tax settings), social security (for example, housing-related transfer payments), and immigration (a crucial component of housing demand). In other words, under a holistic conception of 'housing policy', many of the key levers are held at the national level, and not by the states.

Moreover, as increasingly recognised, housing system outcomes can have negative implications for the economy as well as population wellbeing and social cohesion—all important objectives for Australia as a nation. New evidence backs the contention that housing system outcomes are increasingly impairing economic performance through impacts on productivity, financial stability, and inequality (Maclennan et al. 2021). Such concerns can hardly be dismissed as irrelevant to federal administrative obligations.

Even from a narrower 'cost to government' perspective, the Commonwealth cannot afford to disown an interest in the functioning of the housing system. On the current trajectory of falling homeownership, for example, future budgetary challenges will arise in relation to age pension expenditure, as Australia's comparatively low age pension payment rate becomes hard to sustain in the face of more pensioners exposed to rising rents in retirement (Eslake 2017; Coates and Chen 2019). Therefore, on several levels, the Commonwealth's constitutional responsibilities and self-interest create rational imperatives for its active concern with housing.

Nevertheless, as we shall see, over the past 75 years, the federal government's explicit attention to housing has been, at best, episodic—and, at worst, a 'long term abrogation of responsibility and narrowing of the policy agenda' (Milligan and Tiernan 2011: 396).

Before reviewing that story, it is important to emphasise a crucial implication of the housing-related powers held by the Commonwealth. 'Housing policy' in fact encompasses a much broader set of tools and settings than often officially acknowledged. To put this another way, housing policy must be recognised as extending across all the interventions that impact on the production, financing, use, and management of residential property, irrespective of whether these fall within the remit of a government department with 'housing' in its title. At the same time, housing is a complex and interconnected system in which numerous factors affect both demand and supply.

Without treating housing as a system, policy interventions are unlikely to be effective in any fundamental way. Indeed, as in the notorious instances of first home-buyer grants and tax concessions that drive up demand leading to an escalation in house prices, they can prove counterproductive (Freebairn 1999; Eslake 2013).

National housing policy in Australia: A brief review of historical milestones

The postwar impetus

The clearest and, arguably, the only full-blooded assertion of national housing policy in Australia occurred towards the end of World War II via the 1943 Commonwealth Housing Commission (CHC) and its 1944 final report—a document described by Sandercock (1976: 16) as 'remarkable ... perhaps the most imaginative and comprehensive ever presented to an Australian government'. It was issued within the context of national planning for postwar reconstruction—a mission that endowed the Commonwealth Government with authority unprecedented since Federation in 1901 (Howe 2000; Freestone 2012). Accordingly, the CHC's recommendations envisaged a leading peacetime role for the Commonwealth in housing, as part of a much-enlarged influence over urban planning more broadly. Such proposals were even more striking against the backdrop of a prewar status quo in which state governments remained overwhelmingly dominant in domestic policymaking and service provision.

The CHC's overriding concern was the absolute shortage of housing— estimated as 300,000 homes—that the country faced after the war and the preceding depression years. On this basis, the commission called for 50,000 houses to be built in the first year of a postwar housing program, of which 30,000 should be government-funded homes for rent at subsidised rates (CHC 1944; Walter and Holbrook 2015). These aspirations were set within a broader framework that 'envisaged leadership and integrative roles for the Commonwealth in urban and regional planning, housing quality, and land and housing supply' (Milligan and Tiernan 2011: 393).

Perhaps surprisingly, the CHC report 'gave little weight to the Constitutional validity of Commonwealth activity' in this policy area (Troy 2012: 54). This was even though, in proposing the continuance of national security regulations beyond the end of wartime, the commission 'recognised that special … powers were necessary' (Troy 2012: 54).

In practice, reassertion of state government primacy in response to the CHC proposals meant their implementation 'became a test of strength over housing and planning powers within the federal system' (Howe 2000: 83). As a result, while the commission's report is rightly seen as giving birth to the subsequent Commonwealth–State Housing Agreement (CSHA) architecture, this was a far looser arrangement than the CHC had envisaged (Troy 2012). Nevertheless, the resulting compact represented a highly significant vehicle for federal government involvement in housing provision, as maintained through a series of renegotiated agreements for the remainder of the twentieth century and—under different nomenclature—to this day.

Commonwealth State Housing Agreements

In practical terms, the 1945 CSHA and its successors involved Commonwealth funding—initially low-cost loans but, from the 1980s, grants—for state government housing expenditure. This arrangement can be rationalised as recognition of the substantial vertical fiscal imbalance that prevails under Australia's multilevel governance framework whereby state governments are largely responsible for service provision while the Commonwealth possesses the bulk of tax-raising and borrowing (as well as currency-issuing) powers. Thus, in contemporary Australia, the Commonwealth raises more than 80 per cent of total tax revenue— compared, for instance, with Canada, where the comparable proportion is 45 per cent (PM&C 2015). Accordingly, a key dimension of the policy process in housing is 'a search for the appropriate balance between, on the one hand, the Commonwealth's capacity to fund and oversee major redistributive programmes and to establish national standards and, on the other hand, the states' position as the primary service deliverers' (Parkin 1992: 92).

The key significance of the 1945 CSHA and its successors has been as a vehicle for periodic statements of 'national housing policy' via funding conditions or stated preferences. This structure created scope for the Commonwealth to exert a degree of influence over housing policy and practice within each jurisdiction, most effectively through imposition of an array of 'tied funding' programs, matching funding requirements and expenditure rules.

A broad-brush historical review of CSHAs elucidates shifting Commonwealth policy objectives. An overarching policy driver has been the relative priority accorded to public housing versus (assisted access to) homeownership as the best means of enabling satisfactory housing for those in need. For example, the 1945 CSHA stipulated that funded construction should be entirely designated as rental housing, whereas in the 1956 CSHA, the Commonwealth reoriented policy towards enabling homeownership. This shift opened the door to the privatisation of existing homes and public 'build for sale' construction, as well as state government–provided home lending programs that could utilise up to 30 per cent of all CSHA funds (Hayward 1996; Milligan 2003). Subsequent CSHAs until the 1970s embodied tension between policies supporting these two main forms of provision.

From the 1970s, the Commonwealth's view of legitimate state government activity centred on housing assistance as a safety-net function and public housing re-emerged as a primary focus. Under objectives intended to better target public housing, the 1973 and 1978 CSHAs, respectively, proposed adoption of formal income thresholds for public housing eligibility and rents set at market rates—rather than according to historical costs (Yates 2013). And by 1989, the Commonwealth had introduced a requirement that 85 per cent of its general ('untied') grants and state-matching grants be used for investment in public housebuilding and upgrading (Milligan and Persson 1989: 185).

Efforts to project Commonwealth policy influence through CSHA conditions were decisively relaxed from the late 1990s—a stance that will have been welcome to states eager to utilise federal funding to offset public housing operational losses (Hall and Berry 2007). Following significant post-1996 cuts to Commonwealth CSHA funding, the practical effect was to remove the expectation that such funds would necessarily be invested in new public housing construction, thus signalling the end of a routine public housing investment program (Pawson et al. 2020: 94).

The 2009 National Affordable Housing Agreement (NAHA, the renamed CSHA) took devolution a step further by making a virtue of the principle that the federal government would henceforth focus only on state-level housing system 'performance outcomes', rather than seeking any direct influence over each jurisdiction's expenditure of NAHA funding. This was part of the Rudd Government's wider 'outcomes-focused' reform of federal financial relations. The NAHA, nevertheless, failed to adequately specify measurable outcomes and monitoring arrangements (COAG Reform Council 2013). That agreement therefore further diminished Commonwealth influence on housing policy and practice (Milligan and Tiernan 2011; Walter and Holbrook 2015).

Commonwealth Government housing action outside the CSHA

Beyond the CSHAs, successive Commonwealth governments made forays into housing policy throughout the postwar era. Prominent among these, and consistent with the domestic preference for homeownership that is embedded in the Australian welfare-state compact (Castles 1998), was the provision of first-homebuyer grants (1965–90) and the regulation of mortgage lending volumes and costs geared to facilitating home purchase (Dalton 1999). Such programmatic initiatives and regulatory strategies were generally not articulated as part of a coherent and coordinated national housing policy approach.

From 1958, the Commonwealth also introduced a supplementary social security payment, Rent Assistance, for single low-income renters facing housing stress (Ong Viforj et al. 2020). With associated expenditure ramped up from the late 1980s, Rent Assistance became the largest and fastest-growing component of Commonwealth housing assistance outlays (AIHW 2021). The trend has reflected a neoliberal policy preference to assist tenants through private rather than public housing. Despite its growing significance, however, Rent Assistance is not classified in official discourse as a housing policy and, consequently, is not evaluated from the perspective of its housing outcomes. Similarly unclassified as housing outlays are substantial indirect housing-related tax expenditures accrued by private landlords (annually worth $11.7 billion; Daley et al. 2016). These instances illustrate both the concealed and the fragmented nature of Commonwealth housing policy.

The 1991–92 National Housing Strategy

Only after more than four decades of the CSHA regime did the next broadly scoped 'national housing policy' milestone appear. Albeit arguably misnamed, the 1991–92 National Housing Strategy (NHS) initiated under the Hawke Government was effectively a wideranging policy review that generated policy options rather than a policy plan (Parkin 1992). By this time, housing affordability (rather than housing shortage) had emerged as the central policy concern for government, alongside infrastructure and environmental challenges posed by ongoing urban sprawl. These were married with an emerging awareness of economic productivity impairment due to a growing metropolitan mismatch between housing and employment location (Edwards 1991).

Presented as 'a new national housing policy', the prime ministerial statement that followed both the NHS review and the Industry Commission's (1993) review of public housing offered more person-targeted than tenure-targeted housing assistance. This was justified as aiming to achieve 'greater equity between people in the public and private rental markets' (Keating 1995: 2). Under a 'fundamental re-alignment of roles and responsibilities between the Commonwealth and the States, national government would broaden its focus beyond the provision of public housing to improving access to affordable and appropriate housing for low-income households' (Keating 1995: 2). At the same time, however, an intention to distribute CSHA funding on a more rational basis was signalled in the striking commitment that 'commencing in 1996, a national housing needs framework will be developed with the States and Territories against which targets for the levels of public housing required in each State can be established' (Keating 1995: 6).

In practice, a change of government in 1996 meant this agenda fell by the wayside. Ultimately, the retraction of national housing policy ongoing since the 1970s would continue (Dodson 2007).

The 2007–10 Rudd Government

The next noteworthy development in national housing policy, comprising two distinct sets of initiatives, eventuated under the 2007–10 Rudd Government. First, were measures that arose from 2007 election platform commitments (for example, the National Rental Affordability Scheme to increase affordable rental supply through institutional investment).

Alongside these, a second—and quite distinct—batch of housing initiatives was triggered by the Global Financial Crisis (GFC) such as the Social Housing Initiative, aimed at protecting construction industry employment.

While maintaining established national funding for social housing, new spending programs were initiated, albeit of modest dimensions. Moreover, a raft of institutional reforms was instituted in support of the renewed commitment to national housing action. These included re-establishment of a housing minister in the Cabinet and activating the Housing Ministers Council under the Council of Australian Governments (COAG), as well as the creation of several new Commonwealth-level advisory bodies, including the National Housing Supply Council and the Prime Minister's Council on Homelessness. Notably, in the context of the roles and responsibilities debate, the Commonwealth chose to directly administer its biggest initiative, the National Rental Affordability Scheme, rather than devolving management to state governments. Deficiencies in Australian Public Service skills and capacity, however, contributed to the scheme's subsequent underperformance (Milligan and Tiernan 2011: 402).

At the time, the Rudd Government's impetus could be optimistically interpreted as heralding a radical new beginning for Commonwealth housing policy. With hindsight, however, it clearly represented more of a last gasp (to date) of national housing thinking. Impeded by the GFC and domestic political turbulence, little progress was made towards developing 'a coherent vision and strategic plan for achieving a more equitable and sustainable housing system over the medium term, underpinned by more adequate levels of long-term public investment' (Milligan and Pinnegar 2010: 340).

National housing policy in Australia: Recent contestation

Under both the post-2010 Gillard–Rudd governments and the Coalition administrations from 2013, the notion of any coherent or expansive national housing policy again receded. Initially, under the Abbott administration (2013–15), the official narrative shifted to a denial that rising housing unaffordability in fact posed a policy challenge at all—a position (in)famously articulated in treasurer Joe Hockey's comment that 'if housing were unaffordable in Sydney, no one would be buying it' (Bourke 2015).

The most significant post-2013 attention to restructuring national housing governance was prompted by the Abbott Government's 'Reform of the Federation' agenda when serious consideration was given to measures to further distance the Commonwealth Government from an active housing policy interest or responsibility. Housing and homelessness was one of the three policy realms examined in this review, alongside health and education. The wider justification for the exercise was the claim that 'overlap and duplication in our Federation is becoming excessive, leading to wasteful expenditure, a constant "blame game" between governments driving up the cost of public services, and people not really knowing which level of government is responsible for what' (PM&C 2015: 3). Moreover, 'the degree of interference in traditional areas of State and Territory responsibility has now arguably gone too far … [I]n some areas, the States and Territories are no longer sovereign in their own sphere' (PM&C 2015: 3).

In the case of housing and homelessness, however, it is apparent from the preceding discussion that such an argument was misplaced, at least in terms of any claim of growing duplication or illegitimate national interference.

Nevertheless, the preference reportedly favoured by the Abbott Government within this policy realm was 'increased devolution to the states' (Walter and Holbrook 2015: 457), perhaps as envisaged in the formally considered 'reform option' that projected complete Commonwealth withdrawal from social housing and homelessness funding, and from Rent Assistance provision (PM&C 2015).

Once again, this reform debate was terminated by a prime ministerial succession, in 2015—the fall of the Abbott administration. A change of tone under the regimes of Malcolm Turnbull (2015–18) and Scott Morrison (2018–22) saw Coalition governments tending to parry rather than deny the policy challenge posed by housing affordability. Indeed, in response to a senate inquiry into the topic, it was even claimed that the Commonwealth was implementing a 'comprehensive housing affordability plan' (Fierravanti-Wells 2018).

While no plan as such was forthcoming, the 2015–22 period saw flickers of renewed Commonwealth engagement. Perhaps the most significant was the 2018 institutional reform embodied in the creation of the National Housing Finance and Investment Corporation, the primary founding purpose of which was to channel low-cost (government guarantee–backed) debt into not-for-profit social and affordable housing. Although such credit support is insufficient to enable significant development activity without matching subsidy (CFFR 2017), the move indicated a renewed federal government commitment to an active role in non-market housing provision, over and above funding (under the once again renamed National Housing and Homelessness Agreement, NHHA) to state governments.

Such has been the ongoing potency of housing affordability as a popular concern that prime minister Morrison chose to announce eye-catching new housing policy measures in the final weeks of general election campaigns in both 2019 and 2022. Under the 2019 First Home Loan Deposit Guarantee (FHLDG) scheme, qualifying applicants could purchase a dwelling with a deposit of only 5 per cent rather than the 20 per cent normally required by mortgage lenders. Involving little public expenditure, this could be seen as epitomising 'smart policy' consistent with the neoliberal governance paradigm of 'light touch' market-enabling interventions. In common with the 2020 homebuyer grants program, HomeBuilder, initiated in response to the Covid-19 recession, the FHLDG scheme also emphasised Morrison's affinity to homeownership. In 2022, as the election campaign entered its final week, Morrison announced that the Coalition Government, if re-elected, would allow first homebuyers access to up to $50,000 of their retirement savings for a home purchase deposit.

Beyond such electorally salient initiatives, however, the Morrison Government eschewed any more expansive role in housing policy and funding. In particular, then housing minister Michael Sukkar responded to widely voiced calls in 2020 for post-pandemic stimulus investment in social housing by stressing the Commonwealth's reluctance to 'usurp the states and territories' in this policy realm (Coorey 2020). At the same time, as an each-way bet, he also asserted that the Commonwealth 'continues to make significant, ongoing investments into social housing' (Sakkal 2021). However, this reference to continuing NHHA expenditure belied the fact that such funding had long ceased to underpin 'investments' in terms of additional social housing. Rather, it has become a vital source of revenue support for a financially unsustainable public housing system in which operational management and maintenance expenditure now far exceed rental income (Hall and Berry 2007; IPART 2017; Pawson et al. 2020).

Another important strand of the Commonwealth's post-2013 housing narrative is that any housing affordability problem that might exist is largely attributable to 'inadequate supply'—that is, insufficient market housing construction. And, furthermore, that this mainly reflects excessive (state-imposed) regulation as it affects private developers. As noted by Gurran and Phibbs (2015), this proposition is deeply embedded in the national debate. Thus, from the early 2000s, the notion that 'faster land and housing approvals could stimulate private investment in low-cost housing, obviating the need for government funding, began to infuse subsequent national discourse on housing supply and affordability' (Gurran and Phibbs 2015: 719–20). Indeed, such a case was deemed 'incontestable' by then prime minister John Howard in 2006 (Gurran and Phibbs 2015).

Picking up on this theme, Minister Sukkar declared in 2020 that the Commonwealth would 'use all possible levers to encourage states and territories to undertake the politically difficult, but necessary, reforms to increase housing supply and make housing more affordable' (Valic 2021). More pointedly, in 2021, he 'warned that every additional burden placed onto developers by the states is passed onto consumers and exacerbates the affordability challenge' (Thompson and Duke 2021). Thus, it was necessary for state governments to have their 'feet held to the fire' to address rising house prices since it was 'not up to the Commonwealth to fix the problem' (Thompson and Duke 2021). Strikingly, however, then NSW planning minister Rob Stokes countered:

> Let's tear down the myth that supply is the determinant of housing affordability. Planning plays an important and significant role in getting new housing to market but let's not pretend [mainly federally governed] tax rules and interest rates don't also push up prices. (Thompson and Duke 2021)

In late 2021, the federal Treasurer commissioned a new Commonwealth parliamentary inquiry conspicuously slanted to highlighting the adverse impacts of state taxes and regulations on housing supply (and, consequently, on affordability and falling rates of homeownership) (House of Representatives Standing Committee on Tax and Revenue 2022).

Towards a national housing policy

By now it will be apparent that housing policy is a highly contested space in Australia in terms of its breadth, but more particularly its governance. Yet, the growing economic and social stresses attributable to housing system outcomes make a compelling case for stepped-up policymaker attention to the issue. Moreover, as reasoned above, because housing is a complex and interactive system, micromeasures targeted at selected aspects of that system are liable to have minimal or even counterproductive impacts.

Therefore, as argued elsewhere (Pawson et al. 2020), housing logically demands a strategic (rather than an incremental or reactive) policymaking approach. Apparently chiming with this interpretation is the Commonwealth Government's 2017 NHHA requirement that each state government develop 'a publicly available housing strategy' (CFFR 2018: 4). Positively, such strategies are expected to be broadly scoped to encompass diverse dimensions of housing including private rental regulation and homeownership support, as well as social housing provision. Strategies should also detail how 'planning and zoning reform and initiatives' will contribute to NHHA 'housing priority policy areas' (CFFR 2018: 24).

At the time of writing, several of the requisite strategy documents have been published by state governments. Given the NHHA's minimal specification for them, it should be no surprise that their style, form, and content are diverse. A full evaluation is beyond the scope of this chapter. As a case in point, however, the NSW Government's 'Housing 2041' wholly fails to fulfil basic criteria for strategic utility, including: 1) analysis of problems to be tackled, 2) clear and measurable goals, 3) identified actions to achieve goals, and 4) a costed and resourced action plan (Pawson and Milligan 2021).

Meaningful state-level housing strategies—that is, compliant with criteria such as those above—could potentially help to address the kinds of policy challenges listed at the start of this chapter. However, with most of the key housing policy levers held at federal level, state-only plans are inherently highly constrained in their potency. This only goes to emphasise the rational case for a national housing strategy, not least as an overarching framework for state-specific plans. While such a strategy could only be led by the Commonwealth Government, it should be developed collaboratively—not only with the states, territories, and local government, but also with industry and consumer stakeholders. Any endeavour to achieve lasting reform must also garner cross-party political support.

Arguably, such a collaborative approach would fulfil constitutional propriety. Here, it is instructive to note that the 1991–92 NHS papers said little about the constitutionality of national housing leadership. It was, however, stated that 'the NHS believes that it is the Commonwealth's responsibility to implement the Agenda in partnership with other spheres of government and with the coordinated support of industry and community groups' (Edwards 1992: 29). And, as the historical account relayed in this chapter helps to demonstrate, many past Commonwealth housing policy actions have been those of political choice and expediency, and not constitutionally constrained.

As noted above, absolute housing shortage was the key policy challenge addressed by the 1944 CHC report. By the early 1990s, as embodied in the NHS, the focus had shifted to housing affordability and urban form—in terms of both environmental sustainability and economic productivity. By the late 2000s, affordability concerns remained to the fore, albeit briefly eclipsed by housing market slump concerns.

Fast forward to the present and it is questionable whether 2020s Australia in fact continues to face a gross housing shortage in any strict sense (Phillips and Joseph 2017). More certainly, it is a country in which the housing portfolio is used with decreasing efficiency due to rising underutilisation of large dwellings, second homeownership, and short-term lettings (for example, via Airbnb). Nevertheless, assuming such trends remain inviolable, expectations of resumed post-pandemic population growth mean that planning for new supply remains a crucial component of any strategy. All the policy problems identified by the NHS continue to loom large. Incorporating these, along with more recently emerging issues such as intergenerational equity in housing wealth, as a starting point for a discussion about housing strategy goals could be formulated around at least six major objectives:

1. The market functions more smoothly; housing stock is used more efficiently.
2. Housing system impairment of economic productivity and equity is reduced.
3. The energy and environmental performance of the housing stock are enhanced.
4. Housing tax settings are transitioned towards tenure-neutrality.
5. A more diverse range of housing forms enhances consumer choice.
6. Historically rising levels of housing affordability stress are reversed.

It should also be emphasised that even with the political will to attempt such a process, major preparatory steps are required. A wideranging policy review of the kind instituted for the 1991–92 NHS—or the 2009 'Henry Review' of taxation (Henry et al. 2010)—would be essential. And, as discussed in more detail elsewhere (Pawson et al. 2020: 339–58), supporting actions should include institutional reforms such as housing policymaking/domain knowledge capacity-building within governments, integration of what have become dispersed and fragmented housing policy responsibilities across and within spheres of governments, and restoration of a permanent forum for intergovernmental housing policy collaboration.

With the election of a Labor government nationally in 2022, progress on some of these fronts is in prospect. The new administration entered office pledging relatively modest measures on housing. Importantly, however, these included some of the institutional innovations advocated above—notably, the restoration of housing as a Cabinet-level ministerial portfolio and the establishment of a new national housing agency, Housing Australia. Most directly relevant to this chapter—albeit imprecisely specified in the ALP's platform—is the intention to initiate a 'national housing and homelessness plan'. At the time of writing, however, both the ambition and the scope of this initiative remain to be revealed.

Conclusion

Albeit with some discontinuities, the past 75 years have seen the opposite of a trajectory 'towards a national housing policy'. That must be reversed. Part of the argument for the associated policy reset is that while the first two decades of the twenty-first century have seen immense changes to economic, social, and demographic conditions and in the wider public policy backdrop, the bulk of Australia's key housing system settings (for example, on tax and social security) have remained essentially frozen. They are now well overdue for fresh scrutiny.

Since its first dramatic emergence in the 1940s, the scope for a national housing policy has remained highly contested in Australia. Both political cycles and the embedded opposition of central policymakers to broadening housing interventions, especially in Treasury and Finance, help to explain the repeated pattern of policy disintegration. Aborted or stillborn policy reforms have also abounded—notably, around property tax and reform of Commonwealth–state roles and responsibilities.

For the reasons outlined above and elsewhere (Winter 2015), the case that a national housing policy is ruled out by the Australian Constitution is overstated. In delivering some of its key constitutionally assigned responsibilities, the Commonwealth is heavily invested in the effective operation of the housing system over which it, and not the states, in fact wields greatest influence.

Granted, state governments have clear authority to deliver housing programs. Nevertheless, the extent of Australia's vertical fiscal imbalance is a powerful argument for a substantial nationally resourced approach—for example, through redirection of effective taxpayer support currently enjoyed by property owners. Even if this situation could be significantly moderated—for example, by reviving relevant proposals floated in the Henry Review—the case for a nationally led and coordinated approach to housing would remain. The growing economic and social costs incurred by an underperforming housing system present a national challenge that cannot be ducked forever.

References

Australian Bureau of Statistics (ABS). 2019. 'Table 21: Housing Occupancy and Costs, Australia, 2017–18.' In *Housing Occupancy and Costs (2019–20 Financial Year)*. Canberra: ABS. Available from: www.abs.gov.au/statistics/people/housing/housing-occupancy-and-costs/2017-18/41300_table21_2017-18.xls.

Australian Institute of Health and Welfare (AIHW). 2021. *Housing Assistance in Australia*. Sydney: AIHW. Available from: www.aihw.gov.au/reports/housing-assistance/housing-assistance-in-australia/contents/about.

Bourke, L. 2015. 'Joe Hockey's Advice to First Homebuyers: Get a Good Job that Pays Good Money.' *Sydney Morning Herald*, 9 June. Available from: www.smh.com.au/federal-politics/political-news/joe-hockeysadvice-to-first-homebuyers--get-a-good-job-that-pays-goodmoney-20150609-ghjqyw.html.

Castles, F. 1998. 'The Really Big Trade-Off: Home Ownership and the Welfare State in the New World and Old.' *Acta Politica* 33(1): 5–19.

Coates, B., and T. Chen. 2019. 'Fewer Retirees Will Own Their Home in Future, and That Has Big Implications for Policy.' *The Conversation*, 12 April. Available from: theconversation.com/retiree-home-ownership-is-about-to-plummet-soon-little-more-than-half-will-own-where-they-live-115255.

Commonwealth Housing Commission (CHC). 1944. *Final Report*. Canberra: Department of Post-War Reconstruction.

Coorey, P. 2020. 'Housing a Key Plank of Budget.' *Australian Financial Review*, 6 August.

Council of Australian Governments (COAG) Reform Council. 2013. *Lessons for Federal Reform: COAG Reform Agenda 2008–2013*. Sydney: COAG Reform Council.

Council on Federal Financial Relations (CFFR). 2018. *The National Housing and Homelessness Agreement.* Canberra: CFFR. Available from: federalfinancial relations.gov.au/agreements/national-housing-and-homelessness-agreement-0.

Daley, J., B. Coates, and T. Wiltshire. 2018. *Housing Affordability: Re-Imagining the Australian Dream.* Melbourne: Grattan Institute.

Daley, J., D. Wood, and H. Parsonage. 2016. *Hot Property: Negative Gearing and Capital Gains Tax Reform.* Melbourne: Grattan Institute.

Dalton, T. 1999. Making Housing Policy in Australia: Home Ownership and the Disengagement of the State. PhD thesis, RMIT University, Melbourne.

Demographia. 2020. *16th Annual Demographia International Housing Affordability Survey: Rating Middle-Income Housing Affordability.* Belleville, IL: Wendell Cox Consultancy. Available from: www.demographia.com/dhi2020.pdf.

Department of the Prime Minister and Cabinet (PM&C). 2015. *Reform of the Federation.* Discussion Paper, 23 June. Canberra: Commonwealth of Australia. Available from: apo.org.au/node/55457.

Dodson, J. 2007. *Government Discourse and Housing.* Aldershot, UK: Ashgate.

Edwards, M. 1991. *National Housing Strategy: Framework for Reform.* Canberra: AGPS.

Edwards, M. 1992. *National Housing Strategy: Agenda for Action.* Canberra: AGPS.

Eslake, S. 2013. 'Australian housing policy: 50 years of failure. Submission to Senate Economic References Committee Inquiry on Housing Affordability.' Affordable Housing Submission 2, 21 December. Canberra: Parliament of the Commonwealth of Australia. Available from: www.aph.gov.au/Parliamentary _Business/Committees/Senate/Economics/Affordable_housing_2013/ Submissions.

Eslake, S. 2017. *No Place Like Home: The Impact of Declining Home Ownership on Retirement.* AIST Housing Affordability and Retirement Incomes Report, March. Melbourne: Australian Institute of Superannuation Trustees. Available from: apo.org.au/node/74744.

Fierravanti-Wells, C. 2018. Government Response to Report. *Senate Debates,* Wednesday, 28 March 2018, Parliament of Australia. Available from: www. openaustralia.org.au/senate/?id=2018-03-28.172.1.

Freebairn, J. 1999. 'Tax Reform Proposals and Housing.' *Economic Papers* 18(3): 73–84. doi.org/10.1111/j.1759-3441.1999.tb00943.x.

Freestone, R. 2012. 'Post-War Reconstruction and Planning Promotion in 1940s Australia.' Paper presented to Fifteenth International Planning History Society Conference, São Paulo, Brazil, 15–18 July. Available from: www.usp.br/fau/iphs/abstractsAndPapersFiles/FREESTONE%2002.PDF.

Gurran, N., and P. Phibbs. 2015. 'Are Governments Really Interested in Fixing the Housing Problem? Policy Capture and Busy Work in Australia.' *Housing Studies* 30(5): 711–29. doi.org/10.1080/02673037.2015.1044948.

Hall, J., and M. Berry. 2007. *Operating Deficits and Public Housing: Policy Options for Reversing the Trend—2005–06 Update.* Final Report No. 106. Melbourne: AHURI.

Hayward, D. 1996. 'The Reluctant Landlords? A History of Public Housing in Australia.' *Urban Policy and Research* 14(1): 5–36. doi.org/10.1080/08111114960 8551610.

Henry, K., J. Harmer, J. Piggott, H. Ridout, and G. Smith. 2010. *Australia's Future Tax System: Report to the Treasurer.* December. Canberra: Commonwealth of Australia. Available from: www.taxreview.treasury.gov.au/content/downloads/final_report_part_1/00_AFTS_final_report_consolidated.pdf.

House of Representatives Standing Committee on Tax and Revenue. 2022. *The Australian Dream: Inquiry into Housing Affordability and Supply in Australia.* March. Canberra: Parliament of the Commonwealth of Australia. Available from: parlinfo.aph.gov.au/parlInfo/download/committees/reportrep/024864/toc_pdf/TheAustralianDream.pdf;fileType=application%2Fpdf.

Howe, R. 2000. 'A New Paradigm: Planning and Reconstruction in the 1940s.' In *The Australian Metropolis: A Planning History*, edited by S. Hamnett and R. Freestone, 80–97. Sydney: Allen & Unwin. doi.org/10.4324/9780203362 518-6.

Independent Pricing and Regulatory Tribunal (IPART). 2017. *Review of Rent Models for Social and Affordable Housing: Final Report.* Sydney: IPART.

Industry Commission. 1993. *Public Housing.* Report No. 34. Canberra: AGPS.

Keating, P. 1995. *Community and Nation.* Canberra: Commonwealth of Australia.

Maclennan, D., L. Crommelin, R. van den Nouwelant, and B. Randolph. 2018. *Making Better Economic Cases for Housing Policies.* A Report to the NSW Federation of Housing Associations, March. Sydney: City Futures Research Centre, University of New South Wales. Available from: cityfutures.be.unsw. edu.au/documents/476/Making_better_economic_cases_for_housing_policies _main_report.pdf.

Maclennan, D., J. Long, H. Pawson, B. Randolph, F. Aminpour, and C. Leishman. 2021. *Housing: Taming the Elephant in the Economy—A Report to the Housing and Productivity Research Consortium*. June. Sydney: City Futures Research Centre, University of New South Wales. Available from: cityfutures.be.unsw. edu.au/documents/644/Synthesis_report-final_version_12.06.pdf.

Milligan, V., and D. Persson. 1989. 'Outcomes of the National Housing Policy Review.' *Urban Policy and Research* 7(4): 183–86. doi.org/10.1080/08111148908551424.

Milligan, V., and S. Pinnegar. 2010. 'The Comeback of National Housing Policy in Australia: First Reflections.' *International Journal of Housing Policy* 10(3): 325–44. doi.org/10.1080/14616718.2010.506747.

Milligan, V., and A. Tiernan. 2011. 'No Home for Housing: The Situation of the Commonwealth's Housing Policy Advisory Function.' *Australian Journal of Public Administration* 70(4): 391–407. doi.org/10.1111/j.1467-8500.2011.00746.x.

Milligan, V.R. 2003. *How Different? Comparing Housing Policies and Housing Affordability Consequences for Low-Income Households in Australia and the Netherlands*. Netherlands Geographical Studies No. 318. Utrecht, Netherlands: Utrecht University.

Ong Viforj, R., H. Pawson, R. Singh, and C. Martin. 2020. *Demand Side Assistance in Australia's Rental Housing Market: Exploring Reform Options*. Final Report, No. 342, 29 October. Melbourne: AHURI. doi.org/10.18408/ahuri8120801.

Organisation for Economic Co-operation and Development (OECD). 2021. 'Household Debt.' *OECD Data*. Paris: OECD. Available from: data.oecd.org/hha/household-debt.htm.

Parkin, A. 1992. 'The Intergovernmental Politics of Housing Policy.' *Australian Journal of Political Science* 29(SI): 91–112.

Pawson, H., and V. Milligan. 2021. 'A Housing Strategy for NSW: A Good Idea, But Housing 2041 Falls Short.' *The Fifth Estate*, [Sydney], 5 May. Available from: thefifthestate.com.au/columns/spinifex/a-housing-strategy-for-nsw-a-good-idea-but-housing-2041-falls-short/.

Pawson, H., V. Milligan, and J. Yates. 2020. *Housing Policy in Australia: A Case for System Reform*. Singapore: Palgrave. doi.org/10.1007/978-981-15-0780-9.

Phillips, B., and C. Joseph. 2017. *Regional Housing Supply and Demand in Australia*. CSRM Working Paper. Canberra: Centre for Social Research and Methods, The Australian National University. Available from: csrm.cass.anu.edu.au/research/publications/regional-housing-supply-and-demand-australia.

Sakkal, P. 2021. 'Calls for Human Right to Shelter in Australia.' *Sydney Morning Herald*, 14 March. Available from: www.smh.com.au/national/calls-for-human-right-to-shelter-in-australia-20210314-p57alf.html.

Sandercock, L. 1976. *Cities for Sale: Property, Politics and Urban Planning in Australia*. Melbourne: Melbourne University Press.

Simons, M. 2011. 'Who Should Look After the Cities?' *Inside Story*, [Melbourne], 2 June. Available from: insidestory.org.au/who-should-look-after-the-cities/.

Thompson, A., and J. Duke. 2021. 'High House Prices "A Risk for All State Governments": Housing Minister Wants Premiers' Feet Held to the Fire.' *Sydney Morning Herald*, 1 May. Available from: www.smh.com.au/politics/federal/high-house-prices-a-risk-for-all-state-governments-housing-minister-wants-premiers-feet-held-to-the-fire-20210430-p57nrr.html.

Troy, P. 1978. *Federal Power in Australian Cities*. Sydney: Hale & Iremonger.

Troy, P. 2012. *Accommodating Australians: Commonwealth Government Involvement in Housing*. Sydney: The Federation Press.

Valic, L. 2021. 'Interview with Michael Sukkar.' *Views from the House*, April. Sydney: Housing Industry Association. Available from: hia.com.au/our-industry/housing/in-focus/2021/04/views-from-the-house.

Walter, J., and C. Holbrook. 2015. 'Housing in a Federation: From Wicked Problem to Complexity Cascade?' *Australian Journal of Public Administration* 74(4): 448–66. doi.org/10.1111/1467-8500.12174.

Whelan, S., H. Pawson, L. Troy, R. Ong Viforj, and J. Lawson. 2023. *Financing First Home Ownership: Opportunities and Challenges*. Final Report. Melbourne: AHURI.

Winter, I. 2015. 'The Federation Review, Housing Policy and the National Interest.' Presentation to Brotherhood of St Laurence, Melbourne, 6 August.

Yates, J. 2013. 'Evaluating Social and Affordable Housing Reform in Australia: Lessons to be Learned from History.' *International Journal of Housing Policy* 13(2): 111–33. doi.org/10.1080/14616718.2013.785717.

19

Planning, housing, and affordability: Lessons from the Covid-19 pandemic

Nicole Gurran and Pranita Shrestha

Introduction

Debates about urban regulation and housing in Australia date from the early introduction of property and building laws (Gurran and Bramley 2017). As such, they are deeply embedded within a settler-colonial context (Jackson 2017), speculative land development (Sisson et al. 2019), and the evolution of urban regulation (Marsden 2000). Since the turn of the millennium, these debates have settled on perceived tensions around the 'costs' of planning versus the supply of residential land and new homes, while dodging foundational questions about the legitimacy of landownership or the ongoing drivers of housing inequality. The politics of land and housing policy in Australia have reinforced this narrative of urban regulation as the cause of house price inflation and falling homeownership (Wetzstein 2021). According to these arguments, urban planning regulation has restricted new housing development, preventing the market from responding to high population growth, and driving house price inflation (Kendall and Tulip 2018; Saunders and Tulip 2020).

These politics persisted throughout the Covid-19 pandemic, even though population growth pressures reversed due to the closure of Australia's international borders. In this chapter, we examine why such politics remain so pervasive in Australia. We contend that urban regulation is neither the cause of nor the solution to Australia's housing crises and that systematic change depends on escaping this discursive binary and the underlying ideological positions it reflects (Pawson 2018). This involves commitment to a whole-of-system housing agenda that responds to population needs and the changing climate. Centring urban and housing policy on post-Covid transition planning, Australia's housing agenda must reassert the role of social, nonprofit, and affordable housing within overall residential supply, and chart a pathway for sustainably renewing the nation's existing dwelling stock.

The social inequalities and fractures revealed by the pandemic, worsened by the housing crisis and combined with seemingly relentless climate-related disasters from the 2019–20 Black Summer bushfires to the unprecedented flooding across the east coast, only underscore the importance of this agenda. The election of a new federal government in 2022 signified a promising shift. The incoming prime minister, Anthony Albanese, grew up in public housing himself, and campaigned on a promise to chart a new national housing and homelessness plan, and increase investment in affordable homes. Yet, the persistence of narrow supply narratives and simplistic planning reform 'solutions' for housing—expounded even by ostensibly independent and well-resourced institutions such as the Productivity Commission (2022)—highlight the extent to which these misconceptions remain entrenched.

We begin the chapter by recapping the drivers of Australia's current housing crisis, including the key debates about planning and housing, before highlighting several lessons emerging from the pandemic. We then outline five fundamental shifts that are needed to realign spatial planning and urban regulation with a comprehensive whole-of-housing-system agenda.

Understanding Australia's contemporary housing crisis

Australia is not alone in witnessing declining homeownership, chronic rental stress, stagnant social housing stock, along with a growing problem of homelessness (Wetzstein 2017). Nor is it the only nation to record extraordinary increases in the value of housing assets alongside deepening inequality based on housing wealth (Dorling 2014).

Explained generally with reference to the wider economic context of neoliberalism encompassing 'financialisation', deregulation, and globalisation (Marcuse and Madden 2016), changes over the past 30 years to Australia's housing system echo shifts in comparable nations such as the United States, Canada, and the United Kingdom (Wetzstein 2017). These changes were slow to take obvious effect, in part because of the success of policies introduced in the wake of the creation in 1943 of the Commonwealth Housing Commission and the urgent postwar housing shortage (Troy 2012). These interventions combined urban policy aspirations for 'slum clearance' and modern town planning laws with funding support for public housing, as well as several initiatives to support homeownership (Dufty-Jones 2018).

Postwar interventions supported a rapid housing boom, significant construction of public housing, and widespread homeownership, which by the 1980s had reached about 70 per cent of all households (Hulse et al. 2012; Pawson et al. 2020). Since then, a series of economic changes with parallels throughout the world has driven house price inflation and structural shifts in Australia's housing system. These include the deregulation of Australia's financial institutions, which resulted in the introduction of non-bank lending and easier access to mortgage finance; rising female participation in the workforce, increasing household incomes; and wage growth more widely (Yates 2011). Alongside favourable tax treatment of the family home and investment properties, these factors increased demand for housing. When interest rates began to fall in the mid-1990s and again in the mid-2010s, these demand-side factors helped propel Australian house price inflation far beyond the rate of wages (Yates 2016).

Beyond these affordability pressures a rising environmental crisis with major implications for the housing sector was looming. Natural disasters—such as the extraordinary bushfires that engulfed eastern Australia in the summer of 2019–20 and, in 2022, a series of extreme flood events across New South Wales and Queensland—drew attention to the vulnerability of much of the nation's housing stock. In part, this vulnerability reflects past planning decisions to allow homes in locations subject to environmental hazards. Revised risk assessments in the context of projected climate change effects—increases in the frequency and intensity of rainfall, storm events, inundation, heat, drought, and bushfires—reveal new urban locations not previously considered prone to environmental hazard (Hurlimann et al. 2021). At the same time, rising energy costs have drawn attention to the poor thermal performance of much of Australia's housing stock, with lower-income renters least able to retrofit their homes or afford high energy bills

(Cornell et al. 2020). Ironically, the foundational role of strong planning in helping Australia's residential communities transition to climate resilience has been largely disregarded within a broader narrative that positions planning solely as a regulatory barrier to new development (Gurran and Ruming 2016).

Debates about planning and housing

Many commentators from industry, government, and beyond have blamed Australia's house price inflation on sluggish rates of new housing production, but this is inconsistent with the evidence (Murray 2021). First, all housing markets are characterised by some 'stickiness' in relation to housing supply responses because new dwellings take time to produce, are fixed in space, and are costly to finance.

Second, local opposition to new housing, reflected in planning regulations such as restrictive land-use zones, oppressive controls on housing density, or lengthy and uncertain decision-making timelines, can further obstruct the development process. However, unlike comparable overseas jurisdictions, Australian states have retained the power to override local controls and resistance by determining targets for new housing supply, tasking local authorities with demonstrating sufficient zoned land to meet these targets, and overruling restrictive development controls to enable more diverse and, in some cases, higher-density developments (Gurran and Ruming 2016; Gilbert and Gurran 2021). Over the past 20 years, a program of urban planning reform has been implemented across all jurisdictions, targeting 'red tape' constraints to new housing supply. Key reforms have included the introduction of strict shorter decision-making time frames; the de-politicisation of development decisions, which are increasingly determined by professional experts rather than local political representatives; and the promulgation of state codes for standardised forms of housing development, which offer simple and certain approvals (Gurran and Ruming 2016; Gilbert and Gurran 2021).

Third, whether a consequence of these reforms or not, over the past 30 years, new housing production has largely kept pace with population growth, although output has increased and contracted with the direction of the market (Phillips and Joseph 2017). Australia's rates of new housing production have been among the highest in the world, adding to the existing stock at a rate of nearly 2 per cent per annum—second only to Iceland and

Türkiye, and well above the average for the OECD (OECD 2021). Fourth, rates of vacancy in the housing stock (that is, dwellings that are empty on census night) have tended to grow over time, even in the major cities, suggesting there is no absolute shortage of houses. Again, on this indicator, Australia has high vacancies in international terms, well above those of the United Kingdom and similar to those in the United States (OECD 2021).

International evidence suggests that even dramatic and sustained increases in housing production do not have significant impacts on overall prices, which are largely determined by the existing housing stock and wider demand factors such as interest rates and access to finance (Bramley 2015). This makes logical sense as private developers are unlikely to increase production within a falling market and therefore will expand and contract production in volumes that maximise profit (Murray 2021). In some contexts, speculative housebuilding in a competitive market could cause discounting, but this is not likely to be the case in Australia, where most dwellings are presold or contracted before construction (Burke and Hulse 2010).

Thus, in Australia, buoyant rates of housing production have not dampened housing prices, with the result that first homebuyers have faced increasing barriers to ownership. As the 'deposit gap' (the number of years needed to save a deposit) grew, so, too, did competition in the private rental market (Hulse et al. 2015). The private rental market itself expanded as access to homeownership and social rental housing declined. Between 2011 and 2016, the size of the private rental sector grew at more than twice the rate of household growth (Hulse et al. 2019). However, rents have risen steadily as well, reflecting the growing number of middle-income earners now excluded from homeownership and forced to seek housing in the private rental sector. Consequently, competition for lower-cost units even among moderate-income households (seeking to minimise their housing costs) has meant a growing shortage of rental homes that are affordable and available to low and very low-income earners, particularly in the major cities.

Approaches to housing assistance for the growing numbers of people unable to access suitable accommodation in the private rental sector changed, too. There was a growing emphasis on market-based solutions to housing need and a winding back of Commonwealth funding for social housing in favour of rental subsidies for very low-income earners and incentives for investment in rental property. Access to social housing was highly targeted with the consequence that the sector became increasingly 'residualised'— a highly stigmatised tenure of last resort (Atkinson and Jacobs 2008). To the extent that social housing has been retained, there are ongoing attempts to 'renew' ageing stock in partnership with private sector developers and community housing providers, who produce mixed-tenure communities (Pawson et al. 2020).

As noted, this evolving situation shares many commonalities with broad policy shifts in other nations where traditional welfare-state approaches to public housing provision have been wound back in favour of market-based and hybrid forms of assistance. However, it is worth noting that Australia's social housing sector is among the smallest among comparable countries: less than 5 per cent of households live in social housing and less than 2 per cent of new housing production is by or on behalf of government (AIHW 2021). By contrast, between 2019 and 2020, about 20 per cent of new housing in the United Kingdom was in the affordable sector, comprising social housing, affordable rental, and affordable homeownership products (Ministry of Housing, Communities and Local Government 2020). In the United States, where the quantum of social housing stock is similar to Australia's, affordable housing is a strong component of new supply thanks to the Low Income Housing Tax Credit program, which has supported construction of more than 2.6 million units since 1987 (McClure 2019), and widespread inclusionary planning requirements (Centre for Housing Policy 2014). But in Australia, neither approach (subsidies for investment in affordable housing or inclusionary planning) has secured a sustained commitment by the Commonwealth or state governments (Rowley et al. 2016; Gurran et al. 2018). Finally, we note the unresolved legacy of colonisation in Australia, which has meant that traditional Indigenous owners, displaced by white settlement less than 250 years ago, continue to experience economic disadvantage, including much lower levels of homeownership than the general population—and, in many cases, enduring very poor-quality housing as well (Pawson et al. 2020).

Lessons from the Covid-19 pandemic

The global public health crisis of the Covid-19 pandemic in many ways presented an opportunity to interrupt Australia's housing trajectory. Government responses—including border closures, increased income assistance, rental protections, and grants for home purchase or construction—presented natural policy experiments in the effects of population growth or decline, rental regulations, and financial settings on the housing market overall and the housing circumstances of low-income earners in particular. Several studies carried out during the pandemic have provided the evidence base on which to make some observations. Leishman et al. (2020), through a scenario-based assessment of the economic impact of Covid-19, concluded that federal government interventions such as increased income support under the JobSeeker scheme and payments to employees of firms affected by the pandemic, known as JobKeeper, considerably reduced housing affordability stress in households: 861,500 households compared with 1,336,000 without intervention.

However, emerging research on private rentals has also produced evidence of uneven impacts across the housing sector. Baker et al. (2020), through their preliminary analysis of a snapshot survey of 15,000 private renters from July until August 2020, have illustrated that half the total surveyed households experienced increased housing stress and anxiety during the first wave of the pandemic. Similarly, research on the impact of Covid-19 on regional housing has shown an exacerbation of existing conditions of increased demand and reduction in housing affordability. A study of Tasmania's housing market highlighted young people, international students, and people with disability or chronic health conditions as key vulnerable groups experiencing housing stress, anxiety, and financial hardship (Verdouw et al. 2021).

Drawing on this emerging body of research evidence and our own analysis of population and migration, housing market trends, and government responses, we identify six lessons arising from the pandemic, which offer pathways through the entrenched politics of housing policy.

First, the abrupt collapse in international migration and overall population growth in Australia during 2020 offered real insights into the impact of growth on housing demand. The National Housing Finance and Investment Corporation (NHFIC 2020) forecast that Australia would experience a surplus of housing units, particularly in the apartment sector, until long after population growth resumed. In fact, the stalled population growth appeared to have no impact on housing demand. House prices continued to rise both in the major cities, even where populations contracted, and in regional areas, which received new residents (NHFIC 2020). The explanation for this counterintuitive outcome is that the drivers of housing demand—primarily financial incentives for property investment and low interest rates—increased as part of the government's pandemic response.

These incentives included generous cash grants for those taking out a new home-building contract or major renovation, as well as assistance for first homebuyers to take out loans with smaller deposits.

Second, Australian housing market trends during the pandemic clarified the distinction between demand and supply pressures in the home purchase and rental markets. Rental markets responded swiftly to population shifts, easing in the major cities but tightening in regional areas. With white-collar urban employees encouraged and, in some cases, mandated to 'work from home' during lockdown periods, many exercised the opportunity to relocate to lower-cost and/or higher-amenity housing markets. It is likely that some took up the opportunity to move into homeownership that had not been accessible within the major metropolitan employment centres of Sydney and Melbourne.

Thus, the changing trade-offs between housing amenity, affordability, tenure, and location—particularly access to employment opportunities— were revealed during the pandemic. This leads to our third observation: that demonstrable preferences for higher-quality/lower-cost housing, or even a different lifestyle in regional areas, suggest an alternative to ongoing economic agglomeration within Australia's major capital cities is possible.

Fourth, the global pandemic has demonstrated the ongoing nexus between housing and health, showing that Australia's most serious housing problems, including overcrowding, emerge because of suppressed household formation and informal rental or share-housing arrangements, which, before the pandemic, were largely invisible. The need to improve housing conditions for Aboriginal and Torres Strait Islander communities was also underscored, with many people forced to 'stay at home' in inadequate dwellings or homes not designed for extended families.

Similarly, the pandemic has highlighted the importance of good housing design, including adequate and flexible space, acoustic and visual privacy, and access to outdoor private areas. Neighbourhood design and amenity have also been shown to matter, implying a future in which people may spend more time within local neighbourhoods and centres, working at or near home.

Finally, government responses to the pandemic demonstrated that there are viable solutions to homelessness, which involve providing accommodation as well as support services. Increased income support through the boost to JobSeeker payments enabled very low-income renters to improve their housing circumstances (Baker et al. 2020). The vulnerability of Australia's private renters and their lack of long-term tenure security were highlighted by the need to impose a national moratorium on rental eviction during the immediate pandemic period. However, the need for more permanent improvements in tenure security remains.

Realigning urban policy, planning, and housing in Australia

Building on the lessons of the Covid-19 pandemic and our wider arguments about housing system failure in Australia, we propose five policy shifts, which are intended to realign spatial planning and urban regulation with a comprehensive whole-of-housing-system agenda that addresses both market and non-market sectors as well as residential design and neighbourhoods.

Prioritising housing and urban policy in post-pandemic transition planning

First, recognising that pivotal periods in history present opportunities for significant policy shifts, we join the many voices calling for housing and urban policy to be prioritised in Australia's post-pandemic transition planning efforts. Just as in the postwar period 70 years ago, the pandemic and the need to plan for its social and economic effects present an opening for significant structural changes in policy. With the changing economic geography made possible by more flexible approaches to work and the inevitable resumption of international migration, it is timely to articulate a national urban policy and settlement plan for Australia. This plan should balance the benefits of urban agglomeration with the opportunities for 'concentrated decentralisation' through regional growth supported by targeted investment in the transportation, health, and education infrastructure known to attract and retain populations as well as economic opportunities. Notably, the opportunity for decentralisation and a 'regional renaissance' accelerated by the Covid-19 pandemic was recognised by Infrastructure Australia in its late-2020 report, marking a shift away from pre-pandemic assumptions about the ongoing centralising forces of urban economic growth (Infrastructure Australia 2018, 2020).

A national settlement strategy is not a new idea; organisations such as the Planning Institute of Australia have been advocating for one for several years and it was the first recommendation of the 2018 parliamentary inquiry into the Australian Government's role in the development of cities (House of Representatives Standing Committee on Infrastructure, Transport and Cities 2018; PIA 2018). But the prospect of uncertain population dynamics combined with an urgent need to reconsider the distribution and location of Australia's existing populations and settlements in the context of climate risk mean that detailed, national-level settlement planning is now a matter of urgency.

A national housing policy

Second, Australia's settlement strategy must be supported by a national housing policy, with a clear set of objectives to ensure that all sectors of the population have access to affordable and appropriate homes. Rather than rhetorical promises to 'solve' house price inflation or moderate property prices through high rates of new housing production, the national housing strategy should emphasise stable rates of housing construction attuned to changing population needs. In this context, better urban regulation to improve the design and amenity of residential housing and improve long-term climate resilience is needed, rather than an ongoing program of deregulatory reform.

Recognising complementary roles for both market and non-market sectors, scaling up the capacity of the nonprofit or limited-profit housing sector is critical to this agenda. This implies both an expansion of the social housing stock and an extension into new models of housing provision such as shared equity and low-cost homeownership. This expansion must be underpinned by government funding to finance construction in the social housing sector and adequate rental assistance to improve the options available to very low-income earners. It should be supported by consistent use of inclusionary planning models to deliver land for affordable homes and genuinely mixed communities.

Diversifying housing across the continuum of need

This leads to our third, related proposition: that the range of diverse housing products available across the continuum of housing must be radically expanded. This involves supporting industry innovation in relation to design and construction methods, the development of new housing typologies, as well as regulatory pathways to enable alternative forms of housing development finance, planning, and tenure. Examples include increasing the use of prefabrication in housing construction to deliver cost savings and faster rates of production.

Rising interest in cooperative housing models and deliberative development approaches should be supported. There is much potential for community land trusts to be demonstrated on public land or for co-living communities to provide alternatives to current modes of residential development. Crabtree (2018) and others have argued for the need to explore the inherent potential of an under-researched cooperative and self-organised housing sector, especially in a move towards repairing market failure (Crabtree et al. 2021) and de-commodifying housing (Marcuse and Madden 2016). Crabtree et al. (2021) have recently provided a comprehensive overview of the benefits of a global cooperative housing sector and its potential future possibilities in Australia. Highlighting six key benefits of cooperative housing, ranging from health and wellbeing to broader economic development outcomes, they strongly argue for the need to diversify Australia's dominant dual housing tenure system beyond *owning* and *renting* (Crabtree et al. 2021). They further argue that the growth of a cooperative housing sector requires 'two interlocked tasks'—that is, demonstrating its benefits and establishing and facilitating a conducive 'regulatory, market and financial environment' (Crabtree et al. 2021: 149).

Similarly, Sharam (2020) has explored the concept of self-organised, multi-residential housing in Australia, also known as 'deliberative development', as an affordable alternative to market-driven speculative development based on the German *Baugruppen* (building groups) concept. Drawing on earlier case studies of eight deliberative developments across Australia, Sharam (2020; Sharam et al. 2015) argues for this concept as a socially diverse and economically viable alternative to combat the affordable housing crisis in Australia.

Indigenous housing

Fourth, there is an urgent need for ongoing policy support and reform in relation to Indigenous housing. This means both support for Aboriginal housing providers and organisations to improve the condition and maintenance arrangements of existing housing stock, particularly in remote communities, and strategies to enable new Aboriginal-led development models across urban and regional Australia. Recognising that many Indigenous people are unable to afford housing within their own communities, despite progress in relation to native title and land rights determinations, Australia's national housing strategy must foreground a process of restitution. This could include a process for reinstating recognition of Aboriginal ownership when land is rezoned or developed, operationalised via a development contribution arrangement or agreement, and/or financial support for local Aboriginal housing funds.

Economic transition

Last, it is critical to wean Australia's economy off house price inflation as a driver of consumer confidence and dependence on new market-driven housing construction as a major source of employment. Recent concerns about Australia's macroeconomic stability centre on seemingly relentless house price growth, with the total value of the housing stock exceeding $9 trillion by October 2021 (CoreLogic 2022). Concerns include the wider economic impacts of inevitable interest rate rises on consumer spending as well as the risks to debt-burdened households, particularly recent first homebuyers, who could face the prospect of negative equity and rising mortgage repayments if rising interest rates cause prices to fall.

At the same time, there has been rising concern that ongoing spending on the existing housing stock is occurring at the expense of alternative, more productive investments (Maclennan et al. 2015). Redirecting housing investment towards longer-term returns from social (public and community), affordable, and long-term rental housing, through more targeted taxation policy and a revival of the incentives for affordable supply under the former National Rental Affordability Scheme, would be important first steps (Rowley et al. 2016). So, too, would be funding to support and incentivise sustainable residential and urban or suburban retrofit and renewal programs responsive to changing climatic conditions and population needs.

Conclusion

The politics of land and housing policy in Australia have long emphasised the role of urban planning as the cause of affordability problems and barriers to homeownership. In countering these arguments, we have drawn on several lessons arising from the Covid-19 pandemic to show that planning neither has caused Australia's housing crises nor is a complete solution to them. These lessons include the disconnect between financial and population drivers of housing demand; the relationships between housing, health, and wellbeing; and the positive impacts of basic interventions like accommodation and adequate income support for people experiencing or at risk of homelessness. Calling for fundamental change rather than ongoing rhetorical debates about regulation, we have outlined a 'whole of housing system' agenda responsive to diverse population needs and the changing climate. By redirecting residential construction towards nonprofit and affordable housing supply, and sustainably renewing the existing housing stock, housing can play an important role in post-pandemic transition planning. Realigning taxation policy and redirecting financial incentives towards investment in affordable and sustainable housing, including new and innovative designs and tenures, would help realign the national economy while better serving Australians across the continuum of housing need.

In calling for this agenda, we recognise the practical hurdles—from our entrenched property politics to the initial costs of reinvesting in a socially and environmentally sustainable housing system. However, we find promise in earlier critical junctures in Australia's housing policy evolution. We are once again at a critical policy juncture whereby the pandemic has not only exposed the entrenched inequalities and failures in Australia's housing system but also highlighted real opportunities for an alternative future. It remains to be seen whether the new Commonwealth Government will navigate the many political and economic changes needed to bring about this promised future.

References

Atkinson, R., and K. Jacobs. 2008. *Public Housing in Australia: Stigma, Home and Opportunity*. Paper No. 01. Hobart: Housing and Community Research Unit, School of Sociology and Social Work, University of Tasmania.

Australian Institute of Health and Welfare (AIHW). 2021. *Home Ownership and Housing Tenure*. Sydney: AIHW. Available from: www.aihw.gov.au/reports/australias-welfare/home-ownership-and-housing-tenure.

Baker, E., R. Bentley, A. Beer, and L. Daniel. 2020. *Renting in the Time of COVID-19: Understanding the Impacts*. Final Report No. 340, 15 October. Melbourne: AHURI. doi.org/10.18408/ahuri3125401.

Bramley, G. 2015. 'Pushing on String: Demand and Supply.' *Built Environment* 41(2): 144–65. doi.org/10.2148/benv.41.2.144.

Burke, T., and K. Hulse. 2010. 'The Institutional Structure of Housing and the Sub-Prime Crisis: An Australian Case Study.' *Housing Studies* 25(6): 821–38. doi.org/10.1080/02673037.2010.511161.

Centre for Housing Policy. 2014. *National Inventory of Inclusionary Housing Programs.* Cambridge, UK: Centre for Housing Policy.

CoreLogic. 2022. 'Australian Housing Market Surpasses $9 Trillion Valuation.' *News & Research*, 7 March. Sydney: CoreLogic Australia. Available from: www.core logic.com.au/news-research/news/archive/australian-housing-market-surpasses-$9-trillion-valuation.

Cornell, C., N. Gurran, and T. Lea. 2020. *Climate Change, Housing, and Health.* Sydney: University of Sydney, NSW Health, and NSW Department of Planning.

Crabtree, L. 2018. 'Self-Organised Housing in Australia: Housing Diversity in an Age of Market Heat.' *International Journal of Housing Policy* 18(1): 15–34. doi.org/10.1080/14616718.2016.1198083.

Crabtree, L., N. Perry, S. Grimstad, and J. McNeill. 2021. 'Impediments and Opportunities for Growing the Cooperative Housing Sector: An Australian Case Study.' *International Journal of Housing Policy* 21(1): 138–52. doi.org/10.1080/19491247.2019.1658916.

Dorling, D. 2014. *All That Is Solid: The Great Housing Disaster.* London: Allen Lane.

Dufty-Jones, R. 2018. 'A Historical Geography of Housing Crisis in Australia.' *Australian Geographer* 49(1): 5–23. doi.org/10.1080/00049182.2017.1336968.

Gilbert, C., and N. Gurran. 2021. 'Can Ceding Planning Controls for Major Projects Support Metropolitan Housing Supply and Diversity? The Case of Sydney, Australia.' *Land Use Policy* 102: 105278. doi.org/10.1016/j.landusepol.2021.105278.

Gurran, N., and G. Bramley. 2017. *Urban Planning and the Housing Market.* London: Palgrave Macmillan. doi.org/10.1057/978-1-137-46403-3.

Gurran, N., C. Gilbert, K. Gibb, R. van den Nouwelant, A. James, and P. Phibbs. 2018. *Supporting Affordable Housing Supply: Inclusionary Planning in New and Renewing Communities.* Final Report No. 297, 10 April. Melbourne: AHURI. doi.org/10.18408/ahuri-7313201.

Gurran, N., and K. Ruming. 2016. 'Less Planning, More Development? Housing and Urban Reform Discourses in Australia.' *Journal of Economic Policy Reform* 19(3): 262–80. doi.org/10.1080/17487870.2015.1065184.

House of Representatives Standing Committee on Infrastructure, Transport and Cities. 2018. *Building Up & Moving Out: Inquiry into the Australian Government's Role in the Development of Cities.* September. Canberra: Parliament of the Commonwealth of Australia. Available from: parlinfo.aph.gov.au/parlInfo/download/committees/reportrep/024151/toc_pdf/BuildingUp&MovingOut.pdf;fileType=application%2Fpdf.

Hulse, K., T. Burke, L. Ralston, and W. Stone. 2012. *The Australian private Rental Sector: Changes and Challenges.* AHURI Positioning Paper No. 149, July. Melbourne: AHURI. Available from: www.ahuri.edu.au/sites/default/files/migration/documents/AHURI_Positioning_Paper_No149_The-Australian-private-rental-sector-changes-and-challenges.pdf.

Hulse, K., M. Reynolds, C. Nygaard, S. Parkinson, and J. Yates. 2019. *The Supply of Affordable Private Rental Housing in Australian Cities: Short-Term and Longer-Term Changes.* Final Report No. 323, 11 December. Melbourne: AHURI. doi.org/10.18408/ahuri-5120101.

Hulse, K., M. Reynolds, W. Stone, and J. Yates. 2015. *Supply Shortages and Affordability Outcomes in the Private Rental Sector: Short and Longer Term Trends.* Final Report No. 241, 9 June. Melbourne: AHURI. Available from: www.ahuri.edu.au/research/final-reports/241.

Hurlimann, A., S. Moosavi, and G.R. Browne. 2021. 'Urban Planning Policy Must Do More to Integrate Climate Change Adaptation and Mitigation Actions.' *Land Use Policy* 101: 105188. doi.org/10.1016/j.landusepol.2020.105188.

Infrastructure Australia. 2018. *Future Cities: Planning for Our Growing Population.* Canberra: Infrastructure Australia. Available from: www.infrastructureaustralia.gov.au/publications/future-cities-planning-our-growing-population.

Infrastructure Australia. 2020. *Infrastructure beyond COVID-19: A National Study on the Impacts of the Pandemic On Australia.* Canberra: Infrastructure Australia. Available from: www.infrastructureaustralia.gov.au/publications/Infrastructure-beyond-COVID#:~:text=Infrastructure%20beyond%20COVID%2D19%3A%20A,to%20be%20released%20next%20year.

Jackson, S. 2017. 'The Colonial Technologies and Practices of Australian Planning.' In *Planning in Indigenous Australia*, edited by S. Jackson, L. Porter, and L.C. Johnson, 72–91. London: Routledge. doi.org/10.4324/9781315693668-6.

Kendall, R., and P. Tulip. 2018. *The Effect of Zoning on Housing Prices.* RBA Research Discussion Paper, 2018-03. Sydney: Reserve Bank of Australia. doi.org/10.2139/ssrn.3149272.

Leishman, C., R. Ong, L. Lester, and W. Liang. 2020. *Supporting Australia's Housing System: Modelling Pandemic Policy Responses.* Final Report No. 346, 26 November. Melbourne: AHURI. doi.org/10.18408/ahuri3125701.

McClure, K. 2019. 'What Should Be the Future of the Low-Income Housing Tax Credit Program?' *Housing Policy Debate* 29(1): 65–81. doi.org/10.1080/10511482.2018.1469526.

Maclennan, D., R. Ong, and G. Wood. 2015. *Making Connections: Housing, Productivity and Economic Development.* Final Report No. 251, 29 October. Melbourne: AHURI. Available from: www.ahuri.edu.au/research/final-reports/251.

Marcuse, P., and D. Madden. 2016. *In Defense of Housing: The Politics of Crisis.* London: Verso.

Marsden, S. 2000. 'The Introduction of Order.' In *A History of European Housing in Australia*, edited by P. Troy, 26–41. Melbourne: Cambridge University Press.

Ministry of Housing, Communities and Local Government. 2020. *Affordable Housing Supply: April 2019 to March 2020, England.* London: UK Government.

Murray, C.K. 2021. 'The Australian Housing Supply Myth.' *Australian Planner* 57(1): 1–12. doi.org/10.1080/07293682.2021.1920991.

National Housing Finance and Investment Corporation (NHFIC). 2020. *State of the Nation's Housing 2020.* Sydney: NHFIC.

Organisation for Economic Co-operation and Development (OECD). 2021. 'Housing Stock and Construction.' *OECD Affordable Housing Database.* Paris: Directorate of Employment, Labour and Social Affairs Social Policy Division, OECD. Available from: www.oecd.org/els/family/HM1-1-Housing-stock-and-construction.pdf.

Pawson, H., V. Milligan, and J. Yates. 2020. *Housing Policy in Australia: A Case for System Reform.* Singapore: Springer Nature. doi.org/10.1007/978-981-15-0780-9.

Pawson, I. 2018. 'Reframing Australia's Housing Affordability Problem: The Politics and Economics of Negative Gearing.' *Journal of Australian Political Economy* 81: 121–43.

Phillips, B., and C. Joseph. 2017. *Regional Housing Supply and Demand in Australia*. CSRM Working Paper No. 1/2017. Canberra: Centre for Social Research & Methods, The Australian National University.

Planning Institute of Australia (PIA). 2018. *Through the Lens: The Tipping Point Identifies the Factors*. Canberra: PIA.

Productivity Commission. 2022. *In Need of Repair: The National Housing and Homelessness Agreement*. Study Report, August. Canberra: Productivity Commission. Available from: www.pc.gov.au/inquiries/completed/housing-homelessness/report/housing-homelessness.pdf.

Rowley, S., A. James, C. Gilbert, N. Gurran, R. Ong, P. Phibbs, D. Rosen, and C. Whitehead. 2016. *Subsidised Affordable Rental Housing: Lessons from Australia and Overseas*. Final Report No. 267, 3 August. Melbourne: AHURI. doi.org/10.18408/ahuri-8104301.

Saunders, T., and P. Tulip. 2020. 'A Model of the Australian Housing Market.' *Economic Record* 96: 1–25. doi.org/10.1111/1475-4932.12537.

Sharam, A. 2020. '"Deliberative Development": Australia's Baugruppen Movement and the Challenge of Greater Social Inclusion.' *Housing Studies* 35(1): 107–22. doi.org/10.1080/02673037.2019.1594712.

Sharam, A., L.E. Bryant, and T. Alves. 2015. 'Identifying the Financial Barriers to Deliberative, Affordable Apartment Development in Australia.' *International Journal of Housing Markets and Analysis* 8(4): 471–83. doi.org/10.1108/IJHMA-10-2014-0041.

Sisson, A., D. Rogers, and C. Gibson. 2019. 'Property Speculation, Global Capital, Urban Planning and Financialisation: *Sydney Boom, Sydney Bust* Redux.' *Australian Geographer* 50(1): 1–9. doi.org/10.1080/00049182.2018.1464365.

Troy, P. 2012. *Accommodating Australians: Commonwealth Government Involvement in Housing*. Sydney: The Federation Press.

Verdouw, J., M. Belen Yanotti, J. De Vries, K. Flanagan, and O. Ben Haman. 2021. *Pathways to Regional Housing Recovery from COVID-19*. Final Report No. 354, 22 April. Melbourne: AHURI. doi.org/10.31235/osf.io/rbx49.

Wetzstein, S. 2017. 'The Global Urban Housing Affordability Crisis.' *Urban Studies* 54(14): 3159–77. doi.org/10.1177%2F0042098017711649.

Wetzstein, S. 2021. 'Toward Affordable Cities? Critically Exploring the Market-Based Housing Supply Policy Proposition.' *Housing Policy Debate* 32(3): 506–32. doi.org/10.1080/10511482.2021.1871932.

Yates, J. 2011. 'Housing in Australia in the 2000s: On the Agenda Too Late?' In *Conference—2011: The Australian Economy in the 2000s*, edited by H. Gerard and J. Kearns. Sydney: Reserve Bank of Australia.

Yates, J. 2016. 'Why Does Australia Have an Affordable Housing Problem and What Can Be Done About It?' *Australian Economic Review* 49(3): 328–39. doi.org/10.1111/1467-8462.12174.

Part 6: Transitional needs and challenges

20

Accelerating low-carbon urban transitions in Australia

Niki Frantzeskaki, Peter Newton, and Fatemeh Shahani[1]

Introduction

Cities play an important role in the design, localisation, and implementation of climate adaptation agendas and experiments with new measures for low-carbon transitions. The global rise of city governments as governance pioneers for climate adaptation actions and for post-pandemic recovery measures exemplifies the fact that cities are the places from which future transitions will originate and accelerate. However, Australia's three-tiered federal, state, and local governance system has inhibited an aligned and coordinated system of governance for policies and programs associated with climate action and decarbonisation of the national electricity grid due to a persistent policy hiatus at the national level over the past 20 years. This explains why only 28 per cent of the national electricity grid is currently renewables-based (and 24 per cent of the total renewable energy generated is from small-scale rooftop solar photovoltaic systems, driven by individual households) (Clean Energy Council 2021). To add to this, there is institutional reluctance by the federal government to participate in national urban planning, where transformational changes are now required if a sustainable urban development transition is to be realised this century.

---

1   The Cooperative Research Centre for Low Carbon Living Limited funded this research as part of the Cooperative Research Centres program, which is an Australian Government initiative.

The magnitude of the challenges Australia's cities face can be summarised as follows (Newton and Doherty 2014):

- There is the need to shrink their world-leading ecological footprints (two to three times the global average) and carbon footprints, which average 15.5 tonnes per capita per annum for domestic emissions—the seventh-highest internationally, and much higher still if embodied carbon emissions in the nation's fossil fuel exports are included (Climate Analytics 2019; World Bank 2020)—representing unsustainable levels of resource consumption and waste generation if the UN Sustainable Development Goals are to be achieved (UN 2015).

- There is an urgent need to reduce the vulnerability of human settlements and the natural environment to climate change pressures and stresses (associated with increased intensities of megafires, rainfall and flooding, drought, and storms).

- There is a challenge to manage rates of annual population growth in the largest cities, which were the highest in the OECD before the Covid-19 pandemic, driven by record levels of immigration aligned with economic policies that are overwhelming metropolitan planning, radically changing demographic composition, and compromising aspirations for inclusive and resilient urban living futures (Levin et al. 2022; Seamer 2019).

- There is an untapped opportunity for low-carbon electrification of cities—principally, buildings and transport, which together represent approximately half of all end-user greenhouse gas emissions from low-density cities—which requires a national energy transition to renewables at scale (NASEM 2021).

- There is an absence of strategies at all levels of government to cope with severe pandemics, as exposed by Covid-19.

Against this backdrop, we identify a *joint transitions challenge* in Australia in relation to decarbonisation and sustainable urban development. This is a multisectoral challenge in which the carbon footprints associated with buildings, transport, and waste generation in the 'built environment' must be radically reduced to compensate for the lag in transitioning to renewable energy and the electrification of cities. Achieving a rapid transition in these areas remains a grand challenge (Kelly and Donegan 2015), requiring programs that can better identify pathways for intervention (Mazzucato 2018). We propose that a transitions approach is needed to provide cross-sectoral and multi-actor collaborations and opportunities for a low-carbon transformation to radically reshape Australian cities for the better.

What we propose in this chapter is theoretically informed by sustainability transitions studies (Frantzeskaki et al. 2017; Newton et al. 2019). Sustainability transitions studies amounts to a theory of change that offers theoretical and interventional frameworks for fundamental changes in the cultures (ways of thinking), structures (ways of organising), and practices (ways of doing) of socio-technical infrastructure systems as well as systems of service provision (Loorbach et al. 2017). The core concept is that, through niche innovations that receive institutional space and nurturing, dominant systems can be overturned, reconfigured, or radically transformed following diverse pathways (Grin et al. 2010). It is a theory of change that emphasises how to unroot deeply entrenched beliefs, practices, and rules, and recent studies point to such changes requiring careful planning and a repertoire of policy and reforms (Kern et al. 2019), curated experimentation at scale (Lam et al. 2019), and capacity for broad diffusion of transformative solutions (Loorbach et al. 2020).

Drawing from transitions studies, we synthesise and build on a scoping literature review of low-carbon people-based urban innovations to identify transformative capacities and potential (Shahani et al. 2021). The concept of transitions pathways illustrates innovative courses of action to guide the 'envisioned' transformation towards a low-carbon urban future in Australia. As such, we extend Westley et al.'s (2011) positioning of innovation as an important driver of dealing with climate change and achieving sustainability. Innovation that is disruptive or catalytic contributes to fundamental changes in systems. Westley et al. (2011: 767) note that 'when innovative ideas are connected to strategic priorities, this produces the cascade of resources required to bring innovation to markets and scale it up'.

The following section presents the core of our analysis in elaborating three interlinked pathways for a low-carbon urban transition in Australian cities derived from a scoping review and previous research by the authors. Section three discusses the crosscutting issues raised by the three pathways, including underlying conditions and their limitations, pointing to future research and practice directions.

Pathways for low-carbon urban transitions in Australia

Samarasinghe et al. (2019) demonstrate the increasing interest in scientific reviews of a fast-growing body of research and knowledge on low-carbon built environments. A critical take on the scientific literature provides insights into new knowledge and practices and gaps for future investigation. We conducted a scoping review of the academic literature in March 2020 according to Preferred Reporting Items for Systematic Reviews and Meta-Analyses (PRISMA) guidelines comprising four categories: identification, screening, eligibility, and included (Arksey and O'Malley 2005). For identification, the following search terms were input into Scopus and Web of Science databases: *ALL ((low-carbon* OR 'low carbon'* AND innovation* AND (urban* OR city*) AND (people* OR social*) AND (wellbeing* OR 'social cohesion'*) AND (limit to published journal articles) AND (exclude non-English articles))*. The records were exported to Mendeley reference management software. After removing duplicates and unrelated publications, the search results were screened independently by two authors (N.F. and F.S.) by reading the title, abstract, and keywords to specify the relevant articles in urban and city subjects. The full article text was assessed for eligibility based on the social aspects of innovations in low-carbon studies. We included 39 articles that were reviewed for qualitative analysis, and relevant information was explicitly gathered by focusing on people-based innovations and initiatives.

From the synthesis of the scoping review, we propose three pathways for transformative shifts in ways of imagining, organising, regenerating, and governing the low-carbon transitions of Australian cities. Our proposals also build on previous research investigating innovations for low-carbon living (Newton et al. 2019) that highlights the importance of an integrated and systemic approach to thinking of ways to address the low-carbon challenge. Specifically, Newton et al. (2019: 10) note:

> There can be no prospect of low-carbon living without a low-carbon built environment that provides the spatial context for resident decision-making and behavior. Livability outcomes are influenced by where people live and the quality and characteristics of the built environment that surrounds them—extending to population health and well-being co-benefits as well as resilience to global warming and local climate change.

In Table 20.1, we provide an overview of the three pathways, the system-level shifts included in each, and the literature review records that support them.

Table 20.1 Overview of proposed pathways for low-carbon urban transitions in Australia

Proposed transition pathway	System-level shifts within pathway	Literature review supporting proposed pathway
Pathway 1: Shift to low-carbon sustainable urban living	From passive to active citizen involvement. From receiving services to self-governed low-carbon initiatives. From participating in to co-designing low-carbon lifestyles and projects. From directive schemes by local governments to learn-by-doing schemes for composting. From regulating to creating institutional space to experiment by and with citizens.	Buijs et al. 2019; Caprotti et al. 2015; Chatterton 2013; Chelleri et al. 2016; Christie and Waller 2019; Eon et al. 2018, 2019; Ghanem et al. 2016; Guillen-Royo et al. 2017; Hagbert and Bradley 2017; Huxley et al. 2019; Huddart Kennedy et al. 2009; Macke et al. 2018, 2019; Newton and Meyer 2011, 2013; Pears and Moore 2019.
Pathway 2: Shift to low-carbon urban infrastructure	From low density to medium density and compact urban living in precincts and cities. From upgrading grey infrastructure to adopting nature-based solutions for urban regeneration. From business-as-usual brownfield, greyfield, and greenfield planning to regenerative urban planning with multifunctionality. From state and privately owned housing to inclusion of cooperatively owned housing and co-housing models. From manicured private and public urban green areas to greenspace incorporating urban farming and agriculture as urban green commons. From reactive energy practices to showcasing renewable energy–powered houses and precincts. From conventional urban materials to materials manufactured from circularly produced low-carbon components. From high-carbon jobs to green jobs in a green economy underpinning new low-carbon urban infrastructure.	Adabre et al. 2020; Arsenio et al. 2018; Burgin 2018; Caprotti et al. 2015; Chatterton 2013; Cuthill et al. 2019; Druckman and Gatersleben 2019; Foster 2020; Hagbert and Bradley 2017; Hasanzadeh et al. 2019; Hausknost et al. 2018; Joffe and Smith 2016; Kilkiş 2016; Landholm et al. 2019; Leporelli and Santi 2019; Liu et al. 2016; Lopes et al. 2018; Macke et al. 2019; Meira et al. 2020; Mindell et al. 2011; Moore and Milkoreit 2020; Plazier et al. 2017; Sandberg 2018; Schäfer et al. 2018; Yu et al. 2021.

Proposed transition pathway	System-level shifts within pathway	Literature review supporting proposed pathway
Pathway 3: Shifting institutional support to unlock low-carbon innovations	From sectoral-only policy to low-carbon policy mixes. From disintegrated or unintegrated environmental policy institutions to adaptive and mission-oriented approaches for low-carbon urban innovations. From fear-driven or fear-inducing marketing campaigns to nudging and inclusive messaging campaigns for low-carbon urban living.	Adabre et al. 2020; Barnes et al. 2018; Chatterton 2013; Chelleri et al. 2016; Christie and Waller 2019; Crowe et al. 2016; Ehnert et al. 2018; Ghanem et al. 2016; Guillen-Royo et al. 2017; Hagbert and Bradley 2017; Harrington and Hoy 2019; Huxley et al. 2019; Landholm et al. 2019; Macke et al. 2018, 2019; Meira et al. 2020; Mindell et al. 2011; Moore and Milkoreit 2020; Newton et al. 2021; Schäfer et al. 2018.

Source: Authors's summary.

Pathway 1: Shift to low-carbon, sustainable urban living

A transition to a low-carbon urban future starts with shifting ways of urban living to sustainable low-carbon practices. There is a significant values/attitude–action gap about sustainable low-carbon living (Newton and Meyer 2013). In designs and proposals for and the facilitation of transformational change, people and their lifestyles must be at the core. This is fundamental for informing, designing, and dealing with the necessary shifts to sustainable urban living that will include civic activation through new modes of co-governance, participation in and inclusiveness of low-carbon initiatives, and adoption of urban design approaches to make low-carbon living in cities attractive and comfortable. As Seamer (2019: 59–60) notes, 'behavioral change in our cities can be nudged rather than forced'. This aligns with the need to address individual and household values related to nature, consumption, and esteem, and to leverage ways to transform social practices and habits in the short and long terms.

Citizen participation in different stages of low-carbon initiatives (from setting up and co-creation to operation and scaling up) is a critical condition for civic ownership and mobilisation of the shift to low-carbon lifestyles (Guillen-Royo et al. 2017). Specifically, engaging with experts and communities in co-designing projects (Caprotti et al. 2015) and finding creative ways to enhance participation in scaling up smart city low-carbon projects (Buijs et al. 2019) are methods to co-govern a pathway to sustainable low-carbon lifestyles. By creating institutional space for citizens to trial new ways of living, urban planning and design can tap into the creative potential of citizens and not only allow new ideas to emerge, but also form new networks that can translate low-impact urban living from idea to reality (Macke et al. 2018), as well as making low-carbon innovations practical at household and neighbourhood scales, such as participation in community projects for reuse and recycling (Christie and Waller 2019). City governments can instigate such a shift through schemes and programs that break the knowledge (and familiarity) barriers to adoption of low-carbon practices. For example, government agencies can support household composting of food scraps to eliminate this significant waste stream to landfill (Hagbert and Bradley 2017), which is developed further in pathway three.

Therefore, it is essential to understand how to motivate, encourage, and lower the resistance to the shift towards low-carbon sustainable living, especially concerns about amenity, comfort, and 'the availability of access to all [the] things that we seek on a day-to-day basis in urban living' (Seamer 2019: 17). The major barriers include a sense of ownership of the problem, lack of relevant information about how to shift to low-carbon practices and behaviours, and time and financial constraints (Newton and Meyer 2011). A way to overcome the information and 'problem ownership' barriers is to promote low-carbon renovations on television shows like *The Block* and among social media influencers. Research by Hulse et al. (2015) and Podkalicka et al. (2016) revealed that to gain traction in the media, the focus must be more on selling points linked to enhanced comfort and liveability than on carbon savings. Changing individual and household behaviours requires a multitude of actions and, foremost, policies and instruments that do not change the meaning of the household practices but rather the ways in which and times when they are performed (Eon et al. 2018, 2019). Breakthroughs are expected to occur via the application of 'smart home' technologies that introduce automation and information feedback to the household (Pears and Moore 2019). This all implies that government actions—local and state—must strive for 'motivation' rather than fear of punishment for noncompliance for the shift to sustainable low-carbon living to be accelerated.

Pathway 2: Low-carbon urban infrastructure

The design of urban infrastructure plays a vital role in shaping urban living. Specifically, urban design concepts and approaches can enable low-carbon living and make it attractive and comfortable, contributing to fast adoption. As Bulkeley and Betsill (2005: 46) argue:

> consolidating urban places and improving design is seen to be beneficial not only from an environmental perspective but also as a means of improving the 'liveability' of urban areas and the provision of services, as well as providing the impetus for economic regeneration.

For example, passive urban design can enable low-carbon leisure activities (Foster 2020), redefine low-carbon behaviour through participation in passive design projects (Chatterton 2013), and enable reductions in energy demand by upgrading insulation in buildings or double-glazing of windows (Yu et al. 2021: 6). Active design can contribute to low-carbon living and better health outcomes (Hadgraft et al. 2021) enabled by enhanced local walking and cycling (Arsenio et al. 2018).

Compact urban designs and forms enable low-carbon living (Newton 2000). Shared journeys using public transport and bike-sharing systems with dedicated bike lanes are enablers of sustainable urban living (Cuthill et al. 2019). In addition, mixed-used urban environments require designs that connect residential locations to functional locations such as those for employment and education, and that create low-carbon mobility options (Leporelli and Santi 2019). With urban infrastructure being intensively used and needing constant upgrading and maintenance as it ages, finding ways to reconfigure it is foundational for charting transition. This second pathway includes a shift to zero-carbon housing; scaled-up adoption of nature-based solutions, including water-sensitive urban design for regenerating greenspaces and water drainage infrastructure; bold investments in low-carbon mobility; and the adoption of new models for planning and development at precinct scale in brownfields, greyfields, and greenfields (Newton 2017).

Housing is the first urban infrastructure in Australia to be targeted with a zero-carbon policy endorsed by the government and industry. Recent research has investigated new modes of housing as well as new ways of constructing built environments for eco-positive performance (Moore and Milkoreit 2020). By providing leaseholder opportunities for cooperatively owned housing (Adabre et al. 2020), co-housing increases community self-governance and democratic control (Hausknost et al. 2018), making it a model for accelerating the uptake of sustainable low-carbon technologies and lifestyles.

There are two significant challenges associated with achieving this transition within 30 years. First, mainstreaming of the construction of net-zero carbon housing (NZCH) in new buildings (which, before Covid-19, typically amounted to about 160,000 dwellings a year) is yet to begin. Despite this, a partnership between the Australian Renewable Energy Agency (ARENA) and Mirvac, one of Australia's largest property groups, was recently struck to build a net-zero energy housing estate of 49 townhouses in Melbourne to demonstrate the feasibility of achieving NZCH at scale. A similar initiative involving collaboration between Sustainability Victoria and three home builders—SJD, Metricon, and Stockland—is part of a government-supported program to design, build, and market NZCH display homes in Melbourne's greenfield estates. These projects are the first of their type, illustrating how far the industry has to go to deliver NZCH without government support. A second challenge concerns the retrofitting of existing housing that has poor operating energy efficiency, which is the bulk of housing in Australia. Research by Newton and Tucker (2010, 2011) demonstrated that five-star-rated housing plus solar photovoltaic technology represented a minimum package capable of achieving carbon-neutral status.

Urban infrastructure can also play an important role in contributing to low-carbon transitions if it is designed or repurposed towards multifunctional use and adopts nature-based solutions. For example, urban parks can be restored towards multifunctional spaces incorporating passive and active designs for climate adaptation such as water drainage pools, rain gardens for passive irrigation of urban trees, and areas with 'renaturing' through the planting of native species to reconnect citizens with nature (Oke et al. 2021). Community-supported urban agriculture can also serve as a nature-based solution to retrofitting brownfields, green in-between spaces, and grey spaces in compact precincts (Burgin 2018; Kingsley et al. 2021).

Charting a low-carbon transition in urban mobility will require bold visions and investments, including rethinking the underlying assumptions of car-dominated strategies, especially in the post-pandemic recovery period. As Seamer (2019: 24–31) notes, there are unquestioned assumptions—or, as he says, 'transport myths'—that underlie the way public urban space is designed for and around the car and accessibility in cities has been measured. Given these entrenched practices and assumptions, it will be essential to have a low-carbon shift in the strategic and statutory planning of cities to promote the use of green public transport, walking, and cycling, and openly address path dependencies and obstacles through innovative urban design and planning alternatives (Meira et al. 2020). New models for retrofitting ageing, low-density, car-dependent suburbs in Australia's largest cities have been developed based on a combination of transit-activated and place-activated greyfield precinct regeneration (Newton et al. 2021). Precinct-scale regeneration projects are well positioned to accommodate a new tranche of green technologies designed to function at this scale: distributed renewable energy and storage, integrated urban water systems, shared mobility, and waste composting.

Showcasing renewable energy–powered houses and precincts is a step towards a broader shift from high-carbon to low-carbon urban energy systems. Alternative approaches to urban energy generation and supply include combined heating and cooling networks, building new houses according to passive heating and cooling principles (Plazier et al. 2017), and green retrofitting schemes to improve the energy efficiency of dwellings (Adabre et al. 2020). Other mitigation actions for low-carbon energy transitions in cities include generating renewable energy from onsite sources, including expanding solar systems at the precinct level, and dealing with measures to curb energy consumption through switching to energy-efficient appliances and behaviour changes (Yu et al. 2021: 6).

Aligned to all these shifts in urban infrastructure systems is the need for a supply chain of new building materials that contribute lower embodied carbon to the built environment. One way to achieve this is to shift to materials produced using biomass rather than fossil fuel–intensive materials (Foster 2020). This must be accompanied by a holistic approach to lower embodied and operational emissions with mitigation measures, including using recycled materials and those produced using circular methods (Yu et al. 2021).

This can be achieved through the circular economy approaches and carbon accounting models now gaining traction in Australia. KPMG Economics (2020) estimates that future circular economy industries could add $20 billion to national GDP by 2025 and $210 billion by 2050, including 17,000 new jobs. They feature new industries relying heavily on creating wealth from the waste streams currently going to landfill or receiving waters and using renewable energy (wind, solar, hydro, and hydrogen) to underpin Australia's future green steel and green aluminium industries. Australia's building product manufacturing industries have long resisted providing declarations of the embodied energy in individual products. Recent decisions by the European Union to impose carbon tariffs on traded goods as part of their COP26 climate action program will drive change in this area. This will allow ready creation of life-cycle analysis databases for all built environment products, which will be essential for making eco-efficiency assessments of building designs an automated process, as demonstrated by prototype tools in the Cooperative Research Centre for Construction Innovation (Seo et al. 2007), enabling regenerative cradle-to-cradle processes for the construction and manufacturing industries (McDonough and Braungart 2002). The Australian Government introduced the Climate Active Carbon Neutral Standards for buildings and precincts in 2011,[2] but it currently excludes embodied energy, known as scope 3 emissions (Wiedmann et al. 2021).

Pathway 3: Shifting institutional support to unlock low-carbon innovations

Institutions play a role in supporting and accelerating urban sustainability transitions. Changing the 'rules of the game' sets the scene for different initiatives and innovations to be generated, supported, and diffused (Barnes et al. 2018). Institutions—including federal and state government policies and schemes, statutory and strategic planning, and city and community programs supported by public funding—must shift from reinforcing existing practices and structures to unlocking and incentivising low-carbon practices and innovations. Kashima et al. (2021) point to the importance of public policies for cultivating low-carbon readiness in societies. In Australia, policy compliance is high, indicating that the role of the state is paramount for leading and driving behavioural shifts and shaping the socioeconomic landscape for new businesses, knowledge, and innovations to emerge.

Institutional support to unlock low-carbon innovations in Australian cities can take the shape of policies (Russo and Pavone 2021) for low-carbon transitions, incentive schemes for low-carbon practices, and disincentives for unsustainable practices (Rogge et al. 2020; Sovacool et al. 2021). Such support could include policy actions targeting different infrastructure and sectors, such as:

---

2   Available from: www.dcceew.gov.au/sites/default/files/documents/climate-active-carbon-neutral-standard-precincts.pdf; www.dcceew.gov.au/sites/default/files/documents/climate-active-carbon-neutral-standard-buildings.pdf.

- reform of building regulations to design out carbon-intensive elements in district/precinct developments (Schäfer et al. 2018)
- support for green retrofitting initiatives targeting aged housing to extend building life and enhance environmental performance (Adabre et al. 2020)
- subsidies for the use of public transport for people on low incomes or with disabilities to ensure equal access to services (Macke et al. 2018)
- reversing the investment hierarchy to put pedestrian infrastructure first and automobile infrastructure last (Mindell et al. 2011)
- providing discounts for electric or hybrid vehicles (Meira et al. 2020)
- offering low-carbon mobility scholarships to students who commute daily on foot, by bike, public transport, or school bus (Hagbert and Bradley 2017)
- revising the building code, lifting the minimum performance regulations for low-carbon buildings (Moore and Milkoreit 2020).

Low-carbon policy mixes will require adaptive institutional designs that could differ across states, so an interdisciplinary approach to institutional design may be critical to avoid misfit institutions and failed implementation. As Alexander (2020: 23) points out, 'institutional design means designing institutions: devising and realizing rules, procedures, and organizational structures to enable and constrain behavior and action and make them conform to held values, achieve desired objectives or execute given tasks'. Such institutional shifts must be accompanied by a change in the policy narrative, away from protecting existing high-carbon systems. Transformation narratives are powerful governance instruments, however, they come with a dual character: they can motivate and instigate change agendas, but at the same time, they can present an unattainable or even idealistic future, meaning many citizens may feel powerless to contribute or be part of such a transition or even afraid that their lifestyle choices and welfare will be compromised. To avoid such social and governance backlash, local and state governments must show that low-carbon transitions are happening in cities, are easy to adopt, and can enhance lifestyles while still being comfortable.

A case in point is the institutional and policy pathway for minimising food waste in metropolitan Melbourne. Australia generates about 7.3 million tonnes of food waste annually, accounting for more than 5 per cent of the nation's greenhouse gas emissions from landfill (DEE 2021). The Victorian Government has implemented several strategies and regulatory frameworks in the past decade to reduce food waste and support the Australian National Food Waste Strategy (DEE 2017). In metropolitan Melbourne, three documents have influenced the direction of policymaking for managing food waste: the Metropolitan Waste and Resource Recovery Implementation Plan (Recycling Victoria 2016), the Victorian Waste Education Strategy (Sustainability Victoria 2016), and the Waste and Resource Recovery Strategy 2030 (City of Melbourne 2019). An analysis of these strategies reveals the critical role of community involvement and empowerment in managing food waste at different levels of government. The importance of education, of learning about waste reduction and separation, and of waste-reduction campaigns has been highlighted, and can further inform or shape a planning policy mix for waste reduction targets.

Effective implementation of low-carbon urban strategies can happen through information campaigns 'to inform people about what behaviors are effective at curtailing greenhouse gasses emissions' (Kashima et al. 2021: 180), platforms for information and knowledge-sharing (Ghanem et al. 2016), and by creating powerful storytelling and symbols to shape cultural and cognitive beliefs (Huxley et al. 2019). Policies, knowledge, and information schemes must establish a new environmental identity for Australian urban citizens that aligns with their values or, as Kashima et al. (2021) define it, a person's low-carbon readiness. In addition, information must be understandable to all users and distributed equally to avoid creating information divides (Guillen-Royo et al. 2017).

Progressing institutional change to unlock the potential of low-carbon innovations in Australian cities must put justice at the heart of the transition. This means 'no citizen is left behind' in facilitating transformative changes and creating institutional spaces for emerging low-carbon innovations and there is no deepening of existing socioeconomic and literacy divides. Wachsmuth et al. (2016: 392) write: 'Socially, policymakers should incorporate equity into every stage of the urban-policy process, from research to formulation to implementation.' As post-pandemic recovery agendas are under discussion, rethinking how our institutions operate and how they must change should be guided by the compass of justice and a low-carbon urban future.

Conclusion

Cities lead the way in positive transitions to a more sustainable, resilient, and liveable future. As our planet becomes increasingly urbanised, the roles of urban science and sustainability transitions scholarship grow in significance (Kalantari 2021). Our scan of the state of play in Australia's sustainability transition in energy and urban systems indicates that the rate of progress is too slow. The urgency for change has not diminished since the publication of *Transitions* more than a decade ago (Newton 2008). We conclude that the shift to low-carbon urbanism requires concerted and open-ended transformative actions through social, technological, and governance innovations that promote community-based approaches, policies, and trust in the creativity of citizens and interdisciplinary science teams.

Specifically, the three pathways advocated here provide innovative ways to transform existing infrastructure, urban living, and institutional schemes and incentives. Our contribution has two theoretical and conceptual limitations that could be avenues for future research on low-carbon urban transitions. First, broader societal changes (including to perceptions and mindsets) and conceptual paradigms of alternative urbanism have not been investigated or integrated into our proposed pathways. Alternative urbanism concepts such as localisation of cities (Seamer 2019) and biophilic urbanism (Soderlund and Newman 2020) could be compared through urban planning scenarios and against the UN Sustainable Development Goals to inform future planning for low-carbon cities and precincts. Second, the proposed pathways must directly connect transformative shifts with future strategic programs. Future research on the policy context for the pathways must juxtapose them with existing strategies or policies—demonstrating a 'From → To' vision. For example, the Urban Forestry Strategy of the City of Melbourne exemplifies a metropolitan-scale strategy that can reinforce the restoration of urban ecosystems to deal with the combined climate change and biodiversity crises. Future research can enrich the proposed pathways and connect global research on urban low-carbon innovations with existing policies and programs towards more 'transformative' implementation plans.

Australia must invest effort and science in institutional development to shift to a low-carbon future. New adaptive, agile, and cross-sectoral institutions are needed that will also require an innovative approach to development and coordination. In earlier work, we noted the need to scale up a national innovation platform that can drive citywide and nationwide collaboration and experimentation (Newton and Frantzeskaki 2021). With our proposed pathways as starting points for such development and dialogue between science, policy, and industry, we call for a national effort to create scaled-up strategies for a low-carbon urban future in Australia.

References

Adabre, M.A., A.P.C. Chan, A. Darko, R. Osei-Kyei, R. Abidoye, and T. Adjei-Kumi. 2020. 'Critical Barriers to Sustainability Attainment in Affordable Housing: International Construction Professionals' Perspective.' *Journal of Cleaner Production* 253: 119995. doi.org/10.1016/j.jclepro.2020.119995.

Alexander, E.R. 2020. 'Complexity, Institutions, and Institutional Design.' In *Handbook on Planning and Complexity*, edited by G. De Roo, C. Yamu, and C. Zuidema, 19–34. Cheltenham, UK: Edward Elgar.

Arksey, H., and L. O'Malley. 2005. 'Scoping Studies: Towards a Methodological Framework.' *International Journal of Social Research Methodology* 8(1): 19–32. doi.org/10.1080/1364557032000119616.

Arsenio, E., J.V. Dias, S. Azeredo Lopes, and H. Iglésias Pereira. 2018. 'Assessing the Market Potential of Electric Bicycles and ICT for Low Carbon School Travel: A Case Study in the Smart City of ÁGUEDA.' *European Transport Research Review* 10(13). doi.org/10.1007/s12544-017-0279-z.

Barnes, J., R. Durrant, F. Kern, and G. MacKerron. 2018. 'The Institutionalisation of Sustainable Practices in Cities: How Initiatives Shape Local Selection Environments.' *Environmental Innovation and Societal Transitions* 29: 68–80. doi.org/10.1016/j.eist.2018.04.003.

Buijs, A., R. Hansen, S. Van der Jagt, B. Ambrose-Oji, B. Elands, E. Lorance Rall, T. Mattijssen, S. Pauleit, H. Runhaar, A. Stahl Olafsson, and M. Steen Møller. 2019. 'Mosaic Governance for Urban Green Infrastructure: Upscaling Active Citizenship from a Local Government Perspective.' *Urban Forestry and Urban Greening* 40: 53–62. doi.org/10.1016/j.ufug.2018.06.011.

Bulkeley, H., and M. Betsill. 2005. 'Rethinking Sustainable Cities: Multilevel Governance and the "Urban" Politics of Climate Change.' *Environmental Politics* 14(1): 42–63. doi.org/10.1080/0964401042000310178.

Burgin, S. 2018. 'Sustainability as a Motive for Leisure-Time Gardening: A View from the "Veggie Patch".' *International Journal of Environmental Studies* 75: 1000–10. doi.org/10.1080/00207233.2018.1464277.

Caprotti, F., C. Springer, and N. Harmer. 2015. '"Eco" for Whom? Envisioning Eco-Urbanism in the Sino-Singapore Tianjin Eco-City, China.' *International Journal of Urban and Regional Research* 39: 495–517. doi.org/10.1111/1468-2427.12233.

Chatterton, P. 2013. 'Towards an Agenda for Post-Carbon Cities: Lessons from LILAC, the UK's First Ecological, Affordable Cohousing Community.' *International Journal of Urban and Regional Research* 37: 1654–74. doi.org/10.1111/1468-2427.12009.

Chelleri, L., H.W. Kua, J.P. Rodríguez Sánchez, K.M. Nahiduzzaman, and G. Thondhlana. 2016. 'Are People Responsive to a More Sustainable, Decentralized, and User-Driven Management of Urban Metabolism?' *Sustainability* 8(3): 275. doi.org/10.3390/su8030275.

Christie, B., and V. Waller. 2019. 'Community Learnings Through Residential Composting in Apartment Buildings.' *Journal of Environmental Education* 50(2): 97–112. doi.org/10.1080/00958964.2018.1509289.

City of Melbourne. 2019. *Waste and Resource Recovery Strategy 2030*. Melbourne: City of Melbourne. Available from: www.melbourne.vic.gov.au/about-melbourne/sustainability/Pages/waste-and-resource-recovery-strategy-2030.aspx.

Clean Energy Council. 2021. *Clean Energy Australia Report*. Melbourne: Clean Energy Council. Available from: www.cleanenergycouncil.org.au/resources/resources-hub/clean-energy-australia-report.

Climate Analytics. 2019. 'Australia on Track to Become One of the World's Major Climate Polluters.' *News*, 8 July. Berlin: Climate Analytics. Available from: climateanalytics.org/latest/australia-on-track-to-become-one-of-the-worlds-major-climate-polluters/.

Crowe, P.R., K. Foley, and M.J. Collier. 2016. 'Operationalizing Urban Resilience Through a Framework for Adaptive Co-Management and Design: Five Experiments in Urban Planning Practice and Policy.' *Environmental Science and Policy* 62: 112–19. doi.org/10.1016/j.envsci.2016.04.007.

Cuthill, N., M. Cao, Y. Liu, X. Gao, and Y. Zhang. 2019. 'The Association between Urban Public Transport Infrastructure and Social Equity and Spatial Accessibility Within the Urban Environment: An Investigation of Tramlink in London.' *Sustainability* 11(5): 1229. doi.org/10.3390/su11051229.

Deng, G., and P. Newton. 2017. 'Assessing the Impact of Solar PV on Domestic Electricity Consumption: Exploring the Prospect of Rebound Effects.' *Energy Policy* 110: 313–24. doi.org/10.1016/j.enpol.2017.08.035.

Department of the Environment and Energy (DEE). 2017. *National Food Waste Strategy: Halving Australia's Food Waste by 2030*. November. Canberra: Commonwealth of Australia. Available from: www.environment.gov.au/protection/waste/publications/national-food-waste-strategy.

Department of the Environment and Energy (DEE). 2021. *Tackling Australia's Food Waste*. Canberra: Commonwealth of Australia. Available from: www.environment.gov.au/protection/waste/food-waste.

Druckman, A., and B. Gatersleben. 2019. 'A Time-Use Approach: High Subjective Wellbeing, Low Carbon Leisure.' *Journal of Public Mental Health* 18: 85–93. doi.org/10.1108/JPMH-04-2018-0024.

Ehnert, F., N. Frantzeskaki, J. Barnes, S. Borgström, L. Gorissen, F. Kern, L. Strenchock, and M. Egermann. 2018. 'The Acceleration of Urban Sustainability Transitions: A Comparison of Brighton, Budapest, Dresden, Genk, and Stockholm.' *Sustainability* 10(3): 612. doi.org/10.3390/su10030612.

Eon, C., J. Breadsell, G. Morrison, and J. Byrne. 2019. 'Shifting Home Energy Consumption Through a Holistic Understanding of the Home System of Practice.' In *Decarbonising the Built Environment: Charting the Transition*, edited by P. Newton, D. Prasad, A. Sproul, and S. White, 431–47. Singapore: Palgrave Macmillan. doi.org/10.1007/978-981-13-7940-6_23.

Eon, C., X. Liu, G.M. Morrison, and J. Byrne. 2018. 'Influencing Energy and Water Use Within a Home System of Practice.' *Energy and Buildings* 158: 848–60. doi.org/10.1016/j.enbuild.2017.10.053.

Foster, G. 2020. 'Circular Economy Strategies for Adaptive Reuse of Cultural Heritage Buildings to Reduce Environmental Impacts.' *Resources, Conservation and Recycling* 152: 104507. doi.org/10.1016/j.resconrec.2019.104507.

Frantzeskaki, N., V. Castán Broto, L. Coenen, and D. Loorbach, eds. 2017. *Urban Sustainability Transitions*. New York, NY: Routledge. doi.org/10.4324/9781315228389.

Ghanem, D.A., S. Mander, and C. Gough. 2016. '"I Think We Need to Get a Better Generator": Household Resilience to Disruption to Power Supply During Storm Events.' *Energy Policy* 92: 171–80. doi.org/10.1016/j.enpol.2016.02.003.

Grin, J., J. Rotmans, and J. Schot. 2010. *Transitions to Sustainable Development: New Directions in the Study of Long Term Transformative Change*. New York, NY: Routledge.

Guillen-Royo, M., J. Guardiola, and F. Garcia-Quero. 2017. 'Sustainable Development in Times of Economic Crisis: A Needs-Based Illustration from Granada (Spain).' *Journal of Cleaner Production* 150: 267–76. doi.org/10.1016/j.jclepro.2017.03.008.

Hadgraft, N., M. Chandrabose, B. Bok, N. Owen, I. Woodcock, P. Newton, N. Frantzeskaki, and T. Sugiyama. 2021. 'Low-Carbon Built Environments and Cardiometabolic Health: A Systematic Review of Australian Studies.' *Cities & Health* 6(2): 418–31. doi.org/10.1080/23748834.2021.1903787.

Hagbert, P., and K. Bradley. 2017. 'Transitions on the Home Front: A Story of Sustainable Living Beyond Eco-Efficiency.' *Energy Research & Social Science* 31: 240–48. doi.org/10.1016/j.erss.2017.05.002.

Harrington, P., and V. Hoy. 2019. 'The Trajectory to a Net Zero Emissions Built Environment: The Role of Policy and Regulation.' In *Decarbonising the Built Environment: Charting the Transition*, edited by P. Newton, D. Prasad, A. Sproul, and S. White, 193–207. Singapore: Palgrave Macmillan. doi.org/10.1007/978-981-13-7940-6_10.

Hasanzadeh, K., M. Czepkiewicz, J. Heinonen, M. Kyttä, S. Ala-Mantila, and J. Ottelin. 2019. 'Beyond Geometries of Activity Spaces: A Holistic Study of Daily Travel Patterns, Individual Characteristics, and Perceived Wellbeing in Helsinki Metropolitan Area.' *Journal of Transport and Land Use* 12(1): 149–77. doi.org/10.5198/jtlu.2019.1148.

Hausknost, D., W. Haas, S. Hielscher, M. Schäfer, M. Leitner, I. Kunze, and S. Mandl. 2018. 'Investigating Patterns of Local Climate Governance: How Low-Carbon Municipalities and Intentional Communities Intervene in Social Practices.' *Environmental Policy and Governance* 28(6): 371–82. doi.org/10.1002/eet.1804.

Huddart Kennedy, E., T.M. Beckley, B.L. McFarlane, and S. Nadeau. 2009. 'Why We Don't "Walk the Talk": Understanding the Environmental Values/Behaviour Gap in Canada.' *Human Ecology Review* 16(2): 151–60. www.jstor.org/stable/24707539.

Hulse, K., A. Podkalicka, E. Milne, T. Winfree, and G. Melles. 2015. *'I'd Just Google It': Media and Home Renovation Practices in Australia*. RP3021 Report 1: Media/Home Renovations. Low Carbon Living Cooperative Research Centre. Available from: research.monash.edu/en/publications/rp3021-report-1-id-just-google-it-media-and-home-renovation-pract.

Huxley, R., A. Owen, and P. Chatterton. 2019. 'The Role of Regime-Level Processes in Closing the Gap Between Sustainable City Visions and Action.' *Environmental Innovation and Societal Transitions* 33: 115–26. doi.org/10.1016/j.eist.2019.04.001.

Infrastructure Sustainability Council of Australia, ClimateWorks Australia, and Australian Sustainable Built Environment Council. 2021. *Reshaping Infrastructure for a Net Zero Emissions Future.* Issues Paper, March. Melbourne: ClimateWorks Australia. Available from: www.asbec.asn.au/wordpress/wp-content/uploads/2020/03/200304-CWA-ISCA-ASBEC-Reshaping-Infrastructure-Issues-Paper.pdf.

Joffe, H., and N. Smith. 2016. 'City Dweller Aspirations for Cities of the Future: How Do Environmental and Personal Wellbeing Feature?' *Cities* 59: 102–12. doi.org/10.1016/j.cities.2016.06.006.

Kalantari, Z. 2021. 'Enlivening Our Cities: Towards Urban Sustainability and Resilience.' *Ambio* 50: 1629–33. doi.org/10.1007/s13280-021-01518-w.

Kashima, Y., L. O'Brien, I. McNeill, M. Ambrose, G. Bruce, C.R. Critchley, P. Dudgeon, P. Newton, and G. Robins. 2021. 'Low Carbon Readiness in Social Context: Introducing the Social Context of Environmental Identity Model.' *Asian Journal of Social Psychology* 24(2): 169–83. doi.org/10.1111/ajsp.12454.

Kelly, J.-F., and P. Donegan. 2015. *City Limits: Why Australia's Cities Are Broken and How We Can Fix Them.* Melbourne: Melbourne University Publishing.

Kern, F., K.S. Rogge, and M. Howlett. 2019. 'Policy Mixes for Sustainability Transitions: New Approaches and Insights Through Bridging Innovation and Policy Studies.' *Research Policy* 48(10). doi.org/10.1016/j.respol.2019.103832.

Kilkiş, Ş. 2016. 'Sustainable Development of Energy, Water and Environment Systems Index for Southeast European Cities.' *Journal of Cleaner Production* 130: 222–34. doi.org/10.1016/j.jclepro.2015.07.121.

Kingsley, J., M. Egerer, S. Nuttman, L. Keniger, P. Pettitt, N. Frantzeskaki, T. Gray, A. Ossola, B. Lin, A. Bailey, D. Tracey, S. Barron, and P. Marsh. 2021. 'Urban Agriculture as a Nature-Based Solution to Address Socio-Ecological Challenges in Australian Cities.' *Urban Forestry & Urban Greening* 60: 127059. doi.org/10.1016/j.ufug.2021.127059.

KPMG Economics. 2020. *Potential Economic Payoff of a Circular Economy.* Report, 28 April. Melbourne: KPMG. Available from: assets.kpmg.com/content/dam/kpmg/au/pdf/2020/potential-economic-pay-off-circular-economy-australia-2020.pdf.

Lam, D.P., A.I. Horcea-Milcu, J. Fischer, D. Peukert, and D.J. Lang. 2019. 'Three Principles for Co-Designing Sustainability Intervention Strategies: Experiences from Southern Transylvania.' *Ambio* 49: 1451–65. doi.org/10.1007/s13280-019-01302-x.

Landholm, D.M., A. Holsten, F. Martellozzo, D.E. Reusser, and J.P. Kropp. 2019. 'Climate Change Mitigation Potential of Community-Based Initiatives in Europe.' *Regional Environmental Change* 19: 927–38. doi.org/10.1007/s10113-018-1428-1.

Leporelli, E., and G. Santi. 2019. 'From Psychology of Sustainability to Sustainability of Urban Spaces: Promoting a Primary Prevention Approach for Well-Being in the Healthy City Designing. A Waterfront Case Study in Livorno.' *Sustainability* 11. doi.org/10.3390/su11030760.

Levin, I., C.A. Nygaard, and P.W. Newton, eds. 2022. *Migration and Urban Transitions in Australia*. Global Diversities Series. Singapore: Springer Nature. doi.org/10.1007/978-3-030-91331-1.

Liu, M., Y. Huang, R. Hiscock, Q. Li, J. Bi, P.L. Kinney, and C.E. Sabel. 2016. 'Do Climate Change Policies Promote or Conflict with Subjective Wellbeing: A Case Study of Suzhou, China.' *International Journal of Environmental Research and Public Health* 13(3): 344. doi.org/10.3390/ijerph13030344.

Loorbach, D., N. Frantzeskaki, and F. Avelino. 2017. 'Sustainability Transitions Research: Transforming Science and Practice for Societal Change.' *Annual Review of Environment and Resources* 42: 599–626. doi.org/10.1146/annurev-environ-102014-021340.

Loorbach, D., J. Wittmayer, F. Avelino, T. von Wirth, and N. Frantzeskaki. 2020. 'Transformative Innovation and Translocal Diffusion.' *Environmental Innovation and Societal Transitions* 35: 251–60. doi.org/10.1016/j.eist.2020.01.009.

Lopes, A.M., S. Healy, E. Power, L. Crabtree, and K. Gibson. 2018. 'Infrastructures of Care: Opening Up "Home" As Commons in A Hot City.' *Human Ecology Review* 24(2): 41–59. doi.org/10.22459/HER.24.02.2018.03.

McDonough, W., and M. Braungart. 2002. *Cradle to Cradle: Remaking the Way We Make Things*. New York, NY: North Point Press.

Macke, J., R.M. Casagrande, J.A.R. Sarate, and K.A. Silva. 2018. 'Smart City and Quality of Life: Citizens' Perception in a Brazilian Case Study.' *Journal of Cleaner Production* 182: 717–26. doi.org/10.1016/j.jclepro.2018.02.078.

Macke, J., J.A. Rubim Sarate, and S. de Atayde Moschen. 2019. 'Smart Sustainable Cities Evaluation and Sense of Community.' *Journal of Cleaner Production* 239. doi.org/10.1016/j.jclepro.2019.118103.

Mazzucato, M. 2018. *Mission-Oriented Research & Innovation in the European Union: A Problem-Solving Approach to Fuel Innovation-Led Growth*. Directorate-General for Research and Innovation, European Commission. Brussels: Publications Office. Available from: data.europa.eu/doi/10.2777/360325.

Meira, L.H., C.A. de Mello, Y.M. Castro, L.K. Oliveira, and C.D.O.L Nascimento. 2020. 'Measuring Social Effective Speed to Improve Sustainable Mobility Policies in Developing Countries.' *Transportation Research Part D: Transport and Environment* 78: 102200. doi.org/10.1016/j.trd.2019.12.002.

Mindell, J.S., J.M. Cohen, S. Watkins, and N. Tyler. 2011. 'Synergies Between Low-Carbon and Healthy Transport Policies.' *Proceedings of the Institution of Civil Engineers: Transport* 64(3): 127–39. doi.org/10.1680/tran.2011.164.3.127.

Moore, M.-L., and M. Milkoreit. 2020. 'Imagination and Transformations to Sustainable and Just Futures.' *Elementa: Science of the Anthropocene* 8(1). doi.org/10.1525/elementa.2020.081.

National Academies of Sciences, Engineering, and Medicine (NASEM). 2021. *Accelerating Decarbonization of the US Energy System.* Washington, DC: The National Academies Press. doi.org/10.17226/25932.

Newton, P. 2000. 'Urban Form and Environmental Performance.' In *Achieving Sustainable Urban Form*, edited by E. Burton, M. Jenks, and K. Williams, 46–53. London: Routledge. doi.org/10.4324/9780203827925.

Newton, P. 2017. 'Framing New Retrofit Models for Regenerating Australia's Fast Growing Cities.' In *Retrofitting Cities for Tomorrow's World*, edited by M. Eames, T. Dixon, M. Hunt, and S. Lannon, 183–206. Hoboken, NJ: Wiley-Blackwell. doi.org/10.1002/9781119007241.ch12.

Newton, P., and N. Frantzeskaki. 2021. 'Creating a National Urban Research and Development Platform for Advancing Urban Experimentation.' *Sustainability* 13(2): 530. doi.org/10.3390/su13020530.

Newton, P., and D. Meyer. 2011. 'Who Cares? An Exploration of Attitudes and Behaviour Towards the Conservation of Resources.' In *Urban Consumption*, edited by P. Newton, 267–89. Melbourne: CSIRO Publishing.

Newton, P., and D. Meyer. 2013. 'Exploring the Attitudes–Action Gap in Household Resource Consumption: Does "Environmental Lifestyle" Segmentation Align with Consumer Behaviour?' *Sustainability* 5(3): 1211–33. doi.org/10.3390/su5031211.

Newton, P., P.W.G. Newman, S. Glackin, and G. Thomson. 2021. *Greening the Greyfields: New Models for Regenerating the Middle Suburbs of Low-Density Cities.* Singapore: Palgrave Macmillan. doi.org/10.1007/978-981-16-6238-6.

Newton, P., A. Pears, J. Whiteman, and R. Astle. 2012. 'The Energy and Carbon Footprints of Urban Housing and Transport: Current Trends and Future Prospects.' In *Australia's Unintended Cities: The Impact of Housing on Urban Development*, edited by R. Tomlinson, 153–89. Melbourne: CSIRO Publishing.

Newton, P., D. Prasad, A. Sproul, and S. White. 2019. *Decarbonising the Built Environment: Charting the Transition.* Singapore: Palgrave Macmillan. doi.org/10.1007/978-981-13-7940-6.

Newton, P.W. 2008. *Transitions: Pathways Towards Sustainable Urban Development in Australia.* Melbourne: CSIRO Publishing. doi.org/10.1071/9780643097995.

Newton, P.W., and P. Doherty. 2014. 'The Challenges to Urban Sustainability and Resilience.' In *Resilient Sustainable Cities*, edited by L. Pearson, P. Newton, and P. Roberts, 19–30. New York, NY: Routledge.

Newton, P.W., and S.N. Tucker. 2010. 'Hybrid Buildings: A Pathway to Carbon Neutral Housing.' *Architectural Science Review* 53(1): 95–106. doi.org/10.3763/asre.2009.0052.

Newton, P.W., and S.N. Tucker. 2011. 'Pathways to Decarbonizing the Housing Sector: A Scenario Analysis.' *Building Research & Information* 39(1): 34–50. doi.org/10.1080/09613218.2010.531085.

Oke, C., S.A. Bekessy, N. Frantzeskaki, J. Bush, J.A. Fitzsimons, G.E. Garrard, M. Grenfell, L. Harrison, M. Hartigan, D. Callow, B. Cotter, and S. Gawler. 2021. 'Cities Should Respond to the Biodiversity Extinction Crisis.' *npj Urban Sustainability* 1(1): 1–4. doi.org/10.1038/s42949-020-00010-w.

Pears, A., and T. Moore. 2019. 'Decarbonising Household Energy Use: The Smart Meter Revolution and Beyond.' In *Decarbonising the Built Environment: Charting the Transition*, edited by P. Newton, D. Prasad, A. Sproul, and S. White, 99–115. Singapore: Palgrave Macmillan. doi.org/10.1007/978-981-13-7940-6_6.

Plazier, P.A., G. Weitkamp, and A.E. van den Berg. 2017. '"Cycling Was Never So Easy!" An Analysis of e-Bike Commuters' Motives, Travel Behaviour and Experiences Using GPS-Tracking and Interviews.' *Journal of Transport Geography* 65: 25–34. doi.org/10.1016/j.jtrangeo.2017.09.017.

Podkalicka, A.M., E. Milne, K. Hulse, T. Winfree, and G. Melles. 2016. *Hashtag Sustainability? Home Renovators' Media World.* RP3021 Report: Media & Home Renovations. Low Carbon Living Cooperative Research Centre. Available from: apo.org.au/node/75050.

Recycling Victoria. 2016. *The Metropolitan Waste and Resource Recovery Implementation Plan.* Melbourne: Victorian Government. Available from: www.vic.gov.au/strengthening-our-waste-and-recycling-system.

Rogge, K.S., B. Pfluger, and F.W. Geels. 2020. 'Transformative Policy Mixes in Socio-Technical Scenarios: The Case of the Low-Carbon Transition of the German Electricity System (2010–2050).' *Technological Forecasting and Social Change* 151: 119259. doi.org/10.1016/j.techfore.2018.04.002.

Russo, M., and P. Pavone. 2021. 'Evidence-Based Portfolios of Innovation Policy Mixes: A Cross-Country Analysis.' *Technological Forecasting and Social Change* 168. doi.org/10.1016/j.techfore.2021.120708.

Samarasinghe, G., M. Lagisz, M. Santamouris, K. Yenneti, A.K. Upadhyay, F. De La Peña Suarez, B. Taunk, and S. Nakagawa. 2019. 'A Visualized Overview of Systematic Reviews and Meta-Analyses on Low-Carbon Built Environments: An Evidence Review Map.' *Solar Energy* 186: 291–99. doi.org/10.1016/j.solener. 2019.04.062.

Sandberg, M. 2018. 'Downsizing of Housing: Negotiating Sufficiency and Spatial Norms.' *Journal of Macromarketing* 38(2): 154–67. doi.org/10.1177/ 0276146717748355.

Schäfer, M., S. Hielscher, W. Haas, D. Hausknost, M. Leitner, I. Kunze, and S. Mandl. 2018. 'Facilitating Low-Carbon Living? A Comparison of Intervention Measures in Different Community-Based Initiatives.' *Sustainability* 10(4): 1047. doi.org/10.3390/su10041047.

Seamer, P. 2019. *Breaking Point: The Future of Australian Cities*. Melbourne: Black Inc.

Seo, S., S. Tucker, and P. Newton. 2007. 'Automated Material Selection and Environmental Assessment in the Context of 3D Building Modelling.' *Journal of Green Building* 2(2): 51–61. doi.org/10.3992/jgb.2.2.51.

Shahani, F., M. Pineda-Pinto, and N. Frantzeskaki. 2021. 'Transformative Low-Carbon Urban Innovations: Operationalising Transformative Capacity for Urban Planning.' *Ambio* 51: 1179–98. doi.org/10.1007/s13280-021-01653-4.

Soderlund, J., and P. Newman. 2020. 'How the Biophilic Design Social Movement Informs Planning, Policy and Professional Practice.' 16 September, Preprint (Version 1). Available from: doi.org/10.21203/rs.3.rs-66814/v1.

Sovacool, B.K., L.F. Cabeza, A.L. Pisello, A.F. Colladon, H.M. Larijani, B. Dawoud, and M. Martiskainen. 2021. 'Decarbonizing Household Heating: Reviewing Demographics, Geography and Low-Carbon Practices and Preferences in Five European Countries.' *Renewable and Sustainable Energy Reviews* 139: 110703. doi.org/10.1016/j.rser.2020.110703.

Sustainability Victoria. 2016. *Victorian Waste Education Strategy*. Melbourne: Victorian Government. Available from: www.sustainability.vic.gov.au/about-us/our-mission/our-strategies/victorian-waste-education-strategy.

United Nations (UN). 2015. *Transforming Our World: The 2030 Agenda for Sustainable Development.* New York, NY: Division for Sustainable Development Goals, United Nations. Available from: sustainabledevelopment.un.org/post 2015/transformingourworld/publication.

Wachsmuth, D., D.A. Cohen, and H. Angelo. 2016. 'Expand the Frontiers of Urban Sustainability.' *Nature News* 536: 391–93. doi.org/10.1038/536391a.

Westley, F., P. Olsson, C. Folke, T. Homer-Dixon, H. Vredenburg, D. Loorbach, J. Thompson, M. Nilsson, E. Lambin, J. Sendzimir, B. Banerjee, V. Galaz, and S. van der Leeuw. 2011. 'Tipping Toward Sustainability: Emerging Pathways of Transformation.' *Ambio* 40(7): 762–80. doi.org/10.1007/s13280-011-0186-9.

Whiteman, J. 2010. 'Transport and Stationary Energy and Greenhouse Gas Emissions Scenarios for Melbourne 2031.' In *Australasian Transport Research Forum Proceedings.* Canberra, 29 September – 1 October. Available from: australasiantransportresearchforum.org.au/wp-content/uploads/2022/03/2010 _Whiteman.pdf.

Wiedmann, T., G. Chen, A. Owen, M. Lenzen, M. Doust, J. Barrett, and K. Steele. 2021. 'Three-Scope Carbon Emission Inventories of Global Cities.' *Journal of Industrial Ecology* 25(3): 735–50. doi.org/10.1111/jiec.13063.

World Bank. 2020. 'CO2 emissions (Metric Tons Per Capita—Australia).' In *Climate Watch: GHG Emissions.* Washington, DC: World Resources Institute. Available from: data.worldbank.org/indicator/EN.ATM.CO2E.PC?locations=AU.

Yu, G., H. Yang, D. Luo, X. Cheng, and M.K. Ansah. 2021. 'A Review on Developments and Researches of Building Integrated Photovoltaic (BIPV) Windows and Shading Blinds.' *Renewable and Sustainable Energy Reviews* 149: 111355. doi.org/10.1016/j.rser.2021.111355.

21

Australian urban transport: Generating solidarity in a landscape of crisis and change

Crystal Legacy and Rebecca Clements

Introduction

Transforming the dominant forms of mobility in Australian cities is imperative to achieving sustainable and equitable cities, yet much transport planning and infrastructure delivery remains opaque and mismatched to public needs and place contexts. While the urban morphology of Australia's capital cities poses challenges for urban transport policy, some research locates the main source of problems within the realm of governance and politics. As Mees (2000, 2009a, 2009b) explored, the provision of quality public transport infrastructure and services across these complex metropolitan regions has more to do with the integration, transparency, and accountability of Australian urban transport governance and policy than with urban form—insights gleaned while working as a postdoctoral fellow with Patrick Troy at The Australian National University.

Mees' work critically examined the role of policy and transport institutions— work that was later built on by Curtis and Low (2016) in their research into the institutional barriers to sustainable transport, which revealed the challenges of path dependency, deepening the importance of policy institutions in transport planning. Yet, as this research lamented, and as more recent research continues to show, the rigidity of transport policy has done little to slow the privatisation of land, service delivery, and infrastructural assets (Ashmore et al. 2019). In some cases, this governance landscape is giving rise to newfound public and private partnerships formalised through what Rogers and Gibson (2021) describe as unsolicited urbanism, whereby democratic public participation in infrastructure governance is displaced through closed-door elite dealmaking.

The privatisation of transport infrastructure assets has fragmented planning and current policy settings have done little to curtail the worst outcomes of what Dodson (2009) has called 'the infrastructure turn'. These trends have had serious consequences for transport policy, as observed in recent independent reports. For instance, a Victorian Auditor-General's Office (VAGO 2021) report critiqued the state of Victoria's strategic transport planning as fragmented and ineffective. Citing the absence of an integrated transport plan, VAGO claimed the Victorian State Government was in breach of its responsibilities under the *Integrated Transport Act 2010* to deliver a fully integrated and transparent plan that could guide the state's planning efforts. While independent reports critiquing the state of transport planning are not rare, they are joined by independent critical assessments by the Grattan Institute (Terrill 2021) and urban transport academics (Woodcock et al. 2017). Together, these reports cast attention to what is at stake for transport policy in Australian cities: the continued use of exclusionary decision-making processes, opaque managerial governance settings, and elite actors subverting strategic planning—all of which put at risk planning's capacity to act in the public interest. Critically, the public interest in transport planning includes collective responses to the climate emergency (Meerow and Woodruff 2020) and tackling structural social inequalities (Sheller 2018), which means further delays or reversals in the capacity of planning to make meaningful and effective changes raise deeply ethical concerns.

At the heart of these critical reviews of urban transport policy is a systematic disavowal of transport planning's political content. Research by Legacy (2016) and Haughton and McManus (2019) has described a post-political condition shaping transport policy and governance. Taking cues from post-foundational scholarship (Rancière 1999, 2010), post-politics is where the state is designed with techno-managerial processes that render planning otherwise de-political. In other words, the state forecloses the political in traditional or formal planning arenas, meaning the political must find new spaces in which to be expressed (for example, as a form of citizen resistance). The post-political urban condition impacts the ability of planning to consider the political questions that lie at its heart. For decades, critical planning scholars have lamented neoliberalism's ability to remove, or at least conceal, the political from planning's content (Porter 2011). Gatekeeping of what counts as transport planning and the knowledge systems available to transport planners prevents them from speaking fearlessly to the full social, cultural, economic, and ecological impacts of decisions which have overwhelmingly been limited to the technical and addressed through managerial processes (Grange 2017). Even the economic aspects of transport planning have borne little consideration in decisions, as transport infrastructure projects are approved with neither sound business cases nor clear articulation of costs and benefits.

Whether this disavowal has led to a reckoning of sorts in planning remains a compelling and open question. In some quarters, critical reflection has begun. A rejection of the Victorian transport planning system by longstanding transport engineer William McDougall (2018) joins a powerful critique from senior transport planning academic Carey Curtis (2017). These moments of public refusal to accept the terms in which contemporary transport planning is being conducted are rare, but nonetheless inspiring. Refusals of these kinds give grounds to the question of refusal at wider, and potentially collective, scales. To what extent is scholarship prepared to step into the spaces of dissent to generate new political possibilities for transport planning?

We begin this chapter by exploring in greater depth the paradox besetting transport policy and governance, establishing a case for a more political scholarship. In the first section, we establish the ways transport policy and governance have been impacted by post-politics, with attention given to the ways planning has been de-politicised by design through different instruments and approaches, such as market-led proposals, technology capital, and 'black box' modelling. This shift in power has created a deeply challenging paradoxical landscape for public policy. To address these challenges, we look to solidarity as a conceptual framework. In the penultimate section, we explore the potential individual and collective practices required to rethink the focus and direction from the bottom up, and the role of transport planners and researchers in those processes. In the conclusion, we consider the political possibilities that transport planning can cultivate. At the heart of this question lies a deeper reckoning: *what is* transport planning, *who does it*, and *in whose interest*? While the idea of solidarity may seem ill suited to a discipline that has its foundations in technical knowledge, we argue that solidarity possesses a political power that opens transport planning to the social processes of change, to the deeply political aspects of transport planners' work, and to the diverse knowledge systems that must inform transport policies.

A political paradox

Transport planning occurs in a paradoxical landscape. On the one hand, the ethical responsibility of planning is to make cities and regions more accessible for diverse populations (Creutzig et al. 2020). Improving accessibility to urban places and services is not simply about social equity but also deeply connected to the capacities for human flourishing (Sturup 2019). Ostensibly, this ethical practice is conducted to serve the public interest. On the other hand, transport planning is conducted within a landscape where powerful commercial interests are brought to bear on decisions about mobility and accessibility. The public interest claims made are framed through the prism of sustainability, jobs creation, and productivity (Haughton and McManus 2019; Searle and Legacy 2021) and are rarely tested within a planning system that is beholden to the interests of capital. These settings have not just limited the spaces for dialogue about the social, spatial, and cultural harms attached to projects, but also bounded where those discussions take place, and who is involved.

The de-politicisation of transport planning is achieved by design. This context de-politicises transport planning both through the privileging of technical and managerial competencies and through the capacities of elite actors to control the narratives of transport policy and the frames through which transport projects are justified (Haughton and McManus 2019; Murphy 2019). The foreclosing of the political in transport planning extends across practice, policy, and procedural landscapes and it is systemic in its ability to control the frames and ways of knowing available to transport planners (Reardon and Marsden 2020). Looking to Australia, the Grattan Institute (Daley 2021) has described a landscape that makes reform under current conditions challenging and in which reformist policymaking is plagued by a weakening of the public service and of independent agencies that can produce evidence-based advice. This weakening of public and independent oversight has led to the empowerment of ministerial advisors over the frank and fearless advice offered by public servants, and the erosion of controls regulating decision-makers, political parties, ministerial advisors, and vested interests.

Adding to these challenges, planning itself is stripped of its political content through the introduction of instruments that conceal the decision-making power of the private sector. Such instruments, particularly the market-led or unsolicited proposals, have formalised private sector leadership and displaced decision-making arenas to those possessing elite status as powerful corporate entities. The latter has been described by Rogers and Gibson (2021: 543) as those 'targeted and incremental amendments' that are manipulating 'existing systems that centralise power with business interests and evade democratic governance or critical scrutiny; and the normalisation of planning-as-deal-making'.

The ways in which that de-politicisation is enshrined are deeply troubling. De-politicisation is a political-economic project conditioned under neoliberalism that pushes well beyond 'forward looking and government-led strategic planning' to enable the participation of elite coalitions. As Rogers and Gibson (2021: 542) describe it:

> Unsolicited urbanism attempts to side-step, re-scale, and obfuscate decision-making with new in-house processes and monopolistic determinations. Money and power indeed reshape cities. But new regulatory-technical processes are reconfigured to make this possible, and only for distinctive constellations of actors.

Further change is afoot with the rise of global corporate actors who are claiming the spaces of transport planning. The technologists and the futurists are generating new technologies that are not only revolutionising the way we move, but also reshaping who is doing transport planning and who is claiming the spaces of strategic planning. Technology capital has urbanised, seeking to own and control greater realms of urban governance, city operations and spaces, and the scope of urban futures (Sadowski 2021). While concerns about data privacy and control remain intractable problems, less focus has been given to the changing political economy of transport planning that is altering knowledge systems and determining who has access to knowledge, as well as the spaces through which that knowledge can be challenged and scrutinised.

De-politicisation cannot foreclose transport planning from its political content. In fact, re-politicisation is a common practice. From street protests and occupation of space through to community-led meetings and grassroots strategic planning exercises, the re-politicisation of transport includes the ignition of protest against an undesired transport decision. Acts of re-politicisation have been seen against undesired projects such as the East West Link and West Gate Tunnel in Melbourne, Roe 8 in Perth, and WestConnex in Sydney. Re-politicisation can also be observed as an act of resistance against prevailing transport planning practices and processes (Legacy 2016). Resistance to projects can reveal insights into public values and expose injustices, such as who is being excluded from the discussion, and the narrow ways in which knowledge is created and applied to the decisions affecting people's mobility.

To offer one example of how transport knowledge is narrowly scoped and defined, we turn to transport modelling. Often derided for being largely a 'black box' exercise, the privileging of modelling as a knowledge-creation tool available to transport planners places singular emphasis on technical solutions. While modelling is an important tool, this knowledge is silent on the social, political, cultural, ecological, or even economic variables that a society must also confront in thinking about the future city. Nor does this technical knowledge engage with the values from which such decisions find guidance. Engaging with these more social questions is the domain of non-transport planners, but engagement is relatively rare and largely occurs in a tightly controlled environment (Legacy 2016, 2017).

Towards a more political urban transport scholarship

The political paradox described above presents a challenging landscape for urban transport scholarship. Calls to engage with transport's political economy expose power relationships and the processes through which de-politicisation is practised and secured (Reardon and Marsden 2020). In equal measure, a plethora of academic research into the processes of change in transport planning reveal future possibilities through political action and savvy policymaking by documenting the actions and strategies that lead to projects being defeated and cancelled (Legacy 2016; Murphy 2019), and the formation of new power configurations in government that can open spaces for reformist policies and transformational urban ambitions (Stone 2009).

Facing the complex challenges of climate change (which present ever greater levels of urgency with each successive Intergovernmental Panel on Climate Change report) and expanding spatial and social injustices, one must ask what this period demands from public policy and urban scholarship.

From academics, perhaps it is to conduct research and teach with radical intention; to be purposeful in a way that allows the evidence base to expose planning's complicity in oppression (Porter 2011) and ecological degradation (Oke et al. 2021); and to reveal the fractures that can make change challenging to achieve. Intentionality in our practice, scholarship, and pedagogy could also imply joining existing community grassroots efforts in ways that allow research to serve those communities, facilitate new practices, and draw from new knowledge systems. Using transport scholarship to nurture solidarities can inspire new political possibilities and pathways towards change. Prefiguring new planning contexts through purposeful research, teaching, as well as policy and community engagement can expose the deleterious politics of transport planning and support conditions for change.

Solidarity: A new conceptual foundation for politically engaged transport planning?

In this section, we bring ideas of solidarity formation into conversation with the vexed challenges afflicting transport policy and research. Grounded in justice claims, solidarity-based action runs against the kind of self-interest cultivated under neoliberalism (George 2018) and focuses the imperatives informing one's actions on the unjust conditions of others. Solidarity formation also demands a higher degree of intentionality forged through normative goals (for example, the just city, the good city, the public city), an ethics of care, and careful engagement with place, Country, and each other. Drawing from long-established work in bioethics, solidarity is characterised as 'reaching out through moral imagination and responsive action across social and/or geographic distance and asymmetry to assist other people who are vulnerable, and to advance justice' (Eckenwiler 2018: 562). In short, solidarity is about building a constituency through which to resist and refuse and, through the establishment of such collectivism, to define actors practising *in common* towards political change.

There are connections to be made through political action generated by solidarity in times of complex crises. Under neoliberal economic austerity such as in the years after the GFC, solidarity networks and movements typically arose demanding greater equality (Kallianos 2018), to make visible urban fragmentation (Cesafsky 2017), or in response to contexts of oppression (Bosworth 2018; Temper 2019). Solidarity movements can represent forms of bottom-up collective provision within vacuums of institutional care and welfare. They can also set the conditions to collectively assert political demands for justice, such as community recognition or liberation. Solidarity can also be a principle for meaningful recognition and action founded on shared or similar injustices. It may invoke empathetic engagement with, and enact responsibility towards, the political interests of others, involving confronting 'layers of shared vulnerabilities and histories of silencing and erasures' (Tschakert 2020: 277).

Community solidarity within and across groups is strengthened through collective practices that engender a sense of empowerment, involving large or small democratic experiences of forging futures together, such as organising together for political ends or social provision (Wamuchiru 2017). Expressions of solidarity are also seen through collective resistance to harmful policies, such as infrastructure approaches that represent unjust outcomes for vulnerable groups (Monstadt and Coutard 2019). For example, new coalitions of political anarchist groups and indigenous communities resisting pipeline projects in Canada helped to redirect the anger of certain groups towards common structures and institutions, bringing them into solidarity with the aims of decolonisation (Bosworth 2018).

This perspective reveals solidarity practices to be processes of relationship-building, political reorganising, and future visioning, as new commonalities are forged through political alliance. Bosworth (2018: 248) disagrees that solidarity must be based on common experiences, and instead posits that 'alliance and solidarity across difference can shift the horizons of the possible', including through negotiated arrangements based on principles of respect that connect plural concerns and struggles. Solidarity can also be enacted through a sense of ethical responsibility to use one's relative power and privilege to support others within politically entangled relationships. To act in solidarity with others is an attempt to create collective empowerment through expanded relations and aligned goals, and to overcome boundaries of personal or group self-interest.

What is distinctive about solidarity?

To intentionally enact practices of solidarity generation through transport research and policymaking, it is important to reflect on what makes solidarity meaningful and powerful. While solidarity principles are conceptually intertwined with the notions of representation and advocacy, more central to recent understandings of solidarity practices is an alignment of one's own actions with the political interests of others, including some personal sacrifice when necessary (Arnsperger and Varoufakis 2003). Acting in solidarity with others involves questioning for whom and what purposes one's practices serve, and what relations of power they help or fail to legitimise (Jon 2021). This notion also implicates understanding whose interests are excluded or whose interests you are acting against, such as powerful players with unethical interests (Hankins and Martin 2019).

The arenas of placemaking and governance are often seen as important and fertile spaces for nurturing solidaristic relations over time, and as central terrain for care, health, and collective bonds (Eckenwiler 2018). Transport research and policy can also be grounds for such solidarity practices. In the context of the ongoing Covid-19 pandemic, for example, many challenging questions about socioeconomic care, collective urban interdependencies, and collective commitment to different forms of immobility in cities have come to the fore of public debate.

Engendering solidarity around how we live and move in cities has potentially opened unexpected windows for change by calling into question existing assumptions about possible futures (Osborne 2019). Going further, the ethos of solidarity enables radical bottom-up urban change (for example, new mobility practices that can be understood at the level of individuals and collectives) through the development of a sense that the urban and our experiences within it are not fixed and can (and should) be transformed. Similarly, drawing out new understandings of mutual interdependencies and obligations around movement can forge new political commitments and future orientations, and potentially challenge the hegemonic narratives of future transport policy being predicated on responding to emerging technologies, over new ways of moving and living in cities.

The creation of a transport policy and politics that are grounded in place-based research methodologies can be a productive space for solidarity formation. For instance, as a feminist research approach, situated solidarity (Nagar and Geiger 2007) is engaged scholarly activism rooted in the reflexivity and positionality of the researcher and, by extension, the planner. It is proposed as a way of 'locating political struggle in place' and reflecting on how academic resources and policymaking can be mobilised around the questions relevant to grounded social justice movements (Goldfischer et al. 2020: 8) and then scaled up to inform urban and transport policy. Beyond traditional diagnosis and analysis, this solidarity-based approach seeks to 'meet people where they are' (Goldfischer et al. 2020: 8), listening to and learning from experiences of struggle and transformation situated in place contexts, and forging new alliances and commitments through engaging with conflicts and contradictions to seek 'workable compromises' (Larner 1995: 187–88). Here, transport research and policy are grounded in the everyday experiences of diverse communities, which can be imagined as an entirely radical form of planning that shifts from the de-political policy arenas described earlier, while dismantling the power wielded by those with elite access to policymaking and decision-makers.

In seeking practices of solidarity in the transport arena that can meaningfully contribute to just outcomes within placemaking and research contexts, it is important to be mindful of structural limitations to, or cynical manifestations of, solidarity. There can be gaps between the rhetoric of solidarity among communities impacted by transport decisions and the capacity to act collectively or in the interest of others in more precarious contexts (Simone 2013). Facades of common interest or camaraderie across different geographies of the city and between planners, academics, and diverse community members can obscure diverging political or material interests that may simply be untested publicly. For example, 'performances of solidarity' within place-based communities can generate ironic and contradictory behaviours among different groups that are simply displaced to a different spatiality and out of sight (Simone 2013). Structural forces and material interests can create critical constraints for solidarity-based movements, such as dependence on funding sources or critical ideological differences between networks (Zajontz and Leysens 2015). These are important tensions of which to be mindful and, at times, to face directly in research and policy, particularly in complex urban transport governance and planning that are wrought with unequal power relationships. Solidarity formation can be empowering and inspiring, but it is often challenging and confronting, served by optimism, but not political naivety.

Conclusion

Solidarity formation as a conceptual lens available to transport planners, scholars, and policymakers raises interesting questions and even provocations for the field. As we write in the wake of the tabling the Sixth Intergovernmental Panel on Climate Change Assessment Report in August 2021, we use this concluding section to invite an unsettling of contemporary transport planning. We look to reframe transport planning as a practice engaged in the social, economic, and political processes shaping cities and regions. Also, we centre solidarity formation as a conceptual lens through which to rethink the practice of transport planning and policymaking in a way that connects it to Country, the lived experiences of diverse communities, and climate change action. Thinking through what solidarity invites, we also look to a recent paper by Ihnji Jon (2021: 321), who writes that academics have responsibilities to commit to active change in the public interest. In seeking to strategically reinvigorate planning scholarship's social responsibilities, Jon (2021) puts forth a critical agenda for researchers that includes redefining the scales of possible and pragmatic public solidarities and, in so doing, making visible the intangible values behind city-making, and elevating alternative values (that is, beyond profit maximisation) through which new urban logics can be advanced.

In these final paragraphs, we outline several ways in which transport planners, policymakers, and scholars could embrace solidarity formation as a lens through which to generate or prefigure alternative logics, values, and practices in transport planning. To begin, reconnecting transport planning with Country and treaty processes through partnership with Indigenous communities must be central to this effort. In Australia, transport planning is conducted on unceded First Nations lands. If we are to address the fault lines in transport governance and prefigure a more climate-just form of transport planning, settler Australians must self-critically ask whose transport planning are we seeking to improve and to what ends?

Solidarity formation demands attention be paid to scale. Typically, transport planning embraces aggregate information to think through the distribution of infrastructure and transport resources. Little attention is paid to the local and the lived experience of diverse populations. To reconcile this tension, and to work in efforts to build solidarities and connection with communities, ethnographic methodologies must be explored as legitimate knowledge-creation practices available to transport planning. Building closer connections with communities through ethnographic knowledge formation has the potential to cultivate new possibilities for co-designing urban transport futures. At the forefront of thinking through new practices of solidarity is situating this work in a political context that is largely controlled through elite actors in government and the private sector. Doing so demands a level of political participation in the knowledge-generation process so that alternative ways of knowing transport are advanced. Policy and planning academics can play an integral role in the knowledge-creation process and, with the relative independence granted through university employment, can help speak truth to power and support the prefiguration of new landscapes for knowledge creation.

There is much scope for change in transport planning. Who engages in transport planning and the dominant ways of knowing the problems of and solutions to transport require ongoing critical engagement. The urgency of this agenda is clear. The climate emergency demands new forms of mobility and the end of carbon-intensive transport and infrastructure. The urgency has also been created by the changing political economy of transport planning that has given way to strategic intervention from elite actors. The historical pathways available for change—namely, well-communicated evidence bases that can inform policy, as communicated by Pat Troy—do not hold enough power to ignite the kinds and levels of change needed today. Instead, a more political form of engagement with enduring social, spatial, and cultural injustices demands recognition of the importance of different knowledge of and approaches to transport planning and the roles that policymakers and academics can play in prefiguring new practices and processes. This revival of planning principles and politics demands a refusal of the practices and processes that continue to exclude and oppress. This moment demands bold action and forging solidarities with communities, policy actors, and transport scholars to enable this change through the building of collective action and the establishment of a new political paradigm for Australian transport policy.

References

Arnsperger, C., and Y. Varoufakis. 2003. 'Toward a Theory of Solidarity.' *Erkenntnis* 59(2): 157–88. doi.org/10.1023/A:1024630228818.

Ashmore, D.P., J. Stone, and Y. Kirk. 2019. 'The Need for Greater Transparency When Assessing the Performance and Prospects of Melbourne's Rail Franchise Contracts.' *Urban Policy and Research* 37(1): 82–96. doi.org/10.1080/08111146. 2018.1486296.

Bosworth, K. 2018. The People Versus the Pipelines: Energy Infrastructure and Liberal Ideology in North American Environmentalism. PhD thesis, University of Minnesota, Saint Paul.

Cesafsky, L. 2017. 'How to Mend a Fragmented City: A Critique of "Infrastructural Solidarity".' *International Journal of Urban and Regional Research* 41(1): 145–61.

Creutzig, F., A. Javaid, Z. Soomauroo, S. Lohrey, N. Milojevic-Dupont, A. Ramakrishnan, M. Sethi, L. Liu, L. Niamir, C. Bren d'Amour, U. Weddige, D. Lenzi, M. Kowarsch, L. Arndt, L. Baumann, J. Betzien, L. Fonkwa, B. Huber, E. Mendez, A. Misiou, C. Pearce, P. Radman, P. Skaloud, and J.M. Zausch. 2020. 'Fair Street Space Allocation: Ethical Principles and Empirical Insights.' *Transport Reviews* 40(6): 711–33. doi.org/10.1080/01441647.2020.1762795.

Curtis, C. 2017. 'Transport Planning Decision-Making.' In *Never Again: Reflections on Environmental Responsibility After Roe 8*, edited by A. Ganor, P. Newman, and P. Jennings, 165–87. Perth: UWA Publishing.

Curtis, C., and N. Low. 2016. *Institutional Barriers to Sustainable Transport.* London: Routledge. doi.org/10.4324/9781315588827.

Daley, J. 2021. *Gridlock: Removing Barriers to Policy Reform.* Grattan Institute Report No. 2021-08, July. Melbourne: Grattan Institute. Available from: grattan.edu. au/wp-content/uploads/2021/07/Gridlock-Grattan-Report.pdf.

Dodson, J. 2009. 'The "Infrastructure Turn" in Australian Metropolitan Spatial Planning.' *International Planning Studies* 14(2): 109–23. doi.org/10.1080/13563470903021100.

Eckenwiler, L. 2018. 'Displacement and Solidarity: An Ethic of Place-Making.' *Bioethics* 32(9): 562–68. doi.org/10.1111/bioe.12538.

George, J. 2018. The Contribution of Community Governance Towards the Sustainable Planning and Management of Urban and Regional Green Infrastructure. PhD thesis, Curtin University, Perth.

Goldfischer, E., J.L. Rice, and S.T. Black. 2020. 'Obstinate Curiosity and Situated Solidarity in Urban Political Ecology.' *Geography Compass* 14(2): e12479. doi.org/10.1111/gec3.12479.

Grange, K. 2017. 'Planners: A Silenced Profession? The Politicisation of Planning and the Need for Fearless Speech.' *Planning Theory* 16(3): 275–95. doi.org/10.1177/1473095215626465.

Hankins, K.B., and D.G. Martin. 2019. 'Contextualizing Neighbourhood Activism: Spatial Solidarity in the City.' In *Handbook of Urban Geography*, edited by T. Schwanen and R. van Kempen, 411–27. Cheltenham, UK: Edward Elgar. doi.org/10.4337/9781785364600.00040.

Haughton, G., and P. McManus. 2019. 'Participation in Postpolitical Times: Protesting Westconnex in Sydney, Australia.' *Journal of the American Planning Association* 85(3): 321–34. doi.org/10.1080/01944363.2019.1613922.

Jon, I. 2021. 'The City We Want: Against the Banality of Urban Planning Research.' *Planning Theory & Practice* 22(2): 321–28. doi.org/10.1080/14649357.2021.1893588.

Kallianos, Y. 2018. 'Infrastructural Disorder: The Politics of Disruption, Contingency, and Normalcy in Waste Infrastructures in Athens.' *Environment and Planning D: Society and Space* 36(4): 758–75.

Larner, W. 1995. 'Theorising "Difference" in Aotearoa/New Zealand.' *Gender, Place and Culture* 2(2): 177–90. doi.org/10.1080/09663699550022008.

Legacy, C. 2016. 'Transforming Transport Planning in the Postpolitical Era.' *Urban Studies* 53(14): 3108–24. doi.org/10.1177/0042098015602649.

Legacy, C. 2017. 'Is There a Crisis of Participatory Planning?' *Planning Theory* 16(4): 425–42. doi.org/10.1177/1473095216667433.

McDougall, W. 2018. 'Our Ridiculous Frenzy of Road Construction Will Swallow Up Resources for Two Decades.' *Sydney Morning Herald*, 5 January, [Updated 6 January]. Available from: www.smh.com.au/opinion/our-ridiculous-frenzy-of-road-construction-will-swallow-up-resources-for-two-decades-20180105-h0dwd0.html.

Meerow, S., and S.C. Woodruff. 2020. 'Seven Principles of Strong Climate Change Planning.' *Journal of the American Planning Association* 86(1): 39–46. doi.org/10.1080/01944363.2019.1652108.

Mees, P. 2000. *A Very Public Solution: Transport in the Dispersed City*. Melbourne: Melbourne University Press.

Mees, P. 2009a. 'How Dense Are We? Another Look at Urban Density and Transport Patterns in Australia, Canada and the USA.' *Road and Transport Research: A Journal of Australian and New Zealand Research and Practice* 18(4): 58–67.

Mees, P. 2009b. *Transport for Suburbia: Beyond the Automobile Age*. London: Earthscan. doi.org/10.4324/9781849774659.

Monstadt, J., and O. Coutard. 2019. 'Cities in an Era of Interfacing Infrastructures: Politics and Spatialities of the Urban Nexus.' *Urban Studies* 56(11): 2191–206. doi.org/10.1177/0042098019833907.

Murphy, J. 2019. The Making and Unmaking of East-West Link. PhD thesis, Swinburne University of Technology, Melbourne.

Nagar, R., and S. Geiger. 2007. 'Reflexivity and Positionality in Feminist Fieldwork Revisited.' In *Politics and Practice in Economic Geography*, edited by A. Tickell, E. Sheppard, J. Peck, and T. Barnes, 267–68. Los Angeles, CA: SAGE. doi.org/10.4135/9781446212240.n23.

Oke, C., S. Bekessy, N. Frantzeskaki, J. Bush, J. Fitzsimons, G. Garrard, M. Grenfell, L. Harrison, M. Hartigan, D. Callow, B. Cotter, and S. Gawler. 2021. 'Cities Should Respond to the Biodiversity Extinction Crisis.' *npj Urban Sustainability* 1(1): 1–4. doi.org/10.1038/s42949-020-00010-w.

Osborne, N. 2019. 'For Still Possible Cities: A Politics of Failure for the Politically Depressed.' *Australian Geographer* 50(2): 145–54. doi.org/10.1080/00049182.2018.1530717.

Porter, L. 2011. 'The Point Is to Change It.' *Planning Theory & Practice* 12(4): 477–80. doi.org/10.1080/14649357.2011.626296.

Rancière, J. 1999. *Disagreement: Politics and Philosophy.* Minneapolis, MN: University of Minnesota Press.

Rancière, J. 2010. *Dissensus: On Politics and Aesthetics.* London: Bloomsbury. doi.org/10.5040/9781472547378.ch-001.

Reardon, L., and G. Marsden. 2020. 'Exploring the Role of the State in the Depoliticisation of UK Transport Policy.' *Policy & Politics* 48(2): 223–40. doi.org/10.1332/030557319X15707904263616.

Rogers, D., and C. Gibson. 2021. 'Unsolicited Urbanism: Development Monopolies, Regulatory-Technical Fixes and Planning-As-Deal-Making.' *Environment and Planning A: Economy and Space* 53(3): 525–47. doi.org/10.1177/0308518X20952421.

Sadowski, J. 2021. 'Who Owns the Future City? Phases of Technological Urbanism and Shifts in Sovereignty.' *Urban Studies* 58(8): 1732–44.

Searle, G., and C. Legacy. 2021. 'Locating the Public Interest in Mega Infrastructure Planning: The Case of Sydney's WestConnex.' *Urban Studies* 58(4): 826–44. doi.org/10.1177/0042098020927835.

Sheller, M. 2018. *Mobility Justice: The Politics of Movement in an Age of Extremes.* New York, NY: Verso.

Simone, A. 2013. 'Cities of Uncertainty: Jakarta, the Urban Majority, and Inventive Political Technologies.' *Theory, Culture & Society* 30(7–8): 243–63. doi.org/10.1177/0263276413501872.

Stone, J. 2009. 'Contrasts in Reform: How the Cain and Burke Years Shaped Public Transport in Melbourne and Perth.' *Urban Policy and Research* 27(4): 419–34. doi.org/10.1080/08111140903342411.

Sturup, S. 2019. 'What Does Our Transport System Make Us Capable Of?' Paper presented to Ninth State of Australasian Cities National Conference, Perth, 30 November – 5 December. Available from: apo.org.au/node/306034.

Temper, L. 2019. 'Blocking Pipelines, Unsettling Environmental Justice: From Rights of Nature to Responsibility to Territory.' *Local Environment* 24(2): 94–112. doi.org/10.1080/13549839.2018.1536698.

Terrill, M. 2021. *How to Get Better Bang for Transport Bucks: Submission to House of Representatives Standing Committee on Infrastructure, Transport and Cities Inquiry into Procurement Practices for Government-Funded Infrastructure.* Submission 8. Melbourne: Grattan Institute. Available from: grattan.edu.au/wp-content/uploads/2021/07/How-to-get-better-bang-for-transport-bucks-submission.pdf.

Tschakert, P. 2020. 'More-Than-Human Solidarity and Multispecies Justice in the Climate Crisis.' *Environmental Politics* 31(2): 277–96. doi.org/10.1080/09644016.2020.1853448.

Victorian Auditor-General's Office (VAGO). 2021. *Integrated Transport Planning: Independent Assurance Report to Parliament.* August. Melbourne: VAGO. Available from: www.audit.vic.gov.au/sites/default/files/2021-08/20210804-Integrated-Transport_0.pdf.

Wamuchiru, E. 2017. 'Beyond the Networked City: Situated Practices of Citizenship and Grassroots Agency in Water Infrastructure Provision in the Chamazi Settlement, Dar es Salaam.' *Environment and Urbanization* 29(2): 551–66. doi.org/10.1177/0956247817700290.

Woodcock, I., S. Sturup, J. Stone, N. Pittman, C. Legacy, and J. Dodson. 2017. *West Gate Tunnel: Another Case of Tunnel Vision?* Case Study Report, 8 December. Melbourne: Centre for Urban Research, RMIT University. Available from: apo.org.au/sites/default/files/resource-files/2017-12/apo-nid122421.pdf.

Zajontz, T., and A. Leysens. 2015. 'Civil Society in Southern Africa: Transformers from Below?' *Journal of Southern African Studies* 41(4): 887–904. doi.org/10.1080/03057070.2015.1060091.

22

Inequality, sustainability, and public policy: Historical and spatial perspectives

Frank Stilwell

Introduction

Should the Australian Government develop urban policies that seek to enhance equity and sustainability? This chapter explores this question by comparing the experience of urban policies during the Whitlam Government's period of office in the 1970s with the subsequent decades of policy drift. Can we learn lessons from the former period that are relevant to the situation now with a new ALP federal government in office? What is the potential for a program of reforms in which urban policies are a central feature? What would it take for a policy package of that type to be more enduring than previously? These are questions that require consideration from historical and spatial perspectives.

This chapter probes what is possible and potentially effective. It begins with a section on methodology that seeks to clarify how, in general, knowledge can be framed to enhance its relevance for public policy purposes. Then come sections reviewing the Whitlam Government's urban and regional policy initiatives and the subsequent decades of relative policy inaction. The penultimate section turns to consideration of a reform agenda targeted at current concerns about employment, equity, and the environment. The chapter concludes with discussion of relationships between past experiences and current challenges.

Framing knowledge and policy

Public policy operates in the political space between the perception of problems and the practicalities of solving them. Awareness of problems does not of itself generate remedial policies. Systematic study of the possibilities and pitfalls is also needed, helping to build bridges between theorists and practitioners. Analytically, the process has three interrelated aspects: 1) understanding the problems 'out there' that must be addressed; 2) developing remedial policies; and 3) trying to attain effective outcomes.

The first stage requires recognition of social problems and research to illuminate their character, causes, and possible remedies. Only then do governments usually become actively engaged. Seen in this light, researchers are not marginal players, because their work can be crucial in framing problems and pointing to potentially effective policy responses.

The second stage—the public policy process itself—relates directly to the state, broadly defined to include all levels of government and public services. Here is where the choice between alternative policy approaches and the development and implementation of specific policies occurs. The public policy process converts what *might* be done into active interventions.

Then comes the third stage: policy implementation and its outcomes. Overall policy effectiveness—or lack thereof—depends on state capacity to drive effective change and the economic, environmental, and social factors that constrain what is achieved in practice. Policies—however well intentioned and carefully crafted—may be ineffective because of unforeseen obstacles. Political considerations are ever present, of course, because no policy operates in a vacuum, separate from other policies or from changes to the political-economic context.

Of course, all three aspects have strong interconnections and interdependencies. The policy process is seldom linear and requires feedback loops and modifications in the light of experience. The ultimate test is whether the problems are resolved, or at least ameliorated, by the policies pursued. For urban analysis, historical and spatial perspectives are integral to such assessments. To distinguish between what is unique to specific times and places and what can be usefully generalised is the key element in effective social science.

Urban policies in political-economic context

Public policies tend to reflect the general social concerns of each era. In Australia during the years after World War II, for example, a dominant concern was to address the housing shortage that had resulted from the housebuilding doldrums during the Great Depression and subsequent war years. There was a pressing need to create 'homes fit for heroes', for newly formed households, and increasingly, for immigrants arriving as 'new Australians'. State and territory governments, as well as many highly motivated households, sought to meet the challenge (Troy 2012). The macroeconomic conditions were propitious, with buoyant economic growth and the development of new manufacturing industries leading to almost continuous full employment over two decades. The federal government's novel commitment to Keynesian macroeconomic priorities was conducive to buoyant employment conditions and steadily rising incomes, though an array of other policies, including industry policies and tariff protection, also contributed (Jones 2021). The surge in housebuilding was a significant driver of economic growth, leading to the subsequent long boom and increasingly widespread urban prosperity.

Yet, not all was well, particularly in the bigger cities, where, by the 1960s, public attention was shifting to the problems arising from rapid urban expansion, much of it in poorly serviced dormitory suburbs. The growth in automobile ownership during that era, combining with 'urban sprawl', had resulted in traffic congestion and long journey times. Pioneering research by the leading Australian urban economist Max Neutze (1965) sought to identify an optimum city size, placing primary emphasis on those congestion costs. However, building more and wider roads for bigger cities remained the dominant practice. Some grumbling came from 'regional and rural Australia' about the absence of policies for more balanced regional development, but the dominant political-economic paradigm and policy practice seemed largely untroubled.

Substantial stirrings of discontent were evident within the cities, however. Looking at the cities from a critical aesthetic and architectural perspective, Robin Boyd's book *The Australian Ugliness* (1960) was a landmark contribution. Ten years later, the historian and political scientist Hugh Stretton produced his *Ideas for Australian Cities* (1970), which became renowned as the springboard for modern concerns about urban policies aiming to redress social inequalities. Then, Lois Bryson and Faith Thompson's

An Australian Newtown (1972) pointed to the social stresses arising from inadequate provision of the necessary infrastructure to accompany the new housing in the outer suburbs. These and other academic contributions fed into the yet deeper discontent being expressed by growing waves of urban social movements. Of special note was the cooperation between resident action groups and the Builders Labourers Federation in New South Wales in the early 1970s, forming a 'green bans' movement to stop proposed urban development projects that prioritised the pursuit of profits over the wellbeing of urban residents and the environment (Mundey 1981; Iveson 2021).

Indeed, there was no shortage of topics for urban and regional researchers to study during that era, including concerns about social-spatial inequality and the growing imbalance between metropolitan and non-metropolitan areas. Some mild policy stirrings, including the establishment of the National Urban and Regional Development Authority, occurred during the last few years of the 23-year reign of Liberal–Country Party Coalition governments. It was not until the advent in 1972 of the federal Labor government led by Gough Whitlam, however, that more coherent policy emerged.

Whitlam's government established the Department of Urban and Regional Development (DURD) as a vehicle for realising the potential synergies between research, policy development, and implementation. Its minister was Tom Uren, a leading light in the ALP's Left faction, with the urbane Bob Lansdown as its senior public servant, and engineer-turned-urbanist Pat Troy as the major internal driving force. Unusually, the department's personnel were recruited largely from outside the existing federal bureaucracy. The team that Troy assembled—including key participants such as Michael Eyers, Peter Till, Joan Vipond, Michael Keating, David Wilmoth, Murray Geddes, and Henry Wardlaw—put prodigious efforts into developing new policies to tackle the urban and regional problems that had proliferated during the preceding decades (Wilmoth 2021).

The principal programs of DURD included formulation of a national urban and regional strategy; plans for development of new growth centres; formation of land commissions; provision of funds for area improvement schemes; creating a regional employment development program; changing the Commonwealth Grants Commission processes; and developing public housing projects in inner-city areas like Sydney's Glebe and Woolloomooloo. Redressing the backlog in the provision of sewerage to the expanding suburbs of the big cities was another program that Whitlam himself often—

and wittily—described as one of his most pleasing signature achievements. DURD's impact was significant, not only because of what was directly achieved 'on the ground' but also because it heralded overdue recognition of the need for a coherent national approach to the development and management of Australia's cities and regions.

Expertise from outsiders was helpful, too. For example, the distinguished US urban economist William Alonso was invited to visit DURD as an advisor on policy development. It was Alonso's proposed quartet of assessment criteria—efficiency, equity, environment, and quality of life— that helped set the standards by which the effectiveness of policies would be judged. Two underlying beliefs, reflected in the DURD policy agenda, were that each of these four criteria was being violated by the prevailing spatial socioeconomic arrangements and that progressive, research-based public policies could fundamentally change the situation for the better. Pursuing this theme, I used those four criteria to frame how my first book on Australian urban and regional development addressed the issues (Stilwell 1974). In other advice to DURD, Alonso emphasised the need for urban analysts and policymakers to take account of the *implicit* urban policies embedded in other government policies, such as those relating to taxation, trade, industry, money, and banking (Alonso 1971; Wilmoth 2021). This usefully highlighted the necessity for urban and regional policy to reach beyond explicitly spatial policy instruments, such as land-use controls. Not surprisingly, it also made other government departments, particularly Treasury, alarmed that the upstart DURD would be 'meddling' in their policy areas.

This DURD experience is worth recalling because, while it created tensions and faced practical impediments to progress, it was a bold step towards coherence in urban and regional policies. It showed that the federal government *could* develop and implement policies to deal with stresses that the six state governments had manifestly failed to resolve. The initiative was short-lived, however, ending when the conservative Coalition parties recaptured government after the controversial 'constitutional coup' of 1975 (Lloyd and Troy 1981; Wilmoth 2021). The new government led by Malcolm Fraser amalgamated DURD into the Department of Environment, Housing and Community Development, which had only a brief life before being disbanded by subsequent departmental restructuring. So ended the 'short flowering of national urban policy' (Wilmoth 2021: 31). The dominance of business and landed property interests over the broader public interest was re-established. Capital accumulation resumed as the main game in town, portending the later turn to neoliberalism in public policy formulation. That is why it is better to regard the DURD experiment not as a watershed in the development of urban policy but as an interregnum in the longstanding 'rule of capital'.

In terms of this chapter's earlier analytical framing of 'understanding', 'policies', and 'outcomes', DURD can be seen in retrospect as a bold experiment that scored well in the first two respects but poorly in relation to the third. While it was innovative in mobilising knowledge about cities and in the formulation of policy, its short life produced only glimpses of transformed practical outcomes. The essentially 'grounded' character of cities and regions requires effective policy over decades, not just a few years.

An era of public policy drift

Following DURD's demise, macroeconomic problems dominated the Australian Government's policy agenda, particularly as the pressures of unemployment and inflation coalesced into seemingly intractable 'stagflation'. The switch to a neoliberal approach in public policy gained increasing traction during the 1980s and continued for the next four decades, interrupted by brief interludes of revived Keynesianism to deal with the economic crises that erupted in 2008 and 2020. A brief flurry of federal government interest in explicitly urban policies occurred in the 1990s when Brian Howe, then deputy prime minister, implemented the Building Better Cities Program; but urban policy was generally left to the state and territory governments to manage as they saw fit. To the extent that there was any attempted coherence in spatial policies during this era, it was the increasing emphasis on 'urban consolidation' policies to increase urban density, sometimes accompanied by TINA ('there is no alternative') rhetoric. Pat Troy, back in his academic role at The Australian National University, was among the trenchant critics of this policy turn, pointing to its adverse consequences for equity and the environment (Troy 1996).

The growing socio-spatial inequalities and stresses made it more difficult to achieve the necessary transition to a sustainable economy and society (as argued in Troy 1999). In transport policy, for example, the emphasis on building yet more freeways to 'serve' cities by continuing their outward expansion—notwithstanding the concurrent policy push for urban consolidation—has been extraordinarily energy-intensive. On neoliberal principles, the primary emphasis has been on accommodating the preferences for travel modes expressed 'in the market', while constraining public transport provision through funding models in which the sale of public assets and the adoption of public–private partnerships have been recurring features.

Housing policy is another example. During the past half-century, both state and federal governments have substantially changed the character of public housing policy. An original ambition to provide decent, affordable housing for low and middle-income people has been transformed into a policy of providing welfare housing for people in dire straits. Seen in relation to the longer history of active federal government engagement in housing (as recorded in Troy 2012), the growing emphasis on private provision has had perverse effects. Housing outcomes have been increasingly stratified by income inequalities (Pawson et al. 2020), thereby compounding *wealth* inequalities over time as increasingly valuable housing assets—or the lack thereof—are passed on intergenerationally. One could not imagine a clearer example of 'circular and cumulative causation' in the intensification of socioeconomic inequalities (Stilwell 2019). The greater emphasis on housing as tradeable *property*, rather than as a home, has become a pervasive feature of the political economy of housing. The use of real estate as a vehicle for further capital accumulation by already wealthy people and tax-advantaged investors has worsened housing affordability and prioritised capitalistic values over social needs.

Indeed, the development of an 'asset economy' in which housing's primary function, for many people, is capital accumulation rather than the direct provision of housing services has been one of the most striking features of the past four decades (Konings et al. 2021). It is a process that has contributed to an ever-deeper gulf between those with a stake in property inflation and those simply trying to 'put a roof over their head'. Increased wealth in real estate and increased problems of housing affordability have been the twin outcomes, particularly in the major cities where the process has been most marked. Sydney is the extreme case, as revealed by data on household income inequalities that show it to be the most unequal city in Australia (Pearce and Hitchcock 2019). This is not purely a 'natural' market outcome; rather, as Scanlon (2019) indicates, public institutions have also buttressed policies that prioritise processes of capital accumulation over concerns about inequality and unsustainability.

The economic crises beginning in 2007 and 2020 highlighted the socioeconomic vulnerabilities that result from this neoliberal orientation. In both instances—the GFC and the economic crisis triggered by the onset of the Covid-19 pandemic—the severity of the downturns made the switch to a more stimulatory Keynesian approach to fiscal management a political-economic imperative. Even the Morrison-led conservative Coalition government—notorious for its rhetoric about 'getting the budget back to surplus'—followed suit, rightly fearing the prospect of unemployment. Its economic legacy is huge public deficits and debt that are projected to continue for many years. Yet, returning to policies of economic austerity is not really an option. Dealing with the widespread public concerns about the social and environmental stresses that intensified during the neoliberal era requires more, not less, government spending. Alongside growing awareness of climate change, questions about urban ecological resilience are increasingly gaining attention, including the energy policy requirements for creating more sustainable cities, housing, and transport. This is why concerns about equity and sustainability have become part of the dominant global discourse—evident in statements by presidents and prime ministers in many nations and by heads of international agencies such as the International Monetary Fund.

Does this signal the possibility as well as desirability of a sea-change in public policy? Many social commentators have argued that governments should aim for much more than a 'snap back' to the pre-pandemic norms, making the case for more ambitious programs that would rebuild for a better future (for example, Dawson and McCalman 2020; Macklin 2020; Stilwell 2020). Seen in this light, it is pertinent to probe how urban policies could form part of a broader program of radical economic and social reform that would address macroeconomic concerns in conjunction with restructuring for equity and sustainability.

Having a new federal government elected in 2022 and dependent on the Greens and progressive independents to advance its legislative agenda bodes well for the prospects for some such policy shift. The ALP government, with an eye to the possibility of having two or more terms in office, faces a political context in which sustained long-term policy commitments are needed. Prime Minister Anthony Albanese, with a personal background and keen interest in urban political economy, is well placed to lead that reform process. Of course, systemic and structural impediments exist, too, because self-interested economic actors and powerful institutional forces continue to propel processes that fuel inequality and inhibit sustainability.

Indeed, it is this tension between the market-focused capital accumulation processes and broader public concerns about equity and sustainability that creates awareness of the need for fundamental political-economic change. It is timely to recognise the exhaustion of the old paradigm and grasp the opportunity to create a new one.

A Labor 'Green Deal' and its spatial policy aspects

The current challenges of growing inequality and unsustainability require policy responses that go well beyond the normal reliance on market forces augmented by some tinkering at the edges. The wellbeing of the planet and our capacity to live in harmony on it are at stake. The principal alternative to business as usual is what has come to be known as the Green New Deal. The 'new deal' terminology has a distinctively US origin, stemming from President Franklin D. Roosevelt's employment-creation policies during the Great Depression of the 1930s (Chomsky and Pollin 2020; Stilwell 2021). The 'green' element, of course, signals the need to ensure that the policy program also responds to the challenges of dealing with climate change and other environmental stresses. In the current Australian political context, rather more appropriate local terminology could be a 'Labor Green Deal'.

How would a comprehensive approach to public policy for jobs and the environment integrate urban and regional policies into the broader program of reforms? Broadly, five interacting elements can be identified, relating to green jobs, just transition, redistribution, recognition, and empowerment.

The first policy element is the development of green jobs to reconcile concerns about employment and the environment. This is the principal link between the conventional Keynesian job-creation aspect of a fiscally expansionary program and the economic restructuring that is needed for more ecologically sustainable industries and employment. This element in the reform program requires detailed plans for developing industry sectors that use renewable energy sources, recycle waste, and have minimal climate change impacts, coupled with planned transition of labour and capital out of industries that cannot meet these criteria (Pearce and Stilwell 2008). Developing industry policies of this sort necessarily has an explicit *spatial* dimension, taking account of where industries are located and the needs and human and natural resource capacities of different localities. Detailed spatial specificity is required because industry policies for the development of green jobs are 'joined at the hip' to urban (and regional) policies.

The second element is policies to ensure a just transition, including workforce training and retraining that enable displaced workers to get new jobs. Provision of improved technical and further education is essential for this purpose, as acknowledged by the Jobs and Skills Summit held by the Albanese-led Labor government shortly after taking office in 2022. In practice, there is a crucial spatial dimension to the policy process, too, because attention to the *locations* of the existing workforce and places of work is essential. Developing regional transition plans, particularly for areas currently specialising in ecologically unsustainable industries, is essential. Not everyone in regions with 'sunset' industries will voluntarily relocate to where employment opportunities are being created in 'sunrise' industries. Making a 'just transition' requires organised relocation and retraining assistance for workers who are vulnerable to structural changes in employment conditions.

The third element is economic and social policies emphasising redistribution. The fiscal costs of transition falling on the public sector must be paid for by those individuals and institutions with the greatest capacity to do so. Seen in this way, the concern with equity is a corollary of the quest for sustainability. More than just progressive income taxation is implied. An expanded system of *land taxation*, for example, would more directly ensure that the increases in land values resulting from urban developments or investment in new transport infrastructure are *publicly*, rather than privately, appropriated. A major expansion of *social housing*—linked with green building design and retrofitting for ecological sustainability—is also potentially a key element in this context. Because housing markets, as well as labour and capital markets, have been driving the growth of socio-spatial inequalities, a major refocusing on social housing could help to break the vicious cycle of housing unaffordability, while also creating substantial employment. Concurrently, it would extend the policy instruments by which government exerts influence on patterns of urban and regional development.

A fourth element concerns processes of recognition and engagement of First Nations peoples in policy development and implementation. This is also fundamental to any 'new deal' process, as emphasised by the Australian Greens when making their policy commitment (Di Natale 2019). The Labor government's strong commitment to the Indigenous 'Voice' process should extend beyond the failed 2023 Referendum. The policy formulation process should not only seek to redress the longstanding marginalisation of Indigenous peoples but also provide an overdue opportunity for learning from their traditional knowledge of sustainability. After all, having lived here for more than 60,000 years, Indigenous Australians have the world's best sustainability credentials. Given the distinctive spatial distribution and community structures of First Nations peoples, such processes of recognition and engagement necessarily have a *regional* focus.

Finally, broader community empowerment can give the policy development and implementation processes a bottom-up character. The durability and potential success of any 'new deal' are likely to depend substantially on the development of processes for widespread public participation. This is best done at a scale with which people personally identify, which most often means their *locality*. The value of a communitarian approach that encourages and harnesses urban grassroots activism is increasingly emphasised in Australian urban studies (for example, Alexander and Gleeson 2019). Bridging the top-down and bottom-up elements, *local governments* can also play a significant role, as can be seen in the UK context where local 'community wealth-building' programs have injected renewed vitality into previously depressed urban areas and empowered urban communities to take control of their future (Guinan and O'Neill 2020; Brown and Jones 2021).

Seen in this way, the potential effectiveness of a Labor Green Deal depends substantially on policies applied at the urban and regional scales. It is a point that echoes Alonso's (1971) advice to the architects of DURD's policies half a century ago: all policies are spatial, whether explicitly and implicitly. Explicitly spatial policies directly target locations to enhance their prospects for making sustainable transitions, taking account of their resources and distinctive needs. But the *implicitly* spatial impacts of all policies must be considered if the policy reforms are to be turned into grounded outcomes across different cities and regions. A big research agenda is implied, the surface of which is barely scratched by outlining the foregoing five features.

Is it worth the bother? Or is it a utopian fantasy to which research programs and policy analyses cannot sensibly be pinned? Green New Deal advocacy has been a controversial position in many countries, even among advocates of radical reform (Chomsky and Pollin 2020; Sturman and Heenan 2021; Tsuda 2021). Moreover, the conditions conducive to its adoption and implementation are profoundly uncertain. Even the policy's name could be an obstacle to getting started: Labor parliamentarians might think the label 'Labor Green Deal' concedes too much to a minority party that they regard as a political competitor, perhaps preferring Jenny Macklin's (2020) proposed 'jobs and climate accord' because it echoes the accord between the ALP government and trade unions during the 1980s. Indeed, terminology does matter, even though it should not be an obstacle when so much is at stake.

Deeper problems to be anticipated relate to political opposition. On the right flank, a proposed policy package like this would inevitably have powerful critics who adhere to neoliberal views, cling to pro-market orthodoxies, advocate more austerity to rein in post-pandemic budget deficits, and warn that policies to reduce the effects of climate change will have intolerable economic costs. Concurrently, on the left flank, proponents of a more ambitiously transformational program for achieving a 'circular economy', a 'steady state economy', or 'ecological socialism' (Baer 2019) will be critical of any incrementally reformist program, positing bolder ambitions for an economy that recycles all resources, jettisons ongoing economic growth ambitions, and challenges capitalists' power. Indeed, such aspirations are pertinent to any prospect of political economic transformation. However, the immediate challenge is to start the process of change. As Chomsky and Pollin (2020) argue, the urgency of dealing with climate change requires the first steps to be taken within the existing structures of corporate and state power. How the policy program develops in the longer term would then depend on the evolving balance of interests, ideologies, and social forces, interacting in an 'arena of struggle' (Stilwell 2020, 2021). A pullback on the expansionary Keynesian aspects, relative to the redistributive and 'deeper green' aspects of the program, could become a stronger feature in the medium term, depending on the shifting balance of political forces and the as-yet-unknown environmental and economic outcomes.

The possibility that a radical reform program might not survive such contestation cannot be discounted. A parallel with DURD's premature demise is not difficult to envisage. Yet, the circumstances now are different, particularly because of the growing recognition of the challenges posed by climate change. Unless a 'political tipping point' towards radical reform precedes an irreversible ecological tipping point in the climate change process, all is otherwise futile. Seen in this way, the *precautionary principle* justifies the embrace of a new policy direction even though there are still many unknowns among the environmental, economic, and policy variables. Acting on that principle, gaining an initial policy 'toehold' could initiate a more thoroughgoing process of social democratic reform that strengthens the emphasis on 'just transition', redistribution, further engagement with First Nations peoples, and broader community empowerment, facilitated by newly developed institutional arrangements at local, urban, and regional scales. Starting on a process of comprehensive political-economic reform widens the future possibilities for yet more fundamental change.

The future is never a simple extrapolation of the past: successive social, economic, and ecological stresses generate continually evolving political expressions. The barrier that climate change denialism has imposed to progress in Australian public policy is already in the process of being overcome. The Covid-19 pandemic has precipitated awareness of the need and possibilities for ongoing political-economic changes. This creates the potential for a different policy direction to be taken, addressing the systemic roots of inequality, environmental damage, and economic insecurity. Seen in this way, the political-economic context could be regarded as comparable with that which spawned the DURD initiatives, albeit with public policies now more directly related to dealing with global ecological and socioeconomic crises.

Conclusion

On current trends, Australia will become a much more deeply unequal and environmentally unsustainable society unless a policy program of radical reform is initiated. If the waiting time for that policy shift is comparable with the half-century since the Whitlam Government's DURD initiatives, it will surely be too little, too late. Urban and regional analysts have an important role, alongside a broader array of concerned citizens, in driving the necessary political-economic changes. Laying the necessary analytical foundations for changes in public policy requires explicit attention to the 'framing' introduced at the start of this chapter and targeted research. A historically informed analysis can strengthen the connections between our understanding of the problems to be tackled, the possible public policy options, and the broader political-economic considerations that shape outcomes, for better or worse. Concurrently, a spatially informed analysis strengthens awareness of how local and global concerns interact across cities and regions.

Retrospective consideration of the DURD experience offers significant lessons in this context. It shows what can be done to create innovative policy initiatives if there is clarity about the social concerns to be addressed and willingness to draw on a continuously improving knowledge base. Even more, it is also a potent reminder that the reform process can be vulnerable to changing economic conditions and political conflicts. Looking through a similar lens shows the adverse effects arising from the dearth of comparable government policy interventions during recent decades, including the growing stresses relating to inequality and unsustainability. Recognising the impoverished political-economic legacy of the neoliberal era may imply a pessimistic conclusion; yet pessimism of the intellect always needs, as its companion, optimism of the will. Among the grounds for the latter is the prospect that ongoing research and more widely disseminated knowledge will help to pave the way for progressive political responses.

Making the case for radical reform like a Labor Green Deal, not just as a policy program but also as a framing for research that includes urban and regional analysis, fits well into this way of seeing policy development and social change. Thus, the advocacy of radical reform in the latter half of this chapter may be regarded as part of a process of laying foundations for remedial action to deal with inequality and unsustainability. It has an agenda-setting role that is especially important for researchers and practitioners in a field such as this. As we have seen, research and writing by Boyd, Neutze, Stretton, and Troy, among others, helped to pave the way for DURD's major policy push. New analyses of policies for combating the current problems of inequality and unsustainability, especially from an urban and regional policy perspective, are both necessary and timely. Taking this journey, following in Pat Troy's footsteps, is a good path to tread, linking academic research in urban studies with careful consideration and advocacy of public policy. Pat's contributions (such as Troy 1981a, 1981b, 1999, 2000) exemplified a similar concern to link critique, research, and policy development. His approach was both visionary and practical, dealing with the big picture and the devilish details. The best tribute to him would be to proceed purposefully with the task at hand, engaging with the challenge to create a more equitable and sustainable future for our cities and regions. Onward …

References

Alexander, S., and B. Gleeson. 2019. *Degrowth in the Suburbs: A Radical Urban Imaginary*. Singapore: Palgrave Macmillan. doi.org/10.1007/978-981-13-2131-3.

Alonso, W. 1971. 'Problems, Purposes and Implicit Policies for a National Strategy of Urbanisation.' Paper prepared for the National Commission on Population Growth and The American Future. Mimeo.

Baer, H.A. 2019. *Democratic Socialism as Real Utopia: Transitioning to An Alternative World System*. New York, NY: Berghahn Books.

Boyd, R. 1960. *The Australian Ugliness*. Melbourne: Cheshire.

Brown, M., and R.E. Jones. 2021. *Paint Your Town Red: How Preston Took Back Control and How Your Town Can Too*. London: Repeater Books.

Bryson, L., and F. Thompson. 1972. *An Australian Newtown*. Harmondsworth, UK: Penguin.

Chomsky, N., and R. Pollin. 2020. *Climate Crisis and the Green New Deal*. New York, NY: Verso.

Dawson, E., and J. McCalman, eds. 2020. *What Happens Next? Restructuring Australia after COVID-19*. Melbourne: Melbourne University Press. doi.org/10.2307/jj.1640569.

Di Natale, R. 2019. 'The Time Has Come for a Green New Deal.' Speech to National Conference, Canberra, 22 November, [delivered by Adam Bandt]. Canberra: Australian Greens. Available from: greens.org.au/magazine/time-has-come-green-new-deal.

Guinan, J., and M. O'Neill. 2020. *The Case for Community Wealth Building*. Cambridge, UK: Polity Press.

Iveson, K. 2021. 'The Sydney "Green Bans" Show How We Can Transform Our Cities.' *Jacobin Magazine*, [New York], 7 October. Available from: www.jacobinmag.com/2021/07/australia-sydney-urbanism-construction-builders-labourers-federation-nsw-green-labor-militancy.

Jones, E. 2021. 'Macroeconomic and Structural Policies: Economic Policies in Post–World War II Australia.' *Journal of Australian Political Economy* 88: 98–123.

Konings, M., L. Adkins, G. Bryant, S. Maalsen, and L. Troy. 2021. 'Lock-In and Lock-Out: COVID-19 and the Dynamics of the Asset Economy.' *Journal of Australian Political Economy* 87: 20–47.

Lloyd, C., and P.N. Troy. 1981. *Innovation and Reaction: The Life and Death of the Federal Government's Department of Urban and Regional Development*. Sydney: George Allen & Unwin.

Macklin, J. 2020. 'An Emissions and Employment Accord.' In *What Happens Next? Restructuring Australia after COVID-19*, edited by E. Dawson and J. McCalman, 33–42. Melbourne: Melbourne University Press. doi.org/10.2307/jj.1640569.7.

Mundey, J. 1981. *Green Bans and Beyond.* Sydney: Angus & Robertson.

Neutze, G.M. 1965. *Economic Policy and the Size of Cities.* Canberra: Urban Research Unit, The Australian National University.

Pawson, H., V. Milligan, and J. Yates. 2020. *Housing Policy in Australia: A Case for System Reform.* Singapore: Springer Verlag.

Pearce, A., and F. Stilwell. 2008. '"Green-Collar" Jobs: Employment Impacts of Climate Change Policies.' *Journal of Australian Political Economy* 62: 120–38.

Pearce, R., and J.N. Hitchcock. 2019. *The Sydney Inequality Indicators Framework: Measures for a Just City.* Sydney Policy Lab Report for the City of Sydney. Sydney: University of Sydney.

Scanlon, R. 2019. 'Capital Accumulation, Urban Planning and the Greater Sydney Commission.' *Journal of Australian Political Economy* 83: 115–39.

Stilwell, F. 1974. *Australian Urban and Regional Development.* Sydney: ANZ Book Co.

Stilwell, F. 2019. *The Political Economy of Inequality.* Cambridge, UK: Polity Press.

Stilwell, F. 2020. '"Snap Back" or "Press On": From the Current Crisis to a Green New Deal.' *Journal of Australian Political Economy* 85: 219–27.

Stilwell, F. 2021. 'From Green Jobs to Green New Deal: What Are the Questions?' *Economic and Labour Relations Review* 32(2): 155–69. doi.org/10.1177/10353046211009774.

Stretton, H. 1970. *Ideas for Australian Cities.* Melbourne: Georgian House.

Sturman, A., and N. Heenan. 2021. 'Introduction: Configuring the Green New Deal.' *Economic and Labour Relations Review* 32(2): 149–54. doi.org/10.1177/10353046211017601.

Troy, P.N., ed. 1981a. *A Just Society? Essays on Equity in Australia.* Sydney: Allen & Unwin.

Troy, P.N., ed. 1981b. *Equity in the City.* Sydney: Allen & Unwin.

Troy, P.N. 1996. *The Perils of Urban Consolidation.* Sydney: The Federation Press.

Troy, P.N., ed. 1999. *Serving the City.* Sydney: Pluto Press.

Troy, P.N., ed. 2000. *Equity, Environment, Efficiency: Ethics and Economics in Urban Australia.* Melbourne: Melbourne University Press.

Troy, P.N. 2012. *Accommodating Australians: Commonwealth Government Involvement in Housing*. Sydney: The Federation Press.

Tsuda, K. 2021. 'Naive Questions on Degrowth.' *New Left Review* 128(March–April): 111–30. doi.org/10.2139/ssrn.3837997.

Wilmoth, D. 2021. *The Promise of the City: Adventures in Learning Cities and Higher Education*. Melbourne: Laneway Press.

Part 7: Conclusion

23

Australian urban policy futures

Wendy Steele, Robert Freestone, and Bill Randolph

Introduction

Contemporary understandings of urban policy in twenty-first-century Australia reflect not just 'a nation of city dwellers' (Hamilton 1976)—although this is important—but also the fact that our cities and towns, while situated on unceded Indigenous land, must be understood within the context of dynamic and interconnected cultural and natural hinterlands. Within the context of anthropogenic climate change, 'the urban' is something not 'out there', but deeply embedded in the patterns and processes of settler colonialism, neoliberalism, and globalisation that continue to shape and frame Australian settlements. Urban policy, like its close corollary urban research, reflects this hybridity and the need for an interdisciplinary approach to better understand 'how to make cities tick' (Neutze 1978), but also how urban society can flourish and be more regenerative.

Over the past half-century, urban policy across different levels of government has had a strong, selective, interventionist agenda focused on housing, transport infrastructure, telecommunications, water, and international competitiveness. More recent themes have been the lived experience of cities and regions, more transparent and participatory decision-making, the complexities of metropolitan governance in a federal system, the evolving morphology of Australian suburbanisation, the reciprocal links to social and economic polarisation (including public housing and energy poverty), and urban design. Alongside the impacts of severe biodiversity loss, damage, and degradation—some of which is now irreversible within the context of climate change—this amounts to a profound refocusing of urban policy on addressing sustainability as a politics of redistribution, resilience, and equity.

This policy reorientation was recognised in the *Australian State of Environment Report 2021* (DCCEEW 2021, held back until its release in 2022), which draws explicit attention to urban policy and the urban dimensions of public policy. The impacts of fossil fuel burning, land clearing, and other activities linked to the growth and development of cities have had a devastating effect on the health and biodiversity of the environment, including air, land, and waterways. This affects not just native species—of which Australia has higher rates of extinction than anywhere else in the world—but also the vitality, liveability, and sustainability of human health and urban habitats (Johnston et al. 2022). Ross Garnaut critiques the inability of public policy to address urban energy and water consumption, waste, and pollution as an agenda of national significance:

> [T]oday, public policy based on marshalling knowledge through research and analysis, and then nurturing public understanding of the issues, seems a distant dream … If Australia is to realise its immense opportunity in a zero-carbon world economy, it will require a different policy framework. (Garnaut 2019: 9–10)

In this final chapter, we draw together the insights that have emerged from across the different contributions assembled in this volume, as well as outline emergent priority areas that point to what a 'different policy framework' could begin to address. This is intended to be not a prescriptive or instrumental agenda, but rather a focus on the prospects for urban policy based on the three key questions that underpinned this book within the context of Australian urban policy challenges and prospects: What has been delivered in enhancing productive, sustainable, and liveable cities and regions? What aspirations have fallen short or produced counterintuitive outcomes because of governance, financial, and political reasons? And finally, what can be identified as matters of emergent concern in both recalibrating existing and devising new policy settings to address the quality of urban Australian life in the mid to late twenty-first century?

The conclusion is thus organised in two parts. The first addresses some key themes that have surfaced in the chapters as collective concerns for Australian cities and regions, including path dependency and connectedness;

the relationship between critical infrastructure and urban policy, known as the new Australian urbanism; emerging meta-themes of climate and decarbonisation; Indigenous sovereignty and reconciliation; and the ongoing disruptions caused by Covid-19. The second part looks ahead to new policy settings for moving to a more sustainable future. Eclectic rather than systematic in focus and scale, the shared focus of the contributors is the need to challenge orthodoxy, commit to transition planning and management, and better recognise the principles of subsidiarity and equity, national leadership, and Australia's international environmental and humanitarian obligations. Urban policy matters, but it emerges as contested and often misused and misrepresented by vested interests, although still with largely unrealised transformative potential, particularly at the research–policy nexus within the Australian context.

Urbanising policy or urban policy?

Australian settlement trajectories extend far beyond the moment of the city—even recognition of global cities such as Sydney and Melbourne—to work across diverse coalitions of actors, sectors, and scales. Although often positioned as 'flat' landscapes, contemporary constructs of cities and urban regions increasingly recognise their multidimensional nature even in physical terms from, say, the subterranean underground of tunnels and sewers through surface rail networks and toll roads to the airspace of drones, planes, and helicopters—in effect, from 'satellites to bunkers' (Graham 2016). Despite the political and material complexity of modern urban contexts, the two-dimensional 'flat earth' viewpoint is still dominant in urban policy and planning.

The legacy of public policy that is 'fit for urban purpose' is mixed across the chapters. References range from an urban policy void or vacuum through reductive and piecemeal applications to the prospects for a more integrated, interdisciplinary, and holistic policy framework to guide the planning and development of towns, cities, and urban regions. But a common theme woven through the diverse thematic chapters was that urban policy has reached a major juncture requiring critical appraisal and action, national leadership, innovative and ethical governance frameworks, and a commitment to address the twin agendas of sustainability and equity.

This is evident in the simplistic and often siloed approaches to complex urban issues identified and the need for more innovative and integrative public policy approaches and solutions. As Prime Minister Anthony Albanese highlighted in a major speech on 'The future of our cities', from which we also quoted in the Introduction, there is a 'need to reinvigorate cities policy' given that cities are 'where so many Australians live, work and do business' (Albanese 2021). As captured in this book, this requires sophisticated governance tools and solutions, as well as strategic policy interventions and entry points at different scales. Pauline McGuirk and colleagues (2022) draw attention to five key research agendas for contemporary urban governance and public policy innovation: reconfiguring states and governance authorities; shifting forms and dynamics of power; constituting urban governance as a political project; implementing innovative techniques; and the shifting spatiality of urban governance. We would concur fully with these statements.

The great paradox for urban policy is that rhetoric around the need to be equal, fair, transparent, well-resourced, and progressive is rarely matched in policy practices. Not all policy innovation is ethical, useful, or even needed. Addressing the 'let it rip' mentality and bipartisan political impulse to 'build something big' requires a strategic vision to replace policy drift with policy drive and dynamism. To achieve the necessary transition to a low-carbon, equitable future, urban policy needs vision and practicality, participatory development, and of course 'on the ground' resourcing and implementation.

For example, housing is a recurring theme in several chapters, with calls for a more holistic and human approach to housing as urban policy. Housing is a basic need and remains inadequate and unaffordable for many, with deepening inequality creating a new generation of precarity. People's access to housing is directly or indirectly affected by action across all three tiers of government and, despite promises to address the problem through improving the supply, funding, and allocation of public housing and/or subsidised private housing, this has not been realised in practice. With Australia having one of the highest debt-to-income ratios globally and 'Generation Rent' navigating housing unaffordability and income security, piecemeal policy interventions that fail to recognise the deeply integrated nature of housing are unlikely to be successful.

The inadequacy and inaccessibility of the housing stock in Australia, public or otherwise, threaten to derail urban prospects and point to the need for a different mix of policy levers, underpinned by cultures, structures, and practices that support equity and affordability. At one level, this is about the need to 'build better' through good design and participatory governance, and this is important. However, speculative land development, contested ownership, and property rights are as much about banking, taxation, immigration, social security, and Indigenous reconciliation as they are about construction and low-carbon technology. Australia can do better than this and recent calls for a national housing policy and an agency to drive such policy emphasise the urgent need for a strategic and holistic focus for a critical urban infrastructure (Maclennan et al. 2021).

Part of the challenge lies in making clearer the links between urban policy and critical infrastructure as connected frameworks for coordinated and strategic action. This includes a more nuanced approach to the natural environment as critical to the national urban policy agenda. Access to clean water, for example, is vital to the liveability and sustainability of Australia's urban regions, yet policy is often disconnected from these lifelines and driven by vested interests rather than evidenced-based or informed research. As Garnaut (2019: 3) has recently commented: 'The tragedy of the Murray–Darling [Basin] is a consequence of denial, and of knowledge not being applied to public policy.' Alongside housing systems, the networks of water systems, transportation, sewerage, energy, and greenspace are vital to the functioning of urban regions, yet their interdependencies are inadequately understood and poorly reflected in policy decision-making processes and practices.

A critical focus on the compact city, for example, stresses the need for more nuanced understandings of the impact and efficacy of urban densification policies, and to move beyond simplistic representations of suburban settlement and its discontents. Several chapters in the book call explicitly for a more robust discussion about compact city policies and their rationale and the expectations that have at times been politically cultivated. The focus is an equity and justice question about who benefits most from consolidation policies. This includes a greater interrogation of the evidence that, first, consolidation reduces sprawl and lowers requirements for public sector investment in infrastructure through more efficient use of services—water, sewerage, power, transportation, and communication—and, second, that higher urban density will lower the cost of housing and energy usage.

There is growing recognition of a new and distinctly Australian urbanism that has grown in the wake of the Covid-19 and climate emergencies. Settlement patterns are shifting in response to uneven geographies and socio-spatial and economic inequity. The 'exodus' (a somewhat hyperbolic term) from the cities during the global pandemic nevertheless underscores a rural drift and repopulation trend that has developed over the past two decades. Within major cities themselves an urban inversion has seen the suburban settlement dream challenge the inner city as a site of speculative development and its attendant twin bedfellows of urban displacement and gentrification. Yet, this dispersal of urban development and growth and the rise of new satellite city models and narratives remain out of step with infrastructure funding mechanisms for basic services. Out of touch with community needs and aspirations, the danger is urban policy that veers chaotically from the visionary to the farcical.

Meta-themes that emerge from this book include equity, sustainability, population distribution and density, and the importance of public commons in Australian urban policy. This is underpinned by the trio of climate and decarbonisation, Indigenous sovereignty, and the global Covid-19 pandemic. Addressing anthropogenic climate change is an inherently urban problem that goes to the heart of the sustainability of Australian society. The basic form and structure of the nation's urban regions were made possible by low-cost fossil fuels, yet as the chapters here indicate, there are other ways of arranging the distribution of people and their activities to require lower levels of energy consumption and produce less pollution. This requires a radical reimagining of systems for our land, water, carbon, and mineral use, and for the role and nature of housing, transport, and 'smart' systems.

Recognition of the unsustainable nature of business-as-usual urban development requires reckoning with the ongoing acts of dispossession and de-politicisation that surround policy and practices. The settler-colonial city is premised in Australia on a Eurocentric construction of non-Western, non-modern, non-industrialised ways of life as inferior and in need of development, devaluing other forms of social existence. The construction of alternative urban futures requires reimagining these structures of power and policy as something very different from what First Nations scholar Glen Coulthard (2014: 176) describes as *Urbs nullius*: 'urban space void of Indigenous sovereign presence'. The Uluru Statement from the Heart, for example, offers a powerful pathway for shared futures—urban or otherwise—on unceded Country.

Current urban growth trajectories cannot be sustained, and the critiques being raised of both the lived experience and the legacy of contemporary urban society reflect their settler-colonial origins and the prioritisation of profit and financial return over the sustainability of local communities and natural systems. As many of the contributors in the book highlight, new approaches to urban policy and planning are needed as existing threats such as climate change intensify along with new threats exemplified by Covid-19 that emerge to challenge the resilience of cities and regions. Urban policy conceived in these terms has the capacity to direct strategic change: to 'scale out' to empower practices horizontally; to 'scale up' to encourage the formal embedding of structures and practices vertically; and to 'scale deep' so that new ideas and practices help transform the status quo to achieve more sustainable growth and settlement futures (Moore et al. 2015; Steele et al. 2021).

Transforming cities and urban regions

What might these new policy approaches be? The unsustainability of Australian cities and urban regions within the context of climate change signals the need for participatory, transformative change at multiple scales. To be transformative, policies and practices must be enabling not disabling, participatory rather than hierarchical, and have the capacity to constructively disrupt the status quo when needed. The prospect of intentional transformational change requires a critical capacity to go beneath surface appearances to challenge existing structural patterns and norms that support power imbalances and the layered injustices that impact the sustainability of society and communities. To address this, Stephen Dovers (2022) offers four critical observations: urban inequalities require an integrated, systemic policy response; more evidence-based research to support policy is needed; this evidence and messaging must be promoted by a broad coalition of advocates; and urban policy and reform are hard, but are possible.

The emphasis here, following the seminal work of Patrick Troy, is that we do not have to accept the present urban context or continue with the policy prescriptions that have failed to engender sustainability or adequately address this climate of change. The growth and management strategies that have been supported and pursued have devastated Indigenous communities and compromised the capacity and stability of the ecosystems on which Australian society and its settlements depend. What is needed is to continue and further develop a civic debate about the size, nature, form, and structure of Australian cities. Is it appropriate? How would we know? What would we do to change? What are the alternatives? How might they be achieved? As Troy highlighted:

> We have created a high level of dependence and low degrees of self-sufficiency in our cities. We are dependent on others for our jobs, our entertainments and diversions, the service[s] we use and the removal of the wastes we produce. We are dependent on the importation of energy in the form of electricity and petroleum products. Very little of the food of city residents is produced by them; even less will be as we pursue policies of consolidation. The hydraulic services we develop make little use of the water which falls naturally on the city and our form of development converts it into a 'problem' which is expensive to solve. All these features of our cities have implications for energy consumption and provide clues as to ways in which we might reduce it. (Troy 2012: 156)

Transformative change to Australian cities and urban regions requires policy and practices that are firmly grounded in social and environmental equity and the politics of redistribution and reconciliation. This includes recognition of the inheritance and influence of spatial, social, and governance structures, and the path-dependent policy trajectories that pose ongoing challenges for transitional politics, reform, and innovation. At the same time, Australian cities, suburbs and urban regions are functioning differently than in the past as economic, social, and political structures have shifted. In particular, neoliberalism in its various guises has both directly and indirectly created new Australian settlements that are more unequal and precarious and therefore less likely to be resilient to future system shocks.

Across the chapters in this volume the interconnectedness of policy trajectories under the urban banner is a conceptual strength yet to be realised in the stubbornly unyielding silos of policy, planning, and practice. This further underscores the importance of seeing cities and regions holistically and as alive to co-benefits, rather than devoid of indirect impacts. This includes recognising international responsibilities and commitments such as the 2015 Paris Agreement to reduce greenhouse gas emissions to well below 2 degrees Celsius of warming, the achievement of the Sustainable Development Goals by 2030, and the 2007 UN Declaration on the Rights of Indigenous Peoples. If we continue to fall short of coherent evidence-based urban policy initiatives at the national level, the nation could be in breach of international environmental agreements. At the very least there must be recognition that cities and urban regions are powerful instruments for realising these international obligations.

Overall, there is a clear sense from our contributors that many current orthodox programs are not working well at local, state, and federal levels and bolder actions are called for. The role of the Commonwealth was identified in strategic national leadership, coordination, support, and resourcing, leaving the 'how to' of more explicit statements of policy targets and adaptation to circumstances in practice to local and state contexts. While a national urban policy framework exists in the Turnbull–Morrison legacy of the *Smart Cities Plan*, it goes nowhere near encompassing the diverse social and environmental equity concerns raised in this book, let alone the aspirations of the government's own 2018 inquiry into the role of the Commonwealth in the cities (House of Representatives Standing Committee on Infrastructure, Transport and Cities 2018). The prospects for both a national settlement strategy and a national housing policy were raised to address the need for interventions that are more likely to be effective.

The principle of subsidiarity was invoked in managing the interplay between all three tiers of government, indicating the need for reform in better linking the common/wealth at the federal level to needs at the local and subregional scales. This includes lines of sight, with cascading and stronger complementarity of aims and means from larger to smaller jurisdictions, as well as more participatory—that is, democratic—processes of policy formation that are less dependent on big corporate consultants and more open to research alliances with community groups: an alternative coalition of the heterodox. Others have termed this the imperative of co-design and co-production of knowledge to guide selection of desired transition pathways (Bai et al. 2018; Webb et al. 2018). While Covid-19 was unavoidable, it reinforced the sense that Australians experience the built environment very differently and must adapt accordingly. The global health crisis flowed into concerns about social, environmental, and spatial inequality and the concomitant role of urban policy as public policy that supports and promotes the flourishing of people and the planet.

This book—an outcome of an Australian Academy of Social Sciences workshop—offers a multi-voice, cross-disciplinary, policy-orientated, and nongovernmental forum on Australian urban policy. Several key focuses of urban policy emerged: sustainability, the environment, and conservation; populations, settlement, and urban form; justice and wellbeing; productivity and infrastructure; and transition needs and challenges. Collectively the chapters offer new cross-generational ideas to challenge policymakers to think outside the current policy box and the dominant voices and vested interests who currently 'own' the ideas about cities. This is also a challenge to the urban research community broadly defined—that is, whether in academia, the private or the public sector—to work to reimagine the urban policy–research nexus and the future impact on culture that this entails (Kokshagina et al. 2021).

Prospects and pathways

Existing dominant approaches to conventional research and policy impact are not adequately meeting societal and planetary needs, nor are they meeting community expectations or building the public trust needed to achieve transformational urban change. However, multiple pathways are available that complement academic rigour by demonstrating the relevance of research, increasing its reach, and encouraging end users to adopt it. Working collaboratively and across disciplines helps to ensure that research is legitimate and generates value where needed. This includes finding better ways to assemble, assess, and find integrative synergies, enhance learning, evaluate net effects around what is most important, and demonstrate adaptability in how urban policy is imagined and produced through democratic processes.

In the face of crisis and change, the prospects and challenges for urban policy and its attendant coalitions to transform the pathways and practices of Australian cities and urban regions with the speed required are both necessary and daunting. Established path-dependent ways of understanding urban issues and failing policy orthodoxies must be reassessed and redefined where needed. To counter the impacts of technological determinism, exclusionary practices, opaque power structures, and the dominance of elite market-driven actors, a different kind of politics of solidarity, sustainability, and resilience is required. Transformative practices will not be achieved without creative experimentation and transition, but this is a nonlinear pathway that also necessitates debate and at times dissent. Understanding and responding to complex urban challenges are wicked problems that require ethical and innovative solutions (Head 2022). A transformative urban policy agenda is not just the identification of problems and solutions, but also recognition of the vulnerability and interconnectedness of urban places, and the need for more regenerative policy practices that involve communities from the ground up.

References

Albanese, A. 2021. 'The future of our cities.' Speech to the Australian Financial Review's Business Summit 2021, Sydney, 10 March. Available from: anthonyalbanese. com.au/media-centre/the-future-of-our-cities-10-march-2021.

Bai, X., R.J. Dawson, D. Ürge-Vorsatz, G.C. Delgado, A.S. Barau, S. Dhakal, D. Dodman, L. Leonardsen, V. Masson-Delmotte, D.C. Roberts, and S. Schultz. 2018. 'Six Research Priorities for Cities and Climate Change.' *Nature* 555(7694): 23–25. doi.org/10.1038/d41586-018-02409-z.

Coulthard, G. 2014. *Red Skin, White Masks: Rejecting the Colonial Politics of Recognition*. Minneapolis, MN: University of Minnesota Press. doi.org/10.5749/minnesota/9780816679645.001.0001.

Department of Climate Change, Energy, the Environment and Water (DCCEEW). 2021. *Australian State of Environment Report 2021*. Canberra: Commonwealth of Australia.

Dovers, S. 2022. 'Inequality in Australia: The Persistence of Policy Hopes and Failures.' *Urban Policy and Research* 40(3): 186–89. doi.org/10.1080/08111146. 2022.2060960.

Garnaut, R. 2019. *Superpower: Australia's Low-Carbon Opportunity*. Melbourne: La Trobe University Press.

Graham, S. 2016. *Vertical*. London: Verso.

Hamilton, P. 1976. *A Nation of City Dwellers*. Melbourne: Thomas Nelson.

Head, B. 2022. *Wicked Problems in Public Policy: Understanding and Responding to Complex Challenges*. London: Palgrave Pivot. doi.org/10.1007/978-3-030-94580-0.

House of Representatives Standing Committee on Infrastructure, Transport and Cities. 2018. *Building Up & Moving Out: Inquiry into the Australian Government's Role in the Development of Cities*. September. Canberra: Parliament of the Commonwealth of Australia. Available from: parlinfo.aph.gov.au/parlInfo/download/committees/reportrep/024151/toc_pdf/BuildingUp&MovingOut. pdf;fileType=application%2Fpdf.

Johnston, E., I. Creswell, and T. Janke. 2022. 'This is Australia's Most Important Report on the Environment's Deteriorating Health. We Present Its Grim Findings.' *The Conversation*, 19 July. Available from: theconversation.com/this-is-australias-most-important-report-on-the-environments-deteriorating-health-we-present-its-grim-findings-186131.

Kokshagina, O., L. Rickards, W. Steele, and O. Moraes. 2021. 'Futures Literacy for Research Impact in Universities.' *Futures* 132: 102803. doi.org/10.1016/j.futures.2021.102803.

McGuirk, P., T. Baker, A. Sisson, R. Dowling, and S. Maalsen. 2022. 'Innovating Urban Governance: A Research Agenda.' *Progress in Human Geography* 46(6): 1391–412. doi.org/10.1177/03091325221127298.

Maclennan, D., J. Long, H. Pawson, B. Randolph, F. Aminpour, and C. Leishman. 2021. *Housing: Taming the Elephant in the Economy. A Report to the Housing and Productivity Research Consortium*. June. Sydney: City Futures Research Centre, University of New South Wales. Available from: cityfutures.ada.unsw.edu.au/documents/644/Synthesis_report-final_version_12.06.pdf.

Moore, M.-L., D. Riddell, and D. Vocisano. 2015. 'Scaling Out, Scaling Up, Scaling Deep.' *Journal of Corporate Citizenship* 58: 67–84. doi.org/10.9774/GLEAF.4700.2015.ju.00009.

Neutze, M. 1978. *Australian Urban Policy*. Sydney: George Allen & Unwin.

Steele, W., J. Hillier, D. MacCallum, J. Byrne, and D. Houston. 2021. *Quiet Activism: Climate Action at the Local Scale*. Cham, Switzerland: Palgrave Macmillan. doi.org/10.1007/978-3-030-78727-1.

Troy, P.N. 2012. 'The Greenhouse Effect and the City.' *Australian Planner* 49(2): 153–60. doi.org/10.1080/07293682.2012.684435.

Webb, R., X. Bai, M. Stafford Smith, R. Costanza, D. Griggs, M. Moglia, M. Neuman, P. Newman, P. Newton, B. Norman, C. Ryan, H. Schandl, W. Steffen, N. Tapper, and G. Thomson. 2018. 'Sustainable Urban Systems: Co-Design and Framing for Transition.' *Ambio* 47: 57–77. doi.org/10.1007/s13280-017-0934-6.

Index

Page numbers in **bold** text represent images.

North South Rail Link 53
Sydney Metro–Western Sydney
  Airport 53
see also high-speed railway, Very
  Fast Train
rainwater, *see* water—rainwater
RAISE Toolkit 259
Register of the National Estate 130
remote working, *see* Covid-19
  pandemic—and working from
  home
renewable energy 389, 398, 437
  offsets 115
  targets 68
  transition 390, 393, 398, 402
  see also energy
rental housing 213, 214, 339, 342,
  354, 356, 373
  affordable 54, 209, 356, 357, 373,
    374, 380
  build-to-rent 211, 212, 213, 214
  dominance of 16, 206, 336, 340,
    341, 343, 373
  eviction 342, 377
  'Generation Rent' 330, 335, 452
  informal 376
  investors 212, 334, 339, 341, 373
  market 206, 340, 376
  private 16, 206, 334–5, 336, 339,
    373, 375
  reform 212, 342
  regulation 212, 361, 374, 377
  stress 355, 370, 371, 375
  subsidies 355, 358, 373, 376, 378
  see also National Rental
    Affordability Scheme
Rent Assistance 355, 358, 378
Research for Development Impact
  Network (RDI) 32
Reserve Bank of Australia 44
resilience
  community 212
  ecological 436
  to disasters 94

to heat 228
urban 23, 64, 89, 93, 136, 249,
  259, 390, 402, 450, 455, 456,
  458
see also climate change resilience
Resilience NSW 76
resilient
  buildings 94
  regeneration 185
Richmond Valley 118
Ripley 170, 172
RMIT 11–12, 97, 258
roads 5, 116, 274, 289, 291
  and climate change 64, 434
  cost of 270, 271, 272
  funding 50, 270, 273, 277, 278
  provision of 91, 270
  safety 93, 94
  toll roads 51, 451
  upgrades 55, 75, 431
  see also car dependency, congestion,
    transport
Robert, Stuart 36
Rocky Creek Dam 119
Roosevelt, Franklin D. 437
Rous County Council 118, 119
Royal Australian Institute of
  Architects, *see* Australian Institute
  of Architects
Royal Australian Planning Institute, *see*
  Planning Institute of Australia
Rudd Government 41, 49, 56, 70, 71,
  171, 278, 355, 356–7
Rudd–Gillard governments 8, 100,
  357
Rudd, Kevin 44, 49

Salvado 168, 170
Sandercock, Leonie 182, 194, 352
Sanders, Will 288
Scotland 139
second Sydney airport, *see* Sydney—
  second airport
sewage 111, 121

www.ingramcontent.com/pod-product-compliance
Lightning Source LLC
Chambersburg PA
CBHW050328270326
41926CB00016B/3357